PROJECTS

Planning, Analysis, Selection, Financing, Implementation, and Review

Ninth Edition

About the Author

Dr Prasanna Chandra, Director of Centre for Financial Management, is an MBA, PhD (Finance). He has nearly five decades of teaching experience in postgraduate and executive education programmes. He was a professor of finance at Indian Institute of Management, Bangalore for nearly two decades. He was a visiting professor of finance at Southern Illinois University, USA for two years. He was appointed as a member of several committees including the Capital Issues Advisory Committee, the High Powered Committee on Insurance Sector Reforms, and the SEBI Committee on Derivatives. He has served on the boards of a number of organizations including Torrent Pharmaceuticals, Power Finance Corporation, UTIIAS, ICFAI, SDMIMD, IFCI, IIM (B), Templeton Mutual Fund, Bangalore Stock Exchange Limited, and Karnataka Soaps and Detergents Limited. He has been a consultant to many organizations.

Dr Chandra has conducted executive seminars for a number of organizations like TCS, Infosys, Tata Motors, ITC, NIIT, Tata Steel, Sasken Communications, BHEL, Bharat Shell, ANZ Grindlays, HMT, Canara Bank, Vysya Bank, ONGC, Wipro, GAIL, Microsoft, Motorola, and Tata Power.

He has published ten other books – *Strategic Financial Management: Managing for Value Creation; Financial Management: Theory and Practice; Investment Analysis and Portfolio Management; Investment Game; Corporate Valuation; Finance Sense; Fundamentals of Financial Management; Behavioural Finance and Valuation of Equity Shares* and has authored over 70 articles in professional journals and business periodicals. He has been a Fulbright Scholar and a UNDP Fellow. He has received several honours including the Best Teacher Award from the Association of Indian Management Schools.

PROJECTS

Planning, Analysis, Selection, Financing, Implementation, and Review

Ninth Edition

Prasanna Chandra
Director
Centre for Financial Management (CFM)
Bangalore

McGraw Hill Education (India) Private Limited

Published by McGraw Hill Education (India) Private Limited
Registered Office: Anjana Complex No: 5/90 A, Butt Road, St. Thomas Mount, Chennai – 600016

Projects, 9e

Third reprint 2022
RCBXYDLJDCLRB

Print Book Edition:
ISBN-13: 978-81-941138-3-6
ISBN-10: 81-941138-3-0

E-Book Edition:
ISBN-13: 978-81-941138-4-3
ISBN-10: 81-941138-4-9

04 05 06 07 08 RAJ 26 25 24 23 22

Managing Director: *Lalit Singh*
Head of HED Portfolio: *Nikhil Wadhera*
Senor Content Developer: *Sachin Kumar*
Project Manager—Production Services: *Atul Gupta*
General Manager—Production: *Rajender P Ghansela*
Manager—Production: *Reji Kumar*

Typeset at APS Compugraphics, 4G, PKT 2, Mayur Vihar Phase – III, Delhi 110096, and Printed and bound in India at Rajkamal Electric Press, Kundli, Sonepat, Haryana

Cover Image Source: Shutterstock
Cover Designer: Creative Designer

Visit us at: www.mheducation.co.in; Phone (Toll free in India): **1800 103 5875**
Write to us at: info.india@mheducation.com

CIN: U80302TN2010PTC111532

To

Prashant and Pranav

Contents

PART 3 SELECTION I

PART 4 SELECTION II

PART 6 INFRASTRUCTURE PROJECTS

Part 7 Implementation

Part 8 Review

Preface to the Ninth Edition

This book is now four decades old. Its longevity can be attributed to the growing number of academics and practitioners who have found it useful, relevant, and readable.

My effort has been to present the key principles and techniques for evaluating capital expenditure proposals that have been developed primarily by financial economists. The book explains the rationale behind these principles and suggests ways and means to improve project appraisal and capital budgeting in practice.

The book spans the entire gamut of capital budgeting, defined in its broadest sense. Beginning with project planning, it concludes with the review of projects undertaken. In this respect, it is wider in coverage than other books in the field.

Numerous examples have been included to illustrate the principles and techniques. Where necessary, two or more examples in the ascending order of complexity have been included. Apart from analytical methods, the book discusses strategic, qualitative, and organisational considerations which impinge on capital budgeting decisions. It also describes and evaluates business practices in various areas.

The book is primarily designed for two categories of readers — students and practitioners. Students of professional programmes (like MBA, CFA, ACA, and ACMA) and post graduate courses in Commerce, Finance, and Economics will benefit from this book. The book will also prove to be a valuable reference to corporate policy makers who formulate and shape corporate investment strategies; to consultants and others who prepare project feasibility studies; to executives who have a say in the selection of projects and development of the firm's capital budget; to officials of banks and financial institutions who evaluate projects as lenders and investors; and to managers who are concerned with implementing as well as reviewing projects.

The key guidelines relevant to project planning, analysis, selection, financing, implementation, and review discussed in this book are:

- Develop a strategy that leads to sustainable competitive advantage.
- Sharpen the ability of the firm to identify promising investment opportunities.
- Formulate the project, considering the interrelationships among various aspects.
- Forecast realistically the incremental cash flows attributable to the project.
- Establish a hurdle rate that is consistent with the risk exposure of the project.
- Calculate the net present value of the project and value the real options.
- Blend judgment with analytical reasoning.

- Choose a financing structure that lowers the cost of capital, preserves financial flexibility, and mitigates agency costs.
- Formulate the project adequately, assign specific responsibilities to project managers, and use network techniques for project planning and control.
- Conduct post-audit and periodically review project performance.

ORGANISATION OF THE BOOK

Organised in terms of the broad phases of capital budgeting, this book is divided into eight parts:

Part 1 *Planning*: Part 1 covers the planning phase of capital budgeting. Chapter 1 provides an overview of capital budgeting. Chapter 2 discusses the key concepts, models, and considerations that are helpful in articulating the capital allocation strategy of a firm. Chapter 3 looks at the ways and means of generating project ideas and screening them at a preliminary level.

Part 2 *Analysis*: Part 2 focuses on gathering and analysing basic information about the project. Chapter 4 discusses the key steps involved in market and demand analysis. Chapter 5 dwells on the various facets of technical analysis. Chapter 6 explains how financial estimates and projections relating to a project are developed.

Part 3 *Selection-I*: The content on the selection phase is very extensive. It has thus been split into two parts, Selection-I (Part 3) and Selection-II (Part 4). Part 3 consists of Chapters 7–11. Chapter 7 discusses the principles of compounding and discounting. Chapter 8 covers extensively the various investment appraisal criteria. Chapter 9 shows how project cash flows are defined. Chapter 10 explains the concept and measurement of cost of capital. Finally, Chapter 11 expounds the techniques for measuring and evaluating the stand-alone risk of a project.

Part 4 *Selection-II*: Concerned with more advanced techniques of selection or broader methodologies of evaluation, Part 4 consists of Chapters 12–17. Chapter 12 discusses how the project rate of return can be fine tuned. Chapter 13 looks at how capital budgeting decisions may be made in certain special situations. Chapter 14 presents the methodology of social cost benefit analysis. Chapter 15 shows how the capital budget may be drawn up in face of constraints, using the technique of mathematical programming. Chapter 16 explains the key insights provided by the option pricing theory and how the same may be employed for valuing the options embedded in capital projects. Chapter 17 explores the behavioural, strategic, and organisational issues relating to capital budgeting.

Part 5 *Financing*: Consisting of Chapters 18–19, Part 5 discusses how projects may be financed. Chapter 18 discusses various sources of finance used for setting up a project. Chapter 19 explains the concept and practice of venture capital and private equity.

Part 6 *Infrastructure Projects:* Consisting of Chapters 20 and 21, Part 6 focuses on infrastructure projects. Chapter 20 looks at the characteristics of infrastructure projects and the features of public private partnership. Chapter 21 discusses the evaluation and financing of infrastructure projects.

Part 7 *Implementation:* Part 7 includes two chapters which look at the implementation of the selected projects. Chapter 22 discusses various aspects of project management. Chapter 23 explains how network techniques (PERT, CPM and Network Cost System) may be employed for project planning, scheduling and control.

Part 8 *Review:* Part 8 discusses various issues involved in project review (Chapter 24). It also covers the administrative aspects of capital budgeting.

CHANGES IN THE NINTH EDITION

Encourage by the response to the previous edition, I revised and updated several chapters and appendixes.

To strengthen the book further, the following additions have been made:

- Given the growing importance of infrastructure projects, a new section titled *Infrastructure Projects* (Part 6) has been added.
- Nine new appendixes have been added: Appendix 2C—Five Principles of Capital Allocation; Appendix 2D—Personality Traits and Capital Management; Appendix 7B—Microsoft as a Financial Calculator; Appendix 7C—XNPV and XIRR; Appendix 10B—Cost of Capital in Practice; Appendix 12A—Getting More Out of Projects; Appendix 14A—Social Impact Analysis; Appendix 16A—Slow Adoption of Real Options; Appendix 21A—A Case Study of Indira Gandhi International Delhi Airport.

ANCILLARY MATERIAL

To enhance the utility of the book for students and instructors, the following ancillary materials are available on the companion website of the book. It can be accessed at **www.mhhe.com/chandra/projects9e**. The 'Student Edition' of the resources can be freely accessed and used; the 'Instructor Edition' can be provided on special request.

Spreadsheets Mr. Venugopal Unni developed Excel spreadsheets for all the major numerical exhibits in the book.

Solved Problems A number of solved problems have been prepared for various chapters of the book.

Additional Problems and Minicases To enable students to practice more, a number of additional problems and minicases have been prepared.

Solutions Manual, Powerpoint Presentations and Quizzes A solutions manual containing solutions to problems at the end of the chapters and cases, quizzes, and powerpoint presentations of all chapters are hosted on the website.

I look forward to receiving suggestions from the readers for further improving the content of this book.

Prasanna Chandra
chandra@cfm-india.com

Acknowledgements

I am indebted to my students and the participants of executive development programmes conducted by me for providing the stimulus for writing this book. They pointed to me the need for a comprehensive book, akin to a manual, on managing capital expenditures.

In writing this book I have drawn on materials from a variety of disciplines that have a bearing on different facets of project appraisal and capital budgeting. I owe a profound intellectual debt to numerous authors whose ideas and contributions have shaped my thinking on this subject.

I am extremely thankful to Venugopal Unni for thoroughly combing the book and adding useful material. I am grateful to Prof. G. Sabarinathan, Prof. Padmini Srinivasan, Prof. V. Nagadevara, Dr. T.V. Ramachandra, Suman Saha, Prof. Naganna, Prof. Y.L.R. Murthy, Prof. Pratap Subramanyam, Pradeep Lath and Dr. P.S.S. Murthy for their valuable contributions to this book. I am indebted to a number of practitioners who have generously shared their views with me and to Nikhil Wadhera, Shivkant Singhal, Sachin Kumar, Atul Gupta, and others of McGraw Hill Education for their interest in this book. I am thankful to Pushpa for her help in preparing the manuscript of this book. My deepest gratitude is to my wife, Padma, for her unstinted support.

At places I have drawn on my articles published in *Indian Management, Chartered Accountant, Management Accountant, Decision, Chartered Financial Analyst,* and *Lok Udyog*. I am grateful to the editors of these journals.

Prasanna Chandra
chandra@cfm-india.com

Planning

PART ONE

CHAPTER 1

Overview

CHAPTER 2

Strategy and Resource Allocation

CHAPTER 3

Generation and Screening of Project Ideas

Chapter 1 Overview

LEARNING OBJECTIVES

After studying this chapter you should be able to

- Appreciate the importance and difficulties associated with capital investments.
- Describe the broad phases of capital budgeting.
- Discuss the important facets of project analysis.
- Explain the rationale for maximising the value of the firm.
- Understand the common weaknesses in capital budgeting.

A mini steel plant is considering building a new arc furnace; an insurance company is planning to install a computer system for information processing; the Government of India is thinking of an ambitious plan to link the Ganges and Cauvery rivers; Gautam, a graduate student, is planning to buy a mobike. All these situations involve a capital expenditure decision. Essentially, each of them represents a scheme for investing resources which can be analysed and appraised reasonably independently. The basic characteristic of a capital expenditure (also referred to as a capital investment or capital project or just project) is that it typically involves a current outlay (or current and future outlays) of funds in the expectation of a stream of benefits extending far into the future.

This definition of a capital expenditure is not necessarily synonymous with how a capital expenditure is defined in accounting. A capital expenditure, from the accounting point of view, is an expenditure which is shown as an asset in the balance sheet. This asset, except in the case of a non-depreciable asset like land, is depreciated over its life. In accounting, the classification of an expenditure as a capital expenditure or a revenue expenditure is governed by certain conventions, by some provisions of law, and by the management's desire to enhance or depress reported profits. Often, outlays on research and development, major advertising campaigns, and reconditioning of plant and machinery may be treated as revenue expenditures for accounting purposes, even though they are expected to generate a stream of benefits in the future and, therefore, qualify for being capital expenditures.

This chapter provides a broad overview of the field of project appraisal and capital budgeting.

1.1 CAPITAL INVESTMENTS: IMPORTANCE AND DIFFICULTIES

Importance Capital expenditure decisions often represent the most important decisions taken by a firm. Their importance stems from three inter-related reasons:

- *Long-Term Effects* The consequences of capital expenditure decisions extend far into the future. The scope of current manufacturing activities of a firm is governed largely by capital expenditures made in the past. Likewise, current capital expenditure decisions provide the framework for future activities. Capital investment decisions have an enormous bearing on the basic character of a firm.
- *Irreversibility* The market for used capital equipment in general is ill-organised. Further, for some types of capital equipment, custom-made to meet specific requirements, the market may virtually be non-existent. Once such an equipment is acquired, reversal of decision may mean scrapping the capital equipment. Thus, a wrong capital investment decision often cannot be reversed without incurring a loss.
- *Substantial Outlays* Capital expenditures usually involve substantial outlays. An integrated steel plant, for example, involves an outlay of several thousand crore rupees. Capital costs tend to increase with advanced technology.

Difficulties While capital expenditure decisions are extremely important, they also pose difficulties which stem from three principal sources:

- *Measurement Problems* Identifying and measuring the costs and benefits of a capital expenditure proposal tend to be difficult. This is more so when a capital expenditure has a bearing on some other activities of the firm (like cutting into the sales of some existing product) or has some intangible consequences (like improving the morale of workers).
- *Uncertainty* A capital expenditure decision involves costs and benefits that extend far into the future. It is impossible to predict exactly what will happen in the future. Hence, there is usually a great deal of uncertainty characterising the costs and benefits of a capital expenditure decision.
- *Temporal Spread* The costs and benefits associated with a capital expenditure decision are often spread out over a long period of time, usually 10–20 years for industrial projects and 20–50 years for infrastructural projects. Such a temporal spread creates some problems in estimating discount rates and establishing equivalences.

1.2 TYPES OF CAPITAL INVESTMENTS

Capital investments may be classified in different ways. At the simplest level, capital investments may be classified as physical, monetary, or intangible. Physical assets are tangible investments like land, building, plant, machinery, vehicles, and computers. Monetary assets are financial claims against some parties. Deposits, bonds, and equity shares are examples of monetary assets. Intangible assets are not in the form of physical assets or financial claims. They represent outlays on research and development, training, market development, franchises, and so on that are expected to generate benefits over a period of time.

Capital investments may also be classified as strategic investments and tactical investments. A strategic investment is one that has a significant impact on the direction of the firm. Tata Motor's decision to invest in a passenger car project may be regarded as a strategic investment. A tactical investment is meant to implement a current strategy as efficiently or as profitably as possible. An investment by Tata Motors to replace an old machine to improve productivity represents a tactical investment.

Capital investments are often classified by companies in different categories for planning and control. While the system of classification may vary from one firm to another, the following categories are found in most classifications: mandatory investments, replacement investments, expansion investments, diversification investments, R&D investments, and miscellaneous investments. A mandatory investment is a capital expenditure required to comply with statutory requirements. Examples of such investments are a pollution control equipment, a fire fighting equipment, a medical dispensary, and a créche in the factory. A replacement investment is meant to replace worn out equipment with new equipment to reduce operating costs, increase the yield, and improve quality. An expansion investment is meant to increase the capacity to cater to a growing demand. A diversification investment is aimed at producing new products or services or entering into new geographical areas. R&D investments are meant to develop new products and processes which would sharpen the technological edge of the firm. Finally, miscellaneous investments represent a catch-all category that includes items like interior decoration, recreational facilities, and landscaped gardens.

1.3 PHASES OF CAPITAL BUDGETING

Capital budgeting is a complex process which may be divided into six broad phases: planning, analysis, selection, financing, implementation, and review. Exhibit 1.1 portrays the relationship among these phases. The solid arrows reflect the main sequence: planning precedes analysis; analysis precedes selection; and so on. The dashed arrows indicate that the phases of capital budgeting are not related in a simple, sequential manner. Instead, there are several feedback loops reflecting the iterative nature of the process.

Exhibit 1.1 ***Capital Budgeting Process***

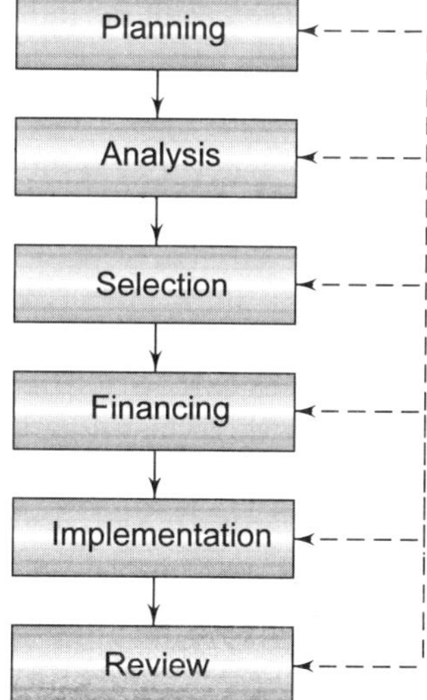

Planning The planning phase of a firm's capital budgeting process is concerned with the articulation of its broad investment strategy and the generation and preliminary screening of project proposals. The investment strategy of the firm delineates the broad areas or types of investments the firm plans to undertake. This provides the framework which shapes, guides, and circumscribes the identification of individual project opportunities.

Once a project proposal is identified, it needs to be examined. To begin with, a preliminary project analysis is done. A prelude to the full blown feasibility study, this exercise is meant to assess (i) whether the project is prima facie worthwhile to justify a feasibility study and (ii) what aspects of the project are critical to its viability and hence warrant an in-depth investigation.

Analysis If the preliminary screening suggests that the project is prima facie worthwhile, a detailed analysis of the marketing, technical, financial, economic, and ecological aspects is undertaken. The questions and issues raised in such a detailed analysis are described in a subsequent section. The focus of this phase of capital budgeting is on gathering, preparing, and summarising relevant information about various project proposals which are being considered for inclusion in the capital budget. Based on the information developed in this analysis, the stream of costs and benefits associated with the project can be defined.

Selection Selection follows, and often overlaps, analysis. It addresses the question—Is the project worthwhile? A wide range of appraisal criteria have been suggested to judge the worthwhileness of a project. They are divided into two broad categories, viz., non-discounting criteria and discounting criteria. The principal non-discounting criteria are the payback period and the accounting rate of return. The key discounting criteria are the net present value, the internal rate of return, and the benefit cost ratio. The selection rules associated with these criteria are as follows:

Criterion	*Accept*	*Reject*
Payback period (*PBP*)	*PBP* < target period	*PBP* > target period
Accounting rate of return (*ARR*)	*ARR* > target rate	*ARR* < target rate
Net present value (*NPV*)	$NPV > 0$	$NPV < 0$
Internal rate of return (*IRR*)	*IRR* > cost of capital	*IRR* < cost of capital
Benefit cost ratio (*BCR*)	$BCR > 1$	$BCR < 1$

To apply the various appraisal criteria, suitable cut-off values (hurdle rate, target rate, and cost of capital) have to be specified. These are essentially a function of the mix of financing and the level of project risk. While the former can be defined with relative ease, the latter truly tests the ability of the project evaluator. Indeed, despite a wide range of tools and techniques for risk analysis (sensitivity analysis, scenario analysis, simulation analysis, decision tree analysis, portfolio theory, capital asset pricing model, and so on), risk analysis remains the most intractable part of the project evaluation exercise.

Financing Once a project is selected, suitable financing arrangements have to be made. The two broad sources of finance for a project are equity and debt. Equity (referred to as shareholders' funds on balance sheets in India) consists of paid-up capital, share premium, and retained earnings. Debt (referred to as loan funds on balance sheets in India) consists of term loans, debentures, working capital advances and so on.

Flexibility, risk, income, control, and taxes (referred to by the acronym FRICT) are the key business considerations that influence the capital structure (debt-equity ratio) decision and the choice of specific instruments of financing.

Implementation The implementation phase for an industrial project, which involves setting up of manufacturing facilities, consists of several stages: (i) project and engineering designs, (ii) negotiations and contracting, (iii) construction, (iv) training, and (v) plant commissioning. What is done in these stages is briefly described below:

Stage	*Concerned with*
Project and engineering designs	Site probing and prospecting, preparation of blueprints, and plant designs, plant engineering, selection of specific machineries and equipments.
Negotiations and contracting	Negotiating and drawing up of legal contracts with respect to project financing, acquisition of technology, construction of building and civil works, provision of utilities, supply of machinery and equipment, marketing arrangements, etc.
Construction	Site preparation, construction of buildings and civil works, erection and installation of machinery and equipment.
Training	Training of engineers, technicians, and workers. (This can proceed simultaneously along with the construction work.)
Plant commissioning	Start up of the plant. (This is a brief but technically crucial stage in the project development cycle.)

Translating an investment proposal into a concrete project is a complex, time-consuming, and risk-fraught task. Delays in implementation, which are common, can lead to substantial cost overruns. For expeditious implementation at a reasonable cost, the following are helpful:

1. *Adequate Formulation of Projects* A major reason for the delay is inadequate formulation of projects. Put differently, if the necessary homework in terms of preliminary studies and comprehensive and detailed formulation of the project is not done, many surprises and shocks are likely to spring on the way. Hence, the need for adequate formulation of the project cannot be over-emphasised.
2. *Use of the Principle of Responsibility Accounting* Assigning specific responsibilities to project managers for completing the project within the defined time-frame and cost limits is helpful in expeditious execution and cost control.
3. *Use of Network Techniques* For project planning and control two basic techniques are available – PERT (Programme Evaluation Review Technique) and CPM (Critical Path Method). These techniques have, of late, merged and are being referred to by a common terminology, that is network techniques. With the help of these techniques, monitoring becomes easier.

Review Once the project is commissioned, the review phase has to be set in motion. Performance review should be done periodically to compare actual performance with projected performance. A feedback device, it is useful in several ways: (i) It throws light on how realistic were the assumptions underlying the project; (ii) It provides a documented log of experience that is highly valuable in future decision making; (iii) It suggests corrective action to be taken in the light of actual performance; (iv) It helps in uncovering judgmental biases; (v) It induces a desired caution among project sponsors.

1.4 LEVELS OF DECISION MAKING

In addition to looking at the various phases of capital budgeting, researchers have also examined different levels of decision making. Gordon, Miller, and Mintzberg, for example, defined three levels of decision making: operating, administrative, and strategic. The key characteristics of decisions at these levels are described below:

	Operating decisions	*Administrative decisions*	*Strategic decisions*
■ Where is the decision taken	Lower level management	Middle level management	Top level management
■ How structured is the decision	Routine	Semi-structured	Unstructured
■ What is the level of resource commitment	Minor resource commitment	Moderate resource commitment	Major resource commitment
■ What is the time horizon	Short-term	Medium-term	Long-term

The three levels (operating, administrative, and strategic) of decision making can be readily applied to capital budgeting decisions. Examples are given below:

Operating capital budgeting decision	:	Minor office equipment
Administrative capital budgeting decision	:	Balancing equipment
Strategic capital budgeting decision	:	Diversification project

While the methods and techniques covered in this book are applicable to all levels of capital budgeting decisions, our discussion will mainly be oriented towards administrative and strategic capital budgeting decisions.

1.5 FACETS OF PROJECT ANALYSIS

The important facets of project analysis are:

- Market analysis
- Technical analysis
- Financial analysis
- Economic analysis
- Ecological analysis

Market Analysis Market analysis is concerned primarily with two questions:

- What would be the aggregate demand for the proposed product/service in the future?
- What would be the market share of the project under appraisal?

To answer the above questions, the market analyst requires a wide variety of information and appropriate forecasting methods. The kinds of information required are:

- Consumption trends in the past and the present consumption level
- Past and present supply position
- Production possibilities and constraints
- Imports and exports
- Structure of competition
- Cost structure
- Elasticity of demand
- Consumer behaviour, intentions, motivations, attitudes, preferences, and requirements
- Distribution channels and marketing policies in use
- Administrative, technical, and legal constraints

Technical Analysis Analysis of the technical and engineering aspects of a project needs to be done continually when a project is formulated. Technical analysis seeks to determine whether the prerequisites for the successful commissioning of the project have been considered and reasonably good choices have been made with respect to location, size, process, etc. The important questions raised in technical analysis are:

- Whether the preliminary tests and studies have been done or provided for?
- Whether the availability of raw materials, power, and other inputs has been established?
- Whether the selected scale of operation is optimal?
- Whether the production process chosen is suitable?
- Whether the equipment and machines chosen are appropriate?
- Whether the auxiliary equipments and supplementary engineering works have been provided for?
- Whether provision has been made for the treatment of effluents?
- Whether the proposed layout of the site, buildings, and plant is sound?
- Whether work schedules have been realistically drawn up?
- Whether the technology proposed to be employed is appropriate from the social point of view?

Financial Analysis Financial analysis seeks to ascertain whether the proposed project will be financially viable in the sense of being able to meet the burden of servicing debt and whether the proposed project will satisfy the return expectations of those who provide the capital. The aspects which have to be looked into while conducting financial analysis are:

- Investment outlay and cost of project
- Means of financing
- Cost of capital
- Projected profitability
- Break-even point
- Cash flows of the project
- Investment worthwhileness judged in terms of various criteria of merit
- Projected financial position
- Level of risk

Economic Analysis Economic analysis, also referred to as social cost benefit analysis, is concerned with judging a project from the larger social point of view. In such an evaluation the focus is on the social costs and benefits of a project which may often be different from its monetary costs and benefits. The questions sought to be answered in social cost benefit analysis are:

- What are the direct economic benefits and costs of the project measured in terms of shadow (efficiency) prices and not in terms of market prices?
- What would be the impact of the project on the distribution of income in the society?
- What would be the impact of the project on the level of savings and investment in the society?
- What would be the contribution of the project towards the fulfillment of certain merit wants like self-sufficiency, employment, and social order?

Ecological Analysis In recent years, environmental concerns have assumed a great deal of significance — and rightly so. Ecological analysis should be done particularly for major projects which have significant ecological implications (like power plants and irrigation schemes) and environment-polluting industries (like bulk drugs, chemicals, and leather processing). The key questions raised in ecological analysis are:

- What is the likely damage caused by the project to the environment?
- What is the cost of restoration measures required to ensure that the damage to the environment is contained within acceptable limits?

Exhibit 1.2 summarises the key issues considered in different types of analysis:

Exhibit 1.2 ***Key Issues in Project Analysis***

Feasibility Study: A Schematic Diagram We have looked at the six broad phases of capital budgeting and examined the key facets of project analysis. The feasibility study is concerned with the first four phases of capital budgeting, viz., planning, analysis, selection (evaluation), and financing, and involves market, technical, financial, economic, and ecological analysis. The schematic diagram of the feasibility study is shown in Exhibit 1.3.

Exhibit 1.3 ***Feasibility Study: A Schematic Diagram***

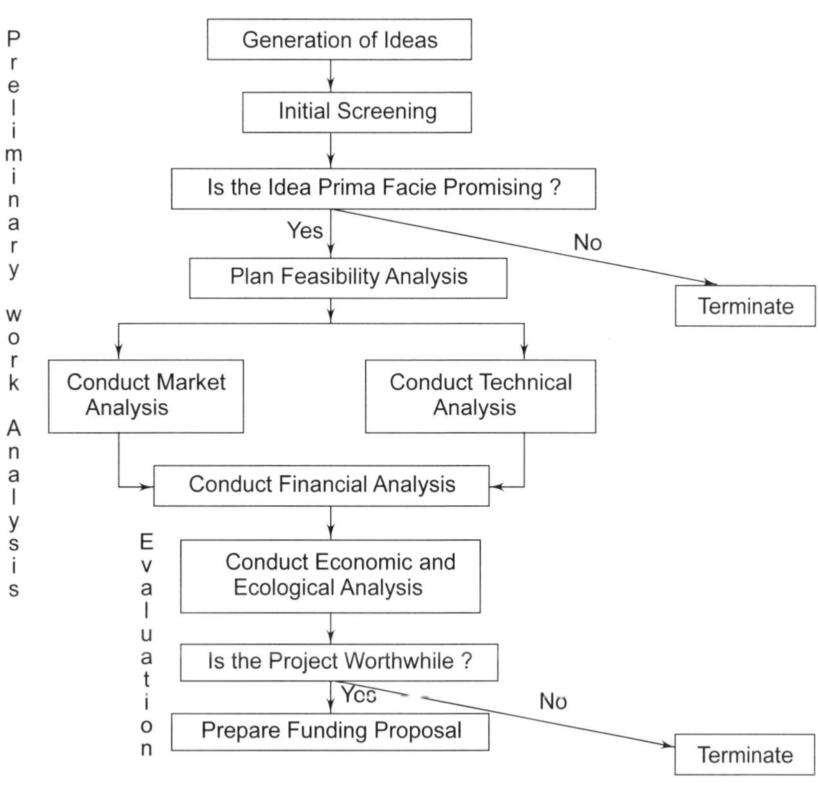

1.6 KEY ISSUES IN MAJOR INVESTMENT DECISIONS[1]

While making a major investment decision, the following key issues are examined.

Investment Story Before the firm commits to a project, the investment story must make sense to the management. This essentially means that the management must be convinced that the firm enjoys a comparative advantage vis-à-vis its competitors, in investing in the project. Remember that a positive NPV stems from a sustainable comparative advantage.

Risks Capital investments invariably are risky propositions. Hence the firm must carefully assess the risks associated with the project and its ability to handle the same.

DCF Value Discounted cash flow (DCF) criteria like net present value and internal rate of return are commonly employed to judge the financial attractiveness of projects.

[1] Sherid Titman, John D. Martin, and V. Ravi Anshuman, *Valuation*, Section 1.2, Pearson Education Inc., 2008.

Financing There may be different ways of financing a major investment project. The financing mix chosen should result in a low cost of capital and yet provide enough flexibility.

Impact on Short-term EPS Apart from looking at a discounted cash flow measure like net present value, managers are also concerned about the impact of the project on near-term EPS (earnings per share). Why? Investors and equity analysts consider EPS as a key indicator of a firm's performance. Equally, or even more important, the incentive compensation of managers is often linked to some measure of earnings like profit after tax or EPS.

Options The traditional DCF model does not fully capture the value of a capital project, as it does not reflect the value of options embedded in it. The important types of real options embedded in a capital project are the option to delay, the option to expand, the option to change the outputs or inputs of the project, and the option to contract or abandon the project. As these options give managers flexibility to amplify gains or to reduce losses, they are valuable.

1.7 OBJECTIVE OF CAPITAL BUDGETING

Finance theory rests on the premise that managers should manage their firm's resources with the objective of enhancing the firm's market value. This goal has been eloquently defended by distinguished finance scholars, economists, and practitioners. Here is a sampling of their views:

> "In a market-based economy which recognises the rights of private property, the only social responsibility of business is to create value and do so legally and with integrity. It is a profound error to view increases in a company's value as a concern just for its shareholders. Enlightened managers and public officials recognise that increases in stock prices reflect improvement in competitiveness—an issue which affects everyone who has a stake in the company or economy."[2]
>
> "Should a firm maximise the welfare of employees, or customers, or creditors? These are bogus questions. The real question is: What should a firm do to maximise its contribution to the society? The contribution to the society is maximised by maximising the value of the firm".[3]
>
> "The quest for value drives scarce resources to their most productive uses and their most efficient users. The more effectively resources are deployed, the more robust will be the economic growth and the rate of improvement in our standard of living. Adam Smith's 'invisible hand' is at work when investors' private gain is a public value."[4]

[2] Rappaport, Alfred, "Let's Let Business be Business", *New York Times*, February 4, 1990.

[3] Jensen, Michael, Economist, 1997.

[4] Stewart, Bennett, *The Quest for Value: A Guide to Senior Management*, New York: Harper & Row, 1991.

You may ask why are we overlooking the interests of customers, employees, and suppliers. No company can succeed unless it offers value for money to its customers, provides satisfactory employment conditions to its employees, and treats its suppliers fairly. Hence the question of neglecting the interests of these constituencies to promote the welfare of shareholders simply does not arise. More value for shareholders does not imply less value for customers, employees, or suppliers. On the contrary, only by focusing on creating value for its shareholders can a firm ensure that it has durable and mutually beneficial relationships with their customers, employees, and suppliers. As Jack Welch, arguably the most outstanding CEO of our times, said, "A proper balance between shareholders, employees, and communities is what we all try to achieve. But it is a tough balancing act because, in the end, if you don't satisfy shareholders, you don't have the flexibility to do the things you have to do to take care of employees or communities. In our society, whether we like it or not, we have to satisfy shareholders."

1.8 COMMON WEAKNESSES IN CAPITAL BUDGETING

A key factor that distinguishes value-creating firms from value-destroying firms is the quality of investment decisions, which, in turn, depends considerably on how sound is the capital budgeting system of the firm. Unfortunately, the quality of investment decisions is often impaired due to various deficiencies in capital budgeting. The common weaknesses found in capital budgeting systems in practice are discussed below.

Poor Alignment between Strategy and Capital Budgeting Most companies seem to draw up a vision statement and a strategy to accomplish their goals. However, the capital budgeting system may not be well integrated with the strategy. For example, the strategy of a company may be to grow aggressively through new product introductions. Yet, the erosion of revenues of old products caused by the introduction of new products is viewed seriously in capital budgeting practice.

Deficiencies in Analytical Techniques Companies often employ flawed techniques and procedures. The commonly observed deficiencies are:

The Base Case Is Poorly Identified For evaluating a project, the base case or the status quo scenario which reflects "what happens to the firm without the project" has to be specified. Obviously, the worse the base case, the more attractive the project looks. This may prompt project sponsors to portray a bleak base case scenario so that their pet proposals look attractive.

Risk Is Treated Inadequately Capital projects are characterised by various risks which are assessed somewhat naively. A common practice is to develop low, medium, and high risk scenarios to gauge the range of future outcomes. Such simplistic characterisations are usually not enough for informed decision making.

Options Are not Properly Evaluated When a firm undertakes a project it is likely to enjoy certain options in the future. It can expand its commitments; it can put the facilities to some other use; it can modify the scope of the project; it may truncate or even abandon the project prematurely. These options are often not properly assessed and captured in the capital budgeting analysis.

There Is Lack of Uniformity in Assumptions In many multidivisional companies, project proposals coming from different divisions tend to make varying assumptions about economy growth rate, inflation rate, residual value, capital cost, and so on. Top management has to wrestle with non-uniform assumptions while evaluating capital investment proposals.

Side Effects Are Ignored A project is likely to have important side effects. It may enhance the profitability of some of the existing activities of the firm because it has a complementary relationship with them; or, it may detract from the profitability of some of the existing activities of the firm because it has a competitive relationship with them. These side effects are often not fully considered properly during project evaluation.

No Linkage between Compensation and Financial Measures Companies often use discounted cash flow criteria like net present value (NPV) and internal rate of return (IRR) for project selection, but link compensation to accounting measures like profit or average rate of return. In such a situation, managers may salute discounted cash flow criteria but walk in the direction of accounting measures.

A possible reason for such a misalignment is that NPV is a stock measure and not a flow measure. Further, it is a summary measure reflecting projected cash flows and not actual performance. To overcome this problem, a flow measure like economic value added (EVA), which is linked to NPV, may be used instead of accounting measures like profit or average rate of return.

Reverse Financial Engineering Capital investment analysis is often afflicted by a subtle malaise in the form of reverse financial engineering. This involves twisting the figures and projections to fulfill certain criteria laid down by the firm.

Every project sponsor is keen to get his project included in the capital budget. So he is inclined to doctor the figures and dress up the proposal. For example, if the policy of the firm, stated or unstated, is to consider only those projects that have an IRR of more than 20 per cent or a payback period of less than five years, operating managers while submitting their project proposals will ensure that the financial estimates and projections are massaged to produce an IRR of more than 20 per cent or a payback period of less than 5 years. Thus, the quality of information used in capital budgeting is compromised.

Weak Integration between Capital Budgeting and Expense Budgeting Capital budgeting and expense budgeting are often done somewhat independently. For example, the projected profitability of a capital project may be based on the assumption that the firm would incur certain outlays on advertising and sales promotion. However, these outlays form part of the expense budget. Often, people approving the capital budget and the expense budget may not ensure consistency between the two. Even if the two budgets are developed in a mutually consistent manner, the pressure to perform in the short run may lead to a cutback in expense budgets. This may impair the performance of the capital budget and also induce skepticism about future capital investment proposals.

Inadequate Post-audits The post-audit of a project involves comparison of its actual performance vis-à-vis its planned performance. It is meant to document the sources of discrepancy, provide useful feedback, facilitate continual improvement, and induce healthy caution among project sponsors. However, in many companies, post-audit is not handled properly. It often ends up as a policing device, leading to skepticism and distrust.

SUMMARY

- Essentially a capital project represents a scheme for investing resources that can be analysed and appraised reasonably independently.
- The basic characteristic of a capital project is that it typically involves a current outlay (or current and future outlays) of funds in the expectation of a stream of benefits extending far into the future.
- Capital expenditure decisions often represent the most important decisions taken by a firm. Their importance stems from three inter-related reasons: long-term effects, irreversibility, and substantial outlays.
- While capital expenditure decisions are extremely important, they pose difficulties which stem from three principal sources: measurement problems, uncertainty, and temporal spread.
- Capital budgeting is a complex process which may be divided into six broad phases: planning, analysis, selection, financing, implementation, and review.
- One can look at capital budgeting decisions at three levels: operating, administrative, and strategic.
- The important facets of project analysis are: market analysis, technical analysis, financial analysis, economic analysis, and ecological analysis.
- While making a major investment decision, the following key issues are examined: investment story, risks, DCF value, financing, impact on short-term EPS, and options.
- Financial theory, in general, rests on the premise that the goal of financial management should be to maximise the present wealth of the firm's equity shareholders.
- The common weaknesses found in capital budgeting systems in practice are: poor alignment between strategy and capital budgeting; deficiencies in analytical techniques; no linkage between compensation and financial measures; reverse financial engineering; weak integration between capital budgeting and expense budgeting; inadequate post-audits.

QUESTIONS

1. Why are capital expenditures often the most important decisions taken by a firm?
2. Explain the difficulties faced in capital expenditure decisions.
3. Discuss the six broad phases of capital budgeting.
4. Define the levels of decision making. What are their key characteristics?
5. What are the key questions raised in market analysis?
6. What are the important questions raised in technical analysis?

7. What aspects are looked into while conducting financial analysis?
8. What questions are sought to be answered in economic and ecological analysis?
9. Present a schematic diagram of the feasibility study.
10. What key issues are examined while making a major investment decision?
11. What is the rationale for the goal of shareholder wealth maximisation?
12. Discuss the weaknesses found in capital budgeting systems in practice.

Chapter 2 Strategy and Resource Allocation

LEARNING OBJECTIVES

After studying this chapter you should be able to

- Show schematically how strategies are formulated.
- Describe different types of strategies.
- Explain how conglomerates can add value.
- Discuss various tools of portfolio planning.
- Show how the corporate centre can add value.
- Describe the various ways in which businesses compete.

If you look at any organisation today what you see is mainly the result of capital allocation decisions made in the past. Its strategic assets, tangible or intangible, are traceable to the investment decisions of yesteryears. Hence, it is scarcely surprising that the key responsibility of top management is concerned with capital allocation decisions. And this seems to be more so in large divisionalised companies (which are the norm currently) where a central concern of top management at the corporate head office is to allocate capital across strategic business units and manage the investment decision making activity in the entire group.

Capital is scarce and must be allocated across competing claims very judiciously. As Mike Kaufman says: "The selection of the investment projects and the allocation of corporate capital to them are among top management's primary responsibilities to shareholders. A good corporate investment program can mean sustained growth; failure to invest wisely can impede growth or threaten company survival."

Capital budgeting is not the exclusive domain of financial analysts and accountants. Rather, it is a multifunctional task linked to a firm's overall strategy. As Richard Bower has said in his perceptive work *Managing the Resource Allocation Process* that the set of problems firms refer to as capital budgeting is "a task for general management rather than financial specialists."

Capital budgeting may be viewed as a two-stage process. In the first stage promising growth opportunities are identified through the use of strategic planning techniques and in the second stage individual investment proposals are analysed and evaluated in detail to determine their worthwhileness.

This chapter discusses strategic planning techniques and approaches aimed at identifying promising growth opportunities.

Warren Buffett on Capital Allocation

... The heads of many companies are not skilled in capital allocation. Their inadequacy is not surprising. Most bosses rise to the top because they have excelled in an area such as marketing, production, engineering, administration — or, sometimes institutional politics.

... CEOs who recognize their lack of capital allocation skills (which not all do) will often try to compensate by turning to their staffs, management consultants or investment bankers. Charlie and I have frequently observed the consequences of such "help." On balance, we feel it is more likely to accentuate the capital allocation problem than to solve it.

... In the end, plenty of unintelligent capital allocation takes place in corporate America (that's why you hear so much about "restructuring").

2.1 CONCEPT OF STRATEGY

Alfred. D. Chandler, Jr, a Harvard professor, defined strategy as "the determination of the basic long-term goals and objectives of an enterprise, and the adoption of courses of action and the allocation of resources necessary for carrying out those goals."

Strategy involves matching a firm's capabilities with the opportunities present in the external environment. Exhibit 2.1 shows schematically how strategies are formulated based on a concept advanced by Kenneth R. Andrews.[1]

Apart from looking at the optimal fit between the capabilities of the firm and the opportunities in the environment, strategic planning also considers the following:

- The complementarities and synergies between the existing assets and growth opportunities (the cross-sectional relationships).
- The relationship between current growth opportunities and future growth opportunities (the time-series relationships).
- The impact of new investments on the overall riskiness of the firm (the risk profile of the firm).

[1] Andrews, Kenneth R., The Concept of Corporate Strategy, Homewood, Ill: Dow-Jones-Irwin, 1971.

Exhibit 2.1 ***Formulation of Strategies***

Environmental Analysis

Customers
Competitors
Suppliers
Regulation
Infrastructure
Social/political environment

Internal Analysis

Technical knowhow
Manufacturing capacity
Marketing and distribution capability
Logistics
Financial resources

Opportunities and Threats

Identify opportunities

Strengths and Weaknesses

Determine core capabilities

Find the fit between core capabilities and external opportunities

Firm's Strategies

Strategic planning, in essence, lays the framework that helps in identifying valuable investment opportunities — opportunities that have positive NPV.

2.2 GRAND STRATEGY

The thrust of the overall strategy or 'grand strategy' of the firm may be on growth, stability, or contraction as shown in Exhibit 2.2.

Growth Strategies

Generally, companies strive for growth in revenues, assets, and profits. The important growth strategies are concentration, vertical integration, and diversification.

Concentration When a company anticipates growth in the market size of its product range or an increase in the market share enjoyed by it in its product range, expansion of the capacity of the existing product range would have great appeal. Such an expansion offers several advantages: familiarity with the technology, production methods, and market conditions; lower capital costs due to the existence of surplus capacity in certain sections of the factory; reduction in unit overhead costs because of larger volume of production. These advantages, however, should be weighed against the possibility of market saturation and risk of excessive dependence on the existing product range.

Examples of companies which have aggressively pursued this strategy are McDonald's in fast food business, Michelin Tyres in tyres, Microsoft in computer software and related products, Asian Paints in paints, and Hero Motors in two wheelers.

Exhibit 2.2 ***The Thrust of Grand Strategy***

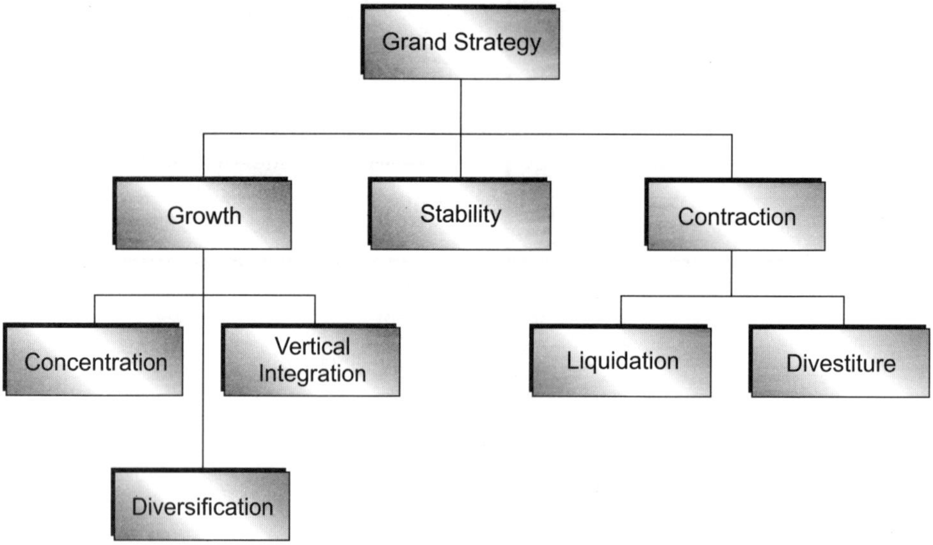

Vertical Integration Vertical integration may be of two types: backward integration and forward integration. Backward integration involves manufacture of raw materials and components required for the existing operations of the company. For example, Reliance Industries Limited set up a unit for the manufacture of polyester filament yarn required for its textile units. Forward integration involves the manufacture of products which use the existing products of the company as input. For example, Bharat Forge Company set up an automotive axles unit which uses its forgings as input. Vertical integration, backward or forward, provides greater stability to the existing as well as proposed operations, ensures better coordination between the supplying and consuming units, brings about savings in indirect taxes, and enhances the market power of the combined entity.

Internationally, most of the oil companies are vertically integrated. Companies like Exxon-Mobil and British Petroleum are engaged in oil exploration and production, refining, and marketing through their own outlets.

Diversification Diversification involves entering a new business that is different from the current businesses. There are two broad types of diversification: concentric diversification and conglomerate diversification.

Concentric diversification involves getting into a related business. For example, a detergent manufacturer may get into soap business (Nirma chemicals), a scooter manufacturer may enter the field of motor cycles (Bajaj Auto), and a truck manufacturer may go in for passenger cars (Tata Motors). Such diversification offers several advantages: (i) The company can leverage its core competencies and capabilities. (ii) Certain manufacturing facilities may be better utilised. (iii) All products may benefit from the market image of the company. (iv) A common distribution network may be employed.

Conglomerate diversification means that a firm gets into a new business which is unrelated to its existing business. For example, ITC Limited, traditionally a cigarette manufacturer, entered the field of hotels, Bharat Vijay Mills, a textile manufacturer, diversified into synthetic tanks, and Escorts, a tractor company, set up a dry dock. The principal motivations underlying conglomerate diversification are to: (i) overcome the limited growth opportunities in the existing line of business; (ii) enter newly emerging and promising sectors, and (iii) reduce the overall risk exposure of the firm.

Stability Strategy

While growth strategies are most commonly pursued, occasionally firms may pursue a stability strategy. A firm may follow a stability strategy if it is satisfied in serving the same product market segment and has no inclination to expand or diversify.

Small, privately owned businesses, which have established clientele and which prefer status quo, are likely to follow a stability strategy.

Contraction Strategies

Contraction is the opposite of growth. It may be effected through divestiture or liquidation.

Divestiture Divestiture involves sale of a business unit or plant of one firm to another. From the seller's perspective, it is a form of contraction; from the buyer's point of view, it is a form of expansion. For example, when Coromandal Fertilisers Limited sold its cement division to India Cement Limited, the size of Coromandal Fertilisers Limited contracted whereas the size of India Cements Limited expanded.

A divestiture may be prompted by a variety of motives. One motive for divestiture may be to raise capital. CEAT, for example, sold its nylon tyre cord to shore up its liquidity. Another motive may be to bring about a desired strategic realignment. ICI, for example, sold its fibre, fertilisers, and seeds division to focus on paints and industrial chemicals, in line with its parent's global strategy. Yet another motive may be to divest a unit earning a sub-normal rate of return.

Liquidation When a business is consistently under-performing and there is no hope of reviving or rehabilitating it within a reasonable period, liquidation may be the only option. When the business is "better dead than alive", steps must be taken to liquidate it expeditiously.

Motivations and Likely Outcomes

The principal motivations and likely impact of various strategies on profitability, growth, and risk are summarised in Exhibit 2.3.

Exhibit 2.3 ***Strategies, Principal Motivations, and Likely Outcomes***

Strategy	*Principal Motivations*	*Likely Outcomes*		
		Profitability	*Growth*	*Risk*
■ Concentration	- Ability to serve a growing market - Familiarity with technology and market - Cost leadership	High	Moderate	Moderate
■ Vertical integration	- Greater stability for existing and proposed operations - Greater market power	High	Moderate	Moderate
■ Concentric diversification	- Improved utilisation of resources	High	Moderate	Moderate
■ Conglomerate diversification	- Limited scope in the present business	Moderate	High	Low
■ Stability	- Satisfaction with status quo	High	Low	Low
■ Divestment	- Inadequate profit - Poor strategy	High	Low	Low

2.3 DIVERSIFICATION DEBATE

The main engines of corporate activity around the world are individual corporations that are organised as portfolios of business units. General Electric, Procter & Gamble, Merck, Berkshire Hathaway, Unilever, Sony Corporation, and Reliance Industries are some of the well-known portfolio companies. They owe their success to the dynamism of their portfolio units.

Notwithstanding the success of these portfolio companies, portfolio companies in general have had a patchy record and conglomerate diversification is considered to be a highly controversial investment strategy. This section examines various facets of conglomerate diversification.

Pros and Cons of Conglomerate Diversification

The proponents of conglomerate diversification argue that it helps a company in reducing its overall risk exposure. As most of the businesses are characterised by cyclicality it is desirable that there are at least two to three distinct lines of business in a firm's portfolio. As someone put it vividly: "If you have three legs to your firm, you enjoy a reasonable degree of stability." This is simply another way of saying that don't put all your eggs in the same basket. The risk-reduction benefit of conglomerate diversification is depicted pictorially in Exhibit 2.4. This exhibit shows the behaviour of ROI (return on investment, which is simply profit divided by investment) for (i) business A, (ii) business B (whose ROI is perfectly negatively correlated with that of business A), and (iii) a portfolio consisting of A and B with equal weightages for them.

Another advantage claimed for conglomerate diversification is that it expands opportunities for growth. If the opportunities in the existing business are limited because of some kind of saturation, it is natural to look at other businesses where growth opportunities exist. Typically, such opportunities are more in newly emerging industries and hence there may be a justification to diversify into these fields which may be very different from the firm's existing businesses. While the prospects of succeeding in the new line of business are often uncertain, the immense potential acts as an irresistible bait. It naturally allures firms which have strong growth-orientation. Such firms continually look for opportunities to 'widen their options' in a dynamic industrial environment.

Exhibit 2.4 ***Diversification and Risk Reduction***

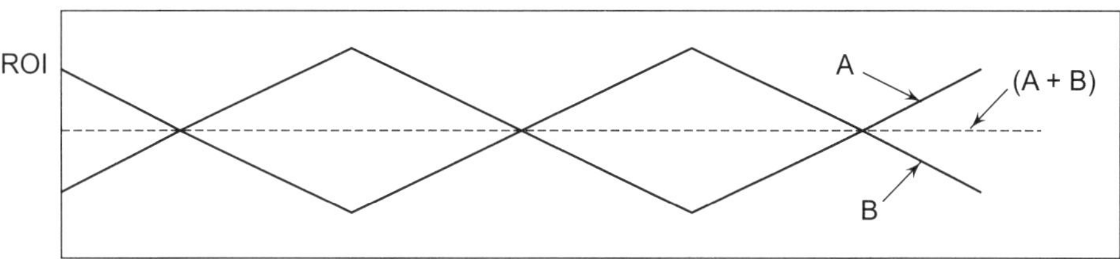

Though a good device for reducing risk exposure and widening growth possibilities, conglomerate diversification more often than not tends to dampen average profitability. Michael Gort[2] who conducted a study for the National Bureau of Economic Research in the US found that unrelated diversification is not positively correlated with profitability. In their classic work, Peters and Waterman[3] argued that organisations which stick very close to their original business outperform others and organisations which diversify into unrelated areas tend to underperform others. Echoing a similar view, Richard Rumelt in a widely quoted research study[4] reached the following conclusion: "Companies which branch out somewhat yet stick very close to their central skill, outperform all others."

• International Experience in Conglomerate Diversification

In 1960s and 1970s, the wave of diversification swept the industrial world in the western countries. During this period the proportion of Fortune 500 companies which were diversified or outright conglomerates increased from 50 percent to 80 percent. Likewise, in the US, this proportion went up from 40 percent to 60 percent. The factors which seemed responsible for this swing in favour of diversification were:

- A desire to add second and third legs to one's company to overcome cyclical fluctuations.

---

[2] Gort, Michael, *Diversification and Integration in American Industry*, Princeton, New Jersey: Princeton University Press, 1962.

[3] Peters, Thomas J. and Robert H. Waterman, Jr., *In Search of Excellence: Lessons from America's Best-run Companies*, New York: Harper and Row, 1982.

[4] Rumelt, R.P., Strategy, *Structure and Economic Performance*, Boston: Harvard Business School, 1974.

- The argument of the Boston Consulting group that no company was safe unless it had a portfolio consisting of at least three different kinds of businesses.
- An inexorable desire of many companies to gradually get out of certain industries and move into newer ones.
- Existence of role models like Harold Geneen who presided over a gigantic corporate conglomerate.
- Influence of Theodore Levitt's doctrine that a company should redefine its business in a broad sense.

Back to Basics What happened in 1980s? The experience of most of the companies which pursued the strategy of diversification in the 1960s and 1970s was that while they succeeded in related (or allied) diversification, they failed in unrelated (or conglomerate) diversification. Guided by this experience, many companies, particularly from the beginning of 1980s, began shedding their once-coveted activities. Thirty three large US companies sold off by the middle of 1980s, more than one-half of their diversifications (via the takeover route) made between 1950 and 1980. Many companies seem to be pursuing the strategy of going "back to basics" Here are some examples:

- United Biscuits dropped its fast food restaurants to concentrate on biscuits and food products.
- British Petroleum sold its world coal interests to concentrate on oil.
- Exxon divested Zilog, the last remnant of its decade long abortive attempt to expand in electronics.

Revival of Diversification Interestingly, from 1990s onward corporates, the world over, have begun to adopt the strategy of diversification. As Goold and Luchs observed in a 1993 article that appeared in *Academy of Management Executives*: "In the 1990s, the corporations have once again taken an interest in using diversification to grow. But unlike the unrelated diversification that took place in the 1960s, the trend in the 1990s is to diversify into related businesses or at least into businesses in which the strengths of a particular management team fits the need of the new business being added to the corporations."

Why Conglomerates Can Add Value in Emerging Markets

In western economies, corporate strategists have argued from the 1980s that the days of conglomerate companies are over and have preached the virtues of core competence and focus. Many conglomerates created in the 1960s and 1970s have been dismantled and restructured. By and large these initiatives have significantly enhanced corporate performance.

Management consultants and foreign investors have been persuading diversified business groups in emerging markets to imitate the practice of western companies, reduce the scope of their activities, and focus on a few core businesses. Many Indian business groups have begun restructuring their business portfolio in conformity with this advice.

Tarun Khanna and Krishna Palepu[5], however, believe that while focus makes eminent sense in the west, conglomerates may have certain advantages in emerging markets which are characterised by many institutional shortcomings.

What are the institutional weaknesses in emerging markets? How can conglomeration help in overcoming these shortcomings? The following discussion addresses these issues:

Product Markets Buyers and sellers in the emerging markets suffer from informational handicaps because of the following reasons: (a) The infrastructure for communication (postal services and telecommunication services) is often underdeveloped. (b) There are no reliable mechanisms in the form of independent consumer research outfits and governmental agencies to verify the claims of sellers. (c) Consumers do not have satisfactory redressal mechanisms when a product fails on its promises.

Due to lack of information, companies have to incur substantial costs for establishing credible brands. In such an environment, a conglomerate with a good track record has a natural advantage. As Tarun Khanna and Krishna Palepu argue: "A conglomerate with a reputation for quality products and services can use its group name to enter new businesses, even if those businesses are completely unrelated to its current lines." The cost incurred by a group to build a brand can be spread across multiple lines of businesses. Of course, the group will have strong incentive not to spoil its brand quality in any business as it can negatively impact on other businesses.

Capital Markets Capital markets in developing countries are underdeveloped in several ways: (a) Venture capital mechanisms are weak and inadequate (b) The regulatory apparatus is deficient. (c) The quality of financial reporting is poor. (d) The community of investment analyst is small and not so well trained. (e) Financial press is often not very objective and professional.

In such an environment where investors may be reluctant to provide capital to new ventures, diversified groups with a good track record have an advantage as they can inspire confidence in investors. They enjoy superior ability to raise capital and this gives them a great edge over smaller companies.

Labour Markets The major deficiencies characterising the labour markets in developing countries are: (a) There is often a shortage of well trained people. (b) Rigid laws prevent companies from retrenching manpower.

A conglomerate group can overcome problems by instituting training programmes to develop human capital, by shifting manpower from declining ventures to growing businesses, and by allocating scarce talent to units where it can be used optimally.

Regulation Despite liberalisation initiatives in recent years, governmental regulation over business activity is fairly extensive in developing countries. Often regulatory provisions give considerable discretion to bureaucrats.

A diversified conglomerate seems to have an advantage in coping with such a regulatory environment. Its experience and connections give it an advantage. The larger the conglomerate, the easier it is to maintain government relationship.

[5] Khanna, Tarun and Krishna Palepu "Why Focused Strategies may be Wrong for Emerging Markets," *Harvard Business Review*, July-August 1997.

Contract Enforcement Developing countries often lack effective contract enforcement mechanisms. Judicial processes are inordinately slow and may be vitiated or capricious. As a consequence, companies may not be able to resolve disputes satisfactorily through the normal legal channel.

In such an environment conglomerates who have built a reputation have an edge. As Khanna and Palepu argue: "In such situations, conglomerates can leverage reputations established.... Because the misdeeds of one company in a group will damage the prospects of the others, all the groups companies have credibility when they promise to honour their agreements with any single partner."

Conglomerate Diversification in the Indian Context

In India, the appropriate question to ask is 'How diversified is a business house?' and not 'How diversified is a particular company of a business house? For example, the business house of Tata is extremely diversified with presence in steel, information technology, automobiles, power, hospitality, tea, watches, telecommunications, salt, and so on. However, individual companies in the business house of Tata are fairly focused. For example, Tata Steel is focused on steel, TCS on information technology, Tata Power on power, and so on.

Diversification and Value Creation

Firms operate in markets for inputs such as capital, products, services, and other resources. The markets in which these goods and services are traded are subject to failure as it may not be always possible for firms to buy what they need at prices at which vendors are ready to sell them.

According to economists and management scholars, firms resort to different types of diversification to cope with different kinds of market failure. More specifically, unrelated diversification is a response to the failure of **capital markets**; vertical integration is a means to deal with the failure of **product or information markets**; related diversification is a response to the failure of **resource markets**; and strategic diversification is a way of coping with the failure of **risk markets**.

Unrelated Diversification Agency costs arise because managers, who have privileged access to inside information, may misrepresent the facts about investment possibilities to advance their personal gains. Aware of this, investors will require a higher rate of return than what they would earn if they were assured of managerial truthfulness. As a consequence, the cost of capital goes up and worthwhile projects (positive NPV projects) languish for want of funds. This represents a failure of the capital markets.

In his insightful book *Markets and Hierarchies*, Oliver Williamson argues that the corporate office can monitor divisional management better than external investors. Corporate office can easily obtain privileged information, monitor closely divisional managers, and take corrective action expeditiously. Put differently, the corporate structure can potentially improve governance. Thus, companies like General Electric and Berkshire Hathaway have succeeded in unrelated diversification because of *governance economies*.

Vertical Integration Around the turn of twentieth century, many U.S. firms were compelled to diversify by way of vertical integration because there were no outside suppliers of critical products and services. Put differently, 'missing markets' prodded vertical integration.

The gradual emergence of markets for products and services led to vertical de-integration in some cases. Nevertheless, vertical integration persists in many sectors. (For example, major oil companies are engaged in exploration and production, refining, and distribution) Why? There are two reasons: opportunism and unspecifiability. If an input supplier or an output buyer resorts to opportunistic behaviour, it makes sense to become vertically integrated.

When it is not possible to specify precisely the parameters of a contract for supply of products and services because the technology is immature, it pays to be vertically integrated. Vertical integration facilitates better coordination. Put differently, it captures *coordination economies.*

Related Diversification There are three general categories of resources in an organisation: physical resources (land, buildings, plants, equipments, raw materials, and so on), intangible assets (patents, copyrights, trademarks, brand name recognition, business designs, and so on), and human resources (manual workers, clerical staff, managerial personnel, and so on).

When a firm assembles the complement of resources required to do business, it is likely to find that some of its resources are under-employed. For example, the research and development capabilities of the organisation may exceed its manufacturing capacity or the manufacturing capacity may exceed the marketing and distribution capability. The imbalance occurs because resources often come in fairly discrete units and hence are not infinitely divisible.

If the research and development capability exceeds the firm's manufacturing capacity, the firm may resort to related diversification to fully exploit its research and capability in a certain domain. As Michael E Raynor put it: "Diversification motivated by the desire to exhaust fully the productive opportunities available to all of a firm's resources is likely to spiral outward from the 'epicentre' of the firm's original complement of resources." Such diversification is typically related diversification.

Thus, related diversification helps a firm overcome a failure in the *resource* markets (remember that resources come in fairly discrete units and are not infinitely divisible). Since related diversification involves broadening the scope of a firm's activities, it captures *scope economies.*

Strategic Diversification Strategic diversification involves creating real options that enable a firm to pursue new strategic opportunities. Microsoft's sustained success over a long period may be attributed mainly to its ability to manage a portfolio of real options to deal with strategic uncertainty.

Creating a portfolio of real options has a cost associated with it as some of the options will expire worthless. Still, it seems worthwhile. As Michael E. Raynor put it: "To the extent that the firm balances the cost of real options with their risk-mitigating and opportunity-enhancing value, shareholders will enjoy a higher risk-adjusted return than firms that do not engage in strategic diversification."

Thus, strategic diversification compensates for a failure in the risk market and generates *option economies.*

To sum up, diversification, in different forms, can help in creating value by addressing different kinds of market failure as shown below:

Market Failure	*Form of Diversification*	*Source of Value Addition*
Capital markets	Unrelated diversification	Governance economies
Product markets	Vertical integration	Coordination economies
Resource markets	Related diversification	Scope economies
Risk markets	Strategic diversification	Option economies

Diversification — A Mixed Bag

Growth through diversification, related diversification in particular, can create value for shareholders, thanks to the following factors:

- **Managerial Economies of Scale** Porter, Rappaport, and others believe that diversification can utilise managerial talent more effectively.
- **Higher Debt Capacity** Lewellen argues that because of the coinsurance effect, a diversified company has a higher debt capacity than a focused company.
- **Lower Tax Burden** Majd and Myers argue that by combining businesses that have imperfectly correlated cash flows, a diversified firm can avail of tax shelters better.
- **Larger Internal Capital** In a diversified company, cash-producing businesses provide funds to cash-consuming businesses. Thanks to its internal capital market, a diversified company is less dependent on the external capital market. This reduces its cost of capital.

Of course, diversification is not an unmixed blessing. It can lead to erosion of shareholder value on account of the following:

- **Unprofitable Investment** Michael Jensen has argued persuasively that the ready availability of surplus cash generated by some businesses may tempt managers to invest in unprofitable (negative NPV) projects.

• Compulsions for Conglomerate Diversification in India

Over the last two and half decades or so, a large number of business houses in India have invested substantially in areas different from their traditional lines of business. The factors responsible for large scale moves in unrelated areas appear to be as follows:

- Restriction in growth in the existing line of business, often arising from governmental refusal to expansion proposals.
- Vulnerability to changes in governmental policies with respect to imports, duties, pricing, and reservations.

- Opening up of newer areas of investments in the wake of liberalisation.
- Cyclicality of the main line of business leading to wide fluctuations in sales and profits from year to year.
- Bandwagon mentality which has been induced by years of close regulation of industrial activity.
- Desire to avail of tax incentives mainly in the form of investment allowance and large initial depreciation write-offs.
- A self-image of venturesomeness and versatility prodding companies to prove themselves in newer fields.
- A need to widen future options by entering newly emerging industries where the potential seems enormous.

How to Reduce the Risks in Diversification?

Diversification, like other major business decisions, involves uncertainty. To reduce the risk of diversification, it has to be approached systematically and rationally. Markides[6] argues that the risk of diversification can be mitigated if managers ask the following questions:

What Can Our Company Do Better than any of Our Competitors in Our Current Markets? Diversification is often based on a vague definition of business rather than on a systematic evaluation of what distinguishes a company from its competitors. By identifying what it excels at, a company can improve the prospects of its success in new markets. The diversification decision has to be made on the basis of strategic assets like excellent distribution capabilities, or superior technical know-how, or talented and motivated manpower.

What Strategic Assets Do We Need in Order to Succeed in the New Market? If a company excels in one market it does not mean that its success is assured in a new and related market. Managers evaluating a diversification proposal must ascertain whether their company has all the strategic assets required to gain a competitive advantage in the new market. Often companies assume that having some of the necessary strategic assets is enough to pursue diversification. But success often calls for having all of them.

Can We Catch up to or Leapfrog Competitors at their Own Game? A company need not despair if it lacks some critical strategic asset. It can perhaps buy what it lacks, or develop it, or even render it redundant by altering the rules of competition. As an example, Markides cites the history of Sharp Corporation. To diversify into the field of television, Sharp licensed the television technology from RCA; to enter the business of microwave, Sharp acquired the technology by working with Litton; to manufacture the electronic calculator, Sharp bought the technology from Rockwell.

Will Diversification Break up Strategic Assets that Need to be Kept Together? Often companies employ their proven strategic assets in a new market and yet flounder. This generally happens because strategic assets that need to reinforce each other for producing results are separated.

---

[6] Markides, Constantinos C., "To Diversify or not to Diversify", *Harvard Business Review*, November-December, 1997.

Will We be Simply a Player in the New Market or will We Emerge a Winner? Competitors are likely to out-manoeuver a diversifying company. They may imitate, or purchase, or even render unnecessary strategic assets on which the diversifying company may be betting heavily. As Markides says: "A company's competitive advantage will be short lived, and diversification will fail, if competitors in the new industry can imitate the company's move quickly and cheaply, purchase the necessary strategic assets in the open market, or find an effective substitute for them."

What Can Our Company Learn by Diversifying, and Are we Sufficiently Organised to Learn it? Smart companies derive valuable lessons from their diversification initiatives. They use new businesses to improve existing businesses, to serve as launching pads for other business forays, and to enhance organisational efficiency.

Guidelines for Conglomerate Diversification Conglomerate diversification, in general, dampens profitability and in some cases jeopardises the existence of the firm as it happened in the case of Metal Box. Yet there are many compulsions and inducements in India prompting companies to pursue the path of conglomerate diversification. Since it involves a journey into a relatively unfamiliar terrain it should be viewed with circumspection. Here are some practical guidelines in this respect:

1. If you lack financial sinews to sustain the new project during the 'learning period', avoid grandiose diversification projects.
2. Realistically examine whether you have the critical skills and resources to succeed in the new line of business.
3. Ensure that the diversification project has a good fit in terms of technology and market with the existing business.
4. Try to be the first or a very early entrant in the field you are diversifying into. This will protect you from serious competitive threat in the initial years.
5. Where possible, adopt the following sequence — substantial sub-contracting — full blown manufacturing.
6. Seek partnership of other firms in areas where you are vulnerable or competitively weak.
7. If the failure of the new project can threaten the company's existence, float a separate company to handle the new project.
8. Remember that meaningful conglomerate diversification represents the greatest challenge to corporate vision and leadership.
9. Guard against bandwagon mentality and empire-building tendencies.

Emerging Scenario in India Historically most business groups in India diversified into a number of sectors, thanks to various inducements, compulsions, and temptations. The heightening competition from the mid-1990s has forced many business houses to review and restructure their business portfolios. Given the benefits of diversification in an emerging market, the existence of shallow markets, and the obstacles in the way of selling and purchasing companies, it is unlikely that Indian firms will fully embrace the 'focus' model which has gained currency in the western world from the early 1980s onward. Barring exceptions like Bajaj Auto, Asian Paints, and Sun Pharmaceuticals, most of the other companies will perhaps shed peripheral businesses, and focus on a few areas. Put differently, moderate diversification may become more common. Incidentally, Neil Harper and Patrick Vigueri support this stance in the following words: "While a tendency toward focus usually leads to superior performance, we've found that the ongoing processes of moderate diversification — ensuring an appropriate balance among growth potential, current performance, and the intensity of management focus — can help deliver significant additional growth and superior shareholder value." This is also reflected in the following views:

Harsh Goenka: "My view is that we are all moving towards moderate focus: that is, a sizeable presence in four to six sectors. Not a vast array, but not just one or two."

B.K. Modi: "One cannot achieve any kind of global size in a single product or sector; our markets are not big enough. You also run the risk of being swamped by global competition in a single sector."

Conglomerates can Misallocate Capital

An often-cited reason for conglomerate diversification is that the cash surpluses generated by mature businesses can be deployed effectively to support growing businesses. However, conglomerates can destroy value if managers use the flexibility in transferring resources to subsidise loss-making businesses. Robert D. Kennedy, former chairman of Union Carbide, a company that made a number of conglomerate acquisitions, stated this point as follows: "All that stuff about balancing the cash generators and the cash users sounded great on paper. But it never worked: When corporate management gets into the business of allocating resources between businesses crying for cash, it makes mistakes."

2.4 PORTFOLIO STRATEGY

In a multi-business firm, allocation of resources across various businesses is a key strategic decision. Portfolio planning tools have been developed to guide the process of strategic planning and resource allocation. Three such tools are the BCG matrix, the General Electric's stoplight matrix, and the McKinsey matrix.

• BCG Matrix

Developed by Boston Consulting Group, the BCG matrix classifies the various businesses in a firm's portfolio on the basis of relative market share and relative market-growth rate. As shown in Exhibit 2.5, the BCG matrix consists of four cells with market share on the horizontal axis and market growth rate on the vertical axis.

Exhibit 2.5 ***BCG Matrix***

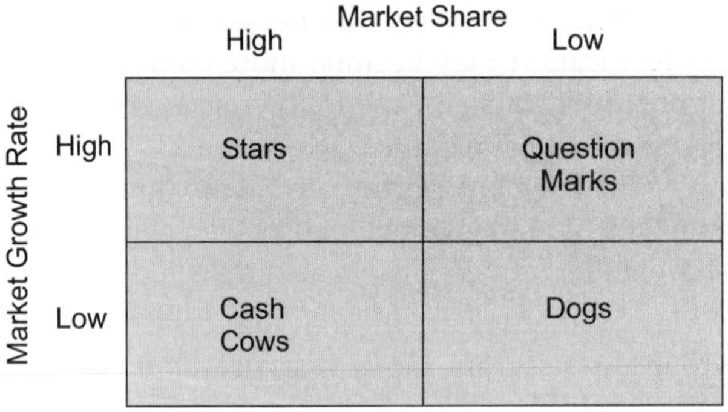

Market Growth Rate	Market Share: High	Market Share: Low
High	Stars	Question Marks
Low	Cash Cows	Dogs

The BCG matrix classifies businesses in four categories as described below:

- *Stars* Businesses which enjoy a high market share and a high growth rate are referred to as stars. Though they earn high profits, they require additional commitment of funds because of the need to make further investments for expanding their production and sales. Eventually, as growth declines and additional investment needs diminish, stars become cash cows.
- *Question marks* Businesses with high growth potential but low present market share are called question marks. Additional resources are required to improve their market share and potentially convert them into stars. Of course, there is no guarantee that this would happen — that is why they are called 'question marks'.
- *Cash cows* Businesses which enjoy a relatively high market share but low growth potential are called cash cows. They generate substantial profits and cash flows but their investment requirements are modest. The cash surpluses provided by them are available for use elsewhere in the business.
- *Dogs* Businesses with low market share and limited growth potential are referred to as dogs. Since the prospects for such products are bleak, it is advisable to phase them out rather than continue with them.

From the above description, it is broadly clear that cash cows generate funds and dogs, if divested, release funds. On the other hand, stars and question marks require further commitment of funds. Hence, the suggested pattern of capital allocation should be as shown in Part A of Exhibit 2.6. Conscious efforts should be made to avoid the pattern of capital allocation depicted in Part B of Exhibit 2.6. Some firms unwittingly adopt this pattern which leads to the neglect of stars and question marks and misdirection of surplus funds generated by cash cows into futile efforts to revive dogs.

General Electric's Stoplight Matrix

The General Electric Company is highly admired for the sophistication, maturity, and quality of its planning system. It uses a 3×3 matrix called the General Electric's Stoplight

Matrix to guide the allocation of resources. This matrix calls for evaluating the businesses of a firm in terms of two key issues:

- *Business strength* How strong is the firm vis-à-vis its competitors?
- *Industry attractiveness* What is the attractiveness or potential of the industry?

The commitment of resources to various businesses is guided by how they are rated in terms of the above two dimensions. As shown in Exhibit 2.7, businesses which are favourably placed justify substantial commitment of funds; businesses which are unfavourably placed call for divestment; and businesses which are placed in between qualify for modest investment.

Exhibit 2.6 ***Pattern of Capital Allocation***

Part A

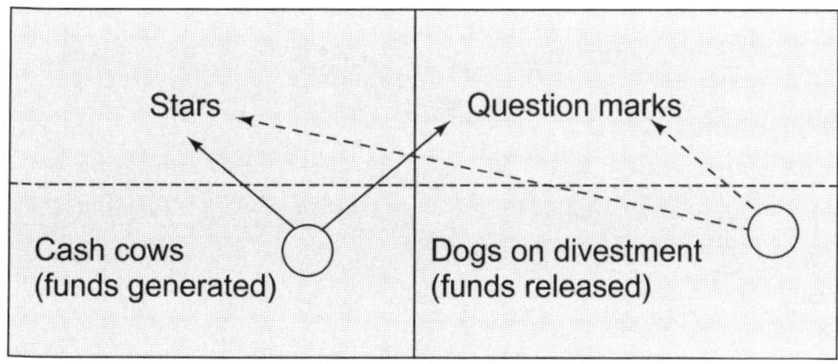

Part B

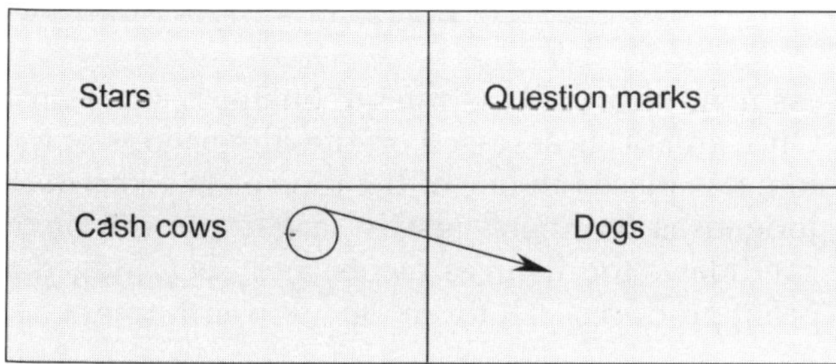

• McKinsey Matrix

Very similar to the General Electric Matrix, the McKinsey matrix has two dimensions viz., competitive position and industry attractiveness. The criteria or factors used for judging industry attractiveness and competitive position along with suggested weights for them are shown below:

Industry Attractiveness		*Competitive Position*	
Criteria	*Weight*	*Key Success Factors*	*Weight*
Industry size	0.10	Market share	0.15
Industry growth	0.30	Technological knowhow	0.25

Industry profitability	0.20	Product quality	0.15
Capital intensity	0.05	After-sales service	0.20
Technological stability	0.10	Price competitiveness	0.05
Competitive intensity	0.20	Low operating costs	0.10
Cyclicality	0.05	Productivity	0.10

Exhibit 2.7 ***General Electric's Stoplight Matrix***

Industry Attractiveness \ Business Strength	Strong	Average	Weak
High	Invest	Invest	Hold
Medium	Invest	Hold	Divest
Low	Hold	Divest	Divest

An illustrative assessment of an SBU (strategic business unit) on these dimensions is shown in Exhibit 2.8. Once an SBU is assessed on the dimensions of industry attractiveness and competitive position, it is placed in one of the nine cells given in the 3x3 matrix shown in Exhibit 2.9. SBUs judged as 'winners' justify larger commitment of resources, SBUs judged as 'losers' are candidates for disinvestments, and SBUs judged as 'question mark' or 'average business' or 'profit producer' call for moderate commitment of resources.

Exhibit 2.8 ***Assessment of the SBU Factory Automation***

	Industry Attractiveness		
Criteria	*Weight*	*Rating*	*Weighted Score*
Industry size	0.10	4	0.40
Industry growth	0.30	4	1.20
Industry profitability	0.20	3	0.60
Capital intensity	0.05	2	0.10
Technological stability	0.10	1	0.10
Competitive intensity	0.20	3	0.60
Cyclicality	0.05	2	0.10
			3.10

(Contd.)

	Competitive Position		
Key Success Factors	*Weight*	*Rating*	*Weight Score*
Market share	0.15	4	0.60
Technological know how	0.25	5	1.25
Product quality	0.15	4	0.60
After-sales service	0.20	3	0.60
Price competitiveness	0.05	4	0.20
Low operating costs	0.10	4	0.40
Productivity	0.10	5	0.50
			4.15

Exhibit 2.9 ***The McKinsey Matrix***

Competitive Position

Industry Attractiveness	Good	Medium	Poor
High	Winner	Winner	Question Mark
Medium	Winner	Average Business	Loser
Low	Profit Producer	Loser	Loser

Evaluation Though widely used, portfolio planning models, like the BCG matrix, tend to over-simplify the analysis of alternatives. For example, issues become more complex if the matrix is expanded to cover the possibilities of moderate market share and moderate potential market growth rate. Likewise, if factors other than profit returns and investment requirements are considered, greater complications arise. Notwithstanding these limitations, the basic idea of classifying products in terms of market share and potential market growth rate is very powerful. It helps the management in asking the right questions and examining relevant strategies.

• Parenting Advantage

The classic approach to business portfolio management, as exemplified by the BCG matrix or the McKinsey matrix, focuses on the overall attractiveness of the industry and the business's competitive position within the industry. While the classic approach is inherently sound, it suffers from a limitation. It ignores the synergies between different businesses in the firm's portfolio and assumes that the firm is the right owner for all its businesses.

Since different skills are required for managing different businesses, it is necessary to go beyond business positioning and consider whether there is a good fit between the parent and the business unit.

McKinsey and Company recommends a more sophisticated approach to business portfolio management that considers parenting advantage along with the business unit's inherent value creation potential. Their approach is illustrated in Exhibit 2.10.

Exhibit 2.10 ***Market-Activated Corporate Strategy (MACS) Framework***

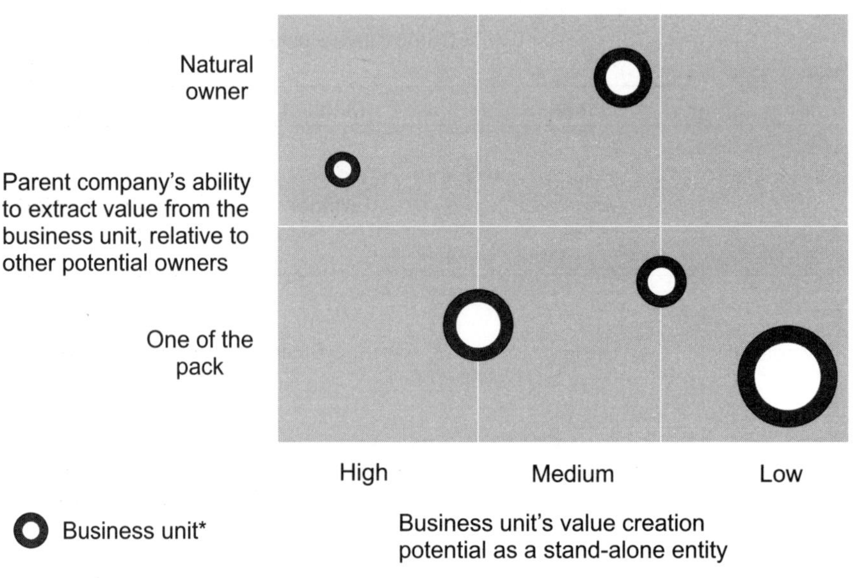

Source: McKinsey and Company

* A business unit's radius can be proportional to its sales, invested capital, or value added, relative to other business units.

The horizontal axis of this approach reflects the business unit's potential to create value as a stand-alone enterprise. This captures both the dimensions of the classical approach viz., the overall attractiveness of the industry and the business's competitive position in the industry. The vertical axis reflects the ability of the parent company to extract value from the business unit.

A natural parent, compared to other possible owners, can extract more value. Parenting advantage stems from certain core competencies. Most companies have a few core competencies (such as project management, cost management, product development, manufacturing excellence, brand management, performance management, human resources management, and so on). A core competency represents a world class skill or process that gives the company an edge over competitors, creates value, and is durable.

• Portfolio Configuration

Identifying the appropriate configuration of business portfolio is perhaps the most important task of top management. It calls for an insightful assessment of the logic of relatedness among various businesses in the portfolio.

How the Corporate Centre Can Add Value*

According to Tom Copeland, Tim Koller, and Jack Murrin, the corporate centre in a multibusiness company or group can add value in the following ways:

Industry Shaper It acts proactively to shape an emerging industry to its advantage.

Deal Maker It spots and executes deals based on its superior insights.

Scarce Asset Allocator It allocates capital and other resources efficiently across different businesses.

Skill Replicator It facilitates the lateral transfer of distinctive resources.

Performance Manager It instills a high performance ethic with appropriate measurement systems and incentive structures.

Talent Agency It attracts, retains, and develops talent.

Growth Asset Allocator It leads innovation in multiple businesses.

*Adapted from Tom Copeland, Tim Koller, and Jack Murrin, *Valuation: Measuring and Managing the Value of Companies*, New York: John Wiley and Sons, 2000.

According to C.K. Prahalad[7] and Yves Doz there are different ways of thinking about relatedness as discussed below:

1. *Business Selection* An important cornerstone of General Electric's strategy has been to choose only those businesses in which the company has a leading position. This logic was vividly encapsulated in Jack Welch's "1 or 2 or out" formula.
   Business selection can also be founded on the principle of industry consolidation. In highly fragmented industries characterised by low investment in technology, mediocre general management skills, and an inability to capture the economies of scale, industry consolidation may be the way out. It has been used in industries such as cement, retailing, telecom, entertainment, and airlines. ABB's strategy of consolidation in the electrical power business and Mittal Steel Corporation strategy of consolidation in the steel business are good examples of this approach.
2. *Parenting Similarities* Value may be created from a diverse corporate portfolio when businesses share common strategic and managerial characteristics. For example, Hanson Trust manages diverse businesses such as coal, brick making, chemicals,

[7] Adapted from C.K. Prahalad and Y. Doz, "The CEO: A Visible Hand in Wealth Creation?" *Journal of Applied Corporate Finance*, Fall 2000.

and jaccuzis that appear prima facie unrelated. Yet, Hanson's managers believe that their businesses share the following characteristics that require similar management skills, (a) basic businesses providing essential products (and not high-tech, people intensive businesses), (b) good operating management, (c) stable rate of change, (d) satisfactory asset backing, and (e) strong and predictable cash flows.

3. *Core Competencies* Cargill has a highly diversified portfolio consisting of seeds, salt, commodity trading, meat processing, fertilizer, ministeel mills, financial services, orange juice, and animal feeds. Outsiders may view this portfolio as "unrelated." Yet the firm's top management thinks differently, as Cargil'ls CEO Whitney MacMillan reported:
"Experience in the handling of bulk commodities, knowledge of trading, processing expertise, international understanding, risk management; these are the attributes of Cargill that underpin all our businesses. These core competencies represent the collective learning and judgment of our 125 years of experience in all our businesses."
As C.K. Prahalad and Y. Doz put it: "The concept of relatedness at Cargill is based not on product-market configuration or technology similarities, but on shared competencies and knowledge."
4. *Interbusiness Linkages* In some portfolios interbusiness linkages are a source of value. For example, General Electric uses its financial service business to support the deals of its operating businesses. Procter & Gamble manages to get better terms with retailers like Wal-Mart by negotiating collectively on behalf of its various stand-alone businesses. As C.K. Prahalad and Y. Doz put it: "Thus, P & G and G E have to manage their businesses differently from Hanson, which deliberately sacrificed any benefits from coordination in order to emphasize accountability for performance."
5. *Complex Strategic Integration* According to C.K. Prahalad and Y. Doz "Competencies that transcend individual businesses in the portfolio not only create the basis of value creation by enabling the discovery of valuable new interlinkages, they also help identify new business opportunities that draw on competencies from multiple units and reconfigure them in creative ways." They cite the example of Hewlett-Packard with its thrust on creating businesses at the intersection of Measurement, Computing, and Communications, its so-called MC^2 strategy.

Enhancing the Effectiveness of Portfolio Management

Corporate portfolio management is mainly concerned with deciding which businesses to own and which businesses to divest. A central issue in capital allocation, corporate portfolio management perhaps has the greatest impact on value creation.

Despite its significance, many companies do not manage their business portfolios optimally. It appears that there are three major barriers to effective portfolio management: measurement and information problems, behavioural factors, and corporate governance and incentive problems.

Measurement and Information Problems In theory a firm should exit a business when the expected rate of return from continuing the business is less than the cost of capital.

However, implementing this rule is difficult in practice because of measurement and information problems. The returns that are expected from a business change dynamically over time. Assuming that the growth pattern of a business is an "S" curve, the growth is slow in the first stage, explosive in the second stage, slow in the third stage, and possibly slightly negative in the fourth stage. The slope at any point of the S curve may be regarded as a proxy for the expected return from that point on. The practical problem, of course, is that it is very difficult to establish that you are at an inflection point.

Behavioural Factors Implementation of effective portfolio management practices is hindered by behavioural factors such as "sunk cost thinking," "loss aversion," "endowment effect," and "status quo bias." Sunk costs are not relevant for decision making. Yet people often do not overlook sunk costs. Behavioural economists Kahneman and Tversky have documented the phenomenon called "loss aversion." According to them the utility of gaining a rupee is much less than the utility of avoiding the loss of a rupee. Hence, people are reluctant to divest assets at prices less than what they deem to be worth. There is empirical evidence in support of "endowment effect," which is a tendency on the part of people to place greater value on what belongs to them relative to the value they would place on the same thing if it belonged to someone else. Finally, there is a "status quo bias" which means that people are comfortable with the familiar and would like to keep things the way they have been.

Corporate Governance and Incentives Most corporate boards and senior managements understand the logic of shareholder value maximisation. Yet they may commit to objectives that come in the way of maximising shareholder value.

Firms interested in enhancing the effectiveness of portfolio management will find the following suggestions helpful.

1. **Create a team of independent people for portfolio review** Most companies foster cultures and build incentive systems to reward successful growth, but often have an institutional bias against selling businesses at the right time.
   To counter this bias, it may be necessary to set up a team of people who are independent of the existing corporate units and are inclined to shake things up, if required.
2. **Improve the quality of information** While companies keep track of revenues and margins of their business segments (such as operating divisions, product lines, or brand names), they often have sketchy information about cash flows, capital employed, and return on capital of various business segments.
   By improving the quality of information on business segments, companies can enhance effectiveness of their portfolio management.
3. **Develop processes for thinking about alternatives** Generally companies that are good at portfolio management have a well-developed process for evaluating alternative ways of deploying capital. Steve Munger describes this process vividly: "I like to describe this process by comparing it to what happens during an eye examination. It's tough to describe to you the level of clarity of a given letter on a screen in isolation; but when you see one letter alongside another, it's much easier to identify comparative levels." He continues "And the same is true when looking at different strategies and capital projects, particularly when comparing levels of risk and uncertainty."

4. **Look outside the company** Effective corporate portfolio managers look outside their own company to see what their competitors, current and potential, are doing and anticipate the likely changes in the regulatory landscape. As Steve Munger puts it: "People who spend less time at corporate headquarters and more time on the road tend to be more alert to the kind of changes that might suggest an inflection point change that may not be visible inside the business."

Capital Allocation: Indian Business Houses vs PE Firms

Thanks to liberalisation initiatives, many new sectors such as telecommunications, airlines, airports, roads, and so on have been opened to the private sector. So, business houses such as the Tatas, Reliance, and the Aditya Birla Group have to deal with greater complexity in capital allocation.

In some ways, there is a similarity between Indian business houses and private equity (PE) firms. Both have to manage a portfolio of diverse businesses. Representatives of Indian business houses, however, argue that their approach is different from that of PE firms.

They claim to have an indefinitely long horizon, unlike their PE counterparts who have time horizons of 3 to 7 years. As Kishor Chaukar, managing director of Tata Industries, an investment vehicle for the Tata Group, puts it: "We do not start companies with the intention of exiting or selling out. While we do have targets for rate of return, they are normal business returns such as through dividends and not exit returns."

The most common model in India is for a leading group company to promote new ventures and eventually spin them off as listed companies. Reliance Industries Limited, for example, has promoted the telecommunications business, the retail business, the Haryana SEZ. The telecommunications business has been spun off and listed separately (Reliance Communications Limited). A similar thing may happen to the retail business and the SEZ business.

Thanks to their new found riches, promoters of Indian business houses have started investing in mega projects in their personal capacity. Mukesh Ambani, along with his associates such as Anand Jain promoted the famous SEZ near Mumbai. Likewise, Kumar Mangalam Birla has invested in his personal capacity in the retail business called More. Such forays can lead to potential conflict of interests between shareholders (of existing publicly listed companies) and promoters.

2.5 BUSINESS LEVEL STRATEGIES

Diversified firms don't compete at the corporate level. Rather, a business unit of one firm competes with a business unit of another.

Among the various models that can be used as frameworks for developing a business level strategy, the Porter's generic model is perhaps the most popular. According to Michael

Porter, there are three generic strategies that can be adopted at the business unit level: cost leadership, differentiation, and focus. Another strategy that has gained recognition in recent years is the network effect strategy.

• Cost Leadership

A business unit may seek to achieve a position of cost leadership as its principal weapon of competition. Cost leadership may be gained by exploiting economies of scale, improving capacity utilisation, exercising tight control across the entire value chain, enhancing the productivity of R&D and marketing outlays, deriving advantage from cumulative learning, and simplifying the product/service design.

Does cost leadership mean sacrifice of quality? Usually, not. The typical motto of a cost leader is to "offer a product of acceptable quality at a low cost."

Firms that have successfully followed this strategy include Hero Motors in motorcycles, Reliance Industries in petrochemicals, Walmart in discount retailing, Mittal Steel in steel, and Dell Computers in computers.

Strategy of Cost Leadership: Dell Computer Corporation

In the highly competitive personal computer industry, Dell Computers achieved a very respectable market share and high profitability by effectively pursuing the strategy of cost leadership. The key elements of Dell's strategy are as follows:

Direct selling Dell sells most of its computers directly to its customers, thereby saving the retailer's margin.

Built-to-order manufacturing Dell sells machines which are built to order. It relies on an efficient and flexible supply chain of component makers and just-in-time assemblers. This enables it to avoid locking funds in working capital and reduce inventory obsolescence costs which can be substantial in the rapidly changing computer industry.

Low-cost service Dell uses the following low-cost approaches to after sales service: (a) telephone-based service offered by its technical support representatives who use a comprehensive electronic maintenance system and (b) third-party service for on-site maintenance.

Negative working capital Dell carries minimal inventories because of its built-to-order manufacturing and Dell has low receivables as it encourages customers to pay by credit card at the time of purchase or immediately thereafter through electronic payment. Its low investment in inventories and receivables along with the credit that it gets from its suppliers means that Dell has a negative working capital.

Thanks to the above strategy, Dell achieved a significant cost edge over its competitors. This enabled it to expand market share, grow rapidly, and achieve high profitability.

• Differentiation

A differentiation strategy involves offering a product or service that is perceived by customers as distinctive or unique so that they are expected to pay a higher price. To succeed in this strategy the firm must identify some attributes of a product or service that customers really value, position itself to serve the customer need in a unique manner, and offer the differentiated product or service profitably.

Differentiation may be achieved through product quality, product range, bundled services, brand image, delivery convenience, and reputation. Differentiation strategies call for investments in R&D, engineering capabilities, and marketing skills. Firms that pursue differentiation strategies build organisational structures and control systems that nurture creativity and innovation.

While a differentiated offering may be very pricey in some cases, it is not always so. Many firms that pursue this strategy seek to "offer a superior product or service at an affordable price."

Firms that have pursued the differentiation strategy include Intel in microchips, Maytag in electrical appliances, Coca-Cola in beverages, Rolex in wrist-watches, and Raymond in textiles.

• Focus

A strategy of focus involves concentrating on a narrow line of products or a limited market segment. In the selected target market the company seeks to gain a competitive edge through cost leadership (cost focus) or product differentiation (differentiation focus).

Cost Focus A firm which pursues this strategy, concentrates on a narrow line of products or limited market segment. Within this domain, it achieves cost leadership through sustained efforts. McDonalds, for example, pursues a strategy of cost focus by offering limited menus to achieve economies of scale.

Differentiation Focus A strategy of differentiation focus involves concentrating on a limited market segment wherein the firm can offer a differentiated product based on its innovative capabilities. Porsche, for example, specialises in sports car, a market segment in which it competes with the likes of General Motors and Nissan. As a focused differentiator, it relies on its ability to innovate faster than a large differentiator.

Exhibit 2.11 shows the various generic competitive strategies suggested by Michael Porter in his classic work *Competitive Strategy*.[8]

---

[8] Porter, Michael, *Competitive Strategy*, New York; Free Press, 1980.

Exhibit 2.11 ***Porter's Generic Competitive Strategies***

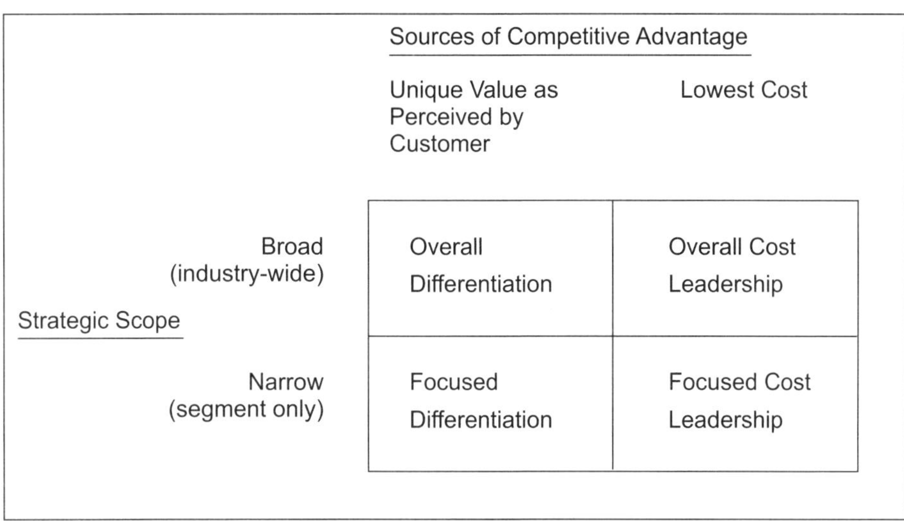

Source: Porter, op.cit.

Network Effect Strategy

Telephones, first introduced in the US in late 19th century, were not very useful initially. A person could just talk to few others who had a telephone. But as more and more homes and offices joined the telephone network, the utility of telephones increased. This phenomenon is referred to as the network effect: the value of a product or service increases as more and more people use it.

Success with the network strategy depends on the ability of a company to lead the charge and establish a dominant position. When a company does so, there is very little space available for others. That is why the network effect strategy is also called the winner-take-all strategy. For example, eBay dominates the online auction industry. Buyers flock to eBay as it has the most sellers, and sellers list their items as it has the most buyers. This virtuous circle established eBay as the dominant online auction site. Likewise, Microsoft enjoys a dominant position with its Window operating system. As Richard Luecke put it: "Thus, since most PCs operated with Windows, most new software was developed for Windows machines. And because most software was Windows-based, more people bought PCs equipped with the Windows operating system. To date no one has broken this virtuous circle."

Achieving and Sustaining Competitive Advantage

A firm does not achieve and sustain competitive advantage by merely choosing a competitive strategy. It has to make necessary commitments to develop the required core competencies and structure its value chain efficiently. Core competencies are the key economic assets or resources of the firm and value chain is the linked set of activities performed to transform inputs into outputs. As Palepu et. al put it: "The uniqueness of a firm's core competencies and its value chain and the extent to which it is difficult for competitors to imitate them determines the sustainability of a firm's competitive advantage."

2.6 STRATEGIC PLANNING AND CAPITAL BUDGETING

Capital expenditures, particularly the major ones, are supposed to subserve the strategy of the firm. Hence, the relationship between strategic planning and capital budgeting must be properly recognised. Exhibit 2.12 presents a way of defining this relationship. As emphasised in this exhibit, capital budgeting should be squarely related to corporate strategy.

Exhibit 2.12 ***Strategic Planning and Capital Budgeting***

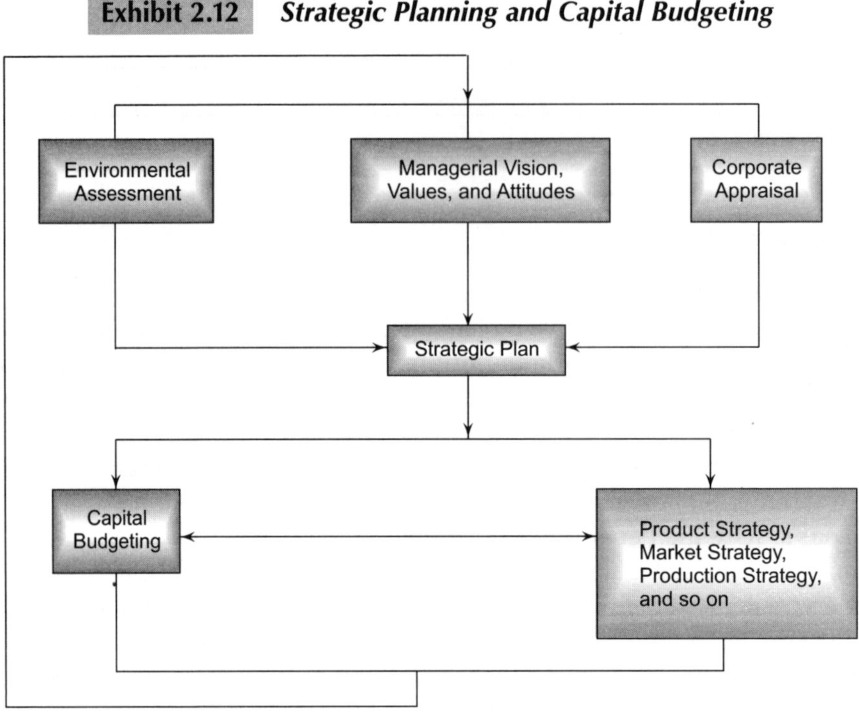

SUMMARY

- Capital budgeting is not the exclusive domain of financial analysts and accountants. Rather, it is a multifunctional task linked to a firm's overall strategy.
- Capital budgeting may be viewed as a two-stage process. In the first stage promising growth opportunities are identified through the use of strategic planning techniques

and in the second stage individual investment proposals are analysed and evaluated in detail to determine their worthwhileness.

- Strategy involves matching a firm's capabilities to the opportunities in the external environment.
- The thrust of the overall strategy or 'grand strategy' of the firm may be on growth, stability, or contraction.
- Generally, companies strive for growth in revenues, assets, and profits. The important growth strategies are concentration, vertical integration, and diversification.
- While growth strategies are most commonly pursued, occasionally firms may pursue a stability strategy.
- Contraction is the opposite of growth. It may be effected through divestiture or liquidation.
- Conglomerate diversification, or diversification into unrelated areas, is a very popular but highly controversial investment strategy. Although a good device for reducing risk exposure and widening growth possibilities, conglomerate diversification more often than not tends to dampen average profitability.
- In Western economies, corporate strategists have argued from the 1980s that the days of conglomerates are over and have preached the virtues of core competence and focus. Many conglomerates created in the 1960s and 1970s have been dismantled and restructured. Tarun Khanna and Krishna Palepu, however, believe that while focus makes eminent sense in the west, conglomerates may have certain advantages in emerging markets which are characterised by many institutional shortcomings.
- In a multi-business firm, allocation of resources across various businesses is a key strategic decision. Portfolio planning tools have been developed to guide the process of strategic planning and resource allocation. Three such tools are the BCG matrix, the General Electric's stoplight matrix, and the McKinsey matrix.
- Diversified firms don't compete at the corporate level. Rather, a business unit of one firm competes with a business unit of another. Among the various models that can be used as frameworks for developing a business level strategy, the Porter's generic model is perhaps the most popular. According to Michael Porter, there are three generic strategies that can be adopted at the business unit level: cost leadership, differentiation, and focus.
- Capital expenditures, particularly the major ones, are supposed to subserve the strategy of the firm. Hence, the relationship between strategic planning and capital budgeting must be properly recognised.

QUESTIONS

1. Show schematically how strategies are formulated based on a concept advanced by Kenneth R. Andrews.
2. Discuss various strategies for growth, stability, and contraction.

3. What are the principal motivations and likely impact of various strategies on profitability, growth, and risk?
4. What are the pros and cons of conglomerate diversification?
5. What has been the international experience in conglomerate diversification?
6. How can conglomeration help in overcoming the institutional weaknesses in emerging markets?
7. Discuss how diversification, in different forms, can help in creating value by addressing different kinds of market failure.
8. How can the risks of diversification be reduced?
9. What guidelines should be borne in mind while pursuing the path of conglomerate diversification?
10. Explain the tools of portfolio planning: BCG matrix, General Electric's stoplight matrix, and Mckinsey matrix.
11. What are the ways in which the corporate centre can add value in a multibusiness company or group? What are the barriers to effective portfolio management?
12. Discuss the following generic strategies that can be adopted at the business unit level: cost leadership, differentiation, focus, and network effect strategy.
13. Define the link between strategic planning and capital budgeting.

APPENDIX 2A

STRATEGIC POSITION AND ACTION EVALUATION (SPACE)

SPACE is an approach to hammer out an appropriate strategic posture for a firm and its individual businesses. An extension of the two-dimensional portfolio analysis, SPACE involves a consideration of four dimensions:

- Company's competitive advantage
- Company's financial strength
- Industry strength
- Environmental stability

The basic strategic postures associated with the SPACE approach are as follows:

Aggressive Posture This is appropriate for a company which (i) enjoys a competitive advantage and considerable financial strength and (ii) belongs to an attractive industry that operates in a relatively stable environment. An aggressive posture means that the firm must fully exploit opportunities available to it, seriously look for acquisition possibilities in its own or related industries, concentrate resources to maintain its competitive edge, and enhance its market share. The aggressive posture is similar to the generic strategy of *overall cost leadership* suggested by Michael Porter.

Competitive Posture This is suitable for a company which (i) enjoys a competitive advantage but has limited financial strength, and (ii) belongs to an attractive industry operating in a relatively unstable environment. The key planks of the competitive posture are as follows: maintain and enhance competitive advantage by product improvement and differentiation, widen the product line, improve marketing effectiveness, and augment financial resources. There is a great deal of commonality between the competitive posture described here and the generic strategy of *product differentiation* suggested by Michael Porter.

Conservative Posture This is appropriate for a company which (i) enjoys financial strength but has limited competitive advantage, and (ii) belongs to a not-so-attractive industry operating in a relatively stable environment. A conservative posture calls for the following actions: prune non-performing products, reduce costs, improve productivity, develop new products, and access more profitable markets. The conservative posture described here is somewhat similar to the generic strategy of focus suggested by Michael Porter.

Defensive Posture This is suitable for a company which (i) lacks competitive advantage as well as financial strength, and (ii) belongs to a not-so-attractive industry operating in an unstable environment. A defensive posture involves the following actions: discontinue unviable products, control costs aggressively, monitor cash flows strictly, reduce capacity, and postpone or limit investments. The defensive posture so defined may be likened to gamesmanship which calls for employing manoeuvres to keep the company afloat, check the onslaught of competition, and eventually facilitate withdrawal or exit.

The generic strategies and the key options associated with them are shown below. This is drawn from the book *Strategic Management — A Methodological Approach* by A.J. Rowe, R.O. Mason, and K.E.Dickel (Reading, Massachusetts, Addison-Wesley Publishing Company, 1986).

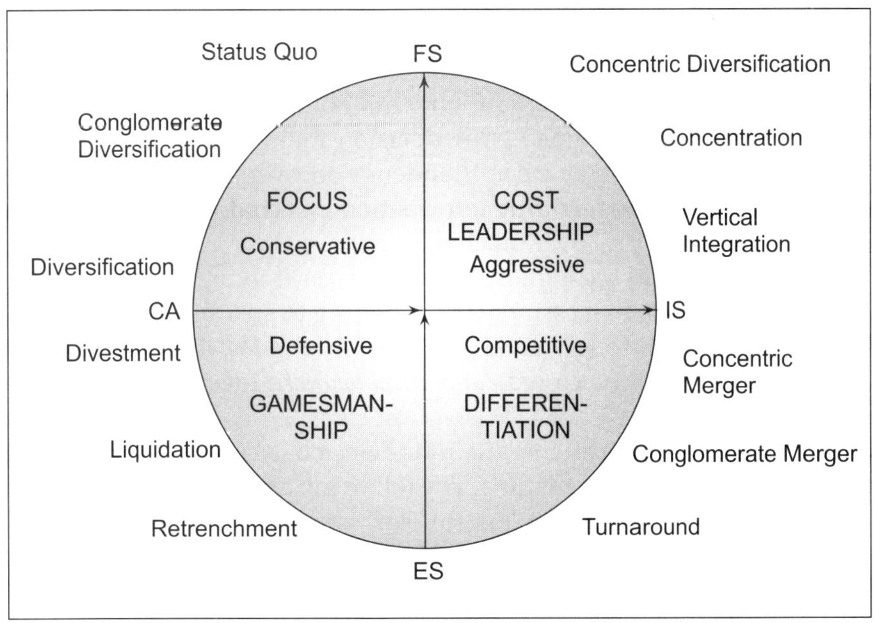

APPENDIX 2B
CASE FOR BEHAVIORAL STRATEGY

Once regarded as heretical, behavioral economics is now gaining acceptance, particularly in the fields of finance and marketing. However, not many corporate strategists consciously consider cognitive biases. This may be because in fields such as finance and marketing, insights of behavioral economics can be used to exploit the biases of others. But in strategic decision-making leaders need to understand their own biases and that seems difficult.

This does not, however, mean that executives think their strategic decisions are perfect. A *McKinsey Quarterly* survey of 2,207 executives found that only 28 percent regarded the quality of strategic decisions in their companies as generally good, 60 percent said that bad decisions were about as frequent as good ones, and the balance 12 percent said good decisions were altogether infrequent. In many candid conversations, senior executives admit unease with the quality of strategic decisions. No wonder, mergers routinely fail to produce the expected synergies, strategic plans often overlook competitive responses, and large investment projects typically exceed their time and cost budget.

An important business decision such as a large acquisition, a major capital expenditure, a new product launch, or a key technological choice typically entails the following. It involves some fact-gathering and analysis; it relies on the insights and judgement of a number of persons (sometimes the number can be as small as one); it is arrived at after a process-ranging from highly informal to very formal – that converts the data and judgment into a decision. Since the process can be contaminated by various cognitive biases, a conscious effort has to be made to mitigate the effects of such biases.

The human brain is a wondrous organ, but it is not a rational calculating machine as neoclassical economists have assumed. Our decision making is affected by a number of biases. The major ones are: *overconfidence* (tendency to overestimate the accuracy of our forecasts), *confirmation bias* (overweighting information that confirms our opinions), *illusion of control* (exaggerating one's control over outcomes), *representativeness bias* (forming judgments on the basis of stereotypes and analogues), *availability bias* (relying overly on easily available information), *anchoring* (linking assessment of something to an arbitrary reference point), *loss aversion* (feeling much more strongly about the pain from a loss than the pleasure from an equal gain), *herding* (following the crowd), and *affect heuristic* (deciding mostly on what feels right emotionally and viscerally).

Since these behavioural biases often remain undetected, a conscious and deliberate effort has to be made to "de-bias" decision making. The following are helpful in this task. (a) Develop multiple hypotheses and potential solutions. (b) Use a checklist for evaluating the quality and independence of information. (c) Specify objective decision criteria in advance and examine the possibility of being wrong. A technique like 'premortem assessment' (imagining yourself in future where your decision has turned out to be wrong and identifying the reasons for the same) can be helpful.

APPENDIX 2C
FIVE PRINCIPLES OF CAPITAL ALLOCATION

Capital allocation is a key responsibility of top management. Unfortunately, many CEOs, though well-intentioned, do not know how to allocate capital effectively. Warren Buffett observed perceptively in his 1987 letter to shareholders: "The point can be important because the heads of many companies are not skilled in capital allocation. Their inadequacy is not surprising. Most bosses rise to the top because they have excelled in an area such as marketing, production, engineering, administration or, sometimes, institutional politics. In the end, plenty of unintelligent capital allocation takes place in corporate America (That's why you hear so much about 'restructuring.')"

Capital Misallocation

There are many reasons for misallocation of capital. The more common ones are mentioned below.

- Investment in ambitious projects due to overconfidence.
- Excessive diversification due to herd mentality.
- Overpayment for acquisitions on account of winner's curse.
- Throwing good money after bad due to sunk cost fallacy.
- Steering investments to initiatives that offer the most tangible and immediate returns and short-changing investments in initiatives that are crucial to long- term health.
- Hoarding of cash for the comfort of liquidity.
- Considering internally generated funds as very cheap.
- Incorrect appreciation of the value of real options.

Five Principles of Capital Allocation

The five key principles of capital allocation are as follows:

1. **Zero-based Capital Allocation** Capital in most companies is allocated on an incremental basis. For example, a McKinsey study of more than 1,600 U.S. companies found that the correlation between how much capital a business unit received in one year and the next was 0.99. It appears that inertia plays a large role in capital allocation.

   Zero-based approach is the proper approach to capital allocation. This approach determines the right amount of capital to support the strategy that will create the most wealth. The thrust is on determining how much should be invested without any reference to how much has been already invested.

   McKinsey research suggests that companies that follow a zero-based approach to capital allocation deliver superior total shareholder return than companies that take more of an incremental approach.

2. **Fund Strategies, not Projects** Capital allocation should be concerned with assessing and approving strategies and determining the projects that support the strategies, rather than assessing and approving projects in isolation. This is a critical distinction. There can be value-destroying projects within a sound strategy and value-creating projects within a flawed strategy.
   One must be wary of a project approach, as it is easy to manipulate the numbers of a project to make it look good. As Warren Buffett noted: "Any business craving of the leader, however foolish, will be quickly supported by detailed rate-of-return and strategic studies prepared by his troops." As Richard Brealey et al. observed: "Here is a riddle. Are projects proposed because they have positive NPVs, or do they have positive NPVs because they are proposed? No prizes for the correct answer."
   It must be recognised that a business strategy entails a bundle of projects and what really matters is the value of the bundle. As Michael Mauboussin said, "The CEO and board must evaluate alternative strategies and consider the financial prospects of each."
3. **No Capital Rationing** Many companies limit their investments to internally generated funds which are considered "scarce but free." This "scarce but free" mindset must be replaced by "plentiful but costly" mindset. After all, a company can always raise external capital to support valuable investments. Hence no worthwhile investment must be rejected just because there is inadequacy of internally generated capital. Further, it must be recognised that capital, irrespective of whether it is internally generated or externally obtained, has an opportunity cost associated with it.
4. **Zero Tolerance for Bad Growth** Companies that want to grow will invariably make bad investments. Failed investments are no sin; in fact they are essential to the process of value creation. What is sin, however, is to remain committed to a bad strategy that drains human and financial resources.
   Companies have an opportunity to create value by promptly exiting businesses where they lack advantage. This will reduce cross-subsidisation and direct managerial energies to businesses that create the most value.
5. **Know the Value of Assets and Act Accordingly** Capital allocation is similar to portfolio management. An intelligent portfolio manager has a good sense of how the value of a security compares with its price. Likewise, an intelligent capital allocator knows the difference between the value and price of each asset. As Warren Buffett famously said, "I am a better investor because I am a manager and I am a better manager because I am an investor."
   With a good sense of value and price, management should be ready to take action to create value. As Michael Mauboussin put it, "Sometimes that means acquiring, other times that means divesting, and frequently there are no clear gaps between value and price. As we have seen, managers tend to prefer to buy or sell, even though the empirical record shows quite clearly that sellers fare better than buyers, on average."

APPENDIX 2D

PERSONALITY TRAITS AND CAPITAL MANAGEMENT

A study done at Perth Leadership Institute found the following relationship between personality traits and capital management:

- A visionary CEO, on balance, is less likely to manage capital well.
- A highly altruistic CEO may not manage capital well.
- Introverted CEOs and extroverted CEOs tend to manage capital differently. If there is a good (poor) match between the CEO and the company, capital will be managed well (poorly).
- Analytical CEOs and intuitive CEOs manage capital differently. If there is a good (poor) match between the CEO and the company and its needs, capital will be managed well (poorly).
- In a sales-focused (product-focused) company, CEOs with a sales (product) background will tend to be poor managers of capital.
- A CEO with a financial background is likely to be a better manager of capital, compared to a CEO with an operations background.
- Very impatient as well as very deliberative CEOs are likely to manage capital poorly.

Chapter 3

Generation and Screening of Project Ideas

LEARNING OBJECTIVES

After studying this chapter you should be able to

- List the important aspects to be studied in monitoring the environment.
- List the broad areas of corporate appraisal.
- Describe the popular tools or frameworks helpful in identifying promising investment opportunities.
- Discuss the key aspects to be considered for a preliminary screening of investment ideas.
- Explain how a project rating index is developed.
- Understand the sources of positive NPV.
- Describe the qualities and traits of a successful entrepreneur.

The search for promising project ideas is the first step towards establishing a successful venture. As the traditional adage goes, the key to success lies in getting into the right business at the right time. While this advice is simple, its accomplishment is difficult because good business opportunities tend to be elusive. Identification of such opportunities requires imagination, sensitivity to environmental changes, and realistic assessment of what the firm can do. The task is partly structured, partly unstructured; partly dependent on 'convergent thinking', partly dependent on 'divergent thinking'; partly requiring objective analysis of quantifiable factors, partly requiring subjective evaluation of qualitative factors; partly amenable to control, and partly dependent on fortuitous circumstances.

Identification is often the outcome of a triggering process rather than an analytical exercise. While the notion of identification is simple, it is difficult to develop methods or procedures for accomplishing it as there is no well defined theory to guide this task. And as Gordon and Pinches observed: "These difficulties become more severe as one moves up the hierarchy of organisational decision-making levels because of the relative uniqueness (non-routineness) of higher level decisions as compared to lower level decisions".[1]

[1] Gordon, Lawrence A. and George E. Pinches, Improving Capital Budgeting: A Decision Support System Approach, Reading, Massachusetts: Addison-Wesley Publishing Co., 1984.

With this caveat, this chapter discusses certain broad considerations and guidelines helpful in the generation and screening of project ideas. The objective is to identify investment opportunities which are prima facie feasible and promising and which merit further examination and appraisal.

3.1 GENERATION OF IDEAS

Barring truly new ideas which are based on significant technological breakthrough, most of the project ideas involve combining existing fields of technology or offering variants of present products or services. The typical route may be described as follows. Someone with specialised technical knowledge or marketing expertise or some other competence feels that he can offer a product or service which can cater to a presently unmet need or serve a market where demand exceeds supply or effectively compete with similar products or services because of certain favourable features like better quality or lower prices. His ideas are endorsed by his associates who encourage him and even show willingness to collaborate with him on the proposal. Finally he receives support from financial institutions and banks who approve his project and show readiness to finance it.

Stimulating the Flow of Ideas Often firms adopt a somewhat casual and haphazard approach to the generation of project ideas. To stimulate the flow of ideas, the following are helpful:

SWOT Analysis SWOT is an acronym for strengths, weaknesses, opportunities, and threats. SWOT analysis represents a conscious, deliberate, and systematic effort by an organisation to identify opportunities that can be profitably exploited by it. Periodic SWOT analysis facilitates the generation of ideas.

Clear Articulation of Objectives The operational objectives of a firm may be one or more of the following :

- Cost reduction
- Productivity improvement
- Increase in capacity utilisation
- Improvement in contribution margin
- Expansion into promising fields

A clear articulation and prioritisation of objectives helps in channelising the efforts of employees and prods them to think more imaginatively.

Fostering a Conducive Climate To tap the creativity of people and to harness their entrepreneurial urges, a conducive organisational climate has to be fostered. Two conspicuous examples of organisations which have been exceptionally successful in tapping the creativity of employees are the Bell Telephone Laboratory and 3 M Corporation. While the former has succeeded in harnessing creativity by providing an unconstrained environment the latter has effectively nurtured the entrepreneurial urges of its employees. At a more mundane level, many organisations (Hindustan Unilever is a prominent example in India), have successfully used suggestion schemes to motivate employees to think more creatively.

3.2 MONITORING THE ENVIRONMENT

Basically a promising investment idea enables a firm (or entrepreneur) to exploit opportunities in the environment by drawing on its competitive strengths. Hence, the firm must systematically monitor the environment and assess its competitive abilities. This section looks at the monitoring of environment and the following at corporate appraisal. For purposes of monitoring, the business environment may be divided into six broad sectors, as shown in Exhibit 3.1. The important aspects studied in monitoring the key sectors of the environment are as follows:

Exhibit 3.1 ***Business Environment***

Economic Sector

- State of the economy
- Overall rate of growth
- Growth rate of primary, secondary, and tertiary sectors
- Cyclical fluctuations
- Linkages with the world economy
- Interest rates and exchange rates
- Balance of payment situation

Governmental Sector

- Industrial policy
- Government programmes and projects
- Tax framework
- Subsidies, incentives , and concessions
- Import and export policies
- Financing norms
- Lending conditions of financial institutions and commercial banks

Technological Sector

- Emergence of new technologies
- Access to technical know-how, foreign as well as indigenous
- Receptiveness on the part of industry

Socio-demographic Sector

- Population trends
- Age shifts in population
- Income distribution
- Educational profile
- Employment of women
- Attitudes toward consumption and investment

Competition Sector

- Number of firms in the industry and the market share of the top few (four or five)
- Degree of homogeneity and differentiation among products
- Entry barriers
- Comparison with substitutes in terms of quality, price, appeal, and functional performance
- Marketing policies and practices

Supplier Sector

- Availability and cost of raw materials and sub-assemblies
- Availability and cost of energy
- Availability and cost of money

3.3 CORPORATE APPRAISAL

A realistic appraisal of corporate strengths and weaknesses is essential for identifying investment opportunities which can be profitably exploited. The broad areas of corporate appraisal and the important aspects to be considered under them are as follows:

Marketing and Distribution

- Market image
- Product line
- Market share
- Distribution network
- Customer loyalty
- Marketing and distribution costs

Production and Operations

- Condition and capacity of plant and machinery
- Availability of raw materials, sub-assemblies, and power
- Degree of vertical integration
- Locational advantages
- Cost structure

Research and Development

- Research capabilities of the firm
- Track record of new product developments
- Laboratories and testing facilities
- Coordination between research and operations

Corporate Resources and Personnel

- Corporate image
- Clout with governmental and regulatory agencies
- Dynamism of top management
- Competence and commitment of employees
- State of industrial relations

Finance and Accounting

- Financial leverage and borrowing capacity
- Cost of capital
- Tax situation
- Relations with shareholders and creditors
- Accounting and control system
- Cash flows and liquidity

3.4 TOOLS FOR IDENTIFYING INVESTMENT OPPORTUNITIES

There are several useful tools or frameworks that are helpful in identifying promising investment opportunities. The more popular ones are the Porter model, life cycle approach, and experience curve.

Porter Model: Profit Potential of Industries

Michael Porter[2] has argued that the profit potential of an industry depends on the combined strength of the following five basic competitive forces:

- Threat of new entrants
- Rivalry among existing firms
- Pressure from substitute products
- Bargaining power of buyers
- Bargaining power of sellers

Exhibit 3.2 diagrammatically shows the forces that drive competition and determine industry profit potential.

Threat of New Entrants New entrants add capacity, inflate costs, push prices down, and reduce profitability. Hence, if an industry faces the threat of new entrants, its profit potential would be limited. The threat from new entrants is low if the entry barriers confer an advantage on existing firms and deter new entrants. Entry barriers are high when:

- The new entrants have to invest substantial resources to enter the industry.
- Economies of scale are enjoyed by the industry.
- Existing firms control the distribution channels, benefit from product differentiation in the form of brand image and customer loyalty, and enjoy some kind of proprietary experience curve.
- Switching costs—these are essentially one-time costs of switching from the products of one supplier to another—are high.
- The government policy limits or even prevents new entrants.

[2] Porter, Michael E., *Competitive Strategy: Techniques for Analysing Industries and Competitors*, The Free Press, 1980.

Exhibit 3.2 ***Forces Driving Industry Competition***

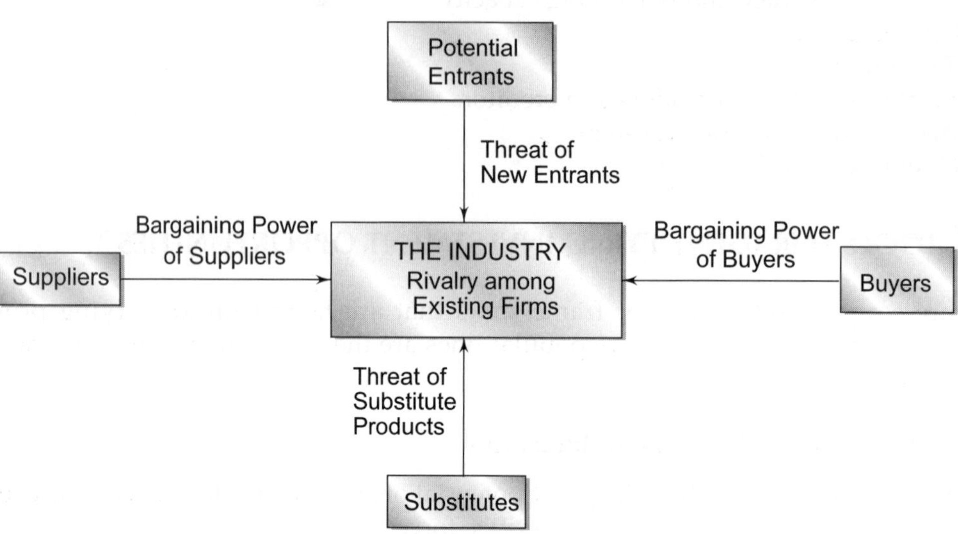

Rivalry between Existing Firms Firms in an industry compete on the basis of price, quality, promotion, service, warranties, and so on. Generally, a firm's attempts to improve its competitive position provoke retaliatory action from others. If the rivalry between the firms in an industry is strong, competitive moves and countermoves dampen the average profitability of the industry. The intensity of rivalry in an industry tends to be high when:

- The number of competitors in the industry is large.
- At least a few firms are relatively balanced and capable of engaging in a sustained competitive battle.
- The industry growth is sluggish, prodding firms to strive for a higher market share.
- The level of fixed costs is high, generating strong pressures for all firms to achieve a higher capacity utilisation level.
- There is chronic over capacity in the industry.
- The industry's product is regarded as a commodity or near-commodity, stimulating strong price and service competition.
- The industry confronts high exit barriers.

Pressure from Substitute Products In a way, all firms in an industry face competition from industries producing substitute products. Performing the same function as the original product, substitute products may limit the profit potential of the industry by imposing a ceiling on the prices that can be charged by the firms in the industry. The threat from substitute products is high when:

- The price-performance trade off offered by the substitute products is attractive.
- The switching costs for prospective buyers are minimal.
- The substitute products are being produced by industries earning superior profits.

Bargaining Power of Buyers Buyers are a competitive force. They can bargain for price cut, ask for superior quality and better service, and induce rivalry among competitors. If they are powerful, they can depress the profitability of the supplier industry. The bargaining power of a buyer group is high when:

- Its purchases are large relative to the sales of the seller.
- Its switching costs are low.
- It poses a strong threat of backward integration.

Bargaining Power of Suppliers Suppliers, like buyers, can exert a competitive force in an industry as they can raise prices, lower quality, and curtail the range of free services that they provide. Powerful suppliers can hurt the profitability of the buyer industry. Suppliers have strong bargaining power when:

- A few suppliers dominate and the supplier group is more concentrated than the buyer group.
- There are hardly any viable substitutes for the products supplied.
- The switching costs for the buyers are high.
- Suppliers do present a real threat of forward integration.

Life Cycle Approach

Many industrial economists believe that most products evolve through a life cycle which has four stages: pioneering stage, rapid growth stage, maturity and stabilisation stage, and decline stage.

Pioneering Stage During this stage, the technology and or the product is relatively new. Lured by promising prospects, many entrepreneurs enter the field. As a result, there is keen, and often chaotic, competition. Only a few entrants may survive this stage.

Rapid Growth Stage Once the period of chaotic developments is over, the rapid growth stage arrives. Thanks to a relatively orderly growth during this period, firms which survive the intense competition of the pioneering stage, witness significant expansion in their sales and profits.

Maturity and Stabilisation Stage After enjoying an above-average rate of growth during the rapid growth, the industry enters the maturity and stabilisation stage. During this stage, when the industry is more or less fully developed, its growth rate is comparable to that of the economy as a whole.

Decline Stage With the satiation of demand, encroachment of new products, and changes in consumer preferences, the industry eventually enters the decline stage, relative to the economy as a whole. In this stage, which may continue indefinitely, the industry may grow slightly during prosperous periods, stagnate during normal periods, and decline during recessionary periods.

Each stage presents investment opportunities that exhibit different characteristics. Investment in the pioneering stage, per se, may have a low return and negative NPV. However, it may possibly create options for participating in the growth stage. Investment in the growth stage is likely to earn a high return and generate positive NPV. Investment in the maturity stage may earn average return and be NPV-neutral. Finally, investment in the decline stage may earn meagre returns and produce negative NPV.

The Experience Curve

Investments aimed at reducing costs are essential to the long-term survival and profitability of the firm. The experience curve is a useful tool for planning such investments.

The experience curve shows how the cost per unit behaves with respect to the accumulated volume of production. The accumulated volume of production is the total number of units produced cumulatively from the very beginning - it should not be confused with the annual rate of production.

In general, the cost per unit declines with the accumulated volume of production. Exhibit 3.3 shows an illustrative experience curve. In this exhibit the cost per unit has been calculated in present value terms, which means that it has been adjusted for the inflation factor. As per this exhibit, the unit cost declines by 20 percent for each doubling of the accumulated volume. Hence, such a curve is called an "80 percent curve".

Exhibit 3.3 ***An 80% Experience Curve***

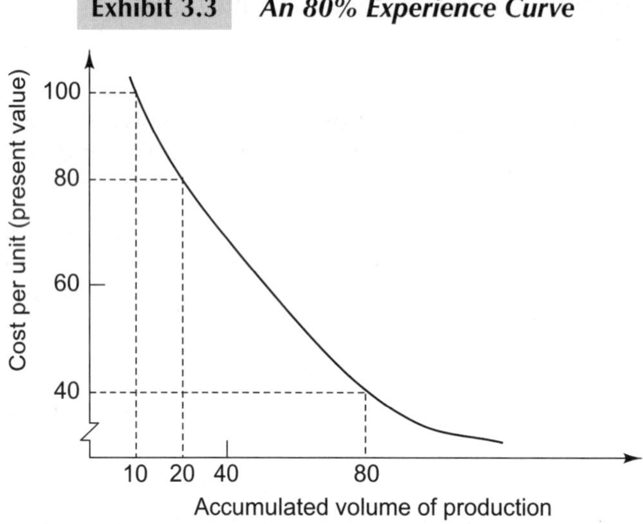

What factors contribute to decline in unit cost with respect to the accumulated volume of production? The key factors are learning effects, technological improvements, and economies of scale.

- *Learning Effects* With more and more of production, labour skills improve and productivity increases, leading to lower costs.
- *Technological Improvements* Increased volume makes it possible to deploy improved production techniques and processes that lower costs.
- *Economies of Scale* As the capacity increases, the cost per unit decreases, thanks to the economies of scale. Generally, if the capacity doubles, the investment outlay increases by 2^n where n varies between 60 percent and 80 percent. This means that a 100 percent capacity increase entails an additional investment between 52 and 74 percent.

3.5 SCOUTING FOR PROJECT IDEAS

Good project ideas — the key to success — are elusive. So a wide variety of sources should be tapped to identify them. Here are some suggestions in this regard.

Analyse the Performance of Existing Industries A study of existing industries in terms of their profitability and capacity utilisation can indicate promising investment opportunities – opportunities which are profitable and relatively risk-free. An examination of capacity utilisation of various industries provides information about the potential for further investment. Such a study becomes more useful if it is done region-wise, particularly for products which have high transportation costs.

Examine the Inputs and Outputs of Various Industries An analysis of the inputs required for various industries may throw up project ideas. Opportunities exist when (i) materials, purchased parts, or supplies are presently being procured from distant sources with attendant time lag and transportation cost, and (ii) several firms produce internally some components/parts which can be supplied at a lower cost by a single manufacturer who can enjoy economies of scale. Similarly, a study of the output of the existing industries may reveal opportunities for adding value through further processing of main outputs, by-products, as well as waste products. (Remember that one person's trash can be another person's treasure.)

Review Imports and Exports An analysis of import statistics for a period of five to seven years is helpful in understanding the trend of imports of various goods and the potential for import substitution. Indigenous manufacture of goods currently imported is advantageous for several reasons: (i) it improves the balance of payments situation, (ii) it generates employment, and (iii) it provides market for supporting industries and services. Likewise, an examination of export statistics is useful in learning about the export possibilities of various products.

Study Plan Outlays and Governmental Guidelines The government plays a very important role in our economy. Its proposed outlays in different sectors provide useful pointers toward investment opportunities. They indicate the potential demand for goods and services required by different sectors.

A valuable source of information to understand the scope for investment in India is the publications and policies of the Department of Industrial Policy and Promotion, Ministry of Commerce and Industry, Government of India. Of particular relevance are the Foreign Direct Investment Policy, Industrial Policy, and National Manufacturing Policy.

While the governmental projections are often a good starting point, they must be viewed with some caution. Often they are not well-grounded. It is helpful to remember the words of Alvin Hanson: "No one reading the plans can fail to be impressed by the frequent unrealism of these assumptions. So much appears to be contingent on the realisation of the unrealisable."

Look at the Suggestions of Financial Institutions and Developmental Agencies In a bid to promote development of industries in their respective states, state financial corporations, state industrial development corporations, and other developmental bodies conduct studies, prepare feasibility reports, and offer suggestions to potential entrepreneurs. The suggestions of these agencies are helpful in identifying promising projects.

Investigate Local Materials and Resources A search for project ideas may begin with an investigation into local resources and skills. Various ways of adding value to locally available materials may be examined. Similarly, the skills of local artisans may suggest products that may be profitably produced and marketed.

The National Council of Applied Economic Research (NCAER) and other bodies publish surveys of various regions showing the potential for industrial development in various regions. These surveys assess the resources (human and material), infrastructural facilities, and markets for various products.

Analyse Economic and Social Trends A study of economic and social trends is helpful in projecting demand for various goods and services. Changing economic conditions and consumer preferences provide new business opportunities. For example, a greater awareness of the value of time is dawning on the public. Hence, the demand for time-saving products like prepared food items, ovens, and powered vehicles has been increasing. Another change that can be seen is the increasing desire for leisure and recreational activities. This has caused a growth in the market for recreational products and services.

Study New Technological Developments There is a large network of research laboratories in India under the umbrella of the Council of Scientific and Industrial Research and other bodies. New products or new processes and technologies for existing products developed by research laboratories may be examined for profitable commercialisation.

Draw Clues from Consumption Abroad Entrepreneurs willing to take higher risks may identify projects for the manufacture of products or supply of services which are new to the country but extensively used abroad. Automatic vending machines, entertainment parks, pre-fabricated houses, and robots are examples of projects belonging to this category.

Explore the Possibility of Reviving Sick Units Industrial sickness is rampant in the country. There are innumerable units which have been characterised as sick. These units are either closed or face the prospect of closure. A significant proportion of sick units, however, can be nursed back to health by sound management, infusion of further capital, and provision of complementary inputs. Hence, there is a fairly good scope for investment in this area. Such investments typically have a shorter gestation period because one does not have to begin from scratch. Indeed, in many cases marginal efforts would suffice to revive such units.

Identify Unfulfilled Psychological Needs For well-established, multi-brand product groups like bathing soap, detergents, cosmetics, and toothpaste, the question to be asked is not whether there is an opportunity to manufacture something to satisfy an actual physical need but whether there are certain psychological needs of consumers which are presently unfulfilled. To find out whether such an opportunity exists, the technique of spectrum analysis is useful. This analysis is done in the following manner: (i) Important factors influencing brand choice are identified. (ii) Existing brands in the market are positioned on a continuum in respect of the factors identified in step (i). (iii) Gaps which exist in relation to consumer psychological needs are identified.

Attend Trade Fairs National and international trade fairs provide an excellent opportunity to get to know about new products and developments.

Stimulate Creativity for Generating New Product Ideas New product ideas may be generated by thinking along the following lines: Modification, Rearrangement, Reversal, Magnification, Reduction, Substitution, Adaptation, and Combination.

Hope that the Chance Factor will Favour You[3] Identification of investment opportunity may be influenced by the chance factor. Two examples may be given here.

- Nrupendar Rao and KVK Raju on a visit to Bokaro Steel Plant learnt that the steel plant was about to lose a 60,000 tonne order for hot rolled coils from a subsidiary of General Motors mainly because of sub-standard packaging. General Motors had then suggested to Bokaro managers that they use Signode packaging systems. This incident led to a plan to set up a project to cater to packaging needs.
- Joseph Kamoo, while he was employed in Zurich, once witnessed two Muslims almost come to blows over the correct direction to face while offering their prayers. Triggered by this incident, Kamoo thought of manufacturing a Mecca-finder.

3.6 PRELIMINARY SCREENING

By using the suggestions made in the preceding section, it is possible to develop a long list of project ideas. Some kind of preliminary screening is required to eliminate ideas which *prima facie* are not promising. For this purpose, the following aspects may be looked into:

- Compatibility with the promoter
- Consistency with governmental priorities
- Availability of inputs
- Adequacy of market
- Reasonableness of cost
- Acceptability of risk level

Compatibility with the Promoter The idea must be compatible with the interest, personality, and resources of the entrepreneur. According to Murphy, a real opportunity has three characteristics: (i) It fits the personality of the entrepreneur – it squares with his abilities, training, and proclivities. (ii) It is accessible to him. (iii) It offers him the prospect of rapid growth and high return on invested capital.

Consistency with Governmental Priorities The project idea must be feasible given the national goals and governmental regulatory framework. The questions to be raised in this context are:

- Is the project consistent with national goals and priorities?
- Are there any environmental effects contrary to governmental regulations?
- Can the foreign exchange requirements of the project be easily accommodated?
- Will there be any difficulty in obtaining the license for the project?

[3] I wish you best of luck!

Availability of Inputs The resources and inputs required for the project must be reasonably assured. To assess this, the following questions need to be answered:

- Are the capital requirements of the project within manageable limits?
- Can the technical know-how required for the project be obtained?
- Are the raw materials required for the project available domestically at a reasonable cost? If the raw materials have to be imported, will there be problems?
- Is the power supply for the project reasonably obtainable from external sources and captive power sources?

It may be noted here that Indian business has been traditionally faced with: (i) shortages of certain inputs like power, foreign exchange, and important raw materials, and (ii) fluctuating supplies of agricultural raw materials like cotton, jute and oil seeds.

Of course, in recent times the situation has improved in many ways: (i) power generation has increased significantly, (ii) foreign exchange is now available more easily, and (iii) supplies of certain basic industrial raw materials have been augmented substantially. However, the supply situation of power, coal, and transport facilities still needs to improve a great deal.

Adequacy of the Market The size of the present market must offer the prospect of adequate sales volume. Further, there should be a potential for growth and a reasonable return on investment. To judge the adequacy of the market the following factors have to be examined.

- Total present domestic market
- Competitors and their market shares
- Export markets
- Quality-price profile of the product vis-à-vis competitive products
- Sales and distribution system
- Projected increase in consumption
- Barriers to the entry of new units
- Economic, social, and demographic trends favourable to increased consumption
- Patent protection

It may be emphasised here that barring recessionary aberrations, the demand for most of the products in India has been growing secularly. This trend would continue because of the low levels of per capita consumption in India. Fortunately, from the point of view of entrepreneurs, the Indian economy, unlike most developed western economies, is not a "share shift" economy wherein the growth in demand for a product is likely to be at the expense of the demand for others.

Reasonableness of Cost The cost structure of the proposed project must enable it to realise an acceptable profit with a price. The following should be examined in this regard.

- Costs of material inputs
- Labour costs
- Factory overheads
- General administration expenses

- Selling and distribution costs
- Service costs
- Economies of scale

Acceptability of Risk Level The desirability of a project is critically dependent on the risk characterising it. In the assessment of risk — a difficult task, indeed — the following factors should be considered:

- Vulnerability to business cycles
- Technological changes
- Competition from substitutes
- Competition from imports
- Governmental control over price and distribution[4]
- Shifts in consumer preferences

3.7 PROJECT RATING INDEX

When a firm evaluates a large number of project ideas regularly, it may be helpful to streamline the process of preliminary screening. For this purpose, a preliminary evaluation may be translated into a project rating index. The steps involved in determining the project rating index are as follows:

- Identify factors relevant for project rating
- Assign weights to these factors (the weights are supposed to reflect their relative importance)
- Rate the project proposal on various factors, using a suitable rating scale. (Typically a 5-point scale or a 7-point scale is used for this purpose)
- For each factor multiply the factor rating with the factor weight to get the factor score
- Add all the factor scores to get the overall project rating index

Exhibit 3.4 illustrates the determination of the project rating index. Once the project rating index is determined, it is compared with a pre-determined hurdle value to judge whether the project is *prima facie* worthwhile or not.

[4] The present approach of the Indian government — it may be noted that the history of controls imposed by the government reveals a varied and chequered pattern-appears to have three main features: 1) The government is not as control-conscious as it was in the past. This is evident from the relaxation — total or partial — of several controls in recent years. 2) The government seems to favour partial controls. In many cases a part of production is being reserved to be supplied to certain sectors at a fixed, concessional price and the remaining is allowed to be sold at market price. 3) In price fixation, the government has shown a better responsiveness to inflationary forces.

Exhibit 3.4 ***Construction of a Rating Index***

Factor	*Factor Weight*	*Rating*					*Factor Score*
		VG 5	*G* 4	*A* 3	*P* 2	*VP* 1	
Input availability	0.25			✓			0.75
Technical know-how	0.10		✓				0.40
Reasonableness of cost	0.05		✓				0.20
Adequacy of market	0.15	✓					0.75
Complementary relationship with other products	0.05		✓				0.20
Stability	0.10		✓				0.40
Dependence on firm's strength	0.20	✓					1.00
Consistency with governmental priorities	0.10			✓			0.30
				Rating Index			4.00

3.8 SOURCES OF POSITIVE NET PRESENT VALUE

It is often taken for granted that there is an abundance of positive NPV projects which can be identified rather easily. However, note that choosing positive NPV projects is akin to selecting under-valued securities using fundamental analysis. The latter is possible if there are imperfections in the financial market that cause a discrepancy between security prices and their equilibrium values (intrinsic values). Likewise, imperfections in real markets (product and factor markets) lead to entry barriers which cause positive NPVs. Hence, an understanding of entry barriers is helpful in identifying positive NPV projects.

It appears that there are six main entry barriers that result in positive NPV projects which are as follows:

- Economies of scale
- Product differentiation
- Cost advantage
- Marketing reach
- Technological edge
- Government policy

Economies of Scale Economies of scale means that an increase in the scale of production, marketing, or distribution results in a decline in the cost per unit. When substantial economies of scale are present, the existing firms are likely to be large in size. The more pronounced the economies of scale, the greater the cost advantage of the existing firms.

In order to exploit the economies of scale, new entrants require substantial investments in plant and machinery, research and development, and market development. Such capital needs serve as an entry barrier. The greater the capital requirement, the higher the barrier to entry. This seems to be especially true in industries like petroleum refining, mineral extraction, iron and steel, and aluminium.

Product Differentiation A firm can create an entry barrier by successfully differentiating its products from those of its rivals. The basis for differentiation may be one or more of the following:

- Effective advertising and superior marketing
- Exceptional service
- Innovative product features
- High quality and dependability

Cost Advantage If a firm can enjoy cost advantage vis-à-vis its competitors, it can be reasonably assured of earning superior returns. Cost advantage may stem from one or more of the following:

- Accumulated experience and comparative edge on the learning curve
- Monopolistic access to low cost materials
- A favourable location
- More effective cost control and cost reduction

Marketing Reach A penetrating marketing reach is an important source of competitive advantage. Two examples illustrate this:

- Avon Products markets its products through a worldwide network of 1,300,000 independent sales representatives. Avon's competitors find it almost impossible to replicate this. Thanks to such a nonpareil marketing network, Avon has been able to earn superior returns in a highly competitive industry.
- The breadth and depth of Hindustan Unilever's distribution network is miles ahead of its competitors. Such a marketing reach has contributed to the superior returns earned by Hindustan Unilever.

Technological Edge Technological superiority enables a firm to enjoy excellent returns. Firms like IBM and Intel earned superior returns over extended periods of time due to, inter alia, the technological edge they had over their rivals. On the Indian scene, firms like BHEL and Hero Honda have substantially outperformed their competitors because of their technological strength.

Government Policy A government policy which shelters a firm from the onslaught of competition enables it to earn superior returns. Government policies that create entry barriers, partial or absolute, include the following:

- Restrictive licensing
- Import restrictions
- High tariff walls
- Environmental controls
- Special tax reliefs

A number of firms in India benefited substantially from restrictive government policies which offered considerable protection to them from potential competition, domestic as well as foreign, for many years. The liberalisation measures of recent years have, of course, dismantled, partly or substantially, entry barriers stemming from earlier government policies. Remember what government can give, it can also take away.

3.9 ON BEING AN ENTREPRENEUR

Many persons have an entrepreneurial urge to set up their own project and be on their own. Hence, it may not be out of place here to discuss the questions every entrepreneur must answer and the qualities and traits of a successful entrepreneur.

The Questions Every Entrepreneur Must Answer According to Amar Bhide[5] the following are the questions that every entrepreneur must answer:

(i) Are my goals well defined?
- Personal aspirations
- Business sustainability and size
- Tolerance for risk

(ii) Do I have the right strategy?
- Clear definition
- Profitability and potential for growth
- Durability
- Rate of growth

(iii) Can I execute the strategy?
- Resources
- Organisational infrastructure
- The founder's role

Qualities and Traits of a Successful Entrepreneur What qualities and traits are required to be a successful entrepreneur? While it is difficult to answer this question definitively, it appears that a successful entrepreneur has the following qualities and traits:

- Willingness to make sacrifices
- Leadership
- Decisiveness
- Confidence in the project
- Marketing orientation
- Strong ego

Willingness to Make Sacrifices A new venture is often plagued with numerous difficulties and unanticipated problems. To nurture it in such an inhospitable environment, the entrepreneur has to be prepared to sacrifice his time, energy, and resources. He must be willing to struggle, sacrificing personal comforts and conveniences, against seemingly endless odds. An entrepreneurial job is not like a typical nine-to-five executive job. It tends to be far more demanding, requiring total commitment — and sometimes, even obsessive preoccupation — on the part of the entrepreneur.

---

[5] Bhide, Amar, "The Questions Every Entrepreneur Must Answer", *Harvard Business Review*, 1996.

Leadership Successful entrepreneurs generally have strong leadership qualities. They are able to inspire ordinary persons to accomplish great feats. Even though outwardly they may show bizarre signs (they may be whimsical, timid, or even cantankerous) they are able to fire people with their zeal. They have the flair for galvanising their team to successfully cope with the challenges and frustrations inherent in a new venture.

Decisiveness A fledgling enterprise has to accomplish many things in an atmosphere of uncertainty. Numerous decisions have to be taken in quick succession on the basis of limited information. The firm does not have a history to fall back on or a well-organised data base to rely upon. Unless the entrepreneur is decisive by nature, he would not be able to cope with the enormous burden of decision making. If he procrastinates, he may court disaster; if he dilly-dallies, he may miss valuable opportunities. The fluid situation of a new enterprise calls not only for an ability to decide quickly but also an ability to revise the decisions to adapt the enterprise to an environment in which it has not established proper moorings.

Confidence in the Project An entrepreneur should have unbounded faith in his project. This helps him in instilling confidence in suppliers, investors, customers, employees, and others. Without unflinching conviction in the project, it would be difficult for the entrepreneur to withstand the failures and frustrations that form the new venture diet.

Marketing Orientation A strong marketing orientation is critical to a new venture. An entrepreneur who is skillful in exploiting market opportunities has the best chance of success. Irrespective of the professional guise he wears (whether it be that of an engineer, inventor, production technologist, accountant, or any other), the entrepreneur must have marketing talent. Edwin Land of Polaroid is widely recognised as an ideal example of disguised marketing talent. Land, an engineering genius, had superior marketing skills and perhaps this was the most critical factor in the outstanding success of Polaroid under his leadership. Land could inspire the technical and financial world, thanks to his marketing abilities. If an entrepreneur lacks marketing skills, he must find a partner who can remedy this deficiency. Otherwise the venture will be severely handicapped because of its inability to exploit the marketing opportunities.

Strong Ego Setting up a new enterprise is like riding an emotional roller coaster. There are days which bring jubilation and there are days which cause despondency, as the enterprise is buffeted by environmental forces, which tend to have a strong influence on the nascent venture. The entrepreneur needs a strong ego to bear with such ups and downs. To endure periods of adversity and to maintain proper perspective when events cast shadow over the enterprise, the entrepreneur needs a strong identity and self-image.

On Entrepreneurship

An internationally acknowledged authority on development economics, Nobel Laureate Sir Arthur Lewis commented as follows on the role of entrepreneurship.

"I have devoted a lifetime to the study of developing economies. I have examined strategies of development, the role of foreign trade, of savings and investment, the most helpful role of government, and a myraid of other factors. I am now convinced that nothing matters more than the work ethic and entrepreneurial spirit of the population."

SUMMARY

- Identification of promising investment opportunities requires imagination, sensitivity to environmental changes, and a realistic assessment of what the firm can do.
- To stimulate the flow of investment ideas, the following are helpful: (i) SWOT analysis, (ii) clear articulation of objectives, and (iii) conducive climate
- The business environment which needs to be monitored regularly to identify investment opportunities may be divided into six broad sectors: economic sector, government sector, technological sector, socio-demographic sector, competition sector, and supplier sector.
- A realistic appraisal of corporate strengths and weaknesses is essential for identifying investment opportunities which can be profitably exploited.
- According to Michael Porter the profit potential of an industry depends on the combined strength of the following five basic competitive forces (i) threat of new entrants, (ii) rivalry among existing firms, (iii) pressure from substitute products, (iv) bargaining power of buyers, and (v) bargaining power of sellers.
- Good project ideas — the key to success — are elusive. So a wide variety of sources should be tapped to identify them.
- When a firm evaluates a large number of project ideas regularly, it may be helpful to streamline the process of preliminary screening by employing a project rating index.
- It appears that there are six main entry barriers which result in positive NPV projects: economies of scale, product differentiation, cost advantage, marketing reach, technological edge, and government policy.
- Every entrepreneur must answer the following questions: Are my goals well defined? Do I have the right strategy? Can I execute the strategy?
- It appears that a successful entrepreneur has the following qualities and traits: willingness to make sacrifices, leadership, decisiveness, confidence in the project, marketing orientation, and strong ego.

QUESTIONS

1. What can a firm do to stimulate the flow of project ideas?
2. Describe briefly the aspects of business environment that need to be monitored?
3. Discuss the five forces that shape the profit potential of an industry.
4. What key issue would you examine in a preliminary screening exercise?
5. Discuss how a project rating index may be developed.
6. What qualities and traits are required to be a successful entrepreneur?
7. Discuss the sources of positive NPV.

Analysis

PART TWO

Market and Demand Analysis

LEARNING OBJECTIVES

After studying this chapter you should be able to

- List the important sources of secondary information useful for market and demand analysis.
- Describe the steps in a sample survey.
- Discuss the key dimensions along which the market is characterised.
- Explain the various methods of demand forecasting.
- Understand the uncertainties in demand forecasting.
- Explain how the market plan for a new product is prepared.

In most cases, the first step in project analysis is to estimate the potential size of the market for the product proposed to be manufactured (or service planned to be offered) and get an idea about the market share that is likely to be captured. Put differently, market and demand analysis is concerned with two broad issues: What is the likely aggregate demand for the product/service? What share of the market will the proposed project enjoy?

These are very important, yet difficult, questions in project analysis. Intelligent and meaningful answers to them call for an in-depth study and assessment of various factors like patterns of consumption growth, income and price elasticity of demand, composition of market, nature of competition, availability of substitutes, reach of distribution channels, so on and so forth. Yet, sometimes project feasibility studies seem to make a short shrift of market and demand analysis. One finds cursory statements like "the market is attractive" or "the demand is expected to exceed supply" as substitutes for a thorough market and demand analysis in project evaluation exercises.

Given the importance of market and demand analysis, it should be carried out in an orderly and systematic manner. The key steps involved in market and demand analysis are depicted in Exhibit 4.1. This chapter discusses these steps in some detail.

4.1 SITUATIONAL ANALYSIS AND SPECIFICATION OF OBJECTIVES

In order to get a "feel" for the relationship between the product and its market, the project analyst may informally talk to customers, competitors, middlemen, and others in the industry. Wherever possible, he may look at the experience of the company to learn about the preferences and purchasing power of customers, actions and strategies of competitors, and practices of the middlemen.

If such a situational analysis generates enough data to measure the market and get a reliable handle over projected demand and revenues, a formal study need not be carried out, particularly when cost and time considerations so suggest. In most cases, of course, a formal study of the market and demand is warranted. To carry out such a study, it is necessary to spell out its objectives clearly and comprehensively. Often this means that the intuitive and informal goals that guide situational analysis need to be expanded and articulated with greater clarity. A helpful approach to spell out objectives is to structure them in the form of questions. Of course, in doing so, always bear in mind how the information generated will be relevant in forecasting the overall market demand and in assessing the share of the market that the project will capture. This will ensure that questions not relevant to the market and demand analysis will not be asked unnecessarily.

Exhibit 4.1 ***Key Steps in Market and Demand Analysis and Their Inter-relationship***

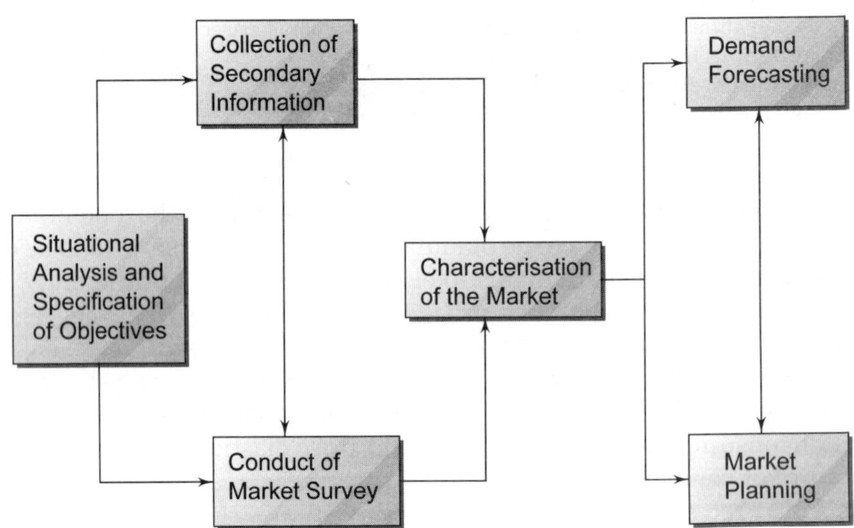

To illustrate, suppose that a small but technologically competent firm has developed an improved air cooler based on a new principle that appears to offer several advantages over the conventional air cooler. The chief executive of the firm needs information about where and how to market the new air cooler. The objectives of market and demand analysis in this case may be to answer the following questions:

- Who are the buyers of air coolers?
- What is the total current demand for air coolers?
- How is the demand distributed temporally (pattern of sales over the year) and geographically?
- What is the break-up of demand for air coolers of different sizes?
- What price will the customers be willing to pay for the improved air cooler?
- How can potential customers be convinced about the superiority of the new cooler?

- What price and warranty will ensure its acceptance?
- What channels of distribution are most suited for the air cooler? What trade margins will induce distributors to carry it?
- What are the prospects of immediate sales?

4.2 COLLECTION OF SECONDARY INFORMATION

In order to answer the questions listed while delineating the objectives of the market study, information may be obtained from secondary and/or primary sources. Secondary information is information that has been gathered in some other context and is already available. Primary information, on the other hand, represents information that is collected for the first time to meet the specific purpose on hand. Secondary information provides the base and the starting point for the market and demand analysis. It indicates what is known and often provides leads and cues for gathering primary information required for further analysis. This section looks at the secondary information and the following at the primary information.

General Sources of Secondary Information The important sources of secondary information useful for market and demand analysis in India are mentioned below:

Census of India A decennial publication of the Government of India, it provides, inter alia, information on population, demographic characteristics, household size and composition, and maps.

National Sample Survey Reports Issued from time to time by the Cabinet Secretariat, Government of India, these reports present information on various economic and social aspects like patterns of consumption, distribution of households by the size of consumer expenditure, distribution of industries, and characteristics of the economically active population. The information presented in these reports is obtained from a nationally representative sample by the interview method.

Plan Reports Issued by the Planning Commission usually at the beginning, middle and end of the five-year plans, these reports and documents provide a wealth of information on plan proposals, physical and financial targets, actual outlays, accomplishments, etc.

Statistical Abstract of the Indian Union An annual publication of the Central Statistical Organisation, it provides, inter alia, demographic information, estimates of national income, and agricultural and industrial statistics.

India Year Book An annual publication of the Ministry of Information and Broadcasting, it provides a wide range of information on economic and other aspects.

Statistical Year Book An annual publication of the United Nations, it provides world statistics relating to various aspects like population, demography, gross domestic production, industrial production, international trade, etc.

Economic Survey An annual publication of the Ministry of Finance, it provides the latest data on industrial production, wholesale prices, consumer prices, exports, agricultural production, national income etc.

Guidelines to Industries This is an annual publication of the Ministry of Industrial Development.

Annual Survey of Industries An annual publication of the Central Statistical Organisation, it contains information on various aspects of industry: number of units and statewise distribution, average number of working days, employment, materials consumption, quantity of products, etc.

Annual Reports of the Development Wing, Ministry of Commerce and Industry An annual publication, it gives a detailed review of industries under the purview of the wing. It also provides information about new items manufactured for the first time in India and the list of protected industries.

Annual Bulletin of Statistics of Exports and Imports An annual publication of the Ministry of Commerce, it provides data on imports and exports for a very large number of items and as per international classification.

Techno-Economic Surveys The National Council of Applied Economic Research has conducted and published techno-economic surveys for various states.

Industry Potential Surveys The Industrial Development Bank of India in consortium with other financial institutions has conducted and published industrial potential surveys for several backward areas.

The Stock Exchange Directory This directory, published by the Bombay Stock Exchange, provides a ten-year picture of performance and financial statements for all listed companies and other important companies. It contains very valuable information for comparative analysis. It is periodically updated.

Monthly Studies of Production of Selected Industries A monthly publication of the Central Statistical Organisation, it provides all-India data on production, number of units installed, capacity, state-wise break-up, stock level, etc., for several selected industries.

Monthly Bulletin of Reserve Bank of India This provides information on production indices, prices, balance of payment position, exchange rates, etc.

Publications of Advertising Agencies The leading advertising agencies like Clarion, McCann and Thompson have published test markets, marketing rating indices of towns of India, consumer indices of markets, and other studies which throw valuable light on Indian markets.

Other Publications Among other publications, a mention may be made of the following: (i) Weekly bulletin of Industrial Licenses, Import Licenses and Export Licenses (published by the Government of India); (ii) Studies of the State Trading Corporation; (iii) Commodity reports and other studies of the Indian Institute of Foreign Trade; (iv) Studies and reports of export promotion councils and commodity boards; and (v) Annual Report on Currency and Finance (issued by the Reserve Bank of India).

ETIG (Economic Times Intelligence Group) has a subscription service for providing macro-economic, sectoral, and company level information.

Corporate Databases Centre for Monitoring Indian Economy (CMIE) and Capitalline publish extensive information on companies. CMIE's prowess database has data on about 10,000 companies.

Industry Associations like Confederation of Indian Industries (CII), the Associated Chambers of Commerce and Industry of India (ASSOCHAM), and Federation of Indian Chamber of Commerce and Industries (FICCI) publish reports on different aspects of the economy and industry verticals.

Consultancy Firms like McKinsey, BCG, Bain, and Booz publish forward looking reports on different aspects of the economy and industry verticals.

World Bank prepares studies and reports on the world economy and different economies.

Brokerage Reports Brokerage firms like Motilal Oswal, Kotak Securities, Edelweiss, Indiabulls, Goldman Sachs, Morgan Stanley, and so on regularly produce reports on different companies, sectors, and industry verticals. Several of these are available on free websites like moneycontrol, moneyrediff, myiris, and indiainfoline.

Industry Specific Sources of Secondary Information The important industry specific sources of secondary information are given in Exhibit 4.2.

Exhibit 4.2 ***Some Important Industry Specific Sources of Secondary Information***

Industry	*Publication*
Automobiles	*Annual Report of the Association of Indian Automobile Manufacturers*
Fertilisers	*Fertiliser Statistics*
Chemicals	*Chemical Age of India*
Pharmaceuticals	*Annual Report of Organisation of Pharmaceuticals Producers of India*
Electrical	*Annual Report of Indian Electrical Manufacturers Association*
Electronics	*Electronics Information and Planning*
Industrial Machinery	*Annual Report of Indian Machine Tools Manufacturers Association*
Mettalurgical	*JPC Bulletin of Iron and Steel Minerals and Metals Review*
Textiles	*Indian Textile Bulletin, Manmade Fibers*
Other Industries	*Cement, Glass Udyog, India Rubber World*

Evaluation of Secondary Information While secondary information is available economically and readily (provided the market analyst is able to locate it) its reliability, accuracy, and relevance for the purpose under consideration must be carefully examined. The market analyst should seek to know:

- Who gathered the information? What was the objective?
- When was the information gathered? When was it published?
- How representative was the period for which the information was gathered?

- Have the terms in the study been carefully and unambiguously defined?
- What was the target population?
- How was the sample chosen?
- How representative was the sample?
- How satisfactory was the process of information gathering?
- What was the degree of sampling bias and non-response bias in the information gathered?
- What was the degree of misrepresentation by respondents?
- How accurately was the information edited, tabulated, and analysed?
- Was statistical analysis properly applied?

4.3 CONDUCT OF MARKET SURVEY

Secondary information, though useful, often does not provide a comprehensive basis for market and demand analysis. It needs to be supplemented with primary information gathered through a market survey, specific to the project being appraised.

The market survey may be a census survey or a sample survey. In a census survey the entire population is covered. (The word 'population' is used here in a particular sense. It refers to the totality of all units under consideration in a specific study. Examples are: all industries using milling machine, all readers of the Economic Times). Census surveys are employed principally for intermediate goods and investment goods when such goods are used by a small number of firms. In other cases a census survey is prohibitively costly and may also be infeasible. For example, it would be inordinately expensive-nay, impossible — to cover every user of Lifebuoy or every person in the income bracket ₹10,000 – ₹15,000.

Due to the above mentioned limitations of the census survey, the market survey, in practice, is typically a sample survey. In such a survey a sample of population is contacted or observed and relevant information is gathered. On the basis of such information, inferences about the population may be drawn.

The information sought in a market survey may relate to one or more of the following:

- Total demand and rate of growth of demand
- Demand in different segments of the market
- Income and price elasticities of demand
- Motives for buying
- Purchasing plans and intentions
- Satisfaction with existing products
- Unsatisfied needs
- Attitudes toward various products
- Distributive trade practices and preferences
- Socio-economic characteristics of buyers

Steps in a Sample Survey Typically, a sample survey consists of the following steps:

Define the Target Population In defining the target population the important terms should be carefully and unambiguously defined. The target population may be divided into various segments which may have differing characteristics. For example, all television owners may be divided into three to four income brackets.

Select the Sampling Scheme and Sample Size There are several sampling schemes: simple random sampling, cluster sampling, sequential sampling, stratified sampling, systematic sampling, and non-probability sampling. Each scheme has its advantages and limitations. The sample size, other things being equal, has a bearing on the reliability of the estimates – the larger the sample size, the greater the reliability.

Develop the Questionnaire The questionnaire is the principal instrument for eliciting information from the sample of respondents. The effectiveness of the questionnaire as a device for eliciting the desired information depends on its length, the types of questions, and the wording of questions. Developing the questionnaire requires a thorough understanding of the product/service and its usage, imagination, insights into human behaviour, appreciation of subtle linguistic nuances, and familiarity with the tools of descriptive and inferential statistics to be used later for analysis. It also requires knowledge of psychological scaling techniques if the same are employed for obtaining information relating to attitudes, motivations, and psychological traits. Industry and trade market surveys, in comparison to consumer surveys, generally involve more technical and specialised questions.

Since the quality of the questionnaire has an important bearing on the results of market survey, the questionnaire should be tried out in a pilot survey and modified in the light of problems/difficulties noted.

Recruit and Train the Field Investigators Recruiting and training of field investigators must be planned well since it can be time-consuming. Great care must be taken for recruiting the right kind of investigators and imparting the proper kind of training to them. Investigators involved in industry and trade market survey need intimate knowledge of the product and technical background particularly for products based on sophisticated technologies.

Obtain Information as per the Questionnaire from the Sample of Respondents Respondents may be interviewed personally, telephonically, or by e-mail or snail mail for obtaining information. Personal interviews ensure a high rate of response. They are, however, expensive and likely to result in biased responses because of the presence of the interviewer. Mail surveys by snail mail or e-mail are economical and evoke fairly candid responses. The response rate, however, is often low. Telephonic interviews, common in western countries, have not for various reasons become popular in India.

Scrutinise the Information Gathered Information gathered should be thoroughly scrutinised to eliminate data which are internally inconsistent and which are of dubious validity. For example, a respondent with a high income and large family may say that he lives in a one-room tenement. Such information, probably inaccurate, should be deleted. Sometimes data inconsistencies may be revealed only after some analysis.

Analyse and Interpret the Information Information gathered in the survey needs to be analysed and interpreted with care and imagination. After tabulating it as per a plan of analysis, suitable statistical investigation may be conducted, wherever possible and necessary. For purposes of statistical analysis, a variety of methods are available. They may be divided into two broad categories: parametric methods and non-parametric methods. Parametric methods assume that the variable or attribute under study conforms to some known distribution. Non-parametric methods do not presuppose any particular distribution.

Results of data based on sample survey will have to be extrapolated to the target population. For this purpose, appropriate inflationary factors, based on the ratio of the size of the target population to the size of the sample studies, will have to be used.

The statistical analysis of data should be directed by a person who has a good background in statistics as well as economics.

It may be emphasised that the results of the market survey can be vitiated by: (i) non-representativeness of the sample, (ii) imprecision and inadequacies in the questions, (iii) failure of the respondents to comprehend the questions, (iv) deliberate distortions in the answers given by the respondents, (v) inept handling of the interviews by the investigators, (vi) cheating on the part of the investigators, (vii) slip-shod scrutiny of data, and (viii) incorrect and inappropriate analysis and interpretation of data.

Some Problems A market researcher in India has to contend with the following problems:

Heterogeneity of the Country Since it is well-nigh impossible to cover all the states in an all-India survey, the country has to be divided into broad territories going beyond the state boundaries. However, the heterogeneity of the country makes the task difficult. Presently the research agencies seem to divide the country the way they think it is appropriate. This causes problems in comparing the findings of different research agencies.

Multiplicity of Languages Related to the above difficulty is the problem of multiplicity of languages confronted by a research agency interested in conducting an all-India survey.

Design of Questionnaire Scaling techniques, commonly recommended in marketing research literature, involve a 5-point scale or a 7-point scale. Such refined scales are not easily amenable to translation in regional languages. More important, they are often not comprehensible to a vast majority of respondents who may lack the education and sophistication to understand them. Hence, when refined scaling techniques are used, answers tend to be erratic and inconsistent. It is perhaps desirable to rely more on open-ended questions and less on pre-coded questions on definite scales.

4.4 CHARACTERISATION OF THE MARKET

Based on the information gathered from secondary sources and through the market survey, the market for the product/service may be described in terms of the following:

- Effective demand in the past and present
- Breakdown of demand
- Price
- Methods of distribution and sales promotion
- Consumers
- Supply and competition
- Government policy

Effective Demand in the Past and Present To gauge the effective demand in the past and present, the starting point typically is apparent consumption which is defined as :

Production + Imports – Exports – Changes in stock level

The figure of apparent consumption has to be adjusted for consumption of the product by the producers and the effect of abnormal factors. The consumption series, after such adjustments, may be obtained for several years.

In a competitive market, effective demand and apparent consumption are equal. However, in most of the developing countries, where competitive markets do not exist for a variety of products due to exchange restrictions and controls on production and distribution, the figure of apparent consumption may have to be adjusted for market imperfections. Admittedly, this is often a difficult task.

Breakdown of Demand To get a deeper insight into the nature of demand, the aggregate (total) market demand may be broken down into demand for different segments of the market. Market segments may be defined by (i) nature of product, (ii) consumer groups, and (iii) geographical division.

Nature of Product One generic name often subsumes many different products: steel covers sections, rolled products, and various semi-finished products; commercial vehicles cover trucks and buses of various capacities; so on and so forth.

Consumer Groups Consumers of a product may be divided into industrial consumers and domestic consumers. Industrial consumers may be sub-divided industry wise. Domestic consumers may be further divided into different income groups.

Geographical Division A geographical breakdown of consumers, particularly for products which have a small value-to-weight relationship and products which require regular, efficient after-sales service is helpful.

Why is segmental analysis required? Segmental information is helpful because the nature of demand tends to vary from one segment to another. The demand from consumers in high income brackets may not be sensitive to price variations whereas the demand from consumers in low income brackets may be very sensitive to price variations and different marketing strategies may be appropriate to different market segments.

Price Price statistics must be gathered along with statistics pertaining to physical quantities. It may be helpful to distinguish the following types of prices: (i) manufacturer's price quoted as FOB (free on board) price or CIF (cost, insurance, and freight) price, (ii) landed price for imported goods, (iii) average wholesale price, and (iv) average retail price.

Methods of Distribution and Sales Promotion The methods of distribution may vary with the nature of product. Capital goods, industrial raw materials or intermediates, and consumer products tend to have differing distribution channels. Likewise, methods used for sales promotion (advertising, discounts, gift schemes, etc.) may vary from product to product.

The methods of distribution and sales promotion employed presently and their rationale must be specified. Such a study may explain certain patterns of consumption and highlight the difficulties that may be encountered in marketing the proposed products.

Consumers Consumers may be characterised along two dimensions as follows:

Demographic and sociological	Attitudinal
Age	Preferences
Sex	Intentions
Income	Habits
Profession	Attitudes
Residence	Responses
Social background	

Supply and Competition It is necessary to know the existing sources of supply and whether they are foreign or domestic. For domestic sources of supply, information along the following lines may be gathered: location, present production capacity, planned expansion, capacity utilisation level, bottlenecks in production, and cost structure.

Competition from substitutes and near-substitutes should be specified because almost any product may be replaced by some other product as a result of relative changes in price, quality, availability, promotional effort, and so on.

Government Policy The role of government in influencing the demand and market for a product may be significant. Governmental plans, policies, legislations, and fiats which have a bearing on the market and demand for the product under examination should be spelt out. These are reflected in: production targets in national plans, imports and export trade controls, import duties, export incentives, excise duties, sales tax, industrial licensing, preferential purchases, credit controls, financial regulations, and subsidies/penalties of various kinds.

4.5 DEMAND FORECASTING

After gathering information about various aspects of the market and demand from primary and secondary sources, an attempt may be made to estimate future demand. A wide range of forecasting methods is available to the market analyst. These may be classified into three broad categories as shown in Exhibit 4.3. The methods listed in this exhibit are described in some detail below:

Exhibit 4.3 *Methods of Demand Forecasting*

I **Qualitative Methods** These methods rely essentially on the judgment of experts to translate qualitative information into quantitative estimates. The important qualitative methods are:

- Jury of executive method
- Delphi method

II **Time Series Projection Methods** These methods generate forecasts on the basis of an analysis of the historical time series. The important time series projection methods are:

- Trend projection method
- Exponential smoothing method
- Moving average method

III **Causal Methods** More analytical than the preceding methods, causal methods seek to develop forecasts on the basis of cause-effect relationships specified in an explicit, quantitative manner. The important causal methods are:

- Chain ratio method
- Consumption level method
- End use method
- Bass diffusion model
- Leading indicator method
- Econometric method

Jury of Executive Opinion Method This method, which is very popular in practice, involves soliciting the opinions of a group of managers on expected future sales and combining them into a sales estimate.

The advantages of this method are: (i) It is an expeditious method for developing a demand forecast. (ii) It permits consideration of a variety of factors like economic climate, competitive environment, consumer preferences, technological developments, and so on, to be included in the subjective estimates provided by the experts. (iii) It has immense appeal to managers who tend to prefer their judgment to mechanistic forecasting procedures. The disadvantages of this method are: (i) The biases underlying subjective estimates cannot be unearthed easily. (ii) The reliability of this technique is questionable.

Delphi Method This method is used for eliciting the opinions of a group of experts with the help of a mail survey. The steps involved in this method are:

1. A group of experts is sent a questionnaire by mail and asked to express their views.
2. The responses received from the experts are summarised without disclosing the identity of the experts, and sent back to the experts, along with a questionnaire meant to probe further the reasons for extreme views expressed in the first round.
3. The process may be continued for one or more rounds till a reasonable agreement emerges in the views of the experts.

Delphi method appeals to many organisations for the following reasons: (i) It is intelligible to users. (ii) It has a fancy name. (iii) It seems to be more accurate and less expensive than the traditional face-to-face group meetings.

While the Delphi method is appealing, there are certain questions: What is the value of expert opinion? What is the contribution of additional rounds and feedback to accuracy?

Trend Projection Method The trend projection method involves (a) determining the trend of consumption by analysing past consumption statistics and (b) projecting future consumption by extrapolating the trend.

When the trend projection method is used, the most commonly employed relationship is the linear relationship.

$$Y_t = a + bt \tag{4.1}$$

where Y_t is the demand for year t, t is the time variable, a is the intercept of the relationship, and b is the slope of the relationship.

To estimate the parameters a and b of the linear relationship, the least squares method is used. To illustrate the use of this method, the following demand data for a product will be used as shown in Exhibit 4.4.

Exhibit 4.4 *Demand Data*

Year	Demand	Year	Demand
2005	10*	2012	20
2006	13	2013	22
2007	14	2014	23
2008	17	2015	22
2009	18	2016	24
2010	18	2017	24
2011	19	2018	25

* in thousand units

For purposes of linear trend analysis, it is convenient to change the time axis as shown in Exhibit 4.5.

Exhibit 4.5 *Change in Time Axis*

Actual Year	Year for Analysis	Actual Year	Year for Analysis
2005	0	2012	7
2006	1	2013	8
2007	2	2014	9
2008	3	2015	10
2009	4	2016	11
2010	5	2017	12
2011	6	2018	13

According to the least squares method, the linear relationship is chosen in such manner that the sum of the squared deviations of the observations from the line is minimised. The parameters, a and b, of the linear relationship are estimated with the help of the following equations:[2]

$$b = \frac{\Sigma\, TY - n\,\overline{T}\,\overline{Y}}{\Sigma\, T^2 - n\,\overline{T}^2} \tag{4.2}$$

[2] The equations for a and b are derived as follows. The sum of squared deviations is

$$\Sigma\,(Y - a - bT)^2 \tag{1}$$

To minimise this with respect to a and b, the partial derivatives of this sum with respect to a and b are set equal to zero. This gives:

$$\frac{\partial}{\partial a}\,(Y - a - bT)^2 = -\,2\,\Sigma\,(Y - a - bT) = 0 \tag{2}$$

$$a = \overline{Y} - \overline{T} \tag{4.3}$$

The calculation of *a* and *b*, for our example, is shown in Exhibit 4.6. The least squares line is shown in Exhibit 4.7.

Exhibit 4.6 ***Calculations in the Least Square Method***

T	Y	TY	T^2
0	10	0	0
1	13	13	1
2	14	28	4
3	17	51	9
4	18	72	16
5	18	90	25
6	19	114	36
7	20	140	49
8	22	176	64
9	23	207	81
10	22	220	100
11	24	264	121
12	24	288	144
13	25	325	169
$\Sigma T = 91$	$\Sigma Y = 269$	$\Sigma TY = 1988$	$\Sigma T^2 = 819$
$\overline{T} = 6.5$	$\overline{Y} = 19.21$		

$$b = \frac{\Sigma\, TY - n\,\overline{T}\,\overline{Y}}{\Sigma\, T^2 - n\,\overline{T}^2} = \frac{1988 - 1748.11}{819 - 591.5} = 1.054$$

$$a = \overline{Y} - b\overline{T} = 19.21 - 1.054 \times 6.5 = 12.36$$

where T is the time, Y is the demand, n is the number of observations, $\overline{T}$ is mean of T, $\overline{Y}$ is the mean of Y, a is the intercept, and b is the slope.

$$\frac{\partial}{\partial b}\,(Y - a - bT)^2 = -\,2\,T\,\Sigma\,(Y - a - bT) = 0 \tag{3}$$

From the above equations we get the following:

$$\Sigma\, Y = \Sigma\,(a + bT) \tag{4}$$

$$\Sigma\, TY = \Sigma\,(aT + bT^2) \tag{5}$$

Solving these two equations, referred to as normal equations, we get the values of a and b given in Eqns (4.2) and (4.3).

Exhibit 4.7 ***Least Squares Fitting***

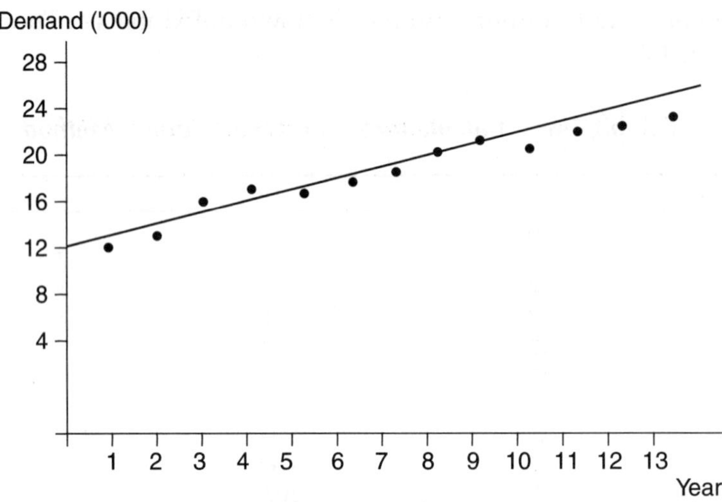

The advantages of the least squares method are: (i) It uses all the observations. (ii) The straight line is derived by an objective, statistical procedure. (iii) A measure of goodness of fit is available. The limitations of the least squares method are: (i) The method is somewhat more complicated than the methods discussed earlier. (ii) The results of such an analysis are valid only when certain conditions are satisfied.

Apart from the linear relationship, the following relations are also used:

Exponential Relationship: $Y_t = a\,e^{bt}$ (4.4)

On logarithmic transformation this becomes:

$$\log Y_t = \log a + bt \quad (4.4a)$$

Polynomial Relationship: $Y_t = a_0 + a_1\,t + a_2\,t^2 + \ldots + a_n\,t^n$ (4.5)

A polynomial of the second degree in t is:

$$Y_t = a_0 + a_1\,t + a_2\,t^2 \quad (4.5a)$$

Cobb Douglas Relationship: $Y_t = a\,t^b$ (4.6)

On logarithmic transformation this becomes:

$$\log Y_t = \log a + b \log t \quad (4.6a)$$

In the above equations Y_t represents demand for year t, t is the time variable, and a, b and a_ts are constants.

Exponential Smoothing Method In exponential smoothing, forecasts are modified in the light of observed errors. If the forecast value for year t, F_t, is less than the actual value for year t, S_t, the forecast for the year $t + 1$, F_{t+1}, is set higher than F_t. If $F_t > S_t$, F_{t+1} is set lower than F_t. In general

$$F_{t+1} = F_t + \alpha\,e_t \quad (4.7)$$

where F_{t+1} is the forecast for year t+1, α is the smoothing parameter (which lies between 0 and 1), and e_t is the error in the forecast for year $t = S_t - F_t$.

Exhibit 4.8 shows how the forecasts would be arrived at, given an initial forecast of $F_1 = 29$ and $\alpha = 0.2$ (The choice of these will be discussed later.)

Exhibit 4.9 shows the plot of the forecasts versus the data. The plot shows that the forecasts have the desirable property of being stable.

How should the first forecast (F_1) and the smoothing parameter (α) be chosen? A simple and reasonably satisfactory rule of thumb is to choose F_1 as the mean of the warm-up sample (The warm-up sample consists of several observations preceding the period for which the forecasting exercise is begun.)

For choosing α, consider several values in the range of 0 to 1 and choose the value which minimises the MSE (mean squared error) in the warm-up period. The mean squared error is defined as

$$\frac{\Sigma (S_i - F_i)^2}{n} \tag{4.8}$$

where S_i is actual value of sales in period i, F_i is forecast value of sales in period i, and n is number of periods in the "warm-up" sample.

Exhibit 4.8 ***Derivation of Forecasts***

t	(S_t)	Data (F_t)	Forecast ($e_t = S_t - F_t$)	Error Forecast for t +1 $F_{t+1} = F_{t+1} + \alpha\, e_t$
1	28.0	29.0	–1.0	F_2 = 29.0 + 0.2 (–1.0) = 28.8
2	29.0	28.8	0.2	F_3 = 28.8 + 0.2 (0.2) = 28.8
3	28.5	28.8	–0.3	F_4 = 28.8 + 0.2 (–0.3) = 28.7
4	31.0	28.7	2.3	F_5 = 28.7 + 0.2 (2.3) = 29.2
5	34.2	29.2	5.0	F_6 = 29.2 + 0.2 (5.0) = 30.2
6	32.7	30.2	2.5	F_7 = 30.2 + 0.2 (2.5) = 30.7
7	33.5	30.7	2.8	F_8 = 30.7 + 0.2 (2.8) = 31.3
8	31.8	31.3	0.5	F_9 = 31.3 + 0.2 (0.5) = 31.4
9	31.9	31.4	0.5	F_{10} = 31.4 + 0.2 (0.5) = 31.5
10	34.3	31.5	2.8	F_{11} = 31.5 + 0.2 (2.8) = 32.1
11	35.2	32.1	3.1	F_{12} = 32.1 + 0.2 (3.1) = 32.7

Moving Average Method As per the moving average method of sales forecasting, the forecast for the next period is equal to the average of the sales for several preceding periods.

In symbols,

$$F_{t+1} = \frac{S_t + S_{t-1} + \ldots + S_{t-n+1}}{n} \tag{4.9}$$

where F_{t+1} is the forecast for the next period, S_t is the sales for the current period, and n is the period over which averaging is done.

Exhibit 4.9 ***Forecasts versus Data***

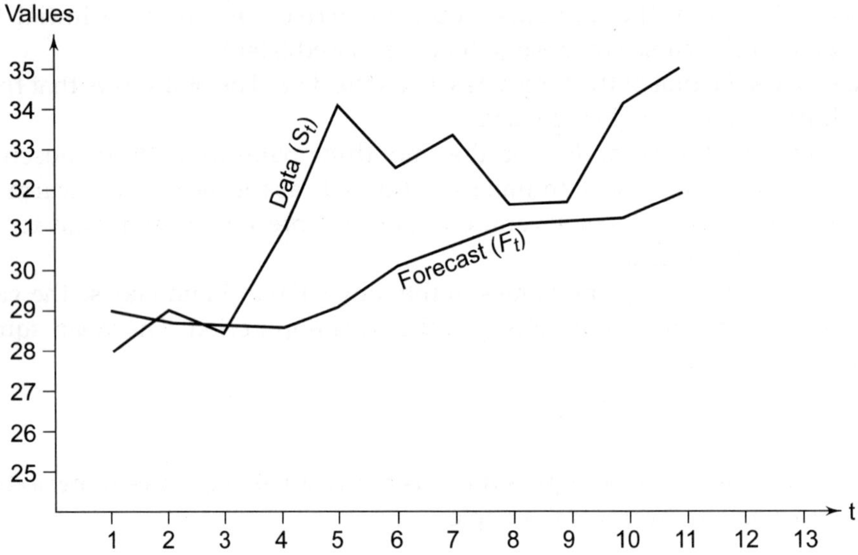

To illustrate the use of the moving average technique, consider the following time series.

Year	Sales
1	28.0
2	29.0
3	28.5
4	31.0
5	34.2
6	32.7
7	33.5
8	31.8
9	31.9
10	34.3
11	35.2
12	36.0

If n is set equal to 4 (*n* has to be specified by the forecaster), the forecast for period 5 will be equal to

$$(28.0 + 29.0 + 28.5 + 31.0)/4 = 29.1$$

(It may be noted that if *n* is equal to 4, the first forecast can be made only for period 5.)

The forecast for period 6 is equal to

$$(S_5 + S_4 + S_3 + S_2)/4 = (34.2 + 31.0 + 28.5 + 29.0)/4 = 30.7$$

Other forecasts follow as shown in Exhibit 4.10.

Exhibit 4.10 ***Forecasts***

t	Data S_t	Forecast F_t	Forecast for t +1 $F_{t+1} = (S_t + S_{t-1} + S_{t-2} + S_{t-3})/4$
1	28.0		
2	29.0		
3	28.5		
4	31.0		
			F_5 = (28.0 + 29.0 + 28.5 + 31.0) / 4 = 29.1
5	34.2	29.1	F_6 = (29.0 + 28.5 + 31.0 + 34.2) / 4 = 30.7
6	32.7	30.7	F_7 = (28.5 + 31.0 + 34.2 + 32.7) / 4 = 31.6
7	33.5	31.6	F_8 = (31.0 + 34.2 + 32.7 + 33.5) / 4 = 32.9
8	31.8	32.9	F_9 = (34.2 + 32.7 + 33.5 + 31.8) / 4 = 33.1
9	31.9	33.1	F_{10} = (32.7 + 33.5 + 31.8 + 31.9) / 4 = 32.5
10	34.3	32.5	F_{11} = (33.5 + 31.8 + 31.9 + 34.3) / 4 = 32.9
11	35.2	32.9	F_{12} = (31.8 + 31.9 + 34.3 + 35.2) / 4 = 33.3
12	36.0	33.3	

In the above illustration, we set n equal to 4. Why should not n be set equal to 3, 5, 6 or any other number? There seems to be no *a priori* way to determine n; it can best be arrived at by experimentation. Another issue may be raised. In Eq. (4.9), which is based on a simple arithmetic average, all preceding values of sales are weighted equally. Should the more recent data not be accorded higher weightage? For example, it may make more sense to assign weights of 0.1, 0.2, 0.3, and 0.4 to the years t–3, t–2, t–1, and t respectively. Here again experimentation seems to be the only way to decide the system of weights.

Chain Ratio Method The potential sales of a product may be estimated by applying a series of factors to a measure of aggregate demand. For example, the General Foods of the U. S. estimated the potential sales for a new product, a freeze-fried instant coffee (Maxim), in the following manner:

- Total amount of coffee sales : 174.5 million units
- Proportion of coffee used at home : 0.835
- Coffee used at home : 145.7 million units
- Proportion of non-decaffeinated coffee used at home : 0.937
- Non-decaffeinated coffee used at home : 136.5 million units
- Proportion of instant coffee : 0.400
- Instant non-decaffeinated coffee used at home : 54.6 million units
- Estimated long-run market share for Maxim : 0.08
- Potential sales of Maxim : 4.37 million units

Another example of the chain ratio method may be given. Many years ago a firm planning to manufacture stainless steel blades in India tried to estimate its potential sales in the following manner:

- Adult male population in the country : 150 million
- Proportion of adult male population using shaving blades : 0.60

- Adult male population using shaving blades : 90 million
- Number of times in a year a person, who uses shaving blades, shaves : 100
- Total shavings done per year : 9,000 million
- Proportion of shavings done with stainless steel blades : 0.40
- Average number of shavings per stainless steel blade : 6
- Number of stainless steel blades used per year (9000 million × 0.40)/6 : 600 million
- Proportion of the stainless steel blade market the firm could capture : 0.20
- Potential sales : 120 million

The chain ratio method uses a simple analytical approach to demand estimation. However, its reliability is critically dependent on the ratios and rates of usage used in the process of determining the sales potential. While some of these ratios and rates of usage may be based on objective proportions, others will have to be subjectively defined.

Consumption Level Method Useful for a product which is directly consumed, this method estimates consumption level on the basis of elasticity coefficients, the important ones being the income elasticity of demand and the price elasticity of demand.

Income Elasticity of Demand The income elasticity of demand reflects the responsiveness of demand to variations in income. It is measured as follows:

$$E_I = \frac{Q_2 - Q_1}{I_2 - I_1} \times \frac{I_1 + I_2}{Q_2 + Q_1} \tag{4.10}$$

where E_I is the income elasticity of demand, Q_1 is the quantity demanded in the base year, Q_2 is the quantity demanded in the following year, I_1 is the income level in the base year, and I_2 is the income level in the following year.

Example The following information is available on quantity demanded and income level: $Q_1 = 50$, $Q_2 = 55$, $I_1 = 1{,}000$ and $I_2 = 1{,}020$. What is the income elasticity of demand? The income elasticity of demand is:

$$E_I = \frac{55 - 50}{1{,}020 - 1{,}000} \times \frac{1{,}000 + 1{,}020}{55 + 50} = 4.81$$

The information on income elasticity of demand along with projected income may be used to obtain a demand forecast. To illustrate, suppose the present per capita annual demand for paper is 1 kg and the present per capita annual income is 840,000. The income elasticity of demand for paper is 2. The projected per capita annual income three years hence is expected to be 10 per cent higher (in real terms) than what it is now. The projected per capita demand for paper three years hence will be:

$$\begin{pmatrix} \text{Present per} \\ \text{capita} \\ \text{demand} \end{pmatrix} \begin{pmatrix} & \text{Per capita} & & \text{Income} \\ 1 + & \text{change in} & \times & \text{elasticity} \\ & \text{income level} & & \text{of demand} \end{pmatrix}$$

$$= (1)\,(1 + 0.10 \times 2) = 1.2 \text{ kg.}$$

The aggregate demand projection for paper will simply be:

Projected per capita demand × Projected population

The income elasticity of demand differs from one product to another. Further, for a given product, it tends to vary from one income group to another and from one region to another. Hence, wherever possible, disaggregative analysis should be attempted.

Price Elasticity of Demand The price elasticity of demand measures the responsiveness of demand to variations in price. It is defined as:

$$E_p = \frac{Q_2 - Q_1}{P_2 - P_1} \times \frac{P_1 + P_2}{Q_2 + Q_1} \qquad (4.11)$$

where E_p is the price elasticity of demand, Q_1 is the quantity demanded in the base year, Q_2 is the quantity demanded in the following year, P_1 is the price per unit in the base year, and P_2 is the price per unit in the following year.

Example The following information is available about a certain product: P_1 = ₹600, Q_1 = 10,000, P_2 = ₹800, and Q_2 = 9,000. What is the price elasticity of demand? The price elasticity of demand is:

$$E_p = \frac{9{,}000 - 10{,}000}{800 - 600} \times \frac{600 + 800}{9{,}000 + 10{,}000} = -\,0.37$$

The price elasticity of demand is a useful tool in demand analysis. The future volume of demand may be estimated on the basis of the price elasticity coefficient and expected price change. The price elasticity coefficient may also be used to study the impact of variations in prices in future on the economic viability of the project. In using the price elasticity measure, however, the following considerations should be borne in mind: (i) The price elasticity coefficient is applicable to only small variations. (ii) The price elasticity measure assumes that the pattern of consumer behaviour remains unchanged.

End Use Method Suitable for estimating the demand for intermediate products, the end use method, also called the consumption coefficient method, involves the following steps:

1. Identify the possible uses of the product.
2. Define the consumption coefficient of the product for various uses.
3. Project the output levels for the consuming industries.
4. Derive the demand for the product.

This method may be illustrated with an example. A certain industrial chemical, Indchem, is used by four industries, Alpha, Beta, Gamma, and Kappa. The consumption coefficients for these industries, the projected output levels for these industries for the year X, and the projected demand for Indchem are shown in Exhibit 4.11.

Exhibit 4.11 ***Projected Demand for Indchem***

	*Consumption Coefficient**	*Projected Output in Year X*		*Projected Demand for Indchem in year X*
Alpha	2.0	10,000		20,000
Beta	1.2	15,000		18,000
Kappa	0.8	20,000		16,000
Gamma	0.5	30,000		15,000
			Total	69,000

* This is expressed in tonnes of Indchem required per unit of output of the consuming industry.

As is clear from the foregoing discussion, the key inputs required for the application of the end-use method are: (i) projected output levels of consuming industries (units), and (ii) consumption coefficients. It may be difficult to estimate the projected output levels of consuming industries (units). More important, the consumption coefficients may vary from one period to another in the wake of technological changes and improvements in the methods of manufacturing. Hence, the end-use method should be used judiciously.

Bass Diffusion Model Developed by Frank Bass, the Bass diffusion model seeks to estimate the pattern of sales growth for new products, in terms of two factors:

p: The coefficient of innovation. It reflects the likelihood that a potential customer would adopt the product because of its innovative features.

q: The coefficient of imitation. It reflects the tendency of a potential customer to buy the product because many others have bought it. It can be regarded as a network effect.

According to a linear approximation of the model:

$$n_t = pN + (q - p)\, N_{t-1} + (q/N) \times (N_{t-1})^2 \qquad (4.12)$$

where n_t is the sales in period t, p is the coefficient of innovation, N is the potential size of the market, q is the coefficient of imitation, and N_t is the accumulative sales made until period.

Example A new product has a potential market size of 1,000,000. There is an older product that is similar to the new product. $p = 0.030$ and $q = 0.080$ describe the industry sales of this older product. The sales trend of the new product is expected to be similar to the older product.

Applying the Bass diffusion model, we get the following estimates of sales in year 1 and year 2.

$$n_1 = 0.03 \times 1000{,}000 + (0.08 - 0.03) \times 0 + \frac{0.080}{1{,}000{,}000} \times 0^2 = 30{,}000$$

$$n_2 = 0.03 \times 1{,}000{,}000 + (0.08 - 0.03) \times 30{,}000 + (0.08/1{,}000{,}000) \times (30{,}000)^2$$

$$= 31{,}572$$

Following the iterative procedure, we can get the estimates of sales for year 3, 4, 5, and so on.

Leading Indicator Method Leading indicators are variables which change ahead of other variables, the lagging variables. Hence, observed changes in leading indicators may be used to predict the changes in lagging variables. For example, the change in the level of urbanisation (a leading indicator) may be used to predict the change in the demand for air conditioners (a lagging variable).

Two basic steps are involved in using the leading indicator method: (i) First, identify the appropriate leading indicator(s). (ii) The lead-lag relationship may not remain stable over time. In view of these problems this method has limited use.

Econometric Method An econometric model is a mathematical representation of economic relationship(s) derived from economic theory. The primary objective of econometric analysis is to forecast the future behaviour of the economic variables incorporated in the model.

Two types of econometric models are employed: the single equation model and the simultaneous equation model. The single equation model assumes that one variable, the dependent variable (also referred to as the explained variable), is influenced by one or more independent variables (also referred to as the explanatory variables). In other words, one-way causality is postulated. An example of the single equation model is given below:

$$D_t = a_0 + a_1 P_t + a_2 N_t \tag{4.13}$$

where D_t is the demand for a certain product in year *t*, P_t is price for the product in year t, and N_t = income in year t.

The simultaneous equation model portrays economic relationships in terms of two or more equations. Consider a highly simplified three-equation econometric model of Indian economy.

$$GNP_t = G_t + I_t + C_t \tag{4.14}$$

$$I_t = a_0 + a_1 GNP_t \tag{4.15}$$

$$C_t = b_0 + b_1 GNP_t \tag{4.16}$$

where GNP_t is gross national product for year *t*, G_t is governmental purchases for year *t*, I_t is gross investment for year *t*, and C_t is consumption for year t.

In the above model, Eq. (4.14), is just a definitional equation which says that the gross national product is equal to the sum of government purchases, gross investment, and consumption. Eq. (4.15) postulates that investments is a linear function of gross national product; Eq. (4.16) posits that consumption is a linear function of gross national product.

The construction and use of an econometric model involves four broad steps.

Specification This refers to the expression of an economic relationship in a mathematical form.

Estimation This involves the determination of the parameter values and other statistics by a suitable method such as the least squares method.

Verification This step is concerned with accepting or rejecting the specification as a reasonable approximation to truth on the basis of the results of estimation.

Prediction This involves projection of the value of the explained variables(s).

The econometric method offers certain advantages: (i) The process of econometric analysis sharpens the understanding of complex cause-effect relationships. (ii) The econometric model provides a basis for testing assumptions and for judging how sensitive the results are to changes in assumptions.

The limitations of the econometric method are: (i) It is expensive and data-demanding. (ii) To forecast the behaviour of the dependent variable, one needs the projected values of independent variables(s). The difficulty in obtaining these may be the main limiting factor in employing the econometric method for forecasting purposes.

Improving Forecasts

Two Baruch professors argue that you can improve forecasts by following some simple guidelines:

- *Check assumptions.* Many forecasts fail because the world changes.
- *Stress fundamentals.* Focus on simple questions. Who are the customers? What is the size of the market? What benefits does the proposed product offer to consumers over the existing products? Are they worth the price?
- *Beware of history.* Seemingly immutable trends may change suddenly and dramatically. Remember that a trend is a trend only until it bends.
- *Watch out for euphoria.* Customer preferences may change quickly, by the time you enter the market.
- *Don't be dazzled by technology.* Its application in the market is more important than the wizardry of the products it makes possible.
- *Stay flexible.* Be ready to enter and leave a market quickly, especially when growth opportunities are elusive.

4.6 UNCERTAINTIES IN DEMAND FORECASTING

Demand forecasts are subject to error and uncertainty which arise from three principal sources:

- Data about past and present market
- Methods of forecasting
- Environmental change

Data About Past and Present Market The analysis of past and present market, which serves as the springboard for the projection exercise, may be vitiated by the following inadequacies of data:

Lack of Standardisation Data pertaining to market features like product, price, quantity, cost, income, etc., may not reflect uniform concepts and measures.

Few Observations Observations available to conduct meaningful analysis may not be enough.

Influence of Abnormal Factors Some of the observations may be influenced by abnormal factors like war or natural calamity.

Methods of Forecasting Methods used for demand forecasting are characterised by the following limitations.

Inability to Handle Unquantifiable Factors Most of the forecasting methods, quantitative in nature, cannot handle unquantifiable factors which sometimes can be of immense significance.

Unrealistic Assumptions Each forecasting method is based on certain assumptions. For example, the trend projection method is based on the 'mutually compensating effects' premise and the end-use method is based on the constancy of technical coefficients. Uncertainty arises when the assumptions underlying the chosen method tend to be unrealistic and erroneous.

Excessive Data Requirement In general, the more advanced a method, the greater the data requirement. For example, to use an econometric model one has to forecast the future values of explanatory variables in order to predict the explained variable. Clearly, predicting the future value of explanatory variables is a difficult and uncertain exercise.

Environmental Changes The environment in which a business functions is characterised by numerous uncertainties. The important sources of uncertainty are mentioned below:

Technological Change This is a very important but hard-to-predict factor which influences business prospects. A technological advancement may create a new product which performs the same function more efficiently and economically, thereby cutting into the market for the existing product. For example, electronic watches encroached on the market for mechanical watches.

Shift in Governmental Policy In India, governmental regulations of business is extensive. Changes in governmental policy, which may be difficult to anticipate, could have a telling effect on business environment: granting of licenses to new companies, particularly foreign companies, may alter the market situation significantly; relaxation of price and distribution controls may widen the market considerably.

Developments on the International Scene Developments on the international scene may have a profound effect on industries. The most classic example of recent decades is the OPEC price hike in 1970s which led to a near-stagnation in the Indian automobile industry for a few years.

Discovery of New Sources of Raw Material Discovery of new sources of raw materials, particularly hydrocarbons, can have a significant impact on the market situation of several products.

Vagaries of Monsoon Monsoon, which plays an important role in the Indian economy, is somewhat unpredictable. The behaviour of monsoon influences, directly or indirectly, the demand for a wide range of products.

Coping with Uncertainties Given the uncertainties in demand forecasting, adequate efforts, along the following lines, may be made to cope with uncertainties.

- Conduct analysis with data based on uniform and standard definitions.
- In identifying trends, coefficients, and relationships, ignore the abnormal or out-of-the-ordinary observations.
- Critically evaluate the assumptions of the forecasting methods and choose a method which is appropriate to the situation.

- Adjust the projections derived from quantitative analysis in the light of unquantifiable, but significant, influences.
- Monitor the environment imaginatively to identify important changes.
- Consider likely alternative scenarios and their impact on market and competition.
- Conduct sensitivity analysis to assess the impact on the size of demand for unfavourable and favourable variations of the determining factors from their most likely levels.

4.7 MARKETING PLAN[3]

A marketing plan usually has the following components:

- Current marketing situation
- Opportunity and issue analysis
- Objectives
- Marketing strategy
- Action programme

We will demonstrate the preparation of marketing plan for a new product. ABC Limited already has a successful five-year old shampoo addressing the South and East markets in India. ABC now plans to launch a toilet soap named Alpha in the same geographical markets. ABC's current year sales are ₹100 million. Its gross contribution margin is 18.4 percent and net profit 4.4 percent. The gross and net margins have been roughly the same in the last 5 years. (Note: The company and the brands are fictitious. They are meant to illustrate the development of a marketing plan.)

Current Marketing Situation This part of the marketing plan deals with the different dimensions or facts of the current situation. It examines the market situation, competitive situation, distribution situation, and the macro-environment. In other words, it paints a pen-picture of the present.

Market Situation This deals with size, the growth, the consumer aspirations, and buying behaviour in the market under consideration. The toilet soap market has a size of about 5.5 lakh tons. There are three price-based segments in this market. The low priced segment consists of Lifebuoy and Nirma Bath. The medium priced segment has brands like Jai, Breeze, Santoor, and Hamam. The premium segment features soaps like Mysore Sandal, Pears, and Dove. The medium priced segment is growing at the expense of the low priced segment.

Competitive Situation This dwells on the major competitors, their objectives, strategies, strengths etc. Alpha's important competitors are brands of Hindustan Unilever (HUL) and Nirma. HUL's marketing prowess is well known. It has more than 50 percent share of the toilet soap market. Its objective would be retaining overall control of the market. It could

[3] This section has been contributed by Dr. Y. L. R. Murthy of Indian Institute of Management, Bangalore. It has been adapted from Philip Kotler, Marketing Management-Millennium Edition, 2000 published by Prentice-Hall Inc.

use the profit from its successful soaps like Lux, Hamam, and Rexona to subsidise its new launches. Nirma, the other competitor, is a challenger and a price fighter. After struggling for 6 years it established its toilet soaps in the market. The competition from both these companies is formidable. Besides, there are other competitors like Godrej, Reckitt-Coleman, and Wipro to contend with.

Distribution Situation This compares the distribution capabilities of the competitors. There are an estimated 9 million retail outlets in the country. These are spread across 570,000 villages, besides towns and cities. Very few companies reach these outlets effectively. HUL, Eveready, and ITC are the few companies that have made a name for themselves in distribution. Nirma, by contrast, is strong at the wholesale level. It retains the loyalty of trade by paying them very handsome margins. Recently it launched a brand called Nirma to strengthen its retail presence. The questions before ABC are therefore (a) How many retail outlets should it aim to stock in? (b) What kind of margins should it be paying to its trade? (c) What special schemes can it offer trade, to keep them loyal to Alpha?

Macroenvironment This describes the effect of social, political, economic, technological, and other external variables on the market. For instance, when there is an economic downturn, consumption moves towards low priced soaps. Most Indian population is young (as opposed to American, European, and Japanese which is middle aged). Therefore there is likely to be demand for more fashionable and contemporary soaps. The liberalisation of Indian economy may bring in cheap raw material. But it will also usher in stiff competition. Thus the macro environment also points to enhanced competition as the competitive situation does.

Opportunity and Issue Analysis In this section a SWOT (Strength, Weakness, Opportunity, Threat analysis) is conducted for Alpha and the core issues before the product identified. Alpha's strength is that its parent ABC has to its credit the successful launch of a shampoo in the current market. Its weakness is probably its limited resources. The **opportunity** for Alpha could be the growth witnessed in the medium-priced segment of the toilet soap market at the expense of low priced soaps. The threat might be the growing acceptance of new launches like Nirma which are already exhausting the opportunities available in the market.

In the light of this analysis, the issues before Alpha are:

- Given ABC's limited resources should Alpha be marketed first in South and then East or should it be launched simultaneously in both the markets.
- Given that its shampoo is already successful should ABC use a new brand name Alpha or should it extend its shampoo's brand name to the soap.

Objectives Objectives have to be clear-cut, specific, and achievable. The following objectives have been set:

- Achieve break-even in 3 years for Alpha.
- Attain sales of ₹20 million in the first year, ₹80 million in the second, and ₹120 million in the third.
- Achieve a top-of-mind recognition of 75 percent in the target segment for Alpha in the first year and 90 percent in the second.

- Reach 300,000 retail outlets in the first year, 900,000 in the second, and 1,500,000 in the third.

> **Kotler on Marketing Plans**
>
> My experience with marketing plans is that most of them are poorly done. Some are overloaded with number and ads, but lack a compelling strategy. Or the strategy is there but the tactics are unrelated to the strategy. Or the targets are unrealistic. Or the budget is unrealistic. Or the controls are not adequate for feedback plan revision.

Marketing Strategy The marketing strategy covers the following: target segment, positioning, product line, price, distribution, sales force, sales promotion, and advertising.

Target Segment The target segment from the point of view of income is middle class (as defined by NCAER). But the segment needs to be described more clearly in terms of its psychographics. This is to make the soap distinct from its competitors. For instance, Alpha could specifically target students or teenagers or entry level executives.

Positioning Positioning is how a product is placed in the mind of the customer. Having decided on targeting students, Alpha could be positioned as "romantic" or "rugged". Similarly, if entry level executives are targeted, the positioning could be "self confidence" or "daylong freshness". An important issue here is, as to which of the above positioning statements dovetail with the shampoo's positioning if a brand extension is attempted.

Product Line Would ABC like to launch a single variant or more than one variant? What fragrance goes with a "romantic" soap (lavender!) and what fits if the positioning is "rugged" (cologne!)?

Price Will Alpha be launched in the mid-price segment because the segment is growing? Whose pricing will it be closest to, ranging from Breeze at the lower end of this segment to Hamam at the higher end? Will the price decision change depending on whether the positioning is "romantic" or "rugged"?

Distribution Alpha may like to confine its distribution to important consumption centres in South and East. It may drop out ineffective outlets.

Sales Force The sales force may be marginally increased. In fact Alpha is likely to press for an increase in the efficiency of its individual salesmen to boost sales.

Sales Promotion Direct consumer promotion is usually expensive because it covers thousands of individual consumers. As a small organisation ABC may like to promote dealers because their number is limited. It may aim at spending 60 percent of the promotion money on dealer schemes and the balance on consumer schemes. (A larger organisation may do the opposite.)

Advertising Unconventional and creative advertising options (balloons, advertising behind bus tickets, pamphlets in newspapers, hoarding in high visibility locations like bus stations etc) may be allocated 60 percent of the budget. The balance goes into mainstream advertising like newspapers and TV. This is because mainstream advertising is expensive and not affordable.

Action Programme Action programmes operationalise the strategy. The following steps give an idea of how Alpha might like to roll out its marketing plan in the next one year.

Quarter 1 Alpha should attain a top-of-mind-awareness of 60 percent in the target segment. This is done by spending 60 percent of Alpha's advertising budget on unconventional media and the rest on conventional media as mentioned above. Alpha shall reach 100,000 retail outlets by ensuring that all the outlets that currently stock shampoo, stock the soap also.

Quarter 2 Alpha shall reach 200,000 retail outlets. This means doubling the number of outlets stocking Alpha. The outlets that are not stocking shampoo currently shall also be pursued aggressively. Alpha's turnover shall reach ₹10 million by the second quarter. Display money and stock incentives shall be given to retailers to achieve the required turn over.

Quarter 3 Alpha shall reach 300,000 retail outlets. The aggressive drive for distribution started in the second quarter shall be continued. Top-of-mind awareness should reach 75 percent. Since what is being reached now is incremental audience, promotional programmes shall be more focused. 20 percent of the promotional budget is to be spent in this quarter.

Quarter 4 Alpha shall consolidate its position in 300,000 retail outlets. Dip-stick tests to be conducted on customer preferences to determine whether the strategies adopted have been successful.

4 Ps to 4Cs of Marketing Planning

The 4 Ps (Product, Price, Place and Promotion) is a useful framework for marketing planning. Phillip Kotler argues that the 4 Ps which represent the seller's thinking more than buyer's thinking can be translated into the 4Cs (Customer value, Customer costs, Customer convenience, Customer communication) as follows.

- Product becomes Customer value
- Price becomes Customer costs
- Place becomes Customer convenience
- Promotion becomes Customer communication

SUMMARY

- Given the importance of market and demand analysis, it should be carried out in an orderly and systematic manner. The key steps in such analysis are (i) situational analysis and specification of objectives, (ii) collection of secondary information, (iii) conduct of market survey, (iv) characterisation of the market, (v) demand forecasting, and (vi) market planning.
- The project analyst may do an informal situational analysis which in turn may provide the basis for a formal study.
- For purposes of market study, information may be obtained from secondary and/or primary sources.

- Secondary information is information that has been gathered in some other context and is already available. While secondary information is available economically, its reliability, accuracy, and relevance for the purpose under consideration must be carefully examined.
- Secondary information, thought useful, often does not provide a comprehensive basis for market and demand analysis. It needs to be supplemented with primary information gathered through a market survey, specific to the project being appraised. It is likely to be a sample survey.
- Typically, a sample survey consists of the following steps: (i) Define the target population. (ii) Select the sampling schemes and sample size. (iii) Develop the questionnaire. (iv) Scrutinise the information gathered. (vii) Analyse and interpret the information.
- Based on the information gathered from secondary sources and through market survey, the market for the product/service may be described in terms of the following: effective demand in the past and present; break-up of demand; price; methods of distribution and sales promotion; consumers; supply and competition; and government policy.
- After gathering information about various aspects of the market and demand from primary and secondary sources, an attempt may be made to estimate future demand. A wide range of forecasting methods is available to the market analyst. These may be divided into three broad categories, viz., qualitative methods, time series projection methods, and causal methods.
- Qualitative methods rely essentially on the judgment of experts to translate qualitative information into quantitative estimates. The important qualitative methods are: jury of executive method and Delphi method.
- Time series projection methods generate forecasts on the basis of an analysis of the historical time series. The important time series projection methods are: trend projection methods, exponential smoothing method, and moving average method.
- The Bass diffusion model seeks to estimate the pattern of sales growth for new products in terms of two factors p, the coefficient of innovation and q, the coefficient of imitation.
- Causal methods seek to develop forecasts on the basis of cause-effect relationships specified in an explicit, quantitative manner. The important causal methods are: chain ratio method, consumption level method, end use method, leading indicator method, and econometric method.
- To enable the product to reach a desired level of market penetration, a suitable marketing plan, covering pricing, distribution, promotion, and service, needs to be developed.

QUESTIONS

1. Describe briefly the general sources of secondary information available in India?
2. List the important industry-specific sources of secondary information in India.
3. How would you evaluate secondary information?

4. Discuss the key steps in a sample survey.
5. How would you characterise the market?
6. What are the pros and cons of the jury of executive opinion method?
7. What steps are involved in the Delphi Method?
8. What are the different kinds of relationships commonly used in the trend projection method?
9. Describe the exponential smoothing method?
10. Discuss the moving average method.
11. Give an example of the chain ratio method.
12. How is income elasticity of demand measured?
13. How is price elasticity of demand measured?
14. What steps are involved in the end use method?
15. Describe the Bass diffusion model.
16. Describe the leading indicator method.
17. What is an econometric model? What steps are involved in constructing an econometric model? What are the pros and cons of the econometric method?
18. Discuss the uncertainties in demand forecasting. How can one cope with these uncertainties?
19. Describe the aspects covered in market planning.

PROBLEMS

1. The sales of a certain product during a fourteen-year period have been as follows:

Period	Sales	Period	Sales
1	2,000	8	4,000
2	2,200	9	3,900
3	2,100	10	4,000
4	2,300	11	4,200
5	2,500	12	4,300
6	3,200	13	4,900
7	3,600	14	5,300

Find the least squares regression line for the data given.

2. For the data given in Problem 1 assume that the forecast for period 1 was 2,100. If α is equal to 0.3, derive the forecasts for the periods 2 to 14 using the exponential smoothing method?
3. For the data given in Problem 1, set n equal to 3 and develop forecasts for the periods 4 to 14 using the moving average method.
4. The following information is available on quantity demanded and income level:
   $Q_1 = 60$, $Q_2 = 70$. $I_1 = 1000$ and $I_2 = 1200$. What is the income elasticity of demand?
5. The following information is available on price and quantity for a certain product:
   $P_1 = ₹40$, $Q_1 = 100{,}000$, $P_2 = ₹50$, $Q_2 = 95{,}000$. What is the price elasticity of demand?
6. A new product has a potential market size of 500,000. There is an older product that is similar to the new product. p = 0.020 and q = 0.075 describe the industry sales of this older product.

   What will be the estimates of sales in years 1, 2, and 3 for the new product, according to the Bass diffusion model?

MINICASE

Amalgamated Enterprises is a broadly diversified company with presence in a variety of sectors such as cement, textiles, apparel, and industrial chemicals.

After a thorough review of various capital projects undertaken in the last five years, the executive committee of Amalgamated Enterprises felt that the quality of market and demand analysis of most of the projects was somewhat patchy.

As a marketing analyst, you have been invited by Abhijit Ghosh, the managing director of Amalgamated Enterprises, to do a seminar on market and demand analysis for the business heads of the company. Among other things, he wants you to address the following issues.

1. How should one evaluate secondary information?
2. Discuss the steps in a sample survey.
3. Briefly describe the various methods of demand forecasting.
4. The sales of a certain product during a 15 year period have been as follows:

Period	Sales	Period	Sales	Period	Sales
1	1,000	6	2,050	11	2,950
2	1,150	7	1,900	12	3,500
3	1,320	8	2,400	13	4,050
4	1,600	9	2,650	14	4,250
5	1,750	10	3,040	15	4,600

   (i) Find the least squares regression line for the data given.

   (ii) For the data given in this problem, assume that the forecast for period 11 was 3,250. If α is equal to 0.4, derive the forecasts for the periods 12 to 15, using the exponential smoothing period.

   (iii) For the data given in this problem, set n equal to 4 and develop forecasts for the periods 12 to 15, using the moving averages method.

5. (i) What is income elasticity of demand? How is it measured?

   (ii) What is price elasticity of demand? How is it measured?

6. What are the sources of uncertainties in demand? What can be done to cope with these uncertainties?

Chapter 5 Technical Analysis

LEARNING OBJECTIVES

After studying this chapter you should be able to

- Discuss the considerations that have a bearing on the choice of technology.
- Describe the various material inputs and utilities required for a project.
- Discuss the factors that have a bearing on the capacity decision.
- List the important charts and layouts that define the scope of the project.
- Show the inter-linkages among the key facets of a project.

Analysis of technical and engineering aspects is done continually when a project is being examined and formulated. Other types of analyses are closely intertwined with technical analysis.

The broad purpose of technical analysis is (a) to ensure that the project is technically feasible in the sense that all the inputs required to set up the project are available and (b) to facilitate the most optimal formulation of the project in terms of technology, size, location, and so on.

While technical analysis is essentially the preserve of the technical expert, the financial analyst participating in the project appraisal exercise should be able to raise basic issues relating to technical analysis using common sense and economic logic.

5.1 MANUFACTURING PROCESS/TECHNOLOGY

For manufacturing a product/service, often two or more alternative technologies are available. For example:

- Steel can be made either by the Bessemer process or the open hearth process.
- Cement can be made either by the dry process or the wet process.
- Soda can be made by the electrolysis method or the chemical method.
- Paper, using bagasse as the raw material, can be manufactured by the kraft process or the soda process or the Simon Cusi process.
- Vinyl chloride can be manufactured by using one of the following reactions: acetylene on hydrochloric acid or ethylene on chlorine.
- Soap can be manufactured by semi boiled process or fully boiled process

Choice of Technology The choice of technology is influenced by a variety of considerations:

- Plant capacity
- Principal inputs
- Investment outlay and production cost
- Use by other units
- Product mix
- Latest developments
- Ease of absorption

Plant Capacity Often, there is a close relationship between plant capacity and production technology. To meet a given capacity requirement, perhaps only a certain production technology may be viable.

Principal Inputs The choice of technology depends on the principal inputs available for the project. In some cases, the raw materials available influence the technology chosen. For example, the quality of limestones determines whether the wet or dry process should be used for a cement plant.

Investment Outlay and Production Cost The effect of alternative technologies on investment outlay and production cost over a period of time should be carefully assessed.

Use by Other Units The technology adopted should be proven by successful use by other units, preferably in India.

Product Mix The technology chosen must be judged in terms of the total product-mix generated by it, including saleable by-products.

Latest Developments The technology adopted must be based on latest developments in order to ensure *inter alia* that the likelihood of technological obsolescence in the near future, at least, is minimised.

Ease of Absorption The ease with which a particular technology can be absorbed can influence the choice of technology. Sometimes a high-level technology may be beyond the absorptive capacity of a developing country which may lack trained personnel to handle that technology.

Appropriateness of Technology Appropriate technology refers to those methods of production which are suitable to local economic, social, and cultural conditions. In recent years the debate about appropriate technology has been sparked off mainly by Schumacher and others. The advocates of appropriate technology urge that the technology should be evaluated in terms of the following questions:

- Whether the technology utilises local raw materials?
- Whether the technology utilises local manpower?
- Whether the goods and services produced cater to the basic needs?
- Whether the technology protects ecological balance?
- Whether the technology is harmonious with social and cultural conditions?

5.2 TECHNICAL ARRANGEMENTS

Satisfactory arrangements must be made to obtain the technical know-how needed for the proposed manufacturing process. When collaboration is sought, *inter alia*, the following aspects of the agreement must be worked out in detail.

- The nature of support to be provided by the collaborators during the designing of the project, selection and procurement of equipment, installation and erection of the plant, operation and maintenance of the plant, and training of project personnel.
- Process and performance guarantees in terms of plant capacity, product quality, and consumption of raw materials and utilities.
- The price of technology in terms of one-time licensing fee and periodic royalty fee.
- The continuing benefit of research and development work being done by the collaborator.
- The period of collaboration agreement.
- The assistance to be provided and the restrictions to be imposed by the collaborator with respect to exports.
- The level of equity participation and the manner of sharing of management control, especially if the technical collaboration is backed by financial collaboration.
- Assignment of the agreement by either side in case of change of ownership.
- Termination of the agreement or other remedies when either party fails to meet its obligation.
- Approach to be adopted in *force majeure* situations.

5.3 MATERIAL INPUTS AND UTILITIES

An important aspect of technical analysis is concerned with defining the materials and utilities required, specifying their properties in some detail, and setting up their supply programme. There is an intimate relationship between the study of materials and utilities and other aspects of project formulation, particularly those concerned with location, technology, and equipments.

Material inputs and utilities may be classified into four broad categories: (i) raw materials, (ii) processed industrial materials and components, (iii) auxiliary materials and factory supplies, and (iv) utilities.

Raw Materials Raw materials (processed and/or semi-processed) may be classified into four types: (i) agricultural products, (ii) mineral products, (iii) livestock and forest products, and (iv) marine products.

Agricultural Products In studying agricultural products the quality must first be examined. Then, an assessment of quantities available, currently and potentially, is required. The questions that may be raised in this context are: What is the present marketable surplus? What is the present area under cultivation? What is the likely increase in yield per acre?

Mineral Products In assessing mineral raw materials, information is required on the quantum of exploitable deposits and the properties of raw materials. The study should provide details of the location, size, and depth of deposits and the viability of open cast or underground mining. In addition, information should be generated on the composition of the ore, level of impurities, need for beneficiation, and physical, chemical and other properties.

Livestock and Forest Products Secondary sources of data on livestock and forest products often do not provide a dependable basis for estimation. Hence, in general, a specific survey may be required to obtain more reliable data on the quantum of livestock produce and forest products.

Marine Products Assessing the potential availability of marine products and the cost of collection is somewhat difficult. Preliminary marine operations, essential for this purpose, have to be provided for in the feasibility study.

Processed Industrial Materials and Components Processed industrial materials and components (base metals, semi-processed materials, manufactured parts, components, and sub-assemblies) represent important inputs for a number of industries. In studying them the following questions need to be answered: In the case of industrial materials, what are their properties[1]? What is the total requirement of the project? What quantity would be available from domestic sources? What quantity can be procured from foreign sources? How dependable are the supplies? What has been the past trend in prices? What is the likely future behaviour of prices?

Auxiliary Materials and Factory Supplies In addition to the basic raw materials and processed industrial materials and components, a manufacturing project requires various auxiliary materials and factory supplies like chemicals, additives, packaging materials, paints, varnishes, oils, grease, cleaning materials, etc. The requirements of such auxiliary materials and supplies should be taken into account in the feasibility study.

Utilities A broad assessment of utilities (power, water, steam, fuel, etc.) may be made at the time of input study though a detailed assessment can be made only after formulating the project with respect to location, technology, and plant capacity. Since the successful operation of a project critically depends on adequate availability of utilities, the following questions should be raised while conducting the inputs study. What quantities are required? What are the sources of supply? What would be the potential availability? What are the likely shortages/bottlenecks? What measures may be taken to augment supplies?

5.4 PRODUCT MIX

The choice of product mix is guided by market requirements. In the production of most of the items, variations in size and quality are aimed at satisfying a broad range of customers.

[1] The analysis here may have to cover the following properties: a. Physical properties: dimensions, form, specific gravity, viscosity, porosity, state (gas, liquid, solid), and melting and boiling points. b. Mechanical properties: formability, machinability, tensile strength, shearing strength, elasticity, fatigue resistance, hardness, and anneal. c. Chemical properties: form (suspension, emulsion), composition, purity, inflammability, and oxidising and reducing potentials. d. Electrical and magnetic properties: magnetisation, conductance, and resistance.

For example, a garment manufacturer may have a wide range in terms of size and quality to cater to different customers. It may be noted that variation in quality can enable a company to expand its market and enjoy higher profitability. For example, a toilet soap manufacturing unit may, by variation in raw material, packaging, and sales promotion, offer a high profit margin soap to consumers in upper-income brackets.

While planning the production facilities of the firm, some flexibility with respect to the product mix must be sought. Such flexibility enables the firm to alter its product mix in response to changing market conditions and enhances the power of the firm to survive and grow under different situations. The degree of flexibility chosen may be based on a careful analysis of the additional investment requirement for different degrees of flexibility.

5.5 PLANT CAPACITY

Plant capacity (also referred to as production capacity) refers to the volume or number of units that can be manufactured during a given period. Plant capacity may be defined in two ways: feasible normal capacity (FNC) and nominal maximum capacity (NMC). The feasible normal capacity refers to the capacity attainable under normal working conditions. This may be established on the basis of the installed capacity, technical conditions of the plant, normal stoppages, downtime for maintenance and tool changes, holidays, and shift patterns. The nominal maximum capacity is the capacity which is technically attainable and this often corresponds to the installed capacity guaranteed by the supplier of the plant. Our discussion will focus on the feasible normal capacity. Several factors have a bearing on the capacity decision.

- Technological requirement
- Input constraints
- Investment cost
- Market conditions
- Resources of the firm
- Governmental policy

Technological Requirement For many industrial projects, particularly in process type industries, there is a certain minimum economic size determined by the technological factor. For example, a cement plant should have a capacity of at least 300 tonnes per day in order to use the rotary kiln method; otherwise, it has to employ the vertical shaft method which is suitable for lower capacity.

Input Constraints In a developing country like India, there may be constraints on the availability of certain inputs. Power supply may be limited; basic raw materials may be somewhat scarce; foreign exchange available for imports may be inadequate. Constraints of these kinds should be borne in mind while choosing the plant capacity.

Investment Cost When serious input constraints do not obtain, the relationship between capacity and investment cost is an important consideration. Typically, the investment cost per unit of capacity decreases as the plant capacity increases. This relationship may be expressed as follows:

$$C_2 = C_1\left(\frac{Q_2}{Q_1}\right)^{\alpha} \tag{5.1}$$

where C_2 is the derived cost for Q_2 units of capacity, C_1 is the known cost for Q_1 units of capacity, and α is a factor reflecting capacity-cost relationship. This is usually between 0.2 and 0.9.

Example Suppose the known investment cost for 5,000 units of capacity for the manufacturer of a certain item is ₹1,000,000. What will be the investment cost for 10,000 units of capacity if the capacity-cost factor is 0.6.

The derived investment cost for 10,000 units of capacity may be obtained as follows:

$$C_2 = 1{,}000{,}000 \times \left(\frac{10{,}000}{5{,}000}\right)^{0.6} = ₹1{,}516{,}000$$

Market Conditions The anticipated market for the product/service has an important bearing on plant capacity. If the market for the product is likely to be very strong, a plant of higher capacity is preferable. If the market is likely to be uncertain, it might be advantageous to start with a smaller capacity. If the market, starting from a small base, is expected to grow rapidly, the initial capacity may be higher than the initial level of demand – further additions to capacity may be effected with the growth of market.

Resources of the Firm The resources, both managerial and financial, available to a firm define a limit on its capacity decision. Obviously, a firm cannot choose a scale of operations beyond its financial resources and or managerial capability.

Government Policy The capacity level may be influenced by the policy of the government. Traditionally, the policy of the government was to distribute the additional capacity to be created in a certain industry among several firms, regardless of economies of scale. This policy has been substantially modified in recent years and the concept of 'minimum economic capacity' has been adopted in several industries.

5.6 LOCATION AND SITE

The choice of location and site follows an assessment of demand, size, and input requirements. Though often used synonymously, the terms 'location' and 'site' should be distinguished. Location refers to a fairly broad area like a city, an industrial zone, or a coastal area; site refers to a specific piece of land where the project would be set up.

The choice of location is influenced by a variety of considerations: proximity to raw materials and markets, availability of infrastructure, labour situation, governmental policies, and other factors.

Proximity to Raw Materials and Markets An important consideration for location is the proximity to sources of raw materials and nearness to the market for final products. In terms of a basic locational model, the optimal location is one where the total cost (raw material transportation cost plus production cost plus distribution cost for the final product) is minimised. This generally implies that: (i) a resource-based project like a cement plant or a steel mill should be located close to the source of basic material (for example, limestone in the case of a cement plant and iron-ore in the case of a steel plant); (ii) a project based on imported material may be located near a port; and (iii) a project manufacturing a perishable product should be close to the centre of consumption.

However, for many industrial products proximity to the source of raw material or the centre of consumption may not be very important. Petrochemical units or refineries, for example, may be located close to the source of raw material, or close to the centre of consumption, or at some intermediate point.

Availability of Infrastructure Availability of power, transportation, water, and communications should be carefully assessed before a location decision is made.

Adequate supply of power is a very important condition for location – insufficient power can be a major constraint, particularly in the case of an electricity-intensive project like an aluminium plant. In evaluating power supply the following should be looked into: the quantum of power available, the stability of power supply, the structure of power tariff, and the investment required by the project for a tie-up in the network of the power supplying agency.

For transporting the inputs of the project and distributing the outputs of the project, adequate transport connections – whether by rail, road, sea, inland water, or air – are required. The availability, reliability, and cost of transportation for various alternative locations should be assessed.

Given the plant capacity and the type of technology, the water requirement for the project can be assessed. Once the required quantity is estimated, the amount to be drawn from the public utility system and the amount to be provided by the project from surface or sub-surface sources may be determined. For doing this the following factors may be examined: relative costs, relative dependabilities, and relative qualities.

In addition to power, transport, and water, the project should have adequate communication facilities like telephone and internet.

Labour Situation In labour-intensive projects, the labour situation in a particular location becomes important. The key factors to be considered in evaluating the labour situation are:

- Availability of labour, skilled, semi-skilled and unskilled
- Prevailing labour rates
- Labour productivity
- State of industrial relations judged in terms of the frequency and severity of strikes and lockouts
- Degree of unionisation

Governmental Policies Government policies have a bearing on location. In the case of public sector projects, location is directly decided by the government. It may be based on a wider policy for regional dispersion of industries.

In the case of private sector projects, location is influenced by certain governmental restrictions and inducements. The government may prohibit the setting up of industrial projects in certain areas which suffer from urban congestion. More positively, the government offers inducements for establishing industries in backward areas. These inducements consist of subsidies, concessional finance, reliefs from indirect taxes, income tax benefits, lower promoter contribution, and so on.

Other Factors Several other factors have to be assessed before arriving at a location decision:

- Climatic conditions
- General living conditions
- Proximity to ancillary units
- Ease in coping with pollution

Climatic Conditions The climatic conditions like temperature, humidity, wind, sunshine, rainfall, snowfall, dust, flooding, and earthquakes have an important influence on location decision. They have a bearing on cost as they determine the extent of air-conditioning, de-humidification, refrigeration, special drainage, and so on required for the project.

General Living Conditions The general living conditions like the cost of living, housing situation, safety, and facilities for education, health care, transportation and recreation need to be assessed carefully.

Proximity to Ancillary Units Most firms depend on ancillary units for components and parts. If the ancillary units are located nearby, coordination becomes easy, transportation costs are lower, and inventory requirements become considerably less.

Ease in Coping with Environmental Pollution A project may cause environmental pollution in various ways: it may throw gaseous emissions; it may produce liquid and solid discharges; it may cause noise, heat, and vibrations. The location study should analyse the cost of mitigating environmental pollution to tolerable levels at alternative locations.

Site Selection Once the broad location is chosen, attention needs to be focused on the selection of a specific site. Two to three alternative sites must be considered and evaluated with respect to cost of land and cost of site preparation and development.

The cost of land tends to differ from one site to another in the same broad location. Sites close to a city cost more whereas sites away from the city cost less. Sites in an industrial area developed by a governmental agency may be available at a concessional rate.

The cost of site preparation and development depends on the physical features of the site, the need to demolish and relocate existing structures, and the work involved in obtaining utility connections to the site. The last element, viz., the work involved in obtaining utility connections and the cost associated with it should be carefully looked into. It may be noted in this context that the cost of the following may vary significantly from site to site: power transmission lines from the main grid, railway siding from the nearest railroad, feeder road connecting with the main road, transport of water, and disposal of effluents.

5.7 MACHINERIES AND EQUIPMENTS

The requirement of machineries and equipments is dependent on production technology and plant capacity. It is also influenced by the type of project. For a process-oriented industry, like a petrochemical unit, machineries and equipments required should be such that the various stages are matched well. The choice of machineries and equipments for a manufacturing industry is somewhat wider as various machines can perform the same function with varying degrees of accuracy. For example, the configuration of machines required for the manufacture of refrigerators could take various forms. To determine the kinds of machinery and equipment required for a manufacturing industry, the following procedure may be followed: (i) Estimate the likely levels of production over time. (ii) Define the various machining and other operations. (iii) Calculate the machine hours required for each type of operation. (iv) Select machineries and equipments required for each function.

The equipments required for the project may be classified into the following types: (i) plant (process) equipments, (ii) mechanical equipments, (iii) electrical equipments, (iv) instruments, (v) controls, (vi) internal transportation system, and (vii) others.

In addition to the machineries and equipments, a list should be prepared of spare parts and tools required. This may be divided into: (i) spare parts and tools to be purchased with the original equipment, and (ii) spare parts and tools required for operational wear and tear.

Constraints in Selecting Machineries and Equipments In selecting the machineries and equipments certain constraints should be borne in mind: (i) there may be a limited availability of power to set up an electricity-intensive plant like, for example, a large electric furnace; (ii) there may be difficulty in transporting a heavy equipment to a remote location; (iii) workers may not be able to operate, at least in the initial periods, certain sophisticated equipments such as numerically controlled machines; and (iv) the import policy of the government may preclude the import of certain machineries and equipments.

Procurement of Plant and Machinery For procuring plant and machinery, orders for different items of plant and machinery may be placed with different suppliers or a turnkey contract may be given for the entire plant and machinery to a single supplier. The factors to be considered in selecting the supplier(s) of plant and machinery are the desired quality of machinery, the level of technological sophistication, the relative reputation of various suppliers, the expected delivery schedules, the preferred payment terms, and the required performance guarantee[2]. If inhouse technical expertise is inadequate, external consultant(s) may be employed to select plant and machinery and supervise the installation of the same.

5.8 STRUCTURES AND CIVIL WORKS

Structures and civil works may be divided into three categories: (i) site preparation and development, (ii) buildings and structures, and (iii) outdoor works.

Site Preparation and Development This covers the following: (i) grading and levelling of the site, (ii) demolition and removal of existing structures, (iii) relocation of existing pipelines, cables, roads, power lines, etc., (iv) reclamation of swamps and draining and removal of

[2] Performance guarantees provided by machinery suppliers are of three types: mechanical guarantees, input guarantees, and output guarantees.

standing water, (v) connections for the following utilities from the site to the public network: electric power (high tension and low tension), water for drinking and other purposes, communications (telephone, telex, internet etc.), roads, railway sidings, and (vi) other site preparation and development work.

Buildings and Structures Buildings and structures may be divided into: (i) factory or process buildings; (ii) ancillary buildings required for stores, warehouses, laboratories, utility supply centres, maintenance services, and others; (iii) administrative buildings; (iv) staff welfare buildings, cafeteria, and medical service buildings; and (v) residential buildings.

Outdoor Works Outdoor works cover (i) supply and distribution of utilities (water, electric power, communication, steam, and gas); (ii) handling and treatment of emission, wastages, and effluents; (iii) transportation and traffic signals; (iv) outdoor lighting; (v) landscaping; and (vi) enclosure and supervision (boundary wall, fencing, barriers, gates, doors, security posts, etc.)

5.9 ENVIRONMENTAL ASPECTS

A project may cause environmental pollution in various ways: it may throw gaseous emissions; it may produce liquid and solid discharges; it may cause noise, heat, and vibrations.

Projects that produce physical goods like cement, steel, paper, and chemicals by converting natural resource endowments into saleable products are likely to cause more environmental damage. Hence the environmental aspects of these projects have to be properly examined. The key issues that need to be considered in this respect are:

- What are the types of effluents and emissions generated?
- What needs to be done for proper disposal of effluents and treatment of emissions?
- Will the project be able to secure all environmental clearances and comply with all statutory requirements?

5.10 PROJECT CHARTS AND LAYOUTS

Once data are available on the principal dimensions of the project – market size, plant capacity, production technology, machineries and equipments, buildings and civil works, conditions obtaining at plant site, and supply of inputs to the project – project charts and layouts may be prepared. These define the scope of the project and provide the basis for detailed project engineering and estimation of investment and production costs.

The important charts and layouts drawings are briefly described below.

1. *General Functional Layout* This shows the general relationship between equipments, buildings, and civil works. In preparing this layout, the primary consideration is to facilitate smooth and economical movement of raw materials, work-in-process, and finished goods. This means that:

(a) The layout should seek to allow traffic flow in one direction to the extent possible, with a minimum of crossing.

(b) Godowns, workshops, and other services must be functionally situated with respect to the main factory buildings.

2. *Material Flow Diagram* This shows the flow of materials, utilities, intermediate products, final products, by-products, and emissions. Along with the material flow diagram, a quantity flow diagram showing the quantities of flow may be prepared.
3. *Production Line Diagrams* These show how the production would progress along with the main equipments.
4. *Transport Layout* This shows the distances and means of transport outside the production line.
5. *Utility Consumption Layout* This shows the principal consumption points of utilities (power, water, gas, compressed air, etc.) and their required quantities and qualities. These layouts provide the basis for developing specifications for utility supply installations.
6. *Communication Layout* This shows how the various parts of the project will be connected with telephone, internet, intercom, etc.
7. *Organisational Layout* This shows the organisational set-up of the project along with information on personnel required for various departments and their inter-relationship.
8. *Plant Layout* The plant layout is concerned with the physical layout of the factory. In certain industries, particularly process industries, the plant layout is dictated by the production process adopted. In manufacturing industries, however, there is much greater flexibility in defining the plant layout. The important considerations in preparing the plant layout are:
   - Consistency with production technology
   - Smooth flow of goods from one stage to another
   - Proper utilisation of space
   - Scope for expansion
   - Minimisation of production cost
   - Safety of personnel

5.11 SCHEDULE OF PROJECT IMPLEMENTATION

As part of technical analysis, a project implementation schedule is also usually prepared. For preparing the project implementation schedule the following information is required:

- List of all possible activities from project planning to commencement of production.
- The sequence in which various activities have to be performed.
- The time required for performing various activities.
- The resources normally required for performing various activities.
- The implications of putting more resources or less resources than are normally required.

For small projects with few activities, a bar chart showing when a particular activity would begin and when it would end is a fairly simple tool for drawing up the implementation schedule. For most real life projects which have numerous activities and are fairly large, PERT/CPM analysis is required. PERT is an acronym for Programme Evaluation Review Technique and CPM is an acronym for Critical Path Method. These are network planning techniques that can handle innumerable activities, complex interdependency relationships, resource constraints, probabilistic estimates, and cost-time tradeoffs. Lending institutions often insist on the use of network techniques by the project sponsors.

Work Schedule The work schedule, as its name suggests, reflects the plan of work concerning installation as well as initial operations. The purpose of the work schedule is:

- To anticipate problems likely to arise during the installation phase and suggest possible means for coping with them.
- To establish the phasing of investments taking into account the availability of finances.
- To develop a plan of operations covering the initial period (the running-in period).

Sometimes, it is found that the required inputs like raw material and power are not available in adequate quantities when the plant is ready for commissioning, or the plant is not ready when the raw material arrives.

In the first case the plant remains idle and in the second the material may tend to deteriorate and/or pose problems of storage. To avoid losses arising from idle capacity and deterioration of stocks of material, work schedule should be drawn up with care and realism so that the commissioning of plant is reasonably synchronised with the availability of the basic inputs.

5.12 NEED FOR CONSIDERING ALTERNATIVES

The need for considering alternatives has been touched upon earlier. This point, however, needs to be emphasised. There are alternative ways of transforming an idea into a concrete project. These alternatives may differ in one or more of the following aspects:

- Nature of project
- Production process
- Product quality
- Scale of operation and time phasing
- Location

Nature of Project The project may envisage the manufacture of all the parts and components in a vertically integrated unit or it may be an assembly type unit which obtains the bulk of the parts and components from outside suppliers. The project may consist of processing up to the finished stage or may stop at a semi-finished stage. These alternatives are available depending on the nature of project.

Production Process There may be several alternatives with respect to the production process. The availability and characteristics of raw materials, the cost structure, and the nature of markets served are factors that have to be borne in mind while deciding about the process.

Product Quality Barring a few products like clinical thermometers where a certain standard has to be maintained, the choice with respect to quality is fairly wide. This is particularly true in the case of consumer products like textiles, footwear, etc. The quality and product range decisions would depend on the characteristics of the market, the elasticity of demand, consumer preferences, and the nature of competition.

Scale of Operation and Time Phasing In many cases several scales of operation are feasible technically and financially. The choice of a particular scale would depend on the financial resources available, the nature of competition, the nature of demand, and the economies of scale.

Further, a given capacity may be installed in one stage or in phases. The capital cost of capacity installation is usually lower when it is done in one stage. The cost of idle capacity, however, is higher when it is built in a single stage. The trade-off between these costs would determine the optimal pattern of time phasing.

Location Location and size are closely interrelated. Perhaps the same demand could be satisfied by: (i) a single plant for the entire market; or (ii) one large plant for the bulk of the market with a few smaller plants for the remaining market; or (iii) several plants of similar size spread over the market areas. The choice would depend mainly on the trade-off between economies of scale in manufacturing and economies of distribution.

Key Project Inter-linkages

While evaluating various alternatives, the inter-linkages among key factors of the project like product (or service), demand, plant capacity, production technology, location, investment outlay, financial resources, production costs, selling price, and profitability must be borne in mind. Exhibit 5.1 shows these inter-linkages pictorially.

Exhibit 5.1 ***Key Project Inter-linkages***

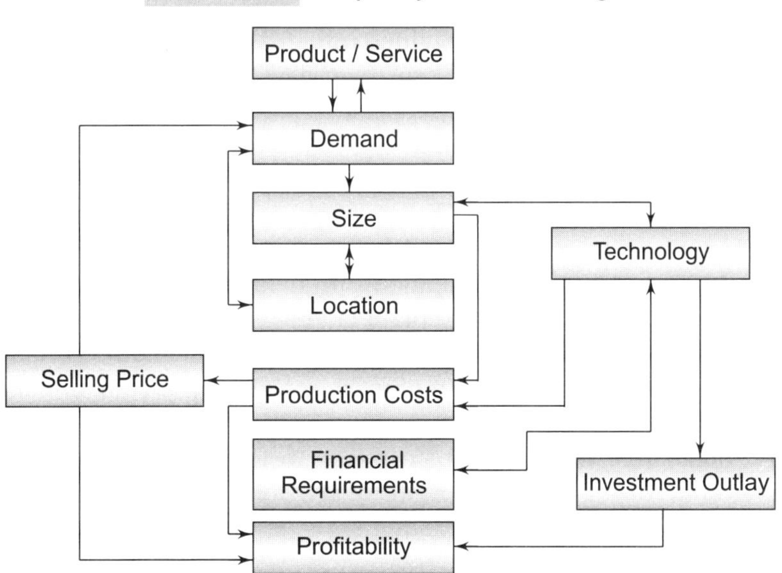

SUMMARY

- For manufacturing a product/service often two or more alternative technologies are available. The choice of technology is influenced by a variety of considerations: plant capacity, principal units, investment outlay, production cost, use by other units, product mix, latest developments, and ease of absorption.
- Satisfactory arrangements have to be made to obtain the technical know-how needed for the proposed manufacturing process
- An important aspect of technical analysis is concerned with defining the materials and inputs required, specifying their properties in some detail, and setting up their supply programme. Materials may be classified into four broad categories: (i) raw materials, (ii) processed industrial materials and components, (iii) auxiliary materials and factory supplies, and (iv) utilities.
- The acquisition of technology from some other enterprise may be by way of (i) technology licensing, (ii) outright purchase, or (iii) joint venture arrangement.
- Appropriate technology refers to those methods of production which are suitable to local economic, social, and cultural conditions.
- Several factors have a bearing on the plant capacity decision: technological requirements, input constraints, investment cost, market conditions, resources of the firm, and governmental policy.
- The choice of location is influenced by a variety of considerations: proximity to raw materials and markets, availability of infrastructure facilities, and other factors. Once a broad location is chosen, the attention needs to be focused on the selection of site – a specific piece of land where the project would be set up.
- The requirement of machinery and equipment is dependent on production technology and plant capacity. Further, it is influenced by the type of product.
- Structures and civil works may be divided into three categories: (i) site preparation and development, (ii) buildings and structures, and (iii) outdoor works.
- A project may cause environmental pollution in various ways. Hence the environmental aspects have to be properly examined.
- Once data are available on the principal dimensions of the project, project charts and layouts may be prepared. The important charts and layout drawings are: (i) general functional layout, (ii) material flow diagrams, (iii) production line diagram, (iv) transport layout, (v) utility consumption layout, (vi) communication layout, (vii) organisational layout, and (viii) plant layout
- As part of technical analysis, a project implementation schedule is also prepared.
- The work schedule reflects the plan of work concerning installation as well as initial operation.
- There are alternative ways of transforming an idea into a concrete project. These alternatives may differ in one or more of the following aspects: nature of project, production process, quality of products, scale of operation, time phasing, and location.

QUESTIONS

1. What aspects are considered in technical analysis?
2. What factors have a bearing on choice of technology?
3. List the key issues to be covered in a technical collaboration arrangement.
4. What are the broad types of materials and inputs? What questions would you raise in assessing whether the material and input requirements of the project would be reasonably met?
5. How would you evaluate the appropriateness of a technology?
6. What factors have a bearing on the plant capacity?
7. How would you determine the kinds of machinery and equipments required for a manufacturing industry?
8. Describe the important charts and layout drawings.
9. What information is required for preparing the project implementation schedule?
10. What is a work schedule? What purpose does it serve?
11. Discuss the importance of considering alternative ways of transforming an idea into a concrete project?

Chapter 6 Financial Estimates and Projections

LEARNING OBJECTIVES

After studying this chapter you should be able to

- Describe the key elements of project cost.
- Discuss the means of finance available for financing a project.
- Describe the major components of cost of production.
- Develop profitability projections.
- Develop projected cash flow statements and projected balance sheets.

There are three basic questions to be answered in a project appraisal exercise: Can we produce the goods or services? Can we sell the goods or services? Can we earn a satisfactory return on the investment made in the project?

For answering these questions we have to do a technical appraisal, a market and demand appraisal, and a financial appraisal. The previous two chapters covered technical appraisal and market and demand appraisal. This chapter begins the discussion on financial appraisal which will be covered over several chapters.

In this chapter we will discuss the estimates and projections required for financial appraisal. This exercise culminates in developing projections for three financial statements, viz., profit and loss statement, cash flow statement, and balance sheet.

Before we dwell on the above financial estimates and projections, it is helpful to know how they are interrelated. Exhibit 6.1 presents a schematic diagram showing the interrelationship.

6.1 COST OF PROJECT

Conceptually, the cost of project represents the total of all items of outlay associated with a project which are supported by long-term funds. It is the sum of the outlays on the following:

- Land and site development
- Buildings and civil works
- Plant and machinery
- Technical know-how and engineering fees
- Expenses on foreign technicians and training of Indian technicians abroad

- Miscellaneous fixed assets
- Preliminary and capital issue expenses
- Pre-operative expenses
- Margin money for working capital
- Initial cash losses

Exhibit 6.1 ***Financial Projections***

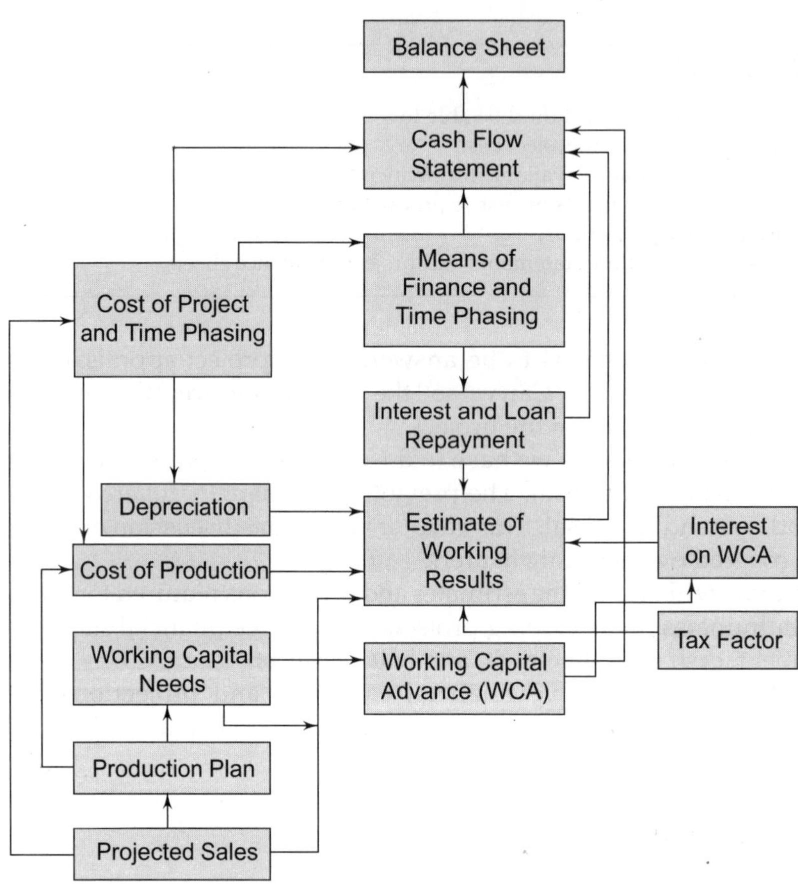

Land and Site Development The cost of land and site development is the sum of the following:

- Basic cost of land including conveyance and other allied charges
- Premium payable on leasehold and conveyance charges
- Cost of levelling and development
- Cost of laying approach roads and internal roads

- Cost of compound wall and gates
- Cost of tube wells

The cost of land varies considerably from one location to another. While it is very high in urban and even semi-urban locations, it is relatively low in rural locations. The expenditure on site development, too, varies widely depending on the location and topography of the land.

Buildings and Civil Works Buildings and civil works cover the following:

- Buildings for the main plant and equipment
- Buildings for auxiliary services like steam supply, workshops, laboratory, water supply, etc
- Godowns, warehouses, and open yard facilities
- Non-factory buildings like canteen, guest houses, time office, excise house, etc
- Quarters for essential staff
- Silos, tanks, wells, chests, basins, cisterns, hoopers, bins, and other structures necessary for installation of the plant and equipment
- Garages
- Sewers, drainage, etc.
- Other civil engineering works

The cost of the buildings and civil works depends on the kinds of structures required which, in turn, are dictated largely by the requirements of the manufacturing process. Once the kinds of structures required are specified, cost estimates are based on the plinth area and the rates for various types of structures. These rates, of course, vary with the location to some extent.

Plant and Machinery The cost of the plant and machinery, typically the most significant component of the project cost, consists of the following:

- Cost of imported machinery: This is the sum of (i) FOB (free on board) value, (ii) shipping, freight, and insurance cost, (iii) import duty, and (iv) clearing, loading, unloading, and transportation charges.
- Cost of indigenous machinery: This consists of (i) FOR (free on rail) cost, (ii) sales tax, octroi, and other taxes, if any, and (iii) railway freight and transport charges to the site.
- Cost of stores and spares.
- Foundation and installation charges.

The cost of the plant and machinery is based on the latest available quotation adjusted for possible escalation. Generally, the provision for escalation is equal to the following product: (latest rate of annual inflation applicable to the plant and machinery) × (length of the delivery period).

Technical Know-how and Engineering Fees Often it is necessary to engage technical consultants or collaborators from India and/or abroad for advice and help in various technical matters like preparation of the project report, choice of technology, selection of the plant and machinery, detailed engineering, and so on. While the amount payable for obtaining the technical know-how and engineering services for setting up the project is a component of the project cost, the royalty payable annually, which is typically a percentage of sales, is an operating expense taken into account in the preparation of the projected profitability statements.

Expenses on Foreign Technicians and Training of Indian Technicians Abroad Services of foreign technicians may be required in India for setting up the project and supervising the trial runs. Expenses on their travel, boarding, and lodging along with their salaries and allowances must be shown here. Likewise, expenses on Indian technicians who require training abroad must also be included here.

Miscellaneous Fixed Assets Fixed assets and machinery which are not part of the direct manufacturing process may be referred to as miscellaneous fixed assets. They include items like furniture, office machinery and equipment, tools, vehicles, railway siding, diesel generating sets, transformers, boilers, piping systems, laboratory equipment, workshop equipment, effluent treatment plants, fire fighting equipment, and so on. Expenses incurred for the procurement or use of patents, licences, trademarks, copyrights, etc. and deposits made with the electricity board may also be included here.

Preliminary and Capital Issue Expenses Expenses incurred for identifying the project, conducting the market survey, preparing the feasibility report, drafting the memorandum and articles of association, and incorporating the company are referred to as preliminary expenses.

Expenses borne in connection with the raising of capital from the public are referred to as capital issue expenses. The major components of capital issue expenses are: underwriting commission, brokerage, fees to managers and registrars, printing and postage expenses, advertising and publicity expenses, listing fees, and stamp duty.

Pre-operative Expenses Expenses of the following types incurred till the commencement of commercial production are referred to as pre-operative expenses: (i) establishment expenses, (ii) rent, rates, and taxes, (iii) travelling expenses, (iv) interest and commitment charges on borrowings, (v) insurance charges, (vi) mortgage expenses, (vii) interest on deferred payments, (viii) start-up expenses, and (ix) miscellaneous expenses.

Pre-operative expenses are directly related to the project implementation schedule. So, delays in project implementation, which are fairly common, tend to push up these expenses. Appreciative of this, financial institutions allow for some delay (20 to 25 percent) in the project implementation schedule and accordingly permit a cushion in the estimate for pre-operative expenses.

Pre-operative expenses incurred up to the point of time the plant and machinery are set up may be capitalised by apportioning them to fixed assets on some acceptable basis. Pre-operative expenses incurred from the point of time the plant and machinery are set up are treated as revenue expenditure. The firm may, however, treat them as deferred revenue expenditure and write them off over a period of time.

Provision for Contingencies A provision for contingencies is made to provide for certain unforeseen expenses and price increases over and above the normal inflation rate which is already incorporated in the cost estimates.

To estimate the provision for contingencies the following procedure may be followed: (i) Divide the project cost items into two categories, viz., 'firm' cost items and 'non-firm' cost items (firm cost items are those which have already been acquired or for which definite arrangements have been made). (ii) Set the provision for contingencies at 5 to 10 percent of the estimated cost of non-firm cost items. Alternatively, make a provision of 10 percent for all items (including the margin money for working capital) if the implementation period is one year or less. For every additional one year, make an additional provision of 5 percent.

Margin Money for Working Capital The principal support for working capital is provided by commercial banks and trade creditors. However, a certain part of the working capital requirement has to come from long-term sources of finance. Referred to as the 'margin money for working capital', this is an important element of the project cost.

The margin money for working capital is sometimes utilised for meeting over-runs in capital cost. This leads to a working capital problem (and sometimes a crisis) when the project is commissioned. To mitigate this problem, financial institutions stipulate that a portion of the loan amount, equal to the margin money for working capital, be blocked initially so that it can be released when the project is completed.

Initial Cash Losses Most of the projects incur cash losses in the initial years. Yet, promoters typically do not disclose the initial cash losses because they want the project to appear attractive to the financial institutions and the investing public. Failure to make a provision for such cash losses in the project cost generally affects the liquidity position and impairs the operations. Hence prudence calls for making a provision, overt or covert, for the estimated initial cash losses.

6.2 MEANS OF FINANCE

To meet the cost of the project the following means of finance are available:

- Share capital
- Term loans
- Debenture capital
- Deferred credit
- Incentive sources
- Miscellaneous sources

Share Capital There are two types of share capital - equity capital and preference capital. *Equity capital* represents the contribution made by the owners of the business, the equity shareholders, who enjoy the rewards and bear the risks of ownership. Equity capital being risk capital carries no fixed rate of dividend. *Preference capital* represents the contribution made by preference shareholders and the dividend paid on it is generally fixed.

Term Loans Provided by financial institutions and commercial banks, term loans represent secured borrowings which are a very important source (and sometimes, the major source) for financing new projects as well as for the expansion, modernisation, and renovation schemes of existing firms. There are two broad types of term loans available in India: *rupee term loans* and *foreign currency term loans*. While the former are given for financing land, building, civil works, indigenous plant and machinery, and so on, the latter are provided for meeting the foreign currency expenditures towards the import of equipment and technical know-how.

Debenture Capital Akin to promissory notes, debentures are instruments for raising debt capital. There are two broad types of debentures: non-convertible debentures and convertible debentures. *Non-convertible debentures* are straight debt instruments. Typically they carry a fixed rate of interest and have a maturity period of 5 to 9 years. *Convertible debentures*, as the name implies, are debentures which are convertible, wholly or partly, into equity shares. The conversion period and price are determined in advance.

Deferred Credit Many a time the suppliers of the plant and machinery offer a deferred credit facility under which payment for the purchase of the plant and machinery can be made over a period of time.

Incentive Sources The government and its agencies may provide financial support as an incentive to certain types of promoters or for setting up industrial units in certain locations. These incentives may take the form of *seed capital assistance* (provided at a nominal rate of interest to enable the promoter to meet his contribution to the project), or *capital subsidy* (to attract industries to certain locations), or *tax deferment* or *exemption* (particularly from sales tax) for a certain period.

Miscellaneous Sources A small portion of the project finance may come from miscellaneous sources like unsecured loans, public deposits, and leasing and hire purchase finance. *Unsecured loans* are typically provided by the promoters to bridge the gap between the promoters' contribution (as required by the financial institutions) and the equity capital the promoters can subscribe to. *Public deposits* represent borrowings from the public at large. *Leasing and hire purchase finance* represent a form of borrowing different from the conventional term loans and debenture capital.

Planning the Means of Finance We have described the various means of finance that can be tapped for a project. How should you go about determining the specific means of finance for a given project? The guidelines and considerations that should be borne in mind for this purpose are as follows:

- Norms of regulatory bodies and financial institutions
- Key business considerations

Norms of Regulatory Bodies and Financial Institutions In some countries, the proposed means of finance for a project must either be approved by a regulatory agency or conform to certain norms laid down by the government or financial institutions in this regard. The primary purpose of such regulations is to impart prudence to project financing decisions and provide a measure of protection to investors. In addition, the norms of financial institutions, which often provide substantial assistance to projects significantly shape and circumscribe project financing decisions.

Key Business Considerations The key business considerations which are relevant for the project financing decision are: cost, risk, control, and flexibility.

Cost In general the cost of debt funds is lower than the cost of equity funds. Why? The primary reason is that the interest payable on debt capital is a tax-deductible expense whereas the dividend payable on equity capital is not.

Risk The two main sources of risk for a firm (or project) are: business risk and financial risk. *Business risk* refers to the variability of return on invested capital and arises mainly from fluctuations in demand and variability of prices and costs. *Financial risk* represents the risk arising from financial leverage. It must be emphasised that while debt capital is cheaper source of finance it is also a riskier source of finance because of the fixed financial burden associated with it.

Generally the affairs of the firm are, or should be, managed in such a way that the total risk borne by equity shareholders, which consists of business risk and financial risk, is not unduly high. This implies that if the firm is exposed to a high degree of business risk, its financial risk should be kept low. On the other hand, if the firm has a low business risk profile, it can assume a high degree of financial risk.

Control From the point of view of the promoters of the project, the issue of control is important. They would ordinarily prefer a scheme of financing which enables them to maximise their control, current as well as potential, over the affairs of the firm, given their commitment of funds to the project.

Flexibility This refers to the ability of a firm (or project) to raise further capital from any source it wishes to tap to meet the future financing needs. This provides manoeuvrability to the firm. In most practical situations, flexibility means that the firm does not fully exhaust its debt capacity. Put differently, it maintains reserve borrowing powers to enable it to raise debt capital to meet largely unforeseen future needs.

6.3 ESTIMATES OF SALES AND PRODUCTION

Typically, the starting point for profitability projections is the forecast of sales revenues. In estimating sales revenues, the following considerations should be borne in mind:

1. It is not advisable to assume a high capacity utilisation level in the first year of operation. Even if the technology is simple and the company may not face technical problems in achieving a high rate of capacity utilisation in the first year itself, there are likely to be other constraints like raw material shortage, limited power, marketing problems, etc. It is sensible to assume that capacity utilisation would be somewhat low in the first year and rise thereafter gradually to reach the maximum level in the third or fourth year of operation. A reasonable assumption with respect to capacity utilisation is as follows: 40–50 percent of the installed capacity in the first year, 50–80 percent in the second year, and 80–90 percent from the third year onwards.
2. It is not necessary to make adjustments for stocks of finished goods. For practical purposes, it may be assumed that production would be equal to sales.
3. The selling price considered should be the price realisable by the company net of GST. It shall, however, include dealers' commission which is shown as an item of expense (as part of the sales expenses).
4. The selling price used may be the present selling price - it is generally assumed that changes in selling price will be matched by proportionate changes in cost of production.[1] If a portion of production is saleable at a controlled price, take the controlled price for that portion.

[1] This assumption is commonly used by financial institutions. However, it is not very convincing.

Sales and production are closely inter-related. Hence they may be estimated together. For this purpose, the format given in Exhibit 6.2 may be employed.

Exhibit 6.2 ***Estimates of Production and Sales***

(Details may be furnished separately for each product and until plant reaches maximum capacity utilisation)

	Product				Product			
	1st yr.	*2nd yr.*	*3rd yr.*	*4th yr.*	*1st yr.*	*2nd yr.*	*3rd yr.*	*4th yr.*
1. Installed capacity (qty. per annum)								
2. No. of working days								
3. No. of shifts								
4. Estimated production per day (qty.)								
5. Estimated annual production (qty.)								
6. Estimated output as % of plant capacity								
7. Sales (qty.) (after adjusting stocks)								
8. Value of sales (in '000 of Rs.)								

Note: Production in the initial period should be assumed at a reasonable level of utilisation of capacity increasing gradually to attain full capacity in subsequent years.

6.4 COST OF PRODUCTION

Given the estimated production, the cost of production may be worked out. The major components of cost of production are:

- Material cost
- Utilities cost
- Labour cost
- Factory overhead cost

Materials The most important element of cost, the material cost comprises the cost of raw materials, chemicals, components, and consumable stores required for production. It is a function of the quantities in which these materials are required and the prices payable for them.

While estimating the material cost, the following points should be borne in mind:

1. The requirements of various material inputs per unit of output may be established on the basis of one or more of the following: (a) theoretical consumption norms, (b) experience of the industry, (c) performance guarantees, and (d) specification of machinery suppliers.
2. The total requirement of various material inputs can be obtained by multiplying the requirements per unit of output with the expected output during the year.
3. The prices of material inputs are defined in CIF (cost, insurance, and freight) terms.

4. The present costs of various material inputs is considered. In other words, the factor of inflation is ignored. It may be recalled that the factor of inflation is ignored in estimating the sales revenues too.
5. If seasonal fluctuations in prices are regular, the same must be considered in estimating the cost of material inputs.

Utilities Utilities consist of power, water, and fuel. The requirements of power, water, and fuel may be determined on the basis of the norms specified by the collaborators, consultants, etc. or the consumption standards in the industry, whichever is higher.

The cost of power shown here would include only the cost of bought out power and it may be estimated on the basis of power tariff structure of the concerned electricity boards. The cost of captive power would naturally be reflected in the cost of fuel . The cost payable to local authorities and charges payable to some other firms for water and/or steam supply may be shown separately. Where the entire water requirement is met out of one's own wells, water charges need not be shown separately. The cost of fuel (furnace oil, coal, firewood, bagasse, etc.) often an important item, is somewhat more difficult to estimate.

Labour Labour cost is the cost of all the manpower employed in the factory. Labour cost naturally is a function of the number of employees and the rate of remuneration. The requirement of workers depends on the number of operators/helpers required for operating various machines and manning various services. The number of supervisory personnel and administrative staff may be calculated on the basis of the general norms prevailing in the industry.

In estimating remuneration rates, the prevailing rates in the industry/area should be taken into account. The remuneration should include, besides basic pay, dearness allowance, house rent allowance, conveyance allowance, medical reimbursement, leave travel concession, provident fund contribution, gratuity contribution, and bonus payments. In addition, account should be taken of vacations, overtime work, night work, work on holidays, etc. Sometimes labour cost is estimated by adding a certain percentage, on a global basis, to the basic pay. It is, however, advisable to make a detailed analysis, at least in the beginning. Labour cost estimates may be raised at the rate of 5 percent per annum to allow for annual increment, etc.

Labour cost may be calculated for the year in which the maximum capacity utilisation is first achieved. For the earlier years, when the capacity utilisation tends to be low, somewhat lower labour costs, but not proportionately lower in relation to capacity, may be assumed.

Factory Overheads The expenses on repairs and maintenance, rent, taxes, insurance on factory assets, and so on are collectively referred to as factory overheads. Repairs and maintenance expense depends on the state of the machinery—this expense tends to be lower in the initial years and higher in the later years. Rent, taxes, insurance, etc. may be calculated at the existing rates. A provision should be made for meeting miscellaneous factory expenses. In addition, a contingency margin may be provided on the items of factory overheads.

6.5 WORKING CAPITAL REQUIREMENT AND ITS FINANCING

In estimating the working capital requirement and planning for its financing, the following points have to be borne in mind:

1. The working capital requirement consists of the following: (i) raw materials and components (indigenous as well as imported), (ii) stocks of goods-in-process (also referred to as work-in-process), (iii) stocks of finished goods, (iv) debtors, (v) operating expenses and (vi) consumable stores.
2. The principal sources of working capital finance are: (i) working capital advances provided by commercial banks, (ii) trade credit, (iii) accruals and provisions, and (iv) long term sources of financing.
3. There are limits to obtaining working capital advances from commercial banks. They are in two forms: (i) the aggregate permissible bank finance is specified as per the norms of lending, followed by the lending bank, (ii) against each current asset a certain amount of margin money has to be provided by the firm.
4. The Tandon Committee has suggested three methods for determining the maximum permissible amount of bank finance for working capital. The method that is generally employed now is the second method[2]. According to this method, the maximum permissible bank finance is calculated as follows:

   Current assets as per the norms laid down by the Tandon Committee (0.75) – Non-bank current liabilities like trade credit and provisions

   The implication of this norm is that at least 25 percent of current assets must be supported by long-term sources of finance.
5. The margin requirement varies with the type of current asset. While there is no fixed formula for determining the margin amount, the ranges within which margin requirements for various current assets lie are as follows:

Current Assets	*Margin*
Raw materials	10–25 percent
Work-in-process	20–40 percent
Finished goods	30–50 percent
Debtors	30–50 percent

The format given in Exhibit 6.3, may be used to estimate the working capital requirement, the amount of likely bank finance available, and the margin money for working capital to be provided from long-term sources.

[2] Note that now banks are free to follow their own norms of lending. Yet many of them follow the second method suggested by the Tandon Committee.

Exhibit 6.3 ***Margin Money for Working Capital***

Items	*No. of Months Requirements*	*Bank Margin Availability*	*Amount*	*1 Year**		
				Amount of Bank Finance	*Margin Money Required*	*Amount*
(1)	*(2)*	*(3)*	*(4)*	*(5)*	*(6)*	*(7)*
1. Indigenous raw materials/components						
Less: Trade credits						
Net indigenous raw materials/components						
2. Imported raw materials/components						
3. Consumable stores						
Less: Trade credit						
Net consumable stores						
4. Wages and salaries						
5. Cost of fuel, light and power, taxes, insurance, rent, etc.						
6. Cost of repairs and maintenance						
7. Packing and sales expenses (other than salaries and wages on sales staff which should be included under 4 above)						
8. Stock of finished goods at cost excluding depreciation (to be held for the period between production and realization of sale proceeds)						
9. Stock of goods-in-process (cost of production, excluding depreciation during the period taken for one complete cycle, i.e. from the raw material to the finished goods stage)						
10. Outstanding debtors						
11. Other items of working capital, if any (excise duty payable on 1 month's sale, deposits for utilities, etc.)						
Net working capital**						

6.6 PROFITABILITY PROJECTIONS (OR ESTIMATES OF WORKING RESULTS)

Given the estimates of sales revenues and cost of production, the next step is to prepare the profitability projections or estimates of working results (as they are referred to by term-lending financial institutions in India). The estimates of working results may be prepared along the following lines:

A Cost of production

B	Total administrative expenses
C	Total sales expenses
D	Royalty and know-how payable
E	Total cost of production $(A + B + C + D)$
F	Expected sales
G	Gross profit before interest
H	Total financial expenses
I	Depreciation
J	Operating Profit $(G - H - I)$
K	Other income
L	Preliminary expenses written off
M	Profit/loss before taxation $(J + K - L)$
N	Provision for taxation
O	Profit after tax $(M - N)$
	Less Dividend on
	– Preference capital
	– Equity capital
P	Retained profit
Q	Net cash accrual $(P + I + L)$

Exhibit 6.4 shows a format that may be used for preparing the estimates of working results.

Cost of Production This represents the cost of materials, labour, utilities, and factory overheads as calculated earlier.

Total Administrative Expenses This consists of (i) administrative salaries, (ii) remuneration to directors, (iii) professional fees, (iv) light, postage, telegrams, and telephones, and office supplies (stationery, printing, etc.), (v) insurance and taxes on office property, and (vi) miscellaneous items.

Total Sales Expenses The expenses included under this head are: (i) commission payable to dealers, (ii) packing and forwarding charges, (iii) salary of sales staff (which may be increased at 5 percent per annum), (iv) sales promotion and advertising expenses, and (v) other miscellaneous expenses.

The selling expenses depend mainly on the nature of industry and the kind of competitive conditions that prevail. Typically, selling expenses vary between 5 and 10 percent of sales. The experience of similar firms in the industry may be used as a basic guideline.

Royalty and Know-how Payable Royalty and know-how payable annually may be shown here. The royalty rate is usually 2–5 percent of sales. Further, royalty is payable often for a limited number of years, say 5 to 10 years.

Total Cost of Production This is simply the sum of cost of production, total administrative expenses, total sales expenses, and royalty and know-how payable.

Expected Sales The figures of expected sales are drawn from the estimates of sales and production prepared earlier in the financial analysis and projection exercise.

Exhibit 6.4 *Estimates of Working Results*

(This statement should be prepared for ten years)

(Rupees In thousands)

		Year ending				
	20 × 1	20 × 2	20 × 3	20 × 4	20 × 5	(ten years)
A Cost of Production						
Administrative expenses						
Administrative salaries						
Remuneration to directors						
Professional fees						
Light, postage, telegrams, and telephones, office supplies (stationery, printing, etc.)						
Insurance and taxes on office property						
Miscellaneous						
B Total Administrative Expenses						
C Total Sales Expenses						
D Royalty and Know-how Expenses						
E Total Cost of Production (A+B+C+D)						
F Expected Sales						
G Gross Profit Before Interest (F–E)						
Financial expenses						
Interest on term loans						
Interest on borrowings for working capital						
Guarantee commission						
H Total Financial Expenses						
I Depreciation						
J Operating Profit (G–H–I)						
K Other Income, if any (Given details)						
L Preliminary Expenses Written Off						
M Profit/Loss before Taxation (J+K – L)						
N Provision for Taxation						
O Profit After Tax (M–N)						
Less Dividend on Preference Capital						
P Retained Profit						
Add Depreciation						
Preliminary Expenses Written Off						
Q Net Cash Accruals						

Note: Detailed working shall be provided for the calculation of depreciation (straight line and income tax method), interest, taxation, etc.

Gross Profit Before Interest This represents the difference between expected sales and total cost of production.

Total Financial Expenses Financial expenses consist of interest on term loans, interest on bank borrowings, commitment charges on term loans, and commission for bank guarantees, etc. The principal financial expenses, of course, are interest on term loans and interest on bank borrowings for working capital.

In estimating the interest on term loans, two points should be borne in mind: (i) Interest on term loans is based on the present rate of interest charged by the term lending financial institutions and commercial banks. (ii) Interest amount would decrease according to the repayment schedule of the term loan.

The interest on working capital borrowings from banks may be estimated as follows: (i) determine the total requirement of the working capital, (ii) find out the quantum of bank borrowing that would be available against the total working capital requirement, and (iii) calculate the interest charges on the basis of the prevailing interest rates.

Depreciation This is an important item, particularly for capital-intensive projects. In figuring out the depreciation charge, the following points should be borne in mind:

1. Contingency margin and pre-operative expenses provided in estimating the cost of project should be added to the fixed assets proportionately to ascertain the value of fixed assets for determining the depreciation charge.
2. Preliminary expenses in excess of 5.0 percent of the project cost is included under pre-operative expenses which is subsequently allocated to fixed assets proportionately to ascertain the value of fixed assets for determining the depreciation charge.
3. The Income Tax Act specifies that the written down value method[3] should be used for tax purposes. It further specifies the rate of depreciation applicable to different kinds of assets.
4. For company law (financial reporting) purposes, the method of depreciation may be either the written down value (WDV) method or the straight line (SL) method. From 1988 onwards the depreciation rates under the Companies Act have been delinked from those under the Income Tax Act. The key depreciation rates under the Companies Act are as follows:

	In percentage terms					
	Single Shift		*Double Shift*		*Triple Shift*	
	WDV	*SL*	*WDV*	*SL*	*WDV*	*SL*
1. Building (other than factory buildings)	4.87	1.58				
2. Factory buildings	9.50	3.17				
3. Plant and machinery (general rate)	18.10	6.33	21.87	7.42	27.82	10.34

Other Income This represents income arising from transactions not part of the normal operations of the firm. Examples of such transactions are: sale of machinery, disposal of scrap, etc. Except disposal of scrap, which can be reasonably anticipated and estimated,

[3] According to the written down value method, the depreciation charge is a certain percentage of the written down value of the asset. For example, if an asset costs ₹1 million and the depreciation rate for it is 10 percent, the depreciation charge for the first year would be ₹100,000, the depreciation charge for the second year would be ₹90,000 (10 percent of ₹9,00,000, the written down value after one year), so on and so forth. In general terms, the depreciation charge for the nth year is:

$$D_n = I(1 - d)^{n-1} d \qquad (1)$$

where D_n is the depreciation charge for the nth year, I is the initial cost, and d is the depreciation rate the effects of other non-operating transactions can hardly be estimated. Of course, when non-operating transactions result in a deficit, other income would be negative—put differently, there will be a non-operating loss.

Write-off of Preliminary Expenses Preliminary expenses up to 5.0 percent of the cost of project or capital employed, whichever is higher, can be amortised in five equal annual instalments.

Profit/Loss Before Taxation This is equal to: operating profit + other income - write-off of preliminary expenses.

Provision for Taxation To figure out the tax burden, a sound understanding of the Income Tax Act - a complicated legislation—and relevant case laws is required. While calculating the taxable income, a variety of incentives and concessions have to be taken into account. Once the taxable income, as per the Income Tax Act, is calculated, the tax burden can be figured out fairly easily by applying the appropriate tax rates. The basic framework for tax calculation is discussed in an appendix at the end of the book. Since taxation is a complicated subject, an expert opinion should be sought wherever required.

Profit After Taxation This is simply profit/loss before taxation minus provision for taxation. A part of profit after tax is usually paid out as dividend—dividend on preference capital and dividend on equity capital.

Retained Profit The difference between profit after tax and dividend payment is referred to as retained profit. It is also called ploughed back earnings.

Net Cash Accrual The net cash accrual from operations is equal to: retained profit + depreciation + write-off of preliminary expenses + other non-cash charges.

6.7 PROJECTED CASH FLOW STATEMENT

The cash flow statement shows the movement of cash into and out of the firm and its net impact on the cash balance within the firm. The format for preparing the cash flow statement, which is really a cash flow budget, shown in Exhibit 6.5. While this format calls for preparing the cash flow statement on a half-yearly basis for the construction period and on an annual basis for the operating period (for ten years) for managerial purposes, it may be helpful to prepare it on a quarterly basis for the construction period and on a half-yearly basis for the first 2 to 3 operating years for managerial purposes. This would facilitate better financial planning, project evaluation, and fund control.

Exhibit 6.5 ***Cash Flow Statement***

Sources of Funds

1. Share issue
2. Profit before taxation with interest added back
3. Depreciation provision for the year
4. Development rebate reserve

(*Contd.*)

5. Increase in secured medium and long-term borrowings for the project
6. Other medium/long-term loans
7. Increase in unsecured loans and deposits
8. Increase in bank borrowings for working capital
9. Increase in liabilities for deferred payment (including interest) to machinery suppliers
10. Sale of fixed assets
11. Sale of investments
12. Other income (indicate details)

    Total (*A*)

Disposition of Funds

1. Capital expenditure for the project
2. Other normal capital expenditure
3. Increase in working capital*
4. Decrease in secured medium and long-term borrowings
   - All India Institutions
   - SFCs
   - Banks
5. Decrease in unsecured loans and deposits
6. Decrease in bank borrowings for working capital
7. Decrease in liabilities for deferred payments (including interest) to machinery suppliers
8. Increase in investments in other companies
9. Interest on term loans
10. Interest on bank borrowings for working capital
11. Taxation
12. Dividends
    - Equity
    - Preference
13. Other expenditure (indicate details)

    Total (*B*)
    - Opening balance of cash in hand and at bank
    - Net surplus/deficit (*A* – *B*)
    - Closing balance of cash in hand and at bank

* Working capital here is defined as: (Current assets other than cash) – (Current liabilities other than bank borrowings)

Illustration To illustrate how the projected cash flow statement is prepared let us consider a simple example. The balance sheet of Bhavishya Enterprises at the end of year n (the year which is just over) is as follows:

Liabilities		*Assets*		
Share capital	100	Fixed assets		180
Reserves and surplus	20	Investments		–
Secured loans	80	Current assets		180
Unsecured loans	50	Cash	20	
Current liabilities	90	Receivables	80	
Provisions	20	Inventories	80	
	360			360

The projected income statement and the distribution of earnings for the year $n + 1$ is given below:

Sales	400
Cost of goods sold	300
Depreciation	20
Profit before interest and taxes	80
Interest	20
Profit before tax	60
Tax	30
Profit after tax	30
Dividends	10
Retained earnings	20

During the year $n + 1$, the firm plans to raise a secured term loan of 20, repay a previous term loan to the extent of 5, and increase unsecured loans by 10. Current liabilities and provisions are expected to remain unchanged. Further, the firm plans to acquire fixed assets worth 30 and increase its inventories by 10. Receivables are expected to increase by 15. Other assets would remain unchanged, excepting, of course, cash. The firm plans to pay 10 by way of equity divided.

Given the above information, the projected cash flow statement of Bhavishya Enterprises is shown in Exhibit 6.6.

Exhibit 6.6 ***Projected Cash Flow Statement of Bhavishya Enterprises***

Sources of Funds		
Profit before tax with interest added back		80
Depreciation		20
Increase in secured loans		15
Increase in unsecured loans		10
	Total (*A*)	125
Disposition of Funds		
Capital expenditure		30
Increase in working capital		25
Interest		20
Taxation		30
Dividends – Equity		10
	Total (*B*)	115
Opening balance of cash in hand and at bank		20
Net surplus/deficit (*A* – *B*)		10
Closing balance of cash in hand and at bank		30

6.8 PROJECTED BALANCE SHEET

The balance sheet, showing the balances in various asset and liability accounts, reflects the financial condition of the firm at a given point of time. The horizontal format of balance sheet is given in Exhibit 6.7. It largely conforms to the format prescribed in the Companies Act.

Exhibit 6.7 Format of Balance Sheet

Liabilities	*Assets*
Share capital	Fixed assets
Reserves and surplus	Investments
Secured loans	Current assets, loans and advances
Unsecured loans	Miscellaneous expenditures and losses
Current liabilities and provisions	

The liabilities side of the balance sheet shows the sources of finance employed by the business. A word about its components shown on the left hand side of Exhibit 6.7 is in order. *Share capital* consists of paid-up equity and preference capital. *Reserves and surplus* represent mainly the accumulated retained earnings. They are shown in different accounts like the debenture redemption reserve, dividend equalisation reserve, and the general reserve. Secured loans represent the borrowings of the firm against which security has been provided. The important components of secured loans are debentures, term loans from financial institutions, and loans from commercial banks. *Unsecured loans* represent borrowings against which no specific security has been provided. Examples: fixed deposits from public and unsecured loans from promoters. *Current liabilities* are obligations which mature in the near future, usually a year. These obligations arise mainly from items which enter the operating cycle: payables from acquiring materials and supplies used in production, and accruals of wages, salaries, and rentals. *Provisions* include mainly tax provision, provision for provident fund, provision for pension and gratuity, and provision for proposed dividends.

The assets side of the balance sheet shows how funds have been used in the business. The major asset components may be described briefly. *Fixed assets* are tangible long-lived resources ordinarily used for producing goods and services. They are shown at original cost less accumulated depreciation. *Investments* represent financial securities owned by the firm. *Current assets, loans and advances* consist of cash, debtors, inventories of different kinds, and loans and advances made by the firm. *Miscellaneous expenditures and losses* represent outlays not covered by the previously described asset accounts and accumulated losses, if any.

For preparing the projected balance sheet at the end of year $n + 1$, we need information about the following:

- the balance sheet at the end of year n
- the projected income statement and the distribution of earnings for the year $n + 1$
- the sources of external financing proposed to be tapped in the year $n + 1$
- the proposed repayment of debt capital (long-term, intermediate term, and short-term) during the year $n + 1$
- the outlays and the disposal of fixed assets during the year $n + 1$
- the changes in the level of current assets during the year $n + 1$
- the changes in other assets and certain outlays like preoperative and preliminary expenses (which are capitalised) during the year $n + 1$
- the cash balance at the end of year $n + 1$.

Illustration By way of illustration, the projected balance sheet of Bhavishya Enterprises may be prepared. Based on the information provided in the previous section (where we introduced Bhavishya Enterprises), the projected balances in various asset and liability accounts are worked out in Exhibit 6.8.

Exhibit 6.8 ***Projected Balances in Liabilities and Assets Accounts***

Account Category	*Opening Balance*	*Changes During the Year*	*Closing Balance*
Liabilities			
Share capital	100	–	100
Reserves and surplus	20	+ 20 (Retained earnings)	40
Secured loans	80	+ 20 (Additional term loan)	
		– 5 (Repayment)	95
Unsecured loans	50	+10 (Proposed increase)	60
Current liabilities	90		90
Provisions	20		20
			405
Assets			
Fixed assets	180	+30 (Additional outlay)	190
		– 20 (Depreciation)	
Investments	-		-
Current assets	180		215
Cash	20		30*
Inventories	80	+10 (Proposed increase)	90
Receivables	80	+15 (Expected increase)	95
			405

* This is the balancing item.

6.9 MULTI-YEAR PROJECTIONS

Having learnt the basics of projection, we shall now look at an illustration wherein financial projections are made over a longer time frame.

A new firm, ABC Limited, is being set up to manufacture alloy steel. The expected outlays and proposed financing during the construction and the first two operating years are shown in Exhibit 6.9.

The projected revenues and costs for the first two operating years are shown in Exhibit 6.10. It may be assumed that (i) the tax rate for the firm will be 60 percent, (ii) no deductions (reliefs) are available, (iii) preliminary and pre-operative expenses will not be written off during the first two operating years, and (iv) no dividend will be paid in the first two operating years.

Based on the above information, the projected profit and loss statements, projected cash flow statements, and projected balance sheets may be prepared as shown in Exhibits 6.11, 6.12, and 6.13.

Exhibit 6.9 ***Proposed Outlays and Financing of ABC Limited***

			(₹ in millions)
	Construction Period	1st Operating Year	2nd Operating Year
Outlays			
Preliminary and preoperative expenses	2	-	-
Fixed assets	20	20	10
Current assets (other than cash)	-	20	10
Financing			
Share capital	10	15	-
Term loan	15	15	7.5
Short-term bank borrowing	-	12	6

Exhibit 6.10 ***Projected Revenues and Costs***

		(₹ in millions)
	1st Operating Year	2nd Operating Year
Sales 30	60	
Cost of sales (excluding interest and depreciation)	30	40
Interest	4.8	6.4
Depreciation	2	2.8

Exhibit 6.11 ***Projected Profit and Loss Statements of ABC Limited***

		(₹ in millions)
	1st Operating Year	2nd Operating Year
Sales	30	60
Cost of sales (excluding depreciation and interest)	30	40
Interest	4.8	6.4
Depreciation	2	2.8
Losses (absorbed)	-	6.8
Profit before tax	(6.8)	4
Tax	-	2.4
Profit after tax	(6.8)	1.6

Exhibit 6.12 ***Projected Cash Flow Statements for ABC Limited***

(₹ in millions)

	Construction Period	1st Operating Year	2nd Operating Year
Sources of Funds			
Share issue	10	15	
Profit before taxation and interest added back*		(2)	17.2
Depreciation provision for the year		2	2.8
Increase in secured medium and long-term borrowings for the project	15	15	7.5
Increase in bank borrowings for working capital	-	12	6
Total (A)	25	42	33.5
Disposition of Funds			
Capital expenditure for the project	20	20	10
Increase in current assets	-	20	10
Interest	-	4.8	6.4
Other expenditure (preliminary and preoperative expenses)	2	-	-
Taxes	-	-	2.4
Total (B)	22	44.8	28.8
Opening balance of cash in hand and cash at bank	-	3	0.2
Net surplus/deficit (A – B)	3	(2.8)	4.7
Closing balance of cash in hand and at bank	3	0.2	4.9

* This does not, of course, take into account losses absorbed.

Exhibit 6.13 ***Projected Balances Sheets of ABC Limited***

(₹ in millions)

Liabilities	*End of Construction Period*	*End of 1st Operating Year*	*End of 2nd Operating Year*	*Assets*	*End of Construction Period*	*End of 1st Operating Year*	*End of 2nd Operating Year*
Share capital	10	25	25	Fixed assets	20	38	45.2
Reserves and surplus			1.6	Current assets			
Secured loan				Cash	3	0.2	4.9
				Others	–	20	30
Term loan	15	30	37.5	Miscellaneous expenditures	–	20	30
Short-term bank borrowings	–	12	18				

(*Contd.*)

(₹ in millions)

Liabilities	*End of Construction Period*	*End of 1st Operating Year*	*End of 2nd Operating Year*	*Assets*	*End of Construction Period*	*End of 1st Operating Year*	*End of 2nd Operating Year*
				Preliminary and pre-operative expenses	2	2	2
				Profit and loss account balance	–	6.8	–
Total	25	67	82.1	Total	25	67	82.1

6.10 FINANCIAL MODELING USING SPREADSHEET

We will now create a template for multi-year projections using Microsoft Excel™ spreadsheet. A brief introduction to Excel follows.

When you open Excel, you will see a worksheet which has cells for inputting data. Each cell is uniquely specified by reference to the row and column on which it lies. The rows are numbered 1,2,3,4...from top and the columns have the headings A,B,C,D... from left. Thus, A1 is the very first cell. The one immediately to its right is B1, the one immediately below it is A2 etc. Once you finish typing a word or number inside a cell, say A1, either press enter or click on some other cell, to come out of A1. If you again type anything inside A1, the earlier matter will get overwritten, unless before typing, you press the key F2 or double click inside the cell.

If you want to widen a column width, say of column A, place the cursor on the small line separating the headings A and B (the cursor will turn into a cross), left click and drag the line to the right to the extent needed. Follow a similar procedure for changing the height of cells. If you wish to merge cells, align or wrap the text after typing, convert a number into percentage, specify the number of decimals etc. go to menu 'Format' and follow the directions in the drop-down menu.

Suppose you have filled in a value in cell A1 (say 7) and want the value in cell B4 to be equal to the value in cell A1 multiplied by 3. What you do is, without leaving any gap, type inside that cell = A1*3 and press enter and the result 21 will appear inside B4. In the formula, after typing = you may either type A1 or point the cursor on A1 and left click, and that cell no., i.e. A1, will appear after =. Change the value in A1 to, say 8 and the value in B4 will automatically change to 24.

Now, in the cell immediately below A1, i.e. in A2, enter the number 4. Copy the contents of B4 into the cell immediately below it, i.e. on to cell B5 (copy paste as in MS Word), and the number 12 will appear in B5. This is because what you have copied is the formula, which in its new position has correspondingly changed to = A2*3 due to the relative change in cell from A1 to A2.

There is an easy way to copy a formula to an adjacent cell to the right or below. Click on B4 and look at the right bottom corner of the cell to see a tiny dark rectangle, This is called a fill handle. Place the cursor on the fill handle (it will turn into a cross), and drag it onto the right bottom corner of B5 and release the mouse. The new formula value 12 will appear in B5.

If for some reason, you do not wish a cell reference number, say A1, to change while copying a formula, press the key F4 immediately after A1 in the original formula. By doing this, A1 will change to A1 (Alternatively you can type these $ signs). This is called making the cell A1 absolute. Most of the other features are as in MS Word. Spend some time exploring the various features of Excel and you should be ready for the following exercise.

Use the data in Exhibit 6.14 and 6.15 for the projections. For this, open a new Excel worksheet and first type out the various given assumptions and projected figures in Exhibits 6.14 and 6.15 as shown below. To prepare the projected profit and loss statements, fill in the text part of Exhibit 6.16 as shown below. Copy the sales figure from C15 on to C23 by typing there in the formula =C15. Drag this formula to D23 to get the corresponding figure for operating year 2. Similarly copy the cost of sales, interest and depreciation figures for the two years from the given data in Exhibit 6.15. Leave cell C27 blank, as there is no previous year loss.

To get profit before tax figure of -6.8 in cell C28, type therein the formula =C23-C24-C25-C26-C27. For the tax figure use IF function in Excel as follows: Type inside Cell C29, =IF(C28>0,C28*H5,"0"). This function says, if the condition C28>0 is true, then give the result C28*H5 and if it is not true, give the result 0. In this particular case, this condition is not true, as it is a loss, and you will get the value 0 inside C29. (You can find a list of various such functions: statistical, logical, financial etc. If you go to menu Insert>Function......)

Instead of typing out a formula, you may choose to select the formula/function from the menu list, if available there, and insert in a cell). Here you would have noted that we have made the reference to cell H5 absolute, as we do not wish the tax rate to change. Next, type the formula =C28-C29 inside C30 to get the profit after tax. Go to cell D27 and type the formula =IF(C30<0,-C30,"0"). The magnitude of the previous year loss figure will appear in that cell. Fill the cells D28, D29 and D30 by dragging the formulae from the respective cells to their left.

You can complete Exhibits 6.17 and 6.18 using the formulae indicated in the adjacent shaded portion. These formulae shown are only for your easy reference and may be deleted once the templates are ready. Note that for totaling work, you can use the SUM function. If you have to total the values in cells F36 to F40, use the formula = SUM(F36:F40).

The templates are now ready. Change the set of given data and all the statements will get suitably altered automatically. A condition is that the input data should be internally consistent. For instance, the uses should not exceed the sources, or else you will get odd statements with negative cash figure! Also note that for simplicity, we have made certain assumptions, like, no loan repayments, no dividend payments etc. during these years of projection. The template will have to be suitably modified if the assumptions change.

	A	B	C	D	E	F	G	H
1	**Exhibit 6.14** ***Proposed Outlays and Financing of ABC Limited***							
2				***(₹ in million)***				
3		*Construction Period*	*1st Operating year*	*2nd Operating year*				
4	**Outlays**				***Assumptions***			
5	Preliminary and preoperative expenses	2			Tax rate		=	60%
6	Fixed assets	20	20	10				
7	Current assets (other than eash)		20	10	Non deductions (reliefs) are available			
8	**Financing**							
9	Share capital	10	15		No. of operating years from the beginning during which no preliminary and preoperative expenses will be written off			
10	Term loan	15	15	7.5				
11	Short-term bank borrowing		12	6			=	2
12	**Exhibit 6.15** ***Projected Revenues and Costs***							
13				***(₹ in million)***				
14			*1st Operating year*	*2nd Operating year*	No. of operating years from the beginning in which no dividend will be paid		=	2
15	Sales		30	60				
16	Cost of sales (excluding interest and depreciation		30	40				
17	Interest		4.8	6.4				
18	Depreciation		2	2.8				
19								
20	**Exhibit 6.16** ***Projected Profit and Loss Statements of ABC Limited***							
21				***(₹ in million)***				
22			*1st Operating year*	*2nd Operating year*	Formula used in C column		Formula used in D column	
23	Sales		30	60	= C15		=D15	
24	Cost of sales (excluding interest and depreciation)		30	40	= C16		=D16	
25	Interest		4.8	6.4	= C17		=D17	
26	Depreciation		2	2.8	= C18		=D18	
27	Losses (abosorbed)			6.8			=IF(C30<0,-C30,"0")	
28	Profit before tax		-6.8	4	=C23-C24-C25-C26-C27		=D23-D24-D25-D26-	
29	Tax		0	2.4	=IF(C28>0,C28"H5,"0")		=IF(D28>0,D28"H5,"0	
30	Profit after tax		-6.8	1.6	=C28-C29		=D28-D29	
31								

32	***Exhibit 6.12 Projected Cash Flow Statements of ABC Limited***						
33							*(₹ in million)*
34	Formula Used in columns	F	G	H	*Construction Period*	*1nd Operating year*	*2nd Operating year*
35	**Sources of Funds Exhibit 6.17**						
36	Share issue	=B9	=C9	=D9	10	15	0
37	Profit before taxation and interest added back*		=C28+C27+C25	=D28+D27+D25		-2	17.2
38	Depreciation provision for the year		=C26	=D26		2	2.8
39	Increase in secured medium and long-term borrowings for the project	=B10	=C10	=D10	15	15	7.5
40	Increase in bank borrowing for working capital		=C11	=D11		12	6
41	Total (*A*)	=SUM(F36:F40)	=SUM(G36:G40)	=SUM(H36:H40)	25	42	33.5
42	**Disposition of Funds**						
43	Capital expenditure for the project	=B6	=C6	=D6	20	20	10
44	Increase in current assets		=C7	=D7		20	10
45	Interest		=C17	=D17		4.8	6.4
46	Other expenditure (preliminary and preoperative expenses)	=B5			2		
47	Taxes		=C29	=D29		0	2.4
48	Total (*B*)	=SUM(F43:F47)	=SUM(G43:G47)	=SUM(H43:H47)	22	44.8	28.8
49	Opening balance of cash in hand and cash at bank		=F51	=G51		3	0.2
50	Net surplus/deficit (*A-B*)	=F41-F48	=G41-G48	=H41-H48	3	-2.8	4.7
51	Closing balance of cash in hand and at bank	=F49+F50	=G49+G50	=H49+H50	3	0.2	4.9
52	* This does not, of course, take into account losses absorbed						

	A	B	C	D	E	F	G	H
53								
54	**Exhibit 6.18** ***Projected Balance Sheets of ABC Limited***							
55								*(₹ in million)*
56	***Liabilities***	*End of Construction Period*	*End of 1st Operating year*	*End of 2nd Operating year*	***Assets***	*End of Constructi-on Period*	*End of 1st Operating year*	*End of 2nd Operating year*
57	Share capital	10	25	25	Fixed assets	20	38	45.2
58	Reserves and surplus		0	1.6	Current assets			
59	Secured loan				Cash	3	0.2	4.9
60	Term loan	15	30	37.5	Others		20	30
61	Short-term bank borrowing		12	18	Miscellaneous expenditures and losses			
62					Preliminary and preoperative expenses	2	2	2
63					Profit and loss account balance		6.8	0
64	Total	25	67	82.1	Total	25	67	82.1

FORMULAE USED

56	***Liabilities***	*End of Construction Period*	*End of 1st Operating Year*	*End of 2nd Operating Year*	***Assets***	*End of Constructi-on Period*	*End of 1st Operating year*	*End of 2st Operating year*
57	Share capital	=B9	=B57+C9	=C57+D9	Fixed assets	=B6	=F57+C6-C18	=G57+C6-D18
58	Reserves and surplus		=IF(C30>0, C30,"0")	=C58+D30	Current assets			
59	Secured loan				Cash	=F51	=G51	=H51
60	Term loan	=B10	=B60+C10	=C60+D10	Others		=C7	=G60+D7
61	Short-term bank borrowings		=B61+C11	=C61+D11	Miscellaneous expenditures and losses			
62					Preliminary and preoperative expenses	=B5	=F62+C5	=G62+D5
63					Profit and loss account balance		=IF(C30<0, -C30,"0")	=IF(D30<0, -D30,"0")
64	Total	=SUM(B57: B6 1)	=SUM(C57 :C61)	=SUM(D57: D61)	Total	=SUM(F57: F63)	=SUM(G57: G63)	=SUM(H57: H63)

SUMMARY

- To judge a project from the financial angle, we need information about the following: (i) cost of project, (ii) means of financing, (iii) estimates of sales and production, (iv) cost of production, (v) working capital requirement and its financing, (vi) estimates of working results (profitability projections), (vii) break-even point, (viii) projected cash flow statements, and (ix) projected balance sheets.
- The cost of project represents the sum of all items of outlay associated with a project which are supported by long-term funds. It is the sum of outlays on the following: (i) land and site development, (ii) buildings and civil works, (iii) plant and machinery, (iv) technical know-how and engineering fees, (v) expenses on foreign technicians and training of Indian technicians abroad, (vi) miscellaneous fixed assets, (vii) preliminary and capital issue expenses, (viii) pre-operative expenses, (ix) provision for contingencies, (x) margin money for working capital, and (xi) initial cash losses.
- To meet the cost of project, the following sources of finance (referred to commonly as the means of finance) may be available: share capital (equity capital and preference capital), term loans (rupee term loans and foreign currency term loans), debenture capital (non-convertible debentures and convertible debentures), deferred credit, incentive sources (seed capital assistance, capital subsidy, and tax deferment or exemption), and miscellaneous sources (unsecured loans, public deposits, and lease and hire purchase finance).
- To determine the specific means of finance for a given project, the following should be borne in mind: (i) norms of regulatory bodies and financial institutions, and (ii) key business considerations, namely, cost, risk, control, and flexibility.
- Typically, the starting point for profitability projections is the forecast for sales revenues. In estimating sales it is reasonable to assume that capacity utilisation would be somewhat low in the first year and rise thereafter gradually to reach the maximum level in the third or fourth year of operation.
- The major components of cost of production are: material cost, utilities cost, labour cost, and factory overhead cost. The material cost comprises the cost of raw materials, chemicals, components, and consumable stores required for production. The cost of utilities is the sum of the cost of power, water, and fuel. The labour cost includes the cost of all manpower employed in the factory. The expenses on repairs and maintenance, rent, taxes and insurance on factory assets, and so on are collectively referred to as factory overheads.
- In estimating the working capital requirement and planning for its financing, the following must be borne in mind: the build up of current assets till the rated level of capacity utilisation is reached, the maximum permissible bank finance (often arrived as per the second method of lending recommended by the Tandon Committee), and the margin requirements against various current assets.
- The profitability projections or estimates of working results (as they are referred to by term-lending financial institutions) are prepared along the following lines: (i) cost of production, (ii) total administrative expenses, (iii) total sales expenses, (iv) royalty and know-how payable, (v) total cost of production, (vi) expected sales, (vii) gross profit

before interest, (viii) total financial expenses, (ix) depreciation, (x) operating profit, (xi) other income, (xii) preliminary expenses written off, (xiii) profit/loss before taxation, (xiv) provision for taxation, (xv) profit after tax, (xvi) dividend, (xvii) retained profit, and (xviii) net cash accrual.

- The cash flow statement shows the movement of cash into and out of the firm and its net impact on the cash balance with the firm.
- The balance sheet, showing the balance in various asset and liability accounts, reflects the financial condition of the firm at a given point of time.

QUESTIONS

1. Show how various financial estimates and projections are inter-related.
2. What are the components of cost of project? Discuss them in detail.
3. Describe briefly the various means of financing a project.
4. Discuss the key business considerations relevant for a project financing decision.
5. What considerations should be borne in mind while estimating sales revenues?
6. Discuss in detail the major components of cost of production.
7. What points should be kept in mind while estimating the working capital requirement and planning for its financing?
8. Discuss the items that are considered in estimating the working results.
9. What are the items found in a cash flow statement?
10. Discuss the contents of a balance sheet.

PROBLEMS

1. The balance sheet of Swaraj Limited at the end of year n (the year which is just over) is as follows:

(₹ in millions)

Liabilities		Assets	
Share capital	5	Fixed assets	11
Reserves and surplus	4	Investments	0.5
Secured loans	4	Current assets	11.5
Unsecured loans	3	■ Cash	1
Current liabilities	6	■ Receivables	4
Provisions	1	■ Inventories	6.5
	23		23

The projected income statement and the distribution of earnings is given below:

(₹ in millions)

Sales	25
Cost of goods sold	19
Depreciation	1.5
Profit before interest and tax	4.5

(Contd.)

Interest	1.2
Profit before tax	3.3
Tax	1.8
Profit after tax	1.5
Dividends	1.0
Retained earnings	0.5

During the year n+1, the firm plans to raise a secured term loan of ₹1 million, repay a previous term loan to the extent of ₹0.5 million. Current liabilities and provisions would increase by 5 percent. Further, the firm plans to acquire fixed assets worth ₹1.5 million and raise its inventories by ₹0.5 million. Receivables are expected to increase by 5 percent. The level of cash would be the balancing amount in the projected balance sheet.
Given the above information, prepare the following:

(i) Projected cash flow statement
(ii) Projected balance sheet

2. Hitek Limited is being set up to manufacture plastic window frames. The expected outlays and proposed financing during the construction and the first operating year are shown below:

Outlays	**Construction period**	**1st operating year**
Land	120	—
Building	630	—
Plant and machinery	2700	—
Miscellaneous fixed assets	450	—
Preliminary expenses	150	—
Pre-operative expenses	600	—
Current assets (other than cash)	—	2400
	4650	2400
Financing		
Equity capital	1800	—
Term loan	3000	600
Short-term bank borrowing	—	1800
	4800	2400

The following information is available:

(a) The construction period will last for one year, beginning on 1st April of year n and ending on 31st march of year $n + 1$.

(b) The first operating period will begin on 1st April of year $n + 1$ and end on 31st March of year $n + 2$.

(c) The term loan will carry an interest of 20 percent. It is repayable in 16 equal semi-annual instalments after a grace period of 2 years. The interest on term loan during the construction period is included in *pre-operative expenses*. The term loan financing of 600 in the *first operating period* will occur right in the beginning of that year.

(d) Short-term bank borrowing of 1800 will occur right in the beginning of the first operating year. It will carry an interest rate of 14 percent.

(e) Pre-operative expenses may be allocated to land, building, plant and machinery, and miscellaneous fixed assets in proportion of their values. Preliminary expenses may be written off in ten equal annual instalments.

(f) The expected revenues and cost of sales (excluding depreciation, other amortisation, and interest) for the first operating year are 4500 and 3000 respectively.

(g) The depreciation rates for company law purposes will be as follows:

Building	...	3.34 percent
Plant and machinery	...	7.42 percent
Miscellaneous fixed assets	...	7.42 percent

(h) There will be no tax liability for the first operating year.

Given the above information, complete the following projected statements:

Projected Income Statement for the 1st Operating Year

Sales	4500
Cost of sales	3000
Depreciation	—
Interest	—
Write-off of preliminary expenses	15
Net profit	—

Projected Cash Flow Statements

Sources	Construction period	1st operating year
Share capital	1800	...
Term loan	3000	...
Short-term bank borrowing		...
Profit before interest and tax		...
Depreciation		...
Write-off of preliminary expenses		...
	4800	...
Uses		
Capital expenditure	3900	...
Current assets (other than cash)	—	...
Preliminary expenses	150	...
Pre-operative expenses	600	...
Interest	—	...
	4650	...
Opening cash balance	0	...
Net surplus/deficit	150	...
Closing balance	150	...

Projected Balance Sheets

Liabilities	31/3/n + 1	31/3/n + 2	Assets	31/3/n + 1	31/3/n + 2
Share Capital	1800	...	Fixed Assets (Net)	4500	...
Reserves and Surplus	—	...			
Secured Loans:			Current Assets:		
— Term loan	3000	...	— Cash	150	...
— Short-term borrowing		...	— Other Current Assets		...
Unsecured Loans	—	...			
Current Liabilities and Provisions	—	...	Miscellaneous Expenditures and Losses		
			— Preliminary Expenses	150	...
	4800	...		4800	...

APPENDIX 6A

VEGETRON LIMITED: A CASE STUDY ON FINANCIAL PROJECTIONS

• Background

Vegetron Limited is a newly set up public limited company, promoted by Mr Muthaiah, Mr Balasubramaniam, and Mr Krishna. Mr Muthaiah, the managing director of the company, is a food technologist with over twenty years of experience in some of the well-known companies in the food sector. Mr Balasubramaniam, the finance director, is a qualified chartered accountant with over twenty-five years of industrial experience. Mr Krishna, the marketing director, has over fifteen years of experience in marketing food products.

Vegetron proposes to set up a plant to manufacture Textured Vegetable Protein (TVP), at a location not far from Bangalore. TVP is a high protein instant food mix, which is considered to be a substitute for meat. Due to its texture, TVP has an appeal for both vegetarians and non-vegetarians. So it is expected to enjoy a growing market. There are only two other units in the country manufacturing TVP, located near Bhopal and Delhi. Both of them are now doing reasonably well, though they had some problems initially.

• Technical and Marketing Aspects

The process know-how for TVP is proposed to be supplied by Spectra Machines Private Limited, a project engineering company, which will supply the main extrusion plant. The indigenous extrusion plant developed by Spectra Machines is a cost-effective alternative to imported extrusion plants. While the extrusion plant of Spectra Machines costs ₹55 million, a similar imported plant costs ₹90 million (inclusive of customs duty). Spectra Machines have supplied similar plants to the other two manufacturers of TVP and they are running satisfactorily. Vegetron proposes to give a turn-key contract of Spectra Machines that covers supply and commissioning of the unit along with a guarantee for a satisfactory trial run for a consideration of ₹62 million. A condition will stipulate that the last 25 percent of the amount is to be released only after a satisfactory trial run.

Vegetron will require about 2000 TPA (tonnes per annum) of defatted soya as the raw material at its optimum capacity utilisation. Enquiries in Bhopal, which is the major centre for defatted soya, suggest that there is no problem whatsoever in procuring this quantity.

Vegetron plans to market its product in two forms: bulk TVP and branded TVP. While the former is sold as a commodity the latter is marketed as a branded product. The bulk TVP requires very little marketing effort as well as expenses but the margin on its sales is low. The branded TVP, on the other hand, entails considerable marketing effort and expenditure and the margin on its sales is high. It is expected that the revenues from bulk TVP and branded TVP will be in the ratio 80:20. Given this mix, the sales expenses are expected to be 10 percent of net sales.

Cost of Project and Means of Finance

The cost of the project is estimated at ₹121 million as follows:

	(₹ in millions)
Land and site development	10
Building	15
Plant and machinery	62
Miscellaneous fixed assets	4
Preliminary expenses	2
Pre-operative expenses (including interest during construction)	11.5
Contingency margin	8
Working capital margin	8.5
	121

The proposed means of finance for the project are as follows:

	(₹ in millions)
Share capital	50
Term loans	60
State governments' special incentive loan (Repayable in 6 instalments after 12 years)	11
	121

The discussions with state level financing agencies and a commercial bank suggest that it should be feasible to get term loans and working capital finance for the project.

• Basic Assumptions Underlying Financial Projections

The profitability and other projections may be prepared on the basis of the following assumptions:

1. The construction period will last for one year.
2. The company would work for 300 days per year on a 2 shift basis. The installed capacity on this basis works out to 2880 TPA.
3. The company will start commercial production on April 1, of year 1. The expected capacity utilisation will be 50 percent in the first year, 60 percent in the second year, and 70 percent for the third year and beyond.
4. The average sales realisation per kilogram of TVP will be ₹120, net of GST.
5. The cost of raw materials and consumables will be 65 percent of sales; the cost of power will be 4 percent of sales.
6. Wages and salaries are expected to be ₹9 million, ₹10 million, and ₹12 million for the first, second, and third operating years respectively. Thereafter, they would rise at the rate of 5 percent per year.
7. Factory overhead expenses will be ₹0.5 million for the first year. They will increase at the rate of 6 percent per year subsequently.
8. Administration expenses will be ₹1 million per year.
9. Selling expenses will be 10 percent of sales.
10. The term loan will be repaid in 16 equal half-yearly instalments, with the first instalment falling due at the end of the second operating year. The interest rate on the outstanding term loan will be 12 percent.
11. The current asset requirements are expected to be as follows:

Raw materials (including consumables)	:	1.50 months
Stock-in-process	:	0.03 month
Finished goods	:	0.50 month
Book debt	:	1.00 month

12. The suppliers of raw materials and consumables will provide trade credit for half a month.
13. The bank finance for working capital will cost 13 percent.
14. The depreciation rates[1] for company law purposes are as follows:

Building	:	3.34 percent
Plant and machinery	:	7.24 percent
Miscellaneous fixed assets	:	7.24 percent

15. The depreciation rates for income tax[2] purposes are as follows, under the written down value method:

Building	:	10 percent
Plant and machinery and miscellaneous fixed assets	:	15 percent

[1,2] Note that these were the rates when this project was set up.

16. The preliminary expenses may be written off in 10 equal annual instalments.
17. The income tax rate applicable is 30 percent.
18. The firm plans to pay dividend from the second year. The dividend rate is proposed to be 12 percent for the second year. Thereafter, it would be enhanced by 2 percent every alternate year.

• Financial Projections

In order to prepare the profitability estimates (estimates of working results), the projected cash flow statements, and the projected balance sheets, we need information about

(a) interest on term loan,
(b) working capital requirements,
(c) depreciation schedule, and
(d) sales realisation.

This is developed in Exhibits 6A.1, 6A.2, and 6A.3 and 6A.4 respectively.

Putting together all the above information, the following projections have been prepared:

Exhibit 6A.5 : Profitability Estimates
Exhibit 6A.6 : Tax Calculation
Exhibit 6A.7 : Projected Cash Flow Estimates
Exhibit 6A.8 : Projected Balance Sheets

The spreadsheet templates for all the exhibits are given on the website of McGraw Hill Education (India) Private Limited.

Exhibit 6A.1 ***Interest on Term Loans***

(₹ *in millions*)

Year	*Loan o/s at the Beginning*	*Loan o/s at the End of the First Half Year*	*Loan o/s at the End of the Second Half Year*	*Interest for the First Half Year*	*Interest for the Second Half Year*	*Total Interest for the Term Loan*
1	60	60	60	3.60	3.60	7.20
2	60	60	56.25	3.60	3.60	7.20
3	56.25	52.5	48.75	3.38	3.15	6.53
4	48.75	45	41.25	2.93	2.70	5.63
5	41.25	37.5	33.75	2.48	2.25	4.73
6	33.75	30	26.25	2.03	1.80	3.83
7	26.25	22.5	18.75	1.58	1.35	2.93
8	18.75	15	11.25	1.13	0.90	2.03
9	11.25	7.5	3.75	0.68	0.45	1.13
10	3.75	0	0	0.23	0.00	0.23

Exhibit 6A.2 *Working Capital Requirements*

(₹ *in millions*)

Item	*Norms in Months*	*Year* 1	2	3
Raw Materials (including consumables)	1.5	14.04	16.85	19.66
Stock-in-Process	0.03	0.32	0.38	0.45
Finished Goods	0.5	5.34	6.38	7.46
Book Debts	1	14.40	17.28	20.16
Total Current Assets		34.10	40.89	47.72
Less: Margin for working capital from long-term sources (25% of total current assets)		8.53	10.22	11.93
Less: Trade credit for raw materials and consumables stores	0.5	4.68	5.62	6.55
Bank Finance for Working Capital		20.90	25.05	29.24

Exhibit 6A.3 *Depreciation Schedules*

(₹ *in millions*)

Asset Valuation for Depreciation Purposes

Asset	*Basic Cost*	*Share of Preoperative Cost*	*Share of Contingency Margin*	*Total*
Land	10	1.26	0.88	12.14
Building	15	1.90	1.32	18.21
Plant and machinery	62	7.84	5.45	75.29
Miscellaneous fixed assets	4	0.51	0.35	4.86

Depreciation schedule for company law purposes

(₹ *in millions*)

Building	3.34%	0.61
Plant and machinery	7.42%	5.59
Misc. fixed assets	7.42%	0.36
Annual depreciation		6.55

Depreciation schedule for income tax purposes (Written down value method)

(₹ *in millions*)

Year	*1*	*2*	*3*	*4*	*5*	*6*	*7*	*8*	*9*	*10*
Building	1.821	1.639	1.475	1.328	1.195	1.076	0.968	0.871	0.784	0.706
Plant and machinery and misc. fixed assets	12.021	10.218	8.685	7.383	6.275	5.334	4.534	3.854	3.276	2.784
Total	13.843	11.858	10.161	8.710	7.470	6.410	5.502	4.725	4.060	3.490

Exhibit 6A.4 ***Sales Realisation***

Year	*1*	*2*	*3*	*4*	*5*	*6*	*7*	*8*	*9*	*10*
Installed Capacity(TPA)	2880	2880	2880	2880	2880	2880	2880	2880	2880	2880
Production(TPA)	1440	1728	2016	2016	2016	2016	2016	2016	2016	2016
Capacity utilisation	50%	60%	70%	70%	70%	70%	70%	70%	70%	70%
Sales realisation (Rs. million)	172.80	207.36	241.92	241.92	241.92	241.92	241.92	241.92	241.92	241.92

Exhibit 6A.5 ***Profitability Estimates (Estimates of Working Results)***

(*₹ in millions*)

	1	*2*	*3*	*4*	*5*	*6*	*7*	*8*	*9*	*10*
A. Sales realisation	172.80	207.36	241.92	241.92	241.92	241.92	241.92	241.92	241.92	241.92
B. Cost of production										
■ Raw materials	112.32	134.78	157.25	157.25	157.25	157.25	157.25	157.25	157.25	157.25
■ Power	6.91	8.29	9.68	9.68	9.68	9.68	9.68	9.68	9.68	9.68
■ Wages and salaries	9.00	10.00	12.00	12.60	13.23	13.89	14.59	15.32	16.08	16.89
■ Factory overheads	0.50	0.53	0.56	0.60	0.63	0.67	0.71	0.75	0.80	0.84
C. Administration & selling expenses										
■ Administration expenses	1.00	1.00	1.00	1.00	1.00	1.00	1.00	1.00	1.00	1.00
■ Selling expenses	17.28	20.74	24.19	24.19	24.19	24.19	24.19	24.19	24.19	24.19
D. Gross profit before interest	25.79	32.02	37.24	36.61	35.94	35.24	34.51	33.74	32.93	32.07
E. Total financial expenses										
■ Interest on term loans	7.20	7.20	6.53	5.63	4.73	3.83	2.93	2.03	1.13	0.23
■ Interest on bank borrowing	2.72	3.26	3.80	3.80	3.80	3.80	3.80	3.80	3.80	3.80
F. Depreciation	6.55	6.55	6.55	6.55	6.55	6.55	6.55	6.55	6.55	6.55
G. Operating profit	9.32	15.00	20.36	20.63	20.86	21.06	21.23	21.36	21.44	21.49
H. Preliminary expenses written off	0.20	0.20	0.20	0.20	0.20	0.20	0.20	0.20	0.20	0.20
I. Profit /Loss before tax	9.12	14.80	20.16	20.43	20.66	20.86	21.03	21.16	21.24	21.29
J. Provision for tax	0.55	2.85	4.97	5.48	5.92	6.30	6.62	6.90	7.12	7.31
K. Profit after tax	8.57	11.95	15.19	14.95	14.74	14.56	14.40	14.26	14.12	13.99

(*Contd.*)

(₹ *in millions*)

	1	2	3	4	5	6	7	8	9	10
L. Less: Dividend		6	6	7	7	8	8	9	9	10
M. Retained profit	8.57	5.95	9.19	7.95	7.74	6.56	6.40	5.26	5.12	3.99
N. Add: Depreciation	6.55	6.55	6.55	6.55	6.55	6.55	6.55	6.55	6.55	6.55
Preliminary expenses written off	0.2	0.2	0.2	0.2	0.2	0.2	0.2	0.2	0.2	0.2
O. Net cash accruals	15.32	12.71	15.95	14.70	14.49	13.31	13.16	12.01	11.88	10.74

Exhibit 6A.6 *Tax Calculation*

(₹ *in millions*)

	1	2	3	4	5	6	7	8	9	10
▪ Profit/loss before tax	9.12	14.80	20.16	20.43	20.66	20.86	21.03	21.16	21.24	21.29
Add: depreciation for company law purposes	6.55	6.55	6.55	6.55	6.55	6.55	6.55	6.55	6.55	6.55
	15.67	21.36	26.72	26.98	27.22	27.42	27.58	27.71	27.80	27.85
▪ Less: depreciation for tax purposes	13.84	11.86	10.16	8.71	7.47	6.41	5.50	4.72	4.06	3.49
	1.83	9.50	16.55	18.27	19.75	21.01	22.08	22.99	23.74	24.36
▪ Less: unabsorbed depreciation of earlier years	-	-	-	-	-	-	-	-	-	-
▪ Gross total income	1.83	9.50	16.55	18.27	19.75	21.01	22.08	22.99	23.74	24.36
▪ Total income	1.83	9.50	16.55	18.27	19.75	21.01	22.08	22.99	23.74	24.36
Income tax @ 30%	0.55	2.85	4.97	5.48	5.92	6.30	6.62	6.90	7.12	7.31

Exhibit 6A.7 *Projected Cash Flow Statements*

(₹ *in millions*)

Year	*Construction Period*	*1*	*2*	*3*	*4*	*5*	*6*	*7*	*8*	*9*	*10*
Sources of Funds											
Share issue	50										
Profit before taxation with interest added back		19.03	25.26	30.49	29.85	29.19	28.49	27.75	26.98	26.17	25.32
Depreciation		6.55	6.55	6.55	6.55	6.55	6.55	6.55	6.55	6.55	6.55
Preliminary expenses written off		0.2	0.2	0.2	0.2	0.2	0.2	0.2	0.2	0.2	0.2

(Contd.)

(₹ *in millions*)

Year	*Construction Period*	*1*	*2*	*3*	*4*	*5*	*6*	*7*	*8*	*9*	*10*
Increase in secured medium and long-term borrowings	60										
Increase in bank borrowings for working capital		20.90	4.15	4.19							
Increase in the State Govt's Special Incentive Loan	11										
Total (A)	121.00	46.69	36.17	41.43	36.61	35.94	35.24	34.51	33.74	32.93	32.07
Disposition of Funds											
Capital expenditure for the project	110.50										
Increase in working capital		29.42	5.85	5.89							
Preliminary expenses	2.00										
Decrease in secured medium & long term borrowings			3.75	7.50	7.50	7.50	7.50	7.50	7.50	7.50	3.75
Interest on term loans		7.20	7.20	6.53	5.63	4.73	3.83	2.93	2.03	1.13	0.23
Interest on bank borrowings for working capital		2.72	3.26	3.80	3.80	3.80	3.80	3.80	3.80	3.80	3.80
Taxation		0.55	2.85	4.97	5.48	5.92	6.30	6.62	6.90	7.12	7.31
Dividend		0.00	6.00	6.00	7.00	7.00	8.00	8.00	9.00	9.00	10.00
Total (B)	112.50	39.89	28.91	34.69	29.41	28.95	29.43	28.85	29.22	28.55	25.08
Opening balance of cash in hand and at bank		8.50	15.30	22.56	29.30	36.50	43.49	49.31	54.97	59.48	63.86
Net surplus/ deficit(A-B)	8.50	6.80	7.26	6.74	7.20	6.99	5.81	5.66	4.51	4.38	6.99
Closing balance of cash in hand and at bank	8.50	15.30	22.56	29.30	36.50	43.49	49.31	54.97	59.48	63.86	70.85

Exhibit 6A.8 ***Projected Balance Sheets***

(₹ *in millions*)

	At the End of the Construction Period	*Years* 1	2	3	4	5	6	7	8	9	10
Liabilities											
Share capital	50	50	50	50	50	50	50	50	50	50	50
Reserves and surplus		8.57	14.52	23.72	31.66	39.40	45.96	52.36	57.62	62.74	66.73
Secured loans											
Term loans	60	60.00	56.25	48.75	41.25	33.75	26.25	18.75	11.25	3.75	0.00
Working capital advance		20.90	25.05	29.24	29.24	29.24	29.24	29.24	29.24	29.24	29.24
Unsecured loans											
State Govt. loan	11	11	11	11	11	11	11	11	11	11	11
Current liabilities and provisions											
Trade credit		4.68	5.62	6.55	6.55	6.55	6.55	6.55	6.55	6.55	6.55
Total	121.00	155.15	162.44	169.25	169.70	169.94	169.00	167.90	165.66	163.28	163.52
Assets											
Fixed assets											
Gross block	110.50	110.50	110.50	110.50	110.50	110.50	110.50	110.50	110.50	110.50	110.50
Less: Accumulated depreciation		6.55	13.11	19.66	26.22	32.77	39.33	45.88	52.44	58.99	65.55
Net fixed assets	110.50	103.95	97.39	90.84	84.28	77.73	71.17	64.62	58.06	51.51	44.95
Investments											
Current assets, loans and advances											
Raw materials		14.04	16.85	19.66	19.66	19.66	19.66	19.66	19.66	19.66	19.66
Stock-in-process		0.32	0.38	0.45	0.45	0.45	0.45	0.45	0.45	0.45	0.45
Finished goods		5.34	6.38	7.46	7.46	7.46	7.46	7.46	7.46	7.46	7.46
Book debts		14.40	17.28	20.16	20.16	20.16	20.16	20.16	20.16	20.16	20.16
Cash and bank balances	8.50	15.30	22.56	29.30	36.50	43.49	49.31	54.97	59.48	63.86	70.85
Misc. expenditure and losses											
Preliminary expenses	2.00	1.80	1.60	1.40	1.20	1.00	0.80	0.60	0.40	0.20	0.00
Total	121.00	155.15	162.44	169.25	169.70	169.94	169.00	167.90	165.66	163.28	163.52

MINICASE

Magna Industries Ltd. is being set up to manufacture industrial gears. The expected outlays and proposed financing during the construction and the first two operating years are shown below.

Outlays	*Construction Period*	*Operating Year*	
		I	*II*
Land	1220	—	—
Building	6110	—	—
Plant & machinery	24440	—	—
Miscellaneous fixed assets	4720	—	—
Preliminary expenses	860	—	—
Pre-operative expenses	4800	—	—
Current assets (Other than cash)		22804	2500
	42140	22804	2500
Financing			
Equity capital	16300	—	—
Term loan	29000	5704	500
Short-term bank borrowing		17100	2000
	45300	22804	2500

The following information is available:

(a) The construction period will last for one year, beginning on 1st April of year n and ending on 31st March of year n+1.

(b) The first operating period will begin on 1st April of year n+1 and end on 31st March of year n+2. This will be immediately followed by the second operating year which will end on 31st March of year n+3.

(c) The term loan will carry an interest rate of 10 percent. Each amount disbursed is repayable in 16 equal semi-annual instalments, the first such repayment commencing from the end of the I operating year. The interest on term loan during the construction period is included in pre-operative expenses. Interest due in each subsequent half year is payable at the end of the same half year. The term loan disbursals in each operating year will at beginning.

(d) Short-term bank borrowings in the two operating years will occur right in the beginning of those years and carry an interest rate of 8 percent which is payable at the end of the respective operating year.

(e) Pre-operative expenses will be allocated to land, building, plant and machinery, and miscellaneous fixed assets in proportion of their values. Preliminary expenses will be written off in ten equal annual instalments.

(f) For the first two operating years the expected revenues are 42000 and 60000 and the expected cost of sales (excluding depreciation, other amortisation, and interest) are 280000 and 40000 respectively. There is no tax liability in these years.

(g) The depreciation rates for company law purposes will be as follows: buildings (3.34%); other assets (10.34%). The method of depreciation will be the straight line method.

Required Prepare the following: (a) Projected income statements for the first two operating years, (b) Projected cash flow statements for the construction period and the first two operating years, and (c) Projected balance sheets as on 31/3/n+1, 31/3/n+2, and 31/3/n+3.

Selection I

CHAPTER 7

The Time Value of Money

CHAPTER 8

Investment Criteria

CHAPTER 9

Project Cash Flows

CHAPTER 10

The Cost of Capital

CHAPTER 11

Project Risk Analysis

PART THREE

The Time Value of Money

LEARNING OBJECTIVES

After studying this chapter you should be able to

- Calculate the future value and present value of a single amount.
- Calculate the future value and present value of an annuity.
- Compute the present value of a growing annuity.
- Show the impact of compounding frequency on the effective rate of interest.

Money has time value. A rupee today is more valuable than a rupee a year hence. Why? There are several reasons:

- Individuals, in general, prefer current consumption to future consumption.
- Capital can be employed productively to generate positive returns. An investment of one rupee today would grow to (1 + *r*) a year hence (*r* is the rate of return earned on the investment).
- In an inflationary period a rupee today represents a greater real purchasing power than a rupee a year hence.

Most financial problems involve cash flows occurring at different points of time. These cash flows have to be brought to the same point of time for purposes of comparison and aggregation. Hence you should understand the tools of compounding and discounting which underlie most of what we do in finance – from valuing securities to analysing projects, from determining lease rentals to choosing the right financing instruments, from setting up the loan amortisation schedules to valuing companies, so on and so forth.

This chapter discusses the methods for dealing with the time value of money. The material covered in this chapter will serve as a foundation for understanding the discounted cash flow techniques – the most important techniques for investment evaluation – which are discussed in the following chapter.

7.1 TIME LINES AND NOTATION

When cash flows occur at different points in time, it is easier to deal with them using a time line. A time line shows the timing and the amount of each cash flow in a cash flow stream. Thus, a cash flow stream of ₹10,000 at the end of each of the next five years can be depicted on a time line like the one shown in Part A of Exhibit 7.1.

Exhibit 7.1 ***Time Line***

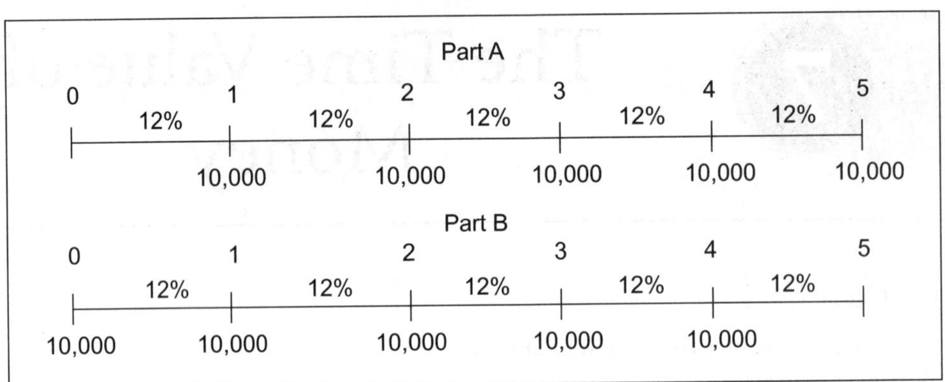

In Exhibit 7.1, 0 refers to the present time. A cash flow that occurs at time 0 is already in present value terms and hence does not require any adjustment for time value of money. You must distinguish between a *period of time* and a *point of in time*. Period 1 which is the first year is the portion of time line between point 0 and point 1. The cash flow occurring at point 1 is the cash flow that occurs at the end of period 1. Finally, the discount rate, which is 12 percent in our example, is specified for each period on the time line and it may differ from period to period. If the cash flow occurs at the beginning, rather than the end, of each year, the time line would be as shown in Part B of Exhibit 7.1. Note that a cash flow occurring at the end of year 1 is equivalent to a cash flow occurring at the beginning of year 2.

Cash flows can be positive or negative. A positive cash flow is called a *cash inflow*; a negative cash flow, a *cash outflow*.

The following notation will be used in our discussion:

PV	:	Present value
FV_n	:	Future value n years hence
C_t	:	Cash flow occurring at the end of year t
A	:	A stream of constant periodic cash flows over a given time
r	:	Interest rate or discount rate
g	:	Expected growth rate in cash flows
n	:	Number of periods over which the cash flows occur.

7.2 FUTURE VALUE OF A SINGLE AMOUNT

Suppose you invest ₹1,000 for three years in a savings account that pays 10 percent interest per year. If you let your interest income be reinvested, your investment will grow as follows:

First year	:	Principal at the beginning	1,000
		Interest for the year (₹1,000 × 0.10)	100
		Principal at the end	1,100

Second year	:	Principal at the beginning	1,100
		Interest for the year (₹1,100 × 0.10)	110
		Principal at the end	1,210
Third year	:	Principal at the beginning	1,210
		Interest for the year (₹1,210 × 0.10)	121
		Principal at the end	1,331

Formula The process of investing money as well as reinvesting the interest earned thereon is called compounding. The future value or compounded value of an investment after n years when the interest rate is r percent is:

$$FV_n = PV(1 + r)^n \tag{7.1}$$

In this equation $(1 + r)^n$ is called the future value interest factor or simply the future value factor.

To solve future value problems you have to find the future value factors. You can do it in different ways. In the example given above, you can multiply 1.10 by itself three times or more generally $(1 + r)$ by itself n times. This becomes tedious when the period of investment is long.

Fortunately, you have an easy way to get the future value factor. Most calculators have a key labelled "y^x". So all that you have to do is to enter 1.10, press the key labelled y^x, enter 3, and press the "=" key to obtain the answer.

Alternatively, you can consult a future value interest factor (FVIF) table. Exhibit 7.2 presents one such table showing the future value factors for certain combinations of periods and interest rates. A more comprehensive table is given in Appendix A at the end of the book.

Suppose you deposit ₹1,000 today in a bank which pays 10 percent interest compounded annually, how much will the deposit grow to after 8 years and 12 years?

$$₹1{,}000\ (1.10)^8 = ₹1{,}000\ (2.144)$$
$$= ₹2{,}144$$

The future value, 12 years hence, will be:

$$₹1{,}000\ (1.10)^{12} = ₹1{,}000\ (3.138)$$
$$= ₹3{,}138$$

Exhibit 7.2 ***Value of $FVIF_{r,n}$ for Various Combinations of r and n***

n/k	6%	8%	10%	12%	14%
2	1.124	1.166	1.210	1.254	1.300
4	1.262	1.360	1.464	1.574	1.689
6	1.419	1.587	1.772	1.974	2.195
8	1.594	1.851	2.144	2.476	2.853
10	1.791	2.159	2.594	3.106	3.707
12	2.012	2.518	3.138	3.896	4.817

While tables are easy to use they have a limitation as they contain values only for a small number of interest rates. So often you may have to use a calculator.

Graphic View Exhibit 7.3 shows graphically how one rupee would grow over time for different interest rates. Naturally the higher the interest rates, the faster the growth rate. We have plotted the growth curves for three interest rates: 0 percent, 6 percent, and 12 percent. Growth curves can be readily plotted for other interest rates.

Exhibit 7.3 ***Graphic View of Compounding***

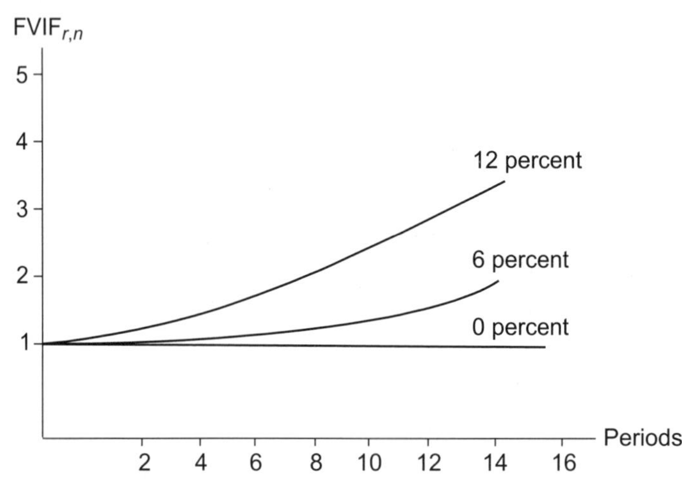

Compound and Simple Interest So far we assumed that money is invested at compound interest which means that each interest payment is reinvested to earn further interest in future periods. By contrast, if no interest is earned on interest the investment earns only simple interest. In such a case the investment grows as follows:

$$\text{Future value} = \text{Present value} [\, 1 + \text{Number of years} \times \text{Interest rate}\,]$$

For example, an investment of ₹1,000, if invested at 12 percent simple interest rate will in 5 years time become:

$$1{,}000\,[1 + 5 \times 0.12\,] = ₹1{,}600$$

Exhibit 7.4 shows how an investment of ₹1,000 grows over time under simple interest as well as compound interest when the interest rate is 12 percent. From this exhibit you can feel the power of compound interest. As Albert Einstein once remarked: "I don't know what the seven wonders of the world are, but I know the eighth – compound interest". You may be wondering why your ancestors did not display foresight. Hopefully, you will show concern for your posterity.

Exhibit 7.4 ***Value of ₹1000 Invested at 12 Percent Simple and Compound Interest***

Year	Simple Interest						Compound Interest					
	Starting Balance	+	Interest	=	Ending Balance		Starting Balance	+	Interest	=	Ending Balance	
1	1000	+	100	=	1100		1000	+	100	=	1100	
5	1400	+	100	=	1500		1464	+	146	=	1610	
10	1900	+	100	=	2000		2358	+	236	=	2594	
20	2900	+	100	=	3000		6116	+	612	=	6728	
50	5900	+	100	=	6000		106,718	+	10672	=	117,390	
100	10,900	+	100	=	11000		12,527,829	+	1,252,783	=	13,780,612	

Doubling Period Investors usually ask the question: How long would it take to double the amount at a given rate of interest? To answer this question we may look at the future value interest factor table. Looking at Exhibit 7.2 we find that when the interest rate is 12 percent it takes about 6 years to double the amount, when the interest is 6 percent it takes about 12 years to double the amount, so on and so forth. Is there a rule of thumb which dispenses with the use of the future value interest factor table? Yes, there is one and it is called the rule of 72. According to this rule of thumb, the doubling period is obtained by dividing 72 by the interest rate. For example, if the interest rate is 8 percent, the doubling period is about 9 years (72/8). Likewise, if the interest rate is 4 percent the doubling period is about 18 years (72/4). Though somewhat crude, it is a handy and useful rule of thumb.

If you are inclined to do a slightly more involved calculation, a more accurate rule of thumb is the rule of 69. According to this rule of thumb, the doubling period is equal to:

$$0.35 + \frac{69}{\text{Interest Rate}}$$

As an illustration of this rule of thumb, the doubling period is calculated for two interest rates, 10 percent and 15 percent.

Interest Rate	*Doubling Period*
10 percent	$0.35 + \frac{69}{10} = 7.25$ years
15 percent	$0.35 + \frac{69}{15} = 4.95$ years

Finding the Growth Rate The formula we used to calculate future value is quite general and it can be applied to answer other types of questions related to growth. Suppose your company currently has 5,000 employees and this number is expected to grow by 5 percent per year. How many employees will your company have in 10 years? The number of employees 10 years hence will be:

$$5{,}000 \times (1.05)^{10} = 5000 \times 1.629 = 8{,}145$$

Consider another example. Phoenix Limited had revenues of ₹100 million in 2000 which increased to ₹1000 million in 2010. What was the compound growth rate in revenues? The compound growth rate may be calculated as follows:

$$100\,(1+g)^{10} = 1{,}000$$

$$(1+g)^{10} = \frac{1000}{100} = 10$$

$$(1+g) = 10^{1/10}$$

$$g = 10^{1/10} - 1$$

$$= 1.26 - 1 = 0.26 \text{ or } 26 \text{ percent}$$

7.3 PRESENT VALUE OF A SINGLE AMOUNT

Suppose someone promises to give you ₹1,000 three years hence. What is the present value of this amount if the interest rate is 10 percent? The present value can be calculated by discounting ₹1,000, to the present point of time, as follows:

$$\text{Value three years hence} = ₹1{,}000$$

$$\text{Value two years hence} = ₹1{,}000\left(\frac{1}{1.10}\right)$$

$$\text{Value one year hence} = ₹1{,}000\left(\frac{1}{1.10}\right)\left(\frac{1}{1.10}\right)$$

$$\text{Present value} = ₹1{,}000\left(\frac{1}{1.10}\right)\left(\frac{1}{1.10}\right)\left(\frac{1}{1.10}\right)$$

Formula The process of discounting, used for calculating the present value, is simply the inverse of compounding. The present value formula can be readily obtained by manipulating the compounding formula:

$$FV_n = PV\,(1+r)^n \tag{7.2}$$

Dividing both the sides of Eq. (7.2) by $(1+r)^n$, we get:

$$PV = FV_n\,[1/(1+r)^n] \tag{7.3}$$

The factor $1/(1+r)^n$ in Eq. (7.3) is called the discounting factor or the present value interest factor ($PVIF_{r,n}$). Exhibit 7.5 gives the value of $PVIF_{r,n}$ for several combinations of r and n. A more detailed table of $PVIF_{r,n}$ is given in Appendix A at the end of this book.

What is the present value of ₹1,000 receivable 6 years hence if the rate of discount is 10 percent?

The present value is:

$$₹1{,}000 \times PVIF_{10\%,6} = ₹1{,}000(0.565) = ₹565$$

What is the present value of ₹1,000 receivable 20 years hence if the discount rate is 8 percent? Since Exhibit 7.5 does not have the value of $\text{PVIF}_{8\%,20}$ we obtain the answer as follows:

$$
\begin{aligned}
₹1{,}000 \left(\frac{1}{1.08}\right)^{20} &= ₹1{,}000 \left(\frac{1}{1.08}\right)^{10} \left(\frac{1}{1.08}\right)^{10} \\
&= ₹1{,}000\ (\text{PVIF}_{8\%,10})(\text{PVIF}_{8\%,10}) \\
&= ₹1{,}000\ (0.463)(0.463) = ₹214
\end{aligned}
$$

Exhibit 7.5 ***Value of $PVIF_{r,n}$ for Various Combinations of r and n***

n/r	*6%*	*8%*	*10%*	*12%*	*14%*
2	0.890	0.857	0.826	0.797	0.770
4	0.792	0.735	0.683	0.636	0.592
6	0.705	0.630	0.565	0.507	0.456
8	0.626	0.540	0.467	0.404	0.351
10	0.558	0.463	0.386	0.322	0.270
12	0.497	0.397	0.319	0.257	0.208

Graphic View of Discounting Exhibit 7.6 shows graphically how the present value interest factor varies in response to changes in interest rate and time. The present value interest factor declines as the interest rate rises and as the length of time increases.

Exhibit 7.6 ***Graphic View of Discounting***

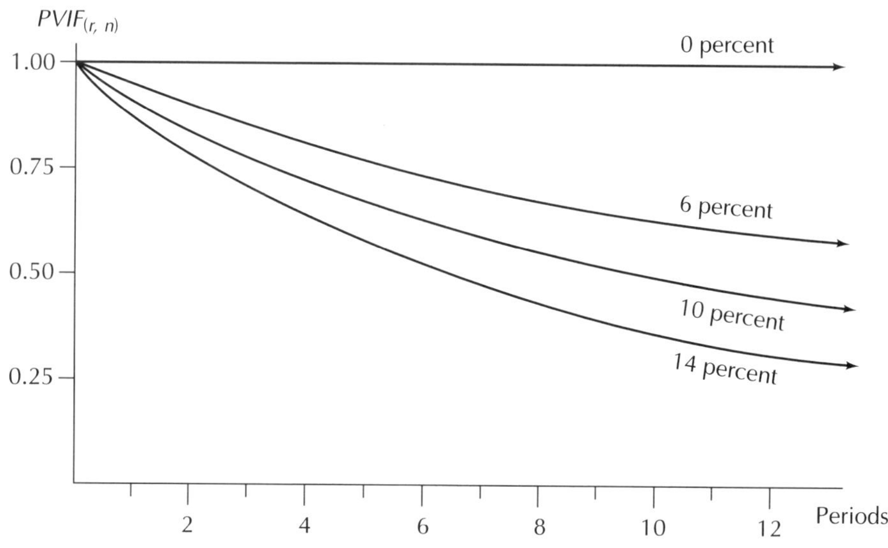

Present Value of an Uneven Series In financial analysis we often come across uneven cash flow streams. For example, the cash flow stream associated with a capital investment project is typically uneven. Likewise, the dividend stream associated with an equity share is usually uneven and perhaps growing.

The present value of a cash flow stream - uneven or even - may be calculated with the help of the following formula:

$$PV_n = \frac{A_1}{(1+r)} + \frac{A_2}{(1+r)^2} + \ldots + \frac{A_n}{(1+r)^n} = \sum_{t=1}^{n} \frac{A_t}{(1+r)^t} \tag{7.4}$$

where PV_n is the present value of a cash flow stream, A_t is the cash flow occuring at the end of year t, r is the discount rate, and n is the duration of the cash flow stream.

Exhibit 7.7 shows the calculation of the present value of an uneven cash flow stream, using a discount rate of 12 percent.

Exhibit 7.7 ***Present Value of an Uneven Cash Flow Stream***

Year	*Cash Flow (₹)*	$PVIF_{12\%,n}$	*Present Value of Individual Cash Flow*
1	1,000	0.893	893
2	2,000	0.797	1,594
3	2,000	0.712	1,424
4	3,000	0.636	1,908
5	3,000	0.567	1,701
6	4,000	0.507	2,028
7	4,000	0.452	1,808
8	5,000	0.404	2,020
Present Value of the Cash Flow Stream			13,376

7.4 FUTURE VALUE OF AN ANNUITY

An annuity is a stream of constant cash flows (payments or receipts) occurring at regular intervals of time. The premium payments of a life insurance policy, for example, are an annuity. When the cash flows occur at the end of each period the annuity is called an ordinary annuity or a deferred annuity. When the cash flows occur at the beginning of each period, the annuity is called an annuity due. Our discussion here will focus on a deferred annuity - the formulae of course can be applied, with some modification, to an annuity due.

Suppose you deposit ₹1,000 annually in a bank for 5 years and your deposits earn a compound interest rate of 10 percent. What will be the value of this series of deposits (an annuity) at the end of 5 years? Assuming that each deposit occurs at the end of the year, the future value of this annuity will be:

$$\begin{aligned} &₹1{,}000\,(1.10)^4 + ₹1{,}000\,(1.10)^3 + ₹1{,}000\,(1.10)^2 + ₹1{,}000\,(1.10) + ₹1{,}000 \\ &= ₹1{,}000\,(1.4641) + ₹1{,}000\,(1.331) + ₹1{,}000\,(1.21) + ₹1{,}000\,(1.10) + ₹1{,}000 \\ &= ₹6{,}105 \end{aligned}$$

The time line for this annuity is shown in Exhibit 7.8.

Formula In general terms the future value of an annuity is given by the following formula[1]:

$$\text{FVA}_n = A\,(1 + r)^{n-1} + A\,(1 + r)^{n-2} + \ldots + A$$
$$= A\,[(1 + r)^n - 1]/r \qquad (7.5)$$

where FVA_n is the future value of an annuity which has a duration of n periods, A is the constant periodic flow, r is the interest rate per period, and n is the duration of the annuity.

The term $[(1 + r)^n - 1]/r$ is referred to as the future value interest factor for an annuity ($\text{FVIFA}_{r,n}$). The value of this factor for several combinations of r and n is given in Exhibit 7.9. A more detailed table is given in Appendix A at the end of this book.

Exhibit 7.8 ***Time Line for an Annuity***

1	2	3	4	5
1,000	1,000	1,000	1,000	1,000
			(1,000 from year 4) →	+ 1,100
		(1,000 from year 3) →		+ 1,210
	(1,000 from year 2) →			+ 1,331
(1,000 from year 1) →				+ 1,464
				₹6,105

[1] The formula for the future value of an annuity is derived as follows:
The future value of an annuity is:

$$\text{FVA}_n = A\,(1 + r)^{n-1} + A\,(1 + r)^{n-2} + \ldots + A\,(1 + r) + A \qquad (1)$$

Multiplying both the sides of (1) by $(1 + r)$ gives:

$$\text{FVA}_n(1 + r) = A\,(1 + r)^n + A\,(1 + r)^{n-1} + \ldots + A\,(1 + r)^2 + A\,(1 + r) \qquad (2)$$

Subtracting (1) from (2) yields:

$$\text{FVA}_n\, r = A\,[(1 + r)^n - 1] \qquad (3)$$

Dividing both the sides of (3) by r gives:

$$\text{FVA}_n = A\left(\frac{(1+r)^n - 1}{r}\right) \qquad (4)$$

Exhibit 7.9 *Value of $FVIFA_{r,n}$ for Various Combinations of r and n*

n/r	6%	8%	10%	12%	14%
2	2.060	2.080	2.100	2.120	2.140
4	4.375	4.507	4.641	4.779	4.921
6	6.975	7.336	7.716	8.115	8.536
8	9.897	10.636	11.436	12.299	13.232
10	13.181	14.487	15.937	17.548	19.337
12	16.869	18.977	21.384	24.133	27.270

Applications The future value annuity formula can be applied in a variety of contexts. Its important applications are illustrated as follows:

Knowing What Lies in Store for You Suppose you have decided to deposit ₹30,000 per year in your Public Provident Fund Account for 30 years. What will be the accumulated amount in your Public Provident Fund Account at the end of 30 years if the interest rate is 11 percent?

The accumulated sum will be:

$$\text{₹}30{,}000\ (\text{FVIFA}_{11\%,30\text{yrs}})$$

$$= \text{₹}30{,}000 \left(\frac{(1.11)^{30} - 1}{0.11}\right)$$

$$= \text{₹}30{,}000\ [199.02]$$

$$= \text{₹}5{,}970{,}600$$

How Much Should You Save Annually You want to buy a house after 5 years when it is expected to cost ₹2 million. How much should you save annually if your savings earn a compound return of 12 percent?

The future value interest factor for a 5 year annuity, given an interest rate of 12 percent, is:

$$\text{FVIFA}_{n=5,\, r=12\%} = \frac{(1+0.12)^5 - 1}{0.12} = 6.353$$

The annual savings should be:

$$\frac{\text{₹}2000{,}000}{6.353} = \text{₹}314{,}812$$

Annual Deposit in a Sinking Fund Futura Limited has an obligation to redeem ₹500 million worth of bonds 6 years hence. How much should the company deposit annually in a sinking fund account wherein it earns 14 percent interest to cumulate ₹500 million in 6 years time?

The future value interest factor for a 6 year annuity, given an interest rate of 14 percent is:

$$\text{FVIFA}_{n=6,\, r=14\%} = \frac{(1+0.14)^6 - 1}{0.14} = 8.536$$

The annual sinking fund deposit should be:

$$\frac{₹500 \text{ million}}{8.536} = ₹58.575 \text{ million}$$

Finding the Interest Rate A finance company advertises that it will pay a lumpsum of ₹8,000 at the end of 6 years to investors who deposit annually ₹1,000 for 6 years. What interest rate is implicit in this offer?

The interest rate may be calculated in two steps:

1. Find the $FVIFA_{r,6}$ for this contract as follows:

$$₹8,000 = ₹1,000 \times FVIFA_{r,6}$$

$$FVIFA_{r,6} = \frac{₹8,000}{₹1,000} = 8.000$$

2. Look at the $FVIFA_{r,n}$ table and read the row corresponding to 6 years until you find a value close to 8,000. Doing so, we find that

$$FVIFA_{12\%,6} \text{ is } 8.115$$

So, we conclude that the interest rate is slightly below 12 percent.

How Long Should You Wait You want to take up a trip to the moon which costs ₹1,000,000. The cost is expected to remain unchanged in nominal terms. You can save annually ₹50,000 to fulfill your desire. How long will you have to wait if your savings earn an interest of 12 percent?

The future value of an annuity of ₹50,000 that earns 12 percent is equated to ₹1,000,000.

$$50,000 \times FVIFA_{n=?,12\%} = 1,000,000$$

$$50,000 \times \left(\frac{1.12^n - 1}{0.12}\right) = 1,000,000$$

$$1.12^n - 1 = \frac{1,000,000}{50,000} \times 0.12 = 2.4$$

$$1.12^n = 2.4 + 1 = 3.4$$

$$n \log 1.12 = \log 3.4$$

$$n \times 0.0492 = 0.5315$$

$$n = \frac{0.5315}{0.0492} = 10.8 \text{ years}$$

You will have to wait for about 11 years.

7.5 PRESENT VALUE OF AN ANNUITY

Suppose you expect to receive ₹1,000 annually for 3 years, each receipt occurring at the end of the year. What is the present value of this stream of benefits if the discount rate is 10 percent? The present value of this annuity is simply the sum of the present values of all the inflows of this annuity:

$$= ₹1,000\left(\frac{1}{1.10}\right) + ₹1,000\left(\frac{1}{1.10}\right)^2 + ₹1,000\left(\frac{1}{1.10}\right)^3$$

$$= ₹1,000 \times 0.9091 + ₹1,000 \times 0.8264 + ₹1,000 \times 0.7513$$

$$= ₹2,486.8$$

The time line for this problem is shown in Exhibit 7.10.

Exhibit 7.10 ***Time Line***

0	1	2	3
	1,000	1,000	1,000
909.1	← 1,000		
826.4		← 1,000	
751.3			← 1,000
₹2,486.8	Present Value		

Formula In general terms the present value of an annuity may be expressed as follows:

$$PVA_n = \frac{A}{(1+r)} + \frac{A}{(1+r)^2} + \ldots + \frac{A}{(1+r)^{n-1}} + \frac{A}{(1+r)^n}$$

$$= A\left(\frac{1}{(1+r)} + \frac{1}{(1+r)^2} + \ldots + \frac{1}{(1+r)^{n-1}} + \frac{1}{(1+r)^n}\right)$$

$$= A\,[\{1 - (1/1 + r)^n\}/r] \quad (7.6)^2$$

where PVA_n is the present value of an annuity which has a duration of n periods, A is the constant periodic flow, and r is the discount rate.

---

[2] The formula for the present value of an annuity is derived as follows:

$$PVA_n = A\,(1 + r)^{-1} + A\,(1 + r)^{-2} + \ldots + A\,(1 + r)^{-n} \quad (1)$$

Multiplying both the sides of (1) by $(1 + r)$ gives:

$$PVA_n\,(1 + r) = A + A\,(1 + r)^{-1} + \ldots + A\,(1 + r)^{-n+1} \quad (2)$$

Subtracting (1) from (2) yields:

$$PVA_n\, r = A\,[1 - (1 + r)^{-n}] = A\,\{[(1 + r)^n - 1]/(1 + r)^n\} \quad (3)$$

Dividing both the sides of (3) by r results in:

$$PVA_n = A\,\{[(1 + r)^n - 1]/r\,(1 + r)^n\} = A[\{1 - (1/1 + r)^n\}/r] \quad (4)$$

$[(1 + r)^n - 1]/r(1 + r)^n$ is referred to as the present value interest factor for an annuity ($PVIFA_{r,n}$). It is, as can be seen clearly, simply equal to the product of the future value interest factor for an annuity ($FVIFA_{r,n}$) and the present value interest factor ($PVIF_{r,n}$). Exhibit 7.11 shows the value of $PVIFA_{r,n}$ for several combinations of r and n. A more detailed table of $PVIFA_{r,n}$ values is given in Appendix A at the end of this book.

Exhibit 7.11 ***Value of $PVIFA_{r,n}$ for Different Combinations of r and n***

n/r	6%	8%	10%	12%	14%
2	1.833	1.783	1.737	1.690	1.647
4	3.465	3.312	3.170	3.037	2.914
6	4.917	4.623	4.355	4.111	3.889
8	6.210	5.747	5.335	4.968	4.639
10	7.360	6.710	6.145	5.650	5.216
12	8.384	7.536	6.814	6.194	5.660

Applications The present value annuity formula can be applied in a variety of contexts. Its important applications are discussed below.

How Much Can You Borrow for a Car After reviewing your budget, you have determined that you can afford to pay ₹12,000 per month for 3 years toward a new car. You call a finance company and learn that the going rate of interest on car finance is 1.5 percent per month for 36 months. How much can you borrow?

To determine how much you can borrow, you have to calculate the present value of ₹12,000 per month for 36 months at 1.5 percent per month.

Since the loan payments are an ordinary annuity, the present value interest factor of annuity is:

$$PVIFA_{r,n} = \frac{1 - 1/(1+r)^n}{r} = \frac{1 - 1/(1+.015)^{36}}{0.015} = 27.70$$

Hence the present value of 36 payments of ₹12,000 each is:

Present value = ₹12,000 × 27.70 = ₹332,400

You can, therefore, borrow ₹332,400 to buy the car.

Period of Loan Amortisation You want to borrow ₹1,080,000 to buy a flat. You approach a housing finance company which charges 12.5 percent interest. You can pay ₹180,000 per year toward loan amortisation. What should be the maturity period of the loan?

The present value of annuity of ₹180,000 is set equal to ₹1,080,000.

$$180{,}000 \times PVIFA_{n=?,\ r=12.5\%} = 1{,}080{,}000$$

$$180{,}000\ [\{1 - 1/(1.125)^n\}/0.125\ ] = 1{,}080{,}000$$

Given this equality the value of n is calculated as follows:

$$\frac{1 - 1/(1.125)^n}{0.125} = \frac{1{,}080{,}000}{180{,}000} = 6$$

$$\frac{1}{(1.125)^n} = 0.25$$

$$1.125^n = 4$$

$$n \log 1.125 = \log 4$$

$$n \times 0.0512 = 0.6021$$

$$n = \frac{0.6021}{0.0512} = 11.76 \text{ years}$$

You can perhaps request for a maturity of 12 years.

Determining the Loan Amortisation Schedule Most loans are repaid in equal periodic instalments (monthly, quarterly, or annually), which cover interest as well as principal repayment. Such loans are referred to as amortised loans.

For an amortised loan we would like to know (a) the periodic instalment payment and (b) the loan amortisation schedule showing the break up of the periodic instalment payments between the interest component and the principal repayment component. To illustrate how these are calculated, let us look an example.

Suppose a firm borrows ₹1,000,000 at an interest rate of 15 percent and the loan is to be repaid in 5 equal instalments payable at the end of each of the next 5 years. The annual instalment payment A is obtained by solving the following equation.

$$\text{Loan amount} = A \times \text{PVIFA}_{n=5,\ r=15\%}$$

$$1{,}000{,}000 = A \times 3.352$$

$$\text{Hence } A = 298{,}329$$

The amortisation schedule is shown in Exhibit 7.12. The interest component is the largest for year 1 and progressively declines as the outstanding loan amount decreases.

Exhibit 7.12 ***Loan Amortisation Schedule***

Year	*Beginning Amount (1)*	*Annual Instalment (2)*	*Interest (3)*	*Principal Repayment (2)–(3) = (4)*	*Remaining Balance (1)–(4) = (5)*
1	1,000,000	298,329	150,000	148,329	851,671
2	851,671	298,329	127,751	170,578	681,093
3	681,093	298,329	102,164	196,165	484,928
4	484,928	298,329	72,739	225,590	259,338
5	259,338	298,329	38,901	259,428	– 90[1]

a. Interest is calculated by multiplying the beginning loan balance by the interest rate.

b. Principal repayment is equal to annual instalment minus interest.

[1]Due to rounding off error a small balance is shown.

Determining the Periodic Withdrawal Your father deposits ₹300,000 on retirement in a bank which pays 10 percent annual interest. How much can be withdrawn annually for a period of 10 years? Assume that withdrawals occur at the end of each year.

$$A = ₹300{,}000 \times \frac{1}{\text{PVIFA}_{10\%,10}}$$

$$= ₹300{,}000 \times \frac{1}{6.145}$$

$$= ₹48{,}820$$

Finding the Interest Rate Suppose someone offers you the following financial contract: If you deposit ₹10,000 with him he promises to pay ₹2,500 annually for 6 years. What interest rate do you earn on this deposit? The interest rate may be calculated in two steps:

Step 1 Find the $\text{PVIFA}_{r,6}$ for this contract by dividing ₹10,000 by ₹2,500

$$\text{PVIFA}_{r,6} = \frac{₹10{,}000}{₹2{,}500} = 4.000$$

Step 2 Look at the PVIFA table and read the row corresponding to 6 years until you find a value close to 4.000. Doing so, you find that

$$\text{PVIFA}_{13\%,6} \text{ is } 3.998$$

Since 4,000 is very close to 3.998, the interest rate is 13 percent.

Present Value of a Growing Annuity A cash flow that grows at a constant rate for a specified period of time is a growing annuity. The time line of a growing annuity is shown below:

$A(1 + g)$ $A(1 + g)^2$ $A(1 + g)^n$

0 1 2 3 n

The present value of a growing annuity can be determined using the following formula:

$$\text{PV of a Growing Annuity} = A(1 + g)\left(\frac{1 - \dfrac{(1+g)^n}{(1+r)^n}}{r - g}\right) \qquad (7.7)^3$$

---

[3] The formula for the present value of a growing annuity (PVGA) is derived as follows:

$$\text{PVGA} = \frac{A(1+g)}{(1+r)} + \frac{A(1+g)^2}{(1+r)^2} + \ldots + \frac{A(1+g)^n}{(1+r)^n} \qquad (1)$$

Multiplying both the sides of (1) by $(1 + g)/(1 + r)$ gives:

$$\text{PVGA} \times \frac{(1+g)}{(1+r)} = \frac{A(1+g)^2}{(1+r)^2} + \frac{A(1+g)^3}{(1+r)^3} + \ldots + \frac{A(1+g)^{n+1}}{(1+r)^{n+1}} \qquad (2)$$

Subtracting (2) from (1) yields:

$$\text{PVGA}\left[1 - \frac{(1+g)}{(1+r)}\right] = \frac{A(1+g)}{(1+r)} - \frac{A(1+g)^{n+1}}{(1+r)^{n+1}} \qquad (3)$$

This simplifies to:

$$\text{PVGA} = A(1 + g)\left(\frac{1 - \dfrac{(1+g)^n}{(1+r)^n}}{r - g}\right) \qquad (4)$$

The above formula can be used when the growth rate is less than the discount rate ($g < r$) as well as when the growth rate is more than the discount rate ($g > r$). However, it does not work when the growth rate is equal to the discount rate ($g = r$) – in this case, the present value is simply equal to $n A$.

For example, suppose you have the right to harvest a teak plantation for the next 20 years over which you expect to get 100,000 cubic feet of teak per year. The current price per cubic foot of teak is ₹500, but it is expected to increase at a rate of 8 percent per year. The discount rate is 15 percent. The present value of the teak that you can harvest from the teak plantation can be determined as follows:

$$\text{PV of teak} = ₹500 \times 100{,}000\ (1.08) \left(\frac{1 - \dfrac{1.08^{20}}{1.15^{20}}}{0.15 - 0.08} \right)$$

$$= ₹551{,}736{,}683$$

A Note on Annuities Due So far we discussed ordinary annuities in which cash flows occur at the end of each period. There is a variation, which is fairly common, in which cash flows occur at the beginning of each period. Such an annuity is called an annuity due. For example, when you enter into a lease for an apartment, the lease payments may be due at the beginning of the month. The first lease payment is made at the beginning; the second lease payment is due at the beginning of the second month, so on and so forth. The time lines for ordinary annuity and annuity due are shown below:

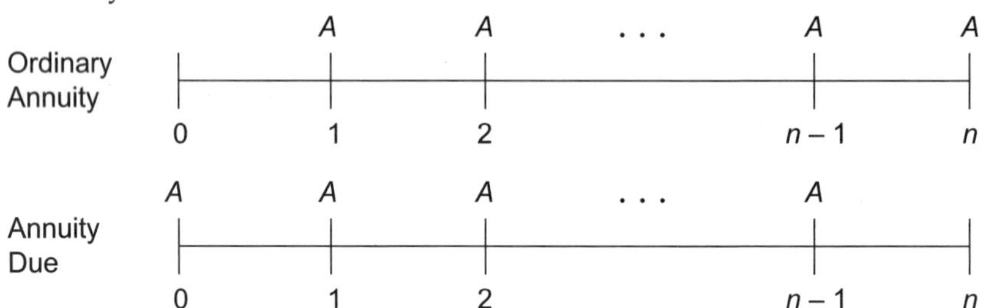

Since the cash flows of an annuity due occur one period earlier in comparison to the cash flows on an ordinary annuity, the following relationship holds:

$$\text{Annuity due value} = \text{Ordinary annuity value} \times (1 + r)$$

This applies for both present and future values. So, two steps are involved in calculating the value of an annuity due. First, calculate the present or future value as though it were an ordinary annuity. Second, multiply your answer by $(1 + r)$.

Present Value of a Perpetuity A perpetuity is an annuity of infinite duration. Hence, the present value of a perpetuity may be expressed as follows:

$$P_{\infty} = A \times \text{PVIFA}_{r,\infty} \tag{7.8}$$

where P_{∞} is the present value of a perpetuity, A is the constant annual payment, and $\text{PVIFA}_{r,\infty}$ is the present value interest factor for a perpetuity (an annuity of infinite duration).

What is the value of $PVIFA_{r,\infty}$? It is equal to:

$$\sum_{t=1}^{\infty} \frac{1}{(1+r)^t} = \frac{1}{r} \qquad (7.9)^4$$

Put in words, it means that the present value interest factor of a perpetuity is simply 1 divided by the interest rate expressed in decimal form. Hence, the present value of a perpetuity is simply equal to the constant annual payment divided by the interest rate. For example, the present value of a perpetuity of ₹10,000 if the interest rate is 10 percent is equal to: ₹10,000/0.10 = ₹100,000. Intuitively this is quite convincing because an initial sum of ₹100,000 would, if invested at a rate of interest of 10 percent, provide a constant annual income of ₹10,000 for ever without any impairment of the capital value.

7.6 INTRA-YEAR COMPOUNDING AND DISCOUNTING

So far we assumed that compounding is done annually. Now we consider the case where compounding is done more frequently. Suppose you deposit ₹1,000 with a finance company which advertises that it pays 12 percent interest semi-annually – this means that the interest is paid every six months. Your deposit (if interest is not withdrawn) grows as follows:

First six months	: Principal at the beginning	=	₹1,000.0
	Interest for 6 months	=	₹60.0
	$₹1{,}000 \times \frac{0.12}{2}$		
	Principal at the end	=	₹1,060.0
Second six months	: Principal at the beginning	=	₹1,060.0
	Interest for 6 months	=	₹63.6
	$₹1{,}060 \times \frac{0.12}{2}$		
	Principal at the end	=	₹1,123.6

---

[4] The formula for $PVIFA_{r,\infty}$ is derived as follows:

$$PVIFA_{r,\infty} = 1(1+r)^{-1} + 1(1+r)^{-2} + \ldots + 1(1+r)^{-\infty} \qquad (1)$$

Multiplying both the sides of (1) by $(1 + r)$ gives:

$$PVIFA_{r,\infty}(1+r) = 1 + 1(1+r)^{-1} + \ldots + (1+r)^{-\infty+1} \qquad (2)$$

Subtracting (1) from (2) yields:

$$PVIFA_{r,\infty} \times r = 1 - 1(1+r)^{-\infty} \qquad (3)$$

Since the second term on the right hand side of (3) vanishes, we get:

$$PVIFA_{r,\infty} \times r = 1 \qquad (4)$$

This results in:

$$PVIFA_{r,\infty} = \frac{1}{r} \qquad (5)$$

Note that if compounding is done annually, the principal at the end of one year would be ₹1,000 (1.12) = ₹1,120. The difference of ₹3.6 (between ₹1,123.6 under semi-annual compounding and ₹1,120 under annual compounding) represents interest on interest for the second half year.

The general formula for the future value of a single cash flow after n years when compounding is done m times a year is:

$$FV_n = PV\left(1+\frac{r}{m}\right)^{m\times n} \tag{7.10}$$

Suppose you deposit ₹5,000 in a bank for 6 years. If the interest rate is 12 percent and the frequency of compounding is 4 times a year your deposit after 6 years will be:

$$₹5{,}000\left(1+\frac{0.12}{4}\right)^{4\times 6} = ₹5{,}000\ (1.03)^{24}$$

$$= ₹5{,}000 \times 2.0328 = ₹10{,}164$$

Effective versus Stated Rate We have seen above that ₹1,000 grows to ₹1,123.6 at the end of a year if the stated rate of interest is 12 percent and compounding is done semi-annually. This means that ₹1,000 grows at the rate of 12.36 percent per annum. The figure of 12.36 percent is called the effective interest rate – the rate of interest under annual compounding which produces the same result as that produced by an interest rate of 12 percent under semi-annual compounding.

The general relationship between the effective interest rate and the stated annual interest rate is as follows:

$$\text{Effective interest rate} = \left(1+\frac{\text{Stated annual interest rate}}{m}\right)^{m} - 1$$

where m is the frequency of compounding per year.

Suppose a bank offers 12 percent stated annual interest rate. What will be the effective interest rate when compounding is done annually, semiannually, and quarterly?

$$\text{Effective interest rate with annual compounding} = \left(1+\frac{0.12}{1}\right)^{1} - 1 = 0.12$$

$$\text{Effective interest rate with semi-annual compounding} = \left(1+\frac{0.12}{2}\right)^{2} - 1 = 0.1236$$

$$\text{Effective interest rate with quarterly compounding} = \left(1+\frac{0.12}{4}\right)^{4} - 1 = 0.1255$$

When compounding becomes continuous, the effective interest rate is expressed as follows[5]:

$$\text{Effective interest rate} = e^{r} - 1 \tag{7.11}$$

where e is the base of natural logarithm, and r is the stated interest rate.

[5] See Appendix 7A.

Exhibit 7.13 shows how compounding frequency impacts on the effective interest rate. From this exhibit is clear that the effect of increasing the frequency of compounding is not as dramatic as some would believe it to be - the additional gains dwindle as the frequency of compounding increases.

Exhibit 7.13 ***Compounding Frequency and Effective Interest Rate***

Frequency	*Rate*	*m*	*Formula*	*Effective Interest Rate*
Annual	12	1	0.12	12 percent
Semi-annual	12	2	$\left[1+\frac{0.12}{2}\right]^2-1$	12.36
Quarterly	12	4	$\left[1+\frac{0.12}{4}\right]^4-1$	12.55
Monthly	12	12	$\left[1+\frac{0.12}{12}\right]^{12}-1$	12.68
Weekly	12	52	$\left[1+\frac{0.12}{52}\right]^{52}-1$	12.73
Daily	12	365	$\left[1+\frac{0.12}{365}\right]^{365}-1$	12.75
Continuous	12		$e^{0.12}-1$	12.75

Shorter Discounting Periods Sometimes cash flows have to be discounted more frequently than once a year — semi-annually, quarterly, monthly, or daily. As in the case of intra-year compounding, the shorter discounting period implies that (i) the number of periods in the analysis increases and (ii) the discount rate applicable per period decreases. The general formula for calculating the present value in the case of shorter discounting period is:

$$\text{PV} = \text{FV}_n\left[\frac{1}{1+r/m}\right]^{mn} \tag{7.12}$$

where PV is the present value, FV_n is the cash flow after n years, m is the number of times per year discounting is done, and r is the annual discount rate.

To illustrate, consider a cash flow of ₹10,000 to be received at the end of four years. The present value of this cash flow when the discount rate is 12 percent (r = 12 percent) and discounting is done quarterly (m = 4) is determined as follows:

$$\begin{aligned}\text{PV} &= ₹10{,}000 \times \text{PVIF}_{r/m,\, m\times n}\\ &= ₹10{,}000 \times \text{PVIF}_{3\%,16}\\ &= ₹10{,}000 \times 0.623 = ₹6{,}230\end{aligned}$$

SUMMARY

- Money has time value. A rupee today is more valuable than a rupee a year hence.
- When cash flows occur at different points in time, it is easier to deal with them using a time line. A time line shows the timing and the amount of each cash flow in a cash flow stream.
- The process of investing money as well as reinvesting the interest earned thereon is called compounding. The future or compounded value of an investment after n years when the interest rate is *r* percent is:

$$\text{Future value}_n = \text{Present value } (1 + r)^n$$

- If no interest is earned on interest the investment earns only simple interest. In such a case the investment grows as follows:

$$\text{Future value} = \text{Present value } [1 + nr]$$

- According to the rule of 72, the doubling period under compounding is obtained by dividing 72 by the interest rate.
- The process of discounting, used for calculating the present value, is simply the inverse of compounding. The present value formula is:

$$\text{PV} = \text{FV}_n[1/(1 + r)^n]$$

- The present value of a cash flow is equal to:

$$\text{PV}_n = \sum_{t=1}^{n} \frac{A_t}{(1+r)^t}$$

- An annuity is a stream of constant cash flows (payments or receipts) occurring at regular intervals of time. When the cash flows occur at the end of each period the annuity is called a regular annuity or a deferred annuity. When the cash flows occur at the beginning of each period, the annuity is called an annuity due.
- The future value of an annuity is given by the formula:

$$\text{FVA}_n = A\ [(1 + r)^n - 1]/r$$

- The present value of an annuity is given by the formula:

$$\text{PVA}_n = A\ \{[(1 + r)^n - 1]/r(1 + r)^n\}$$

- A cash flow that grows at a constant rate for a specified period of time is a growing annuity. The present value of a growing annuity is given by the following formula:

$$\text{PV of a Growing Annuity} = A(1 + g)\ \{[1 - (1 + g)^n/(1 + r)^n]/(r - g)\}$$

- Since the cash flows of an annuity due occur one period earlier in comparison to the cash flows of an ordinary annuity, the following relationship holds:

$$\text{Annuity due value} = \text{Ordinary annuity value} \times (1 + r)$$

- A perpetuity is an annuity of infinite duration. The present value of a perpetuity is:

$$\text{Present value of a perpetuity} = A/r$$

- The general formula for the future value of a single cash flow after n years when compounding is done m times a year is:

$$FV_n = PV\,[1 + r/m]^{mn}$$

- The relationship between effective interest rate and the stated annual interest rate is as follows:

$$\text{Effective interest rate} = \left(1 + \frac{\text{Stated annual interest rate}}{m}\right)^m - 1$$

- When compounding becomes continuous, the effective interest rate is expressed as:

$$\text{Effective interest rate} = e^r - 1$$

- The formula for calculating the present value in the case of shorter compounding period is:

$$PV = FV_n\,[1/(1 + r/m)\,]^{mn}$$

QUESTIONS

1. Why does money have time value?
2. State the general formula for the future value of a single amount.
3. What is the difference between compound and simple interest?
4. Explain the rule of 72.
5. Explain the rule of 69. How does it compare with the rule of 72.
6. State the general formula for calculating the present value of a single amount.
7. What is an annuity? What is the difference between an ordinary annuity and an annuity due?
8. State the formula for the future value of an annuity.
9. State the formula for the present value of an annuity.
10. What is a growing annuity? What is the formula for finding the present value of a growing annuity?
11. What is the formula for the present value of a perpetuity?
12. State the formula for the future value of a single cash flow after n years when compounding is done m times a year.
13. What is the relationship between the effective interest rate and the stated interest rate?
14. State the formula for calculating the present value of a single cash flow when discounting is done m times a year.
15. A firm's earnings grew from ₹1 per share to ₹3 per share over a period of 10 years. The total growth was 200 percent, but the annual compound growth rate was less than 20 percent. Why?

PROBLEMS

1. Calculate the value 5 years hence of a deposit of ₹1,000 made today if the interest rate is (a) 8 percent, (b) 10 percent, (c) 12 percent, and (d) 15 percent.

2. If you deposit ₹5,000 today at 12 percent rate of interest in how many years (roughly) will this amount grow to ₹160,000? Work this problem using the rule of 72 — do not use tables.
3. A finance company offers to give ₹8,000 after 12 years in return for ₹1,000 deposited today. Using the rule of 69, figure out the approximate rate of interest offered.
4. You can save ₹2,000 a year for 5 years, and ₹3,000 a year for 10 years thereafter. What will these savings cumulate to at the end of 15 years, if the rate of interest is 10 percent?
5. Mr Vinay plans to send his son for higher studies abroad after 10 years. He expects the cost of these studies to be ₹1000,000. How much should he save annually to have a sum of ₹1000,000 at the end of 10 years, if the interest rate is 12 percent?
6. A finance company advertises that it will pay a lump sum of ₹10,000 at the end of 6 years to investors who deposit annually ₹1,000. What interest rate is implicit in this offer?
7. Someone promises to give you ₹5,000 after 10 years in exchange for ₹1,000 today. What interest rate is implicit in this offer?
8. Find the present value of ₹10,000 receivable after 8 years if the rate of discount is (i) 10 percent, (ii) 12 percent, and (iii) 15 percent.
9. What is the present value of a 5-year annuity of ₹2,000 at 10 percent?
10. At the time of his retirement, Mr Jingo is given a choice between two alternatives: (a) an annual pension of ₹10,000 as long as he lives, and (b) a lumpsum amount of ₹50,000. If Mr Jingo expects to live for 15 years and the interest rate is 15 percent, which option appears more attractive?
11. Mr X deposits ₹100,000 in a bank which pays 10 percent interest. How much can he withdraw annually (at the end of each year) for a period of 30 years. Assume that at the end of 30 years the amount deposited will whittle down to zero.
12. What is the present value of an income stream which provides ₹1,000 at the end of year one, ₹2,500 at the end of year two, and ₹5,000 during each of the years 3 through 10, if the discount rate is 12 percent?
13. What is the present value of an income stream which provides ₹2,000 a year for the first five years and ₹3,000 a year forever thereafter, if the discount rate is 10 percent?
    Hint: The present value for a perpetual annuity is derived by dividing the constant annual flow by the discount factor.
14. What amount must be deposited today in order to earn an annual income of ₹5,000 beginning from the end of 15 years from now? The deposit earns 10 percent per year.
15. Suppose someone offers you the following financial contract. If you deposit ₹20,000 with him he promises to pay ₹4,000 annually for 10 years. What interest rate would you earn on this deposit?
16. What is the present value of ₹10 receivable 100 years hence at 10 percent discount rate?
17. Suppose you deposit ₹10,000 with an investment company which pays 16 percent interest with quarterly compounding. How much will this deposit grow to in 5 years?
18. How much would a deposit of ₹5,000 at the end of 5 years be, if the interest rate is 12 percent and if the compounding is done quarterly?
19. What is the difference between the effective rate of interest and stated rate of interest in the following cases:

    Case A: Stated rate of interest is 12 percent and the frequency of compounding is six times a year.

    Case B: Stated rate of interest is 24 percent and the frequency of compounding is four times a year.

    Case C: Stated rate of interest is 24 percent and the frequency of compounding is twelve times a year.

20. If the interest rate is 12 percent, how much investment is required now to yield an income of ₹12,000 per year from the beginning of the 10th year and which continues thereafter forever?
21. You have a choice between ₹5,000 now and ₹20,000 after 10 years. Which would you choose? What does your preference indicate?
22. Mr Raghu deposits ₹10,000 in a bank now. The interest rate is 10 percent and compounding is done semi-annually. What will the deposit grow to after 10 years? If the inflation rate is 8 percent per year, what will be the value of the deposit after 10 years in terms of the current rupees?
23. How much should be deposited at the beginning of each year for 10 years in order to provide a sum of ₹50,000 at the end of 10 years?
24. A person requires ₹20,000 at the beginning of each year from 2015 to 2019. How much should he deposit at the end of each year from 2005 to 2010? The interest rate is 12 percent.
25. What is the present value of ₹2,000 receivable annually for 30 years? The first receipt occurs after 10 years and the discount rate is 10 percent.
26. After five years Mr Ramesh will receive a pension of ₹600 per month for 15 years. How much can Mr Ramesh borrow now at 12 percent interest so that the borrowed amount can be paid with 30 percent of the pension amount? The interest will be accumulated till the first pension amount becomes receivable.
27. Mr Prakash buys a scooter with a bank loan of ₹6,000. A monthly instalment of ₹300 is payable to the bank for the next 24 months towards the repayment of the loan with interest. What interest rate does the bank charge?
28. South India Corporation has to retire ₹10 million of debentures each at the end of 8, 9, and 10 years from now. How much should the firm deposit in a sinking fund account annually for 5 years, in order to meet the debenture retirement need? The net interest rate earned is 8 percent.
29. Mr Longman receives a provident fund amount of ₹100,000. He deposits it in a bank which pays 10 percent interest. If he withdraws annually ₹20,000, how long can he do so?
30. Phoenix Company borrows ₹500,000 at an interest rate of 14 percent. The loan is to be repaid in 4 equal annual instalments payable at the end of each of the next 4 years. Prepare the loan amortisation schedule.
31. You want to borrow ₹1,500,000 to buy a flat. You approach a housing company which charges 13 percent interest. You can pay ₹200,000 per year toward loan amortisation. What should be the maturity period of the loan?
32. You are negotiating with the government the right to mine 100,000 tons of iron ore per year for 15 years. The current price per ton of iron ore is ₹3000 and it is expected to increase at the rate of 6 percent per year. What is the present value of the iron ore that you can mine if the discount rate is 16 percent?

MINICASE

As an investment advisor, you have been approached by a client called Ramesh, who wants some help in investment related matters.

Ramesh is currently 45 years old and has ₹600,000 in the bank. He plans to work for 15 more years and retire at the age of 60. Ramesh's present salary is ₹400,000 per year. He expects his salary to increase at the rate of 12 percent per year until his retirement.

Ramesh has decided to invest his bank balance and future savings in a portfolio in which stocks and bonds would be equally weighted. For the sake of simplicity, assume that these proportions will be maintained by him throughout. He also believes that bonds would provide a return of 7 percent and stocks a return of 13 percent. You concur with his assessment.

Once Ramesh retires at the age of 60 he would like to withdraw ₹500,000 per year from his investments for the following 15 years as he expects to live upto the age of 75 years. He also wants to bequeath ₹1000,000 to his children at the end of his life. How much money would he need 15 years from now?

How much should Ramesh save each year for the next 15 years to be able to meet his investment objectives spelt out above? Assume that the savings will occur at the end of each year.

Suppose Ramesh wants to donate ₹200,000 each year in the last three years of his life to a charitable cause. Each donation would he made at the beginning of the year. How much money would he need when he reaches the age of 60 to meet this specific need?

Ramesh recently attended a seminar on human capital where the speaker talked about a person's human capital as the present value of this life time earnings. Ramesh is curious to find out the present value of his lifetime salary. For the sake of simplicity assume that his present salary of ₹400,000 will be paid exactly one year from now, and his salary will be paid in annual instalments. What is the present value of his life time salary, if the discount rate is 8 percent? Remember that Ramesh expects his salary to increase at the rate of 12 percent per year until his retirement.

In answering the above questions, ignore the tax factor.

APPENDIX 7A

CONTINUOUS COMPOUNDING AND DISCOUNTING

In Chapter 7 we have assumed that compounding or discounting takes place at specific intervals (annually, semi-annually, quarterly, and so forth). In this appendix we explore the implications of continuous compounding and discounting.

In Chapter 7, the following relationship was established for a case when compounding occurs m times a year

$$i_e = \left(1+\frac{r}{m}\right)^m - 1 \quad (7A.1)$$

where i_e is the effective interest rate, r is the stated interest rate, and m is the frequency of compounding

Equation (7A.1) may be expressed as:

$$i_e = \left(\left(1+\frac{1}{m/r}\right)^{m/r}\right)^r - 1 \quad (7B.2)$$

Putting $x = m/r$ in Eq. (7B.2), we get

$$i_e = \left(\left(1+\frac{1}{x}\right)^x\right)^r - 1 \quad (7B.3)$$

In continuous compounding $m \to \infty$. This means $x \to \infty$ in Eq. (7B.3). Now,

$$\text{Lim} \left(1+\frac{1}{x}\right)^x = e = 2.71828 \ldots \text{x} \to \infty \quad (7B.4)$$

So from Eq. (7B.3), we get

$$i_e = e^r - 1 \tag{7B.5}$$

This means

$$(1 + i_e) = e^r \tag{7B.6}$$

Given the relationship between the stated (or nominal) interest rate and the effective interest rate, we get the following:

$$\text{FVIF}_{r,n} = e^{rn} \tag{7B.7}$$

$$\text{PVIF}_{r,n} = e^{-rn} \tag{7B.8}$$

$$\text{FVIFA}_{r,n} = \frac{e^{-rn} - 1}{r} \tag{7B.9}$$

$$\text{PVIFA}_{r,n} = \frac{1 - e^{-rn}}{r} \tag{7B.10}$$

APPENDIX 7B

MICROSOFT EXCEL AS A FINANCIAL CALCULATOR

Excel is the greatest financial calculator ever made. All financial calculators have five financial keys, and Excel's basic time value functions are exactly analogous. The following table shows the equivalence between the calculator keys and Excel functions.

Purpose	*Calculator Key*	*Excel Function*
Solve for number of periods	N	**Nper (rate, pmt, pv,** *fv, type*)
Solve for periodic interest rate	I/Yr	**Rate (nper, pmt, pv,** *fv, type, guess*)
Solve for present value	PV	**PV (rate, nper, pmt,** *fv, type*)
Solve for annuity payment	PMT	**PMT (Rate, nper, pv,** *fv, type*)
Solve for future value	FV	**FV (Rate, nper, nper, pmt,** *pv, type*)

To solve a TVM problem in a financial calculator, you have to supply at least three of the variables. Likewise, you have to supply at least three of the arguments to each Excel function. Note that in the table, the bold function arguments are required whereas those in italics are optional.

APPENDIX 7C

XNPV AND XIRR

So far we assumed that cash flows occur periodically (every year, or every half-year, or every quarter, and so on).

In finance, many cash flows, however, do not occur periodically. In such cases the standard functions of NPV and IRR have to be modified to reflect the actual dates when the cash flows occur. These functions are called extended NPV (or XNPV) and extended IRR (or XIRR).

XNPV is defined as:

$$\text{XNPV} = \sum_{t=i}^{N} \frac{C_i}{(1+r)^{(d_i-d_1)/365}}$$

where C_i is the i th cash flow, d_i is the i th cash flow date, d_1 is the O th date, r is the discount rate per year.

XIRR is the interest rate corresponding to XNPV = 0

$$0 = \sum_{i=1}^{N} \frac{C_i}{(1+r)^{(d_j-d_1)/365}}$$

To calculate XNPV and XIRR, use the Microsoft Excel functions XNPV and XIRR. Microsoft Excel stores dates as sequential series numbers so that they can be used in calculations. By default, January 1, 1990 is serial number 1. All subsequent dates are numbered accordingly. For example, January 1, 2008 is serial number 39448 because it is 39,448 days after January 1, 1900.

XNPV and XIRR Illustration

Vishal needed some funds to start a small business. He borrowed an amount of ₹5 lakhs from his close friend Suresh: ₹2 lakhs on 19th March 2014 and ₹3 lakhs on 22nd May 2015. He repaid the loan in parts on various dates: ₹2 lakhs on 1st January 2016, ₹422,000 on 28th November 2017, and ₹480,000 on 31st December 2018. If the cost of capital (discount rate) to Suresh is 15 percent, what is the NPV of the cash flows to him? What is the return earned by him (IRR) on this loan?

The NPV can be obtained as shown below using the XNPV function in Excel:

	A	B	C	D	E	F
1	Date	19-Mar-14	22-May-15	1-Jan-16	28-Nov-17	31-Dec-18
2	Cash flow	–200,000	–300,000	200,000	422,000	480,000
3	Discount rate	0.15	XNPV	=XNPV(B3,B2:F2,B1:F1))→		198,645

The NPV is ₹198,645.

The IRR can be obtained using the XIRR function:

	A	B	C	D	E	F
1	Date	19-Mar-14	22-May-15	1-Jan-16	28-Nov-17	31-Dec-18
2	Cash flow	–200,000	–300,000	200,000	422,000	480,000
3	XIRR	=XIRR(B2:F2,B1:F1)		→		30.13%

The IRR is 30 percent

Chapter 8

Investment Criteria

LEARNING OBJECTIVES

After studying this chapter you should be able to

- List and classify various investment criteria.
- Discuss the properties of the NPV rule.
- Explain the rationale for the NPV rule.
- Discuss the problems associated with internal rate of return.
- Discuss various non-DCF criteria.
- Assess investment evaluation methods in terms of theoretical and practical considerations.
- Describe investment evaluation practice.

The key steps involved in determining whether a project is worthwhile or not are:

- Estimate the costs and benefits of the project
- Assess the riskiness of the project
- Calculate the cost of capital
- Compute the criteria of merit and judge whether the project is good or bad.

For pedagogic purposes, we find it more convenient to start with a discussion of the criteria of merit, referred to as investment criteria or capital budgeting techniques. A familiarity with these criteria will facilitate an easier understanding of costs and benefits, risk analysis, and cost of capital.

There are many criteria that have been suggested by economists, accountants, and others to judge the worthwhileness of capital projects. Indeed, scores of criteria have been proposed, in the extensive literature on this subject. Some are general and applicable to a wide range of investments; others are specialised and suitable for certain types of investments and industries.

The important investment criteria, classified into two broad categories – discounting criteria and non-discounting criteria – are shown in Exhibit 8.1.

This chapter discusses these criteria in some detail. In addition it looks at how investment appraisal is done in practice, both in India and abroad.

Exhibit 8.1 ***Investment Criteria***

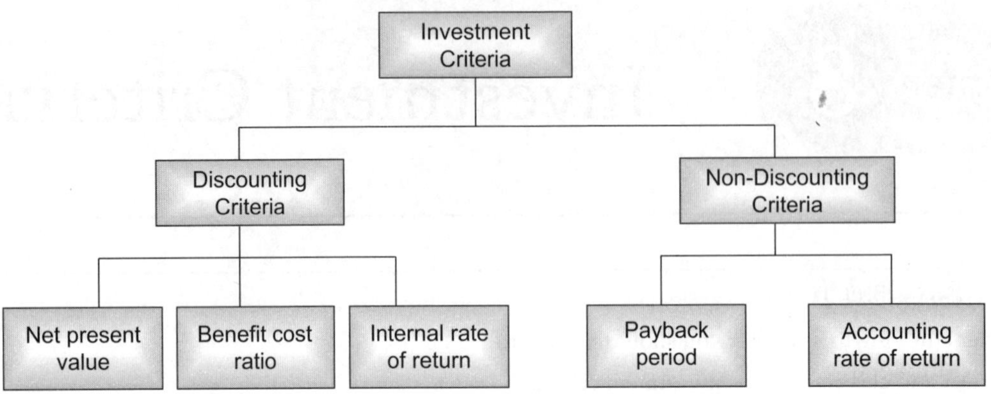

8.1 NET PRESENT VALUE

The net present value (NPV) of a project is the sum of the present values of all the cash flows - positive as well as negative - that are expected to occur over the life of the project. The general formula for NPV is:

$$NPV = \sum_{t=1}^{n} \frac{C_t}{(1+r)^t} - \text{Initial investment} \tag{8.1}$$

where C_t is the cash flow at the end of year t, n is the life of the project, and r is the discount rate.

To illustrate the calculation of net present value, consider a project which has the following cash flow stream:

Year	*Cash Flow*
0	₹(1,000,000)
1	200,000
2	200,000
3	300,000
4	300,000
5	350,000

The cost of capital[1], r, for the firm is 10 percent. The net present value of the proposal is:

$$NPV = -\frac{1,000,000}{(1.10)^0} + \frac{200,000}{(1.10)^1} + \frac{200,000}{(1.10)^2} + \frac{300,000}{(1.10)^3} + \frac{300,000}{(1.10)^4} + \frac{350,000}{(1.10)^5} = ₹5,273$$

[1] The cost of capital must reflect the risk of the project. While the details of how the cost of capital is calculated are discussed in Chapter 10, for the present we assume that the cost of capital figure is given and includes an appropriate premium for risk.

The net present value represents the net benefit over and above the compensation for time and risk. Hence the decision rule associated with the net present value criterion is: Accept the project if the net present value is positive and reject the project if the net present value is negative. (If the net present value is zero, it is a matter of indifference.)

Properties of the NPV Rule The net present value has certain properties that make it a very attractive decision criterion:

Net Present Values are Additive The net present value of a package of projects is simply the sum of the net present values of individual projects included in the package. This property has several implications:

- The value of a firm can be expressed as the sum of the present value of projects in place as well as the net present value of prospective projects:
  Value of a firm = Σ Present value of projects + Σ NPV of expected future projects
  The first term on the right hand side of this equation captures the value of assets in place and the second term the value of *growth opportunities.*
- When a firm terminates an existing project which has a negative NPV based on its expected future cash flows, the value of the firm increases by that amount. Likewise, when a firm undertakes a new project that has a negative NPV, the value of the firm decreases by that amount.
- When a firm divests itself of an existing project, the price at which the project is divested affects the value of the firm. If the price is greater/lesser than the present value of the anticipated cash flows of the project the value of the firm will increase/decrease with the divestiture.
- When a firm takes on a new project with a positive NPV, its effect on the value of the firm depends on whether its NPV is in line with expectation. Hindustan Lever Limited, for example, is expected to take on high positive NPV projects and this expectation is reflected in its value. Even if the new projects taken on by Hindustan Unilever Limited have positive NPV, the value of the firm may drop if the NPV is not in line with the high expectation of investors.
- When a firm makes an acquisition and pays a price in excess of the present value of the expected cash flows from the acquisition it is like taking on a negative NPV project and hence will diminish the value of the firm.

Intermediate Cash Flows Are Invested at Cost of Capital The NPV rule assumes that the intermediate cash flows of a project – that is, cash flows that occur between the initiation and the termination of the project – are reinvested at a rate of return equal to the cost of capital.

NPV Calculation Permits Time Varying Discount Rates So far we assumed that the discount rate remains constant over time. This need not be always the case. The NPV can be calculated using time-varying discount rates. The general formula of NPV is as follows:

$$\text{NPV} = \sum_{t=1}^{n} \frac{C_t}{(1+r_t)^t} - \text{Initial investment} \tag{8.2}$$

where C_t is the cash flow at the end of year t, and r_t is the discount rate for year t

In even more general terms NPV is expressed as follows:

$$\text{NPV} = \sum_{t=1}^{n} \frac{C_t}{\prod_{j=1}^{t}(1+r_j)} - \text{Initial investment} \tag{8.3}$$

where C_t is the cash flow at the end of year t, r_j is the one period discount rate, and n is the life of the project.

The discount rate may change over time for the following reasons: (a) The level of interest rates may change over time - the term structure of interest rates sheds light on expected rates in future. (b) The risk characteristics of the project may change over time, resulting in changes in the cost of capital. (c) The financing mix of the project may vary over time, causing changes in the cost of capital.

To illustrate, assume that you are evaluating a 5-year project involving software development. You believe that the technological uncertainty associated with this industry leads to higher discount rates in future.

	Year 0		Year 1		Year 2		Year 3		Year 4		Year 5
Discount rate		14%		15%		16%		18%		20%	
Investment Cash flow	– 12000		4,000		5,000		7,000		6,000		5,000

The present value of the cash flows can be calculated as follows:

PV of C_1	= 4,000 / 1.14	= 3509
PV of C_2	= 5,000 / (1.14 * 1.15)	= 3814
PV of C_3	= 7,000 / (1.14 * 1.15 * 1.16)	= 4603
PV of C_4	= 6,000 / (1.14 * 1.15 * 1.16 * 1.18)	= 3344
PV of C_5	= 5,000 / (1.14 * 1.15 * 1.16 * 1.18 * 1.20)	= 2322
NPV of project	= 3509 + 3814 + 4603 + 3344 + 2322 – 12000	= ₹5592

NPV of a Simple Project Decreases as the Discount Rate Increases A simple project involves an initial cash outflow, or a series of initial cash outflows, followed by cash inflows. The NPV of a simple project steadily decreases as the discount rate increases. The decrease in NPV, however, is at a decreasing rate.[2]

[2] To demonstrate this point, consider a simple project which has the following cash flow stream.

$$-C_0, C_1, C_2, \ldots, C_N$$

The net present value as a function of the discount rate, r, may be expressed as:

$$\text{NPV}(r) = -C_0 + C_1(1+r)^{-1} + C_2(1+r)^{-2} + \ldots + C_N(1+r)^{-N} \tag{1}$$

Assuming that r is a continuous variable and NPV (r) is a continuous and differentiable function, we get:

$$\frac{d\text{NPV}(r)}{d(1+r)} = -C_1(1+r)^{-2} - 2C_2(1+r)^{-3} - \ldots - NC_N(1+r)^{-(N+1)} \tag{2}$$

This is negative for all values of $-1 < r < \infty$

Hence the net present value of a simple project is steadily decreasing.

The second derivative of the net present value function with respect to $(1 + r)$ is:

$$\frac{d^2\text{NPV}(r)}{d(1+r)^2} = 2C_1(1+r)^{-3} + 6C_2(1+r)^{-4} - \ldots + N(N+1)C_N(1+r)^{-(N+2)} \tag{3}$$

This is positive for all values of $-1 < r < \infty$. Hence the net present value function decreases at a decreasing rate.

Rationale for the NPV Rule The net present value criterion has a sound rationale underlying it. To understand this, let us look at a simple problem concerning a choice between current consumption and future consumption. Suppose you have a cash inflow of *OA* now (year 0) and *OB* in a year from now (year 1) as shown by point *X* in Exhibit 8.2. Further assume that through the capital market you can transfer wealth across time by lending or borrowing. The opportunity for lending or borrowing is represented by the line *CXD*. The slope of this line is $(1 + r)$, where r denotes the 1-year rate of interest. If you lend your present cash inflow of *OA* at an interest rate of r percent, your consumption in year 1 will be augmented by $OA\ (1 + r)$, which is *BD*. Further, if you borrow against your future inflow, you can reach any point on the line *CXD*, by lending or borrowing.

Exhibit 8.2 ***Lending Borrowing Opportunity***

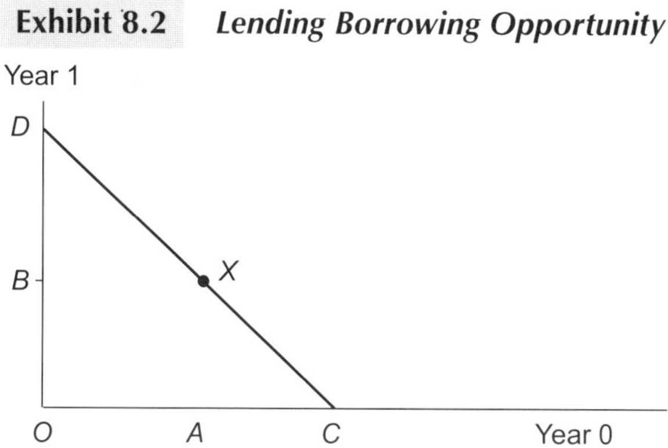

Your investment opportunity, however, is not limited to just lending or borrowing in the capital market. You may also consider investment in land, building, plant, machinery, and other real assets. The investment opportunity line which shows the returns from buying real assets is shown in Exhibit 8.3. This investment opportunity line, unlike the lending or borrowing line of Exhibit 8.2, is not a straight line. Its slope is high to begin with but declines progressively because the marginal return from additional investment in real assets tends to decline.

Exhibit 8.3 ***Investment Opportunity Curve***

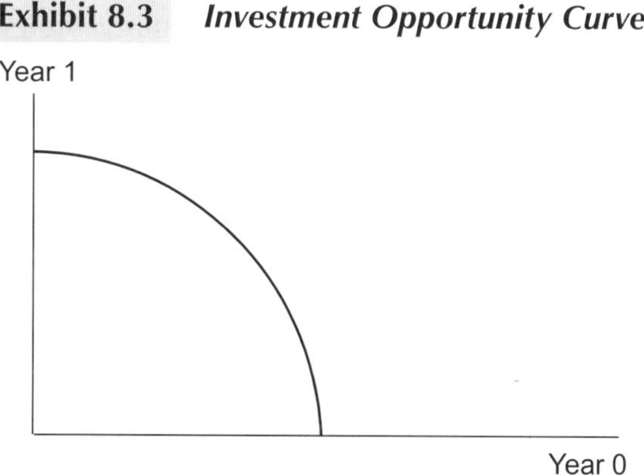

How is your welfare affected by the possibility of investing in real assets along with the possibility of lending or borrowing? To answer this question, we consider the situation illustrated in Exhibit 8.4 in which we assume, for the sake of simplicity, that your initial resources are equal to *OD*. The opportunity to invest in real assets is represented by the line *DXE* and the lending-borrowing opportunity on the capital market is represented by the straight line *DL*.

Exhibit 8.4 ***Investment and Lending-Borrowing Opportunities***

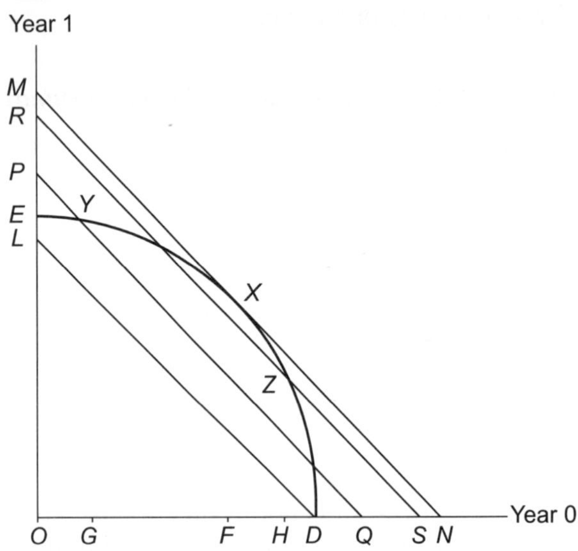

Now let us look at what happens when you invest different amounts in real assets.

- Investment of *DF* in real assets
- Investment of *DG* (an amount greater than *DF*) in real assets
- Investment of *DH* (an amount less than *DF*) in real assets

If you invest *DF* in real assets, a sacrifice of *DF* in year 0 brings a benefit of *FX* in year 1. As a result you move from point *D* to point *X* on the real asset investment opportunity line. From point *X* you can move along the line *MN* by availing of lending-borrowing opportunities (The line *MN*, it may be noted, is parallel to the line *DL* – all lending-borrowing lines are parallel to each other).

If you invest *DG* in real assets you move from *D* to *Y* on the real asset investment opportunity line. From *Y* you can move along the line *PQ* by availing of lending-borrowing opportunities in the capital market.

If you invest *DH* in real assets you move from *D* to *Z* on the real asset investment opportunity frontier. From *Z* you can move along the line *RS* by availing of lending-borrowing opportunities in the capital market.

What do we find when we compare the three cases? If you invest an amount equal to *DF* in real assets you reach the consumption frontier *MN*; if you invest an amount equal to *DG* in real assets you reach the consumption frontier *PQ*; if you invest an amount equal to *DH* in real assets you reach the consumption frontier *RS*. Clearly, investment of an amount equal to *DF* in real assets is the most desirable course of action since it takes you to the highest consumption frontier.

Investment of an amount equal to *DF* in real assets, it may be emphasised, is also the investment which has the highest net present value. This is clear from a comparison of the following:

Net present value of investment *DF* = Present value of benefits – Present value of costs
= $NF - DF = DN$

Net present value of investment *DG* = Present value of benefits – Present value of costs
= $QG - DG = DQ$

Net present value of investment *DH* = Present value of benefits – Present value of costs
= $SH - DH = DS$

Thus, when the net present value is maximised, you reach the highest consumption frontier. This, then, constitutes the rationale for the net present value criterion.

Modified Net Present Value The standard net present value method is based on the assumption that the intermediate cash flows are re-invested at a rate of return equal to the cost of capital. When this assumption is not valid, the re-investment rates applicable to the intermediate cash flows need to be defined for calculating the modified net present value. The steps involved in this process are as follows:

Step 1 Calculate the terminal value of the project's cash inflows using the explicitly defined reinvestment rate(s) which are supposed to reflect the profitability of investment opportunities ahead for the firm.

$$TV = \sum_{t=1}^{n} CF_t (1 + r')^{n-t} \tag{8.4}$$

where TV is the terminal value of the project's cash inflows, CF_t is the cash inflow at the end of year t, and r' is the re-investment rate applicable to the cash inflows of the project.

Step 2 Determine the modified net present value:

$$NPV^* = \frac{TV}{(1 + r)^n} - I \tag{8.5}$$

where NPV^* is the modified net present value, TV is the terminal value, r is the cost of capital, and I is the investment outlay.

To illustrate the calculation of NPV^*, consider two projects, *X* and *Y*:

	Project X	*Project Y*
Investment outlay	₹110,000	₹110,000
Cash inflows		
Year 1	31,000	71,000
Year 2	40,000	40,000
Year 3	50,000	40,000
Year 4	70,000	20,000

The NPV* for X and Y may be calculated for two re-investment rates, 14 percent and 20 percent, assuming a cost of capital of 10 percent.

Step 1 The terminal values of the cash inflows of projects X and Y for the two reinvestment rates are:

$$TV(X)_{14\%} = 31{,}000(1.14)^3 + 40{,}000(1.14)^2 + 50{,}000(1.14) + 70{,}000 = ₹224{,}911$$

$$TV(X)_{20\%} = 31{,}000(1.20)^3 + 40{,}000(1.20)^2 + 50{,}000(1.20) + 70{,}000 = ₹241{,}168$$

$$TV(Y)_{14\%} = 71{,}000(1.14)^3 + 40{,}000(1.14)^2 + 40{,}000(1.14) + 20{,}000 = ₹222{,}774$$

$$TV(Y)_{20\%} = 71{,}000(1.20)^3 + 40{,}000(1.20)^2 + 40{,}000(1.20) + 20{,}000 = ₹248{,}288$$

Step 2 The NPV* of projects X and Y for the two re-investment rates are:

$$\text{NPV}^*(X)_{14\%} = \frac{TV(X)_{14\%}}{(1.10)^4} - 110{,}000 = ₹43{,}614$$

$$\text{NPV}^*(X)_{20\%} = \frac{TV(X)_{20\%}}{(1.10)^4} - 110{,}000 = ₹54{,}717$$

$$\text{NPV}^*(Y)_{14\%} = \frac{TV(Y)_{14\%}}{(1.10)^4} - 110{,}000 = ₹42{,}158$$

$$\text{NPV}^*(Y)_{20\%} = \frac{TV(Y)_{20\%}}{(1.10)^4} - 110{,}000 = ₹59{,}584$$

Limitations Despite its advantages and a direct linkage to the objective of value maximisation, the NPV rule has its opponents who point towards some limitations:

- The NPV is expressed in absolute terms rather than relative terms and hence does not factor in the scale of investment. Thus, project A may have an NPV of 5,000 while project B has an NPV of 2,500, but project A may require an investment of 50,000 whereas project B may require an investment of just 10,000. Advocates of NPV, however, argue that what matters is the surplus value, over and above the hurdle rate, irrespective of what the investment is.
- The NPV rule does not consider the life of the project. Hence, when mutually exclusive projects with different lives are being considered, the NPV rule is biased in favour of the longer term project.

8.2 BENEFIT COST RATIO (OR PROFITABILITY INDEX)

There are two ways of defining the relationship between benefits and costs:

$$\text{Benefit-cost ratio: BCR} = \frac{\text{PVB}}{I} \tag{8.6}$$

$$\text{Net benefit-cost ratio: NBCR} = \frac{\text{PVB} - I}{I} = \text{BCR} - 1 \tag{8.7}$$

where PVB is the present value of benefits, and I is the initial investment.

To illustrate the calculation of these measures, let us consider a project which is being evaluated by a firm that has a cost of capital of 12 percent.

Initial investment:		₹100,000
Benefits:	Year 1	25,000
	Year 2	40,000
	Year 3	40,000
	Year 4	50,000

The benefit cost ratio measures for this project are:

$$\text{BCR} = \frac{\dfrac{25{,}000}{(1.12)} + \dfrac{40{,}000}{(1.12)^2} + \dfrac{40{,}000}{(1.12)^3} + \dfrac{50{,}000}{(1.12)^4}}{100{,}000} = 1.145$$

$$\text{NBCR} = \text{BCR} - 1 = 0.145$$

The two benefit cost ratio measures, because the difference between them is simply unity, give the same signals. The following decision rules are associated with them.

When BCR	*or*	*NBCR*	*Rule is*
>1		>0	Accept
=1		=0	Indifferent
<1		<0	Reject

Evaluation The proponents of benefit cost ratio argue that since this criterion measures net present value per rupee of outlay, it can discriminate better between large and small investments and hence is preferable to the net present value criterion.

How valid is this argument? Weingartner, who examined this criterion theoretically, finds that: (i) Under unconstrained conditions, the benefit-cost ratio criterion will accept and reject the same projects as the net present value criterion. (ii) When the capital budget is limited in the current period, the benefit-cost ratio criterion may rank projects correctly in the order of decreasingly efficient use of capital. However, its use is not recommended because it provides no means for aggregating several smaller projects into a package that can be compared with a large project. (iii) When cash outflows occur beyond the current period, the benefit-cost ratio criterion is unsuitable as a selection criterion.

8.3 INTERNAL RATE OF RETURN

The internal rate of return (IRR) of a project is the discount rate which makes its NPV equal to zero. Put differently, it is the discount rate which equates the present value of future cash flows with the initial investment. It is the value of r in the following equation:

$$\text{Investment} = \sum_{t=1}^{n} \frac{C_t}{(1+r)^t} \tag{8.6}$$

where C_t is the cash flow at the end of year t, r is the internal rate of return (IRR), and n is the life of the project.

In the NPV calculation we assume that the discount rate (cost of capital) is known and determine the NPV. In the IRR calculation, we set the NPV equal to zero and determine the discount rate that satisfies this condition.

To illustrate the calculation of IRR, consider the cash flows of a project being considered by Techtron Limited:

Year	0	1	2	3	4
Cash flow	(100,000)	30,000	30,000	40,000	45,000

The IRR is the value of r which satisfies the following equation:

$$100{,}000 = \frac{30{,}000}{(1+r)^1} + \frac{30{,}000}{(1+r)^2} + \frac{40{,}000}{(1+r)^3} + \frac{45{,}000}{(1+r)^4}$$

The calculation of r involves a process of trial and error. We try different values of r till we find that the right-hand side of the above equation is equal to 100,000. Let us, to begin with, try r = 15 percent. This makes the right-hand side equal to:

$$\frac{30{,}000}{(1.15)} + \frac{30{,}000}{(1.15)^2} + \frac{40{,}000}{(1.15)^3} + \frac{45{,}000}{(1.15)^4} = 100{,}802$$

This value is slightly higher than our target value, 100,000. So we increase the value of r from 15 percent to 16 percent. (In general, a higher r lowers and a smaller r increases the right-hand side value). The right-hand side becomes:

$$\frac{30{,}000}{(1.16)} + \frac{30{,}000}{(1.16)^2} + \frac{40{,}000}{(1.16)^3} + \frac{45{,}000}{(1.16)^4} = 98{,}641$$

Since this value is now less than 100,000, we conclude that the value of r lies between 15 percent and 16 percent. For most of the purposes this indication suffices.

If a more refined estimate of r is needed, use the following procedure:

1. Determine the net present value of the two closest rates of return.
   (NPV/15 percent) 802
   (NPV/16 percent) (1,359)
2. Find the sum of the absolute values of the net present values obtained in step 1:

   802 + 1,359 = 2,161

3. Calculate the ratio of the net present value of the smaller discount rate, identified in step 1, to the sum obtained in step 2:

   $$\frac{802}{2{,}161} = 0.37$$

4. Add the number obtained in step 3 to the smaller discount rate:

   15 + 0.37 = 15.37 percent

To explain IRR we have calculated it by hand. In practice, you will find it convenient to use the EXCEL function IRR.

The decision rule for IRR is as follows:

Accept : If the IRR is greater than the cost of capital
Reject : If the IRR is less than the cost of capital

NPV and IRR By now you may have noticed that the IRR rule is quite similar to the NPV rule. To see the link between them, let us plot the values of NPV for the project of Techtron Limited for different discount rates. The NPV profile is shown in Exhibit 8.5 where the NPV is plotted on the vertical or y-axis and the discount rate on the horizontal or x-axis. The NPV profile provides valuable insights:

Exhibit 8.5 ***NPV Profile***

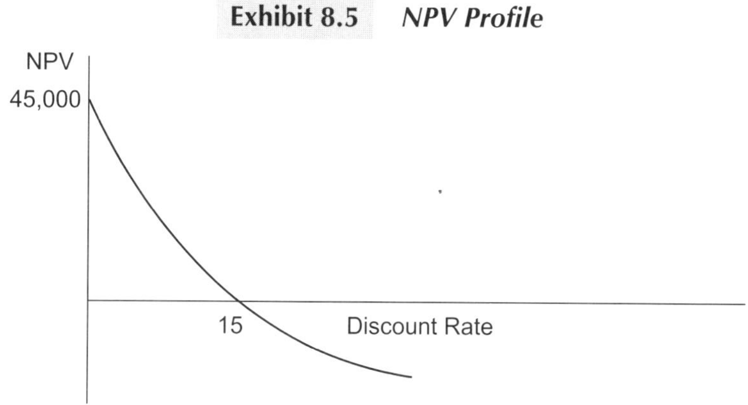

- The IRR is the point at which the NPV profile crosses the x axis.
- The slope of the NPV profile reflects how sensitive the project is to discount rate changes.

Do the IRR and the NPV rules lead to identical decisions? Yes, provided two conditions are satisfied. First, the cash flows of the project must be *conventional*, implying that the initial cash flows are negative and the subsequent cash flows are positive. Second, the project must be *independent*, meaning that the project can be accepted or rejected without reference to any other project.

Problems with IRR There are problems in using IRR when the cash flows of the project are not conventional or when two or more projects are being compared to determine which one is the best. In the first case it is difficult to define 'what is IRR' and in the second case IRR can be misleading. Further IRR cannot distinguish between lending and borrowing. Finally, IRR is difficult to apply when short-term interest rates differ from long-term interest rates.

Non-conventional Cash Flows Consider a project which has the following cash flow stream associated with it:

		Cash Flow	
Project	C_0	C_1	C_2
M	–160,000	+1,000,000	–1,000,000

The IRR equation for this cash flow stream is:

$$-160{,}000 + \frac{1{,}000{,}000}{(1+r)} - \frac{1{,}000{,}000}{(1+r)^2} = 0$$

There are two roots of this equation viz., $r = 0.25$ and $r = 4.00$ which correspond to 25 percent and 400 percent. This is illustrated by the NPV profile shown in Exhibit 8.6.

Exhibit 8.6 ***Multiple Internal Rates of Return***

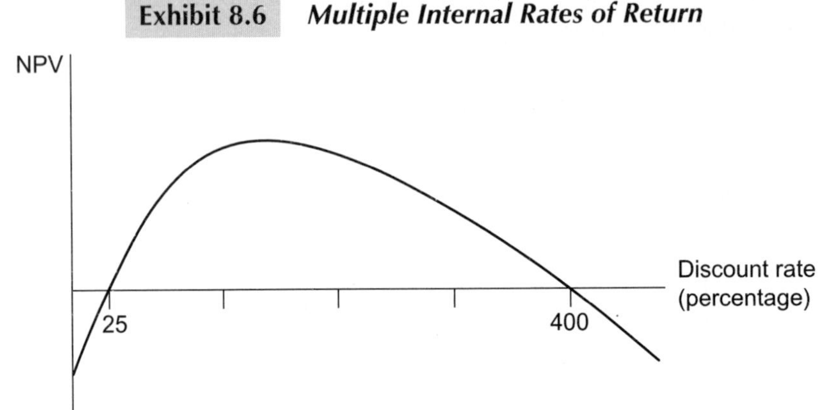

In Exhibit 8.6, the NPV is zero at two discount rates, viz., 25 percent and 400 percent. Which of these is the correct IRR? We can't say. There is no unambiguously correct answer. This is the problem of multiple rates of return and in such cases the IRR rule breaks down.

As if this were not enough, there can also be cases in which no IRR exists. For example, project *P* has a positive NPV for all discount rates and hence no IRR:

	Cash flow				NPV	
Project	C_0	C_1	C_2	IRR, Percent	at 15%	at 30%
P	+15,000	–45,000	+37,500	None	4225	2574

Several modifications of the IRR rule have been suggested for such cases. These modifications are neither adequate nor necessary, for the simple solution lies in using the NPV rule.

Mutually Exclusive Projects Often firms have to choose from two or more mutually exclusive projects. In such cases IRR can be misleading. Consider projects *P* and *Q*.

		Cash flow	*IRR*	*NPV*
Project	C_0	C_1		*(assuming r =12 percent)*
P	–10,000	20,000	100%	7,857
Q	–50,000	75,000	50%	16,964

Both the projects are good, but *Q*, with its higher NPV, contributes more to the value of the firm. Yet from an IRR point of view *P* looks better than *Q*. Hence the IRR rule seems unsuitable for ranking projects of different scale.

The IRR rule, of course, can be salvaged in such cases by considering the IRR on the incremental cash flow. Here is how we do it. Looking at *P*, the project which requires the smaller outlay, we find that it is highly attractive because its IRR is 100 percent, far above the cost of capital which is 12 percent. Now we ask: What is the rate of return on the incremental cash flow if we switch from *P* (the low-outlay project) to *Q* (the high-outlay project)? The incremental cash flow associated with such a switch is:

C_0	C_1
– 40,000	55,000

The IRR of this cash flow stream is 37.5 percent, much above the cost of capital. Hence it is desirable to switch from *P* to *Q*.

Thus, unless you look at the incremental cash flow, IRR is not a reliable rule for ranking projects of different scale.

IRR is also unreliable for ranking projects which have different patterns of cash flow over time. Consider two projects, *X* and *Y*, being evaluated by a firm that has a cost of capital of 10 percent.

Project	C_0	C_1	C_2	C_3	C_4	*IRR*	*NPV at 10%*
X	–110,000	+31,000	+40,000	+50,000	+70,000	22%	36,613
Y	–110,000	+71,000	+40,000	+40,000	+20,000	25%	31,314

Both the projects look good but *X*, with its higher NPV, contributes more to the value of the firm. Yet from an IRR point of view *Y* looks more attractive. Hence the IRR rule can be misleading when a choice has to be made between mutually exclusive projects which have different patterns of cash flow over time.

Of course, in this case too the IRR rule can be salvaged by considering the IRR on the incremental cash flow.

As the previous examples suggest, when mutually exclusive projects are evaluated it is much simpler to use the NPV rule rather than the IRR rule with such involved additional computations.

Lending vs. Borrowing The IRR rule cannot distinguish between lending and borrowing and hence a high IRR need not necessarily be a desirable thing.

To illustrate this point, let us consider two projects *A* and *B*

	Cash flow		*IRR*	*NPV at 10% discount rate*
Project	C_0	C_1		
A	–4000	+6000	50%	1455
B	+4000	–7000	75%	–2364

The IRR for project *A* is 50 percent, whereas the IRR for project *B* is 75 percent. Does this mean that *B* is more attractive than *A*? Certainly not. *A* is a very attractive project, whereas *B* is a highly undesirable project. Why? *A* involves investing 4000 at a rate of return of 50 percent, whereas *B* involves borrowing 4000 at a rate of return of 75 percent. Yet if we go by the IRR figures alone, *B* appears more attractive than *A*.

Differences between Short-term and Long-term Interest Rates Recall our general formula for calculating NPV:

$$\text{NPV} = \sum_{t=1}^{n} \frac{C_t}{(1+r_t)^t} - \text{Initial investment} \tag{8.7}$$

Thus, the cash flow for year 1, C_1, is discounted at the opportunity cost of capital for year 1, r_1; the cash flow for year 2, C_2, is discounted at the opportunity cost of capital for year 2, r_2; so on and so forth.

The IRR rule says that a project should be accepted if its IRR is greater than the opportunity cost of capital. But what should we do when there are several opportunity costs? Should we compare IRR with r_1 or r_2 or r_3 ... or r_n? We have to, in effect, compute a complex weighted average of various rates to get a number comparable to IRR. Given the difficulty in doing so, it makes sense to ignore IRR, when short-term interest rates differ from long-term interest rates, and simply calculate NPV.

What Does IRR Mean? There are two possible economic interpretations of internal rate of return: (i) The internal rate of return represents the rate of return on the unrecovered investment balance in the project. (ii) The internal rate of return is the rate of return earned on the initial investment made in the project.

To understand the nature of these interpretations, consider a project with the following cash flows.

Year	*Cash flow*
0	₹–300,000
1	0
2	417,000
3	117,000

The internal rate of return of this project is the value of r in the expression

$$0 = \frac{-300{,}000}{(1+r)^0} + \frac{0}{(1+r)^1} + \frac{417{,}000}{(1+r)^2} + \frac{117{,}000}{(1+r)^3}$$

The value of r which satisfies the above expression is 30 percent. This figure, according to the first interpretation of internal rate of return, reflects the rate of return on unrecovered investment balance. The unrecovered investment balance is defined as:

$$F_t = F_{t-1}(1+r) + C_t \tag{8.8}$$ [3]

where F_t is the unrecovered investment balance at the end of year t, F_{t-1} is the unrecovered investment balance at the end of year $t-1$, and C_t is the cash flow at the end of year t.

---

[3] Recognising that $F_0 = CF_0$, we may obtain the following by applying the recursive relationship in Eq.(8.8)

$$F_0 = C_0 \tag{1}$$
$$F_1 = F_0(1+r) + C_1 = C_0(1+r) + C_1 \tag{2}$$
$$F_2 = F_1(1+r) + C_2 = C_0(1+r)^2 + C_1(1+r) + C_2 \tag{3}$$

.

.

$$F_n = F_{n-1}(1+r) + C_n = C_0(1+r)^n + C_1(1+r)^{n-1} + .. + C_n \tag{4}$$

Exhibit 8.7 shows that if 30 percent rate of return is applied on the unrecovered investment balance, the balance in the project reduces to 0 at the end of its life.

Exhibit 8.7 ***Unrecovered Investment Balance***

Year	Unrecovered Investment Balance at the Beginning F_{t-1}	Interest for the Year $F_{t-1}\,r$	Cash Flow at the End of the Year C_t	Unrecovered Investment Balance at the End of the Year $F_{t-1}(1+r) + C_t$
1	₹ –300,000	–90,000	0	–390,000
2	₹ –390,000	– 117,000	417,000	–90,000
3	₹ –90,000	–27,000	117,000	0

Now, let us consider the second interpretation, according to which the internal rate of return is the compounded rate of return earned on the initial investment, for the entire life of the project. This means that if a project involves an initial outlay of I, has an internal rate of return of r percent, and has a life of n years, the value of the benefits of the project, assessed at the end of n years, will be $I(1 + r)^n$. In our numerical example, where the initial investment is ₹300,000, the internal rate of return of the project is 30 percent, and the life of the project is three years, the value of the benefits of the project, assessed at the end of three years, will be ₹300,000 $(1 + 0.30)^3$ = ₹659,100.

The second interpretation of internal rate of return is based on the assumption that the intermediate flows of the project are re-invested at a rate of return equal to the internal rate of return of the project. For our numerical example, it means that the intermediate cash inflow of ₹417,000 occurring at the end of the second year (this is the only intermediate cash inflow for the project) can be re-invested at a rate of return equal to 30 percent. Given this assumption, we find that the value of all benefits, assessed at the end of three years, works out to ₹659,100 as follows:

Year	*Benefit (cash inflow)*	*Compounded Value at the End of 3 years*
1		
2	₹417,000	542,100
3	₹117,000	117,000
		Sum = 659,100

Which economic interpretation should we put on internal rate of return? Since it is often not possible for a firm to re-invest intermediate inflows at a rate of return equal to the project's internal rate of return, the first interpretation seems more realistic. Hence, we may view internal rate of return as the rate of return on the time-varying, unrecovered investment balance in the project, rather than the compounded rate of return on the initial investment. *This point deserves to be emphasised because the notion of internal rate of return generally creates the impression that it is the rate of return earned on a sustained basis on the initial investment over the life of the project.*

Redeeming Qualities Despite its deficiencies, IRR is immensely popular in practice, even more than NPV. It perhaps fills a need that NPV does not. Managers as well as financial analysts usually think in terms of rates of return rather than absolute rupee values. Although IRR can be misleading, the result can be readily interpreted by all parties. As Samuel Weaver says: "The resulting IRR can be mentally compared to expected inflation, the current borrowing rates, the cost of capital, an equity's portfolio return, and so on." No wonder surveys suggest that the IRR is the most popular investment evaluation technique.

Further, in certain situations, the IRR offers a practical advantage over NPV. You can't estimate the NPV unless you know the discount rate, but you can still calculate the IRR. Suppose you don't know the discount rate but you find that the project has an IRR of 35 percent. You would perhaps accept the project because it is unlikely that the discount rate would be that high.

The pros and cons of IRR are summarised below:

Pros	*Cons*
■ Closely related to NPV	■ May lead to multiple rates of return
■ Easy to understand and interpret	■ May result into incorrect decisions in comparing mutually exclusive projects

Modified IRR Despite NPV's conceptual superiority, managers seem to prefer IRR over NPV because IRR is intuitively more appealing as it is a percentage measure. Is there a percentage measure that overcomes the shortcomings of the regular IRR? Yes, there is one and it is called the modified IRR or MIRR.

The procedure for calculating MIRR is as follows:

Step 1: Calculate the present value of the costs (PVC) associated with the project, using the cost of capital (r) as the discount rate:

$$\text{PVC} = \sum_{t=0}^{n} \frac{\text{Cash outflow}_t}{(1+r)^t}$$

Step 2: Calculate the terminal value (TV) of the cash inflows expected from the project:

$$\text{TV} = \sum_{t=0}^{n} \text{Cash inflow}_t\,(1+r)^{n-t}$$

Step 3: Obtain MIRR by solving the following equation:

$$\text{PVC} = \frac{TV}{(1+MIRR)^n}$$

To illustrate the calculation of MIRR let us consider an example. Pentagon Limited is evaluating a project that has the following cash flow stream associated with it:

Year	0	1	2	3	4	5	6
Cash flow (₹ in million)	–120	–80	20	60	80	100	120

The cost of capital for Pentagon is 15 percent. The present value of costs is:

$$120 + \frac{80}{(1.15)} = 189.6$$

The terminal value of cash inflows is:

$$20(1.15)^4 + 60(1.15)^3 + 80(1.15)^2 + 100(1.15) + 120$$

$$= 34.98 + 91.26 + 105.76 + 115 + 120 = 467$$

The MIRR is obtained as follows:

$$189.6 = \frac{467}{(1 + \text{MIRR})^6}$$

$$(1+\text{MIRR})^6 = 2.463$$

$$1 + \text{MIRR} = 2.463^{1/6} = 1.162$$

$$\text{MIRR} = 1.162 - 1 = 0.162 \text{ or } 16.2 \text{ percent}$$

The time line diagram for this problem is given in Exhibit 8.8.

Exhibit 8.8 ***Time Line Diagram***

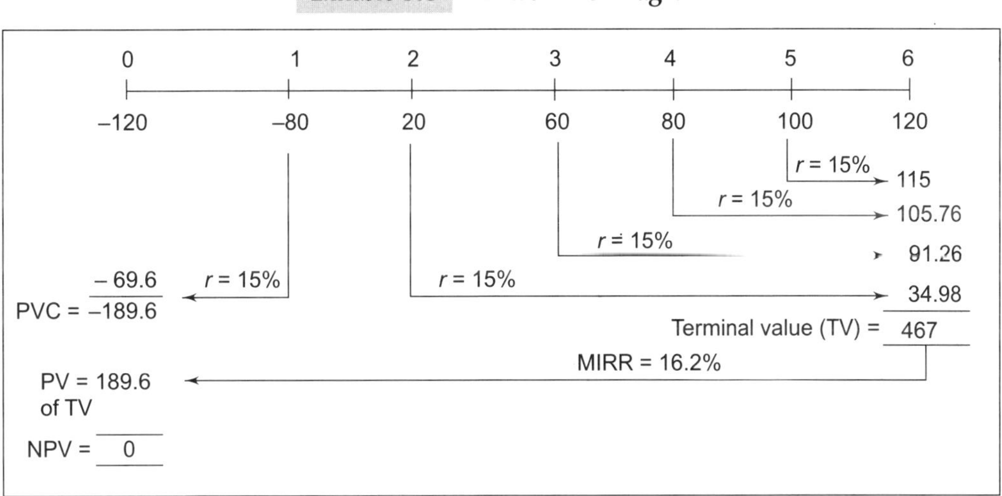

Evaluation MIRR is superior to the regular IRR in two ways. First, MIRR assumes that project cash flows are re-invested at the cost of capital whereas the regular IRR assumes that project cash flows are re-invested at the project's own IRR. Since re-investment at cost of capital (or some other explicit rate) is more realistic than re-investment at IRR, MIRR reflects better the true profitability of a project. Second, the problem of multiple rates does not exist with MIRR.

Thus, MIRR is a distinct improvement over the regular IRR. Is it as good as NPV in choosing between mutually exclusive projects? Without getting into technicalities, let us note the following:

- If the mutually exclusive projects are of the same size, NPV and MIRR lead to the same decision irrespective of variations in life.

- If the mutually exclusive projects differ in size there is a possibility of conflict.

What is the verdict? MIRR is better than the regular IRR in measuring the true rate of return. However, for choosing among mutually exclusive projects of different size, NPV is a better alternative in measuring the contribution of each project to the value of the firm.

8.4 URGENCY

According to this criterion, projects that are deemed to be more urgent get priority over projects that are regarded as less urgent.

The problem with this criterion is: How can the degree of urgency be determined? In certain situations, of course, it may not be difficult to identify really urgent investments. For example, some minor equipment that has failed may have to be replaced immediately to ensure continuity of production. Non-replacement of such equipment may mean considerable losses arising from stoppage in production. It may be futile in such a case to go into detailed analysis and delay decision.

In many situations, however, it is difficult to determine the relative degree of urgency because of the lack of an objective basis. The use of urgency criterion may imply that the persuasiveness of those who propose projects would become a very important factor in investment decisions. Resource allocation may degenerate into a political battle.

In view of these limitations of the urgency criterion, we suggest that in general it should not be used for investment decision making. In exceptional cases, where genuine urgency exists, it may be used provided investment outlays are not large.

8.5 PAYBACK PERIOD

The payback period is the length of time required to recover the initial cash outlay on the project. For example, if a project involves a cash outlay of ₹600,000 and generates cash inflows of ₹100,000, ₹150,000, ₹150,000, and ₹200,000, in the first, second, third, and fourth years, respectively, its payback period is 4 years because the sum of cash inflows during 4 years is equal to the initial outlay. When the annual cash inflow is a constant sum, the payback period is simply the initial outlay divided by the annual cash inflow. For example, a project which has an initial cash outlay of ₹1,000,000 and a constant annual cash inflow of ₹300,000 has a payback period of ₹1,000,000/300,000 $= 3^1/_3$ years.

According to the payback criterion, the shorter the payback period, the more desirable the project. Firms using this criterion generally specify the maximum acceptable payback period. If this is n years, projects with a payback period of n years or less are deemed worthwhile and projects with a payback period exceeding n years are considered unworthy.

Evaluation A widely used investment criterion, the payback period seems to offer the following advantages:

- It is simple, both in concept and application. It does not use involved concepts and tedious calculations and has few hidden assumptions.

- It is a rough and ready method for dealing with risk. It favours projects which generate substantial cash inflows in earlier years and discriminates against projects which bring substantial cash inflows in later years but not in earlier years. Now, if risk tends to increase with futurity – in general, this may be true – the payback criterion may be helpful in weeding out risky projects.
- Since it emphasises earlier cash inflows, it may be a sensible criterion when the firm is pressed with problems of liquidity.

The *limitations* of the payback criterion, however, are very serious:

- It fails to consider the time value of money. Cash inflows, in the payback calculation, are simply added without suitable discounting. This violates the most basic principle of financial analysis which stipulates that cash flows occurring at different points of time can be added or subtracted only after suitable compounding/discounting.
- It ignores cash flows beyond the payback period. This leads to discrimination against projects which generate substantial cash inflows in later years. To illustrate, consider the cash flows of two projects, A and B:

Year	*Cash Flow of A*	*Cash Flow of B*
0	₹(100,000)	₹(100,000)
1	50,000	20,000
2	30,000	20,000
3	20,000	20,000
4	10,000	40,000
5	10,000	50,000
6	-	60,000

  The payback criterion prefers A, which has a payback period of 3 years in comparison to B which has a payback period of 4 years, even though B has very substantial cash inflows in years 5 and 6.

- It is a measure of project's capital recovery, not profitability.
- Though it measures a project's liquidity, it does not indicate the liquidity position of the firm as a whole, which is more important. Weingartner writes: "The usually designated speculative and/or precautionary motive of firms to hold liquid or near liquid funds in order to seize upon unexpected opportunities is a different motive from that which requires each new investment separately to recover its original cost within a short period."[4]

Discounted Payback Period A major shortcoming of the conventional payback period is that it does not take into account the time value of money. To overcome this limitation, the discounted payback period has been suggested. In this modified method, cash flows are first

[4] H.M. Weingartner, "Some Views on the Payback Period and Capital Budgeting Decisions," *Management Science*, vol.15 (August 1969).

converted into their present values (by applying suitable discounting factors) and then added to ascertain the period of time required to recover the initial outlay on the project. Exhibit 8.9 illustrates the calculation of discounted payback period. Looking at the last column in this exhibit, we find that the discounted payback period is between 3 and 4 years.

Reasons for Popularity of Payback Period Despite its serious shortcomings the payback period is widely used in appraising investments. Why? It appears that the payback measure serves as a proxy for certain types of information which are useful in investment decision-making.

- The payback period may be regarded roughly as the reciprocal of the internal rate of return when the annual cash inflow is constant and the life of the project fairly long.[5]
- The payback period is somewhat akin to the break-even point. A rule of thumb, it serves as a useful shortcut in the process of information generation and evaluation.
- The payback period conveys information about the rate at which the uncertainty associated with a project is resolved. The shorter the payback period, the faster the uncertainty associated with the project is resolved. The longer the payback period, the slower the uncertainty associated with the project is resolved. Decision-makers, it may be noted, prefer an early resolution of uncertainty. Why? An early resolution of uncertainty enables the decision-maker to take prompt corrective action, adjust his consumption patterns, and modify/change other investment decisions.

---

[5] The following analysis bears this out:

Let I = initial outlay, c = constant annual cash flow, S = salvage value, and n = life of the project. The internal rate of return is the value of r in the equation.

$$I = \sum_{t=1}^{n} \frac{c}{(1+r)^t} + \frac{S}{(1+r)^n} \qquad (1)$$

Since .

$$\sum_{t=1}^{n} \frac{c}{(1+r)^t} = \frac{c}{r} - \frac{c}{r}\left[\frac{1}{(1+r)}\right]^n \qquad (2)$$

the internal rate of return equation becomes

$$I = \frac{c}{r} - \frac{c}{r}\left[\frac{1}{(1+r)}\right]^n + \frac{S}{(1+r)^n} \qquad (3)$$

When n is very large, the last two terms on the right-hand side of the above expression become negligible.

Hence, $$I \simeq \frac{c}{r} \qquad (4)$$

This means $$r \simeq \frac{c}{I} \qquad (5)$$

In words, the internal rate of return is approximately the inverse of the payback period.

Exhibit 8.9 ***Calculation of Discounted Payback Period***

Year	Cash Flow	Discounting Factor@10%	Present Value	Cumulative Net Cash Flow after Discounting
0	–10,000	1.000	–10,000	–10,000
1	3,000	0.909	2,727	–7,273
2	3,000	0.826	2,478	–4,795
3	4,000	0.751	3,004	–1,791
4	4,000	0.683	2,732	941
5	5,000	0.621	3,105	
6	2,000	0.565	1,130	
7	3,000	0.513	1,539	

8.6 ACCOUNTING RATE OF RETURN

The accounting rate of return, also referred to as the average rate of return on investment, is a measure of profitability which relates income to investment, both measured in accounting terms. Since income and investment can be measured in different ways, there can be a very large number of measures for accounting rate of return.

The measures that are employed commonly in practice are:

A : $$\frac{\text{Average income after tax}}{\text{Initial investment}}$$

B : $$\frac{\text{Average income after tax}}{\text{Average investment}}$$

C : $$\frac{\text{Average income after tax but before interest}}{\text{Initial investment}}$$

D : $$\frac{\text{Average income after tax but before interest}}{\text{Average investment}}$$

E : $$\frac{\text{Average income before interest and taxes}}{\text{Initial investment}}$$

F : $$\frac{\text{Average income before interest and taxes}}{\text{Average investment}}$$

G : $$\frac{\text{Total income after tax but before depreciation} - \text{Initial investment}}{(\text{Initial investment} / 2) \times \text{year}}$$

The computation of various measures of accounting rate of return is shown in Exhibit 8.10 with reference to a hypothetical project.

Exhibit 8.10 ***Various Measures of Accounting Rate of Return***

Year	Investment (book value)	Depreciation	Income before Interest and Taxes	Interest	Income before Tax	Tax	Income after Tax
1	1.00	0.20	0.30	0.10	0.20	0.100	0.100
2	0.80	0.20	0.35	0.10	0.25	0.125	0.125
3	0.60	0.20	0.40	0.10	0.30	0.150	0.150
4	0.40	0.20	0.40	0.10	0.30	0.150	0.150
5	0.20	0.20	0.35	0.10	0.25	0.125	0.125
Sum :	3.00	1.00	1.80	0.50	1.30	0.650	0.650
Average :	0.60	0.20	0.36	0.10	0.26	0.130	0.130

Measures

A: $$\frac{\text{Average income after tax}}{\text{Initial investment}} = \frac{0.13}{1.00} = 13.0\%$$

B: $$\frac{\text{Average income after tax}}{\text{Average investment}} = \frac{0.13}{0.60} = 21.7\%$$

C: $$\frac{\text{Average income after tax but before interest}}{\text{Initial investment}} = \frac{0.13 + 0.10}{1.0} = 23.0\%$$

D: $$\frac{\text{Average income after tax but before interest}}{\text{Average investment}} = \frac{0.13 + 0.10}{0.60} = 38.3\%$$

E: $$\frac{\text{Average income before interest and tax}}{\text{Initial investment}} = \frac{0.36}{1.0} = 36\%$$

F: $$\frac{\text{Average income before interest and tax}}{\text{Average investment}} = \frac{0.36}{0.60} = 60\%$$

G: $$\frac{\text{Total income after tax but before depreciation} - \text{Initial investment}}{(\text{Initial investment} / 2) \times \text{years}} = \frac{0.65 + 1.00 - 1.00}{1/2 \times 5} = 26.0\%$$

Obviously, the higher the accounting rate of return, the better the project. In general, projects which have an accounting rate of return equal to or greater than a pre-specified cut off rate of return – which is usually between 15 percent and 30 percent – are accepted; others are rejected.

Accounting Rate of Return and Internal Rate of Return It is very difficult to generalise if the accounting rate of return is calculated on the basis of average income over the life of the project. However, if the accounting rate of return is calculated for each year using the expected (or actual) net income, the following generalisations may be made:

- The accounting rate of return tends to understate the internal rate of return for earlier years and overstate it for later years.

- The accounting rate of return and the internal rate of return can be the same only if the depreciation schedule is equal to the economic depreciation schedule.
- Inflation and creative accounting tend to create a discrepancy between the accounting rate of return and the internal rate of return.

Evaluation Traditionally a popular investment appraisal criterion, the accounting rate of return has the following virtues:

- It is simple to calculate.
- It is based on accounting information which is readily available and familiar to businessmen.
- It considers benefits over the entire life of the project.
- Since it is based on accounting measures, which can be readily obtained from the financial accounting system of the firm, it facilitates post-auditing of capital expenditures.
- While income data for the entire life of the project is normally required for calculating the accounting rate of return, one can make do even if complete income data is not available. For example, when due to indeterminacy of project life a complete forecast of income cannot be obtained, the accounting rate of return may be calculated on the basis of income for some typical year or income for the first three to five years.

The shortcomings of the accounting rate of return criterion seem to be considerable:

- It is based upon accounting profit, not cash flow.
- It does not take into account the time value of money. To illustrate this point, consider two investment proposals X and Y, each requiring an outlay of ₹100,000. Both the proposals have an expected life of four years after which their salvage value would be nil. Relevant details of these proposals are given below:

	X				Y			
Year	*Book Value*	*Depreciation*	*Profit after Tax*	*Cash Flow*	*Book Value*	*Depreciation*	*Profit after Tax*	*Cash Flow*
0	100,000	0	0	(100,000)	100,000	0	0	(100,000)
1	75,000	25,000	40,000	65,000	75,000	25,000	10,000	35,000
2	50,000	25,000	30,000	55,000	50,000	25,000	20,000	45,000
3	25,000	25,000	20,000	45,000	25,000	25,000	30,000	55,000
4	0	25,000	10,000	35,000	0	25,000	40,000	65,000

  Both the proposals, with an accounting rate of return (measure A) of 40 percent, look alike from the accounting rate of return point of view, though project X, because it provides benefits earlier, is much more desirable. While the payback period criterion gives no weight to more distant benefits, the accounting rate of return criterion seems to give them too much weight.
- There are, as we have seen, numerous measures of accounting rate of return. This can create controversy, confusion, and problems in interpretation.

- Accounting income (whatever particular measure of income we choose) is not uniquely defined because it is influenced by the methods of depreciation, inventory valuation, and allocation of certain costs. Working with the same basic accounting data, different accountants are likely to produce different income figures. A similar problem, though less severe, exists with respect to investment.
- The argument that the accounting rate of return measures facilitate post-auditing of capital expenditure is not very valid. The financial accounting system of a firm is generally designed to report events with respect to accounting periods and for profit centres but not for individual investments.
- The target or hurdle rate of return cannot be specified in relation to the goal of shareholder wealth maximisation.
- The accounting rate of return method can be highly misleading because balance sheet book values reflect neither the earning capacities of assets nor their market values. For example, consider a commercial complex constructed at a cost of ₹20 million 8 years ago producing presently an income of ₹1.8 million. While its book value presently is ₹12 million, its fair market value is ₹40 million. The return on investment based on the book value works out to 15 percent (₹1.8 million in relation to ₹12 million). However, if the income is related to the current value, the return on investment is just 4.5 percent. This example highlights the limitation of using book value figures. It must be stressed that the book value is not relevant as it merely represents sunk costs.

8.7 ASSESSMENT OF VARIOUS METHODS

We have discussed at length the five basic methods of evaluation. It may be helpful at this juncture to do a summary assessment of these methods on the basis of certain theoretical and practical considerations. This is done in Exhibit 8.11.

Exhibit 8.11 ***Assessment of Basic Evaluation Methods***

	Net Present Value	*Benefit Cost Ratio*	*Internal Rate of Return*	*Payback Period*	*Accounting Rate of Return*
Theoretical considerations					
1. Does the method consider all cash flows	Yes	Yes	Yes	No	?
2. Does the method discount cash flows at the opportunity cost of funds?	Yes	Yes	No	No	No
3. Does the method satisfy the principle of value additivity?	Yes	No	No	?	?
4. From a set of mutually exclusive projects, does the method choose the projects which maximise shareholder wealth?	Yes	No	No	?	?

(Contd.)

	Net Present Value	*Benefit Cost Ratio*	*Internal Rate of Return*	*Payback Period*	*Accounting Rate of Return*
Practical considerations					
1. Is the method simple?	Yes	Yes	Yes	Yes	Yes
2. Can the method be used with limited information?	No	No	No	Perhaps	Yes
3. Does the method give a relative measure?	No	Yes	Yes	No	Yes

8.8 INVESTMENT EVALUATION IN PRACTICE

A number of surveys have been conducted to learn about the methods of investment evaluation in practice. This section presents the findings of some of these surveys.

Evaluation Techniques in India A survey of capital budgeting practices in India, conducted by U.Rao Cherukeri, revealed the following:

- Over time, discounted cash flow methods have gained in importance and internal rate of return is the most popular evaluation method.
- Firms typically use multiple evaluation methods.
- Accounting rate of return and payback period are widely employed as supplementary evaluation methods.
- Weighted average cost of capital is the most commonly used discount rate and the most often used discount rate is 15 percent in post-tax terms.
- Risk assessment and adjustment techniques have gained popularity. The most popular risk assessment technique is sensitivity analysis and the most common methods for risk adjustment are shortening of the payback period and increasing the required rate of return.

A survey of corporate finance practices in India by Manoj Anand, reported in the October-December 2002 issue of *Vikalpa,* revealed that the following methods (in order of decreasing importance) are followed by companies to evaluate investment proposals.

Method	*% of Companies Considering as Very Important or Important*
Internal rate of return	85.00
Payback period	67.50
Net present value	66.30
Break-even analysis	58.20
Profitability Index	35.10

Evaluation Techniques in the U.S. To learn about the methods of evaluation used by business firms in the U.S., let us look at the findings of a study conducted by William Petty and David Scott shown in Exhibit 8.12.

Exhibit 8.12 ***Evaluation Techniques***

Technique	Level of Importance None	Slight	Moderate	Fair	High	No Response
■ Accounting return on investment	12.35%	15.29%	17.06%	28.71%	23.65%	2.94%
■ Payback period	1.76	12.35	25.29	28.82	30.00	1.76
■ Net present value	8.82	16.47	20.59	15.29	33.20	5.63
■ Internal rate of return	7.65	9.41	4.71	14.71	59.41	4.12
■ Profitability index or benefit-cost ratio	31.17	18.82	15.29	7.65	11.18	15.88

Evaluation Techniques in Japan Japanese firms appear to rely mainly on two kinds of analysis: (a) one year return on investment analysis and (b) residual investment analysis. While the former needs no explanation, the latter may require some elaboration. The manner in which the residual investment analysis is done is illustrated in Exhibit 8.13. Examining this exhibit we find that the residual investment analysis is similar to the discounted payback analysis. This analysis shows how long it will take for the residual investment in the project to become zero after taking into account the time value of money. This period is conceptually equal to the discounted payback period.

Exhibit 8.13 ***Residual Investment Analysis***

Year	Cash Flow	Imputed Interest @ 10%	Adjusted Cash Flow	Residual Investment
0	(1000)	-	-	-
1	200	100	100	900
2	200	90	110	790
3	300	79	221	569
4	300	57	243	326
5	400	33	367	-
6	400	-	-	-
7	300	-	-	-
8	300	-	-	-

In general, it appears that Japanese firms use methods which are less complicated and sophisticated than the ones used by American firms. Why? Several reasons are offered to explain this difference: (a) Japanese managers, in general, have limited formal business training. (b) There is a great deal of consensus decision making in Japanese firms which necessarily calls for the use of relatively simpler methods. (c) Japanese firms put considerable emphasis on verbal scenario analysis (as opposed to complex calculations) and careful scrutiny of basic assumptions which seems to blend well with a healthy skepticism about the accuracy of quantitative forecasts.

SUMMARY

- A wide range of criteria has been suggested to judge the worthwhileness of investment projects. They fall into two broad categories: discounting criteria and non-discounting criteria. The important discounting criteria are: net present value, benefit cost ratio, and internal rate of return. The major non-discounting criteria are: payback period and accounting rate of return.
- The net present value (NPV) of a project is the sum of the present values of all the cash flows - positive as well as negative - that are expected to occur over the life of the project.
- The decision rule associated with the NPV criterion is: Accept the project if the NPV is positive and reject the project if the NPV is negative.
- NPV has certain properties that make it a very attractive decision criterion: NPVs are additive; the NPV rule assumes that the intermediate cash flows of a project are reinvested at a rate of return equal to the cost of capital; NPV calculation permits time varying discount rates.
- The standard NPV method is based on the assumption that the intermediate cash flows are reinvested at a rate of return equal to the cost of capital. When this assumption is not valid, the reinvestment rates applicable to the intermediate cash flows need to be defined for calculating the modified net present value.
- The benefit cost ratio is defined as the present value of benefits (cash inflows) divided by the present value of costs (cash outflows). A project is considered worthwhile if the benefit cost ratio is more than 1 and not worthwhile if the benefit cost ratio is less than 1.
- The internal rate of return (IRR) of a project is the discount rate which makes its NPV equal to zero. In the NPV calculation we assume that the discount rate is known and determine the NPV. In the IRR calculation, we set the NPV equal to zero and determine the discount rate that satisfies this condition.
- The decision rule for IRR is as follows: Accept the project if its IRR is greater than the cost of capital; reject the project if its IRR is less than the cost of capital.
- The IRR and NPV rules lead to identical decisions provided two conditions are satisfied. First, the cash flows of the project must be conventional, implying that the initial cash flows are negative and the subsequent cash flows are positive. Second, the project must be independent meaning that the project can be accepted or rejected without reference to any other project.
- There are problems in using IRR when the cash flows of the project are not conventional or when two or more projects are being compared to determine which one is the best. In the first case, it is difficult to define 'what is IRR' and in the second case IRR can be misleading. Further, IRR cannot distinguish between lending and borrowing. Finally, IRR is difficult to apply when short-term interest rates differ from long-term interest rates.
- There are two possible economic interpretations of internal rate of return: (i) The internal rate of return represents the rate of return on the unrecovered investment balance in the project. (ii) The internal rate of return is the rate of return earned on the initial investment made in the project.

- Despite NPV's conceptual superiority, managers seem to prefer IRR over NPV because IRR is intuitively more appealing as it is a percentage measure. Is there a percentage measure that overcomes the shortcomings of the regular IRR? Yes, there is one and it is called the modified IRR or MIRR. It is calculated by solving the following equation:

$$\text{Present value of cash outflows} = \frac{\text{Terminal value of cash inflows}}{(1+\text{MIRR})^n}$$

- The payback period is the length of time required to recover the initial cash outlay on the project.
- According to the payback criterion, the shorter the payback period, the more desirable the project. Firms using this criterion generally specify the maximum acceptable payback period.
- Payback period is widely used because it is simple, both in concept and application, and it is a rough and ready method for dealing with risk. However, it has serious limitations: it does not consider the time value of money; it ignores cash flows beyond the payback period; it is a measure of capital recovery, not profitability.
- In the discounted payback period method, cash flows are first converted into their present values (by applying suitable discounting factors) and then added to ascertain the period of time required to recover the initial outlay of the project.
- The accounting rate of return, also called the average rate of return, is defined as

$$\frac{\text{Profit after tax}}{\text{Book value of the investment}}$$

- The accounting rate of return has certain virtues: it is simple to calculate; it is based on accounting information which is readily available and familiar to businessmen; it considers benefits over the entire life of the project. However, it has serious shortcomings as well: it is based upon accounting profit, not cash flow; it does not take into account the time value of money; it is internally inconsistent.
- The most popular methods for evaluating small sized projects are payback method and accounting rate of return method. For larger projects, IRR appears to be the most commonly used method.
- In the U.S., internal rate of return, net present value, accounting rate of return, and payback period are the most popular methods of project appraisal.
- Japanese firms appear to rely mainly on two kinds of analysis: (i) one year return on investment analysis, and (ii) residual investment analysis.

QUESTIONS

1. What is NPV?
2. What are the implications of the additivity property of NPV?
3. Discuss the general formula of NPV when discount rates vary over time.
4. What is the rationale for the NPV rule?

5. How is modified NPV calculated?
6. Show why the NPV of a simple project decreases as the discount rate increases.
7. What are the limitations of NPV?
8. What are the two ways of defining the benefit-cost ratio?
9. Evaluate the benefit-cost ratio as an investment criterion.
10. What is IRR and how is it calculated?
11. Discuss the problems associated with IRR.
12. What are the redeeming qualities of IRR?
13. What does IRR mean?
14. How is MIRR calculated?
15. Why is MIRR superior to the regular IRR?
16. What is payback period?
17. Evaluate payback as an investment criterion.
18. Why is payback so popular, despite its shortcomings?
19. What is discounted payback period?
20. How is accounting rate of return calculated?
21. What are the pros and cons of accounting rate of return?
22. Assess various appraisal criteria on the basis of certain theoretical and practical considerations.
23. Discuss how investment appraisal is done in practice.
24. Describe the evaluation techniques used in the U.S. and Japan.

PROBLEMS

1. Sulabh International is evaluating a project whose expected cash flows are as follows:

Year	*Cash flow*
0	₹(1000,000)
1	100,000
2	200,000
3	300,000
4	600,000
5	300,000

   (a) What is the NPV of the project, if the discount rate is 14 percent for the entire period?
   (b) What is the NPV of the project if the discount rate is 12 percent for year 1 and rises every year by 1 percent?

2. What is the internal rate of return of an investment which involves a current outlay of ₹300,000 and results in an annual cash inflow of ₹60,000 for 7 years?
3. What is the internal rate of return of the following cash flow stream?

Year	*Cash flow*
0	(3,000)
1	9,000
2	(3,000)

4. If an equipment costs ₹500,000 and lasts 8 years, what should be the minimum annual cash inflow before it is worthwhile to purchase the equipment? Assume that the cost of capital is 10 percent.

5. How much can be paid for a machine which brings in an annual cash inflow of ₹25,000 for 10 years? Assume that the discount rate is 12 percent.
6. The cash flows associated with three projects *P*, *Q*, and *R*, are given below:

	Net cash flow		
Year	*P*	*Q*	*R*
0	(2,000)	(2,000)	(2,000)
1	1,400	500	500
2	600	1,100	500
3	400	900	1,600

Calculate the net present value of each project at discount rates of 0 percent, 5 percent, 10 percent, 15 percent, 25 percent, and 30 percent.

7. The expected cash flows of two mutually exclusive projects, P and Q are:

Year	*0*	*1*	*2*	*3*	*4*	*5*
P	(1000)	(1200)	(600)	(250)	2000	4000
Q	(1600)	200	400	600	800	100

(a) Construct the NPV profiles for Projects *P* and *Q*.
(b) What is the IRR of each project?
(c) Which project would you choose if the cost of capital is 10 percent? 20 percent?
(d) What is each project's MIRR if the cost of capital is 12 percent?

8. Your company is considering two mutually exclusive projects, *A* and *B*. Project *A* involves an outlay of ₹100 million which will generate an expected cash inflow of ₹25 million per year for 6 years. Project *B* calls for an outlay of ₹50 million which will produce an expected cash inflow of ₹13 million per year for 6 years. The company's cost of capital is 12 percent.
(a) Calculate the NPV and IRR of each project.
(b) What is the NPV and IRR of the differential project (the project that reflects the difference between Project *B* and Project *A*).

9. Your company is considering two projects, Project *M* and Project *N*, each of which requires an initial outlay of ₹50 million. The expected cash inflows from these projects are:

Year	*Project M*	*Project N*
1	₹11 million	₹38 million
2	19	22
3	32	18
4	37	10

(a) What is the payback period for each of the projects?
(b) What is the discounted payback period for each of the projects if the cost of capital is 12 percent?
(c) If the two projects are independent and the cost of capital is 12 percent, which project(s) should the firm invest in?
(d) If the two projects are mutually exclusive and the cost of capital is 10 percent, which project should the firm invest in?
(e) If the two projects are mutually exclusive and the cost of capital is 15 percent, which project should the firm invest in?
(f) If the cost of capital is 14 percent, what is the modified IRR of each project?

10. Calculate the unrecovered investment balance at the end of each year for the following:

Year	0	1	2	3	4
Cash Flow	–8000	1000	2000	–1000	2000

11. The following financial information is available about a project:

(₹ *in million*)

Year	*1*	*2*	*3*	*4*	*5*	*6*	*7*	*8*
Investment	2.40	2.10	1.80	1.50	1.20	0.90	0.60	0.30
Depreciation	0.30	0.30	0.30	0.30	0.30	0.30	0.30	0.30
Income before interest and taxes	0.60	0.65	0.70	0.70	0.70	0.65	0.60	0.50
Interest	0.25	0.25	0.25	0.25	0.25	0.25	0.25	0.25
Income before tax	0.35	0.40	0.45	0.45	0.45	0.40	0.35	0.25
Tax	-	0.10	0.25	0.25	0.25	0.22	0.19	0.14
Income after tax	0.35	0.30	0.20	0.20	0.20	0.18	0.16	0.11

Compute the various measures of accounting rate of return.

MINICASE

Sona Limited is a leading manufacturer of automotive components. It supplies to the original equipment manufacturers as well as the replacement market. Its projects typically have a short life as it introduces new models periodically.

You have recently joined Sona Limited as a financial analyst reporting to Suresh Gopal, the CFO of the company. He has provided you the following information about three projects, A, B, and C that are being considered by the Executive Committee of Sona Limited:

- Project A is an extension of an existing line. Its cash flow will decrease over time.
- Project B involves a new product. Building its market will take some time and hence its cash flow will increase over time.
- Project C is concerned with sponsoring a pavilion at a Trade Fair. It will entail a cost initially which will be followed by a huge benefit for one year. However, in the year following that a substantial cost will be incurred to raze the pavilion.

The expected net cash flows of the three projects are as follows.

Year	*Project A*	*Project B*	*Project C*
0	(5000)	(5000)	(5000)
1	3500	1000	15000
2	2500	3000	(10000)
3	1500	4000	–

Suresh Gopal believes that all the three projects have risk characteristics similar to the average risk of the firm and hence the firm's cost of capital, viz. 12 percent, will apply to them.

You are asked to evaluate the projects.

(a) What is payback period and discounted payback period? Find the payback periods and the discounted payback periods of Projects A and B.

(b) What is net present value (NPV)? What are the properties of NPV? Calculate the NPVs of projects A, B, and C.

(c) What is internal rate of return (IRR)? What are the problems with IRR? Calculate the IRRs for Projects A, B, and C.

(d) What is modified internal rate of return (MIRR)? What are the pros and cons of MIRR vis-a-vis IRR and NPV? Calculate the MIRRs for projects A, B, and C assuming that the intermediate cash flows can be re-invested at 12 percent rate of return.

MINICASE

Hindustan Hotel Corporation has a prime plot of land in Bangalore acquired years ago for a small amount. Thanks to substantial appreciation in value, the plot, if disposed now, would fetch a post-tax value of ₹100 crore.

Deepak Puri, the CEO of the company, has submitted a proposal to the Board in which two alternative uses of the plot have been suggested:

(a) Construction of a 5-star hotel.

(b) Construction of a commercial complex.

If a 5-star hotel is constructed, it will require two years of construction and begin operation in the third year. In the first year of operation it will incur a cash loss. From the second year of operation onward it will generate positive and rising post-cash flows. At the end of ten years from now, if the hotel property is disposed it will fetch a very substantial post-tax value. Taking into account the opportunity cost of land now, the post-tax cash flows associated with the hotel project are estimated as follows:

₹ *in crore*

Year	0	1	2	3	4	5	6	7	8	9	10
Cash Flow (Post-tax)	–100	–100	–50	–10	20	30	40	50	60	70	70 + 750

If a commercial complex is constructed, it is proposed to sell most of the space to investors and retain a very small space which can be leased out to generate rental income. The substantial sums collected from investors who book the space would cover the construction cost and leave considerable surplus. Taking into account the opportunity cost of land, the post-tax cash flows associated with the project are estimated as follows:

₹ *in crore*

Year	0	1	2	3	4	5............
Cash Flow (Post-tax)	–100	150*	50*	5@	5	5

*Booking amount less construction cost.

@Annual lease rental.

Based on the above cash flows, the IRR of the hotel project was calculated as 19 percent and the IRR of the commercial complex was calculated as 79 percent (for this calculation, cash flows up to the third year were considered).

In his proposal submitted to the board, the CEO recommended the commercial complex project because of its significantly higher IRR. Anuj Srivastava, the chairman of the company, intuitively felt that the hotel alternative was more valuable than the commercial complex alternative. But he was intrigued to see a much higher IRR for the commercial complex alternative. He seeks your help in explaining what is going on. Further, if the cost of capital is 12 percent, what will be your advice.

Chapter 9

Project Cash Flows

LEARNING OBJECTIVES

After studying this chapter you should be able to

- Describe the elements of the project cash flow stream.
- Discuss the basic principles of cash flow stream.
- Calculate the cash flow stream for a replacement project.
- Explain the different perspectives from which a project may be viewed.
- Discuss how financial institutions and the Planning Commission define project cash flows.
- Understand the biases in cash flow estimation.

From the previous discussion it is clear that the estimates of cash flows are a key element in investment evaluation. So far we assumed that cash flows were given because we wanted to focus our discussion on investment criteria. Cash flows, however, are not available on a silver platter.

Estimating cash flows – the investment outlays and the cash inflows after the project is commissioned – is the most important, but also the most difficult step in capital budgeting. Forecast errors can be quite large, particularly in gigantic, complex projects. For example, when several oil majors decided to construct the Alaska Pipeline, the initial cost estimate was about $ 700 million. The final cost, however, was about $ 7 billion. While this may be an extreme example, it highlights the pitfalls of forecasting.

Forecasting project cash flows involves numerous variables and many participate in this exercise. Capital outlays are estimated by engineering and product development departments; revenue projections are provided by the marketing group; and operating costs are estimated by production people, cost accountants, purchase managers, personnel executives, tax experts and others.

The role of the finance manager is to coordinate the efforts of various departments and obtain information from them, ensure that the forecasts are based on a set of consistent economic assumptions, keep the exercise focussed on relevant variables, and minimise the biases inherent in cash flow forecasting.

This chapter discusses how to "spread the numbers" or develop the cash flow forecasts in conformity with certain basic principles.

9.1 ELEMENTS OF THE CASH FLOW STREAM

To evaluate a project, you must determine the relevant cash flows, which are the incremental after-tax cash flows associated with the project.

The cash flow stream of a conventional project – a project which involves cash outflows followed by cash inflows – comprises three basic components: (i) initial investment, (ii) operating cash inflows, and (iii) terminal cash inflow.

The initial investment is the after-tax cash outlay on capital expenditure and net working capital when the project is set up. The operating cash inflows are the after-tax cash inflows resulting from the operations of the project during its economic life. The terminal cash inflow is the after-tax cash flow resulting from the liquidation of the project at the end of its economic life.

Exhibit 9.1 depicts on a time line the cash flows for an illustrative project, with each of the cash flow components labelled.

Exhibit 9.1 ***Cash flow Components***

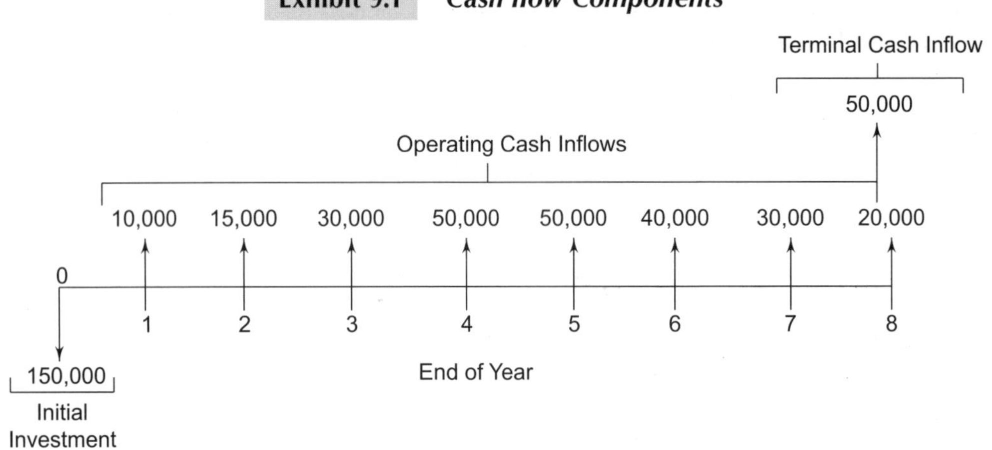

How is the time horizon for cash flow analysis usually established? The time horizon for cash flow analysis is generally the minimum of the following:

Physical Life of the Plant This refers to the period during which the plant remains in a physically usable condition, i.e., the number of years the plant would perform the function for which it had been acquired. This depends on the wear and tear which the plant is subject to. Suppliers of plant may provide information on the physical life under normal operating conditions. While the concept of physical life may be useful for determining the depreciation charge, it is not very useful for investment decision making purposes.

Technological Life of the Plant New technological developments tend to render existing plants obsolete. The technological life of a plant refers to the period of time for which the present plant would not be rendered obsolete by a new plant. It is very difficult to estimate the technological life because the pace of new developments is not governed by any law. While it is almost certain that a new development would occur when it would occur is anybody's guess. Yet an estimate of the technological life has to be made.

Product Market Life of the Plant A plant may be physically usable, its technology may not be obsolete, but the market for its products may disappear or shrink and hence its continuance may not be justified. The product market life of a plant refers to the period for which the product of the plant enjoys a reasonably satisfactory market.

Investment Planning Horizon of the Firm The time period for which a firm wishes to look ahead for purposes of investment analysis may be referred to as its investment planning horizon. It naturally tends to vary with the complexity and size of the investment. For small investments (say, installation of a lathe) it may be five years, for medium-size investments (say, expansion of plant capacity) it may be 10 years, and for large-size investments (say, setting up of a new division) it may be 15 years, and for infrastructure projects it may go up to 30 years.

9.2 BASIC PRINCIPLES OF CASH FLOW ESTIMATION

The following principles should be followed while estimating the cash flows of a project:

- Separation principle
- Incremental principle
- Post-tax principle
- Consistency principle

Separation Principle There are two sides of a project, viz., the investment (or asset) side and the financing side and the cash flows associated with these sides should be separated. A simple example may be given to illustrate how this is done.

Suppose a firm is considering a one-year project that requires an investment of ₹1,000 in fixed assets and working capital at time 0. The project is expected to generate a cash inflow of ₹1,200 at the end of year 1 – this is the only cash inflow expected from the project. The project will be financed entirely by debt carrying an interest rate of 15 percent and maturing after 1 year. Assuming that there are no taxes, the cash flows associated with the investment side of the project, the rate of return on the investment side of the project, the cash flows associated with the financing side of the project, and the cost of capital on the financing side are as follows:

Project

Financing side

Time	Cash flow
0	+ 1,000
1	– 1,150

Cost of capital: 15%

Investment side

Time	Cash flow
0	– 1,000
1	+ 1,200

Rate of return: 20%

Note that the cash flows on the investment side of the project do not reflect financing costs (interest in our example). The financing costs are included in the cash flows on the financing side and reflected in the cost of capital figure (which is 15 percent in our example). The cost of capital is used as the hurdle rate against which the rate of return on the investment side (which is 20 percent in our case) is judged.

The important point to be emphasised is that while defining the cash flows on the investment side, financing costs should not be considered because they will be reflected in the cost of capital figure against which the rate of return figure will be evaluated.

Operationally, this means that interest on debt is ignored while computing profits and taxes thereon. Alternatively, if interest is deducted in the process of arriving at profit after tax, an amount equal to 'Interest (1 – tax rate)' should be added to 'Profit after tax'. Note that:

Profit before interest and tax (1 – tax rate)

= (Profit before tax + Interest) (1 – tax rate)

= (Profit before tax) (1 – tax rate) + Interest (1 – tax rate)

= Profit after tax + Interest (1 – tax rate)

Thus, whether the tax rate is applied directly to the 'Profit before interest and tax' figure or whether the tax-adjusted interest, which is simply 'Interest (1 – tax rate)' is added to the profit after tax figure we get the same result.

Incremental Principle The cash flows of a project must be measured in incremental terms. To ascertain a project's incremental cash flows you have to look at what happens to the cash flows of the firm with the project and without the project. The difference between the two reflects the incremental cash flows attributable to the project. That is,

$$\begin{pmatrix}\text{Project cash flow}\\ \text{for the year } t\end{pmatrix} = \begin{matrix}\text{Cash flow for the firm}\\ \textbf{with} \text{ the project for year } t\end{matrix} - \begin{matrix}\text{Cash flow for the firm}\\ \textbf{without} \text{ the project for year } t\end{matrix}$$

In estimating the incremental cash flows of a project, the following guidelines must be borne in mind:

Consider All Incidental Effects In addition to the direct cash flows of the project, all its incidental effects on the rest of the firm must be considered. The project may enhance the profitability of some of the existing activities of the firm because it has a complementary relationship with them; or it may detract from the profitability of some of the existing activities of the firm because it has a competitive relationship with them – all these effects must be taken into account.

How should **product cannibalisation** – the erosion in the sales of the firm's existing products on account of a new product introduction – be handled? One can argue that the loss of profit resulting from the reduction of sales of existing products may be treated as a negative incremental effect of the new product. This may, however, lead to the possibility of rejecting the new product. If this happens, it is very likely that a competitor may steal a march on the firm and introduce a product similar to what the firm had in mind, leading to an erosion in the sales of the existing products of the firm. This is indeed a highly unwelcome scenario because the firm loses sales to a competitor rather than to itself.

Thus how the loss of sales on account of product cannibalisation is treated will depend on whether or not a competitor is likely to introduce a close substitute to the new product that is being considered by the firm.

If the firm is operating in an extremely competitive business and is not protected by entry barriers, product cannibalisation will occur anyway. Hence the costs associated with it are not relevant in incremental analysis. On the other hand, if the firm is sheltered by entry barriers like patent protection or proprietary technology or brand loyalty, the costs of product cannibalisation should be incorporated in investment analysis.

Ignore Sunk Costs A sunk cost refers to an outlay already incurred in the past or already committed irrevocably. So it is not affected by the acceptance or rejection of the project under consideration. Suppose, for example, a company is debating whether it should invest in a project. The company has already spent ₹10 million for preliminary work meant to generate information useful for this decision. Is this ₹10 million a relevant cost for the proposed project? Clearly not ₹10 million represents a sunk cost as it cannot be recovered irrespective of whether the project is accepted or not. Remember that bygones are bygones and are not relevant for decision making.

Include Opportunity Costs If a project uses resources already available with the firm, there is a potential for an opportunity cost – this is the cost created for the rest of the firm as a consequence of undertaking the project. The opportunity cost of a resource is the benefit that can be derived from it by putting it to its best alternative use. So, to analyse the opportunity cost, ask the question: "Is there any alternative use of the resource if the project is not undertaken?" For most resources, there will be an alternative use:

- The resource may be rented out. In this case the opportunity cost is the rental revenue foregone by undertaking the project. For example, if a project uses a vacant factory building owned by the firm, the revenue that can be derived from renting out this building represents the opportunity cost.
- The resource may be sold. In this case the opportunity cost is the value realised from the sale of the resource after paying taxes. For example, if a project uses an equipment which is currently idle, its opportunity cost is its sales price, net of any tax liability.
- The resource is required elsewhere in the firm. In this case, the cost of replacing the resource represents its opportunity cost. For example, if a project requires the services of some experienced engineers from an existing division of the firm, the cost that is borne by that division to replace those engineers represents the opportunity cost.

What happens when a project uses a resource that has no current alternative use, but some potential alternative use? One example is excess capacity on some machine. Most firms find it impractical to sell or lease excess capacity, but realise that using it for a new product may exhaust capacity much earlier than otherwise. This may call for creating new capacity earlier rather than later or reducing the output of some products in future. If new capacity has to be created earlier than later, the opportunity cost is: Present value of creating capacity earlier – Present value of creating capacity later. If the output of some products is likely to be reduced in future, the opportunity cost is the loss in cash flows that would have otherwise been generated by the sales of those products.

Question the Allocation of Overhead Costs Costs which are only indirectly related to a product (or service) are referred to as overhead costs. They include items like general administrative expenses, managerial salaries, legal expenses, rent and so on. Accountants normally allocate overhead costs to various products on some basis like labour hours, or machine hours, or prime cost which appears reasonable. Hence when a new project is proposed, a portion of the overhead costs of the firm is usually allocated to it. The overhead allocated to it, however, may hardly have any relationship with the incremental overhead costs, if any, associated with it. For purposes of investment analysis, what matters is the incremental overhead costs (along with other incremental costs) attributable to the project and not the allocated overhead costs.

Estimate Net Working Capital Properly Investor funds are required for supporting fixed assets and net working capital. So, the net working capital requirement has to be properly estimated. In this context, the following points must be borne in mind:

- Gross working capital refers to the total of current assets. A portion of gross working capital is supported by non-interest bearing current liabilities (referred to as NIBCLs) such as trade credit, advances from customers, provisions, and so on.
- Net working capital is: Gross working capital-NIBCLs. Net working capital has to be financed by investor claims such as equity, preference, and debt. The requirement of net working capital is likely to change over time as output changes.
- While fixed asset investments are made during the early years of the project and depreciated over time, net working capital is renewed periodically and hence is not subject to depreciation. Thus the net working capital at the end of the project life is assumed to have a salvage value equal to its book value.

Post-tax Principle Cash flows should be measured on an after-tax basis. Some firms may ignore tax payments and try to compensate this by discounting the pre-tax cash flows at a rate that is higher than the cost of capital of the firm. Since there is no reliable way of adjusting the discount rate, you should always use after-tax cash flows along with after-tax discount rate. The important issues in assessing the impact of taxes are: What tax rate should be used to assess tax liability? How should losses be treated? What is the effect of noncash charges?

Tax Rate Let us examine the choices in terms of taxes. The *average tax* rate is the total tax burden as a proportion of the total income of the business. The *marginal tax rate* is the tax rate applicable to the income at margin – the next rupee of income. The marginal tax rate is typically higher than the average tax rate because tax rates are often progressive.

The income from a project typically is marginal. Put differently, it is additional to the income generated by the assets of the firm already in place. Hence, the marginal tax rate of the firm is the relevant rate for estimating the tax liability of the project

Treatment of Losses Because the firm as well as the project can incur losses, let us look at various possible combinations and the ways to deal with them. The different scenarios are summarised below:

Scenario	*Project*	*Firm*	*Action*
1	Incurs losses	Incurs losses	Defer tax savings
2	Incurs losses	Makes profits	Take tax savings in the year of loss
3	Makes profits	Incurs losses	Defer taxes until the firm makes profits
4	Makes profits	Makes profits	Consider taxes in the year of profit
Stand alone	Incurs losses	–	Defer tax saving until the project makes profits

Effect of Noncash Charges Noncash charges can have an impact on cash flows if they affect the tax liability. The most important of such noncash charges is depreciation. The tax benefit of depreciation is:

$$\text{Depreciation} * \text{Marginal tax rate}$$

The depreciation method allowed for tax purposes in India is the written down value method. Under this method the depreciation charge is calculated as follows:

$$DEP_1 = BV_0 r$$

$$DEP_2 = BV_1 r = BV_0 (1-r)\, r$$

$$DEP_t = BV_{t-1} r = BV_0 (1-r)^{t-1}\, r \qquad (9.1)$$

where DEP, BV, and r stand for depreciation charge, book value, and depreciation rate respectively.

For example, if the initial investment (BV_0) is 100 and depreciation rate (r) is 40 percent, the book value and depreciation charge will be as follows for the first three years:

Year	*Beginning book value*	*Depreciation charge*
1	100	100 (0.40) = 40
2	60	100 (1–0.40) 0.40 = 24
3	36	$100\,(1-0.40)^2\,0.40 = 14.4$

Apart from land which is not subject to depreciation, the depreciation rates for various categories of assets, are prescribed under the Income Tax Act. The important rates presently are as follows:

- Factory Buildings : 10%
- Plant and machinery : 15%
- Computers : 60%
- Vehicles on hire : 30%
- Temporary structures : 100%

Deferred Tax Liability and Minimum Alternative Tax To understand the treatment of such items let us note the following:

- Taxable income, which is determined according to income tax regulations, is generally different from accounting profit, which is measured according to generally accepted accounting principles and the accounting policies followed by the firm. The difference may be permanent or temporary.

A permanent difference is caused by an item which is included for calculating either taxable income or accounting profit, but not both. For example, if some income is tax-exempt, it is included in accounting profit but not taxable income. A temporary difference (also called a timing difference) is caused by an item which is included for calculating both taxable income and accounting period, but in different periods. For example, depreciation is charged as per the written down value method for the taxable income but as per the straight line method for calculating the accounting profit. As a result, there are differences in the year-to-year depreciation charges under the two methods, but the total depreciation charges over the life of the asset would be the same under both the methods.

Deferred tax liability (or asset) arises because of the temporary differences between taxable income and accounting profit. A deferred tax liability (asset) is recognised when the charge in the financial statements is less (more) than the amount allowed for tax purposes.

A deferred tax charge in the profit and loss account in a particular year does not mean that there is a tax outflow in that year; likewise, a deferred tax benefit in the profit and loss account in a particular mean does not mean that there is a tax saving in that year.

- In the case of an assessee being a company, if the income-tax payable on the total income is computed under the Income Tax Act is less than 18.5 percent of its book profit, the tax payable for the relevant previous year shall be deemed to be 18.5 percent of the book profits. This tax is called the minimum alternative tax (MAT). It may be noted that the book profit is derived at after making some adjustments to the net profit shown in the profit and loss account prepared for purposes of financial reporting. So it is a variant of accounting profit.

  Under the Income Tax Act, if a company has paid MAT, the difference between MAT and the income tax payable on the total income otherwise, called MAT credit entitlement, can be availed of for seven years. This means, for example, if a company has a MAT credit entitlement of ₹10 million in year 1 and it has a tax liability of ₹20 million in year 2, it will get a MAT credit of ₹10 million in year 2, thereby effectively reducing its tax outgo in year 2 by ₹10 million.

- Given the non-cash nature of deferred tax charge (or benefit) and MAT credit entitlement, the post-tax cash flow is derived from profit after tax as follows:

  Profit after tax + Depreciation and amortisation + Deferred tax charge − MAT credit entitlement

  Remember that depreciation and amortisation and deferred tax charge are debits to the profit and loss account without any corresponding cash outflow in the year. And, MAT credit entitlement is a credit to the profit and loss account without any corresponding cash inflow in the year.

Consistency Principle Cash flows and the discount rates applied to these cash flows must be consistent with respect to the investor group and inflation.

Investor Group The cash flow of a project may be estimated from the point of view of all investors (equity shareholders as well as lenders) or from the point of view of just equity shareholders.

The cash flow of a project from the point of view of all investors is the cash flow available to all investors after paying taxes and meeting investment needs of the project, if any. It is also called as project cash flow. It is estimated as follows:

Cash flow to all investors	=	PBIT (1 – tax rate)
	+	Depreciation and noncash charges
	–	Capital expenditure
	–	Change in net working capital

The cash flow of a project from the point of view of equity shareholders is the cash flow available to equity shareholders after paying taxes, meeting investment needs, and fulfilling debt-related commitments. It is estimated as follows:

Cash flow to equity shareholders	=	Profit after tax
	+	Depreciation and other noncash charges
	–	Preference dividend
	–	Capital expenditures
	–	Change in net working capital
	–	Repayment of debt
	+	Proceeds from debt issues
	–	Redemption of preference capital
	+	Proceeds from preference issue

The discount rate must be consistent with the definition of cash flow:

Cash flow	*Discount rate*
Cash flow to all investors	Weighted average cost of capital
Cash flow to equity shareholders	Cost of equity

Generally, in capital budgeting we look at the cash flow to all investors and apply the weighted average cost of capital of the firm. We will also follow this convention.

Inflation In dealing with inflation, you have two choices. You can incorporate expected inflation in the estimates of future cash flows and apply a nominal discount rate to the same. Alternatively, you can estimate the future cash flows in real terms and apply a real discount rate to the same.

Note that the following relationship holds between nominal and real values:

Nominal cash flow_t = Real cash flow_t (1 + Expected inflation $\text{rate})_t$

Nominal discount rate = (1 + Real discount rate) (1 + Expected inflation rate) – 1

The consistency principle, in essence, suggests the following match up:

Cash flow	*Discount rate*
Nominal cash flow	Nominal discount rate
Real cash flow	Real discount rate

Generally, in capital budgeting analysis nominal cash flows are estimated and nominal discount rate is used. We will also follow this convention, unless mentioned otherwise.

9.3 CASH FLOW ILLUSTRATIONS

To show how cash flows are determined, bearing in mind the principles discussed above, two illustrations are presented in this section.

Illustration I Naveen Enterprises is considering a capital project about which the following information is available:

- The investment outlay on the project will be ₹100 million. This consists of ₹80 million on plant and machinery and ₹20 million on net working capital. The entire outlay will be incurred at the beginning of the project.
- The project will be financed with ₹45 million of equity capital, ₹5 million of preference capital, and ₹50 million of debt capital. Preference capital will carry a dividend rate of 15 percent; debt capital will carry an interest rate of 15 percent.
- The life of the project is expected to be 5 years. At the end of 5 years, fixed assets will fetch a net salvage value of ₹30 million whereas net working capital will be liquidated at its book value.
- The project is expected to increase the revenues of the firm by ₹120 million per year. The increase in costs on account of the project is expected to be ₹80 million per year. (This includes all items of cost other than depreciation, interest, and tax). The effective tax rate will be 30 percent.
- Plant and machinery will be depreciated at the rate of 15 percent per year as per the written down value method. Hence, the depreciation charges will be:

First year	:	₹12.00 million
Second year	:	₹10.20 million
Third year	:	₹8.67 million
Fourth year	:	₹7.37 million
Fifth year	:	₹6.26 million

Given the above details, the project cash flows are shown in Exhibit 9.2.

Exhibit 9.2 ***Project Cash Flows***

(₹ in millions)

	0	*1*	*2*	*3*	*4*	*5*
1. Fixed Assets	(80.00)	-	-	-	-	-
2. Net working Capital	(20.00)	-	-	-	-	-
3. Revenues		120	120	120	120	120
4. Costs (Other than depreciation and interest)		80	80	80	80	80

(Contd.)

	0	1	2	3	4	5
					(₹ in millions)	
5. Depreciation		12.00	10.20	8.67	7.37	6.26
6. Profit before Tax		28.00	29.80	31.33	32.63	33.74
7. Tax		8.40	8.94	9.40	9.79	10.12
8. Profit after Tax		19.60	20.86	21.93	22.84	23.62
9. Net Salvage Value						30.00
10. Recovery of Net Working Capital						20.00
11. Initial Investment	(100.00)					
12. Operating Cash Inflow		31.60	31.06	30.60	30.21	29.88
13. Terminal Flow						50.00
14. Net Cash Flow (11+12+13)	(100.00)	31.60	31.06	30.60	30.21	79.88
Book value of Investment	100.00	88.00	77.80	69.13	61.76	

It may be emphasised that in this illustration the outlay on fixed assets and net working capital occurs only at the beginning. Should there be further outlays on fixed assets and net working capital in future years, the same must be properly accounted for.

In general terms, we refer to net cash flow as free cash flow (FCF). The FCF for any year is defined as:

PAT
\+ DEPRECIATION & AMORTISATION
– Δ FIXED ASSETS
– Δ NET WORKING CAPITAL

Alternatively, it is defined as:

PAT
– Δ NET FIXED ASSETS
Δ NET WORKING CAPITAL

It must be noted that in calculating PAT we ignored interest in conformity with the separation principle. So PAT was effectively equal to:

Profit before interest and taxes (1 – tax rate)
or PBIT (1 – T)

This is also referred to as NOPAT or Net Operating Profit after Tax.

Illustration II India Pharma Ltd is engaged in the manufacture of pharmaceuticals. The company was established in 1998 and has registered a steady growth in sales since then. Presently the company manufactures 16 products and has an annual turnover of ₹2,200 million. The company is considering the manufacture of a new antibiotic preparation, K-cin, for which the following information has been gathered.

1. K-cin is expected to have a product life cycle of five years and thereafter it would be withdrawn from the market. The sales from this preparation are expected to be as follows:

Year	*Sales (₹ in million)*
1	100
2	150
3	200
4	150
5	100

2. The capital equipment required for manufacturing K-cin is ₹100 million and it will be depreciated at the rate of 15 percent per year as per the WDV method for tax purposes. The expected net salvage value after five years is ₹20 million.
3. The net working capital requirement for the project is expected to be 20 percent of sales. At the end of 5 years, the net working capital is expected to be liquidated at par, barring an estimated loss of ₹5 million on account of bad debt. The bad debt loss will be a tax-deductible expense.
4. The accountant of the firm has provided the following cost estimates for K-cin:

Raw material cost	:	30 percent of sales
Variable labour cost	:	20 percent of sales
Fixed annual operating and maintenance cost	:	₹5 million
Overhead allocation (excluding depreciation, maintenance, and interest)	:	10 percent of sales

While the project is charged an overhead allocation, it is not likely to have any effect on overhead expenses as such.
5. The manufacture of K-cin would also require some of the common facilities of the firm. The use of these facilities would call for reduction in the production of other pharmaceutical preparations of the firm. This would entail a reduction of ₹15 million of contribution margin
6. The tax rate applicable to the firm is 30 percent.

Based on the above information, the cash flows for the project have been worked out in Exhibit 9.3. A few points about this exhibit are in order:

- The loss of contribution (item 7) is an opportunity cost.
- Overhead expenses allocated to the project have been ignored as they do not represent incremental overhead expenses for the firm as a whole.
- It is assumed that the level of net working capital is adjusted at the beginning of the year in relation to the expected sales for the year. For example, net working capital at the beginning of year 1 (i.e. at the end of year 0) will be ₹20 million that is 20 percent of the expected revenues of ₹100 million for year 1. Likewise, the level of net working capital at the end of year 1 (i.e. at the beginning of year 2) will be ₹30 million that is 20 percent of the expected revenues of ₹150 million for year 2.

Exhibit 9.3 ***Cash Flows for the K-cin Project***

			Years			*(₹ in Millions)*
	0	*1*	*2*	*3*	*4*	*5*
1. Capital Investment	(100.00)					
2. Level of Net Working Capital (Ending)	20	30	40	30	20	0
3. Revenues		100	150	200	150	100
4. Raw Material Cost		30	45	60	45	30
5. Labour Cost		20	30	40	30	20

(Contd.)

		Years			(₹ Million)	
6. Operating and Maintenance Cost		5	5	5	5	5
7. Loss of Contribution		15	15	15	15	15
8. Depreciation		15.00	12.75	10.84	9.21	7.83
9. Bad Debt Loss						5
10. Profit Before Tax		15.00	42.25	69.16	45.79	17.17
11. Tax		4.50	12.68	20.75	13.74	5.15
12. Profit After Tax		10.50	29.58	48.41	32.05	12.02
13. Net Salvage Value of Equipment						20
14. Recovery of Net Working Capital						15
15. Capital Investment	(100.00)					
16. Operating Cash Inflow (12+8+9)		25.50	42.33	59.25	41.26	24.85
17. Net Working Capital	20.00	10.00	10.00	–10.00	–10.00	
18. Terminal cash inflow (13+14)						35
19. Net cash flow (15+16–17+18)	–120.00	15.50	32.33	69.25	51.26	59.85

9.4 CASH FLOWS FOR A REPLACEMENT PROJECT

Developing cash flows for new projects or expansion projects is relatively straight forward. In such cases, the initial investment, operating cash inflows, and terminal cash inflow are the after-tax cash flows associated with the proposed project. Estimating the relevant cash flows for a replacement project is somewhat complicated because you have to determine the incremental cash outflows and inflows in relation to the existing project. The three components of the cash flow stream of a replacement project are determined as follows:

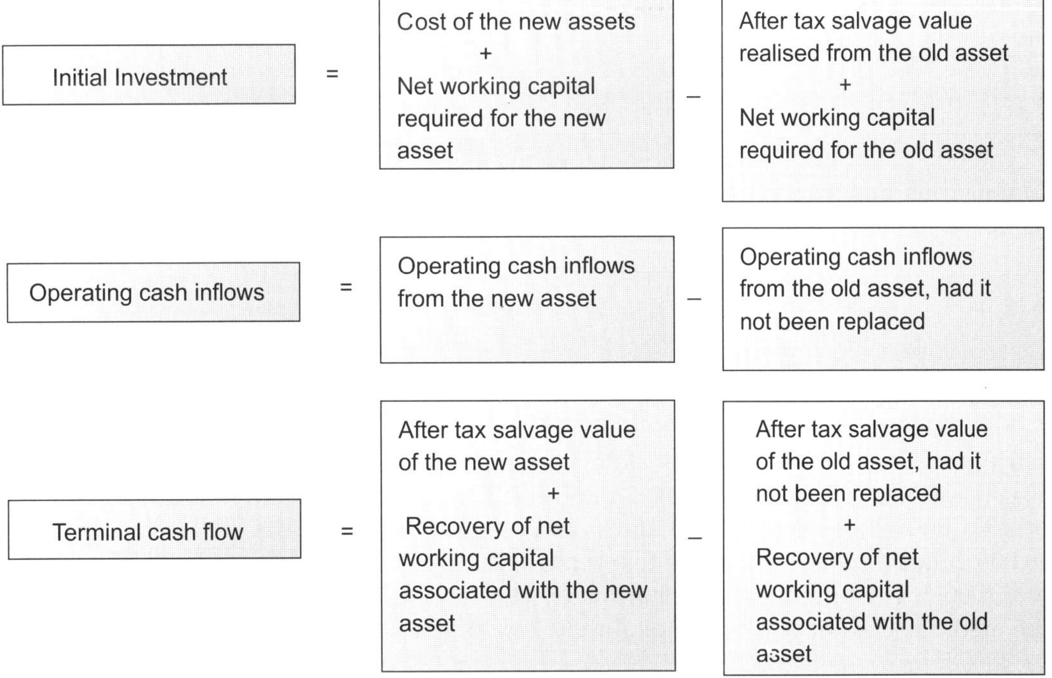

A question often asked is: Once we have assumed that the old asset is replaced, why should we consider the operating cash inflows and terminal cash flow associated with the old asset subsequently? The answer is: If you consider the advantage derived from liquidating the old asset, you should also consider the disadvantage suffered by not having the asset in the future. To illustrate this point, let us consider a very simple example. Suppose you own a plot of land that presently has a market value of ₹1 million. If you keep it for a year it is expected to fetch you ₹1.2 million. You come across another plot of land that will cost you ₹1.5 million now. If you buy this land you hope to sell it for ₹2.0 million a year hence. You are debating whether you should replace the existing plot of land with the new plot that costs ₹1.5 million. If you ignore taxes and assume that there is no operating cash inflow associated with both the plots of land, the cash flows of the replacement proposal are as follows:

Initial investment = Cost of the new plot – After-tax salvage value of the old plot
= ₹1,500,000 – ₹1,000,000
= ₹500,000

Operating cash inflow = Operating cash inflow from the new plot – Operating cash inflow from the old plot
= ₹0 – ₹0
= ₹0

Terminal cash inflow = After tax salvage value of the new plot – After tax salvage value of the old plot, had it been retained
= ₹2,000,000 – ₹1,200,000
= ₹800,000

Thus the relevant cash flow stream of this replacement proposal is:

Year	*Cash Flow*
0	–₹500,000
1	₹800,000

If you don't subtract the salvage value of the existing plot a year from now, you get the following cash flow stream for the replacement proposal:

Thus the relevant cash flow stream of this replacement proposal is:

Year	*Cash Flow*
0	–₹500,000
1	₹2000,000

Clearly this is erroneous and misleading because it considers the advantage from selling the plot today but overlooks the disadvantage expected a year from now.

Illustration Ojus Enterprises is determining the cash flow for a project involving replacement of an old machine by a new machine. The old machine bought a few years ago has a book value of ₹400,000 and it can be sold to realise a post tax salvage value of ₹500,000. It has a remaining life of five years after which its net salvage value is expected to be ₹160,000. It is being depreciated annually at a rate of 15 percent under the written down value method. The net working capital required for the old machine is ₹400,000.

The new machine costs ₹1,600,000. It is expected to fetch a net salvage value of ₹800,000 after 5 years when it will no longer be required. The depreciation rate applicable to it is 15 percent under the written down value method. The net working capital required for the new machine is ₹500,000. The new machine is expected to bring a saving of ₹257,143 annually in manufacturing costs (other than depreciation). The tax rate applicable to the firm is 30 percent.

Given the above information, the incremental after-tax cash flow associated with the replacement project has been worked out in Exhibit 9.4.

Exhibit 9.4 ***Cash Flows for a Replacement Project***

			Year		(₹ in '000)	
	0	1	2	3	4	5
I. Investment Outlay						
1. Cost of New Asset	– 1600					
2. Salvage Value of Old Asset	500					
3. Increase in Net Working Capital	– 100					
4. Total Net Investment	– 1200					
II. Operating Inflows Over the Project Life						
5. After-Tax Savings in Manufacturing Costs		180.00	180.00	180.00	180.00	180.00
6. Depreciation on New Machine		240.00	204.00	173.40	147.39	125.28
7. Depreciation on Old Machine		60.00	51.00	43.35	36.85	31.32
8. Incremental Depreciation (6–7)		180.00	153.00	130.05	110.54	93.96
9. Tax Savings on Incremental Depreciation		54.00	45.90	39.02	33.16	28.19
10. Net Operating Cash Inflow (5+9)		234.00	225.90	219.02	213.16	208.19
III. Terminal Cash Inflow						
11. Net Terminal Value of New Machine						800.00
12. Net Terminal Value of Old Machine						160.00
13. Recovery of Incremental Net Working Capital						100.00
14. Total Terminal Cash Inflow (11–12+13)						740.00
IV. Net Cash Flow (4+10+14)	–1200.00	234.00	225.90	219.02	213.16	948.19

9.5 VIEWING A PROJECT FROM OTHER PERSPECTIVES

There are several perspectives from which a project may be viewed. To understand them, let us look at Exhibit 9.5 which shows the investment and financing sides of a hypothetical project. From this exhibit we find that:

Exhibit 9.5 ***Various Points of View***

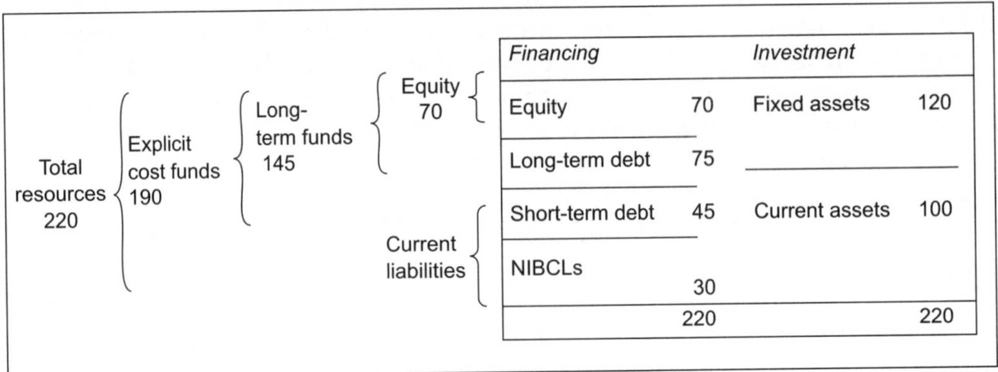

- Long-term funds comprise of equity and long-term debt.
- Current liabilities comprise of short-term debt and non-interest bearing current liabilities or NIBCLs, (trade credit, provisions, etc.)
- Long-term funds (equity and long-term debt) plus short-term debt carry an explicit cost associated with them, whereas NIBCLs carry no explicit cost associated with them. Hence, explicit cost funds comprise of long-term funds and short-term debt. They are also called investor claims.
- Total resources comprise of long-term funds and current liabilities.
- Fixed assets are typically fully supported by long-term funds.
- Current assets are partly supported by long-term funds and partly supported by current liabilities. The portion of current assets that is supported by long-term funds is called working capital margin.

Now, a project can be viewed from four distinct points of view.

- Equity point of view.
- Long-term funds point of view
- Explicit cost funds (investor claims) point of view
- Total resources point of view

In capital budgeting, the explicit cost funds point of view is commonly adopted – that is why our discussion so far defined cash flows from that point of view. However, one can adopt any other point of view as well. What is important is that the measures of cash flow and cost of capital must be consistent with the point of view adopted.

Since the explicit cost funds point of view has already been discussed at length, we will in this section look at how cash flows are defined from the equity point of view, the long-term funds point of view, and the total resources point of view with the help of an illustration.

Magnum Technologies Limited is evaluating an electronics project for which the following information has been assembled:

1. The total outlay on the project is expected to be ₹50 million. This consists of ₹30 million of fixed assets and ₹20 million of current assets.

2. The total outlay of ₹50 million is proposed to be financed as follows: ₹15 million of equity, ₹20 million of term loans, ₹10 million of bank finance for working capital, and ₹5 million of trade credit.
3. The term loan is repayable in five equal annual instalments of ₹4 million each. The first instalment will be due at the end of the first year and the last instalment at the end of the fifth year. The levels of bank finance for working capital and trade credit will remain at ₹10 million and ₹5 million till they are paid back or retired at the end of five years.
4. The interest rates on the term loan and bank finance for working capital will be 10 percent and 12 percent respectively.
5. The expected revenues from the project will be ₹60 million per year. The operating costs, excluding depreciation, will be ₹42 million. The depreciation rate on the fixed assets will be 15 percent as per the written down value method.
6. The net salvage value of fixed assets and current assets at the end of year 5 will be ₹5 million and ₹20 million respectively.
7. The tax rate applicable to the firm is 30 percent.

Cash Flows Relating to Equity The equity-related cash flow stream (also called *free cash flow to equity* stream) reflects the contributions made and benefits accruing to equity shareholders. It may be divided into three components as follows:

- Initial investment : Equity funds committed to the project
- Operating cash flows : Profit after tax – Preference dividend + Depreciation + Other non-cash charges
- Liquidation and retirement cash flow : Net salvage value of fixed assets
  \+
  Net salvage value of current assets
  –
  Repayment of term loans
  –
  Redemption of preference capital
  –
  Repayment of working capital advances
  –
  Retirement of trade credit and other dues

While the first two components, namely, 'initial investment' and 'operating cash inflows' are fairly self-explanatory, the third term, namely, 'liquidation and retirement cash flows' requires a little explanation. It represents the net cash flows accruing to equity shareholders as a result of liquidation of various assets in the project and retirement/redemption of all other claims. Remember that equity shareholders have a residual interest in the project and hence what is left after meeting the claims of all others belongs to equity shareholders.

Exhibit 9.6 works out the net cash flows from the equity point of view for the electronics project of Magnum Technologies Limited.

Exhibit 9.6 ***Net Cash Flows Relating to Equity***

	Years				(₹*million)*	
	0	*1*	*2*	*3*	*4*	*5*
1. Equity Funds	–15.00					
2. Revenues		60.00	60.00	60.00	60.00	60.00
3. Operating Costs		42.00	42.00	42.00	42.00	42.00
4. Depreciation		4.50	3.83	3.25	2.76	2.35
5. Interest on Working Capital Advance		1.20	1.20	1.20	1.20	1.20
6. Interest on Term Loan		2.00	1.60	1.20	0.80	0.40
7. Profit before Tax		10.30	11.38	12.35	13.24	14.05
8. Tax		3.09	3.41	3.70	3.97	4.22
9. Profit after Tax		7.21	7.96	8.64	9.27	9.84
10. Preference Dividend						
11. Net Salvage Value of Fixed Assets						5.00
12. Net Salvage Value of Current Assets						20.00
13. Repayment of Term Loans		4.00	4.00	4.00	4.00	4.00
14. Redemption of Preference Capital						
15. Repayment of Short-term Bank Borrowings						10.00
16. Retirement of Trade Creditors						5.00
17. Initial Investment (1)	–15.00					
18. Operating Cash Inflows (9–10+4)		11.71	11.79	11.90	12.03	12.18
19. Liquidation and Retirement Cash Flows (11+12–13–14–15–16)		–4.00	–4.00	–4.00	–4.00	6.00
20. Net Cash Flow (17+18+19)	–15.00	7.71	7.79	7.90	8.03	18.18

Cash Flows Relating to Long-term Funds As discussed earlier in this chapter, the cash flow stream relating to long-term funds consists of three components as follows:

Initial investment	:	Long-term funds invested in the project. This is equal to: fixed assets + working capital margin
Operating cash inflow	:	Profit after tax + Depreciation + Other non-cash charges + Interest on long-term borrowings (1-tax rate)
Terminal cash flow	:	Net salvage value of fixed assets + Net recovery of working capital margin

Exhibit 9.7 shows the cash flows relating to long-term funds for the electronics project of Magnum Technologies Limited.

Exhibit 9.7 ***Net Cash Flows Relating to Long-term Funds***

	Years			(₹ in millions)		
	0	1	2	3	4	5
1. Fixed Assets	–30.00					
2. Working Capital Margin	–5.00					
3. Revenues		60.00	60.00	60.00	60.00	60.00
4. Operating Costs		42.00	42.00	42.00	42.00	42.00
5. Depreciation		4.50	3.83	3.25	2.76	2.35
6. Interest on Working Capital Advance		1.20	1.20	1.20	1.20	1.20
7. Interest on Term Loan		2.00	1.60	1.20	0.80	0.40
8. Profit before Tax		10.30	11.38	12.35	13.24	14.05
9. Tax		3.09	3.41	3.70	3.97	4.22
10. Profit after Tax		7.21	7.96	8.64	9.27	9.84
11. Net Salvage Value of Fixed Assets						5.00
12. Net Recovery of Working Capital Margin						5.00
13. Initial Investment (1+2)	–35.00					
14. Operating Cash Inflows 9+5+7(1–T)		8.99	8.36	7.80	7.29	6.84
15. Terminal Cash Flow (11+12)						10.00
16. Net Cash Flow (13+14+15)	–35.00	8.99	8.36	7.80	7.29	16.84

Cash Flows Relating to Total Resources The cash flow stream relating to total resources consists of three components as follows:

Initial investment : All the resources committed to the project. This is simply the total outlay on the project consisting of fixed assets plus gross working capital

Operating cash inflow : Profit after tax

+

Depreciation

+

Other non-cash charges

+

Interest on long-term borrowings (1-tax rate)

+

Interest on short-term borrowings (1-tax rate)

Terminal cash flow : Net salvage value of fixed assets

+

Net salvage value of current assets

Exhibit 9.8 shows the net cash flows from the point of view of total resources for the electronics project of Magnum Technologies Limited.

Exhibit 9.8 ***Net Cash Flows Relating to Total Resources***

	Years					(₹ in millions)
	0	*1*	*2*	*3*	*4*	*5*
1. Total Resources	–50.00					
2. Revenues		60.00	60.00	60.00	60.00	60.00
3. Operating Costs		42.00	42.00	42.00	42.00	42.00
4. Depreciation		4.50	3.83	3.25	2.76	2.35
5. Interest on Working Capital Advance		1.20	1.20	1.20	1.20	1.20
6. Interest on Term Loan		2.00	1.60	1.20	0.80	0.40
7. Profit before Tax		10.30	11.38	12.35	13.24	14.05
8. Tax		3.09	3.41	3.70	3.97	4.22
9. Profit after Tax		7.21	7.96	8.64	9.27	9.84
10. Net Salvage Value of Fixed Assets						5.00
11. Net Salvage Value of Current Assets						20.00
12. Initial Investment (1)	–50.00					
13. Operating Cash Inflows [9+4+6(1–T)+5(1–T)]		13.95	13.75	13.58	13.43	13.30
14. Terminal Cash Flow (10+11)						25.00
15. Net Cash Flow (12+13+14)	–50.00	13.95	13.75	13.58	13.43	38.30

9.6 HOW FINANCIAL INSTITUTIONS AND THE PLANNING COMMISSION DEFINE CASH FLOWS

Financial Institutions In evaluating project proposals submitted to them, financial institutions define project cash flows as follows:

Cash outflows

Capital expenditure on the project (net of interest during construction)

\+

Outlays on gross working capital

Cash inflows

Operating inflow	:	Profit after tax[1]
	+	Depreciation
	+	Interest and lease rental
Terminal inflow	:	Recovery of gross working capital (at book value)
	+	Residual value of capital assets (land at 100% and other capital assets at 5% on initial cost)

[1] If there are losses in the initial years the tax shield arising out of losses can be added back to the cash flows only if the existing operations of the company are liable for tax of that amount. In case of new companies, tax shield cannot be added back to the cash flows.

For calculating the IRR the cash flows are considered for a maximum project life of 12 years. For certain industries which are subject to a faster rate of technological obsolescence, a shorter life is considered.

From the above, it is clear that financial institutions look at projects from the point of view of all resources. It is instructive to compare the cash flow stream defined by the financial institutions with the cash flow stream relating to all investors defined by us earlier in this chapter.

	Cash flow stream defined by financial institutions	*Cash flow stream relating to total resources*
Initial investment	Capital expenditure on the project (net of interest during construction period) + Outlay on gross working capital	Capital expenditure on the project (net of interest during construction period) + Outlay on gross working capital
Operating cash inflow	Profit after tax + Depreciation + Interest	Profit after tax + Depreciation + Interest (1-tax rate)[2]
Terminal cash inflow	Recovery of gross working capital (at book value) + Residual value of capital assets (land at 100% and capital assets at 5% of initial cost)	Recovery of gross working capital (at book value) + Expected net salvage value of other assets

From the above, we find that:

- The initial investment is defined identically in both the cases.
- Institutions add back interest without adjusting for taxes whereas in our definition interest is added back after adjusting for the tax factor.
- The residual value of capital assets is defined by the institutions in a very conservative and mechanistic fashion whereas in our definition it is based on expected net salvage value.

Planning Commission As per the *Manual for Preparation of Feasibility Reports* developed by the Planning Commission, the following rules should be observed in defining costs and returns (cash flows in our terminology).

[2] Note that:

$$\begin{aligned} \text{PBIT}\,(1-T) &= (\text{PBT} + I)\,(1-T) \\ &= \text{PBT}\,(1-T) + I\,(1-T) \\ &= \text{PAT} + I\,(1-T) \end{aligned}$$

1. Interest during construction should not be allowed for in the year-wise capital expenditure figures since it is implicitly taken into account by the discounting procedure. If replacement expenditure is likely to be incurred during the life of the project it should be allowed for in the year in which it will occur.
2. Returns should be defined on a gross basis as operating revenues minus operating costs. Depreciation and financial charges on capital expenditures covered by the capital cost figures should not be deducted in defining returns. *They are allowed for implicitly in the discounting procedure.*
3. Capital cost estimates generally do not allow for funds required for working capital purposes, which are assumed to be borrowed, but only for the margin on working capital. In this case the operating cost estimates must include interest payments on funds borrowed for working capital.
4. In some cases involving the use of fixed-interest term loans for capital expenditure, an internal rate of return on own funds (equity) may need to be presented. In such cases the initial capital cost figures should cover only the expenditures out of equity capital. Repayment of term loans and interest due on them should be allowed for in the subsequent years as and when they are expected to arise.
5. Costs and returns should be calculated over the entire life of the project or over 25 years whichever is less. The returns should allow for a salvage value of assets at the end of the period.

Based on the above description, the following observations may be made:

1. A project may be viewed from the point of view of equity capital or long-term funds.
2. Cost and return (benefit) streams have been defined consistently with the point of view adopted. Further, they are defined in pre-tax terms.
3. A fairly long planning horizon is envisaged. This perhaps reflects the fact that the projects considered by the Planning Commission, in general, have a long economic life.

9.7 BIASES IN CASH FLOW ESTIMATION

As cash flows have to be forecast far into the future, errors in estimation are bound to occur. Yet, given the critical importance of cash flow forecasts in project evaluation, adequate care should be taken to guard against certain biases which may lead to over-statement or understatement of the true project profitability.

Overstatement of Profitability In forecasting the outcomes of risky projects, executives often commit planning fallacy, implying that they display overoptimism. Executives' overoptimism results from a variety of cognitive biases (the errors in the way mind processes information) and organisational pressures which are briefly described here.

- *Native optimism* People tend to exaggerate their own talents. They believe that they are above average in being endowed with positive traits and abilities.
- *Attribution error* The native overoptimism gets amplified by the tendency to misperceive the causes of certain events, referred to as attribution errors by psychologists. Typically,

this means that people take credit for positive outcomes and attribute negative outcomes to external factors, irrespective of what the true cause is. Further, people tend to exaggerate their degree of control over things, downplaying the role of luck.

- *Anchoring* After forming an opinion, people are often unwilling to change it, even though they receive new information that is relevant. This is due to anchoring, a very strong cognitive bias. Since the initial proposal for any project emphasises the positive, as it is designed to make a case for the project, the subsequent analysis is skewed toward optimism, thanks to anchoring.
- *Myopic euphoria* Individuals responsible for preparing forecasts may become too involved and lose their sense of proportion. The lack of objectivity in this case is neither intentional nor due to inexperience. It may simply be the effect of 'group psychology' as each person's favourable opinion may be reinforced and magnified by others in the group. Referred to as 'risky shift' or 'group polarisation effect' in social psychology, this phenomenon is widely supported by empirical studies.
- *Competitor neglect* In developing forecasts, executives generally focus on their own abilities and plans, neglecting the abilities and potential actions of competitors.
- *Organisational pressure* In every company, the money and time available for new projects is limited. An awareness of this constraint induces project sponsors to exaggerate the benefits of projects proposed by them. After all, every sponsor is keen that his proposal finds a place in the limited capital budget when there is intense competition among various claimants.
- *Stretch targets* Top managements in most organisations believe in setting stretch targets for various business units. While this can have a salutary effect on motivation, it can skew the forecasts of unit managers toward unrealistically optimistic outcomes. Further, most organisations actively discourage pessimism. As Dan Lovallo and Daniel Kahneman put it in a July-August 2003 HBR article: "The bearers of bad news tend to become pariahs, shunned and ignored by other employees. When pessimistic opinions are suppressed, while optimistic ones are rewarded, an organisation's ability to think critically is undermined."

Tempering the Optimism The human tendency for optimism is inevitable. Likewise, organisational influences that promote optimism will persist. Yet, optimism needs to be tempered.

How can this be done? Dan Lovallo and Daniel Kahneman suggest that decision makers should use the outside view. This calls for looking at the outcomes of similar projects or initiatives and using that evidence to inject greater objectivity in the forecasting exercise. Empirical evidence suggest that when people are asked to take the outside view, their forecasts become more objective and reliable.

The advantage of the outside view is most pronounced for initiatives which have not been attempted earlier such as entering a new market or building a plant using a new technology. Ironically, the inside view is often preferred in such a case. As Dan Lovallo and Daniel Kahneman put it: "Managers feel that if they don't fully account for the intricacies of the proposed project, they would be derelict in their duties. Indeed, the preference for the inside view over the outside view can feel almost like a moral imperative."

In a 1979 article that appeared in *TIMS Studies in Management Science*, Daniel Kahneman and Amos Tversky suggest a five-step procedure for taking the outside view.

1. *Select a reference class.* Identify a reference class of similar past initiatives. This, of course, is not easy. As Kahneman and Tversky put it: "Identifying the right reference class involves both art and science. You usually have to weigh similarities and differences on many variables and determine which are the most meaningful in judging how your own initiative will play out."
2. *Assess the distribution of outcomes.* Document the outcomes of the projects in the reference class and arrange them as a distribution. Determine the average outcome as well as a measure of variability.
3. *Intuitively predict your project's position in the distribution.* Based on how you intutively feel that the project compares with the projects in the reference class, predict where it will fall in the distribution.
4. *Assess the reliability of your prediction.* If there is information on how your past predictions compared with the actual outcomes, the correlation between the two is a reasonable indicator of the reliability of your prediction. In the absence of such information, you may have to subjectively assess the reliability of your predictions.
5. *Correct the intuitive estimate.* Since your intuitive estimate made in step 3 is likely to be optimistic—deviating significantly from the average outcome of the reference class—you have to adjust it toward the average taking into account the reliability of your prediction. The less reliable the prediction, the more the intuitive estimate has to be regressed toward the mean.

Putting Optimism in Place Compared to realism, optimism generates much more enthusiasm and makes people resilient in trying situations. So, it has an important place in any organisation. As Dan Lovallo and Daniel Kahneman put it: "There needs to be a balance between optimism and realism—between goals and forecasts. Aggressive goals can motivate the troups and improve the chance of forecasts, but outside-view forecasts should be used to decide whether or not to make a commitment in the first place".

Understatement of Profitability In the foregoing discussion, we noted the problem of optimistic bias that may lead to an over-statement of project cash flows and profitability. There can be an opposite kind of bias relating to the terminal benefit which may depress a project's true profitability. To understand this bias let us look at how the terminal cash flow is estimated in practice. Typically it is defined as:

Net salvage value of fixed assets + Net recovery of working capital margin.

Generally, the net salvage value of fixed assets, other than land, is put equal to 5 percent of the original cost and the net recovery of working capital margin is set equal to its original book value (under the assumption that current assets do not depreciate).

The above approach almost invariably leads to under-estimation of the terminal benefit of the project, due to the following reasons:

Salvage Values Are Under-Estimated To put the net salvage value of fixed assets equal to just 5 percent (which may more or less correspond to the book value after 8 to 10 years) of the original cost is to ignore the fact that in real life situations fixed assets, even after 8 to 10 years of use, generally command a substantial market value. This is because (a) the rate of physical wear and tear is usually much less than the rate of depreciation for tax or accounting purposes and (b) the secular rate of inflation in India has been around 6 percent.

Intangible Benefits Are Ignored The terminal benefits from a project cannot be equated with just the salvage values of tangible assets left in the project. Apart from investment in tangible assets for which salvage values can be estimated more easily (taking into account the factors mentioned above), major projects are designed to establish a market position, hone research and engineering capability, develop a distribution network, and build brand loyalty. To assume that these benefits are worthless beyond an arbitrarily chosen time horizon is to overlook important business realities. These benefits should not be ignored just because it is difficult to quantify them.

The Value of Future Options Is Overlooked More often than not, a project has a strategic payoff in the form of new investment opportunities that may possibly open up if the project is undertaken. To illustrate, consider the case of a firm which is evaluating a proposal to set up a project for manufacturing scooters. The long-term goal of the firm is to be a market leader in the field of two-wheelers—scooters as well as motorcycles. However, the firm considers entry into the motorcycles market to be infeasible currently as it lacks technical expertise or market image to challenge well-entrenched manufacturers in the field. Thus, the proposal to manufacture motorcycles hinges on the expertise developed and success achieved in the field of scooters. Put differently, it means that the project for manufacturing scooters has a potential payoff in terms of entry into a new field which may generate a large benefit. So, in assessing the scooter project the value of future options generated by it must be taken into account. Since analytical models for doing this are not well developed, judgmental estimation, though subjective in nature, may be done.

Mitigating the Impact of Errors

Forecasting is inherently difficult and subject to large potential errors. To mitigate the impact of these errors, good analysts adopt a three-pronged approach. One, they utilise all the information and technology available to them for developing forecasts. Two, they do post-forecast risk analysis to brace themselves to deal with a wide range of possible outcomes. Three, they try to maintain flexibility in the way the project is implemented so that they can respond to unanticipated future developments.

SUMMARY

- Estimating cash flows—the investment outlays and the cash inflows after the project is commissioned—is the most important, but also the most difficult step in capital budgeting.
- Forecasting project cash flows involves many individuals and departments. The role of the financial manager is to coordinate the efforts of the various departments and obtain information from them, ensure that the forecasts are based on a set of

consistent economic assumptions, keep the exercise focused on relevant variables, and minimise the biases inherent in cash flow forecasting.

- The cash flow stream of a conventional project—a project which involves cash outflows followed by cash inflows—comprises three basic components: (i) initial investment, (ii) operating cash inflows, and (iii) terminal cash inflow.
- The initial investment is the after-tax cash outlay on capital expenditure and net working capital when the project is set up. The operating cash inflows are the after-tax cash inflows resulting from the operations of the project during its economic life. The terminal cash inflow is the after-tax cash flow resulting from the liquidation of the project at the end of its economic life.
- The time horizon for cash flow analysis is usually the minimum of the following: physical life of the plant, technological life of the plant, product market life of the plant, and investment planning horizon of the firm.
- The following principles should be followed while estimating the cash flows of a project: separation principle, incremental principle, post-tax principle, and consistency principle.
- There are two sides of a project, viz., the investment (or asset) side and the financing side. The separation principle says that the cash flows associated with these sides should be separated. While estimating the cash flows on the investment side do not consider financing charges like interest or dividend.
- The cash flows of a project must be measured in incremental terms. To ascertain a project's incremental cash flows you have to look at what happens to the firm **with** the project and **without** the project. The difference between the two reflects the incremental cash flows attributable to the project.
- In estimating the incremental cash flows of a project bear in mind the following guidelines: (i) Consider all incidental effects. (ii) Ignore sunk costs. (iii) Include opportunity costs. (iv) Question the allocation of overhead costs. (v) Estimate working capital properly.
- Cash flows should be measured on an after-tax basis. The important issues in assessing the impact of taxes are: What tax rate should be used to assess tax liability? How should losses be treated? What is the effect of noncash charges?
- Cash flows and the discount rates applied to these cash flows must be consistent with respect to the investor group and inflation.
- The cash flows of a project may be estimated from the point of view of all investors (equity shareholders as well as lenders) or from the point of view of just equity shareholders.
- In dealing with inflation, you have two choices. You can incorporate expected inflation in the estimates of future cash flows and apply a nominal discount rate to the same. Alternatively, you can estimate the future cash flows in real terms and apply a real discount rate to the same.
- Estimating the relevant cash flows for a replacement project is somewhat complicated because you have to determine the incremental cash outflows and inflows in relation to the existing project. The three components of the cash flow stream of a replacement project are: (i) initial investment, (ii) operating cash inflows, and (iii) terminal cash flow.

- Generally, in capital budgeting we look at the cash flow to all investors (equity shareholders as well as lenders) and apply the weighted average cost of capital of the firm. A project can, of course, be viewed from other points of view like the equity point of view, long-term funds point of view, and total funds point of view. Obviously, the project cash flow definition will vary with the point of view adopted.
- Financial institutions look at projects from the point of view of all investors.
- The Planning Commission suggests that a project may be viewed from the point of view of equity capital or long-term funds.
- As cash flows have to go far into the future, errors in estimation are bound to occur. Yet, given the critical importance of cash flow forecasts in project evaluation, adequate care should be taken to guard against certain biases which may lead to over-statement or under-statement of true project profitability.
- Knowledgeable observers of capital budgeting believe that profitability is often overstated because the initial investment is under-estimated and the operating cash inflows are exaggerated. The principal reasons for such optimistic bias are intentional overstatement, lack of experience, myopic euphoria, and capital rationing.
- Terminal benefits of a project are likely to be under-estimated because salvage values are under-estimated, intangible benefits are ignored, and the value of future options is overlooked.

QUESTIONS

1. What are the three elements of the cash flow stream of a project?
2. How is the time horizon for cash flow analysis usually established?
3. What does the separation principle say?
4. Discuss the guidelines to be borne in mind while estimating the incremental cash flows of a project.
5. How will you estimate the tax impact of losses of a project?
6. What is the formula for depreciation under the written down value method?
7. How would you define the cash inflows to all investors and the cash flows to equity shareholders?
8. Discuss the two ways of dealing with inflation.
9. What are the three components of the cash flow stream of a replacement project?
10. Define the cash flows from the point of view of equity, long-term funds, and total funds.
11. How do financial institutions define cash outflows and cash inflows for a project?
12. Describe the rules applicable to the measurement of costs and returns (cash flows) as given in the *Manual for Preparation of Feasibility Reports* developed by the Planning Commission.
13. Explain why there is often an optimistic bias with respect to estimates of initial investment and operating cash inflows.
14. Why is the terminal benefit of a project typically under-estimated?

PROBLEMS

1. Futura Limited is considering a capital project about which the following information is available.
   - The investment outlay on the project will be ₹200 million. This consists of ₹150 million on the plant and machinery and ₹50 million on net working capital. The entire outlay will be incurred in the beginning.
   - The life of the project is expected to be 7 years. At the end of 7 years, fixed assets will fetch a net salvage value of ₹48 million whereas net working capital will be liquidated at its book value.
   - The project is expected to increase the revenues of the firm by ₹250 million per year. The increase in costs on account of the project is expected to be ₹100 million per year (This includes all items of cost other than depreciation, interest, and tax). The tax rate is 30 percent.
   - Plant and machinery will be depreciated at the rate of 25 percent per year as per the written down method.

     (a) Estimate the post-tax cash flows of the project.

     (b) Calculate the IRR of the project.
2. Modern Pharma is considering the manufacture of a new drug, Floxin, for which the following information has been gathered:
   - Floxin is expected to have a product life cycle of seven years and after that it would be withdrawn from the market. The sales from this drug are expected to be as follows:

Year	1	2	3	4	5	6	7
Sales (₹ in million)	80	120	160	200	160	120	80

   - The capital equipment required for manufacturing Floxin is ₹120 million and it will be depreciated at the rate of 25 percent per year as per the WDV method for tax purposes. The expected net salvage value after seven years is ₹25 million.
   - The working capital requirement for the project is expected to be 25 percent of sales. Working capital level is adjusted at the beginning of the year in relation to the expected sales for the year. At the end of 7 years, working capital is expected to be liquidated at par, barring an estimated loss of ₹4 million on account of bad debts which, of course, will be a tax-deductible expense.
   - The accountant of the firm has provided the following estimates for the cost of Floxin:

Raw material cost	:	30 percent of sales
Variable manufacturing cost	:	10 percent of sales
Fixed annual operating and maintenance costs	:	₹10 million
Variable selling expenses	:	10 percent of sales
Overhead allocation (excluding depreciation, maintenance, and interest)	:	10 percent of sales

     The incremental overheads attributable to the new product are, however, expected to be only 5 percent of sales.
   - The manufacture of Floxin will cut into the sales of an existing product thereby reducing its contribution margin by ₹10 million per year.

- The tax rate for the firm is 30 percent.
    (a) Estimate the post-tax incremental cash flows for the project to manufacture Floxin.
    (b) What is the NPV of the project if the cost of capital is 15 percent?

3. Teja International is determining the cash flows for a project involving replacement of an old machine by a new machine. The old machine bought a few years ago has a book value of ₹800,000 and it can be sold to realise a post-tax salvage value of ₹900,000. It has a remaining life of five years after which its net salvage value is expected to be ₹200,000. It is being depreciated annually at a rate of 25 percent under the WDV method.
   The new machine costs ₹3,000,000. It is expected to fetch a net salvage value of ₹1,500,000 after five years. The depreciation rate applicable to it is 25 percent under the WDV method. The new machine is expected to bring a saving of ₹650,000 annually in manufacturing costs (other than depreciation). The incremental working capital associated with this machine is ₹500,000. The tax rate applicable to the firm is 30 percent.
   (a) Estimate the cash flow associated with the replacement project.
   (b) What is the NPV of the replacement project if the cost of capital is 14 percent?
4. A machine costs ₹100,000 and is subject to a depreciation rate of 25 percent under the WDV method. What is the present value of the tax savings on account of depreciation for a period of 5 years if the tax rate is 40 percent and the discount rate is 15 percent?
5. Mahima Enterprises is considering replacing an old machine by a new machine. The old machine bought a few years ago has a book value of ₹90,000 and it can be sold for ₹90,000. It has a remaining life of five years after which its net salvage value is expected to be ₹10,000. It is being depreciated annually at the rate of 20 percent as per the WDV method.
   The new machine costs ₹400,000. It is expected to fetch a net salvage value of ₹25,000 after 5 years. It will be depreciated annually at the rate of 25 percent as per the WDV method. Investment in working capital will not change with the new machine. The tax rate for the firm is 35 percent. Estimate the cash flow associated with the replacement proposal, assuming that other costs remain unchanged.
6. Supreme Industries is evaluating a project for which the following information has been assembled:
   (a) The total outlay of the project is expected to be ₹450 million. This consists of ₹250 million of fixed assets and ₹200 million of gross current assets.
   (b) The proposed scheme of financing is as follows: ₹100 million of equity, ₹200 million of term loans, ₹100 million of working capital advance, and ₹50 million of trade credit.
   (c) The term loan is repayable in 10 equal semi-annual instalments of ₹20 million each. The first instalment will be due after 18 months. The interest rate on the term loan will be 15 percent.
   (d) The levels of working capital advance and trade credit will remain at ₹100 million and ₹50 million respectively till they are paid back or retired at the end of 6 years. The working capital advance will carry an interest rate of 18 percent.
   (e) The expected revenues for the project will be ₹500 million per year. The operating costs (excluding depreciation and interest) are expected to be ₹320 million per year. The depreciation rate on the fixed assets will be $33^1/_3$ percent as per the written down value method.
   (f) The net salvage value of fixed assets and current assets, at the end of year 6 (the project life is expected to be 6 years) will be ₹80 million and ₹200 million respectively.
   (g) The tax rate applicable to the firm is 50 percent.
   Define the cash flows from the point of view of (i) equity funds, (ii) long-term funds, and (iii) total funds.

MINICASE

Metaland is a major manufacturer of light commercial vehicles. It has a very strong R&D centre which has developed very successful models in the last fifteen years. However, two models developed by it in the last few years have not done well and were prematurely withdrawn from the market.

The engineers at its R&D centre have recently developed a prototype for a new light commercial vehicle that would have a capacity of four tons.

After a lengthy discussion, the board of directors of Metaland decided to carefully evaluate the financial worthwhileness of manufacturing this model which they have labelled Meta 4.

You have been recently hired as the executive assistant to Vijay Mathur, Managing Director of Metaland. Vijay Mathur has entrusted you with the task of evaluating the project.

Meta 4 would be produced in the existing factory which has enough space for one more product. Meta 4 will require plant and machinery that will cost ₹400 million. You can assume that the outlay on plant and machinery will be incurred over a period of one year. For the sake of simplicity assume that 50 percent will be incurred right in the beginning and the balance 50 percent will be incurred at the end of year 1. The plant will commence operation after one year.

Meta 4 project will require ₹200 million toward gross working capital. You can assume that the gross working capital investment will occur at the end of year 1.

The proposed scheme of financing is as follows: ₹200 million of equity, ₹200 million of term loan, ₹100 million of working capital advance, and ₹100 million of trade credit. Equity will come right in the beginning by way of retained earnings. Term loan and working capital advance will be raised at the end of year 1.

The term loan is repayable in 8 equal semi-annual instalments of ₹25 million each. The first instalment will be due after 18 months of raising the term loan. The interest rate on the term loan will be 14 percent.

The levels of working capital advance and trade credit will remain at ₹100 million each, till they are paid back or retired at the end of 5 years, after the project commences, which is the expected life of the project. Working capital advance will carry an interest rate of 12 percent.

Meta 4 project is expected to generate a revenue of ₹750 million per year. The operating costs (excluding depreciation and taxes) are expected to be ₹525 million per year.

For tax purposes, the depreciation rate on fixed assets will be 25 percent as per the written down value method. Assume that there is no other tax benefit.

The net salvage value of plant and machinery is expected to be ₹100 million at the end of the project life. Recovery of working capital will be at book value.

The income tax rate is expected to be 30 percent.

Vijay Mathur wants you to estimate the cash flows from three different points of view:

(a) Cash flows from the point of all investors (which is also called the explicit cost funds point of view).

(b) Cash flows from the point of equity investors.

(c) Cash flows as defined by financial institutions.

Chapter 10 The Cost of Capital

LEARNING OBJECTIVES

After studying this chapter you should be able to

- Distinguish between company cost of capital and project cost of capital.
- Show how the cost of debt and the cost of preference are calculated.
- Discuss various methods for estimating the cost of equity.
- Explain the rationale for using the target capital structure weights in market value terms.
- Determine the weighted marginal cost of capital schedule.
- Show how floatation costs should be handled in computing the cost of capital.
- Describe the factors affecting the cost of capital.
- Discuss the misconceptions surrounding cost of capital.

In the previous chapter we learnt that the cash flows of a capital investment may be viewed from various points of view (the equity point of view, the long term funds point of view, the explicit cost funds point of view, and the total funds point of view) and the discount rate applied to the cash flows must be consistent with the point of view adopted. We also mentioned that the standard practice in capital budgeting is to look at the cash flows from the point of view of explicit cost funds (referred to also as investor claims) and apply the weighted average cost of capital of the firm as the discount rate.

The items on the financing side of the balance sheet are called capital components. The major capital components are equity, preference, and debt. Capital, like any other factor of production, has a cost. A company's cost of capital is the average cost of the various capital components (or securities) employed by it. Put differently, it is the average rate of return required by the investors who provide capital to the company.

The cost of capital is a central concept in financial management. It is used for evaluating investment projects, for determining the capital structure, for assessing leasing proposals, for setting the rates that regulated organisations like electric utilities can charge to their customers, so on and so forth. This chapter discusses how a company's cost of capital is calculated.

10.1 SOME PRELIMINARIES

Concept of Average Cost of Capital A firm's cost of capital is the weighted average cost of various sources of finance used by it, viz., equity, preference, and debt.

Suppose that a company uses equity, preference, and debt in the following proportions: 50, 10, and 40. If the component costs of equity, preference, and debt are 16 percent, 12 percent, and 8 percent respectively, the weighted average cost of capital (WACC) will be:

WACC = (Proportion of equity) (Cost of equity)
+ (Proportion of preference) (Cost of preference)
+ (Proportion of debt) (Cost of debt)
= (0.5) (16) + (0.10) (12) + (0.4) (8)
= 12.4 percent

Bear in mind the following in applying the preceding formula:

- For the sake of simplicity, we have considered only three types of capital (equity; nonconvertible, noncallable preference; and nonconvertible, noncallable debt). We have ignored other forms of capital like convertible or callable preference, convertible or callable debt, bonds with payments linked to stock market index, bonds that are puttable or extendable, warrants, so on and so forth. Calculating the cost of these forms of capital is somewhat complicated. Fortunately, more often than not, they are a minor source of capital. Hence, excluding them may not make a material difference.
- Debt includes long-term debt as well as short-term debt (such as working capital loans and commercial paper). Some companies leave out the cost of short-term debt while calculating the weighted average cost of capital. In principle, this is not correct. Investors who provide short-term debt also have a claim on the earnings of the firm. If a company ignores this claim, it will misstate the rate of return required on its investments.
- Non-interest bearing liabilities, such as trade creditors, are not included in the calculation of the weighted average cost of capital. This is done to ensure consistency and simplify valuation. True, non-interest bearing liabilities have a cost. However, this cost is implicitly reflected in the price paid by the firm to acquire goods and services. Hence, it is already taken care of before the free cash flow is determined. While it is possible to separate the implicit financing costs of non-interest bearing liabilities from the cash flow, it will make the analysis needlessly more complex, without contributing to the quality thereof.

Rationale The rationale for using the WACC as the hurdle rate in capital budgeting is fairly straightforward. If a firm's rate of return on its investments exceeds its cost of capital, equity shareholders benefit. To illustrate this point, consider a firm which employs equity and debt in equal proportions and whose cost of equity and debt are 14 percent and 6 percent respectively. The cost of capital, which is the weighted average cost of capital, works out to 10 percent ($0.5 \times 14 + 0.5 \times 6$). If the firm invests ₹100 million, say, on a project which earns a rate of return of 12 percent, the return on equity funds employed in the project will be:

$$\frac{\text{Total return on the project-Interest on debt}}{\text{Equity funds}} = \frac{100(0.12) - 50(0.06)}{50} = 18\%$$

Since 18 percent exceeds the cost of equity (14 percent), equity shareholders benefit.

Conditions for Using the Cost of Capital At the outset we must distinguish between the company cost of capital and the project cost of capital.

The *company cost of capital* is the rate of return expected by the existing capital providers. It reflects the business risk of existing assets and the capital structure currently employed.

The *project cost of capital* is the rate of return expected by capital providers for a new project or investment the company proposes to undertake. Obviously, it will depend on the business risk and the debt capacity of the new project.

If a firm wants to use its company cost of capital, popularly called the weighted average cost of capital (WACC), for evaluating a new investment, two conditions should be satisfied:

- The business risk of the new investment is the same as the average business risk of existing investments. In other words, the new investment will not change the business risk complexion of the firm.
- The capital structure of the firm will not be affected by the new investment. Put differently, the firm will continue to follow the same financing policy.

Thus, strictly speaking the WACC is the right discount rate for an investment which is a carbon copy of the existing firm. This chapter assumes that new investments will be similar to existing investments in terms of business risk and debt capacity.

10.2 COST OF DEBT AND PREFERENCE

Since debt and preference stock entail more or less fixed payments, estimating the cost of debt and preference is relatively easy.

Cost of Debt Conceptually, the cost of a debt instrument is the yield to maturity of that instrument. Let us apply this concept to different types of debt instruments such as debentures, bank loans, and commercial paper.

The *cost of a debenture* is the value of r_D in the following equation.

$$P_0 = \sum_{t=1}^{n} \frac{I}{(1+r_D)^t} + \frac{F}{(1+r_D)^n} \tag{10.1}$$

where P_0 is the current market price of the debenture, I is the annual interest payment, n is the number of years left to maturity, and F is the maturity value of the debenture.

Computation of r_D requires a trial-and-error procedure which was discussed in a previous chapter. If you are not inclined to follow the trial and error procedure, you can employ the following formula which gives a very close approximation to the correct value.

$$r_D = \frac{I + (F - P_0)/n}{0.6\,P_0 + 0.4\,F} \tag{10.2}$$

To illustrate this formula, consider the following debenture of Multiplex Limited.

Face value	:	₹1,000
Coupon rate	:	12 percent
Remaining period to maturity	:	4 years
Current market price	:	₹1040

The approximate yield to maturity of this debenture is:

$$r_D = \frac{120 + (1000 - 1040)/4}{0.6 \times 1040 + 0.4 \times 1000} = 10.7 \text{ percent}$$

Unlike a debenture, a bank loan is not traded in the secondary market. The *cost of a bank loan* is simply the current interest the bank would charge if the firm were to raise a loan now. Suppose that Multiplex Limited has a ₹300 million outstanding bank loan on which it is paying an interest of 13 percent. However, if Multiplex Limited were to raise a loan now the bank would charge 12 percent. This then represents the cost of the bank loan.

A commercial paper is a short-term debt instrument which is issued at a discount and redeemed at par. Hence the *cost of commercial paper* is simply its implicit interest rate. Suppose, Multiplex Limited has outstanding commercial paper that has a balance maturity of 6 months. The face value of one instrument is ₹1,000,000 and it is traded in the market at ₹965,000. The implicit interest rate for 6 month is:

$$\frac{1{,}000{,}000}{965{,}000} - 1 = 0.0363 \text{ or } 3.63 \text{ percent}$$

The annualised interest rate works out to:

$$(1.0363)^2 - 1 = 0.0739 \text{ or } 7.39 \text{ percent}$$

When a firm uses different instruments of debt, the average cost of debt has to be calculated. To illustrate this calculation, let us look at the following data on the debt employed by Multiplex Limited.

Debt Instrument	*Face Value*	*Market Value*	*Coupon Rate*	*YTM or Current Rate*
Non-convertible debentures	₹100 million	₹104 million	12%	10.7%
Bank loan	₹200 million	₹200 million@	13%	12.0%
Commercial paper	₹50 million	₹48.25 million	N.A.	7.39%
		₹352.25 million		

@ Since the bank loan does not have a secondary market we have, for the sake of simplicity, equated market value with face value

The average cost of debt is calculated using the market value proportions and yields (current rates) of various debt instruments.

The average cost of debt for Multiplex Limited works out to:

$$10.7\% \, [104/352.25] + 12.0\% \, [200/352.25] + 7.39\% \, [48.25/352.25] = 10.98\%$$

Note that we use the yields to maturity or the current rates as they reflect the rates at which the firm can raise *new* debt. Put differently, we are interested in calculating the marginal cost of debt. Hence, coupon rates that reflect the *historical* or *embedded* interest rates at the time the debt was originally raised are not relevant for our purposes.

What we have calculated so far is the average pre-tax cost of debt. Since interest on debt is a tax-deductible expense, the pre-tax cost of debt has to be adjusted for the tax factor to arrive at the post-tax cost of debt.

Post-tax cost of debt = Pre-tax cost of debt (1–Tax rate)

The tax rate to be used in this calculation is the marginal tax rate applicable to the company. If we assume that the marginal tax rate for Multiplex Limited is 35 percent, the post-tax cost of debt for Multiplex Limited is:

Post-tax cost of debt = 10.98 percent (1 – 0.35) = 7.14 percent

Cost of Preference Preference capital carries a fixed rate of dividend and is redeemable in nature. Even though the obligations of a company towards its preference shareholders are not as firm as those towards its debenture holders, we will assume that preference dividend will be paid regularly and preference capital will be redeemed as per the original intent.

Thus, preference stock will be considered much like a bond with fixed commitments. However, preference dividend, unlike debt interest, is not a tax-deductible expense and hence does not produce any tax saving[1].

Given the fixed nature of preference dividend and principal repayment commitment and the absence of tax deductibility, the cost of preference is simply equal to its yield. To illustrate, consider the preference stock of Multiplex Limited for which the following data is available:

Face value	:	₹100
Dividend rate	:	11 percent
Maturity period	:	5 years
Market price	:	₹95

The yield on this preference stock, if we apply the approximate yield formula, works out to:

$$\frac{11+(100-95)/5}{0.4\times 100+0.6\times 95} = 12.37 \text{ percent}$$

If a company has more than one issue of preference stock outstanding, the average yield on all preference issues may be calculated, just the way it was done for debt issues.

10.3 COST OF EQUITY: THE CAPM APPROACH

Equity finance may be obtained in two ways: (i) retention of earnings, and (ii) issue of additional equity. The cost of equity or the return required by equity shareholders is the same in both the cases. Remember that when a firm decides to retain earnings, an opportunity cost is involved. Shareholders could receive the earnings as dividends and invest the same in alternative investments of comparable risk to earn a return. So, irrespective of whether a firm raises equity finance by retaining earnings or issuing additional equity shares, the cost of equity is the same. The only difference is in floatation costs. There is no floatation cost for retained earnings whereas there is a floatation cost of 2 to 6 percent or even more for additional equity. This difference is considered separately as explained in Section 10.9. So, in our present discussion, the cost of equity refers to the cost of retained earnings as well as the cost of external equity.

[1] In addition, a company in India presently has to pay a dividend distribution tax. We have ignored this from our calculation.

While the cost of debt and preference can be determined fairly easily, the cost of equity is rather difficult to estimate. The difficulty stems from the fact that equity shareholders have a residual claim on the earnings of the firm. This means that they receive a return when all other claimants (such as lenders and preference shareholders) have been paid. They are not entitled to a promised or predetermined return according to a financial contract.

Several approaches are used to estimate the cost of equity: the capital asset pricing model (CAPM) approach, the bond yield plus risk premium approach, the dividend discount model approach, and the earnings-price approach. This section discusses the CAPM approach, perhaps the most popular approach in practice. The following section discusses the other approaches.

The Intuition Underlying the CAPM Investors are risk-averse. So, they require a higher expected return to bear higher risk.

To understand what is a relevant measure of risk, it is useful to decompose the total risk associated with a security into two components:

$$\text{Total risk} = \text{Unique risk} + \text{Market risk}$$

The **unique risk** of a security represents that portion of its total risk which stems from firm-specific factors like the development of a new product, a labour strike, or the emergence of a new competitor. Events of this nature primarily affect the specific firm and not all firms in general. Hence, the unique risk of a security can be washed away by combining it with other securities. In a diversified portfolio, unique risks of different securities tend to cancel each other - a favourable development in one firm may offset an adverse happening in another and vice versa. Hence, unique risk is also referred to as diversifiable risk or unsystematic risk.

The **market risk** of a security represents that portion of its risk which is attributable to economy-wide factors like the growth rate of GDP, the level of government spending, money supply, interest rate structure, and inflation rate. Since these factors affect all firms to a greater or lesser degree, investors cannot avoid the risk arising from them, however diversified their portfolios maybe. Hence, it is also referred to as systematic risk (as it affects all securities) or non-diversifiable risk.

Since the unique risk of a security can be diversified away, whereas the systematic risk of a security cannot be diversified away, the CAPM suggests that investors are compensated only for bearing the systematic risk.

The CAPM The CAPM is reflected in the following equation that relates the expected rate of return of an investment to its systematic risk.

$$E(R_i) = R_f + (E(R_M) - R_f)\beta_i \tag{10.3}$$

where $E(R_i)$ is the expected return on security i, R_f is the risk-free rate, $E(R_M)$ is the expected return on the market portfolio, and β_i is the systematic risk of the security (it reflects the relative volatility of the security with respect to the market portfolio).

To apply the CAPM, you need estimates of the following factors that determine the CAPM line:

- Risk-free rate
- Market risk premium
- Beta

Risk-free Rate The risk-free rate is the return on a security (or a portfolio of securities) that is free from default risk and is uncorrelated with returns from anything else in the economy. Theoretically, the return on a zero-beta portfolio is the best estimate of the risk-free rate. Constructing zero-beta portfolios, however, is costly and complex. Hence they are often unavailable for estimating the risk-free rate.

In practice, two alternatives are commonly used:

- The rate on a short-term government security like the 364-days Treasury bill.
- The rate on a long-term government bond that has a maturity of 10 to 20 years

It appears that the rate on a long-term bond is a good choice because the duration of a long-term bond is similar to that of the duration of a stock market index. Hence the rate on a long-term bond is consistent with the betas and market risk premiums that are estimated in relation to the stock market index portfolio.

Market Risk Premium The market risk premium is the difference between the expected market return and the risk-free rate. It can be estimated on the basis of historical data or forward looking data.

Historical Risk Premium The historical risk premium is the difference between the average return on stocks and the average risk-free rate earned in the past. Two measurement issues have to be addressed in this context: How long should the measurement period be? Should the arithmetic mean or the geometric mean be used?

The answer to the first question is: Use the longest possible historical period, absent any trends in risk premium over time.

Practitioners seem to disagree over the choice of arithmetic mean versus geometric mean. The arithmetic mean is the average of the annual rates of return over the measurement period whereas the geometric mean is the compounded annual return over the measurement period. The difference between the two may be illustrated with a simple example where we have two years of returns:

Year	*Price*	*Return*
0	100	
1	140	40%
2	154	10%

The arithmetic mean over the two years is 25.0% [(40+10)/2], where as the geometric mean is 24.0% [$1.54^{0.5} - 1 = 0.24$]. The advocates of arithmetic mean argue that it is more consistent with the mean-variance framework and can better predict the premium in the next period. The votaries of geometric mean argue that it takes into account compounding and can better predict the average premium in the long term.

Forward Looking Risk Premium The historical approach assumes that investors expect future results, on average, to be the same as past results. Many investors believe that the future risk premium may not equal the historical risk premium. So they try to develop the forward looking risk premium independently.

A commonly used procedure for estimating the forward looking risk premium is as follows:

Step 1: Estimate the expected market rate of return using the constant growth dividend discount model:

Expected market rate of return = Dividend yield + Constant growth rate

The dividend yield for the market, as measured by some broad stock market index, can be predicted quite accurately. The constant growth rate may be equated with the expected growth rate in corporate earnings.

Step 2: Calculate the market risk premium:

Market risk premium = Expected market rate of return – Risk free rate

Beta The beta of an investment i is the slope of the following regression relationship:

$$R_{it} = \alpha_i + \beta_i R_{Mt} + e_{it} \tag{10.4}$$

where R_{it} is the return on investment i (a project or a security) in period t, R_{Mt} is the return on the market portfolio in period t, α_i is the intercept of the linear regression relationship between R_{it} and R_{Mt} (α is pronounced as alpha), β_i is the slope of the linear regression relationship between R_{it} and R_{Mt} (β is pronounced as beta), and e_{it} is the error term.

To measure the systematic risk of a project, we have to calculate the slope of the regression. The estimate of the slope of the regression model is:

$$\beta_i = \frac{\text{Cov}\,(R_i, R_M)}{\sigma_{M^2}} \tag{10.5}$$

where β_i is the estimate of the slope in the regression model, Cov (R_i, R_M) is the covariance between the return on security i and the return on the market portfolio, and σ_M is the standard deviation of the return on market portfolio.

The calculation of beta may be illustrated with an example. The rates of return on stock A and the market portfolio for 15 periods are given below:

Period	*Return on Stock A (%)*	*Return on Market Portfolio M (%)*	*Period*	*Return on Stock A (%)*	*Return on Market Portfolio M (%)*
1	10	12	9	–9	1
2	15	14	10	14	12
3	18	13	11	15	–11
4	14	10	12	14	16
5	16	9	13	6	8
6	16	13	14	7	7
7	18	14	15	–8	10
8	4	7			

What is the beta for stock A? The beta of stock A is equal to:

$$\frac{\text{Cov}\left(R_A, R_M\right)}{\sigma^2_M}$$

The inputs required for calculating beta are drawn from Exhibit 10.1.

$$\text{Cov}(R_A, R_M) = \frac{\sum(R_A - \bar{R}_A)(R_M - \bar{R}_M)}{n-1} = \frac{221}{14} = 15.79$$

$$\sigma_M^2 = \frac{\sum(R_M - \bar{R}_M)^2}{n-1} = \frac{624}{14} = 44.57$$

So, the beta for stock A is 15.79/44.57 = 0.354

Note that when covariance and variance are calculated on the basis of a sample of observed returns, the divisor is $n - 1$ not n. The reason for subtracting 1 is to correct for what is technically called the loss of 1 degree of freedom.

Exhibit 10.1 ***Calculation of Beta***

Period	*Return on Stock A, R_A*	*Return on Market Portfolio, R_M*	*Deviation of Return on Stock A from its Mean $(R_A - \bar{R}_A)$*	*Deviation of Return on Market Portfolio from its Mean $(R_M - \bar{R}_M)$*	*Product of the Deviations, $(R_A - \bar{R}_A)(R_M - \bar{R}_M)$*	*Square of the Deviation of Return on Market Portfolio from its Mean $(R_M - \bar{R}_M)^2$*
1	10	12	0	3	0	9
2	15	14	5	5	25	25
3	18	13	8	4	32	16
4	14	10	4	1	4	1
5	16	9	6	0	0	0
6	16	13	6	4	24	16
7	18	14	8	5	40	25
8	4	7	-6	-2	12	4
9	- 9	1	-19	-8	152	64
10	14	12	4	3	12	9
11	15	-11	5	-20	-100	400
12	14	16	4	7	28	49
13	6	8	-4	-1	4	1
14	7	7	-3	-2	6	4
15	-8	10	-18	1	-18	1
	$\sum R_A = 150$ $\bar{R}_A = 10$	$\sum R_M = 135$ $\bar{R}_M = 9$			$\sum(R_A - \bar{R}_A)(R_M - \bar{R}_M) = 221$	$\sum(R_M - \bar{R}_M)^2 = 624$

Estimation Issues Estimating the historical beta may appear straightforward. However, there are several issues in practice relating to the length of the estimation period, the return interval, the choice of the market index, and the statistical precision of the estimates.

Estimation Period A longer estimation period provides more data but the risk profile of the firm may change over that period. Given this tradeoff most analysts regard a 5-year period to be reasonable.

Return Interval Returns may be calculated on an annual, monthly, weekly, or daily basis. Using daily returns increases the number of observations, but introduces a bias due to nontrading. Hence analysts prefer weekly or monthly returns to reduce nontrading bias.

Market Index In theory, the market portfolio must include all assets-financial, real as well as human- and not just equity stocks. In practice, the beta of a stock is estimated in relation to the index of stock market to which it belongs. Thus, the betas of Indian stocks are estimated relative to Nifty index (or any other Indian stock market index) and the betas of US Stocks are estimated relative to S&P 500 index (or any other US market index). While this practice provides an acceptable measure of risk for a parochial investor, it may not be appropriate for an international investor.

Statistical Precision The estimate of beta based on stock returns over a particular time period is statistically imprecise. The standard error of the estimated beta reflects the extent of possible mismeasurement. Statisticians set up a confidence interval defined as the estimated value plus or minus two standard errors. For example, if the estimated beta value is 1.4 and the standard error is 0.25, the confidence interval for beta is 1.4 plus or minus 0.5 (2 x 0.25). This means that the true beta lies between 0.9 and 1.90 with a probability of 95 percent.

From the preceding discussion it is clear that while the estimated beta is useful for calculating the required return on stock, it does not give an absolutely correct value. Hence, managers and financial analysts must accept some uncertainty when estimating the cost of capital.

Adjusting Historical Beta The beta calculated above reflects a measure of historical alignment of the price of a stock with that of the market. Hence many regard it as a "measurement" of past relationship that cannot be naively used as an "estimate" of future risk. Why? Two reasons are commonly given:

- The historical alignment may have been significantly influenced by chance factors.
- A company's beta may change over time.

To overcome these limitations, some adjustment may be required. A procedure that is sometimes recommended is to take a weighted average of the historical beta, on the one hand, and 1.0 (the value of market beta) on the other. The weighting scheme should take into account the degree of historical estimation error and the dispersion of individual firms around the average. If the historical estimation error is large, the weight assigned to the historical beta should be small. If the dispersion of individual firms around the average is large, the weight assigned to 1.00 (the market beta) should be small. By balancing these factors, a suitable weighting scheme can be developed. Note that Merill Lynch, in its beta prediction, assigns a weight of 0.66 to historical beta and a weight of 0.34 to average value (see Merill Lynch's booklet *Security Risk Evaluation Service*).

10.4 COST OF EQUITY: OTHER APPROACHES

Besides the CAPM, the following are some of the other approaches used in practice to estimate the cost of equity: bond yield plus risk premium approach, the dividend capitalisation approach, and the earnings-price approach.

Application of CAPM in Practice

In a survey of companies that use CAPM for estimating the cost of equity, Manoj Anand found that the risk-free rate of return, beta, and market risk premium are estimated as follows:

Risk-free Rate

	% of companies
91 days GOI treasury bill rate	15.91
3–7 years GOI treasury bond rate	18.18
10 years GOI treasury bond rate	65.91

Beta

	% of companies
Published source	20.45
CFO's estimate	15.91
Industry average	52.27
Self-calcutated	18.18

Basis for Calculating Beta

- 65.12% of companies use monthly share prices for 5 years
- 30.23% of companies use weekly share prices for 5 years
- 88.10% use BSE Sensex and 16.67% use Nifty as a proxy for market portfolio

Market Risk Premium

	% of companies
Fixed rate: 6% – 8%	6.82
Fixed rate: 8% – 9%	11.36
Fixed rate: 9% – 10%	50.00
Average of historical and implied	18.18
CFO's estimate	13.64

* percentages may not add up to 100 because some companies use more than one method.

Source: Manoj Anand, "Corporate Finance Practice in India: A Survey", *Vikalpa*, October–December 2002, pp 29–56.

Bond Yield Plus Risk Premium Approach Analysts who do not have faith in the CAPM approach often resort to a subjective procedure to estimate the cost of equity. They add a judgmental risk premium to the observed yield on the long-term bonds of the firm to get the cost of equity:

$$\text{Cost of equity} = \text{Yield on long-term bonds} + \text{Risk premium}$$

The logic of this approach is fairly simple. Firms that have risky and consequently high cost debt will also have risky and consequently high cost equity. So it makes sense to base the cost of equity on a readily observable cost of debt.

The problem with this approach is how to determine the risk premium. Should it be 2 percent, 4 percent, or n percent? There seems to be no objective way of determining it. Most analysts look at the operating and financial risks of the business and arrive at a subjectively determined risk premium that normally ranges between 2 percent and 6 percent. While this approach may not produce a precise cost of equity, it will give a reasonable ballpark estimate.

The Dividend Growth Model Approach The price of an equity stock depends ultimately on the dividends expected from it:

$$P_0 = \frac{D_1}{(1+r)^1} + \frac{D_2}{(1+r)^2} + \ldots$$

$$= \sum_{t=1}^{\infty} \frac{D_t}{(1+r)^t} \tag{10.6}$$

where P_0 is the current price of the stock, D_t is the dividend expected to be paid at the end of year t, and r is the equity shareholders' required rate of return.

If dividends are expected to grow at a constant rate of g percent per year, then Eq.(10.6) becomes:

$$P_0 = \frac{D_1}{(1+r)^1} + \frac{D_1(1+g)}{(1+r)^2} + \frac{D_1(1+g)^2}{(1+r)^3} + \ldots\ldots \infty$$

This simplifies to:

$$P_0 = \frac{D_1}{r-g} \tag{10.7}$$

This equation is referred to as the Gordon model as it was proposed by Myron J. Gordon. Solving it for r, we get:

$$r = \frac{D_1}{P_0} + g = \frac{D_0(1+g)}{P_0} + g \tag{10.8}$$

Thus, the expected return of shareholders, which in equilibrium is also the required return, is equal to the dividend yield plus the expected growth rate.

For a publicly traded company, it is fairly easy to determine the dividend yield. However, estimating the expected growth rate, g, is difficult. You can estimate g by using the following methods:

1. You can get a handle over g by relying on analysts' forecasts for the future growth rates. Analysts' forecasts may be available from a variety of sources. Since different sources are likely to give different estimates, a simple approach may be to obtain multiple estimates and then average them.
2. You can look at dividends for the preceding 5–10 years, calculate the annual growth rates, and average them. Suppose you observe the following dividends for some stock.

Year	*Dividend*	*Rupee Change*	*Growth Percentage*
1	₹3.00	-	-
2	₹3.50	₹0.50	16.7
3	₹4.00	₹0.50	14.3
4	₹4.25	₹0.25	6.3
5	₹4.75	₹0.50	11.8

   If you average the four growth rates, the result is 12.3 percent, so you can use this as an estimate of the expected growth rate, g.

3. You can use the retention growth rate method. Here, you first forecast the firm's average retention rate (this is simply 1 minus the dividend payout rate) and then multiply it by the firm's expected future return on equity (ROE).

$$g = (\text{Retention rate})\ (\text{Return on equity})$$

For example, if the forecasted retention rate and return on equity are 0.60 and 15 percent, the expected growth rate is: $g = (0.6)\ (15\%) = 9$ percent.

The dividend growth model is simple. It is easy to understand and easy to apply. However, there are some problems associated with it.

- First, it cannot be applied to companies that do not pay dividends or to companies that are not listed on the stock market. Even for companies that pay dividends, the assumption that dividends will grow at a constant rate may not be valid.
- Second, it does not explicitly consider risk. There is no direct adjustment for the risk associated with the estimated growth. Of course, there is an implicit adjustment for risk as the current stock price is used.

Earnings-Price Ratio Approach According to this approach, the cost of equity is equal to:

$$E_1/P_0 \tag{10.9}$$

where E_1 is the expected earnings per share for the next year, and P_0 is the current market price per share.

E_1 may be estimated as: (Current earnings per share) × (1 + growth rate of earnings per share).

This approach provides an accurate measure of the rate of return required by equity investors in the following two cases:

- When the earnings per share are expected to remain constant and the dividend payout ratio is 100 percent.
- When retained earnings are expected to earn a rate of return equal to the rate of return required by equity investors.

The first case is rarely encountered in real life and the second case is also somewhat unrealistic. Hence, the earnings-price ratio should not be used indiscriminately as the measure of the cost of equity capital. A detailed explanation is provided in Appendix 10A.

How Companies Estimate the Cost of Equity

A survey of corporate finance practices in India by Manoj Anand revealed that the following mehods (in the order of decreasing imporatance) are followed by companies in India to estimate the cost of equity:

	% companies considering as very important or important
Capital asset pricing model	54.3
Gordon's dividend discount model	52.1
Earnings – yield (Earnings per share/Market price per share)	34.2
Dividend-yield	26.2
Multifactor model	7.0

Source: Manoj Anand, "Corporate Finance Practices in India: A Survey," *Vikalpa*, October-December 2002.

10.5 DETERMINING THE PROPORTIONS

For calculating the WACC we need information on the cost of various sources of capital and the proportions (or weights) applicable to them. So far we discussed how to calculate the cost of specific sources of capital. We now look at how the weights should be established.

The appropriate weights are the *target capital structure weights stated in market value terms.* What is the rationale for using the target capital structure? What is the logic for using market values?

The primary reason for using the target capital structure is that the current capital structure may not reflect the capital structure that is expected to prevail in future or the capital structure the firm plans to have in future. While it is conceptually appealing to rely on the target capital structure, there may be some difficulties in using the target capital structure. A company may not have a well-defined target capital structure. Perhaps the changing complexion of its business or the changing conditions in the capital market may make it difficult for the company to articulate its target capital structure. Further, if the target capital structure is significantly different from the current capital structure, it may be difficult to estimate what the component capital costs would be. Notwithstanding these difficulties, finance experts generally recommend that the weights must be based on the target capital structure.

In calculating the weights for the target capital structure, should one use book (balance sheet) values or market values? It is tempting to use the book value weights because they are easy to calculate, they are available for every company (whether it is traded or not), and they are fairly stable.

Finance scholars, however, believe that market values, despite their volatility, are superior to book values, because in order to justify its valuation the firm must earn competitive returns for shareholders and debtholders on the current value (market value) of their investments. An example may be given to illustrate this point. Suppose shareholders invested ₹100 million of initial capital in a company 10 years ago. Over the 10 year period, the book value grew to ₹250 million but the market value increased to ₹450 million. A reasonable return in the present market conditions is 15 percent. Rational investors would expect a return of 15 percent on the current market value of ₹450 million, not the current book value of ₹250 million.

We recommend the use of market value weights unless market values are not available or highly unreliable or distorted due to manipulative trading.

Weights Used by Companies to Compute the Weighted Average Cost of Capital

The frequency with which various weights are used in practice, as found in a survey done by Manoj Anand, reported in the October–December 2002 issue of *Vikalpa* is shown below:

	*% of Use**
Book value weights	41.8
Market value weights	22.8
Target capital structure weights	39.2

*A few respondents use more than one basis of weighting.

10.6 WEIGHTED AVERAGE COST OF CAPITAL (WACC)

Given the cost of specific sources of finance and the scheme of weighting, the WACC can be readily calculated.

$$\text{WACC} = W_E\, r_E + W_p\, r_p + W_D\, r_D\,(1 - t_c) \tag{10.10}$$

where W_E, Wp, and W_D are the proportion of equity, preference, and debt and r_E, r_p and r_D are the component costs of equity, preference, and debt, and t_c, is the corporate tax rate.

For example, the cost of equity, preference, and debt for BPN Limited are 16 percent, 14 percent, and 12 percent respectively and the market value proportions of these sources of finance are 0.60, 0.05, and 0.35 respectively. The tax rate is 30 percent. Given the information, the WACC is:

$$\text{WACC} = 0.60\ (16) + 0.05\ (14) + 0.35\ (12)\ (1\text{-}0.3) = 13.24 \text{ percent}$$

10.7 WEIGHTED MARGINAL COST OF CAPITAL

At the outset we assumed, *inter alia,* that the adoption of new investment proposals will not change either the risk complexion or the capital structure of the firm. Does it mean that the weighted average cost of capital will remain the same irrespective of the magnitude of financing? Apparently not. Generally, the weighted average cost of capital tends to rise as the firm seeks more and more capital. This may happen because the supply schedule of capital is typically upward sloping – as suppliers provide more capital, the rate of return required by them tends to increase. A schedule or graph showing the relationship between additional financing and the weighted average cost of capital is called the weighted marginal cost of capital schedule.

Some Problem Areas in Cost of Capital

Several difficult issues relating to the cost of capital have been ignored or glossed over so far. While they are beyond the scope of this text, they are briefly mentioned below to sensitise you to them.

1. *Privately owned firms* Our discussion focused primarily on the publicly owned companies and the returns required by public shareholders. How should one estimate the cost of equity of a privately owned firm whose stock is not traded? While the same principles of cost of capital estimation apply to both types of firms, obtaining inputs for the privately owned firm is more difficult.
2. *Measurement problems* Estimating the cost of equity is difficult. It is not easy to get accurate inputs for the capital asset pricing model, for the growth rate in the dividend growth model, and for the risk premium in the bond yield plus risk premium approach.
3. *Derivative Securities* Estimating the cost of capital for derivative securities like convertible bonds or callable bonds is complicated. The analyst will have to use sophisticated approaches such as the Black-Scholes option pricing model and numerical techniques. While these approaches are useful, they have their own limitations.
4. *Capital Structure Weights* We assumed a target capital structure to get the weights for calculating the WACC. Determining the target capital structure is a major task in itself.

Determining the Weighted Marginal Cost of Capital Schedule The procedure for determining the weighted marginal cost of capital involves the following steps:

1. Estimate the *cost of each source of financing for various levels of its use* through an analysis of current market conditions and an assessment of the expectations of investors and lenders.
2. Identify the levels of total new financing at which the cost of the new components would change, given the capital structure policy of the firm. These levels, called *breaking points,* can be established using the following relationship.

$$BP_j = \frac{TF_j}{W_j} \tag{10.11}$$

where BP_j is the breaking point on account of financing source j, TF_j is the total new financing from source j at the breaking point, and W_j is the proportion of financing source j in the capital structure.
3. Calculate the WACC for various ranges of total financing between the breaking points.
4. Prepare the weighted marginal cost of capital schedule which reflects the WACC for each level of total new financing.

Illustration To illustrate how the weighted marginal cost of capital schedule is prepared, let us consider an example. Shiva Industries plans to use equity and debt in the following proportions:

Equity	:	40
Debt	:	60

Cost of Each Source of Finance for Various Levels of Use Based on its discussions with its merchant bankers and lenders Shiva Industries estimates the cost of its sources of finance for various levels of usage as follows:

Source of Finance	*Range of New Financing* (*₹ in million*)	*Cost* (%)
Equity	0 – 30	18
	More than 30	20
Debt	0 – 50	10
	More than 50	11

Breaking Points Given the target capital structure proportions and the financing ranges for each source of finance, the breaking point for each source of finance and corresponding ranges of total new financing are given in columns 3 and 4 of Exhibit 10.2.

Weighted Average Cost of Capital for Various Ranges of Total Financing Column 4 of Exhibit 10.2 shows that the firm's weighted average cost of capital will change at ₹75 million and ₹83.3 million of total new financing. Exhibit 10.3 shows the calculation of the weighted average cost of capital over these ranges.

Exhibit 10.2 ***Determination of Breaking Point and the Resulting Range of Total New Financing for Shiva Industries***

Source of Capital	Cost (1)	Range of New Financing (₹ in Million) (2)	Breaking Point (₹ in Million) (3)	Range of Total New Financing (₹ in Million) (4)
Equity	18%	0 – 30	$\frac{30}{0.4} = 75$	0– 75
	20%	Above 30	-	Above 75
Debt	10%	0– 50	$\frac{50}{0.6} = 83.3$	0– 83.3
	11%	Above 50	-	Above 83.3

Exhibit 10.3 ***Weighted Average Cost of Capital for Various Ranges of Total Financing for Shiva Industries***

Range of Total New Financing (₹ in Milliion)	Source of Capital (1)	Proportion (2)	Cost % (3)	Weighted Cost % [(2) X (3)] (4)
0–75	Equity	0.4	0.18	.072
	Debt	0.6	0.10	.060
	Weighted average cost of capital			.132
75 – 83.3	Equity	0.4	0.20	.080
	Debt	0.6	0.10	.060
	Weighted average cost of capital			.140
Above 83.3	Equity	0.4	0.20	.080
	Debt	0.6	0.11	.066
	Weighted average cost of capital			.146

Weighted Marginal Cost of Capital The weighted marginal cost of capital is shown below:

Exhibit 10.4 ***The Weighted Marginal Cost of Capital***

Range of Total Financing (₹ in Million)	Weighted Marginal Cost of Capital (%)
0 – 75	13.2
75 – 83.3	14.0
Above 83.3	14.6

10.8 DETERMINING THE OPTIMAL CAPITAL BUDGET

To determine the optimal capital budget, you have to compare the expected return on proposed capital expenditure projects with the marginal cost of capital schedule.

To illustrate, suppose Shiva Industries is developing its capital budget for the forthcoming year. The company's schedule of proposed capital expenditure projects for the coming year is as follows.

Project	*Amount (₹ in million)*	*Internal Rate of Return*
A	30	18.0%
B	40	16.5%
C	25	15.3%
D	10	13.4%
E	20	12.0%

The expected returns from the proposed capital expenditures are plotted against the cumulative funds required and shown as the *investment opportunity curve* in Exhibit 10.5. In addition, this exhibit shows the *marginal cost of capital* curve for Shiva Industries. The optimal capital budget is reflected by the point at which the investment opportunity curve and the marginal cost of capital curve intersect.

Exhibit 10.5 ***Determining the Optimal Capital Budget***

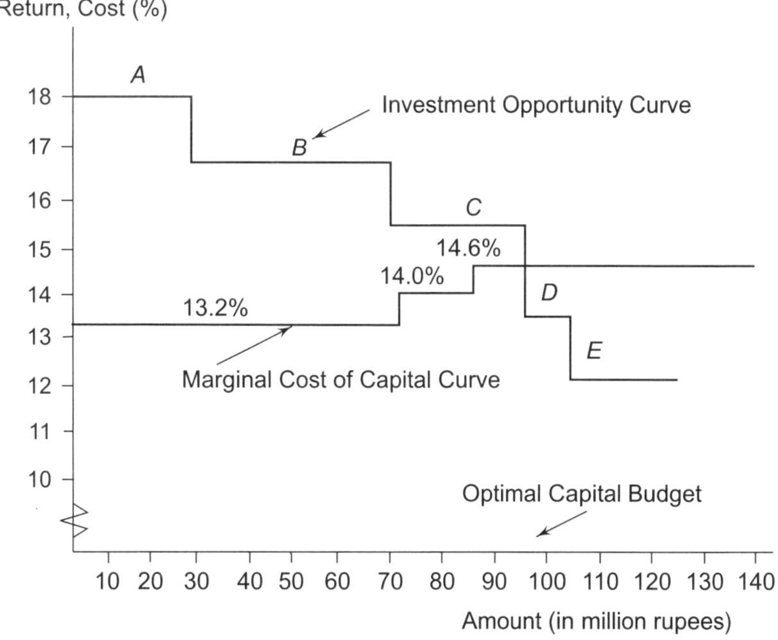

Thus, the optimal capital budget for Shiva Industries totals ₹95 million and includes Projects *A*, *B*, and *C*. Projects *D* and E are excluded as their expected returns are lower than the marginal cost of capital.

The procedure described above assumes that all projects being considered are equal in risk to the average risk of the firm. Indeed, the use of weighted average cost of capital for evaluating a project implies that the project's risk is equal to the average risk of the firm.

10.9 FLOATATION COST AND THE COST OF CAPITAL

So far we have ignored the floatation costs. When a firm raises finance by issuing equity and debt, it almost invariably incurs floatation or issue costs, comprising of items like underwriting costs, brokerage expenses, fees of merchant bankers, advertising expenses, under-pricing cost, so on and so forth. For example, the floatation costs associated with equity issues may be 8 to 10 percent.

How should the floatation costs be handled in computing the cost of capital? One approach is to adjust the WACC to reflect the floatation costs. For example, if the WACC is 12 percent and the average floatation costs are 6 percent, the WACC may be revised as follows:

$$\text{Revised WACC} = \frac{\text{WACC}}{1-\text{Floatation cost}} = \frac{12}{1-0.06} = 12.77 \text{ percent}$$

A better approach is to leave the WACC unchanged but to consider floatation costs as part of the project cost. A simple example may be given to illustrate this approach.

The cost of equity of Prakash Limited, an all equity firm, is 18 percent. Since the firm is financed wholly by equity, its WACC too is 18 percent. Prakash Limited is considering a ₹200 million expansion project which will be funded by selling additional equity. Based on the advice of its merchant banker, Prakash Limited believes that its floatation costs will be 8 percent of the amount issued. This means that the net proceeds will only be 92 percent of the amount of equity raised. What is the cost of expansion, considering the floatation costs?

Prakash Limited has to sell enough equity so that it has ₹200 million after meeting the floatation costs. In other words,

$$₹200 \text{ million} = (1 - .08) \times \text{Amount raised}$$

$$\text{Amount raised} = \frac{₹200 \text{ million}}{(1-.08)} = ₹217.39 \text{ million}$$

Prakash Limited's floatation costs are ₹17.39 million and hence the true cost of the expansion project is ₹217.39 million.

In the previous example, we assumed that a firm raised money only through external equity issue. What happens if the firm relies, as is very common, on a mixture of retained earnings, external equity issue, preference issue, and debt issue? In this case you have to calculate the weighted average floatation cost which is defined as follows:

$$f_A = w_R f_R + w_E f_E + w_P f_P + w_D f_D \tag{10.12}$$

where f_A is the weighted average floatation cost, w_R, w_E, w_p, and w_D are the proportions of retained earnings, external equity, preference capital, and debt capital in the capital structure of the firm, and f_R, f_E, f_p, and f_D are the floatation costs associated with retained earnings, external equity, preference capital, and debt capital.

To illustrate, consider the case of Phoenix Limited which employs retained earnings, external equity, preference capital, and debt capital in the following proportions:

$w_R = 0.2$, $w_E = 0.3$, $w_p = 0.1$, and $w_D = 0.4$. The floatation costs are as follows: $f_R = 0\%$, $f_E = 10\%$, $f_p = 5\%$, and $f_D = 4\%$. The weighted average floatation cost is:

$$f_A = (0.2)0 + (0.3)10 + (0.1)5 + (0.4)4 = 5.1\%$$

This means that for every rupee of financing needed by the firm for its investments, the firm must raise:

$$\frac{1}{1-.051} = ₹1.054$$

While calculating the weighted average floatation costs, use the weights in the existing capital structure (or target capital structure), even though the specific investment under consideration is financed entirely by debt or equity. The fact that a particular project can be financed with debt or equity is not relevant. If a firm has a debt-equity ratio of 3:2, for example, but chooses to finance a given project entirely with debt, it will have to raise additional equity subsequently to maintain its target debt-equity ratio. Taking this into consideration, you should always use weights in the target capital structure.

Floatation Costs and NPV To illustrate how floatation costs are incorporated in an NPV analysis, let us consider an example. Ramesh Engineering is currently at its target debt- equity ratio of 4:5. It is evaluating a proposal to expand capacity which is expected to cost ₹4.5 million and generate after-tax cash flows of ₹1 million per year for the next 10 years. The tax rate for the company is 25 percent. Two financing options are being looked at:

- Issue of equity stock. The required return on the company's new equity is 18 percent. The issuance cost will be 10 percent.
- Issue of debentures carrying a yield of 12 percent. The issuance cost will be 2 percent.

What is the NPV of the expansion project? Since the expansion is in the existing business of the firm, we will use the company's WACC to value it:

$$\begin{aligned}\text{WACC} &= \frac{E}{V} r_E + \frac{D}{V} r_D \ (1 - T_c) \\ &= \frac{5}{9} \times 18\% + \frac{4}{9} \times 12\% \ (1 - 0.25) \\ &= 10\% + 4\% = 14\%\end{aligned}$$

The NPV of the project ignoring the floatation costs is:

NPV = Present value of benefits – Investment

= ₹1,000,000 × PVIFA (14%, 10 years) – ₹4,500,000

$= ₹1,000,000 \times 5.216 - ₹4,500,000$

$= ₹716,000$

What will be the effect of floatation costs? Since the floatation costs of equity and debt are 10 percent and 2 percent respectively and the target debt-equity ratio is 4:5, the weighted average floatation cost, f_A, is:

$$f_A = \frac{E}{V} \times f_E + \frac{D}{V} \times f_d$$

$$= \frac{5}{9} \times 10\% + \frac{4}{9} \times 2\%$$

$$= 6.44 \text{ percent}$$

Note that the fact that Ramesh Engineering can finance the project entirely with equity or debt is irrelevant. What matters is the target capital structure of the firm.

Given that the expansion project needs ₹4,500,000, the true cost, including floatation costs, is ₹4,500,000 / $(1 - f_A)$ = ₹4,500,000 / 0.9356 = ₹4,809,748. Since the present value of cash inflows is ₹5,216,000, the expansion project, after considering the floatation costs, has an NPV of: ₹5,216,000 – ₹4,809,748 = ₹406,252. The project is still worthwhile.

10.10 FACTORS AFFECTING THE WEIGHTED AVERAGE COST OF CAPITAL

The cost of capital is affected by several factors, some beyond the control of the firm and others dependent on the investment and financing policies of the firm.

Factors Outside a Firm's Control The three most important factors, outside a firm's direct control, that have a bearing on the cost of capital are the level of interest rates, the market risk premium, and the tax rate.

The Level of Interest Rates If interest rates in the economy rise, the cost of debt to firms increases and vice versa. Interest rates also have a similar bearing on the cost of preference and cost of equity. Remember that the risk–free rate of interest is an important component of the CAPM, a model widely used for estimating the cost of equity. The general decline in interest rates in India from late 1990s to 2004 had lowered the cost of debt as well as the cost of equity.

Market Risk Premium The market risk premium reflects the perceived riskiness of equity stocks and investor aversion to risk. A factor beyond the control of individual firms, the market risk premium affects the cost of equity directly and the cost of debt indirectly (through a substitution effect).

Tax Rates The tax policy of the government has a bearing on cost of capital. The corporate tax rate has a direct impact on the cost of debt as used in the weighted average cost of capital. The capital gains tax rate relative to the rate on ordinary income has an indirect effect on the cost of equity relative to the cost of debt.

Factors Within a Firm's Control The cost of capital of a firm is affected by its investment policy, capital structure policy, and dividend policy.

Investment Policy To estimate the cost of capital, we start with the rates of return required on the outstanding equity and debt of the firm. These rates reflect how risky the firm's existing assets are. If a firm plans to invest in assets similar to those currently used, then its marginal cost of capital would be more or less the same as its current cost of capital. On the other hand, if the riskiness of its proposed investments is likely to be very different from the riskiness of its existing investments, its marginal cost of capital should also reflect the riskiness of the proposed investments.

Capital Structure Policy To calculate the WACC we assumed a given target capital structure. Of course, a firm can change its capital structure and such a change is likely to affect the cost of capital because the post-tax cost of debt is lower than the cost of equity and equity beta, an input for calculating the cost of equity is a function of financial leverage

Dividend Policy The dividend policy of a firm may affect its cost of equity.

10.11 MISCONCEPTIONS SURROUNDING COST OF CAPITAL

The cost of capital is a central concept in financial management, linking the investment and financing decisions. Hence, it should be calculated correctly and used properly in investment evaluation. Despite this injunction, we find that several errors characterise the application of this concept. The more common misconceptions, along with suggestions to overcome them, are discussed below.

1. **The concept of cost of capital is too academic or impractical** Some companies do not calculate the cost of capital because they regard it as 'academic' or 'impractical' or 'irrelevant' or 'imprecise'. These misgivings about cost of capital appear to be unjustified. Such reservation can be dispelled by emphasising the following points:
   - The cost of capital is an essential ingredient of discounted cash flow analysis. Since discounted cash flow analysis is now widely used, cost of capital can scarcely be considered 'academic' or 'impractical'.
   - Out of the various inputs required for discounted cash flow analysis, viz., project life, project cash flows (consisting of initial investment, operating cash flows, and terminal cash flow) and cost of capital, the last one, viz., the cost of capital can perhaps be calculated most reliably and accurately. So a concern about its imprecision seems to be misplaced.
2. **Current liabilities (accounts payable and provisions) are considered as capital components** Sometimes it is argued that accounts payable and accruals are sources of funding to be considered in the calculation of the WACC. This view is not correct because what is not provided by investors is not capital.

   Current liabilities arise on account of an operating relationship of the firm with its suppliers and employees. They are deducted when the investment requirement of the project is determined. Hence, they should not be considered in calculating the WACC. Of course, current liabilities are not ignored in capital budgeting because they appear in the cash flows of the project. Put differently, current liabilities affect a project's cash flows, but not its WACC.

3. **The coupon rate on the firm's existing debt is used as the pre-tax cost of debt** The coupon rate on the firm's existing debt reflects a historical cost. What really matters in investment decision making is the interest rate the firm would pay if it issues debt today. Hence, use the current cost of debt, not the historical cost of debt.

4. **When estimating the market risk premium in the CAPM method, the historical average rate of return is used along with the current risk-free rate.** Consider the following information:

   - Historical average return on equity stocks = 19 percent
   - Historical return on long-term Treasury bonds = 10 percent
   - Current expected return on equity stocks = 14 percent
   - Current return on long-term Treasury bonds = 7 percent

   Sometimes, the market risk premium is calculated as the difference between the historical average return on equity stocks and the current return on long-term Treasury bonds. This is not correct.

   To calculate the market risk premium, you can use the historical risk premium (19 percent – 10 percent) or the current risk premium (14 percent – 7 percent), but not the difference between the historical average return on equity stocks and the current return on long-term Treasury bonds (19 percent – 7 percent).

5. **The cost of equity is equal to the dividend rate or return on equity** It appears that the cost of equity is often measured incorrectly. Sometimes it is measured as the current dividend rate (dividend per share as a percentage of face value per share) or as return on equity. Only by accident do these measures represent the cost of equity correctly.

   It should be clearly understood that the cost of equity is the rate of return required by equity investors given the risk they are exposed to. It has nothing to do with the current dividend rate or return on equity, which are mere historical numbers.

6. **Retained earnings are either cost free or cost significantly less than external equity** Often firms impute a negligible or low cost to retained earnings under the influence of wrong notions like "retained earnings have no cost because shareholders are satisfied with dividends" or "retained earnings are already with the firm and hence some nominal returns on them may suffice."

   The error in such reasoning stems from ignoring the opportunity cost associated with retained earnings. When a firm retains a portion of its earnings, equity shareholders are denied dividends to that extent. If the same were distributed as dividends, equity shareholders can invest them elsewhere to earn a rate of return comparable to the cost of equity. Hence the opportunity cost of retained earnings is more or less equal to the cost of equity funds.

7. **Depreciation has no cost** Similar to the misconception that retained earnings are more or less cost-free is the notion that depreciation-generated funds are also virtually

cost free. As one manager observed: "Depreciation is capital already in the company. Since it does not have to be raised, even in an indirect sense of retained earnings, it clearly has no cost."

To guard against such an error, invoke the opportunity cost principle once again. Theoretically, the firm can return the depreciation-generated funds to its shareholders and lenders (the parties which provided the finance for asset acquisition) and they, in turn, can invest these funds elsewhere. Hence, the opportunity cost of depreciation-generated funds is the average return the shareholders and lenders would earn on these funds by investing them elsewhere. And this would be more or less equal to the average cost of capital of the firm.

8. **Book value weights may be used to calculate the WACC** Often firms use book value weights in the existing capital structure to calculate the WACC. This is not correct.

   Weights should be based on market values, not book values. Ideally, the target capital structure (in market value terms) should determine the weights for the WACC. If the target capital structure is not specified, use the current market value weights.

9. **The cost of capital for a project is calculated on the basis of the specific sources of finance used for it** If a firm raises debt when it is investing in some project, it may regard the post-tax cost of debt as the relevant cost of capital. Likewise, if it happens to raise equity when it is investing in some other project, it may consider the cost of equity as the relevant cost of capital. In both these cases, the error stems from calculating the WACC on the basis of the immediate sources of finance tapped.

   The immediate sources of funds used for a project do not necessarily determine the hurdle rate. What matters is the contribution made by the project to the overall debt capacity of the firm and not which sources of funds happen to be tapped when the project is undertaken.

10. **The project cost of capital is the same as firm's WACC** Many firms apply a uniform WACC to all projects, irrespective of differences in their risk characteristics. This practice is based on the following reasoning: "While a project may not have the same risk as the firm, its relevant cost of capital is still the firm's WACC because the investors are paid from the cash flows of the firm, not the cash flows of the project."

    The above reasoning is flawed. The return that the investors require from a project is the same as what they would get from an alternative investment with the same risk profile and it has nothing to do with the return that they are currently getting from the firm. For example, if a firm currently engaged in petrochemical business sets up a retailing business, investors will require a return from the retailing business that reflects its riskiness. Note that it is not the WACC of a firm that determines the cost of capital of a project. Rather, it is the other way. Each project has its own cost of capital which reflects its riskiness and its debt capacity. The cost of capital of the firm is the weighted average of the capital costs of various projects undertaken by the firm.

10.12 HOW FINANCIAL INSTITUTIONS CALCULATE COST OF CAPITAL

Financial institutions calculate cost of capital as post-tax weighted average cost of the mix of funds employed for the project.

The cost for different sources of funds are taken as follows:

■ Equity share capital	:	15%
■ Cash accruals/Retained earnings	:	15%
■ Preference share capital	:	Preference dividend rate
■ Subsidy/Incentive loans	:	Zero cost
■ Debt (Long-term loans, non-convertible debentures, deferred credits, bank borrowings for working capital, unsecured loans from public)	:	Post-tax rate of interest
■ Convertible debenture	:	Convertible portion at 15% Non-convertible portion at post-tax interest rate

For calculating the post-tax rate of interest, the interest rate is multiplied by (1-tax rate). The tax rate for this purpose is the average applicable tax rate and not the statutory tax rate. The average applicable tax rate is calculated as follows:

$$\frac{\text{Total tax liability during the life of the project}}{\text{The operating profit over the life of the project}}$$

The average applicable tax rate is generally lower than the prevailing statutory tax rate because of various tax benefits available on account of incentives and losses.

Illustration The means of financing for a project is given below:

■ Equity and cash accruals	:	₹900 million
■ Preference share capital (@10%)	:	₹100 million
■ Rupee term loans from institutions (@14%)	:	₹800 million
■ Non convertible debentures (@12%)	:	₹400 million
■ Convertible portion of convertible debentures	:	₹100 million
■ Non-convertible portion of convertible debentures	:	₹100 million
■ Bank borrowing for working capital (@15%)	:	₹200 million

The average applicable tax rate for the project is estimated at 25 percent.

The cost of capital is calculated in Exhibit 10.6.

Exhibit 10.6 ***Cost of Capital Calculation***

(₹ in millions)

Means of Financing (A)	Amount (₹ in millions) (B)	Cost of Funds (C)	Total Cost (post-tax) (D) = C × B
1. Equity and cash accruals	900	15%	135
2. Preference share capital	100	10%	10
3. Rupee term loans (@14%)	800	10.5%	84
4. Non-convertible debentures (@12%)	400	9%	36
5. Convertible portion of convertible debentures	100	15%	15
6. Non-convertible portion of convertible debentures (@10%)	100	7.5%	7.5
7. Bank borrowing for working capital (@15%)	200	11.25%	22.5
	2600		310

The average cost of capital (post-tax) is: 310 / 2600 = 11.92%

SUMMARY

- Capital, like any other factor of production, has a cost. A company's cost of capital is the weighted average cost of the various sources of finance used by it, viz. equity, preference, long-term debt, and short-term debt.
- Note that many companies leave out the cost of short-term debt while calculating the weighted average cost of capital (WACC). In principle, this is not correct. Investors who provide short-term debt also have a claim on the operating earnings of the firm. So, if a company ignores this claim, it will misstate the rate of return required by its investors.
- WACC is a central concept in financial management. It is used for evaluating investment projects, for determining the capital structure, for setting the rates that regulated organisations like electric utilities can charge to their customers, so on and so forth.
- In general, if a firm uses n different sources of capital its WACC is:

$$\sum p_i r_i$$

- Two basic conditions should be satisfied for using the company's WACC for evaluating new investments: (a) the risk of new investments is the same as the average risk of existing investments; (b) the capital structure of the firm will not be affected by the new investments. Thus, strictly speaking, WACC is the right discount rate for a project that is a carbon copy of the firm's existing business. However, in practice WACC is used as a benchmark hurdle rate that is adjusted for variations in risk and financing patterns.

- Since debt and preference stock entail more or less fixed payments, estimating the cost of debt and preference is relatively easy.
- A company raises debt finance through a variety of instruments like debentures, bank loans, and commercial paper. The cost of debt is the weighted average rate of different kinds of debt employed by it.
- The weighted average rate of debt is calculated using the market values and yields to maturity of various debt instruments. Note that we use the yields to maturity or the current rates as they reflect the rates at which the firm can raise new debt.
- Since interest on debt is a tax-deductible expense, the pre-tax cost of debt has to be adjusted for the tax factor to arrive at the post-tax cost of debt.
- Preference capital carries a fixed rate of dividend and is redeemable in nature. Given the fixed nature of preference dividend and principal repayment commitment and the absence of tax deductibility, the cost of preference is simply equal to its yield.
- Equity earnings may be obtained in two ways: (i) retention of earnings; and (ii) issue of additional equity. The cost of equity or the return required by equity shareholders is the same in both the cases. Remember that when a firm decides to retain earnings, an opportunity cost is involved.
- A popular approach to estimating the cost of equity is the CAPM approach. According to the CAPM, the required return on a company's equity is:

$$r_E = R_f + \beta_i [E(R_M) - R_f]$$

- Analysts who do not have faith in the CAPM approach often resort to a more subjective procedure to estimate the cost of equity. They add a judgmental risk premium to the observed yield on the long-term bonds of the firm to get the cost of equity.
- According to the dividend growth model approach, the cost of equity is equal to:

  Dividend yield + Expected growth rate in dividends

- For calculating the WACC we multiply the cost of each source of capital by the proportion applicable to it. These proportions may be based on book values or target capital structure or market values. Market value proportions are generally recommended unless market values are not available or are highly unreliable or distorted.
- WACC tends to rise as the firm seeks more and more capital. This happens because the supply schedule of capital is typically upward sloping—as suppliers provide more capital, the rate of return required by them tends to increase.
- A schedule or graph showing the relationship between additional financing and WACC is called the weighted marginal cost of capital schedule.
- To determine the optimal capital budget, you have to compare the expected return on proposed capital expenditure projects with the marginal cost of capital schedule.
- When a firm raises finance by issuing equity and debt, it almost invariably incurs floatation or issue costs, comprising of items like underwriting costs, brokerage expenses, fees of merchant bankers, under-pricing costs, so on and so forth.
- There are two ways of handling floatation costs. One approach is to adjust the WACC to reflect the floatation costs. A better approach is to leave the WACC unchanged but to consider floatation costs as part of the project cost.

- The cost of capital is affected by several factors, some beyond the control of the firm and others depending on the investment and financing policies of the firm.
- Despite the importance of cost of capital in financial management, we find that several misconceptions characterise its application in practice. The more serious ones are: (i) the cost of capital is too academic or impractical; (ii) the cost of equity is equal to the dividend rate or return on equity; (iii) retained earnings are either cost free or cost significantly less than external equity; (iv) depreciation has no cost; (v) book value weights may be used to calculate the WACC; (vi) if a project is financed heavily by debt, its WACC is low.

QUESTIONS

1. What are the three steps involved in calculating a firm's WACC?
2. Discuss the conditions that should be satisfied for using a firm's WACC for evaluating new investments.
3. How is the cost of debt calculated?
4. How is the cost of preference calculated?
5. Discuss the application of CAPM to the calculation of cost of equity.
6. What are the pros and cons of using the CAPM approach to calculate the cost of equity?
7. What are the pros and cons of using the bond yield plus risk premium approach to calculate the cost of equity?
8. How is the cost of equity calculated using the dividend growth model approach?
9. What are the pros and cons of using the dividend growth model approach to calculate the cost of equity?
10. Discuss the following bases for determining the proportions (or weights) in the WACC calculation: book values, target capital structure, and market values.
11. Explain the procedure for determining the weighted marginal cost of capital.
12. Describe the procedure for determining the optimal capital budget.
13. How would you handle the floatation costs in computing the cost of capital?
14. Discuss the factors affecting the weighted average cost of capital.
15. What are the common misconceptions surrounding cost of capital in practice? How would you dispel them?
16. How do financial institutions calculate cost of capital?

PROBLEMS

1. Abascus Limited issued 15 year, 14 percent bonds five years ago. The bond which has a face value of ₹100 is currently selling for ₹108.
   a. What is the pre-tax cost of debt?
   b. What is the after-tax cost of debt? (assume a 35 percent tax rate)

2. Omega Enterprises issued 10 year, 9 percent preference shares four years ago. The preference share which has a face value of ₹100 is currently selling for ₹92. What is the cost of preference shares?
3. Rao Corporation has a target capital structure of 60 percent equity and 40 percent debt. Its cost of equity is 18 percent and its pre-tax cost of debt is 13 percent. If the relevant tax rate is 35 percent, what is Rao Corporation's WACC?
4. Unix Limited's equity beta is 1.2. The market risk premium is 7 percent and the risk-free rate is 10 percent. Unix has a debt equity ratio of 2:3. Its pre-tax cost of debt is 14 percent. If the tax rate is 35 percent, what is the WACC?
5. Azeez Corporation's WACC is 12 percent and its tax rate is 35 percent. Azeez's pre-tax cost of debt is 14 percent and its debt-equity ratio is 1:1. The risk-free rate is 11 percent and the market risk premium is 8 percent. What is the beta of Azeez's equity?
6. Satish Kumar, CEO of Vanguard Enterprises is trying to figure out the cost of debt and equity.
   a. Vanguard's balance sheet has total debt of ₹200 million and Vanguard's total interest burden for the forthcoming year will be ₹24 million. Satish argues, "We owe ₹200 million and we will pay ₹24 million interest. So the cost of our debt is 12 percent (24/200)." What is the flaw in this argument?
   b. Vanguard's equity currently sells for ₹100 per share and the dividend per share will probably be ₹6. Satish reasons "Since we plan to pay a dividend of ₹6 per share which has a market price of ₹100 our cost of equity is 6 percent". What is the error in this reasoning?
7. Samanta Company has 20 million equity shares outstanding. The book value per share is ₹40 and the market price per share is ₹120. Samanta has two debenture issues outstanding. The first issue has a face value of ₹300 million, 12 percent coupon, and sells for 90 percent of its face value. It will mature in 5 years. The second issue has a face value of ₹200 million, 14 percent coupon, and sells for 102 percent of its face value. It will mature in 6 years. Samanta also has a bank loan of ₹200 million on which the interest rate is 15 percent.
   a. What are Samanta's capital structure weights on a book value basis and on a market value basis?
   b. Which weights would you use? Why?
8. Suman Corporation manufactures speciality chemicals. Its debt-equity ratio is 0.8. Its WACC is 15 percent and its tax rate is 30 percent.
   a. If Suman's cost of equity is 20 percent, what is its pre-tax cost of debt?
   b. If Suman can issue debt at an interest rate of 13 percent, what is its cost of equity?
9. Panyam Company's capital structure in terms of market value is:

Debt	₹30 million
Equity	₹60 million

   The company plans to maintain this market-value capital structure. The company has a plan to invest ₹15 million next year. This will be financed as follows:

Retained earnings	₹5 million
Additional equity	₹5 million
Debt	₹5 million

   The company's equity stock presently sells for ₹30 per share. The next dividend expected is ₹3.00. The expected rate of dividend growth is 5 percent. Additional equity can be issued at ₹25 per share (net). The interest rate applicable to additional debt would be as follows:

First ₹2.5 million	14 percent
Next ₹2.5 million	15 percent

   The tax rate for the firm is 60 percent.

Required:

(a) At what amounts of new capital will there be breaks in the marginal cost of capital schedule?

(b) What will be the marginal cost of capital in the interval between each of the breaks?

10. Susheel Corporation has the following book value capital structure:

Equity capital (10 million shares, ₹10 par)	₹100 million
Preference capital, 11 percent (100,000 shares, ₹100 par)	₹ 10 million
Retained earnings	₹120 million
Debentures 13.5 percent (500,000 debentures, ₹100 par)	₹ 50 million
Term loans, 12 percent	₹ 80 million
	₹360 million

The next expected dividend per share is ₹1.50. The dividend per share is expected to grow at the rate of 7 percent. The market price per share is ₹20.00. Preference stock, redeemable after 10 years, is currently selling for ₹75.00 per share. Debentures, redeemable after 6 years, are selling for ₹80.00 per debenture. The tax rate for the company is 50 percent.

(a) Calculate the average cost of capital using
   (i) book value proportions, and
   (ii) market value proportions

(b) Define the marginal cost of capital schedule for the firm if it raises ₹100 million next year, given the following information:
   (i) the amount will be raised from equity and debt in equal proportions
   (ii) the firm expects to retain ₹15 million earnings next year
   (iii) the additional issue of equity stock will fetch a net price per share of ₹16.00
   (iv) the debt capital raised by way of term loans will cost 14 percent for the first ₹25 million and 15 percent for the next ₹25 million

11. Microelectronics Corporation is currently at its target debt-equity ratio of 0.5: 1. It is considering a proposal to expand capacity which is expected to cost ₹500 million and generate after-tax cash flows of ₹130 million per year for the next eight years. The tax rate for the firm is 30 percent. Mahesh, the CFO of the company, has considered two financing options: (i) Issue of equity stock. The required return on the company's new equity is 20 percent and the issuance cost will be 12 percent. (ii) Issue of debentures at a yield of 13 percent. The issuance cost will be 3 percent.

   a. What is the WACC for Microelectronics?
   b. What is Microelectronic's weighted average floatation cost?
   c. What is the NPV of the proposal after taking into account the floatation costs?

MINICASE

Suman Joshi, Managing Director of Omega Textiles, was reviewing two very different investment proposals. The first one is for expanding the capacity in the main line of business and the second one is for diversifying into a new line of business.

Suman Joshi asks for your help in estimating Omega's weighted average cost of capital which he believes is relevant for evaluating the expansion proposal. He also wants you to estimate the hurdle rate for the new line of business.

To enable you to carry out your task, he has provided the following data.

- The latest balance sheet of Omega is given below

₹ *in million*

Liabilities		*Assets*	
Equity capital	350	Fixed assets	700
Preference capital	100	Investments	100
Reserves and surplus	200	Current assets, loans and advances	400
Debentures	350		
Current liabilities & provisions	200		
	1200		1200

- Omega's target capital structure has 50 percent equity, 10 percent preference, and 40 percent debt.
- Omega has ₹100 par, 10 percent coupon, annual payment, noncallable debentures with 8 years to maturity. These debentures are selling currently at ₹112.
- Omega has ₹100 par, 9 percent, annual dividend, preference shares with a residual maturity of 5 years. The market price of these preference shares is ₹106.
- Omega's equity stock is currently selling at ₹80 per share. Its last dividend was ₹2.80 and the dividend per share is expected to grow at a rate of 10 percent in future.
- Omega's equity beta is 1.1, the risk-free rate is 7 percent, and the market risk premium is estimated to be 7 percent.
- Omega's tax rate is 30 percent.
- The new business that Omega is considering has different financial characteristics than Omega's existing business. Firms engaged purely in such business have, on overage, the following characteristics: (i) their capital structure has debt and equity in equal proportions, (ii) their cost of debt is 11 percent, (iii) their equity beta is 1.5.

a. What sources of capital would you consider relevant for calculating the weighted average cost of capital?
b. What is Omega's post-tax cost of debt?
c. What is Omega's cost of preference?
d. What is Omega's estimated cost of equity using the dividend discount model?
e. What is Omega's estimated cost of equity using the capital asset pricing model?
f. What is Omega's weighted average cost of capital? Use the capital asset pricing model to estimate the cost of equity.
g. What would be your estimate for the cost of capital for the new business?

APPENDIX 10A

EARNINGS-PRICE (E/P) RATIO AS A MEASURE OF COST OF EQUITY

E/P ratio measures the cost of equity capital in the following cases:

Case A Future earnings are constant and the payout ratio is 100 percent.

Case B The firm invests in projects that earn a rate of return of r_E (the cost of equity capital) forever on the equity portion of financing.

Case A The cost of equity is the value of r_E in the equation.

$$P = \sum_{t=1}^{\infty} \frac{D_t}{(1 + r_E)^t} \tag{10A.1}$$

When future earnings are constant and the payout ratio is 100 percent:

$$E_1 = E_2 = E_3 = ... E = D_1 = D_2 = ... D \tag{10A.2}$$

Putting future earnings as E gives

$$P = \sum_{t=1}^{\infty} \frac{E}{(1 + r_E)^t} \tag{10A.3}$$

This leads to:

$$r_E = E/P \tag{10A.4}$$

Case B For the sake of simplicity, let us assume that the firm has an all-equity capital structure and the retention ratio is b (a constant) in each period.

Since reinvested funds earn a rate of return of r_E percent, earnings, retained earnings, and dividends will be as given in Exhibit 10A.1.

Exhibit 10A.1 ***Earnings, Retained Earnings, and Dividends***

Year	*Earnings*	*Retained Earnings*	*Dividends*
0	E_0	$E_0 b$	$E_0(1—b)$
1	$E_0 + E_0 b r_E = E_0 (1+b r_E)$	$E_0 (1+b r_E) b$	$E_0 (1+b r_E)(1—b)$
2	$E_0 (1+b r_E) + E_0(1+b r_E) b r_E$ $= E_0 (1+b r_E)^2$	$E_0 (1+b r_E)^2 b$	$E_0 (1+b r_E)^2 (1—b)$
.	.	.	.
.	.	.	.
.	.	.	.
n	$E_0 (1+b r_E)^n$	$E_0 (1+b r_E)^n b$	$E_0 (1+b r_E)^n (1—b)$

The cost of equity is the value of r_E in the following equation:

$$P = \sum_{t=1}^{\infty} \frac{D_t}{(1 + r_E)^t} \tag{10A.5}$$

Given the value of D_t in Exhibit 10A.1, we get

$$P = \sum_{t=1}^{\infty} \frac{E_0 (1 + b r_E)^t (1 - b)}{(1 + r_E)^t}$$

$$= \sum_{t=1}^{\infty} E_0 (1 - b) \frac{(1 + b r_E)^t}{(1 + r_E)^t}$$

$$= \frac{E_0 (1 - b)(1 + b r_E)}{r_E (1 - b)} \tag{10A.6}$$

Hence $$r_E = E_1/P \tag{10A.7}$$

APPENDIX 10B

VARYING ASSUMPTIONS UNDERLYING COST OF CAPITAL CALCULATION

A 2012 survey conducted by the Association for Financial Professionals revealed that companies typically use discounted cash flow analysis for evaluating capital investments. In such analysis projected free cash flows are discounted by the weighted average cost of debt and equity. And to estimate the cost of equity, the capital asset pricing model (CAPM) is used predominantly.

But that is where the general argument ends. There seems to be wide variation about assumptions companies in their financial models to quantify investment opportunities as the following tables show:

What's Your Forecast Horizon?

Years	*Respondents (%)*
5	46%
10	34%
15	6%
Other	14%

What's Your Cost of Debt?

Measure	*Respondents (%)*
Current rate on outstanding debt	37%
Forecast rate on new issuance	34%
Average historical rate	29%

What's the Risk-Free Rate?

Rate on U.S Treasuries with Maturity of	*Respondents (%)*
90 days	16%
52 weeks	5%
5 years	12%
10 years	46%
20 years	4%
30 years	11%
Other	6%

What's the Equity–Market Risk Premium?

Risk Premium	*Respondents (%)*
Less than 3%	11%
3%-4%	23%
5%-6%	49%
7% or greater	17%

What's Your Beta Period?

Period	*Respondents (%)*
One year	29%
Two years	13%
Three years	15%
Five years	41%
Other	2%

What's Your Debt-to-Equity Ratio?

Measure	*Respondents (%)*
Current book debt to equity	30%
Targeted book debt to equity	28%
Current market debt to equity	23%
Current book debt to current market equity	19%

The wide variations seem to be a problem. As Michael T. Jacobs and Anil Shivadasani put it: "These tremendous disparities in assumptions profoundly influence how capital is deployed in our economy. Despite record-low borrowing costs and record-high cash balances, capital expenditures by U.S. companies are projected to be flat or to decline slightly in 2012, indicating that most businesses are not adjusting their investment policies to reflect the decline in their cost of capital. They further added, "With $2 trillion at stake, the hour has come for an honest debate among business leaders and financial advisers about how best to determine investment time horizons, cots of capital, and project risk adjustment."

Chapter 11 Project Risk Analysis

LEARNING OBJECTIVES

After studying this chapter you should be able to

- Describe the sources, measures, and perspectives on risk.
- Explain the techniques of sensitivity analysis, scenario analysis, and break-even analysis.
- Discuss the steps involved in simulation analysis.
- Show how decision tree analysis may be used for analysing sequential decision making in face of risk.
- Describe the strategies employed in managing risk.
- Discuss how risk is analysed and assessed in practice.

Risk is inherent in almost every business decision. More so in capital budgeting decisions as they involve costs and benefits extending over a long period of time during which many things can change in unanticipated ways.

For the sake of expository convenience, we have assumed so far that all investments being considered for inclusion in the capital budget had the same risk as those of the existing investments of the firm. Hence the average cost of capital was used for evaluating every project. Investment proposals, however, differ in risk. A research and development project may be more risky than an expansion project and the latter tends to be more risky than a replacement project. In view of such differences, variations in risk need to be evaluated explicitly in capital investment appraisal.

Financial analysts generally evaluate capital investments in two phases. In the first phase, the analyst tries to calculate the NPV, IRR and other measures of investment worth on the basis of what he thinks is most likely to happen. In the second phase, the analyst identifies the underlying sources of risk and explores the consequences thereof. While the preceding three chapters were concerned mainly with the first phase of investment analysis, this chapter focuses on the techniques of risk analysis. At the outset, it must be emphasised that these techniques may give an impression of objectivity and precision. However, the truth is that they rely on information which in inherently subjective.

Risk analysis is one of the most complex and slippery aspects of capital budgeting. Many different techniques have been suggested and no single technique can be deemed as best in all situations. The variety of techniques suggested to handle risk in capital budgeting fall into two broad categories: (i) Techniques that consider the stand-alone risk of a project. (ii) Techniques that consider the risk of a project in the context of the firm or in the context of the market. Exhibit 11.1 classifies various techniques into these broad categories.

This chapter discusses different techniques that consider the stand-alone risk of a project[1], examines ways of managing risk, explores various approaches to project selection under risk, and describes risk analysis in practice.

Exhibit 11.1 ***Techniques of Risk Analysis***

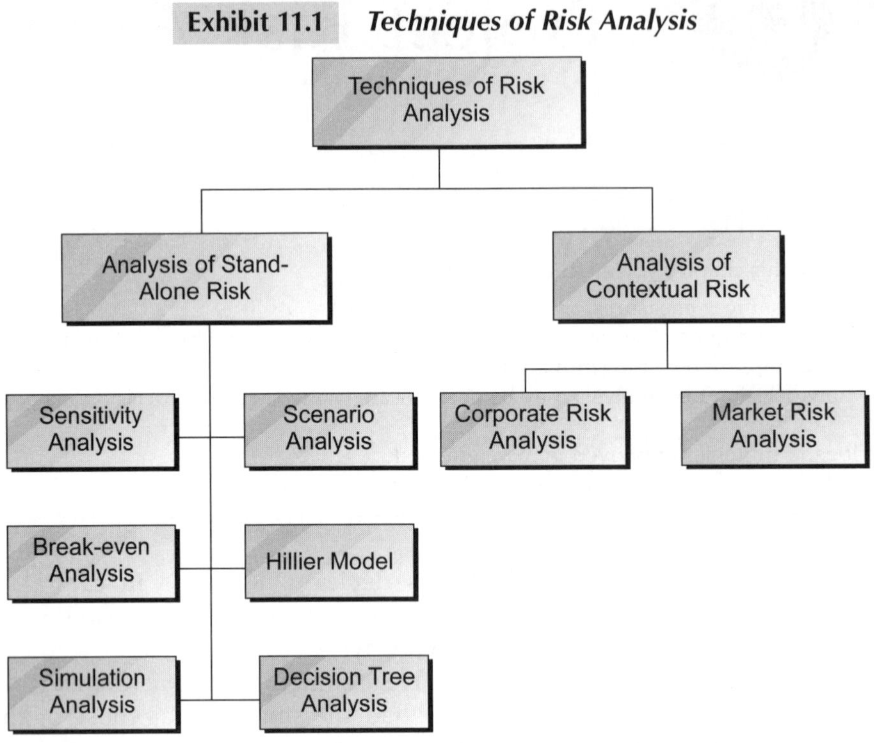

11.1 SOURCES, MEASURES, AND PERSPECTIVES ON RISK

Sources of Risk There are several sources of risk in a project. The important ones are project-specific risk, competitive risk, industry-specific risk, market risk, and international risk.

Project-specific risk The earnings and cash flows of the project may be lower than expected because of estimation error or due to some other factors specific to the project like the quality of management.

Competitive risk The earnings and cash flows of the project may be affected by unanticipated actions of the competitors.

Industry-specific risk Unexpected technological developments and regulatory changes, that are specific to the industry to which the project belongs, will have an impact on the earnings and cash flows of the project as well.

[1] Chapter 12 discusses the techniques that consider the risk of a project in the context of the firm or in the context of the market.

Market risk Unanticipated changes in macroeconomic factors like the GDP growth rate, interest rate, and inflation have an impact on all projects, albeit in varying degrees

International risk In the case of a foreign project, the earnings and cash flows may be different than expected due to the exchange rate risk or political risk.

Measures of Risk Risk refers to variability. It is a complex and multi-faceted phenomenon. A variety of measures have been used to capture different facets of risk. The more important ones are: range, standard deviation, coefficient of variation, and semi-variance.

To illustrate the calculation of these measures, consider a capital investment whose net present value has the following distribution.

NPV	*Probability*
200	0.3
600	0.5
900	0.2

The probability weighted NPV works out to:

$$E\,(\text{NPV}) = \sum_{i=1}^{3} p_i \, \text{NPV}_i$$

$$= 0.3 \times 200 + 0.5 \times 600 + 0.2 \times 900 = 540$$

Now let us look at the various measures of risk.

Range Obviously the simplest measure of risk, the range of a distribution is the difference between the highest value and the lowest value. The range of the above distribution is: 900 – 200 = 700.

Standard Deviation The standard deviation of a distribution is:

$$\sigma = [\Sigma p_i \, (X_i - \overline{X})^2]^{1/2} \qquad (11.1)$$

where σ is the standard deviation, p_i is the probability associated with the *i*th value, X_i is the *i*th value, and $\overline{X}$ is the expected value.

The standard deviation of the NPV distribution presented above is:

$$\sigma = [0.3\,(200 - 540)^2 + 0.5\,(600 - 540)^2 + 0.2\,(900 - 540)^2]^{1/2}$$

$$= [62400]^{1/2} = 249.8$$

The square of standard deviation is called variance

$$\text{Variance} = \sigma^2$$

The variance of the above distribution is 62,400

Coefficient of Variation One problem with standard deviation (or variance) is that it is not adjusted for scale. If you go only by standard deviation, an investment with an expected net present value of ₹10 million and a standard deviation of ₹4 million would be considered more risky than an investment with an expected net present value of ₹1 million and a standard deviation of ₹2 million.

The coefficient of variation (CV) adjusts standard deviation for scale. It is defined as:

$$CV = \frac{\text{Standard deviation}}{\text{Expected Value}}$$

The coefficient of variation for the investment in our illustration is:

$$CV = \frac{249.8}{540} = 0.46$$

Semi-Variance There is yet another problem with standard deviation (or variance). It considers all deviations, positive as well as negative, from the expected value in the same way. Since investors are concerned about only negative deviations, semi-variance seems to be a more suitable measure of risk.

The semi-variance is computed the way the variance is computed, except that only outcomes below the expected value are taken into account. It is defined as:

$$SV = \Sigma\, p_i d_i'^2 \tag{11.2}$$

where d'_i is equal to d_i if $d_i < 0$ and is equal to 0 if $d_i \geq 0$

The semi-variance for the investment in our illustration is:

$$SV = 0.3\,(200 - 540)^2 = 34{,}680$$

The semi-standard deviation is the square root of semi-variance. The semi-standard deviation for the investment in our illustration is:

$$\begin{aligned}\text{Semi-standard deviation} &= (\text{Semi-variance})^{1/2}\\ &= (34680)^{1/2}\\ &= 186.2\end{aligned}$$

The Principal Measure Standard deviation is the most commonly used measure of risk in finance. The main reasons for using standard deviation are as follows:

(i) If a variable is normally distributed, its mean and standard deviation contain all the information about its probability distribution.

(ii) If the utility of money is represented by a quadratic function (a function commonly suggested to represent diminishing marginal utility of wealth), then the expected utility is a function of mean and standard deviation.

(iii) Standard deviation is analytically easily tractable.

Use of Subjective Probabilities For measuring the expected value and dispersion of a variable, its probability distribution is required. In some cases the probability distribution can be defined with a fairly high degree of objectivity on the basis of past evidence. A wildcatter, for example, may be able to define with a high degree of objectivity the probabilities associated with certain states of nature if sufficient records for similar ventures are available. Since such a probability distribution is substantially based on objective facts, it may be referred to as an 'objective' probability distribution.

However, in most real-life situations, such objective evidence may not be available for defining probability distributions. In such cases, knowledgeable persons may pool their experience and judgment to define the probability distribution. Since there is likely to be a high element of subjectivity in these distributions, such distributions are generally referred to as *'subjective'* probability distributions.

Perspectives on Risk Regardless of the risk measure employed, there are different perspectives on risk. You can view a project from at least three different perspectives. These are:

Stand-alone risk This represents the risk of a project when it is viewed in isolation.

Firm risk Also called *corporate risk*, this reflects the contribution of a project to the risk of the firm.

Systematic risk This represents the risk of a project from the point of view of a diversified investor. It is also called *market risk*.

This chapter focuses on stand-alone risk and the following chapter examines firm risk and market risk. There are several reasons for starting with stand-alone risk analysis:

- Measuring a project's stand-alone risk is easier than measuring its corporate risk and far easier than measuring its market risk.
- In most of the cases, stand-alone risk, corporate risk, and market risk are highly correlated. If the overall economy does well, the firm too would do well. Further, if the firm does well, most of its projects would do well. Thanks to this high correlation, stand-alone risk may be used as a proxy for corporate risk and market risk.
- The proponent of a capital investment is likely to be judged on the performance of that investment. Hence he will naturally be concerned about its stand alone risk and not about its contribution to the risk of the firm or the risk of a diversified investor.
- In most firms, the capital budgeting committee considers investment proposals one at a time. The committee often does not have the time or information or expertise to fully consider the interactions of the investments with the other investments of the firm or its shareholders.

11.2 SENSITIVITY ANALYSIS

Since the future is uncertain, you may like to know what will happen to the viability of the project when some variable like sales or investment deviates from its expected value. In other words, you may want to do "what if" analysis or sensitivity analysis.

To understand the nature of sensitivity analysis, let us consider an example. Suppose you are the financial manager of Naveen Flour Mills. Naveen is considering setting up a new flour mill near Bangalore. Based on Naveen's previous experience, the project staff of Naveen has developed the figures shown in Exhibit 11.2 (Note that the salvage value has been assumed to be nil and the cost of capital to be 12 percent).

Exhibit 11.2 *Cash Flow Forecast for Naveen's Flour Mill Project*

		(₹ in thousands)	
		Year 0	*Years 1–10*
1.	Investment	(20,000)	
2.	Sales		18,000
3.	Variable costs ($66^2/_3$% of sales)		12,000
4.	Fixed costs		1,000
5.	Depreciation		2,000
6.	Pre-tax profit		3,000
7.	Taxes		1,000
8.	Profit after taxes		2,000
9.	Cash flow from operation		4,000
10.	Net cash flow	(20,000)	4,000

Since the cash flow from operations is an annuity, the NPV of the flour mill project is:

$$- 20{,}000{,}000 + 4{,}000{,}000 \times PVIFA(r = 12\%, n = 10)$$

$$- 20{,}000{,}000 + 4{,}000{,}000\ (5.650)$$

$$= 2{,}600{,}000$$

The NPV based on the expected values of the underlying variables is positive. You are, however, aware that the underlying variables can vary widely and hence you would like to explore the effect of such variations on the NPV. So you define the optimistic and pessimistic estimates for the underlying variables. These are shown on the left hand side of Exhibit 11.3. With this information, you can calculate the NPV for the optimistic and pessimistic values of each of the underlying variables.

To do this, vary one variable at a time. For example, to study the effect of an adverse variation in sales (from the expected ₹18 million to the pessimistic ₹15 million), you maintain the values of the other underlying variables at their expected levels. (This means that the investment is held at ₹20 million, variable costs as a proportion of sales are held at $66^2/_3$ percent, fixed costs are held at ₹1 million, so on and so forth).

The NPV when the sales are at their pessimistic level and other variables at their expected level is shown on the right hand side of Exhibit 11.3. Likewise you can calculate the effect of variations in the values of the other underlying variables. The NPVs for the pessimistic, expected, and optimistic forecasts are shown on the right hand side of Exhibit 11.3.

Evaluation A very popular method for assessing risk, sensitivity analysis has certain *merits*:

- It shows how robust or vulnerable a project is to changes in values of the underlying variables
- It indicates where further work may be done. If the NPV is highly sensitive to changes in some factor, it may be worthwhile to explore how the variability of that critical factor may be contained.
- It is intuitively very appealing as it articulates the concerns that project evaluators normally have.

Exhibit 11.3 ***Sensitivity of NPV to Variations in the Value of Key Variables***

	Range			NPV		
Key Variable	*Pessimistic*	*Expected*	*Optimistic*	*Pessimistic*	*Expected*	*Optimistic*
Investment (₹ in million)	24	20	18	– 0.65	2.60	4.22
Sales (₹ in million)	15	18	21	– 1.17	2.60	6.40
Variable costs as a percent of sales	70	66.66	65	0.34	2.60	3.73
Fixed costs (₹ in million)	1.3	1.0	0.8	1.47	2.60	3.33

Notwithstanding its appeal and popularity, sensitivity analysis suffers from several *shortcomings*:

- It merely shows what happens to NPV when there is a change in some variable, without providing any idea of how likely that change will be.
- Typically, in sensitivity analysis only one variable is changed at a time. In the real world, however, variables tend to move together.
- The interpretation of results is subjective. The same sensitivity analysis may lead one decision maker to accept the project while another may reject it.

11.3 SCENARIO ANALYSIS

In sensitivity analysis, typically one variable is varied at a time. In scenario analysis, several variables are varied simultaneously. Most commonly, three scenarios are considered: expected (or normal) scenario, pessimistic scenario, and optimistic scenario. In the normal scenario, all variables assume their expected (or normal values); in the pessimistic scenario, all variables assume their pessimistic values; and in the optimistic scenario all variables assume their optimistic values.

The NPV of the project of Naveen Flour Mills under three scenarios is given in Exhibit 11.4.

Scenario Analysis Using a Spreadsheet First, set up the Excel spreadsheet as shown in Exhibit 11.5. The NPV calculation is in C16. Enter the pessimistic values of the key variables, namely, investments, sales, variable costs as a percentage of sales, and fixed costs in B20 to B23. Likewise enter the expected values of the key variables in C20 to C23 and the optimistic values of the key variables in D20 to D23. Then click on Tools and from the drop-down menu select Scenarios. A dialogue box named Scenario Manager appears in which click on the button Add. A new dialogue box appears in which against Scenario name, type Pessimistic and against Changing cells give references of the cells whose values change for the different scenarios, viz.C4, C7, C5, C9 and click on the button OK. Another box named Scenario

Values appears in which fill in the respective values against the changing cells, in this case (24,000), 15,000, 70% and 1,300 respectively. Click on the button OK and the Scenario Manager reappears. Click on the button Add and in the Scenario Name box against name type Expected. The changing cells references remain unchanged but in the next dialogue box the cell values are to be changed to the expected values viz. (20,000), 18,000, 66.67% and 1,000 respectively. Click on the button OK and this time use the Scenario Manager to get the Optimistic scenario by giving the related input values. When the Scenario Manager reappears, click on the button Summary. In the resultant dialogue box, check in the box Scenario summary and in the Result cells give the reference of the cell whose value is needed- in this case C16. Now when we click OK a Scenario Summary appears. This is shown in Exhibit 11.6. In the Result Cell of this summary, we can see the desired result viz. net present value for each of the scenarios, in a neat table, whose labels can be suitably edited if necessary.

Exhibit 11.4 ***Pessimistic, Normal and Optimistic Scenario***

		(₹ in millions)	
	Pessimistic Scenario	Expected Scenario	Optimistic Scenario
1. Investment	24	20	18
2. Sales	15	18	21
3. Variable costs (% of sales)	10.5 (70%)	12 (66.7%)	13.65 (65%)
4. Fixed costs	1.3	1.0	0.8
5. Depreciation	2.4	2.0	1.8
6. Pre-tax profit	0.8	3.0	4.75
7. Tax	0.27	1.0	1.58
8. Profit after tax	0.53	2.0	3.17
9. Annual cash flow from operations	2.93	4.0	4.97
10. Net present value (9) × PVIFA (12%, 10 yrs) – (1)	(7.45)	2.60	10.06

Evaluation Scenario analysis may be regarded as an improvement over sensitivity analysis because it considers variations in several variables together.

However, scenario analysis has its own limitations:

- It is based on the assumption that there are few well-delineated scenarios. This may not be true in many cases. For example, the economy does not necessarily lie in three discrete states, viz., recession, stability, and boom. It can in fact be anywhere on the continuum between the extremes. When a continuum is converted into three discrete states some information is lost.
- Scenario analysis expands the concept of estimating the expected values. Thus, in a case where there are 10 inputs the analyst has to estimate 30 expected values (3×10) to do the scenario analysis.

Exhibit 11.5 *Scenario Analysis*

	A	B	C	D
1	Discount rate	Project life	Tax rate	
2	12%	10	33.33%	
3	**Expected values (₹ in thousands)**			
4	Investment in year 0		(20,000)	
5	Variable costs as a percentage of sales		66 67%	
6	**For years 1 to 10**			
7	Sales		18,000	
8	Variable costs	= C7*C5	12001	
9	Fixed costs		1,000	
10	Depreciation	= -C4/B2	2,000	
11	Pre-tax profit	= C7-C8-C9-C10	2999	
12	Taxes	= C11 * C2	1,000	
13	Profit after taxes	= C11 - C 12	2,000	
14	Cash flow from operation	= C13 + C10	4,000	
15	Present value of the cash flow stream	= PV(A2,B2,-C14)	22,599	
16	Net present value of the project	= C15+C4	2,599	
17				
18				
19	**Key variables**	**Pessimistic**	**Expected**	**Optimistic**
20	Investment	(24,000)	(20,000)	(18,000)
21	Sales	15,000	18,000	21,000
22	Variable costs as a percent of sales	70	66.67	65
23	Fixed costs	1,300	1,000	800

11.4 BREAK-EVEN ANALYSIS

In sensitivity analysis we ask what will happen to the project if sales decline or costs increase or something else happens. As a financial manager, you will also be interested in knowing how much should be produced and sold at a minimum to ensure that the project does not 'lose money'. Such an exercise is called *break-even analysis* and the minimum quantity at which loss is avoided is called the break-even point. The break-even point may be defined in accounting terms or financial terms.

Accounting Break-even Analysis Suppose you are the financial manager of Naveen Flour Mills. Naveen is considering setting up a new flour mill near Bangalore. Based on Naveen's previous experience, the project staff of Naveen has developed the figures shown in Exhibit 11.7.

Exhibit 11.6 ***Scenario Summary***

	A	B	C	D	E	F	G
1	**Scenario Summary**						
2				Current Values:	Pessimistic	Expected	Optimistic
3							
4	Changing Cells:						
5			**C4**	20,000	24,000	20,000	(18,000)
6			**C7**	18,000	15,000	18,000	21,000
7			**C5**	66.67%	70.00%	66.67%	65.00%
8			**C9**	1000	1,300	1000	800
9	Result Cells:						
10			**C16**	2,599	-7,426	2,599	10,064

Note that the ratio of variable costs to sales is 0.667 (12/18). This means that every rupee of sales makes a contribution of ₹0.333. Put differently, the contribution margin ratio is 0.333. Hence the break-even level of sales will be:

$$\frac{\text{Fixed costs} + \text{Depreciation}}{\text{Contribution margin ratio}} = \frac{(1+2)\text{ million}}{0.333} = ₹9 \text{ million}$$

Exhibit 11.7 ***Cash Flow Forecast for Naveen's Flour Mill Project***

	Year 0	('000) Years 1–10
1. Investment	(20,000)	
2. Sales		18,000
3. Variable costs ($66^2/_3$% of sales)		12,000
1. Fixed costs		1,000
2. Depreciation		2,000
3. Pre-tax profit		3,000
4. Taxes		1,000
5. Profit after taxes		2,000
6. Cash flow from operation		4,000
7. Net cash flow	(20,000)	4,000

By way of confirmation, you can verify that the break-even level of sales is indeed ₹9 million.

	₹ in million
Sales	9
Variable costs	6
Fixed costs	1
Depreciation	2
Profit before tax	0
Tax	0
Profit after tax	0

A project that breaks even in accounting terms is like a stock that gives you a return of zero percent. In both the cases you get back your original investment but you are not compensated for the time value of money or the risk that you bear. Put differently, you forego the opportunity cost of your capital. Hence a project that merely breaks even in accounting terms will have a negative NPV.

Financial Break-even Analysis The focus of financial break-even analysis is on NPV and not on accounting profit. At what level of sales will the project have a zero NPV?

To illustrate how the financial break-even level of sales is calculated, let us go back to the flour mill project. The annual cash flow of the project depends on sales as follows:

1. Variable costs	:	66.67 percent of sales
2. Contribution	:	33.33 percent of sales
3. Fixed costs	:	₹1 million
4. Depreciation	:	₹2 million
5. Pre-tax profit	:	(.333 × Sales) – ₹3 million
6. Tax (at 33.3%)	:	.333(.333 Sales – ₹3 million)
7. Profit after tax	:	.667 (.333 × Sales – ₹3 million)
8. Cash flow (4+7)	:	₹2 million + .667 (.333 × Sales – ₹3 million)
		= 0.222 Sales

Since the cash flow lasts for 10 years, its present value at a discount rate of 12 percent is:

PV (cash flows)	=	0.222 Sales × PVIFA (10 years, 12%)
	=	0.222 Sales × 5.650
	=	1.254 Sales

The project breaks even in NPV terms when the present value of these cash flows equals the initial investment of ₹20 million. Hence, the financial break-even occurs when

PV (cash flows)	=	Investment
1.254 Sales	=	₹20 million
Sales	=	₹15.95 million

Thus, the sales for the flour mill must be ₹15.95 million per year for the investment to have a zero NPV. Note that this is significantly higher than ₹9 million which represents the accounting break-even sales.

11.5 HILLIER MODEL

Under certain circumstances, as H. S. Hillier showed, the expected net present value and the standard deviation of net present value may be obtained through analytical derivation. Two cases of such analysis are discussed here: (i) no correlation among cash flows and (ii) perfect correlation among cash flows.

Uncorrelated Cash Flows When the cash flows of different years are uncorrelated, the cash flow for year t is independent of the cash flow for year $t - r$. Put differently, there is no relationship between cash flows from one period to another. In this case the expected net present value and the standard deviation of net present value are defined as follows:

$$\overline{\text{NPV}} = \sum_{t=1}^{n} \frac{\overline{A}_t}{(1+i)^t} - I \tag{11.3}$$

$$\sigma(\text{NPV}) = \left(\sum_{t=1}^{n} \frac{\sigma_t^2}{(1+i)^{2t}} \right)^{1/2} \qquad (11.4)^2$$

where $\overline{\text{NPV}}$ is the expected net present value, $\overline{A}_t$ is the expected cash flow for year t, i is the risk-free interest rate, I is the initial outlay, σ (NPV) is the standard deviation of net present value, and σ_t is the standard deviation of the cash flow for year t.

Note that in the above formulae the discount rate is the risk-free interest rate because we try to separate the time value of money and the risk factor. The risk of the project, reflected in σ (NPV), is considered in conjunction with NPV computed with the risk-free discount rate. If NPV is computed using a risk-adjusted discount rate and then if this is viewed along with σ (NPV), the risk factor would be counted twice.

Example A project involving an outlay of ₹10,000 has the following benefits associated with it:

Year 1		*Year 2*		*Year 3*	
Net cash flow	*Probability*	*Net cash flow*	*Probability*	*Net cash flow*	*Probability*
₹3,000	0.3	₹2,000	0.2	₹3,000	0.3
5,000	0.4	4,000	0.6	5,000	0.4
7,000	0.3	6,000	0.2	7,000	0.3

The cash flows of different years are uncorrelated. Calculate $\overline{\text{NPV}}$ and σ (NPV), assuming that i = 6 percent.

$$\overline{\text{NPV}} = \sum_{t=1}^{3} \frac{\overline{A}_t}{(1+i)^t} - I$$

[2] In Eqs (11.3) and (11.4) we have assumed that the initial investment is known with certainty. The formula can, however, be easily modified to consider the variability of I.

$$= \frac{5,000}{(1.06)} + \frac{4,000}{(1.06)^2} + \frac{5,000}{(1.06)^3} - 10,000 = ₹2,475$$

$$\sigma(\text{NPV}) = \left[\sum \frac{\sigma_t^2}{(1+i)^{2t}}\right]^{1/2}$$

$$= \left[\frac{2,400,000}{(1.06)^2} + \frac{1,600,000}{(1.06)^4} + \frac{2,400,000}{(1.06)^6}\right]^{1/2} = ₹2,258$$

Perfectly Correlated Cash Flows If cash flows are perfectly correlated, the behaviour of cash flows in all periods is alike. This means that if the actual cash flow in one year is α standard deviations to the left of its expected value, cash flows in other years will also be α standard deviations to the left of their respective expected values. Put in other words, cash flows of all years are linearly related to one another. The expected value and the standard deviation of net present value, when cash flows are perfectly correlated, are as follows:

$$\overline{\text{NPV}} = \sum_{t=1}^{n} \frac{\overline{A}_t}{(1+i)^t} - I \quad (11.5)$$

$$\sigma(\text{NPV}) = \sum_{t=1}^{n} \frac{\sigma_t}{(1+i)^t} \quad (11.6)$$

Example An investment project involves a current outlay of ₹10,000. The mean and standard deviation of cash flows, which are perfectly correlated, are as follows:

Year	$\overline{A}_t$	σ_t
1	₹5,000	1,500
2	3,000	1,000
3	4,000	2,000
4	3,000	1,200

Calculate $\overline{\text{NPV}}$ and σ (NPV), assuming a risk-free interest rate of 6 percent.

$$\overline{\text{NPV}} = \sum_{t=1}^{4} \frac{\overline{A}_t}{(1+i)^t} - I$$

$$= \frac{5,000}{(1.06)} + \frac{3,000}{(1.06)^2} + \frac{4,000}{(1.06)^3} + \frac{3,000}{(1.06)^4} - 10,000$$

$$= ₹3,121$$

$$\sigma(\text{NPV}) = \sum_{t=1}^{4} \frac{\sigma_t}{(1+i)^t}$$

$$= \frac{1,500}{(1.06)} + \frac{1,000}{(1.06)^2} + \frac{2,000}{(1.06)^3} + \frac{1,200}{(1.06)^4} = ₹4,935$$

11.6 SIMULATION ANALYSIS

Sensitivity analysis indicates the sensitivity of the criterion of merit (NPV, IRR, or any other) to variations in basic factors and provides information of the following type: If the quantity produced and sold decreases by 1 percent, other things being equal, the NPV falls by 6 percent. Such information, though useful, may not be adequate for decision making. The decision maker would also like to know the likelihood of such occurrences. This information can be generated by simulation analysis which may be used for developing the probability profile of a criterion of merit by randomly combining values of variables which have a bearing on the chosen criterion.

Procedure The steps involved in simulation analysis are as follows:

1. Model the project. The model of the project shows how the net present value is related to the parameters and the exogenous variables. (Parameters are input variables specified by the decision maker and held constant over all simulation runs. Exogenous variables are input variables which are stochastic in nature and outside the control of the decision maker.)
2. Specify the values of parameters and the probability distributions of the exogenous variables.
3. Select a value, at random, from the probability distributions of each of the exogenous variables.
4. Determine the net present value corresponding to the randomly generated values of exogenous variables and pre-specified parameter values.
5. Repeat steps (3) and (4) a number of times to get a large number of simulated net present values.
6. Plot the frequency distribution of the net present value.

Illustration In real life situations, simulation is done only on the computer because of the computational tedium involved. However, to give you a flavour of what goes on in simulation, we will work with a simple example where simulation has been done manually.

Zenith Chemicals is evaluating an investment project whose net present value has been modelled as follows:

$$\text{NPV} = \sum_{t=1}^{n} \frac{\text{Annual Cash Flow}}{(1 + \text{Risk-Free Rate})^t} - \text{Initial Investment} \tag{11.7}$$

In the NPV model embodied in Eq. (11.7), the risk-free rate and the initial investment are parameters with the following values: risk-free rate = 10 percent and initial investment = ₹13,000. The annual cash flow and the project life (n) are stochastic exogenous variables with the following distributions:

Annual Cash Flow		*Project Life*	
Value	*Probability*	*Value*	*Probability*
₹1,000	0.02	3 years	0.05
1,500	0.03	4	0.10
2,000	0.15	5	0.30
2,500	0.15	6	0.25
3,000	0.30	7	0.15
3,500	0.20	8	0.10
4,000	0.15	9	0.03
		10	0.02

The firm wants to perform 10 manual simulation runs for this project. To perform the simulation runs, we have to generate values, at random, for the two exogenous variables: annual cash flow and project life. For this purpose, we have to (i) set up the correspondence between the values of exogenous variables and random numbers, and (ii) choose some random number generating device. Exhibit 11.8 shows the correspondence between various variables and two digit random numbers. Exhibit 11.9 presents a table of random digits that will be used for obtaining two digit random numbers.[3]

Now we are ready for simulation. In order to obtain random numbers from Exhibit 11.9 we may begin anywhere at random in the table and read any pair of adjacent columns (since we are interested in a two-digit random number) and read column-wise or row-wise.

For our example, let us use the first two columns of Exhibit 11.9. Starting from the top, we will read down the column. For the first simulation run we need two two-digit random numbers, one for the annual cash flow and the other for the project life. These numbers are 53 and 97 and the corresponding values for annual cash flow and project life are ₹3,000 and 9 years respectively. We go further in this manner. Exhibit 11.10 shows the random numbers so obtained and the results of simulation.

Exhibit 11.8 ***Correspondence between Values of Exogenous Variables and Two Digit Random Numbers***

Annual Cash Flow				*Project Life*			
Value	*Probability*	*Cumulative probability*	*Two digit random numbers*	*Value*	*Probability*	*Cumulative probability*	*Two digit random numbers*
₹				*Years*			
1,000	0.02	0.02	00 to 01	3	0.05	0.05	00 to 04
1,500	0.03	0.05	02 to 04	4	0.10	0.15	05 to 14
2,000	0.15	0.20	05 to 19	5	0.30	0.45	15 to 44
2,500	0.15	0.35	20 to 34	6	0.25	0.70	45 to 69
3,000	0.30	0.65	35 to 64	7	0.15	0.85	70 to 84
3,500	0.20	0.85	65 to 84	8	0.10	0.95	85 to 94
4,000	0.15	1.00	86 to 99	9	0.03	0.98	95 to 97
				10	0.02	1.00	98 to 99

[3] Extracted from Rand Corporation, *A Million Random Digits with 100,000 Normal Deviates*, Glencoe, Illinois: The Free Press.

Exhibit 11.9 ***Random Numbers***

53479	81115	98036	12217	59526
97344	70328	58116	91964	26240
66023	38277	74523	71118	84892
99776	75723	03172	43112	83086
30176	48979	92153	38416	42436
81874	83339	14988	99937	13213
19839	90630	71863	95053	55532
09337	33435	53869	52769	18801
31151	58925	40823	41330	21093
67619	52515	03037	81699	17106

Exhibit 11.10 ***Simulation Results***

	Annual Cash Flow		*Project Life*		
Run	*Random Number*	*Corresponding Value of Annual Cash Flow*	*Random Number*	*Corresponding Value of Project Life*	*Net Present Value*
1	53	3,000	97	9	4277
2	66	3,500	99	10	8506
3	30	2,500	81	7	(829)
4	19	2,000	09	4	(7660)
5	31	2,500	67	6	(2112)
6	81	3,500	70	7	4039
7	38	3,000	75	7	1605
8	48	3,000	83	7	1605
9	90	4,000	33	5	2163
10	58	3,000	52	6	66

Obtaining Probability Distributions of Basic Variables Defining the probability distributions of basic variables is an important step in simulation. In defining these distributions it must be borne in mind that often it is impossible to find the true distributions. The distributions that are defined in practice are based on the judgment of experts. Great care should be exercised in translating the judgment of experts into probability distributions.

Two approaches may be used for obtaining probability distributions. These may be called the *'portrait'* approach and the *'building block'* approach.

The portrait approach is similar to the portrait method used for identifying suspects. According to this approach a standard probability distribution (normal, beta, chi-square, poisson, uniform, exponential, or any other) is drawn up, usually by a statistician, on the basis of the judgment expressed by the expert (informant). This is shown to the expert for his comments. The expert may suggest changes if the distribution does not conform with his judgment. For example, he may suggest that the probabilities at the tails should be greater or the probability of the modal value should be higher. The statistician modifies the earlier distribution to incorporate the changes suggested by the expert till the latter is satisfied that the probability distribution represents his judgment well.

This method suffers from a major limitation. The expert may accept a smooth distribution because he may be beguiled by the appearance of smooth curves and charmed by complicated formulae.

In the second approach, the 'building block' approach, the probability distribution is defined by the expert. He attempts to quantify his judgment by a procedure which is as follows: (i) he chooses the range encompassing possible values; (ii) he divides the range into intervals which he thinks have different probabilities associated with them; (iii) he assigns probabilities to these intervals such that $\sum p_i = 1$; (iv) he may divide intervals into sub-intervals if he feels that the probabilities within an interval are different; and (v) he continues this process till he arrives at a distribution which represents his judgment well.

This process often leads to a step rectangular distribution and has the following advantages (i) the expert has complete freedom in expressing his judgment; and (ii) it squares well with the principle of using all available information, no more no less.

Some Commonly Used Distributions Defining probability distributions for the variables which reflect expert judgment is a very critical element of risk analysis. It is also regarded as one of the most troublesome aspects of risk analysis. In this context we may ask, how useful are certain distributions in reflecting expert judgments? To answer this question, we will look at the following distributions and consider their utility:

- Uniform distribution
- Triangular distribution
- Step rectangular distribution
- Normal distribution

These distributions are shown graphically in Exhibit 11.11.

Uniform Distribution The uniform distribution makes sense when the expert has an idea about what the range within which a variable is likely to fall, but is unable to differentiate between values within this range. Its practical appeal lies in its simplicity: you need to know just two parameters, viz., the minimum and maximum values, to define the uniform distribution. The mean of this distribution is simply the arithmetic average of the minimum and maximum values.

Triangular Distribution Perhaps the most popular distribution used in practice, the triangular distribution is intuitively very appealing. It is described by three parameters, the minimum, maximum, and most likely value — the mean value of a triangular distribution is the arithmetic average of these three numbers. By adjusting the parameter values, the triangular distribution can be used to represent both symmetric and skewed distributions.

Step Rectangular Distribution A commonly used distribution in practice, the step rectangular distribution may be viewed as a refinement over the triangular distribution. It enables the expert to divide the range of possible values into a few intervals and assign different probabilities to these intervals.

Normal Distribution This is a very important theoretical distribution. However, it is of limited use in risk analysis wherein the variations that are sought to be captured are caused neither by statistical errors nor random disturbances.

Problem of Correlation We considered an example in which it was assumed that the probability distributions of various factors affecting the NPV were independent. In practice, correlations may exist among the distribution of several factors. For example, the number of units sold may be correlated with the price per unit.

When such a dependency exists the factors which are correlated should be considered together. For this purpose, the joint probability distribution of correlated factors has to be developed. This adds immensely to the problem of estimation.

Exhibit 11.11 ***Some Probability Distributions***

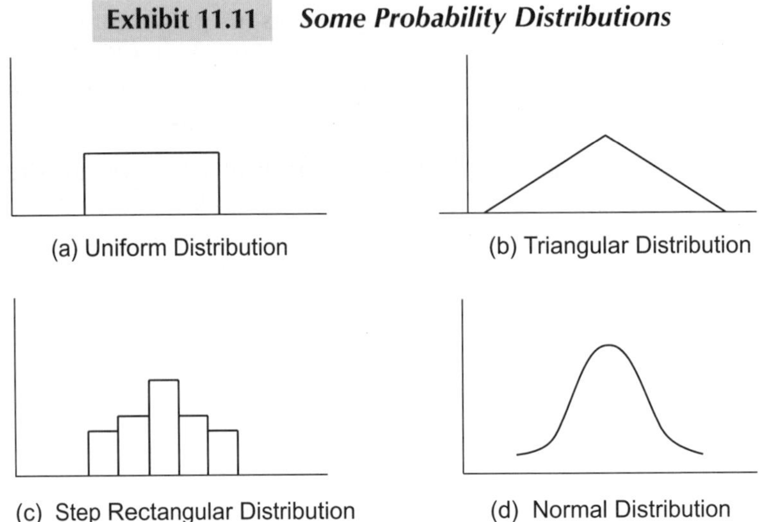

In this context we must consider the choice relating to the level of disaggregation. The nature of this choice may be illustrated with an example. In an investment project the cost of production may be considered at different levels of details as shown in Exhibit 11.12. Now the problem is, to which level of detail should we go? Should we define the probability distribution of cost of production without explicitly considering the probability distribution of various elements like cost of raw materials, cost of fuels and utilities, cost of manpower? Or, should we consider explicitly the distributions of these elements? Should we go further and consider explicitly the distributions of sub-elements like cost of imported raw materials, so on and so forth?

Ideally, the greater the degree of disaggregation, the better it is because it contributes to clarity of judgement. However disaggregated analysis calls for considering correlations explicitly, which is often a difficult task. By limiting the degree of disaggregation we consider correlations implicitly. If we choose to define the probability distribution of cost of production, without doing disaggregated analysis, we do not have to consider explicitly the correlations between, say, cost of raw material and cost of fuel. The distribution of cost of production would implicitly consider this.

The choice of the level of aggregation or disaggregation would be finally based on the trade-off between the advantages of clarity of judgement and the complexities of disaggregated analysis. Since the influence of correlations is more significant than that of the shape of any particular distribution, it may be preferable to limit disaggregation.

Simulation Analysis and Crystal Ball

Crystal Ball, a product of Decisioneering, Inc*. is an "add-in" software package that enables you to build simulation models within Microsoft Excel spreadsheet software.

Excel models are *deterministic*, meaning that the inputs are fixed (one value to a cell). Hence you can get only one solution at a time. If you want to look at alternative results, you have to manually change the inputs in the model. Crystal Ball allows you to dynamically change the inputs to the model in such a manner that the many solutions to the model are calculated and stored for further analysis.

The conversion of a deterministic spreadsheet model into a dynamic simulation model involves three steps:

1. Identify the inputs (such as selling price, quantity, and so on) to the model that are subject to uncertainty and define the distribution for each of them. In Crystal Ball, these uncertain inputs are referred to as *assumptions*.
2. Select a value of each of the *assumptions* in the model, calculate the value of each of the output variables (referred to as *forecast* variables in Crystal Ball), and store the results.
3. Repeat this process for a number of iterations.

The stored values of the forecast variables (such as NPV or IRR) may be summarised using descriptive statistics such as the mean, median, and standard deviation or converted into a histogram or frequency distribution.

*http://www.crystalball.com/index.html

Issues in Applying Simulation Some of the important issues in the application of simulation are:

- What should the output be?
- Is project variability enough?
- How should the extreme values be used?
- How should the results of simulation be used?

What Should the Output Be? Typically the output of simulation is the probability distribution of internal rate of return or net present value. The problem with the probability distribution of internal rate of return is that it only shows what the risk will be in the long run. It does not reflect the risk borne by investors in the capital market, which is captured by the distributions of successive one-period rates of return investors will earn, when investment is made in the project.

Is the probability distribution of net present value a better alternative? Here there is a problem about the discount rate to be used in the net present value calculation. If the cost of capital (which reflects the risk factor) is used as the discount rate, any further risk adjustment would mean double counting. If the risk-free rate of interest is used as the discount rate, then the underlying assumption is that the uncertainty about the project's cash flows would be resolved almost immediately. Since uncertainty is not resolved in this manner, the meaning of the simulated probability distribution is somewhat unclear.

In view of the problems associated with the distributions of internal rate of return and net present value, it perhaps makes sense to look at the distributions of cash flows (or earnings). If a project has an expected economic life of eight years, the project evaluator may examine eight separate cash flow distributions. These distributions may be scaled by their respective expected values for comparisons to be made between the projects.

Exhibit 11.12 ***Levels of Detail***

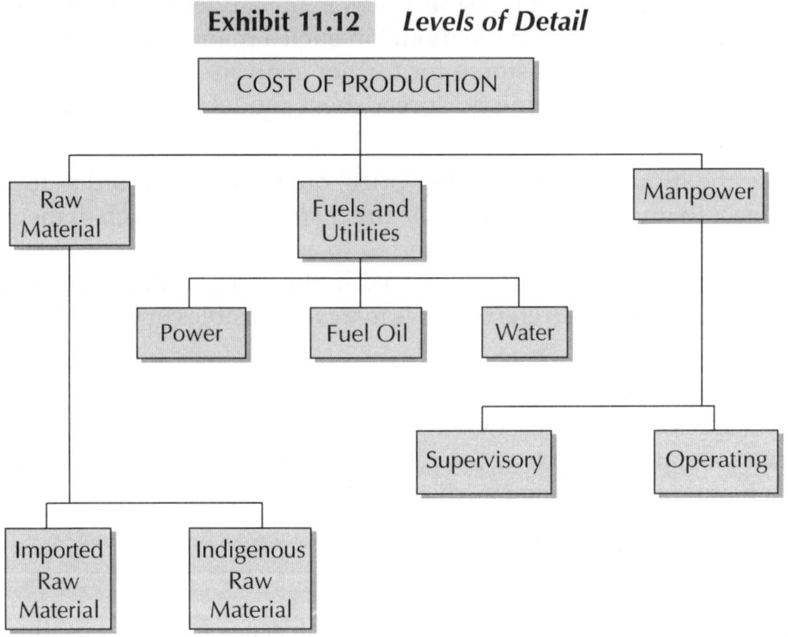

Is Project Variability Enough? According to the Capital Asset Pricing Model what matters is the systematic (non-diversifiable) risk of an investment and not its unsystematic (diversifiable) risk. Simulation can provide information on the total risk (which consists of systematic risk plus unsystematic risk), but it cannot separately show the systematic risk. Hence, a user of simulation must regard total risk as a proxy for systematic risk. Even though this is a strong assumption, it may not be unreasonable because empirical studies show a fairly reliable association between systematic risk and various measures of earnings volatility. Further, systematic risk tends to be proportional to total risk for firms operating in a single homogeneous industry.

How Should the Extreme Values be Interpreted? The proponents of simulation argue that, *inter alia,* it helps in answering questions like "What is the probability that NPV would be less than zero?" or "What is the probability that IRR would be less than x percent?" These questions can be answered satisfactorily when the "tails" of the stimulated distribution are reliable. However, the tails tend to be the least reliable part of the simulated distribution.

There is yet another, and perhaps more fundamental, problem in interpreting the tails of the simulated distribution. When a simulation model is constructed, it is assumed that the management will follow a strategy based on general business conditions it expects to encounter. Hence, the model cranks out numbers on the basis of "business-as-usual" strategy even when it runs into surprises. In real life situations, however, managements modify their strategies to cope with surprises. When adverse developments occur, new actions are likely to be initiated. In extreme cases, the project may be abandoned to save future losses. Thus, the tails of the simulated distribution, which are important elements in risk assessment, are likely to reflect unrealistic management strategies.

How Should the Results of Simulation be Used? Hertz[4] advocated simulation on the grounds that a probability distribution of the criterion of merit (NPV or IRR) leads to better decisions. This implies that a decision maker is able to reach a decision on the basis of the probability distribution. Not many executives, however, may be capable of reviewing the probability distribution of the project's NPV or IRR and deciding confidently whether the project is worthwhile or not. (Of course, there will be some projects which will be sure winners and some projects which will be losers - in these cases, however, simulation itself may be redundant). A better approach to use the results of simulation may call for a two-stage decision making process:

Stage 1 Review the probability distributions of the project (i.e., probability distributions of cash flows, IRR. etc.) along with other factors and make an assessment.

Stage 2 Define the appropriate discount rate to be employed on the basis of the business risk assessment done in stage 1.

World Bank's Experience

It may be instructive here to review the experience of World Bank. The following are its summary remarks on simulation.

1. Simulation is a powerful technique which permits use of a great deal of information which would otherwise be lost.
2. It is a highly efficient medium of communication.
3. It is not a technique which replaces skilled judgment. On the contrary, it often requires the use of far more judgment than the traditional analysis.
4. Despite the method's value, the treatment of correlations between variables remains a major problem. It is clear that results can be completely misleading if correlations are not handled properly.

Evaluation An important tool of risk analysis, simulation offers certain advantages:

- Its principal strength lies in its versatility. It can handle problems characterised by (a) numerous exogenous variables following any kind of distribution, and (b) complex

[4] David B.Hertz, "Risk Analysis in Capital Investment," *Harvard Business Review* (Jan-Feb 1964).

interrelationships among parameters, exogenous variables, and endogenous variables. Such problems often defy the capabilities of analytical methods.

- It compels the decision maker to explicitly consider the interdependencies and uncertainties characterising the project.

Simulation, however, is a controversial tool which suffers from several shortcomings.

- It is difficult to model the project and specify the probability distributions of exogenous variables.
- Simulation is inherently imprecise. It provides a rough approximation of the probability distribution of net present value (or any other criterion of merit). Due to its imprecision, the simulated probability distribution may be misleading when a tail of the distribution is critical.
- A realistic simulation model, likely to be complex, would most probably be constructed by a management scientist, not the decision maker. The decision maker, lacking understanding of the model, may not use it.
- To determine the net present value in a simulation run the risk-free discount rate is used. This is done to avoid prejudging risk which is supposed to be reflected in the dispersion of the distribution of net present value. Thus the measure of net present value takes a meaning, very different from its usual one, that is difficult to interpret.

11.7 DECISION TREE ANALYSIS

So far we assumed that the investment project will be implemented according to a set plan. In reality, firms have some flexibility in the way they proceed with most investment projects, as the example in the following paragraphs demonstrates. When such flexibility exists, decision tree analysis is a useful tool in valuing project flexibility. Another tool for valuing flexibility in projects is the option pricing model. We will discuss decision tree analysis here and option pricing model in Chapter 16.

The scientists at Pharmalab have come up with a new molecule. The firm is ready for pilot production which is estimated to cost ₹8 million and take one year. If the results of pilot production are encouraging the next step would be to test market the product. This will cost ₹3 million and take two months. Based on the outcome of the test marketing, a manufacturing decision may be taken. The firm may, however, skip the test marketing phase and take a decision whether it should manufacture the product or not. If the firm decides to manufacture the product commercially it is confronted with two options: a small plant or a large plant. This decision hinges mainly on the size of the market. While the level of demand in the short run may be gauged by the results of the test market, the demand in the long run would depend on how satisfied the initial users are.

If the firm builds a large plant initially it can cater to the needs of the market when the demand growth is favourable. However, if the demand turns out to be weak, the plant would operate at a low level of capacity utilisation. If the firm builds a small plant, to begin with, it need not worry about a weak market and the consequent low level capacity utilisation.

However, if the market turns out to be strong it will have to build another plant soon (and thereby incur a higher total outlay) in order to save itself from competitive encroachment.

To analyse situations of this kind where sequential decision making in the face of risk is involved, decision tree analysis is a useful tool.

Steps in Decision Tree Analysis The key steps in decision tree analysis are:

1. Identifying the problem and alternatives
2. Delineating the decision tree
3. Specifying probabilities and monetary outcomes
4. Evaluating various decision alternatives

Identifying the Problem and Alternatives To understand the problem and develop alternatives, information from different sources – marketing research, engineering studies, economic forecasting, financial analysis, etc. – has to be tapped. Imaginative effort must be made to identify the nature of alternatives that may arise as the decision situation unfolds itself and assess the kinds of uncertainties that lie ahead with respect to market size, market share, prices, cost structure, availability of raw material and power, technological changes, competitive action, and governmental regulation.

Recognising that risk and uncertainty are inherent characteristics of investment projects, persons involved in analysing the situation must be encouraged to express freely their doubts, uncertainties, and reservations and motivated to suggest contingency plans and identify promising opportunities in the emerging environment.

Delineating the Decision Tree The decision tree, exhibiting the anatomy of the decision situation, shows:

- The decision points (also called decision forks) and the alternative options available for experimentation and action at these decision points.
- The chance points (also called chance forks) where outcomes are dependent on a chance process and the likely outcomes at these points.

The decision tree reflects in a diagrammatic form the nature of the decision situation in terms of alternative courses of action and chance outcomes which have been identified in the first step of the analysis.

A decision tree can easily become very complex and cumbersome if an attempt is made to consider the myriad possible future events and decisions. Such a decision tree, however, is not likely to be a very useful tool of analysis. Over-elaborate, it may obfuscate the critical issues. Hence an effort should be made to keep the decision tree somewhat simple so that the decision makers can focus their attention on major future alternatives without being drowned in a mass of trivia. One must remember the advice of Brealey and Myers: "Decision trees are like grapevines; they are productive only if vigorously pruned."[5]

---

[5] R. Brealey and S. Myers, *Principles of Corporate Finance*, New York; McGraw-Hill Company, 1981.

Specifying Probabilities and Monetary Values for Outcomes Once the decision tree is delineated, the following data have to be gathered:

- Probabilities associated with each of the possible outcomes at various chance forks.
- Monetary value of each combination of decision alternative and chance outcome.

The probabilities of various outcomes may sometimes be defined objectively. For example, the probability of a good monsoon may be based on objective, historical data. More often, however, the possible outcomes encountered in real life are such that objective probabilities for them cannot be obtained. How can you, for example, define objectively the probability that a new product like an electric moped will be successful in the market? In such cases, probabilities have to be necessarily defined subjectively. This does not, however, mean that they are drawn from a hat. To be useful they have to be based on the experience, judgment, intuition, and understanding of informed and knowledgeable executives. Assessing the cash flows associated with various possible outcomes, too, is a difficult task. Again, the judgment of experts play an important role.

Evaluating the Alternatives Once the decision tree is delineated and data about probabilities and monetary values gathered, decision alternatives may be evaluated as follows:

1. Start at the right-hand end of the tree and calculate the expected monetary value at various chance points that come first as you proceed leftward.
2. Given the expected monetary values of chance points in step 1, evaluate the alternatives at the final stage decision points in terms of their expected monetary values.
3. At each of the final stage decision points, select the alternative which has the highest expected monetary value and truncate the other alternatives. Each decision point is assigned a value equal to the expected monetary value of the alternative selected at that decision point.
4. Proceed backward (leftward) in the same manner, calculating the expected monetary value at chance points, selecting the decision alternative which has the highest expected monetary value at various decision points, truncating inferior decision alternatives, and assigning values to decision points, till the first decision point is reached.

A Simple Example The scientists at Spectrum have come up with an electric moped. The firm is ready for pilot production and test marketing. This will cost ₹20 million and take six months. Management believes that there is 70 percent chance that the pilot production and test marketing will be successful. In case of success, Spectrum can build a plant costing ₹150 million. The plant will generate an annual cash inflow of ₹30 million for 20 years if the demand is high or an annual cash inflow of ₹20 million if the demand is low. High demand has a probability of 0.6; low demand has a probability of 0.4. What is the optimal course of action using decision tree analysis. Assume a discount rate of 12 percent.

The decision tree for the electric moped project of Spectrum is shown in Exhibit 11.13.

Exhibit 11.13 ***Decision Tree***

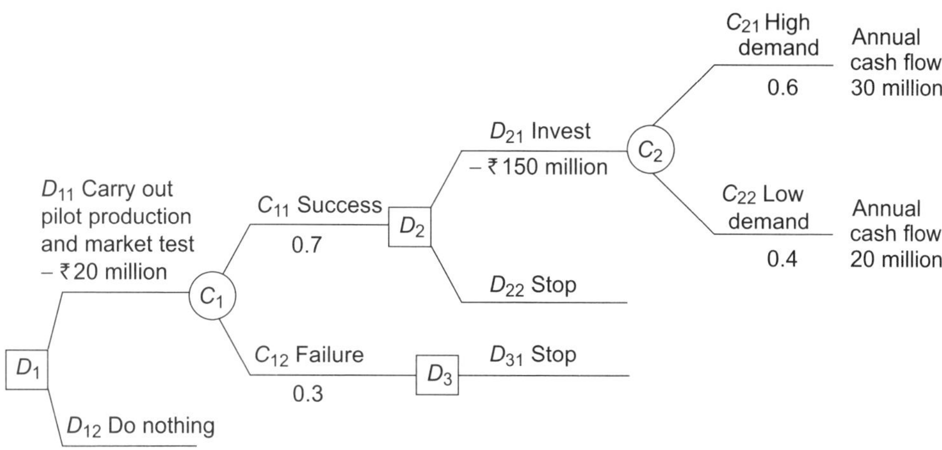

The optimal course of action is determined as follows:

1. Start at the right-hand end of the tree and calculate the expected monetary value (EMV) at chance point C_2 that comes first as you proceed leftward.

$$\text{EMV } (C_2) = 0.6\ [30 \times \text{PVIFA } (20, 12\%)] + 0.4\ [20 \times \text{PVIFA } (20, 12\%]$$
$$= ₹194.2 \text{ million}$$

2. Evaluate the EMV of the decision alternatives at D_2 the last stage decision point.

Alternative	*EMV*
D_{21} (Invest ₹150 million)	₹44.2 million
D_{22} (Stop)	0

3. Select D_{21} and truncate D_{22} as EMV (D_{21}) > EMV (D_{22})
4. Calculate the EMV at chance point C_1 that comes next as we roll backwards.

$$\text{EMV } (C_1) = 0.7\ [44.2] + 0.3\ [0]$$
$$= ₹30.9 \text{ million}$$

5. Evaluate the EMV of the decision alternatives at D_1 the first stage decision point

Alternative	*EMV*
D_{11} (Carryout pilot production and market test at a cost of ₹20 million)	₹10.9 million
D_{12} (Do nothing)	0

Based on the above evaluation, we find that the optimal decision strategy is as follows: Choose D_{11} (carry out pilot production and market test) at the decision point D_1 and wait for the outcome at the chance point C_1. If the outcome at C_1 is C_{11} (success), invest ₹150 million, if the outcome at C_1 is C_{12} (failure) stop.

A Tougher Example[6] Airways Limited has been set up to run an air taxi service in western India. The company is debating whether it should buy a turboprop aircraft or a piston engine aircraft. The turboprop aircraft costs 4000 and has a larger capacity. It will serve if the demand turns out to be high. The piston engine aircraft costs 1800 and has a smaller capacity. It will serve if the demand is low, but it will not suffice if the demand is high.

The company believes that the chances of demand being high and low in year 1 are 0.6 and 0.4. If the demand is high in year 1, there is an 80 percent chance that it will be high in subsequent years (year 2 onward) and a 20 percent chance that it will be low in subsequent years.

The technical director of Airways Limited thinks that if the company buys a piston engine aircraft now and the demand turns out to be high, the company can buy a second-hand piston engine aircraft for 1400 at the end of year 1. This would double its capacity and enable it to cope reasonably well with high demand from year 2 onwards.

The payoffs and the probabilities associated with high and low demand for various decision alternatives are shown in Exhibit 11.14. The payoffs shown for year 1 are the payoffs occurring at the end of year 1 and the payoffs shown for year 2 are the payoffs for year 2 and the subsequent years, evaluated as at the end of year 2, using a discount rate of 12 percent which is the weighted average cost of capital for Airways Limited.

If Airways Limited buys the turboprop aircraft, there are no further decisions to be made. So, the NPV of the turboprop aircraft can be calculated by simply discounting the expected cash flows:

$$\text{NPV} = -4000 + \frac{0.6\,(1000) + 0.4\,(200)}{(1.12)} + \frac{0.6\,[0.8\,(7000) + 0.2\,(1000) + 0.4\,[0.4\,(7000) + 0.6\,(600)]}{(1.12)^2}$$

$$= 389$$

If Airways Limited buys the piston engine aircraft and the demand in year 1 turns out to be high, a further decision has to be made with respect to capacity expansion. To evaluate the piston engine aircraft, proceed as follows:

First, calculate the NPV of the two options viz., 'expand' and 'do no expand' at decision point D_2:

$$\text{Expand: NPV} = \frac{0.8\,(6000) + 0.2\,(600)}{1.12} - 1400 = 2993$$

$$\text{Do not expand: NPV} = \frac{0.8\,(2500) + 0.2\,(800)}{1.12} = 1929$$

Second, truncate the 'do not expand' option as it is inferior to the 'expand' option. This means that the NPV at decision point D_2 will be 2923.

Third, calculate the NPV of the piston engine aircraft option.

---

[6] Adapted from Brealey and Myers *op. cit.*

$$\text{NPV} = -1800 + \frac{0.6\,(500 + 2923) + 0.4\,(300)}{(1.12)} + \frac{0.4\,[0.2\,(2500) + 0.8\,(800)]}{(1.12)^2}$$

$$= 505$$

Exhibit 11.14 ***Decision Tree***

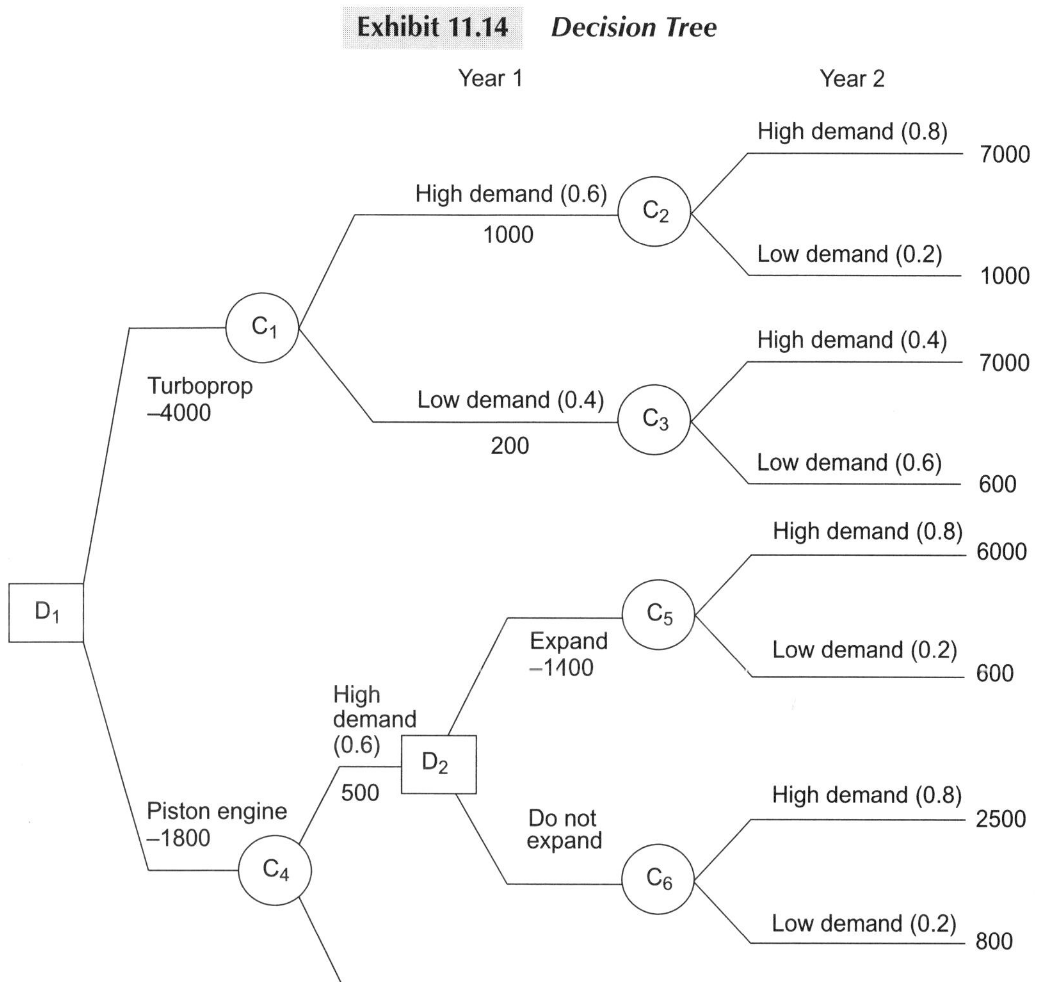

Since the NPV of the piston engine aircraft (505) is greater than the NPV of the turboprop aircraft (389), the former is a better bet. So the recommended strategy for Airways Limited is to invest in the piston engine aircraft at decision point D_1 and, if the demand in year 1 turns out to be high, expand capacity by buying another piston engine aircraft:

Option to Expand Note that if Airways Limited does not have the option of expanding capacity at the end of year 1, the NPV of the piston engine aircraft option would be:

$$NPV = -1800 + \frac{0.6\,(500) + 0.4\,(300)}{(1.12)} + \frac{0.6\,[0.8\,(2500) + 0.2\,(800)] + 0.4\,[0.2\,(2500) + 0.8\,(800)]}{(1.12)^2}$$

$$= -28$$

Thus, the *option to expand* has a value of: 505 – (– 28) = 533.

Option to Abandon So far we assumed that Airways Limited will continue operations irrespective of the state of demand. Let us now introduce the possibility of abandoning the operation and disposing off the aircraft at the end of year 1, should it be profitable to do so. Suppose after 1 year of use the turboprop aircraft can be sold for 3600 and the piston-engine aircraft for 1400.

If the demand in year 1 turns out to be low, the payoffs for 'continuation' and 'abandonment' as at the end of year 1 are as follows.

Turboprop Aircraft		**Piston Engine Aircraft**	
Continuation	0.4 (7000) + 0.6(600)	Continuation:	0.2(2500) + 0.8(800)
	= 3160/(1.12) = 2821		= 1140/(1.12) = 1018
Abandonment:	3600	Abandonment:	1400

Thus in both the cases it makes sense to sell off the aircraft after year 1, if the demand in year 1 turns out to be low.

The revised decision tree, taking into account the abandonment options, is shown in Exhibit 11.15.

Given the decision tree with abandonment possibilities, let us calculate the NPV of the turboprop aircraft and the piston engine aircraft.

NPV (Turboprop)

$$= -4000 + \frac{0.6\,[1000 + \{0.8\,(7000) + 0.2\,(1000)\}\,/\,(1.12)] + 0.4\,(200 + 3600)}{(1.12)}$$

$$= 667$$

NPV (Piston engine)

$$= -1800 + \frac{0.6\,(500 + 2993) + 0.4\,(300 + 1400)}{(1.12)}$$

$$= 678$$

Exhibit 11.15 ***Decision Tree***

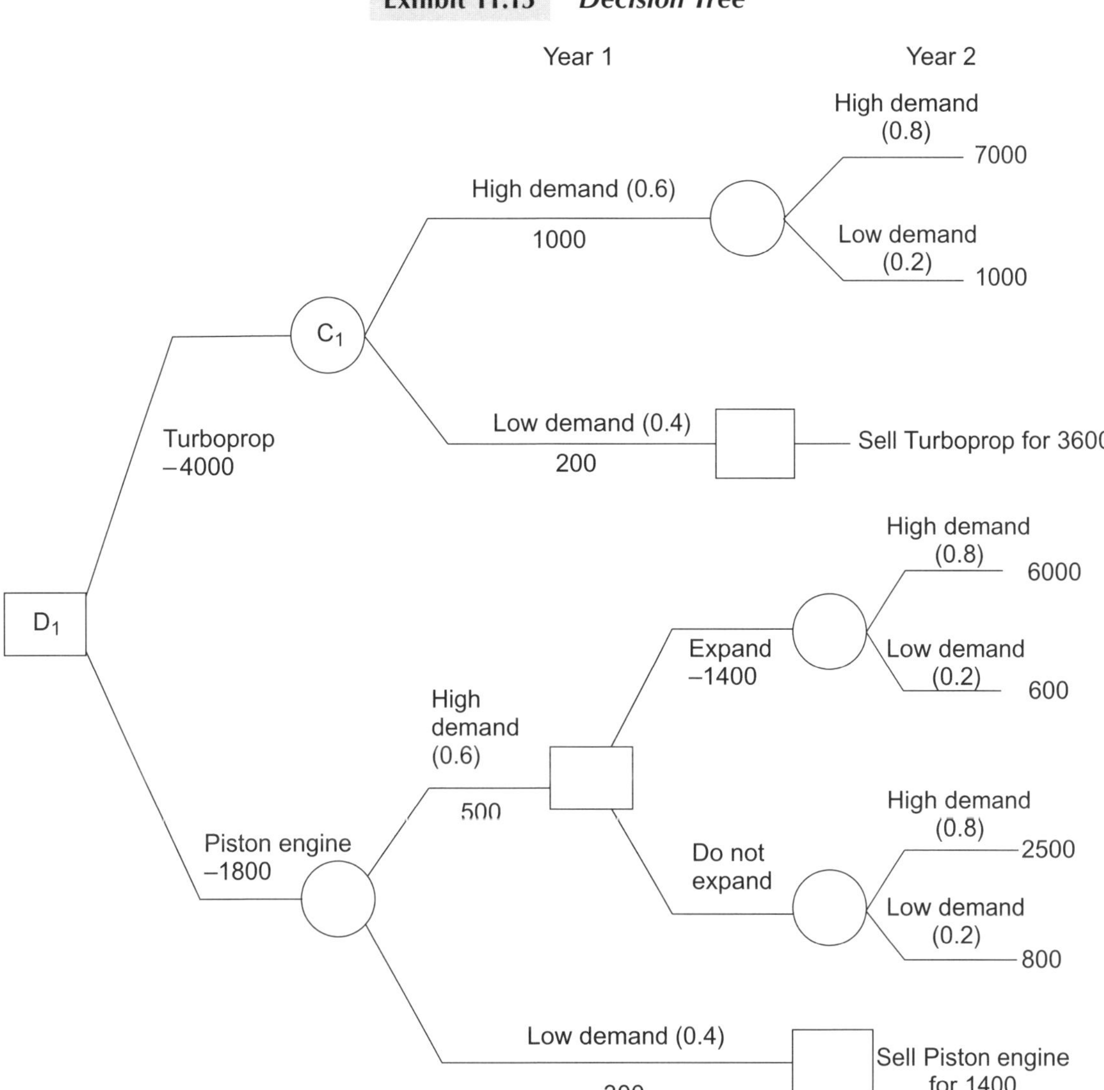

Note that the possibility of abandonment increases the NPV of the turboprop aircraft from 389 to 667. This means that the value of the option to abandon is:

= NPV with abandonment – NPV without abandonment

Value of abandonment option = 667 – 389 = 278

For the piston engine aircraft the possibility of abandonment increases the NPV from 505 to 678. Hence the value of the *abandonment option* is 173.

Evaluation Decision trees are useful for analysing a project that has the following characteristics:

- Decisions on continuing the project are made in well-defined stages.

- The outcomes at each stage fall into a few broad classes.
- The probabilities and the cash flows associated with various outcomes can be specified at the beginning of the project. This means that the firm has experience of doing similar projects in the past.

Obviously, decision tree analysis requires enormous information before it can be applied. In an oil drilling project perhaps the required information may be available. However, it may be much more difficult to apply decision tree analysis to a project where the product or service is new and the firm has very little information on how the market will respond to it. Decision trees are also not easy to apply when investments are gradually made over a period of time rather than in a few well-defined stages.

11.8 MANAGING RISK

Managers are not merely content with measuring risk. They want to explore ways and means of mitigating risk. Some of the ways of doing this are discussed below. These risk reduction strategies have a cost associated with them and whether they are profitable in a given situation will depend on circumstances.

Fixed and Variable Costs A common way to modify the risk of an investment is to change the proportion of fixed and variable costs. For example, in the early 1980s Ford Motor Company restructured its operations. Essentially it decided to buy most of its components from outside suppliers instead of manufacturing them in-house. This decreased its fixed costs and increased its variable costs. The net effect was that its break-even level declined.

Pricing Strategy Pricing strategy is used by many firms to manage risk. A lower price increases potential demand, but also raises the break-even level. This is the reason why publishers first bring out a hard-cover edition at a higher price and then introduce a soft-cover edition at a lower price.

Sequential Investment If you are not sure about the market response to your product or service, you may start small and later expand as the market grows. This strategy may entail higher capital cost per unit because capacity is created in stages. However, it reduces risk exposure. You can employ decision tree analysis to hammer out the optimal sequence of investment in face of risk.

Improving Information An African proverb says *Don't test the depth of a river with both feet.* You may like to gather more information about the market and technology before taking the plunge. Additional study often improves the quality of forecasts but involves direct costs (the cost of the study) as well as opportunity costs of delayed action. You have to weigh the costs and benefits of further study and decide how much of additional information should be gathered.

Financial Leverage We discussed how reducing the proportion of fixed operating costs lowers risk. Likewise reducing the dependence on debt lowers risk. Remember that debt entails a definite contractual commitment whereas equity carries no fixed burden. Hence if the operating risk of the project is high, it makes sense to go for a low level of financial leverage.

Insurance You can get an insurance cover against a variety of risks like physical damage, theft, loss of key person, and so on. Insurance is a pure antidote for such risks. Of course to protect yourself against such risks you have to pay insurance premium.

Long-term Arrangements One way to mitigate risk is to enter into long-term arrangements with suppliers, employees, lenders, and customers. A long-term contract with suppliers ensures availability of inputs at a predictable price; a long-term wage contract with employees removes uncertainty about employee cost; a long term debt contract reduces risk about interest rate; finally, a long-term sales contract with customers eliminates revenue risk.

Often, long-term contracts are indexed. This means that the prices are periodically adjusted in line with the movement of some index which essentially reflects inflation. For example, a supply contract may have an escalator clause that links the supply price to some price index like the Wholesale Price Index. Price indexing protects both the buyer and seller against inflation risk because indexing ensures that the real price (price in terms of purchasing power) is constant.

Strategic Alliance When the resources required for a project or the risks inherent in a project are beyond the capacity of a single company, strategic alliance may be the way out. A strategic alliance, also referred to as a joint venture, represents a partnership between two or more independent companies which join hands to achieve a common purpose. It is usually organised as a newly created company, though the partners may choose any other form of organisation. Typically, the partners partake in the equity of the common enterprise, contribute resources (technology, facilities, distribution networks, brands, key manpower, and so on), and share management and control. The massive resource requirements and huge risks in modern enterprises have compelled many traditional rivals to work together. Competitors are beginning to cooperate leading to a phenomenon called as 'cooptition'.

Derivatives Derivative instruments like options and futures can be used for managing risk. An option gives its owner the right to buy or sell an underlying asset on or before a given date at a predetermined price. An option to buy is a call option. Options give flexibility which is very valuable in volatile markets. For example, a call option embedded in a debt instrument gives the issuing firm the right to prematurely redeem (buy back) the debt instrument at a certain price. Such an option is very valuable when the interest rate falls.

A futures contract is an agreement between two parties to exchange an asset for cash at a predetermined future date for a price that is specified today. Futures contracts eliminate price risk. For example, a refinery may buy an oil futures contract for its oil requirement. Doing so entitles the refinery to get delivery of oil at a specified future date at a price that is fixed today.

11.9 PROJECT SELECTION UNDER RISK

Once information about expected return (measured as net present value, or internal rate of return, or some other criterion of merit) and variability of return (measured in terms of range or standard deviation or some other risk index) has been gathered, the next question is: Should the project be accepted or rejected? There are several ways of incorporating risk in the decision process: judgmental evaluation, payback period requirement, risk profile method, certainty equivalent method, and risk adjusted discount rate method.

Judgmental Evaluation Often, managers look at the risk and return characteristics of a project and decide judgmentally whether the project should be accepted or rejected, without using any formal method for incorporating risk in the decision making process. The decision may be based on the collective view of some group like the capital budgeting committee, or the executive committee, or the board of directors. If judgmental decision making appears highly subjective or haphazard, consider how most of us make important decisions in our personal life. We rarely use formal selection methods or quantitative techniques for choosing a career or a spouse or an employer. Instead, we rely on our judgment.

Payback Period Requirement In many situations companies use NPV or IRR as the principal selection criterion, but apply a payback period requirement to control for risk. Typically, if an investment is considered more risky, a shorter payback period is required even if the NPV is positive or IRR exceeds the hurdle rate. This approach assumes that risk is a function of time.

Ordinarily it is true that the farther a benefit lies in future the more uncertain it is likely to be because economic and competitive conditions tend to change over time. However, risk is influenced by things other than the mere passage of time. Hence the payback period requirement may not be an adequate method for risk adjustment or control.

Risk Adjusted Discount Rate Method The risk adjusted discount rate method calls for adjusting the discount rate to reflect project risk. If the risk of the project is equal to the risk of the existing investment of the firm, the discount rate used is the average cost of capital of the firm; if the risk of the project is greater than the risk of the existing investments of the firm, the discount rate used is higher than the average cost of capital of the firm; if the risk of the project is less than the risk of the existing investments of the firm the discount rate used is less than the average cost of capital of the firm. The risk adjusted discount rate is:

$$r_k = i + n + d_k \tag{11.8}$$

where r_k is the risk-adjusted discount rate for project k, i is the risk-free rate of interest, n is the adjustment for the firm's normal risk, and d_k is the adjustment for the differential risk of project k.

It may be noted that $(i+n)$ measures the firm's cost of capital. d_k may be positive or negative depending on how the risk of the project under consideration compares with the existing risk of the firm.

The adjustment for the differential risk of project k, quite understandably, depends on management's perception of the project risk and management's attitude towards risk (risk-return preference). A large pharmaceutical concern, for example, uses the following risk-adjusted discount rates for various types of investments.

Investment Category	*Risk-adjusted Discount Rate*
Replacement investments	Cost of capital
Expansion investments	Cost of capital + 3%
Investments in related lines	Cost of capital + 5%
Investments in new lines	Cost of capital + 8%

Once the project's risk-adjusted discount rate (r_k) is specified, the project is accepted if its net present value is positive.

$$NPV = \sum_{t=1}^{n} \frac{\overline{A_t}}{(1+r_k)^t} - I \quad (11.9)$$

where NPV is the net present value of project k, $\overline{A_t}$ is the expected cash flow for year t, and r_k is the risk adjusted discount rate for project k.

Example The expected cash flows of a project, which involves an investment outlay of ₹1,000,000, are as follows:

Year	*Cash flow (₹)*
1	₹200,000
2	300,000
3	400,000
4	300,000
5	200,000

The risk-adjusted discount rate for this project is 18 percent. Is the project worthwhile? The net present value of the project, using the risk-adjusted discount rate is:

$$NPV = \frac{200,000}{(1.18)} + \frac{300,000}{(1.18)^2} + \frac{400,000}{(1.18)^3} + \frac{300,000}{(1.18)^4} + \frac{200,000}{(1.18)^5} - 1,000,000 = -₹129,400$$

Since the net present value is negative the project is not worthwhile.

The risk-adjusted discount rate is commonly employed in practice. Firms use different discount rates, presumably related to the risk factor for different types of investment projects. The discount rate is generally low for routine replacement investments, moderate for expansion investments, and high for new investments.

Despite its popularity, the risk-adjusted discount rate method suffers from two serious limitations: (i) It is difficult to estimate d_k consistently – often it is determined in an extremely ad hoc and arbitrary manner. (ii) This method assumes that risk increases with time at a constant rate. This assumption may not be valid.

Certainty Equivalent Method Before describing the certainty equivalent method let us understand the concept of certainty equivalent coefficient. Suppose someone presents you with a lottery the outcome of which has the following probability distribution.

Outcome	*Probability*
₹1,000	0.3
₹5,000	0.7

You are further asked, how much of a certain amount would you accept in lieu of this lottery? Let us say that your reply is: ₹3,000. This amount, ₹3,000, represents the certainty equivalent of the above lottery which has an expected value of ₹3,800 (₹1,000 × 0.3 + ₹5,000 × 0.7) and a given distribution. The factor 3,000/3,800 (= 0.79) is called the certainty equivalent coefficient. It reflects primarily two things: variability of outcomes and your attitude towards risk. Certainty equivalent coefficients transform expected values of uncertain flows into their certainty equivalents.

Under the certainty equivalent method, the net present value is calculated as follows:

$$\text{NPV} = \sum_{t=1}^{n} \frac{\alpha_t \overline{A_t}}{(1+i)^t} - I \tag{11.10}$$

where NPV is the net present value, $\overline{A_t}$ is the expected cash flow for year t, α_t is the certainty equivalent coefficient for the cash flow of year t, i is the risk free interest rate, and I is the initial investment (about which it is assumed that there is no uncertainty).

Example Vazeer Hydraulics Limited is considering an investment proposal involving an outlay of ₹4,500,000. The expected cash flows and certainty equivalent coefficients are:

Year	*Expected cash flow*	*Certainty equivalent coefficient*
1	₹1,000,000	0.90
2	1,500,000	0.85
3	2,000,000	0.82
4	2,500,000	0.78

The risk-free interest rate is 5 percent. Calculate the net present value of the proposal. The net present value is equal to:

$$\frac{1{,}000{,}000\,(0.90)}{(1.05)} + \frac{1{,}500{,}000\,(0.85)}{(1.05)^2} + \frac{2{,}000{,}000\,(0.82)}{(1.05)^3} + \frac{2{,}500{,}000\,(0.78)}{(1.05)^4} - 4{,}500{,}000$$

= ₹534,570

The value of the certainty equivalent coefficient usually ranges between 0.5 and 1. A value of 1 implies that the cash flow is certain or the management is risk neutral. In industrial situations, however, cash flows are generally uncertain and managements usually risk-averse. Hence the certainty equivalent coefficients are typically less than 1. Exhibit 11.16 illustrates typical certainty equivalent coefficients for different types of investments.

Exhibit 11.16 ***Certainty Equivalent Coefficients for Different Types of Investments***

Certainty equivalent coefficients

	Year 1	*Year 2*	*Year 3*	*Year 4*
Replacement investments	0.92	0.87	0.84	0.80
Expansion investments	0.89	0.85	0.80	0.75
New product investments	0.85	0.80	0.74	0.68
Research and development investments	0.75	0.70	0.64	0.58

The certainty equivalent method is conceptually superior to the risk-adjusted discount rate method because it does not assume that risk increases with time at a constant rate. Each year's certainty equivalent coefficient is based on the level of risk characterising its cash flow. Despite its conceptual soundness it is not as popular as the risk-adjusted discount rate method. This is perhaps because it is inconvenient and difficult to specify a series of certainty equivalent coefficients but seemingly simple to adjust the discount rate. Notwithstanding this practical difficulty, the merits of the certainty equivalent method must not be ignored.

11.10 RISK ANALYSIS IN PRACTICE[7]

Several methods to incorporate the risk factor into capital expenditure analysis are used in practice. The most common ones are discussed here.

Conservative Estimation of Revenues In many cases the revenues expected from a project are conservatively estimated to ensure that the viability of the projects is not easily threatened by unfavourable circumstances. The capital budgeting systems often have built-in devices for conservative estimation. This is indicated by the following remarks made by two executives:

> "We ask the project sponsor to estimate revenues conservatively. This checks the optimism common among project sponsors."

> "The capital budgeting committee requires justification for revenue figures given by those who propose capital expenditures. This has a sobering effect on them."

Safety Margin in Cost Figures A margin of safety is generally included in estimating cost figures. This varies between 10 percent and 30 percent of what is deemed as normal cost. The size of the margin depends on what management feels about the likely variation in cost. The following observation suggests this:

> "In estimating the cost of raw material we add about 20 to 25 percent to the current prices as the raw material price is not stable and often we pay a high price to get it. For labour cost we add about 10 to 12 percent as this is the annual increase."

Flexible Investment Yardsticks The cut-off point for an investment varies according to the judgment of management about the riskiness of the project. In one company replacement investments are okayed if the expected post-tax return exceeds 15 percent but new investments are undertaken only if the expected post-tax return is greater than 20 percent. Another company employs a short payback period of three years for new investments. Its decision rule was stated by its financial controller as follows:

> "Our policy is to accept a new project only if it has a payback period of three years. We have never, as far as I know, deviated from this. The use of a short payback period automatically weeds out risky projects."

Acceptable Overall Certainty Index Some companies calculate what may be called the overall certainty index, based on a few crucial factors affecting the success of the project.

---

[7] The discussion in this section is based on a survey conducted by the author which covered 20 firms. The findings of this survey are reported in "Risk analysis in Capital Expenditures," *Indian Management*, October 1975.

The calculation of an overall certainty index may be illustrated by an example drawn from a large engineering concern. The overall index for a capital expenditure considered by this firm was calculated as follows:

	Certainty index %
Raw material availability	70
Power availability	60
Freedom from competition	80

$$\text{Overall certainty } \frac{70 + 60 + 80}{3} = 70$$

This company accepted the project because it regarded a 70 percent level of overall certainty as satisfactory.

Judgment on Three Point Estimates In some companies three estimates are developed for one or more aspects of the proposed investments. The top management or the board of directors decides on the basis of such information. Two examples of this are given below:

In a pharmaceutical company sponsors are required to give three estimates of rate of return: most pessimistic, most likely, and most optimistic.

In a shipping company three estimates, labelled high, medium, and low respectively, are developed for proposed investments.

Evaluation The methods of conservative estimation of revenues, safety margin in cost figures, and flexible investment yardstick, in common practice, do not generally employ explicitly defined probability distributions, which seem alien to current practices. They are based on subjective, implicit evaluations. The three-point estimates method is based on three points in the range of variation and provides some idea of probability distribution. The overall certainty index method is based on two-level discrete probability distributions of important factors affecting the outcome of investments. However, the manner in which these probabilities are used for developing the overall certainty index of a project whose success is dependent on the attainment of three states A, B and C, is $p(\text{A}) \times p(\text{B/A}) \times p(\text{C/A \& B})$ and not $[p(\text{A}) + p(\text{B}) + p(\text{C})]/3$ as defined by the overall certainty index method used in practice.

Room for Improvement A significant improvement in the analysis of the risk factor in practice can be brought about if probability distributions of the key factors underlying investments are developed and information is communicated in this form. This means the use of (i) subjectively understood phrases like the 'most likely return', 'low chances of failure' and (ii) single point estimates will have to be replaced by probability distributions. This has certain advantages:

1. *It would alleviate ambiguity in communication* When judgments about uncertainty are transmitted in qualitative phrases they are likely to be interpreted in a sense different from what the communicator has in mind because of the vagueness of communication. Such vagueness is reduced if judgments are quantified in terms of probability distribution.
2. *It would reduce bias in reporting* When managers and other informants are asked to provide single point estimates (a common practice) they often tend to underestimate

revenues and overestimate costs when performance evaluation emphasises negative variations. If there is no performance evaluation, revenues may be overestimated and costs underestimated for projecting a favourable picture of a project. Such tendencies may be checked to some extent if managers and other informants are asked to provide probability distributions instead of single point estimates.

3. *It utilises more information* When an expert, say, a market analyst, is asked to give an estimate of market demand in terms of a single number, he has to necessarily discard a good deal of his knowledge about the market which otherwise can be communicated in the form of a probability distribution.
4. *It is convenient* With experience it is easy to express judgments in probabilistic terms than in terms of a single-point estimate. Often experts find it convenient to communicate their judgment in terms of probability distribution rather than in the form of a single point estimate.

Relative Importance of Various Methods of Assessing Project Risk

A survey of corporate finance practices in India found the relative importance of various methods of assessing project risk to be as follows:

	% of companies rating it as very important or important
Sensitivity analysis	90.10
Scenario analysis	61.60
Risk-adjusted discount rate	31.70
Decision tree analysis	12.20
Monte Carlo simulation	8.20

Source: Manoj Anand "Corporate Finance Practices in India: A Survey," *Vikalpa*, October-December 2000.

11.11 HOW FINANCIAL INSTITUTIONS ANALYSE RISK

To evaluate the risk dimensions of a project, financial institutions calculate several indicators, the most important ones being the break even point, the debt service coverage ratio, and the fixed assets coverage ratio. In addition, they carry out sensitivity analysis.

The break-even point for a project is calculated with reference to the year when the project is expected to reach its target (or expected) level of capacity utilisation, which is usually the third or the fourth operating year. Further, it is calculated in terms of capacity utilisation. So it is called the break-even point capacity utilisation (BEPCU).

To illustrate the calculation of BEPCU, consider the following data for the third year of a project, when it is expected to reach the target capacity utilisation of 70 percent (the installed capacity of this project is 2880 tonnes per annum and 70 percent of this is 2016 tonnes per annum).

A. Variable Costs

■ Raw materials and consumables	137.2
■ Power, fuel, and water	24.7
■ Variable selling expenses and royalty payments linked to sales	19.2
■ Interest on working capital loans	10.8
■ Other variable expenses	5.0
	196.9

B. Fixed and Semi-fixed Costs

■ Salaries and wages	22.0
■ Repairs and maintenance	2.0
■ Administrative and miscellaneous expenses	2.5
■ Fixed selling expenses	6.3
■ Fixed royalty and know-how payments	3.0
■ Interest on term debt	12.0
■ Depreciation and amortisations	7.5
	55.3

C. Sales Realisation	265.6
D. Contribution	68.7

$$\text{BEPCU (\%)} = \frac{\text{Fixed costs and Semi-fixed costs} \times \text{Percentage capacity utilisation}}{\text{Contribution}}$$

$$= \frac{55.3}{68.7} \times 70\% = 56.3\ \%$$

A variant of BEPCU is the cash BEPCU. It is calculated using the above formula without including depreciation and amortisation as part of fixed costs.

$$\text{Cash BEPCU (\%)} = \frac{47.8}{68.7} \times 70\% = 48.7\%$$

Debt Service Coverage Ratio The debt service coverage ratio (DSCR) is defined as:

$$\text{DSCR} = \frac{\text{Profit after tax} + \text{Depreciation and amortisation} + \text{Interest on term debt} + \text{Lease rentals}}{\text{Repayment of term debt} + \text{Interest on term debt} + \text{Lease rentals}}$$

The average DSCR is computed by taking the total of all values of the numerator and denominator for the entire period of the proposed term loans, commencing from the year in which commercial production starts and not by taking the DSCRs for each year.

The calculation of DSCR is illustrated by an example given in Exhibit 11.17.

Exhibit 11.17 ***Debt Service Coverage Ratio***

Year	1	2	3	4	5	6	7	8	9	10
A. Total Cash Accrual										
1. Profit after tax	0.27	0.81	1.35	1.13	0.99	0.99	0.99	1.01	1.02	1.04
2. Depreciation	0.7	0.7	0.7	0.7	0.7	0.7	0.7	0.7	0.7	0.7
3. Interest on term loan	1.18	1.18	1.07	0.93	0.78	0.64	0.48	0.33	0.19	0.04
Total	2.15	2.69	3.12	2.76	2.47	2.33	2.17	2.04	1.91	1.78
B. Debt Service										
1. Interest on term loan	1.18	1.18	1.07	0.93	0.78	0.63	0.48	0.33	0.19	0.04
2. Repayment of term loan	-	0.4	0.8	0.8	0.8	0.8	0.8	0.8	0.8	0.4
Total	1.18	1.58	1.87	1.73	1.58	1.43	1.28	1.13	0.99	0.44

$$\text{Average DSCR} = \frac{\text{Total cash accrual over the ten year period}}{\text{Total debt service burden over the ten year period}} = \frac{23.42}{13.21} = 1.77$$

Sensitivity Analysis Financial institutions carry out sensitivity analysis to assess the impact of adverse changes in the operating conditions of the project on its viability. The standard sensitivity involves assessing the impact of 10 percent adverse variation in selling price, quantity, and operating costs on internal rate of return (IRR), debt service coverage ratio (DSCR), and break even point (BEP%).

Here is an example of such sensitivity analysis done for a port project:

Case 1 : Fall in cargo handling and storage charges by 10% (This is akin to a fall in selling price)

Case 2 : Fall in cargo by 10% (This is akin to a fall in quantity)

Case 3 : Increase in operating costs by 10%

Case 4 : Combined effect of all the 3 factors

The table showing the sensitivity of IRR, DSCR, and BEP% to the above cases is shown below in Exhibit 11.18.

Exhibit 11.18 ***Sensitivity of IRR, DSCR, and BEP% for Illustrative Cases***

	Revenue (3rd year)	*Operating Profit (3rd year)*	*IRR%*	*DSCR*	*BEP%*	
	(₹ in million)	*(₹ in million)*	*After Tax*	*Avg.*	*Gross*	*Cash*
Base Case	1215.0	566.8	39.89	4.00	39.00	21.13
Case 1	1086.9	438.8	35.24	3.46	44.57	24.15
Case 2	1150.1	519.6	38.02	3.76	40.91	22.17
Case 3	1215.0	538.7	38.82	3.88	40.31	22.11
Case 4	1028.5	371.5	32.50	3.13	48.37	26.53

SUMMARY

- Risk is inherent in almost every business decision. More so in capital budgeting decisions as they involve costs and benefits extending over a long period of time during which many things can change in unanticipated ways.
- Investment proposals, however, differ in risk. A research and development project is typically more risky than an expansion project and the latter tends to be more risky than a replacement project.
- The variety of techniques developed to handle risk in capital budgeting fall into two broad categories: (i) approaches that consider the stand-alone risk of a project (sensitivity analysis, scenario analysis, break-even analysis, Hillier model, simulation analysis, and decision tree analysis); (ii) approaches that consider the contextual risk of a project (corporate risk analysis and market risk analysis).
- Sensitivity analysis or "what if" analysis answers questions like: "What happens to NPV or IRR if sales decline by 5 percent or 10 percent from their expected level?"
- In sensitivity analysis, typically one variable is varied at a time. If variables are inter-related, as they are most likely to be, it is helpful to look at the implications of some plausible scenarios, each scenario representing a consistent combination of variables. Firms often do another kind of scenario analysis called the *best case* and *worst case* analysis.
- As a financial manager, you would be interested in knowing how much should be produced and sold at a minimum to ensure that the project does not 'lose money'. Such an exercise is called break-even analysis and the minimum quantity at which loss is avoided is called the break-even point. The beak-even point may be defined in accounting terms or financial terms.
- Under certain circumstances, the expected NPV and the standard deviation of NPV may be obtained through analytical derivation as proposed by H.S. Hillier.
- Sensitivity analysis indicates the sensitivity of the criterion of merit (NPV, IRR or any other) to variations in basic factors. Though useful, such information may not be adequate for decision making. The decision maker would also like to know the likelihood of such occurrences. This information can be generated by simulation analysis which may be used for developing the probability profile of a criterion of merit by randomly combining values of variables that have a bearing on the chosen criterion.
- Decision tree analysis is a useful tool for analysing sequential decisions in the face of risk. The key steps in decision tree analysis are: (i) identification of the problem and alternatives; (ii) delineation of the decision tree; (iii) specification of probabilities and monetary outcomes; and (iv) evaluation of various decision alternatives.
- Once information about expected return (measured as NPV or IRR or some other criterion of merit) and variability of return (measured in terms of range or standard deviation or some other risk index) has been gathered, the next question is, should the project be accepted or rejected. There are several ways of incorporating risk in the decision process: judgmental evaluation, payback period requirement, risk-adjusted discount rate method, and the certainty equivalent method.
- Often, managers look at the risk and return characteristics of a project and decide judgmentally whether the project should be accepted or rejected. Although judgmental

decision making may appear highly subjective or haphazard, this is how most of us make important decisions in our personal life.

- In many situations companies use NPV or IRR as the principal selection criterion, but apply a payback period requirement to control for risk. If an investment is considered more risky, a shorter payback period is required.
- The risk-adjusted discount rate method calls for adjusting the discount rate to reflect project risk. If the project risk is same as the risk of the existing investments of the firm, the discount rate used is the WACC of the firm; if the project risk is greater (lesser) than the existing investments of the firm, the discount rate used is higher (lower) than the WACC of the firm.
- Under the certainty equivalent method, the expected cash flows of the project are converted into their certainty equivalents by applying suitable certainty equivalent coefficients. Then, the risk-free rate is applied for discounting purposes.
- The methods of risk analysis commonly used in practice are: (i) conservative estimation of revenues, (ii) safety margin in cost figures, (iii) flexible investment yardsticks, (iv) acceptable overall certainty index, and (v) judgment on three-point estimates.
- The analysis of risk factor in practice can be improved if the probability distributions of the key factors underlying an investment project are developed and information is communicated in that form.
- To assess the risk of a project, financial institutions calculate indicators like the break-even point, the debt service coverage ratio and the fixed assets coverage ratio. In addition, they carry out sensitivity analysis.

QUESTIONS

1. List the techniques of risk analysis.
2. Discuss the steps involved in sensitivity analysis.
3. What are the pros and cons of sensitivity analysis?
4. Discuss the steps involved in scenario analysis.
5. What is best and worst case analysis?
6. What are the pros and cons of scenario analysis?
7. How is accounting break-even analysis done?
8. How is financial break-even analysis done?
9. If cash flows of different years are perfectly uncorrelated, how is the standard deviation of NPV defined by the Hillier model?
10. If cash flows of different years are perfectly correlated, how is the standard deviation of NPV defined by the Hillier model?
11. Discuss the procedure for simulation analysis.
12. What are the pros and cons of simulation?
13. Discuss the steps involved in decision tree analysis.
14. What are the pros and cons of decision tree analysis?
15. Discuss the following ways of incorporating risk in the investment decision making process: judgmental evaluation and payback period requirement.

16. Discuss the risk-adjusted discount method.
17. Explain the certainty equivalent method.
18. Critically comment on the methods of risk analysis commonly used in practice.
19. What are the advantages of employing the probability distributions of key factors underlying investment decisions?

PROBLEMS

1. You are the financial manager of Hindustan Extrusion Products Limited (HEPL). HEPL is planning to set up an extrusion plant at Indore. Your project staff has developed the following cash flow forecast for the extrusion plant project.

Cash Flow Forecast for HEPL's Extrusion Plant

		(₹in millions)
	Year 0	*Years 1 – 10*
Investment	(250)	
Sales		200
Variable costs (60% of sales)		120
Fixed costs		20
Depreciation		25
Pre-tax profit		35
Taxes		10
Profit after taxes		25
Cash flow from operations		50
Net cash flow		50

What is the NPV of the project? Assume that the cost of capital is 13 percent. The range of values that the underlying variables can take is shown below:

Underlying Variable	*Pessimistic*	*Expected*	*Optimistic*
Investment (₹ in million)	300	250	200
Sales (₹ in million)	150	200	275
Variable cost as a percent of sales	65	60	56
Fixed costs (₹ in million)	30	20	15
Cost of capital (%)	14	13	12

(a) Calculate the effect of variations in the values of the underlying variables on NPV.
(b) Calculate the accounting break-even point and the financial break-even point for the extrusion plant.

2. Ajeet Corporation is considering the risk characteristics of a certain project. The firm has identified that the following factors, with their respective expected values, have a bearing on the NPV of this project.

	(₹)
Initial investment	30,000
Cost of capital	10%
Quantity manufactured and sold annually	1,400

Price per unit	30
Variable cost per unit	20
Fixed costs	3,000
Depreciation	2,000
Tax rate	50%
Life of the project	5 years
Net salvage value	Nil

Assume that the following underlying variables can take the values as shown below:

Underlying variable	*Pessimistic*	*Optimistic*
Quantity manufactured and sold	800	1800
Price per unit (₹)	20	50
Variable cost per unit (₹)	40	15

(a) Calculate the sensitivity of net present value to variations in (a) quantity manufactured and sold, (b) price per unit, and (c) variable cost per unit.

(b) Calculate the accounting break-even point and the financial break-even point.

3. A project involving an outlay of ₹10 million has the following benefits associated with it.

Year 1		*Year 2*		*Year 3*	
Cash Flow (₹in mln)	*Prob.*	*Cash Flow (₹in mln)*	*Prob.*	*Cash Flow (₹in mln)*	*Prob.*
4	0.4	5	0.4	3	0.3
5	0.5	6	0.4	4	0.5
6	0.1	7	0.2	5	0.2

Assume that the cash flows are independent. Calculate the expected net present value and the standard deviation of net present value assuming that $i = 10$ percent.

4. Janakiram is considering an investment which requires a current outlay of ₹25,000. The expected value and standard deviation of cash flows are:

Year	*Expected Value*	*Standard Deviation*
1	₹12,000	₹5,000
2	10,000	6,000
3	9,000	5,000
4	8,000	6,000

The cash flows are perfectly correlated. Calculate the expected net present value and standard deviation of net present value of this investment, if the risk-free interest rate is 8 percent.

5. Bidhan Corporation is considering the risk characteristics of a project. The firm has identified that the following factors have a bearing on the NPV of this project:

Initial investment	(I)
Cost of capital	(r)
Quantity manufactured and sold annually	(Q)
Price per unit	(P)
Variable cost per unit	(V)
Fixed costs	(F)
Depreciation	(D)
Tax rate	(T)
Life of the project	(n)
Net salvage value	(S)

The relationship between these factors and NPV is as follows:

$$\text{NPV} = \sum_{t=1}^{n} \frac{[Q(P-V)-F-D](1-T)+D}{(1+r)^t} + \frac{S}{(1+r)^n} - I$$

The management of the firm feels that I, r, F, D, T, n, and S, not subject to much variation, may be deemed as constant at the following levels: $I = 30{,}000$, $r = 10\%$, $F = 3{,}000$, $D = 2{,}000$, $T = 0.5$, $n = 5$, $S = 0$.

The probability distributions for Q, P, and V have been defined as follows:

Q		*P*		*V*	
Value	*Prob.*	*Value*	*Prob.*	*Value*	*Prob.*
800	0.10	20	0.4	15	0.3
1000	0.10	30	0.4	20	0.5
1200	0.20	40	0.1	40	0.2
1400	0.30	50	0.1		
1600	0.20				
1800	0.10				

(i) Using a random number table, obtain 50 simulated values of NPV.
(ii) Calculate the mean and standard deviation of NPV from the simulated values.

6. Consider the data given in problem 6. Carry out sensitivity analysis with reference to quantity (Q) and price (P).
7. The expected cash flows of a project are as follows:

Year	*Cash Flow*
0	₹(30,000)
1	7,000
2	8,000
3	9,000
4	10,000
5	8,000

The certainty equivalent factor behaves as per the following equation: $\alpha_t = 1 - 0.06t$
Calculate the net present value of the project if the risk-free rate of return is 8 percent.

MINICASE

Southern Airways has been set up to run an air taxi service in Southern India. The company is debating whether it should buy a turboprop aircraft or a piston engine aircraft. The turboprop aircraft cost 11000 and has larger capacity. It will serve if the demand turns out to be high. The piston aircraft costs 5500 and has a smaller capacity. It will serve if the demand is low, but it will not suffice if the demand is high.

The company believes that the chances of demand being high and low in year 1 are 0.65 and 0.35 respectively. If the demand is high in year 1, there is an 80 percent chance that it will be high in subsequent years (year 2 onward) and 20 percent chance that it will be low in subsequent years.

The CEO of Southern Airways thinks that if the company buys a piston engine aircraft and the demand turns out to be high, the company can buy a second-hand piston engine aircraft for 4400 at the end of year 1. This would double its capacity and enable it to cope reasonably well with high demand for year 2 onwards.

Decision Tree for Southern Airways

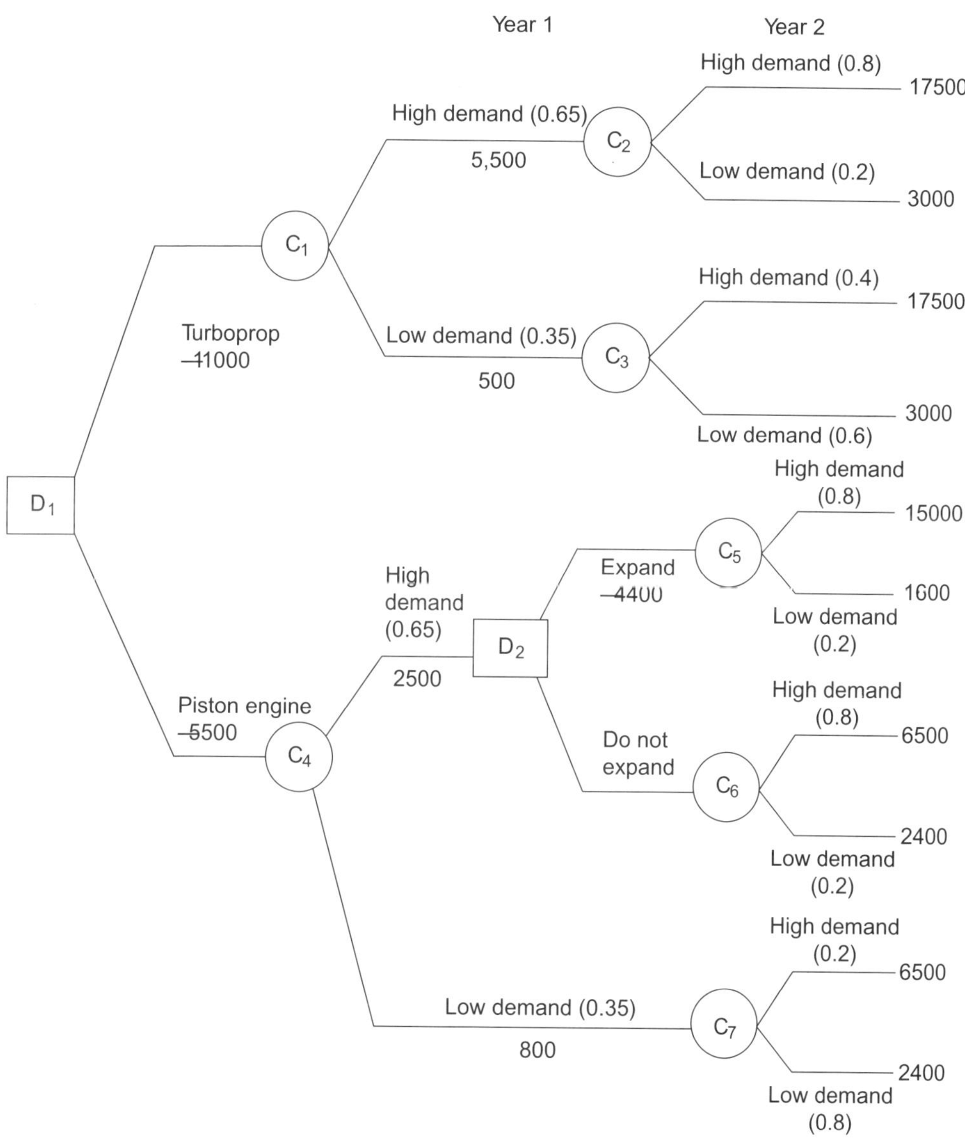

The payoffs and probabilities associated with high and low demand for various decision alternatives are shown in the accompanying decision tree. The payoffs shown for year 1 are the payoffs occurring at the end of year 1 and payoffs shown for year 2 are the payoffs for year 2 and the subsequent years, evaluated at the end of year 2, using a discount rate of 12 percent which is the weighted average cost of capital

1. What is the expected NPV of the turboprop aircraft?
2. What is the expected NPV of the piston engine aircraft?
3. What is the value of the *option to expand* in the case of the piston engine aircraft?
4. If the turboprop aircraft can be sold for 8000 at the end of year 1, what is the value of the *option to abandon*?
5. If the piston engine aircraft can be sold for 4400 at the end of year 1, what is the value of the *option to abandon*?

APPENDIX 11A

CERTAINTY EQUIVALENT METHODS VS. RISK ADJUSTED DISCOUNT RATE METHOD

The expressions of NPV according to the certainty equivalent method and the risk adjusted discount rate method are as follows:

Certainty Equivalent Method

$$\sum_{t=1}^{n} \frac{\alpha_t \overline{A_t}}{(1+i)^t} - I$$

Risk Adjusted Discount Rate Method

$$\sum_{t=1}^{n} \frac{\overline{A_t}}{(1+r)^t} - I$$

From the above expressions, it is clear that the following conditions must be satisfied if the risk adjusted discount rate method is to give the same value for each expected return as the certainty equivalent method.

$$\frac{\alpha_t \overline{A_t}}{(1+i)^t} = \frac{\overline{A_t}}{(1+r)^t} \tag{11C.1}$$

for all values of t

Juggling Eqn. (11C.1) a bit, we get

$$\alpha_t = (1+i)^t / (1+r)^t \tag{11C.2}$$

Likewise we find

$$\alpha_{t+1} = (1+i)^{t+1} / (1+r)^{t+1} \tag{11C.3}$$

Combining Eqns. (11C.2) and (11C.3) we get

$$\frac{\alpha_{t+1}}{\alpha_t} = \frac{(1+i)}{(1+r)} \tag{11C.4}$$

This means that the coefficient α_t, in general, declines at a constant rate of $1 - (1 + i)/(1 + r)$ per period. (For our present purposes, we may ignore the possibility of α_t increasing over time, which, though conceivable, is very unlikely.) This implies that risk increases at a constant rate.

It may be argued that given a stream of expected returns, a value of r can be found which would give the same net present value as obtained by employing the certainty equivalent approach. Compared to the certainty equivalent approach, such a rate would over-estimate the present value of returns in some periods and underestimate in others with the differences cancelling out.

However, it should be borne in mind that the net present value, and not r, is the unknown. Thus, it is difficult to see how r can be interpreted as a reasonable standard for discounting purposes unless Eqn. (11C.2) is satisfied. Hence, on a conceptual level, the certainty equivalent approach is superior to the risk-adjusted discount rate approach.

APPENDIX 11B

VEGETRON SIMULATION[8]

Section 11.6 of the textbook has explained the basic procedure of simulation. The procedure has explained how the random numbers can be mapped to the values of annual cash flows, using the probability distribution. You have also learnt how to carry out simulation manually. This chapter has demonstrated the process by taking you through 10 cycles (runs) of simulation. In reality, the simulation requires us to go through at least few thousands of cycles. While it is not possible to do this manually, we can use the power of computer to carry out this exercise. As a matter of fact, there are many software packages specially designed for simulation. Crystal Ball, as mentioned in chapter 11 is one of them. Another popular software package is @Risk. You can use Excel itself to carry out the simulation exercise. You have to first identify the probability distribution for the variables that you want to use in the simulation. Then, you can use the RAND() function available in Excel to generate random numbers. Once these random numbers are generated, you can map them to the appropriate values of the variables.

The attached Excel sheet uses the case study on Vegetron. The simulation of Vegetron Case Study is available in an EXCEL work book named "Vegetron Simulation".

This simulation exercise uses the data presented in Chapter 6, Appendix 6A. Chapter 6 makes a number of assumptions regarding the Vegetron project. Three of those assumptions have been selected for the simulation exercise. The first one is about the capacity utilisation. The expected utilisation of 50% in the first year and 60% in the second year is considered as fixed. The capacity utilisation from the 3rd year onwards is considered as a random variable. The capacity utilisation can be 65% or 70% or 75% with the probabilities of 15%, 55%, and 30% respectively. Similarly, the average sales realisation is also considered as a random variable with values of ₹115, ₹120 and ₹125. The associated probabilities are 10%, 60%, and

[8] This appendix and the EXCEL workbook (which is available in the web resources of this book) have been developed by Dr. V. Nagadevara, Former Professor, IIM, Bangalore.

30% respectively. The third variable considered for simulation is cost of raw materials. The raw material cost is estimated as a percentage of the sales. This percentage is taken as a random variable with three possible values namely, 60%, 65%, and 70%. The corresponding probabilities are 15%, 60%, and 25% respectively.

The Excel workbook has three worksheets. The first one is named as "Summary Data". The first part of the worksheet contains the values of the three random variables ("Capacity Utilization", "Average Sales Realization" and "Cost of Raw Materials") and their associated probabilities. The second part of this worksheet contains the summary of the simulation results.

The second worksheet is called "Simulated Values". This is the main worksheet where the actual simulation is carried out. Different random numbers are generated with respect to each of the three variables corresponding to each of the ten years (as in Appendix 6A). These random numbers are mapped to different possible values of the respective variables namely, "Capacity Utilisation", "Average Sales Realisation" and "Cost of Raw Materials". These values are then transferred to the third worksheet.

The third worksheet is "Vegetron Data". This worksheet puts together the relationship and calculations as given in Appendix 6A. The year-wise data is presented in sets of columns. Each year is labeled and color-coded in Row 1. This sheet is used to calculate the NPV and IRR for the simulated values. The final calculated values of each simulation for NPV and IRR are presented in columns GK and GL. These results are summarised in two frequency tables located at GO2:GS15. These are titled as probability distributions of NPV and IRR.

The summary results are presented in tables as well as graphs in the first worksheet, "Summary Data". These are reproduced at the end of this appendix.

The random generation function in Excel is dynamic. Hence, whenever you do any operation in any of the cells in the workbook, all the random numbers will be revised and the summary data will change accordingly.

The workbook has included 50 simulations. You can extend this to any number of simulations that you desire. The procedure for extending the number of simulations is as follows.

1. First select the worksheet "Simulated Values". Highlight the area A50:FO52. This area is colored in light green.
2. Copy this area to the desired number by holding the right-hand bottom corner of the highlighted area and drag it to the desired row number. For example, if you want to carry out 2000 simulations, you need to extend this area to row number 2002 by dragging.
3. Now select the worksheet "Vegetron Data". Highlight the area A50:GL52. This area is already colored in light green.
4. Extend this area (as you had done in step 2 above) exactly to the same number of simulations (exactly the same row number as in step 2).

You can also change the probabilities in worksheet "Summary Data" and see the impact on the NPV and IRR. Please change the probabilities corresponding to the first two values only. The third value is automatically calculated. Please keep in mind that the total of the probabilities cannot exceed 1.

Do not change the values under the cumulative probabilities.

For those of you who feel little more adventurous, you can extend the simulation to one more variable. We have made provision to consider the cost of power to be considered as a random variable. Create a probability distribution in the Summary Data sheet. You may use the area Q1:T5. Follow the same pattern as that of any of the other three random variables. Go to Simulated Values sheet and generate another set of random numbers for each of the 10 years. You can use the column immediate right of the RM random numbers column. Map these random numbers to "cost of power as a percentage of sales" under the column "Power". For example, the first year mapping can be done in column E. You can look at the mapping formulas of the other variables in order to do the mapping for cost of power.

The simulation engine will take care of the rest.

Have fun!

Capacity Utilisation				*Average Sales Realisation*				*RM Cost*			
%	*Prob*	*Cum Prob*	*Val*	*Price*	*Prob*	*Cum Prob*	*Val*	*%*	*Prob*	*Cum Prob*	*Val*
65	0.15	0.15	15	115	0.1	0.1	10	60	0.15	0.15	15
70	0.55	0.7	70	120	0.6	0.7	70	65	0.6	0.75	75
75	0.3	1	100	125	0.3	1	100	70	0.25	1	100

Probability Distributions from Simulations

	NPV				*IRR*		
	NPV	*Freq*	*RF*		*IRR*	*Freq*	*RF*
Less Than	–50	0	0.00		0.00%	0.00	0.00
–50 to	–40	0	0.00	0.00% to	2.00%	0.00	0.00
–40 to	–30	0	0.00	2.00% to	4.00%	0.00	0.00
–30 to	–20	0	0.00	4.00% to	6.00%	0.00	0.00
–20 to	–10	10	0.20	6.00% to	8.00%	9.00	0.18
–10 to	0	14	0.28	8.00% to	10.00%	15.00	0.30
0 to	10	21	0.42	10.00% to	12.00%	22.00	0.44
10 to	20	4	0.08	12.00% to	14.00%	4.00	0.08
20 to	30	1	0.02	14.00% to	16.00%	0.00	0.00
30 to	40	0	0.00	16.00% to	18.00%	0.00	0.00
40 to	50	0	0.00	18.00% to	20.00%	0.00	0.00
50 to	60	0	0.00	20.00% to	22.00%	0.00	0.00
	Total	50	1.00			50	1.00

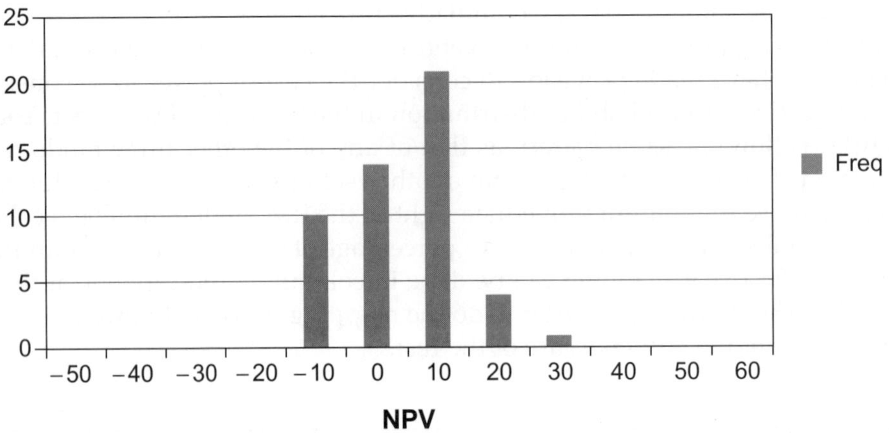
25
20
15
10
5
0
−50
−40
−30
−20
−10
0
10
20
30
40
50
60
NPV
Freq

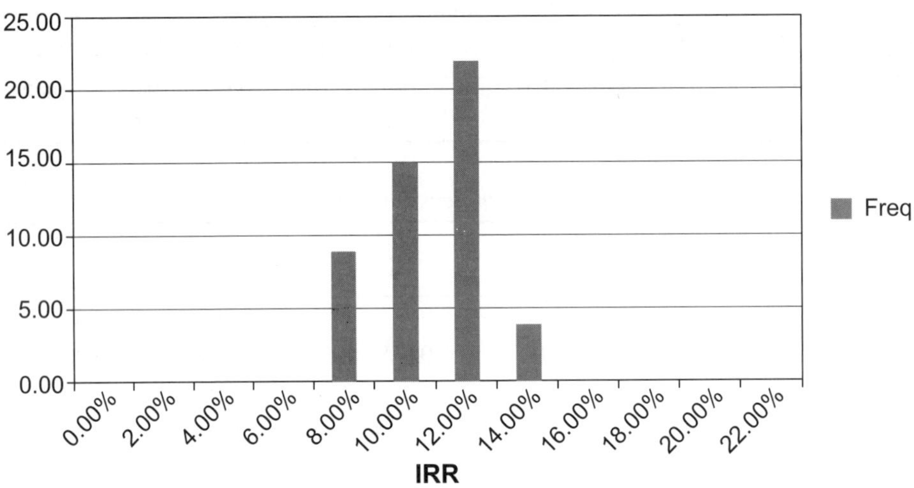
25.00
20.00
15.00
10.00
5.00
0.00
0.00%
2.00%
4.00%
6.00%
8.00%
10.00%
12.00%
14.00%
16.00%
18.00%
20.00%
22.00%
IRR
Freq

Selection II

CHAPTER 12

Project Rate of Return

CHAPTER 13

Special Decisions Situations

CHAPTER 14

Social Cost Benefit Analysis

CHAPTER 15

Multiple Projects and Constraints

CHAPTER 16

Valuation of Real Options

CHAPTER 17

Judgemental, Behavioural, Strategic, and Organisational Considerations

PART FOUR

Chapter 12 Project Rate of Return

LEARNING OBJECTIVES

After studying this chapter you should be able to

- Specify the pros and cons of multiple costs of capital.
- Show how equity beta and asset beta are related.
- Calculate the divisional WACC.
- Explain why firms set a hurdle rate higher than the WACC.
- Discuss how the insights provided by portfolio theory may be applied to capital budgeting.

In Chapter 10 we discussed the concept of a firm's cost of capital (i.e., the weighted average cost of capital, or WACC). In practice, the WACC is widely used for evaluating new investments. However, strictly speaking, the WACC can be applied to a new investment only if its business risk is the same as the average business risk of the existing investments and the capital structure is not affected by the new investment.

When these conditions are not fulfilled, you may have to customise the discount rate, taking into account the specific attributes of the project. You may use the divisional WACC or the project WACC.

This chapter discusses the issues involved in computing and using multiple costs of capital. It also looks at the application of portfolio theory to capital budgeting.

12.1 PROS AND CONS OF MULTIPLE COSTS OF CAPITAL

Should a firm use a single discount rate for all its projects or should it customise the discount rate for different divisions or even specific projects? Each approach has its pros and cons and the decision finally depends on managerial judgment.

• The Justification for Using Multiple Discount Rates

According to finance theory, the appropriate discount rate for a project should reflect its opportunity cost of capital – the rate of return that one can expect from investing in publicly traded securities that have similar risk characteristics. Clearly, when a project is highly risky, it will have a high opportunity cost of capital and when a project is mildly risky, it will have a low opportunity cost of capital.

What happens when a firm uses a single discount rate (WACC) for all its projects, irrespective of their level of risk? The firm will tend to reject a relatively safe project, even though its expected rate of return exceeds its opportunity cost of capital (or risk-adjusted cost of capital) and accept a relatively risky project, even though its expected rate of return is less than its opportunity cost of capital (risk-adjusted cost of capital). Exhibit 12.1 illustrates this bias.

Exhibit 12.1 ***Bias on Account of Using a Single Cost of Capital***

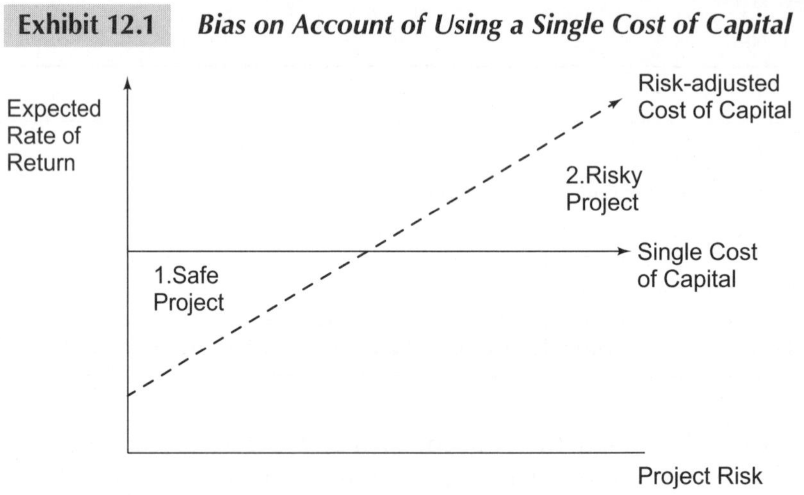

Given the possibility of this bias, conceptually a firm should vary the discount rate, taking into account the risk of the project as shown by the dashed arrow in Exhibit 12.1. Put differently, a firm must use multiple discount rates.

The Rationale for Using a Single Discount Rate

Despite the conceptual argument in favour of varying the discount rate to reflect the project risk, most of the firms use a single discount rate for evaluating all of their investment projects. There are several possible reasons for this practice:

- Many firms engage in a small range of related activities that are perhaps characterised by similar risks.
- It may be somewhat difficult to specify different discount rates for different projects.
- The rationale for multiple discount rates may not be fully understood by persons involved in capital budgeting.
- Opportunistic managers may underestimate project risk and reduce the project cost of capital to get their projects approved.
- The use of a single discount rate reduces the incidence of what economists call *influence costs* (Project advocates spend time and effort in justifying a lower discount rate. Likewise, project evaluators spend time and effort to figure out the extent of bias inherent in the proposals they consider. Influence costs refer to the cost of time and effort spent by project advocates and project evaluators.)

- The use of multiple discount rates increases the possibility of selecting inferior projects, if some managers, who are politically more influential or just more persuasive, are able to use lower discount rates for their project. It may be noted that project advocates tend to inflate cash flow forecasts and ask for low discount rates to justify their projects. However, they have a greater incentive to argue for a lower discount rate. The tendency to inflate cash flow forecasts is somewhat checked by the fact that cash flow forecasts can be compared with the realised cash flows subsequently. However, it is not possible to determine on an ex post basis whether the appropriate discount rate was used at the time of project evaluation.

Weighing the Pros and Cons of Multiple versus Single Discount Rates

Taking into account its circumstances, each firm must properly weigh the pros and cons of multiple versus single discount rates.

Multiple discount rates make more sense when the firm is engaged in diverse businesses or when it operates in different geographies.

A single discount rate makes sense when managers have discretion in specifying discount rates and incentive problems are real. Incentive problems can be mitigated if the cost of capital is estimated, using an objective procedure that relies on market data.

12.2 DIVISIONAL WACC AND PROJECT-SPECIFIC WACC

Most firms are multi-business or multi-divisional firms. For example, Reliance Industries Limited, leaving aside its subsidiaries and associate companies, is engaged in the following businesses: oil and gas, petroleum refining and marketing, petrochemicals, polyester, and textiles. *Inter alia*, Hindustan Unilever Limited is engaged in the following businesses: soaps and detergents, personal products, beverages, and foods.

Since different businesses are likely to have different business risks and debt capacities, it may be worthwhile to compute divisional WACCs. You can apply the capital asset pricing model (CAPM) to figure out the WACC of a division. Before we discuss this procedure, it is helpful to understand the link between equity beta and asset beta.

Equity Beta and Asset Beta

To explore the relationship between equity beta and asset beta, we will initially ignore taxes. Look at Zenith Limited which has the following balance sheet:

Equity	:	50	Assets	:	100
Debt	:	50			

If you buy all the securities of Zenith (its entire equity as well as debt), you will own all its assets. So the beta of your portfolio (β_P) of Zenith's securities is equal to the beta of Zenith's assets (β_A)

$$\beta_P = \beta_A \tag{12.1}$$

Now, the beta of your portfolio is simply the weighted arithmetic average of the betas of its components, viz., equity (E) and debt (D)

$$\beta_P = \beta_E \frac{E}{E+D} + \beta_D \frac{D}{E+D} \tag{12.2}$$

Hence

$$\beta_A = \beta_E \frac{E}{E+D} + \beta_D \frac{D}{E+D} \tag{12.3}$$

Juggling Eq. (12.25) a bit, you get:

$$\beta_E = \beta_A + (\beta_A - \beta_D)\ \frac{D}{E} \tag{12.4}$$

If the beta of debt, β_D, is assumed to be zero (this means that debt is considered to be risk-free)[1]

$$\beta_E = \beta_A + \beta_A\ \frac{D}{E} = \beta_A\left(1+\frac{D}{E}\right) \tag{12.5}$$

So far we assumed that taxes don't exist. What happens in a world of taxes[2] where interest on debt is a tax-deductible expense? In this case, as Robert Hamada[3] and others have shown

$$\beta_E = \beta_A\left(1+\frac{D}{E}(1-T)\right) \qquad (12.6)^4$$

This means

$$\beta_A = \left(\frac{\beta_E}{1+\frac{D}{E}(1-T)}\right) \tag{12.7}$$

Eqns. (12.6) and (12.7) show how equity beta and asset beta are related.

Determinants of Assets Betas

The two key determinants of asset betas are cyclicality and operating leverage.

Cyclicality If a firm's revenues and earnings are strongly dependent on the state of the business cycle, it is likely to have a high asset beta. Cyclicality influences asset beta.

Operating Leverage Just the way financial leverage (implying a commitment to fixed financing costs) increases the beta of an investment portfolio, operating leverage (implying a commitment to fixed operating costs) increases the beta of a capital project.

[1] This is a reasonable assumption for the debt of financially strong companies.

[2] This, indeed, is a more realistic representation of the real world.

[3] Robert Hamada, "Portfolio Analysis, Market Equilibrium, and Corporate Finance," *Journal of Finance*, March 1969.

[4] In Eq. (12.6), T stands for the tax rate.

Procedure for Calculating the Divisional WACC

The procedure for calculating the divisional WACC, as per the CAPM, involves the following steps.

Step 1: *Find a sample of firms engaged in the same line of business* Identify a sample of firms which are engaged wholly or largely in the same line of business.

Step 2: *Obtain equity betas for the sample firms* To calculate the equity beta of a firm, employ the procedure discussed earlier. Regress the monthly return of the equity stock of the firm on the monthly return of the market portfolio for 50 to 60 months. Where 50 to 60 observations of monthly returns are not available, you may use 50–60 observations of fortnightly returns.

Step 3: *Derive asset betas after adjusting equity betas for financial leverage* For each firm in the sample, the asset beta can be derived from its equity beta using the following relationship:

$$\beta_A = \frac{\beta_E}{\left(1 + \frac{D}{E}(1 - T)\right)} \tag{12.8}$$

Step 4: *Find the average of asset betas* Once the asset betas for the sample firms are obtained, the average can be readily calculated.

Step 5: *Figure out the equity beta for the division* The equity beta for the division can be derived by adjusting the average asset beta (obtained in the previous step) for the financial leverage planned for the division. Remember the formula:

$$\beta_E = \beta_A\left(1 + \frac{D}{E}(1 - T)\right) \tag{12.9}$$

Step 6: *Estimate the cost of equity for the division* As per the CAPM, the cost of equity for the proposed project is:

$$r_E = R_f + (\overline{R_M} - R_f)\,\beta_E \tag{12.10}$$

Step 7: Calculate the divisional WACC. The divisional WACC will be:

$$r_A = w_E\, r_e + w_D\, r_D\,(I - T) \tag{12.11}$$

where r_A is the divisional weighted average cost of capital, w_E is the weight associated with divisional equity $[E/(E + D)]$, r_E is the divisional cost of equity, w_D is the weight associated with divisional debt $[D/(E + D)]$, r_D is the pre-tax cost of divisional debt, and T is the tax rate.

Illustration

Diversified Limited is evaluating its granite division for which it uses a debt-equity ratio of 1.5:1. The pre-tax cost of debt is 15 percent and the tax rate is expected to be 30 percent. The risk-free rate is 12 percent and the expected return on the market portfolio is 16 percent. The divisional WACC may be calculated as follows:

Step 1: *Find a sample of firms engaged in similar business* According to the chief executive of Diversified Limited the following firms are engaged wholly in the same line of business:

1. Ankit Granites Limited

2. Bharath Granites Company
3. Modern Granites Limited

Step 2: *Obtain equity betas for the sample of comparable firms* The equity betas of the three firms, obtained by regressing their equity returns on the market portfolio for the past 60 months, are as follows

Ankit Granites Limited	:	1.20
Bharath Granites Company	:	1.10
Modern Granites Limited	:	1.05

Step 3: *Derive asset betas after adjusting equity betas for financial leverage* The debt-equity ratios for the three firms, namely, Ankit Granites Limited, Bharath Granites Company, and Modern Granites Limited are 2.1, 1.6, and 1.3 respectively. The effective tax rate for all of them is 40 percent. Their asset betas are derived by using the formula:

$$\beta_A = \beta_E / [1 + (D/E)(1 - T)]$$

Ankit Granites Ltd : $\dfrac{1.20}{[1 + 2.1\,(0.6)]} = 0.53$

Bharath Granites Co. : $\dfrac{1.10}{[1 + 1.6\,(0.6)]} = 0.56$

Modern Granites Ltd : $\dfrac{1.05}{[1 + 1.3\,(0.6)]} = 0.59$

Step 4: *Find the average of asset betas* The average of asset betas of Ankit Granites Limited, Bharath Granites Company, and Modern Granites Limited is:

$$(0.53 + 0.56 + 0.69)/3 = 0.56$$

Step 5: *Figure out the equity beta for the division.* The equity beta for the granite division is:

$$\beta_E = \beta_A [1 + D/E\,(1 - T)]$$
$$= 0.56\,[1 + 1.5\,(1 - .3)] = 1.148$$

Step 6: *Estimate the cost of equity for the division.* As per the capital asset pricing model, the cost of equity for the granite division is:

$$r_E = R_f + (\overline{R_M} - R_f)\,\beta_E$$
$$= .12 + (.16 - .12)\,1.148 = .166$$

Step 7: *Calculate the divisional WACC.* The weighted average cost of capital (the required rate of return) for the granite project of Diversified Limited is:

$$r_A = W_E\, r_e + W_D\, r_D\,(1 - T)$$
$$= [((1/2.5)\,0.166) + ((1.5/2.5)\,(0.15)\,(0.7))]$$
$$= .1294 = 12.94 \text{ percent}$$

- **Project-specific WACC**

If you want a more refined estimate of the discount rate, you have to estimate the WACC for each individual project, taking into account the risks and financing mix of the project. The procedure for calculating the project-specific WACC would be the same as that for the divisional WACC. However, implementing this procedure for individual projects is difficult because it is not easy to find market proxies for project risk and to define capital structure weights since equity value of individual projects are not observable. Further, the influence costs tend to be high as managers push for their favourite projects.

12.3 HURDLE RATE AND COST OF CAPITAL

We discussed various ways of determining the cost of capital associated with a given investment project. Finance theory suggests that a project must be evaluated on the basis of its NPV, calculated by discounting the project's cash flow at the project cost of capital. In practice, however, firms generally use discount rates, often called hurdle rates, which are greater than the project cost of capital. For example, a firm may use a hurdle rate of 18 percent even when the project WACC is just 12 percent. This means that firms generally require that accepted projects have an adequate NPV cushion or margin of safety.

Why do firms set a hurdle rate that is higher than the WACC? There are several reasons:

1. **Constraints** Most firms believe that the WACC is not the appropriate opportunity cost. The WACC, the opportunity cost of capital calculated from the capital market, is appropriate for firms that face no constraints and can undertake all positive-NPV investments. In reality, firms face constraints – managerial and other – that limit the number of investments that they can accept. When a firm is so constrained, the appropriate opportunity cost of capital is the rate of return foregone on the next best project that is sacrificed for accepting the project that is being evaluated. For example, suppose a firm has to choose between two projects, A and B, that are equally risky. If the expected internal rate of return on A is 18 percent, then the appropriate cost of capital for evaluating B is 18 percent, and not the WACC of the firm.
2. **Incentives** A high hurdle rate motivates project sponsors to find better projects. If the top management sets the hurdle rate at say 15 percent, project sponsors may propose a project that has an IRR of 16 percent. However, if the top management sets up the hurdle rate at 20 percent, project sponsors will put additional efforts and negotiate harder with suppliers, customers, and other partners to develop projects that meet the higher hurdle rate. As it happens with everything in life, in general, the higher the bar, the greater the effort.
3. **Optimistic Forecasts** A higher-than-WACC hurdle rate is meant to counter the optimistic projections and selection bias.
   In general, cash flow forecasts tend to be inaccurate, thanks to uncertainty characterising the future. However, the process used for project selection is such that the cash flow forecasts of the selected projects are coloured by optimistic bias. Hence, it makes sense to use a high hurdle rate to offset the optimistic bias in cash flow forecasts.

To understand the nature of this bias, consider a division of a conglomerate firm which is being auctioned. Several investors are interested in acquiring the division. The investor who bids the highest would bag the division. The highest bidder is likely to value the division the most because it has the most optimistic forecast of the future cash flows of the division.

Likewise, when the top management of a firm selects from a set of proposed investments, it is likely to choose the projects that appear most attractive. Although good projects would appear attractive, some not-so-good projects too, thanks to optimistic forecasts, too would also appear attractive. In this situation, a high hurdle rate can be a good antidote for the optimistic bias in cash flow forecasts.

Survey Evidence on Project Discount Rates

In a survey, CFOs were asked. "How frequently would your company use the following discount rates when evaluating a new project in an overseas market?" The following list of discount rates was given.

- The discount rate for the company as a whole.
- A risk-adjusted discount rate for this particular project.
- A country discount rate.
- A different discount rate for each item of cash flow that has a different risk characteristic (such as depreciation, tax shield, and so on).

The key findings of the survey were:

- 59 percent of the CFOs use the discount rate for the company as a whole.
- 51 percent of the CFOs use a risk adjusted discount rate.
- Large firms are more likely to use risk-adjusted discount rates, compared to small firms.

12.4 PORTFOLIO THEORY AND CAPITAL BUDGETING

Many argue that the risk of a project must not be evaluated in isolation. Rather, it must be judged in the context of the total risk of the firm. This means that the question to be asked is what is the incremental contribution of a project to the risk exposure of the firm as a whole? To answer this question, portfolio theory may be employed.

Portfolio theory was developed by Harry Markowitz to analyse a portfolio of financial securities. However, its broad insights can be applied for analysing a portfolio of real projects.

Basic Ideas

To understand the basic ideas of portfolio theory, let us look at a portfolio consisting of just two assets, A and B.

The expected return and the standard deviation of return for a two-asset portfolio are:

$$E(R_p) = w_A E(R_A) + w_B E(R_B) \quad (12.12)$$

$$\sigma_p = (w_A^2 \sigma_A^2 + w_B^2 \sigma_B^2 + 2 w_A w_B \sigma_{AB})^{1/2} \quad (12.13)$$

where w_A and w_B are the proportions of funds invested in assets A and B ($w_A + w_B = 1$), $E(R_A)$ and $E(R_B)$ are the expected returns on assets A and B, σ_A^2 and σ_B^2 are the variances of returns on assets A and B, and σ_{AB} is the covariance of returns.

Since σ_{AB} (covariance) is equal to the product of ρ_{AB} (coefficient of correlation) and σ_A, σ_B, and the coefficient of correlation of a variable with itself is equal to 1, we can express Eq. (12.13) as follows:

$$\sigma_p = (w_A^2 \rho_{AA} \sigma_A^2 + w_B^2 \rho_{BB} \sigma_B^2 + 2 w_A w_B \rho_{AB} \sigma_A \sigma_B)^{1/2} \quad (12.14)$$

In more general terms, when more than two assets are combined in a portfolio, the expected portfolio return and the standard deviation of portfolio return are:

$$E(R_p) = \Sigma w_i E(R_i) \quad (12.15)$$

$$\sigma_p = \left(\sum_{j=1}^{n} \sum_{i=1}^{n} w_i w_j \rho_{ij} \sigma_i \sigma_j \right)^{1/2} \quad (12.16)$$

Example Three assets, designated A, B, and C have expected returns of 0.12 (or 12 percent), 0.18, and 0.24 respectively. The variances and covariances are as follows:

	A	*B*	*C*
A	.02	.01	–.03
B	.01	.06	0
C	–.03	0	.08

What is the expected return and standard deviation of a portfolio consisting of 40 percent of funds in A, 30 percent of funds in B, and 30 percent of funds in C?

$$E(R_p) = 0.40(0.12) + 0.30(0.18) + 0.3(0.24)$$
$$= 0.174 \text{ or } 17.4 \text{ percent}$$

$$\sigma_p = [(0.40)(0.40)(0.02) + (0.40)(0.30)(0.01)$$
$$+ (0.40)(0.30)(-0.03) + (0.30)(0.40)(0.01) + (0.30)(0.30)(0.06)$$
$$+ (0.30)(0.30)(0) + (0.30)(0.40)(-0.03) + (0.30)(0.30)(0)$$
$$+ (0.30)(0.30)(0.08)]^{1/2}$$
$$= 0.1049$$

• Determination of an Optimal Portfolio

Portfolio theory assumes that investors like returns but dislike risk (which is measured by variance or its square root the standard deviation). Hence, portfolio theory is a mean-variance model.

According to portfolio theory, the optimal portfolio is determined as follows:

1. Identify all feasible portfolios. A feasible portfolio is any portfolio of projects that can be undertaken together. This means that if two projects are mutually exclusive, both of them cannot be included in the same portfolio. Likewise, if a project, say *A*, can be undertaken only if another project, say *B*, is taken up, then a feasible portfolio cannot include *A* without including *B*.
2. Determine the expected return and standard deviation of all the feasible portfolios, using Eqns. (12.15) and (12.16). Exhibit 12.2 shows graphically the expected return and standard deviation of various feasible portfolios. The broken-egg shaped region represents the collection of portfolios comprising the feasible region.
3. Define the efficient frontier. The efficient frontier is the collection of all efficient portfolios. A portfolio is efficient if (and only if) there is no alternative with (i) the same $E(R_p)$ and lower σ_p, or (ii) the same σ and a higher $E(R_p)$, or (iii) a higher $E(R_p)$ and a lower σ_p. The efficient frontier is represented graphically by the thick line representing the northwest frontier of the feasible region in Exhibit 12.2. Note that all other points in the feasible region are dominated by one or more points in the efficient frontier. For example, point *P* is dominated by point *Q* and point *R* is dominated by point *S*.
4. Choose the portfolio on the efficient frontier that offers the highest level of utility (satisfaction) to the decision maker. Referred to as the optimal portfolio, this is the point of tangency between the efficient frontier and the highest attainable utility indifference curve. In Exhibit 12.2, there are three utility indifference curves I_1, I_2, and I_3. All points on a utility indifference curve provide the same level of satisfaction (utility) to the decision maker. The utility indifference curve represents the risk-return tradeoff of the decision maker. The level of satisfaction increases as one moves leftward (or more precisely in the north west direction) because it means higher return and lesser risk. Thus, I_2 represents a higher level of satisfaction than I_1 and I_3 represents a higher level of satisfaction than I_2. In Exhibit 12.2, the optimal portfolio is shown by point *Y*, as it represents the point of tangency between the efficient frontier and the highest attainable utility indifference curve.

Exhibit 12.2 ***Determination of the Optimal Portfolio***

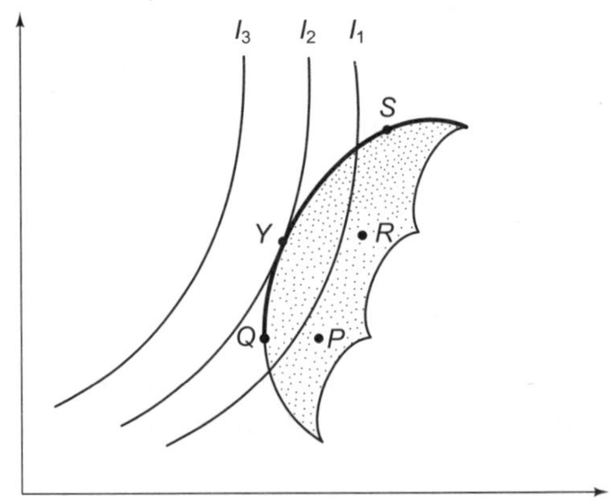

• Application to Capital Budgeting

In applying portfolio theory to capital budgeting we face some special problems. We discuss these problems and then look at some suggestions for applying portfolio concepts to capital budgeting.

Special Problems The special problems encountered in applying portfolio theory to capital budgeting. relate to:

- Indivisibility of assets
- Holding period
- Data requirements

Indivisibility of Assets Unlike securities, which are almost infinitely divisible, capital investments often come in large, indivisible units. They have to be accepted or rejected in toto. Fortunately, the problem of indivisibility can be handled with integer programming.

Holding Period Mean-variance analysis can be used to determine the portfolio of capital investments that has the highest net present value for each level of risk. Unfortunately, it is difficult to interpret such an efficient frontier because asset lives tend to be different. To avoid ambiguity caused by unequal lives, the return should be measured over a common holding period.

One alternative is to define the holding period as the life of the longest asset being considered. In this case we have to identify all investments that will be made between now and the chosen holding period and also impute terminal values to assets which still have a balance economic life at that point. This is indeed a daunting proposition.

To avoid these difficulties, a second alternative is to use a short holding period, say one year. If this alternative is chosen, the value of each asset has to be defined at the end of one year. This too is a difficult proposition because capital assets cannot usually be sold after a short period without incurring losses.

Data Requirements Mean-variance portfolio analysis is highly data-intensive. For a portfolio of n assets, the number of risk and return inputs required is: $0.5n^2 + 1.5n$. For example, if 100 capital assets are being considered the number of inputs required is: $0.5 \times 100^2 + 1.5 \times 100 = 5{,}150$. The difficulty is further compounded by the fact that managers normally are not wonted to think in terms of covariances and correlations.

Simpler Applications Due to the problems discussed above, a full blown application of portfolio theory to capital budgeting seems to be an impractical proposition. The basic ideas of portfolio analysis, however, may be applied in somewhat simpler ways:

- When a large project is being considered, it may be viewed as one asset and the existing firm as a second asset. A portfolio consisting of the existing firm and the new asset may be compared to the existing firm in terms of expected return and standard deviation. The two alternatives may be evaluated subjectively or judged in terms of their reward-to-variability ratios.
- The mean-variance portfolio model may be used to allocate funds across major business divisions which may be few in number, say three to five for most companies. Data requirement of such analysis is quite manageable.

- When a small project is being considered, the beta between the project and the company's existing portfolio may be regarded as the risk measure for incremental decision making.

Developing the Inputs for Portfolio Analysis Estimates of expected return, variance, and covariance are required to apply the mean-variance portfolio model. For security portfolios, historical values can be used as proxies for future values. This is, however, not feasible for proposed capital investments. What is the way out? One method is to identify various states of nature, assign probabilities to them, and estimate the return of each investment in each state of nature. Based on this information, the required inputs for portfolio analysis, viz. expected returns, variances, and covariances, can be generated.

Example Rahul Corporation is considering two new investments, *P* and *Q*, to go with the existing portfolio of the company's assets, designated as *A*. Three possible states of nature have been identified: (a) strong economic growth with a probability of 0.3; (b) moderate economic growth with a probability of 0.5; (c) weak economic growth with a probability of 0.2. The expected returns from *P*, *Q*, and *A* for different states of nature has been estimated as follows:

	Expected Return		
Economic Growth	*P*	*Q*	*A*
Strong (0.30)	0.20	0.07	0.21
Moderate (0.50)	0.15	0.14	0.12
Weak (0.20)	0.08	0.22	0.05

Given the above information, we can compute the expected return, standard deviation, and covariance terms:

$$E(R_P) = 0.30\ (0.20) + 0.50\ (0.15) + 0.20\ (0.08) = 0.151$$

$$E(R_Q) = 0.30\ (0.07) + 0.50\ (0.14) + 0.20\ (0.22) = 0.135$$

$$E(R_A) = 0.30\ (0.21) + 0.50\ (0.12) + 0.20\ (0.05) = 0.133$$

$$\sigma_P = [0.30\ (0.20 - 0.151)^2 + 0.50\ (0.15 - 0.151)^2 + 0.20\ (0.08 - 0.151)^2]^{1/2}$$
$$= 0.041$$

$$\sigma_Q = [0.30\ (0.07 - 0.135)^2 + 0.50\ (0.14 - 0.135)^2 + 0.20\ (0.22 - 0.135)^2]^{1/2}$$
$$= 0.052$$

$$\sigma_A = [0.30\ (0.21 - 0.133)^2 + 0.50\ (0.12 - 0.133)^2 + 0.20\ (0.05 - 0.133)^2]^{1/2}$$
$$= 0.057$$

$$\sigma_{PQ} = 0.30\ (0.20 - 0.151)\ (0.07 - 0.135) + 0.50\ (0.15 - 0.151)(0.140 - 0.135)$$
$$+ 0.20(0.08 - 0.151)(0.22 - 0.135)$$
$$= - 0.001 + 0 - .0012 = - .0022$$

$$\sigma_{PA} = 0.30\ (0.20 - 0.151)(0.21 - 0.133) + 0.50\ (0.15 - 0.151)(0.12 - 0.133) + 0.20$$
$$(0.08 - 0.151)(0.05 - 0.133)$$

$$= .0011 + 0 + 0.0012 = .0023$$

$$\sigma_{QA} = 0.30\ (0.07 - 0.135)(0.21 - 0.133) + 0.50\ (0.14 - 0.135)(0.12 - 0.133) + 0.20\ (0.22 - 0.135)(0.05 - 0.133)$$

$$= -\ .0015 + 0 - .0014 = -.0029$$

SUMMARY

- According to finance theory, the appropriate discount rate for a project should reflect its opportunity cost of capital.
- When a firm uses a single discount rate (WACC) for all its projects, it will tend to reject a relatively safe project, even though its expected rate of return exceeds its opportunity cost of capital (or risk-adjusted cost of capital) and accept a relatively risky project, even though its expected rate of return is less than its opportunity cost of capital (risk-adjusted cost of capital).
- Despite the conceptual argument in favour of varying the discount rate to reflect the project risk, most firms use a single discount rate for evaluating all of their investment projects. This practice is meant to cope with measurement problems, to mitigate influence costs, and check incentive behaviour.
- The relationship between equity beta and asset beta is as follows:

$$\beta_E = \beta_A \left(1 + \frac{D}{E}(1 - T)\right)$$

- The two key determinants of asset betas are cyclicality and operating leverage.
- The procedure for calculating the divisional WACC, as per the CAPM, involves the following steps: (i) Find a sample of firms engaged in the same line of business. (ii) Obtain equity betas for the sample firms. (iii) Derive asset betas after adjusting equity betas for financial leverage. (iv) Find the average of the asset betas. (v) Figure out the equity beta for the division. (vi) Estimate the cost of equity for the division. (vii) Calculate the divisional WACC.
- The procedure for calculating the project-specific WACC would be the same as that for the divisional WACC. However, implementing this procedure for individual projects is difficult because it is not easy to find market proxies for the project risk and to define capital structure weights since equity values of individual projects are not observable.
- Firms typically set a hurdle rate that is higher than the WACC. There are three main reasons for this: (i) Most firms believe that the WACC is not the appropriate opportunity cost. (ii) A higher-than-WACC hurdle rate is meant to incentivise project sponsors to find better projects. (iii) A higher-than-WACC hurdle rate is aimed at countering the optimistic projections and selection bias.
- Although there are various portfolio risk measures, the mean-variance portfolio model is the most widely used. This model assumes that the risk of a portfolio is defined by

the variance or standard deviation of the probability distribution of portfolio returns.

- The expected return and the standard deviation of return for a two-asset portfolio are:

$$E(R_p) = W_A E(R_A) + W_B E(R_B)$$

$$\sigma_p = (W_A^2 \sigma_A^2 + W_B^2 \sigma_B^2 + 2W_A W_B \rho_{A,B} \sigma_A \sigma_B)^{1/2}$$

- The expected return and the standard deviation of return for an n-asset portfolio are:

$$E(R_p) = \sum_{i=1}^{n} W_i E(R_i)$$

$$\sigma_p = \sum_{j=1}^{n} \sum_{i=1}^{n} W_i W_j \sigma_{ij} \sigma_i \sigma_j$$

- A portfolio is efficient if and only if there is no alternative with (i) the same $E(R_p)$ and a lower σ_p, or (ii) the same σ_p and a higher $E(R_p)$, or (iii) a higher $E(R_p)$ and a lower σ_p. The efficient frontier contains all the efficient portfolios.

QUESTIONS

1. Explain the justification for using multiple discount rates.
2. What is the rationale for using a single discount rate?
3. What is the relationship between asset beta and equity beta?
4. Discuss the procedure for calculating the divisional cost of capital.
5. Why do firms generally set a hurdle rate that is higher than the WACC?
6. How is the risk of a 2-asset portfolio defined?
7. How is the risk of an n-asset portfolio defined?
8. What is the efficient frontier?
9. What problems are encountered in applying portfolio theory to capital budgeting?
10. How can basic ideas of portfolio analysis be applied to capital budgeting in simpler ways?

PROBLEMS

1. Magnum Limited is considering a cement project for which it proposes to employ a debt-equity ratio of 2:1. Its pre-tax cost of debt will be 16 percent and its expected tax rate is 30 percent. There are three firms, A, B, and C engaged wholly in cement manufacture. Their equity betas and debt-equity ratios are as follows:

	Equity beta	*Debt-equity ratio*
A	1.25	2.25
B	1.15	2.00
C	1.10	2.10

The risk-free rate is 12 percent and the expected return on the market portfolio is 17 percent. What should be the required rate of return on Magnum's cement project?

2. Pariman Company's equity beta is 1.25. Its debt-equity ratio is 1.60 and its tax rate is 30 percent. What is Pariman Company's asset beta?
3. Growmore Fertiliser Company has a debt-to-equity ratio of 1.25 to 1.0. Its cost of debt funds is 12 percent and it has a marginal tax rate of 40 percent. Growmore is considering a proposal to diversify into petrochemicals, a field that is considerably different from its own. Growmore regards Sunrise Petrochemicals as a good proxy company. Sunrise has a debt-equity ratio of 1.5, a beta of 1.30, and an effective tax rate of 40 percent.
   (a) If Growmore wishes to manufacture petrochemicals, what systematic risk is involved if it intends employing the same amount of leverage in the new project as it currently employs?
   (b) If the risk–free rate is 12 percent and the expected return on the market portfolio is 18 percent, what is the required rate of return for the petrochemicals project as per the CAPM?
4. Three assets, *P*, *Q*, and *R*, have expected returns of 0.15 (or 15 percent), 0.20, and 0.18 respectively. The variances and covariances are as follows:

	P	*Q*	*R*
P	.04	.03	–.04
Q	.03	.05	0
R	–.04	0	.06

   What is the expected return and standard deviation of a portfolio consisting of 30 percent of funds in *A*, 40 percent of funds in *B* and 30 percent of funds in *C*?
5. Surana Corporation is considering two new investments, *B* and *C*, to go with the existing portfolio of the company's assets, designated as *A*. Three possible states of nature have been identified: (a) strong economic growth with a probability of 0.4; (b) moderate economic growth with a probability of 0.3; (c) weak economic growth with a probability of 0.3. The expected returns from *A*, *B*, and *C* for different states of nature has been estimated as follows.

	Expected Return		
Economic Growth	*A*	*B*	*C*
Strong (0.4)	0.21	0.20	0.09
Moderate (0.3)	0.16	0.12	0.15
Weak (0.3)	0.10	0.08	0.24

   Given the above, compute the expected return, standard deviation, and covariance terms.

MINICASE

Shankar Santhanam founded SS Limited about 30 years ago. Initially the company set up a non-ferrous metals division. The profits generated from the metals division were ploughed back for expansion and diversification. Due to a strange turn of events, SS Limited diversified into real estate and finance activities (hire purchase and leasing). Currently, SS Limited has three divisions—metals, real estate, and finance—which function more or less autonomously. The corporate office, with a small staff, exercises financial controls and allocates capital across these divisions. Exhibit 1 presents the balance sheet of SS Limited with assets and loans broken up division-wise.

Exhibit 1 ***Balance Sheet of SS Limited***

Shareholders' Funds		1500	Fixed Assets			2400
Capital	300		Metals	:	900	
Reserves and surplus	1200		Real estate	:	1000	
			Finance	:	500	
Loan Funds		1500	Net Current Asset			600
Term loan	1000		Metals	:	250	
(8% interest)			Real estate	:	50	
Metals	: 200		Finance	:	300	
Real estate	: 500					
Finance	: 300					
Working capital loan						
(10% interest)	500					
Metals	: 200					
Real estate	: 100					
Finance	: 200					
		3000				3000

The revenues and net profits of the three divisions for the just concluded year are as follows.

	Metals	*Real Estate*	*Finance*
Revenues	1300	1500	600
Net Profit	100	200	90

Shankar Santhanam has been applying a cut-off rate of 13 percent for evaluating investment projects in all the divisions. His reasoning is simple: SS Limited uses a debt-equity ratio of 1 : 1; the cost of equity is 18 percent and the cost of debt is 8 percent; so the average cost of funds is 13 percent.

Recently, Shankar Santhanam's son Ravi Santhanam joined the business after graduating from a premier business school. Ravi was surprised that his father applied a uniform cut-off rate across all the three divisions, despite variations in their business risk and financing pattern.

Ravi wants your help in determining the cut-off rates for the three divisions. He has provided you with the summary financial data for Amtex Metals, MLF Realtors, and Nidhi Finance, given in Exhibit 2. These are three pure play competitors to SS Limited's three divisions, namely, metals division, real estate division, and finance division.

Exhibit 2 ***Summary Financial Data for Competitors***

	Amtex Metals	*MLF Realtors*	*Nidhi Finance*
Fixed assets	1200	1600	800
Net current assets	400	200	500
	1600	1800	1300

(Contd.)

Share capital	400	200	300
Reserves and Surplus	900	900	300
Loan funds	300	700	700
	1600	1800	1300
Revenues	2000	2500	400
Net profit	200	300	100
Equity beta	1.1	0.95	1.2

The risk-free rate currently is 7 percent and the general view is that the market risk premium is 7 percent. The corporate tax rate of 30 percent is applicable to all the businesses.

Required

(a) What is the cost of equity applicable to the three divisions, viz, metals, real estate, and finance?
(b) What is the cutoff rate applicable to the three divisions, viz, metals, real estate, and finance?
(c) Explain the justification for using multiple discount rates.
(d) What is the rationale for using a single discount rate?

APPENDIX 12A

GETTING MORE OUT OF CAPITAL BUDGETS

In large capital projects, delays and cost overruns are common. Research suggests that decision biases contribute significantly to the skewing of forecasts and timing as projects are being planned. Inadequate internal discipline at the proposal and management stages too raises costs.

To improve the internal discipline in capital budgeting, the following are helpful:

- A standard comparable model for projects.
- Greater rigour in the scrutiny of capital investment proposals.
- A dedicated multidisciplinary team for managing the capital portfolio.

A Standard Model

In many large firms, the process of developing and managing small capital projects is mostly left to operations and engineering people. As a result, no standardised methodology is used to assess a project's underlying rationale and business case. This creates opacity and makes it difficult to assess the trade-offs of investing in one project over another.

It behooves on the finance organisation to implement a standard model for all projects which defines rules and parameters for key assumptions on exchange rates, inflation, capital costs, product prices, and so on and specifies the parameters to create a business case in terms of financial metrics like net present value and internal rate of return and other non-financial metrics.

• Greater Rigour

Engineers, often the prime movers of capital projects, tend to have a bias towards including costly and inessential refinements in capital projects. They would like to buy the latest models of equipment when a refurbishment would suffice. Business leaders too would like to get a higher capital budget allocated, so that they have flexibility to spend as they deem fit.

The finance organisation has the responsibility to inject a greater rigour into the review and scrutiny of proposals. It has to challenge the business case and the technical case for each project, conduct a detailed review, and compel project teams to single out discrete elements of bundled proposals.

• Dedicated Multidisciplinary Team

A close review and improvement of a large capital portfolio calls for resources and capabilities greater than what are provided by the usual and ad hoc approaches. It requires a dedicated multidisciplinary team that includes members with technical, procurement, and financial skills. Ideally, the committee and process must function under the chief operating officer or a corporate project organisation.

The team remit should be expanded to include the postmortem of projects. Each project, after its completion, must be reviewed at predetermined intervals (typically six months to three years) to determine whether it has delivered the expected value and hold the original sponsor accountable for its outcome.

Chapter 13 Special Decisions Situations

LEARNING OBJECTIVES

After studying this chapter you should be able to

- Compute the uniform annual equivalent of a machine.
- Calculate the adjusted present value (APV) of a project.
- Explain how inflation is considered in capital budgeting.
- Discuss the procedure for evaluating an overseas investment proposal.
- Understand various organisational capabilities.

Our discussion so far assumed that: (i) Every project being considered is independent. This means, among other things, that we don't have a situation where two or more projects are mutually exclusive. (ii) A project is being considered for implementation now or never. (iii) The investment and financing aspects of a project are independent. (iv) The cash flows of a project may be estimated on the basis of current prices.

This chapter discusses decision situations where there are mutually exclusive projects, where a project can be deferred by one or more years, where the investment and financing sides of the project are related, and where inflation is explicitly considered in evaluating the project. In addition it looks at the evaluation of overseas investment proposals, and investment in capabilities.

13.1 CHOICE BETWEEN MUTUALLY EXCLUSIVE PROJECTS AND UNEQUAL LIFE

Alpha Limited is considering two machines, A and B. Though designed differently, they serve the same function. Machine A, a standard model, costs ₹75,000 and lasts for 5 years. Its annual operating costs will be ₹12,000. Machine B, an economy model, costs ₹50,000 but lasts for only 3 years. Its annual operating costs will be ₹20,000. All the figures are expressed in real terms; this means that they represent rupees of constant purchasing power.

How should Alpha Limited choose between the two machines? Since they serve the same function, the choice between them should be based on a comparison of costs. One way of doing this may be to compare the present value of all the costs associated with the two machines. Assuming a discount rate of 12 percent, the present value of all the costs associated with the two machines are:

$$\text{Machine A: } 75{,}000 + \frac{12{,}000}{(1.12)} + \frac{12{,}000}{(1.12)^2} + \frac{12{,}000}{(1.12)^3} + \frac{12{,}000}{(1.12)^4} + \frac{12{,}000}{(1.12)^5} = 118{,}260$$

$$\text{Machine B: } 50{,}000 + \frac{15{,}000}{(1.12)} + \frac{15{,}000}{(1.12)^2} + \frac{15{,}000}{(1.12)^3} = 86{,}030$$

The present value of costs associated with machine B is lower than that of machine A. Based on such a comparison, one may argue that machine B is preferable to machine A. Such an argument, however, is flawed because it overlooks the fact that machine B has a shorter life and has to be replaced earlier.

For a proper comparison of the two alternatives, that have different lives, we have to convert the present value of costs into a uniform annual equivalent (UAE) figure. The UAE is a function of the present value of cost, the life of the asset, and the discount rate. The UAE is simply:

$$\frac{\text{PV Cost}}{\text{PVIFA}_{r,n}}$$

The *UAE* of the two machines is calculated below:

$$\text{Machine } A\text{: } UAE = \frac{118{,}260}{3.605} = 32{,}804$$

$$\text{Machine } B\text{: } UAE = \frac{86{,}030}{2.402} = 35{,}816$$

What does a *UAE* value of ₹32,804 for machine *A* mean? It simply means that incurring a capital outlay and operating costs which have a present value of ₹118,260 for a machine that lasts five years is like incurring an annual cost of ₹32,804 for five years. Likewise a *UAE* value of ₹35,816 for machine *B* implies that incurring a capital outlay and operating costs which have a present value of ₹86,030 for a machine that lasts three years is like incurring an annual cost of ₹35,816 for three years.

The choice between machines *A* and *B* can be made by comparing their *UAE*. Since the *UAE* of machine *A* is lower than the *UAE* of machine *B*, machine *A* is preferable to machine *B*.

13.2 OPTIMAL TIMING

In real life, an investment is rarely a "now or never" proposition. Typically, it can be undertaken now or at some point of time in future. Given this option, the issue of optimal timing assumes significance.

Under conditions of certainty, the optimal timing may be determined by using the following procedure.

1. Examine alternative dates (t) when the investment can be made.
2. Estimate the net future value as of each alternative date and convert the same to its current value.
3. Choose the timing that has the highest current value.

This procedure may be explained with the help of an example. Futuristic Limited is evaluating different dates for investing in a micro-electronics project. The net future value for various dates is as follows:

Time	*Net future value (₹ in million)*
0	20
1	28
2	33
3	36
4	38

The discount rate applicable for the project is 12 percent. Hence the current value for different timing options is as follows:

Time	*Current value (₹ in million)*
0	$\frac{20}{(1.12)^0} = 20.00$
1	$\frac{28}{(1.12)^1} = 25.00$
2	$\frac{33}{(1.12)^2} = 26.30$
3	$\frac{36}{(1.12)^3} = 25.62$
4	$\frac{38}{(1.12)^4} = 24.15$

The optimal timing is year 2 as it maximises the current value.

Thus, determining the optimal timing under conditions of certainty is a fairly easy proposition. Under conditions of uncertainty, however, the problem of optimal timing is very complex. If an investment is not undertaken now ($t = 0$) it may become either more or less valuable in future and there may be no way of figuring that out. Perhaps it may be advantageous to exploit a good opportunity today even though it may become more attractive in future. Or it may be worthwhile to wait for the resolution of some uncertainty to minimise the possibility of an investment blunder. Managerial judgement plays an important role in such a decision.

13.3 DETERMINATION OF ECONOMIC LIFE

A distinction may be made between the physical life and the economic (or optimal) life of an asset. The physical life of an asset represents the number of years it can be used to produce a certain output by regular maintenance and repair (which, of course, tends to cost more and more as the years roll by). The economic life of an asset refers to the number of years the asset should be used to produce a certain output.

The economic life of an asset is influenced by the behaviour of operating and maintenance costs on the one hand and capital costs on the other. Operating and maintenance costs cover labour, material, and power expenses to operate, maintain, and repair the asset. Capital costs, also referred to as ownership costs, represent the decline in the value of the asset over time – this decline occurs as the asset is used up for producing goods and also as it ages with the passage of time.

The economic life of an asset is conceptually defined as the period after which the asset should be replaced to minimise the sum of operating and maintenance costs and capital costs expressed on an annual basis. Put differently, it is the replacement cycle that minimises the uniform annual equivalent total cost, UAE (TC) of operating and owning the asset. The UAE (TC) is simply the sum of the uniform annual equivalent operating and maintenance cost, UAE (OM), and the uniform annual equivalent capital cost, UAE (CC). That is,

$$\text{UAE (TC)} = \text{UAE (OM)} + \text{UAE (CC)}$$

Exhibit 13.1 shows the behaviour of UAE (TC), UAE (OM), and UAE (CC) as the replacement cycle is extended. UAE (OM) increases as the replacement period is lengthened because with aging it costs more and more to operate, maintain, and repair the asset to produce a given quantity and quality of output. The UAE (CC), however declines as the replacement cycle is extended. This happens because, as the asset is used for a longer period, the capital cost per year falls.

Exhibit 13.1 ***Costs Over the Life of Machine***

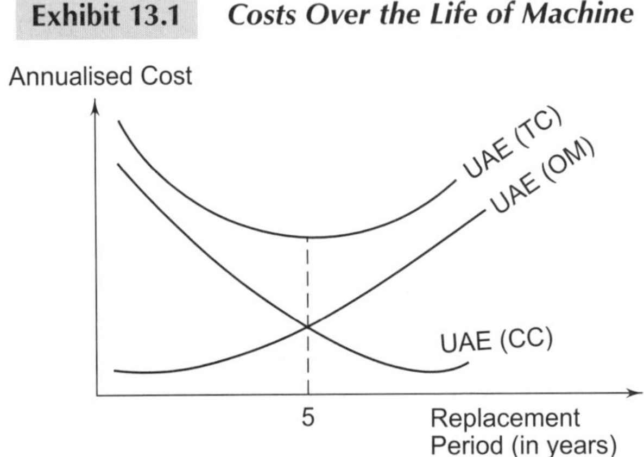

Since UAE (OM) rises and UAE (CC) falls with the lengthening of the replacement period, their sum, UAE (TC), will be minimised for some replacement period. As shown in Exhibit 13.1, UAE (TC) is minimised when the replacement period is 2 years.

The Problem We have discussed conceptually how the economic life of an asset is defined. Its measurement in practice involves a series of calculations, which may be illustrated with the help of an example. Modern Plastics Limited is considering a machine to produce plastic products. It requires an initial outlay of ₹0.6 million and will be depreciated at a rate of 33 1/3 percent per annum as per the written down value method for income tax purposes. The expected operating and maintenance costs and salvage (market) value for the next eight years which represents the maximum physical life of the machine are shown in Exhibit 13.2. The cost of capital appropriate for the machine is 12 percent and the tax rate for Modern Plastics Limited is 40 percent. Not sure of what the economic life of the machine is, the firm seeks your help in determining it.

Exhibit 13.2 ***Operating and Maintenance Costs and Salvage Value for the Machine***

			Year				*₹('000)*	
	1	*2*	*3*	*4*	*5*	*6*	*7*	*8*
Operating and maintenance cost	80.00	100.00	130.00	180.00	240.00	300.00	360.00	450.00
Salvage value at time *t*	400.00	252.00	180.00	100.00	80.00	60.00	50.00	40.00

To determine the economic life of the machine, it is useful to separately consider the operating and maintenance cost and the capital cost. When these are adjusted for taxes and translated into UAE form, the behaviour of UAE (TC) with respect to replacement period can be studied and the economic life determined.

Operating and Maintenance Costs To obtain the UAE (OM) for various replacement periods, the following calculations may be done:

1. Convert the operating and maintenance costs into post-tax terms.
2. Discount the post-tax operating and maintenance costs to obtain their present values.
3. Cumulate the present values for various replacement periods.
4. Calculate the UAE (OM) for various replacement periods by applying suitable annuity factors.

Exhibit 13.3 shows the calculation of UAE (OM) for the various replacement cycles for the machine being considered by Modern Plastics. The first row shows the operating and maintenance costs as taken from Exhibit 13.2; the second row converts the operating and maintenance costs into post-tax terms; the third row gives the present value interest factors, assuming a discount rate of 12 percent; the fourth row translates the post-tax operating and maintenance costs into their present value; the fifth row cumulates the present values for various replacement periods; the sixth row contains the annuity factors (PVIFAs) assuming a discount rate of 12 percent; finally the seventh row displays the UAE (OM) for various replacement periods.

Exhibit 13.3 *Calculation of UAE (OM) for Various Replacement Periods*

₹('000)

	t=1	*t=2*	*t=3*	*t=4*	*t=5*	*t=6*	*t=7*	*t=8*
Operating and maintenance costs	80.00	100.00	130.00	180.00	240.00	300.00	360.00	450.00
Post-tax operating and maintenance costs	48.00	60.00	78.00	108.00	144.00	180.00	216.00	270.00
PVIF (*t*, *r* =12%)	0.893	0.797	0.712	0.636	0.567	0.507	0.452	0.404
Present value of post-tax operating and maintenance costs	42.86	47.82	55.54	68.69	81.65	91.26	97.63	109.08
Cumulative present value	42.86	90.68	146.22	214.91	296.56	387.82	485.45	594.53
PVIFA (*t*, *r* = 12%)	0.893	1.690	2.402	3.037	3.605	4.111	4.564	4.968
UAE (OM)	48.00	53.66	60.87	70.76	82.26	94.34	106.37	119.67

Capital Costs To derive the UAE (CC) for various replacement periods, the following components must be taken into account: the initial outlay (IO), depreciation tax shields (DTS), and the net salvage value (SV). The UAE (CC) for a given replacement period is equal to:

$$\text{UAE (IO)} - [\text{UAE(DTS)} + \text{UAE(SV)}]$$

The calculations of UAE (IO), UAE (DTS), and UAE (SV) are shown in Exhibits 13.4, 13.5, and 13.6 respectively.

Economic Life The economic life represents the replacement period which minimises the UAE (TC). The information required to determine the economic life is summarised in Exhibit 13.7. For each replacement period, column 1 shows UAE (OM) drawn from Exhibit 13.3. Columns 2, 3, and 4 show UAE (IO), UAE (DTS), and UAE (SV) drawn from Exhibits 13.4, 13.5, and 13.6 respectively. Column 5 shows UAE (CC), which is UAE (IO) – [UAE(DTS) + UAE(SV)]. Finally, column 6 represents UAE (TC), which is simply UAE (OM) plus UAE (CC). Looking at the column for UAE (TC) we find that UAE (TC) is minimised when the replacement period is 5 years. So the economic life is 5 years.

Exhibit 13.4 *Calculation of UAE (IO) for Various Replacement Periods*

₹('000)

	t=1	*t=2*	*t=3*	*t=4*	*t=5*	*t=6*	*t=7*	*t=8*
Investment outlay	600.00	600.00	600.00	600.00	600.00	600.00	600.00	600.00
PVIFA (*t*, *r* =12%)	0.893	1.690	2.402	3.037	3.605	4.111	4.564	4.968
UAE (IO)	671.89	355.03	249.79	197.56	166.45	145.95	131.46	120.77

Exhibit 13.5 *Calculation of UAE (DTS) for Various Replacement Periods*

₹('000)

	t=1	t=2	t=3	t=4	t=5	t=6	t=7	t=8
Depreciation charge	200.00	133.33	88.89	59.26	39.51	26.34	17.56	11.70
Depreciation tax shield	80.00	53.33	35.55	23.70	15.80	10.53	7.02	4.68
PVIF (*t*, *r* =12%)	0.893	0.797	0.712	0.636	0.567	0.507	0.452	0.404
Present value of depreciation tax shield	71.44	42.50	25.31	15.07	8.96	5.34	3.17	1.89
Cumulative present value	71.44	113.94	139.25	154.32	163.28	168.62	171.79	173.68
PVIFA (*t*, *r* =12%)	0.893	1.690	2.402	3.037	3.605	4.111	4.564	4.968
UAE (DTS)	80.00	67.42	57.97	50.81	45.29	41.02	37.64	34.96

Exhibit 13.6 *Calculation of UAE (SV) for Various Replacement Periods*

₹('000)

	t=1	t=2	t=3	t=4	t=5	t=6	t=7	t=8
Salvage value	400.00	252.00	180.00	100.00	80.00	60.00	50.00	40.00
PVIF (*t*, *r* =12%)	0.893	0.797	0.712	0.636	0.567	0.507	0.452	0.404
Present value of salvage value	357.20	200.84	128.16	63.60	45.36	30.42	22.60	16.16
PVIFA (*t*, *r* =12%)	0.893	1.690	2.402	3.037	3.505	4.111	4.564	4.968
UAE (SV)	400.00	118.84	53.36	20.94	12.58	7.40	4.95	3.25

Exhibit 13.7 *Summary of Information Required to Determine the Economic Life*

Replacement period in years	*UAE (OM)*	*UAE (IO)*	*UAE (DTS)*	*UAE (SV)*	*UAE (CC)*	*UAE (TC)*
1	48.00	671.89	88.00	400.00	191.89	239.89
2	53.66	355.03	67.42	118.84	168.77	222.43
3	60.68	249.79	57.97	53.36	138.46	199.14
4	70.76	197.56	50.81	20.94	125.81	196.57
5	82.26	166.44	45.29	12.58	108.57	190.83
6	94.34	145.95	41.02	7.40	97.53	191.87
7	106.37	131.46	37.64	4.95	88.87	195.24
8	119.67	120.77	34.96	3.25	82.56	202.23

13.4 INTERRELATIONSHIP BETWEEN INVESTMENT AND FINANCING ASPECTS

The most commonly followed procedure for capital budgeting involves four steps:

1. Forecast the post-tax cash flows of the project.
2. Assess the riskiness of the project.
3. Choose an appropriate discount rate.
4. Calculate the net present value.

Note that the WACC calculated in step 3 reflects the tax shield associated with debt. Thus the above procedure incorporates the value contributed by the financing decision.

Recall that two basic conditions should be satisfied for using WACC for evaluating new investments:

- The risk of new investments is the same as the average risk of existing investments. In other words, the adoption of new investments will not change the risk complexion of the firm.
- The capital structure of the firm will not be affected by the new investments. Put differently, the firms will continue to pursue the same financing policy.
  Thus, strictly speaking WACC is the right discount rate for a project that is a carbon copy of the firm's existing business.

Adjusted Present Value A project may have financing effects that differ from those of the existing investments of the firm[1]. It may have different debt capacity or be entitled to certain subsidies or have some special financial features. In such cases the recommended method is to calculate the adjusted NPV (or APV for short). APV is calculated by first estimating the base-case NPV and then adjusting it to reflect the financing impact of the project.

APV = Base case NPV + Present value of the financing side effects of the project

The base case NPV is the NPV of the project under the following assumptions:

- The project is financed entirely by equity.
- There is no financing effect like issue cost or subsidy.

The present value of financing side effects is equal to:

- Present value of positive financing side effects like tax shield on debt and availability of subsidies
- Present value of negative financing side effects like issue costs.

Illustration The APV calculation may be illustrated with an example. Parimala Company is considering a project requiring ₹5 million of investment. It is expected to generate a net cash flow of ₹1 million per year for 8 years. The opportunity cost of capital is 15 percent - this reflects the return required by equity investors, assuming that the project is entirely financed by equity. The cost of issuing equity is 5 percent. The project enables the firm to raise ₹2.4 million of debt finance. The debt finance will carry 14 percent interest and will be repaid in

[1] For the time being we assume that it does not differ from the existing investments of the firm in terms of risk.

equal annual instalments over an eight year period – the first instalment will be paid at the end of the first year. The tax rate applicable to the firm is 40 percent.

Given the above information about the project, let us calculate its base case NPV. This is equal to:

$$-5000,000 + \sum_{t=1}^{8} \frac{1,000,000}{(1.15)^t} = -₹512,700$$

The base-case NPV has to be adjusted for two factors: (i) issue cost, and (ii) tax-shield associated with debt.

Out of the total financing requirement of the project, ₹2,600,000 will come from the equity sources and ₹2,400,000 will come in the form of debt finance. As the net equity finance required by the project is ₹2,600,000 and issue costs would absorb 5 percent of the gross proceeds of the issue, the firm will have to issue ₹2,736,842 (₹2,600,000/0.95) of equity stock in order to realise a net amount of ₹2,600,000. The difference of ₹136,842 is the cost of underwriting, brokerage, printing, and other issue related expenses. The APV after adjustment for issue cost is:

APV = Base case NPV – Issue cost
= –₹512,700 – ₹136,842
= –₹649,542

Now we consider the adjustment for the tax shield associated with debt finance. The present value of tax shield associated with ₹2,400,000 of debt finance is calculated in Exhibit 13.8. From this exhibit we find that the debt finance associated with the project brings a stream of tax shields which has a present value of ₹403,337. If we make adjustment for this also, we get:

APV = Base case NPV – Issue cost + Present value of tax shield
= –₹512,700 – ₹136,842 + ₹403,337
= –₹246,205

Exhibit 13.8 ***Calculation of the Present Value of Tax Shield***

Year	*Debt Outstanding at the Beginning*	*Interest*	*Tax Shield*	*Present Value of Tax Shield (at 14% discount rate)*
1	2,400,000	336,000	134,400	177,895
2	2,100,000	294,000	117,600	90,489
3	1,800,000	252,000	100,800	68,037
4	1,500,000	210,000	84,000	49,735
5	1,200,000	168,000	67,200	34,902
6	900,000	126,000	50,400	22,962
7	600,000	84,000	33,600	13,428
8	300,000	42,000	16,800	5,889
				Total ₹403,337

The calculation in Exhibit 13.8 assumes that the firm can fully capture the interest tax shield which can be considered safe cash inflows and discounted at the interest rate on debt.

The actual present value of tax shield, however, would almost surely be less than ₹403,267 for the following reasons:

- Few firms can be certain that they will have enough profits in future to avail of interest tax shield fully.
- Apart from the tax that the firm pays on its income, investors (bondholders and shareholders) have to pay personal tax on their debt returns and equity returns. At the personal level debt returns are generally taxed at a higher rate than stock returns.

Opportunity Cost of Capital Recall that the base-case NPV is calculated using the opportunity cost of capital. How is the opportunity cost of capital defined? The opportunity cost of capital, *r*, is the expected rate of return required by the investors if the firm (or project) has no debt. In our illustration *r* was assumed to be 15 percent. How can you estimate *r*? Since you can't get it from any published source, you have to infer it. Under Modigliani-Miller capital structure theory[2]

$$r = r_D \frac{D}{V} + r_E \frac{E}{V} \tag{13.1}$$

where r is the opportunity cost of capital, r_D is the expected return on the debt, r_E is the expected return on the equity of the firm, D/V is the market value weight of debt, and E/V is the market value weight of equity.

How does r, the opportunity cost of capital, compare with WACC, the after-tax weighted average cost of capital? Recall that

$$\text{WACC} = r_D (1 - T_c) \frac{D}{V} + r_E \frac{E}{V} \tag{13.2}$$

Note that when a firm employs debt, WACC is less than r because in WACC's calculation the cost of debt is calculated after-tax. Exhibit 13.9 shows the typical behaviour of r_E, r_D, r and WACC.

Exhibit 13.9 ***Behaviour of r and WACC***

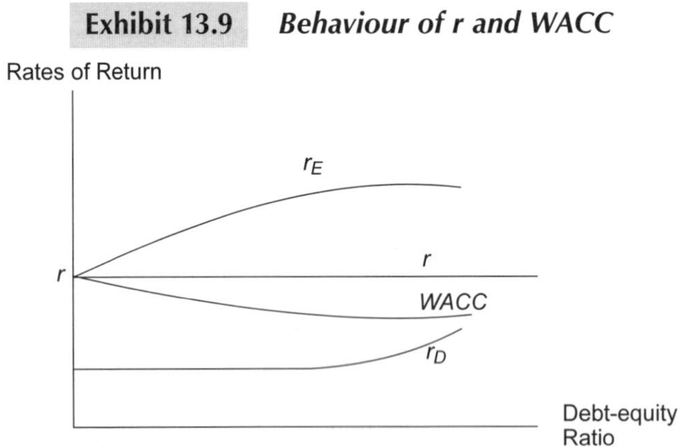

[2] In a seminal contribution made in 1958 Franco Modigliani and Merton H. Miller, who later became Nobel laureates in Economics, argued that in a taxless world the opportunity cost of the capital is independent of the capital structure.

Merits of APV The principle underlying *APV* is to divide and conquer. *APV* does not reflect the side effects of financing in a single calculation. Instead, it captures them in a series of calculations. This makes it more illuminating. You not only know what the *APV* is but also where it is coming from. This is helpful in reformulating the project.

Suppose the *APV* of a project is calculated as follows:

Base case *NPV*	:	₹1,000,000
PV of issue cost	:	₹7,000,000
PV of tax shield	:	₹4,000,000
PV of subsidy	:	₹1,000,000
APV	:	– ₹1,000,000

To salvage the project you may explore ways to reduce issue costs or stake a claim for a higher subsidy with suitable justification.

APV makes more sense for projects that have a capital structure that is different from the rest of the firm or which have a capital structure that changes significantly over time or that enjoy special concessions, incentives, and subsidies. For example, *APV* is eminently suitable for leveraged buyouts (LBOs) or infrastructure projects.

LBOs An LBO is a takeover financed almost entirely with debt. However, the debt employed for an LBO is not meant to be permanent. It is intended to be repaid over time. Obviously you can's use WACC (which presupposes a stable capital structure) to evaluate an LBO.

Infrastructure Projects Infrastructure projects have important financing side effects. They have a high debt ratio which is gradually brought down. Further, debt may be available at concessional rates. Finally, subsidies, incentives, and concessions are often given to such projects.

Adjusted Cost of Capital Though conceptually sound, APV is not very popular because (i) it requires some sophistication to assess the financing side effects, and (ii) it involves a series of adjustments which may be cumbersome.

That is why WACC, which is the cost of capital adjusted for financing effects, is more commonly used in practice. Recall that WACC is:

$$r_D\,(1-T_c)\,\frac{D}{V}+r_E\,\frac{E}{V} \qquad (13.4)$$

There are other formulae of adjusted cost of capital as well. Two of them are:

Modigliani and Miller formula : $r^* = r\,(1-TL)$ (13.5)

Miles and Ezzell formula : $r^* = r - L\,r_D\,T\,\dfrac{1+r}{1+r_D}$ (13.6)

where r^* is the adjusted cost of capital, r is the opportunity cost of capital assuming 100 percent equity financing, T is the tax rate applicable to the firm, L is the marginal contribution of the project to the firm's debt capacity, and r_D is the cost of debt.

Example 1 A firm is considering a project for setting up a captive power plant for which the following information has been gathered.

Investment outlay	:	₹50 million
Annual post-tax savings	:	₹5 million
Life of the project	:	Perpetual
Debt capacity of the project	:	₹25 million
Interest rate on debt	:	10 percent
Nature of debt	:	Perpetual
Tax rate for the firm	:	40 percent
Opportunity cost of capital	:	12 percent

The adjusted cost of capital as per Modigliani–Miller formula is:

$$r^* = r\,(1 - TL) = 0.12\,(1 - 0.4 \times 0.5) = 0.096 \text{ or } 9.6\%$$

The adjusted cost of capital as per Miles and Ezzell formula is:

$$r^* = r - L\,r_D\,T\,\frac{1+r}{1+r_D} = 0.12 - 0.5 \times 0.10 \times 0.4 \times \frac{1.12}{1.10} = 0.100 \text{ or } 10.0\%$$

Example 2 A real estate company is considering the acquisition of a piece of land that it plans to resell after a year. The following information is available:

Investment	:	₹10 million
Net cash flow expected from resale after one year	:	₹11.5 million
Debt capacity	:	₹5 million
Interest rate on debt	:	12 percent
Tax rate of the firm	:	35 percent
Opportunity cost of capital	:	15 percent

The adjusted cost of capital as per Modigliani–Miller formula is:

$$r^* = r\,(1 - TL) = 0.15\,(1 - 0.35 \times 0.5) = 0.12375 \text{ or } 12.375\%$$

The adjusted cost of capital as per Miles and Ezzell formula is:

$$r^* = r - L\,r_D\,T\,\frac{1+r}{1+r_D} = 0.15 - 0.5 \times 0.12 \times 0.35 \times \frac{1.15}{1.12} = 0.1284 \text{ or } 12.84\%$$

The Modigliani–Miller formula is valid when a project generates constant perpetual cash flow and supports permanent debt (these conditions were satisfied by the power project above). The Miles and Ezzell formula requires that the project maintain a constant debt proportion but it does not presuppose any particular cash flow pattern or project life.

13.5 INFLATION AND CAPITAL BUDGETING

Inflation has been a persistent feature of the Indian economy. Hence, it should be properly considered in capital investment appraisal. In practice, however, adjustment for inflation is rarely, if ever, made. The use of current price structure is deemed satisfactory and the reasoning offered runs as follows:

Inflation is expected to raise the revenues and costs of the project in a similar fashion. Hence, net revenues after adjustment for inflation would be equal to net revenues in current terms.

The above argument, however, overlooks the following considerations which cause distortion:

1. The depreciation charge is based on historical costs and hence the tax benefit arising from depreciation charge does not keep pace with inflation.
2. The cost of capital used for investment appraisal contains a premium for anticipated inflation.

13.6 INTERNATIONAL CAPITAL BUDGETING

India Pharma Limited, an India-based multinational company, is evaluating an overseas investment proposal. India Pharma's exports of pharmaceutical products have increased to such an extent that it is considering a project to build a plant in the U.S. The project will entail an initial outlay of $100 million and is expected to generate the following cash flows over its four year life.

Year	*Cash Flow (in millions)*
1	$ 30
2	$ 40
3	$ 50
4	$ 60

The current spot exchange rate is ₹70 per U.S. dollar, the risk-free rate in India is 11 percent and the risk- free rate in the U.S. is 6 percent – these are rates observed in the financial markets.

India Pharma's required rupee return on a project of this kind is 15 percent. Should India Pharma undertake this project? The answer, of course, depends on the NPV of the project. How is the NPV of such a project calculated?

There are two basic ways of doing this:

Home Currency Approach

- Convert all the dollar cash flows into rupees (use the forecasted exchange rates)
- Calculate the NPV in rupees (use the rupee discount rate)

Foreign Currency Approach

- Calculate the NPV in dollars (use the dollar discount rate)
- Convert the dollar NPV into rupees (use the spot exchange rate)

Home Currency Approach To apply the home currency approach we have to come up with the forecasted (or expected) exchange rates. According to the International Fisher Effect, the expected spot exchange rate at time t is:

$$S^e_t = S_o\left(\frac{1+r_h}{1+r_f}\right)^t \qquad (13.10)$$

where S^e_t is the expected spot exchange rate at time t, S_o is the current spot exchange rate, r_h is the nominal risk-free rate in home currency, and r_f is the nominal risk-free interest rate in foreign currency.

In our example, S_o = ₹70, r_h = 8 percent, and r_f = 3 percent. Hence, the forecasted spot exchange rates are as follows

Year	*Forecasted spot exchange rate*		
1	₹70 $(1.08/1.03)^1$	=	₹73.40
2	₹70 $(1.08/1.03)^2$	=	₹76.96
3	₹70 $(1.08/1.03)^3$	=	₹80.70
4	₹70 $(1.08/1.03)^4$	=	₹84.61

Using these forecasted spot exchange rates along with the current spot rate of ₹70, we can convert the dollar cash flows into rupees as shown below:

	(1)	*(2)*	*(3)*
Year	*Cash Flow in Dollar (million)*	*Expected Exchange Rate*	*Cash Flow in Rupees (million) (1) × (2)*
0	–100	₹70.00	–₹7000.0
1	30	73.40	2202.0
2	40	76.96	3078.4
3	50	80.70	4035.0
4	60	84.61	5076.6

Given a rupee discount rate of 15 percent, the NPV in rupees is:

$$\text{NPV} = -7000 + \frac{2202.0}{(1.15)} + \frac{3078.4}{(1.15)^2} + \frac{4035.0}{(1.15)^3} + \frac{5076.6}{(1.15)^4}$$

= ₹2788 million

Foreign Currency Approach To apply the foreign currency approach we have to come up with a risk-adjusted dollar discount rate corresponding to the risk-adjusted rupee discount rate of 15 percent. To do this we have of first find the risk premium implicit in 15 percent:

(1 + Risk-free rupee rate) (1 + Risk premium) = (1 + Risk-adjusted rupee rate)
(1 + 0.8) (1 + Risk premium) = (1 + 0.15)

Hence

$$(1+\text{ Risk premium}) = \frac{(1.15)}{(1.08)} = 1.0648$$

Applying the above risk premium to the risk-free dollar rate of 6 percent, we find that the risk-adjusted dollar rate is:

$$(1 + \text{Risk adjusted dollar rate}) = (1.03)\ (1.0648) = 1.09674$$

Given the dollar cash flows, the NPV in dollars works out to:

$$\text{NPV} = -100 + \frac{30}{(1.09674)} + \frac{40}{(1.09674)^2} + \frac{50}{(1.09674)^3} + \frac{60}{(1.09674)^4}$$

= \$ 39.98 million

Since the spot exchange rate is ₹70 per dollar, the rupee NPV of the project is:

$$NPV = 39.98 \times ₹70 = ₹2798 \text{ million}$$

Expectedly, this is the same as the rupee NPV we obtained earlier using the home currency approach.

Added Complications in Appraising Foreign Projects It is more complicated to evaluate a foreign project than a domestic project on account of the following:

Project Cash Flows versus Parent Cash Flows In the case of a domestic project, the after-tax cash flows generated by the project accrue to the shareholders of the firm. However, this may not be true for a foreign project because the host country may impose restrictions on the amount of profits that can be remitted to the parent company apart from applying withholding taxes. Hence, it may seem natural to consider only remittable cash flows, rather than the after-tax cash flows produced by the project. Of course, one may argue that if the firm regards itself as a true global citizen committed to long-term investment in different countries, exchange controls and restrictions on remittances should not really matter.

Exchange Risk and Segmentation of Capital Market The cash flows of a foreign project are in a foreign currency and hence subject to exchange risk from the point of view of the parent company. How should this risk be incorporated in project evaluation? Further, when the host and home country capital markets are not integrated, what is the appropriate cost of capital?

International Taxation The foreign country may impose withholding taxes on remittances like royalty, license fees, interest, and dividend paid by a subsidiary to its overseas parent. In addition, the home country may also impose taxes on the parent company on the incomes it receives from its foreign subsidiary. If a double taxation avoidance treaty is in place, the parent may receive credit, partial or total, for the taxes paid overseas.

Blocked Funds At times a foreign project becomes attractive because the parent company has some funds accumulated in a foreign country which cannot be repatriated or can be repatriated only after paying heavy penalties. It may make sense to invest such blocked funds in a subsidiary or joint venture in the foreign country.

Risk Premium on Foreign Investment In our discussion so far we assumed that the risk premium on the foreign investment will be the same as the risk premium on a similar domestic investment.

Foreign investments generally involve higher risk which arises from factors like change in currency value, discriminatory treatment of a foreign company, and threat of expropriation. Risk stemming from fluctuations in exchange rate looms constantly on the horizon of foreign investment. In addition, a foreign investment is subject to discriminatory treatment and selective control in various forms, motivated mainly by political considerations. Finally, the threat of expropriation without adequate compensation may exist, particularly in countries where radical nationalistic sentiments are strong.

In view of the higher risk associated with foreign investment, a firm contemplating foreign investment would naturally expect a higher rate of return. Put differently, the discount rate applicable to foreign investment tends to be higher than the discount rate applicable to domestic investment.

A higher-than-normal required rate of return by multinational corporations is often viewed unfavourably by the critics of multinational companies. They hurl accusations of 'profiteering' even when the multinational company may simply be following the sound financial practice of asking for a rate of return commensurate with the risks characterising the project.

Can there be situations where the demand for higher returns by a multinational company can be unreasonable? Yes, when the multinational company invests in several different economies and enjoys the benefit of risk reduction arising from portfolio diversification. In such a case, it may be possible to reduce the overall risk of the firm's portfolio of investments even while accepting a project which individually is highly risky. Of course, this depends on the existence of low or negative correlations between the project under consideration and the other projects within the firm's portfolio of investments.

13.7 INVESTMENT IN CAPABILITIES

Empirical evidence suggests that companies that perform well have organisational capabilities that enable them to exploit opportunities. What are these organisational capabilities? As Carlin Baldwin and Kim Clark[3] say: "Organisational capabilities are combinations of human skills, organisational procedures and routines, physical assets, and the systems of information and incentives that improve performance along particular dimensions. Such capabilities are indeed organisational assets."

They mention five specific capabilities which are briefly described below:

External Integration Capability This is the ability of the firm to link its understanding of customers with engineering design to develop improved products. As Baldwin and Clark say: "Companies with this capability develop products that match customer expectations down to the smallest details. The products not only satisfy customers but often surprise and delight them."

Internal Integration Capability Internal integration makes a company faster and more efficient in performing various functions like new product development, prototyping, facilities engineering, and capacity expansion. Without internal integration, delays occur and costs mount. As Baldwin and Clark say: "In the absence of such internal integration, actions and decisions are taken first by the upstream functions and then by the downstream functions using the up-stream group output. Typically the joint product will require two or more cycles of problem-solving to remedy the initial failures of coordination."

Flexibility Flexibility refers to the ability of the firm to do a variety of things and to respond quickly to changes. As Baldwin and Clark say: "Flexibility comes in many forms.

[3] Baldwin, Carlis Y. and Clark, Kim. B. "Capabilities and Capital Investment: New Perspectives on Capital Budgeting," Journal of Applied Corporate Finance, Summer 1992.

A company may have the capability to manufacture a wide range of products and change its mix on short notice. It may have the ability to respond to changes in volume, or it may have the ability to introduce new products rapidly and efficiently."

The Capacity to Experiment Continuous improvement, a process referred to as *Kaizen* in Japanese, is often the key factor that drives productivity gains. Continuous improvement emanates from organisational learning which in turn requires experimentation. A firm's capacity to experiment depends on the investments it makes in developing knowledge, disseminating knowledge, and adopting the same in practice.

The Capacity to Cannibalise Cannibalisation involves introducing a new product that cuts into the sales of the existing products. An old rule of resource allocation prohibits cannibalisation because it seems to hurt the interest of the firm at least in the short run. However, many established firms have found that their disinclination to cannibalise provided opportunities to other companies to introduce new products. Hence it is imperative for a company to develop its capacity to cannibalise. Since canibalisation is naturally resisted by the established hierarchy, the capacity to cannibalise has to be consciously developed.

Capabilities improve the value of a firm's investment. More specifically, external integration diminishes product risk; internal integration raises the probability of finding opportunities and lowers the cost of exploiting them; flexibility widens the options available to the firm to meet contingencies; the capacity to experiment brings about systematic improvements which reduce the cost over time; and the capacity to cannibalise enables a company to maintain its market position by warding off potential competitors.

Characteristics of Capabilities–Building Investments Investments required to build capabilities have certain special characteristics. These are:

- Many of the outlays required are on things like common language and communication, human training and skill development, and support services. These are not ordinarily regarded as capital expenditure in many firms.
- Investments required to build a capability range widely in scale and scope.
- While costs of building capabilities are visible and appear on someone's budget, the benefits are derived by the company as a whole and occur only after a time lag.

Due to these characteristics, investment in capabilities in most organisations is done outside the financial system of resource allocation. However, this is not a satisfactory arrangement. As Baldwin and Clark say: "Unfortunately overriding the formal resource allocation system creates as many problems as it solves. When top managers short-circuit the system they do little to encourage capabilities investments at lower levels in the organisation."

Allocating Resource to Build Capabilities The challenge for a company lies in developing a capital allocation system that accommodates investment in capabilities without sacrificing the benefits of a formal financial analysis. Towards this end, the following actions are required:

- Identify the capabilities that the firm should develop and ensure that there is a firm organisational commitment to them.

- Develop a capital budget for capabilities and a proper system of authorisation and accounting for expenditures relating to capabilities.
- Translate the desired capabilities into appropriate goals and rewards that are clearly understood and used by people throughout the organisation.
- Link compensation of managers to improvements in speed, quality, and flexibility, which are the outcomes of capabilities.

SUMMARY

- For a proper comparison of two mutually exclusive alternatives, that have different lives, we have to convert the present value of costs into a uniform annual equivalent (UAE) figure. The UAE is simply:

$$\text{PV (Cost)/PVIFA}_{r,n}$$

- In real life, an investment can typically be undertaken now or at some point of time in future. The timing that has the highest current value represents the optimal timing.
- The economic life of an asset is conceptually defined as the period after which the asset should be replaced to minimise the sum of operating and maintenance costs and capital costs expressed on an annual basis.
- Strictly speaking, WACC is the right discount rate for a project that is a carbon copy of the firm's existing business.
- A project may have financing effects that differ from those of the existing investments of the firm. It may have different debt capacity or be entitled to certain subsidies or have some special financial features. In such cases the recommended method is to calculate the adjusted NPV (or APV for short).
- APV is calculated by first estimating the base-case NPV and then adjusting it to reflect the financing impact of the project.

  APV = Base-case NPV + Present value of the financing side effects of the project

- The base-case NPV is the NPV of the project under the following assumptions: (a) The project is financed entirely by equity. (b) There is no financing effect like issue cost or subsidy.
- The present value of financing side effects is equal to: Present value of positive financing side effects like tax subsidies – Present value of negative financing side effects like issue costs.
- Though conceptually sound, APV is not very popular because (i) it requires some sophistication to assess the financing side effects, and (ii) it involves a series of adjustments which may be cumbersome. That is why WACC, which is the cost of capital adjusted for financing effects, is more commonly used in practice.
- WACC is equal to:

$$r_D (1 - T_c) \frac{D}{V} + r_E \frac{E}{V}$$

- There are some other formulae also for calculating the adjusted cost of capital. Two of them are:

  Modigliani and Miller formula : $r^* = r\,(1 - TL)$

  Miles and Ezzell formula : $r^* = r - L\, r_D\, T\, \dfrac{1+r}{1+r_D}$

- The adjustment for inflation should be done properly in practice.
- There are two ways of evaluating an international capital budgeting proposal: the home currency approach and the foreign currency approach. Correctly applied both the approaches yield the same result.

QUESTIONS

1. Explain how you would compare mutually exclusive projects of unequal life.
2. Discuss the procedure for determining optimal timing under conditions of certainty.
3. What is APV? How is it calculated?
4. Show graphically the typical behaviour of r_E, r_D, r, and WACC.
5. What are the merits of APV?
6. What is adjusted cost of capital? Give various formulae for adjusted cost of capital.
7. Discuss the bias when the depreciation charge is based on historical cost.
8. Discuss the bias due to ignoring the inflation factor in project cash flows.
9. Explain the ways of evaluating an international investment proposal.
10. Discuss the organisational capabilities that enable firms to exploit opportunities.
11. What should be done to develop a capital allocation system that accommodates investment in capabilities?
12. How is the economic life of a project determined?

PROBLEMS

1. Plastic emulsion painting for a building costs ₹300,000 and has a life of 7 years. Distemper painting costs ₹180,000 and has a life of 3 years. How does the UAE of plastic emulsion painting compare with that of distemper painting? Assume a discount rate of 10 percent.
2. The initial outlay on an internal transportation system would be ₹1,500,000. The operating costs are expected to be as follows:

Year	*Operating Costs* (₹)
1	300,000
2	360,000
3	400,000
4	450,000
5	500,000

The estimated salvage value at the end of five years is ₹300,000. What is the UAE if the cost of capital is 13 percent?

3. The standard overhaul of an equipment costs ₹0.5 million and is required every 6 years. A less costly overhaul can be done for ₹0.2 million and is required every 2 years. Which one would you recommend if the cost of capital is 14 percent? Why?
4. Shimla Municipality is considering two different snowplows. The Gunning plow has an economic life of 12 years, whereas the Coulter plow has an economic life of 9 years. The Gunning plow costs ₹2.5 million and is expected to have a salvage value of ₹0.8 million at the end of 12 years. The Coulter plow costs ₹1.5 million and is expected to have a salvage value of ₹0.5 million after 9 years. The operating and maintenance costs for the Gunning plow are expected to be ₹0.25 million per year and the same costs for the Coulter plow are expected to be ₹0.32 million per year. The plows have identical capacity. Whichever plow is chosen, Shimla Municipality would continue to replace it with essentially the same machine indefinitely. If the discount rate is 12 percent, which plow should be selected? Ignore taxes.
5. Udyog Limited is evaluating different dates for investing in a drug project. The net future values for various dates are as follows:

Time	*Net future value (₹ in million)*
0	10
1	15
2	19
3	23
4	26

The discount rate applicable to the project is 12 percent. Determine the optimal timing of the project.

6. Zenith Company sews garments for retail stores. The firm is evaluating a new sewing machine costing ₹80,000. The machine has a physical life of five years. The depreciation rate applicable to it is 25 percent as per the written down value method. The estimated operating and maintenance costs and salvage values are as follows:

Year	*Operating and maintenance costs* ₹	*Salvage value* ₹
1	20,000	60,000
2	25,000	45,000
3	35,000	32,000
4	50,000	22,000
5	70,000	15,000

Zenith's cost of capital is 12 percent and its tax rate is 40 percent. What is the economic life of the sewing machine which minimises the uniform annual equivalent cost of buying and operating the machine?

7. Sushant Well Drillers is evaluating a new well-drilling machine costing ₹4 million. Estimates of operating and maintenance costs and salvage values are as follows:

Year	*Operating and maintenance costs (₹ in million)*	*Salvage value (₹ in million)*
1	0.8	2.8
2	1.0	2.0
3	1.3	1.4
4	1.9	1.0
5	2.8	0.8

Sushant has a cost of capital of 12 percent and a tax rate of 30 percent. For tax purposes, Sushant is allowed to depreciate the machine at a rate of 25 percent as per the written down value method.

Determine the economic life for the well-drilling machine that minimises the uniform annual equivalent cost of buying and operating the machine.

8. The contribution of a project which involves an outlay of 100 to the firm's debt capacity is 60. The project's opportunity cost of capital is 16 percent and the tax rate for the firm is 50 percent. The borrowing rate is 15 percent.
   (a) What is the adjusted cost of capital as per Modigliani and Miller formula?
   (b) What is the adjusted cost of capital as per Miles and Ezzell formula?
9. Nimesh Electricals Limited is evaluating a capital project requiring an outlay of ₹12 million. It is expected to generate an annual cash inflow of ₹3 million for 6 years. The opportunity cost of capital is 20 percent. Nimesh Electricals can raise a term loan of ₹8 million for the project. It will carry an interest rate of 18 percent and will be repayable in 8 equal annual instalments, the first instalment falling due at the end of the second year.
   The balance amount required for the project can be raised by issuing external equity. The issue cost is expected to be 12 percent. The tax rate for the company is 30 percent.
   (a) What is the base case NPV?
   (b) What is the adjusted NPV if the adjustment is made only for the issue cost of external equity?
   (c) What is the present value of the tax shield on debt finance?
10. Nikhil Electronics Limited is evaluating a capital project requiring an outlay of ₹8 million. It is expected to generate a net cash inflow of ₹2 million annually for 6 years. The opportunity cost of capital is 18 percent. Nikhil Electronics Limited can raise a term loan of ₹5 million for the project. The term loan will carry an interest rate of 15 percent and would be repayable in 5 equal annual instalments, the first instalment falling due at the end of the second year. The balance amount required for the project can be raised by issuing external equity. The issue cost is expected to be 10 percent. The tax rate for the company is 40 percent.
    (a) What is the base-case NPV?
    (b) What is the adjusted NPV if the adjustment is made only for the issue cost of external equity?
    (c) What is the present value of the tax shield on debt finance?
11. The contribution of a project which involves an outlay of 100 to a firm's debt capacity is 50. The project's opportunity cost of capital is 19 percent and the tax rate for the firm is 50 percent. The borrowing rate is 16 percent.
    (a) What is the adjusted cost of capital as per the Modigliani and Miller formula?
    (b) What is the adjusted cost of capital as per the Miles and Ezzell formula?

12. Videsh Ventures, a Mumbai-based company, is considering a project to be set up in the US. The project will entail an initial outlay of $200 million and is expected to generate the following cash flow over its five year life:

Year	1	2	3	4	5
Cash flow (in million)	$50	$70	$90	$105	$80

The current spot exchange rate is ₹46 per US dollar, the risk-free rate in India is 11 percent and the risk-free rate in the US is 6 percent.
Videsh Venture's required rupee return on a project of this kind is 18 percent. Calculate the *NPV* of the project using the home currency approach.

MINICASE

Venkatraman, the CEO of Vayu Vidyut Nigam Limited, a wind power company, has been looking at a few locations to set up a new wind mill farm. He finally zeroed in on Coimbatore as a government agency in Tamil Nadu was willing to provide an interest-free loan equal to 20 percent of the project cost for a five year period.

You work for Vayu Vidyut Nigam as a senior finance manager. Venkatraman has asked you to evaluate the proposal from a financial point of view.

The proposed wind mill farm will entail an investment outlay of ₹1000 million. It is expected to generate a net cash flow of ₹200 million per year for 5 years. Thereafter Vayu Vidyut Nigam proposes to sell the wind mill farm at an expected post-tax consideration of ₹700 million.

The opportunity cost of capital is 15 percent – this reflects the return required by equity investors, assuming that the project is financed entirely by equity. The cost of issuing equity is 6 percent.

The project is eligible for a 5 year interest free loan equal to 20 percent of the project cost from a government agency. The principal amount of this loan would be repayable in a bullet payment after 5 years.

Further, a bank is willing to provide loan of ₹300 million, carrying an interest rate of 10 percent, the commercial rate applicable to such projects. The loan is repayable in five equal annual installments, the first installment falling due after 1 year. The issue cost associated with the loan will be practically nil.

The tax rate applicable to the project is 30 percent.

Based on the characteristics of the project, you believe that the adjusted present value (APV) analysis may be used.

Venkatraman broadly concurs with you and he has asked you to prepare a note addressing the following issues for the executive committee of Vayu Vidyut Nigam Limited.

(a) What is the base-case NPV?
(b) What is the issue cost associated with equity?
(c) What is the present value of the interest-free loan?
(d) What is the present value of the tax-shield associated with bank loan?
(e) What is the adjusted present value (APV)?
(f) What are the merits of APV?
(g) Why is APV eminently suitable for leverage buyouts (LBOs) or infrastructure projects?
(h) Assuming that the bank loan too is repayable in a bullet amount after 5 years, what is the adjusted cost of capital as per the Miles and Ezzell formula.

Social Cost Benefit Analysis

LEARNING OBJECTIVES

After studying this chapter you should be able to

- Show how social costs and benefits differ from monetary costs and benefits.
- List the stages involved in the UNIDO method of project appraisal.
- Discuss how prices of various resources are calculated.
- Explain how adjustment is made for merit and demerit goods.
- List the similarities and differences between the UNIDO approach and the Little-Mirrlees approach.
- Explain what is meant by economic rate of return, effective rate of protection, and domestic resource cost.
- Discuss the key steps in the public investment decision making process in India.

Social Cost Benefit Analysis (hereafter referred to as SCBA), also called economic analysis, is a methodology developed for evaluating investment projects from the point of view of the society (or economy) as a whole. Used primarily for evaluating public investments (though it can be applied to both private and public investments), SCBA has received a lot of emphasis in the decades of 1960s and 1970s in view of the growing importance of public investments in many countries, particularly in developing countries, where governments have played a significant role in the economic development. SCBA is also relevant, to a certain extent, to private investments as these have now to be approved by various governmental and quasi-governmental agencies which bring to bear larger national considerations in their decisions.

In the context of planned economies, SCBA aids in evaluating individual projects within the planning framework which spells out national economic objectives and broad allocation of resources to various sectors. In other words, SCBA is concerned with tactical decision making within the framework of broad strategic choices defined by planning at the macro level. The perspectives and parameters provided by the macro level plans serve as the basis of SCBA which is a tool for analysing and appraising individual projects.

This chapter discusses various aspects of SCBA.

14.1 RATIONALE FOR SCBA

In SCBA the focus is on the social costs and benefits of the project. These often tend to differ from the monetary costs and benefits of the project. The principal sources of discrepancy are:

- Market imperfections

- Externalities
- Taxes and subsidies
- Concern for savings
- Concern for redistribution
- Merit wants

Market Imperfections Market prices, which form the basis for computing the monetary costs and benefits from the point of view of the project sponsor, reflect social values only under conditions of perfect competition, which are rarely, if ever, realised by developing countries. When imperfections exist, market prices do not reflect social values.

The common market imperfections found in developing countries are: (i) rationing, (ii) prescription of minimum wage rates, and (iii) foreign exchange regulation. Rationing of a commodity means control over its price and distribution. The price paid by a consumer under rationing is often significantly less than the price that would prevail in a competitive market. When minimum wage rates are prescribed, the wages paid to labour are usually more than what the wages would be in a competitive labour market free from such wage legislations. The official rate of foreign exchange in developing countries, which exercise close regulation over foreign exchange, is typically less than the rate that would prevail in the absence of exchange regulations.

Externalities A project may have beneficial external effects. For example, it may create certain infrastructural facilities like roads which benefit the neighbouring areas. Such benefits are considered in SCBA, though they are ignored in assessing the monetary benefits to the project sponsors because they do not receive any monetary compensation from those who enjoy this external benefit created by the project.

Likewise, a project may have a harmful external effect like environmental pollution. In SCBA, the cost of such environmental pollution is relevant, though the project sponsors may not incur any monetary costs. It may be emphasised that externalities are relevant in SCBA because in such analysis all costs and benefits, irrespective of to whom they accrue and whether they are paid for or not, are relevant.

Taxes and Subsidies From the private point of view, taxes are definite monetary costs and subsidies are definite monetary gains. From the social point of view, however, taxes and subsidies are generally regarded as transfer payments and hence considered irrelevant.

Concern for Savings Unconcerned about how its benefits are divided between consumption and savings, a private firm does not put differential valuation on savings and consumption. From a social point of view, however, the division of benefits between consumption and savings (which leads to investment) is relevant, particularly in the capital-scarce developing countries. A rupee of benefits saved is deemed more valuable than a rupee of benefits consumed. The concern of the society for savings and investment is duly reflected in SCBA wherein a higher valuation is placed on savings and a lower valuation is put on consumption.

Concern for Redistribution A private firm does not bother how its benefits are distributed across various groups in the society. The society, however, is concerned about the distribution of benefits across different groups. A rupee of benefit going to an economically poor section is considered more valuable than a rupee of benefit going to an affluent section.

Merit Wants Goals and preferences not expressed in the market place, but believed by policy makers to be in the larger interest, may be referred to as merit wants. For example, the government may prefer to promote an adult education programme or a balanced nutrition programme for school-going children even though these are not sought by consumers in the market place. While merit wants are not relevant from the private point of view, they are important from the social point of view.

14.2 UNIDO APPROACH

Towards the end of the 1960s and in the early 1970s two principal approaches for SCBA emerged: the UNIDO approach and the Little–Mirrlees approach. This section discusses the UNIDO approach; the following discusses the Little–Mirrlees approach.

The UNIDO approach was first articulated in the *Guidelines for Project Evaluation*[1] which provides a comprehensive framework for SCBA in developing countries. The rigour and length of this work created a demand for a succinct and operational guide for project evaluation in practice. To fulfill this need, UNIDO came out with another publication, *Guide to Practical Project Appraisal*[2] in 1978. Our discussion of the UNIDO approach is based largely on the latter publication though at places we will draw on the former publication (generally referred to as *Guidelines*) too.

The UNIDO method of project appraisal involves five stages:

1. Calculation of the financial profitability of the project measured at market prices.
2. Obtaining the net benefit of the project measured in terms of economic (efficiency) prices.
3. Adjustment for the impact of the project on savings and investment.
4. Adjustment for the impact of the project on income distribution.
5. Adjustment for the impact of the project on merit goods and demerit goods whose social values differ from their economic values.

Each stage of appraisal measures the desirability of the project from a different angle.

The measurement of financial profitability of the project in the first stage is similar to the financial evaluation discussed at great length in the previous chapters of this book. So, skipping the first stage, we will discuss the remaining stages here.

14.3 NET BENEFIT IN TERMS OF ECONOMIC (EFFICIENCY) PRICES

Stage two of the UNIDO approach is concerned with the determination of the net benefit of the project in terms of economic (efficiency) prices, also referred to as shadow prices.

Market prices represent shadow prices only under conditions of perfect markets which are often not fulfilled in developing countries. Hence, there is a need for developing shadow prices and measuring net economic benefit in terms of these prices.

[1] UNIDO, *Guidelines for Project Evaluation*, United Nations, 1972.

[2] UNIDO, *Guide to Practical Project Appraisal*, United Nations, 1978.

Shadow Pricing: Basic Issues Before we deal with shadow pricing of specific resources, certain basic concepts and issues must be discussed: choice of numéraire, concept of tradability, source of shadow prices, treatment of taxes, and consumer willingness to pay.

Choice of Numéraire One of the important aspects of shadow pricing is the determination of the numéraire, the unit of account in which the value of inputs or outputs is expressed.

To define the numéraire, the following questions have to be answered: What unit of currency, domestic or foreign, should be used to express benefits and costs? Should costs and benefits be measured in current values or constant values? With reference to which point—present or future—should costs and benefits be evaluated? What use—consumption or investment—will be made of the income from the project? Should the income of the project be measured in terms of consumption or investment? With reference to which group should the income of the project be measured?

The specification of the UNIDO numéraire in terms of the above questions is: "net present consumption in the hands of people at the base level of consumption in the private sector in terms of constant price in domestic accounting rupees."

Concept of Tradability A key issue in shadow pricing is whether a good is tradable or not. For a good that is tradable, the international price is a measure of its opportunity cost to the country. Why? For a tradable good, it is possible to substitute import for domestic production and vice versa; similarly it is possible to substitute export for domestic consumption and vice versa. Hence the international price, also referred to as the border price, represents the 'real' value of the good in terms of economic efficiency.

Sources of Shadow Prices The UNIDO approach suggests three sources of shadow pricing, depending on the impact of the project on national economy. A project, as it uses and produces resources, may for any given input or output (i) increase or decrease the total consumption in the economy, (ii) decrease or increase production in the economy, (iii) decrease imports or increase imports, or (iv) increase exports or decrease exports.

If the impact of the project is on consumption in the economy, the basis of shadow pricing is the *consumer willingness to pay*. If the impact of the project is on production in the economy, the basis of shadow pricing is the *cost of production*. If the impact of the project is on international trade—increase in exports, decrease in imports, increase in imports, or decrease in exports—the basis of shadow pricing is the *foreign exchange value*.

Taxes When shadow prices are being calculated, taxes usually pose difficulties. The general guidelines in the UNIDO approach with respect to taxes are as follows: (i) When a project results in diversion of non-traded inputs which are in fixed supply from other producers or addition to non-traded consumer goods, taxes should be included. (ii) When a project augments domestic production by other producers, taxes should be excluded. (iii) For fully traded goods, taxes should be ignored.

Consumer Willingness to Pay As noted above, if the impact of the project is on consumption in the economy, the basis of shadow pricing is consumer willingness to pay. How is this measured? The measurement of consumer willingness to pay may be explained with the help of Exhibit 14.1. In the graph shown in this exhibit, *DD′* represents the demand schedule, *SS′* the supply schedule, *E* the equilibrium point, *OQ* the quantity bought, and *OP* the price per unit. Looking at the demand schedule we find that the consumer who buys the first unit is willing to pay *OD* for that unit and the consumer who buys the last unit is willing to pay *OP* for that unit. The consumer willingness to pay for various units is indicated by the schedule *DE*. So the total willingness to pay by consumers who buy the product is measured by the area *ODEQ*. The price paid by them, however, is only *OPEQ*. The difference between *ODEQ* and *OPEQ*, namely *DEP*, is referred to as the consumer surplus.

Exhibit 14.1 ***Consumer Willingness to Pay***

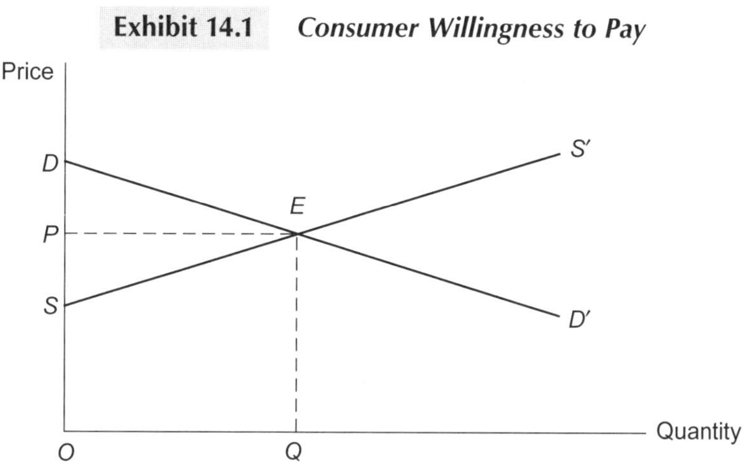

Shadow Pricing of Specific Resources Let us look at how shadow pricing of specific resources is done:

Tradable Inputs and Outputs A good is fully traded when an increase in its consumption results in a corresponding increase in import or decrease in export or when an increase in its production results in a corresponding increase in export or decrease in import. For fully traded goods, the shadow price is the border price, translated in domestic currency at the market exchange rate.

The above definition of a fully traded good implies that domestic changes in demand or supply affect just the level of imports or exports. This means for an imported good, the following conditions should be met: (i) If there is an import quota, it is not restrictive. (ii) The import supply is perfectly elastic over the relevant range of import volume. (iii) There is no surplus capacity in the domestic industry; all additional supply must be imported. If there is surplus domestic capacity it cannot be utilised for want of necessary inputs. (iv) If the additional demand exists inland, the imported goods, even after taking into account the cost of transport from the port of entry to the point of inland demand, cost less than the marginal cost of local production. (v) The imported input costs less than the domestic marginal cost of purchase.

When the above conditions are satisfied, additional demand will be met fully by external trade. Hence, the input is considered fully traded. Similar conditions must be satisfied for importable outputs, exportable inputs, and exportable outputs, if they are to be considered fully traded. In practice, it is reasonable to regard tradable inputs and outputs as fully traded, even if the above-mentioned conditions are not fully satisfied.

A good is not traded if it is tradable but conditions (i) through (iv) above are not fulfilled. For non-traded goods the border price does not reflect its economic value. What then is the value of non-traded goods? The value of a non-traded good should be measured in terms of what domestic consumers are willing to pay, if the output of the project adds to its domestic supplies or if the requirement of the project causes reduction of its consumption by others. The value of a non-traded good should be measured in terms of its marginal cost of production if the requirement of the project induces additional production or if the output of the project causes reduction of production by other units.

Non-tradable Inputs and Outputs A good is non-tradable when the following conditions are satisfied: (i) its import price (CIF price) is greater than its domestic cost of production, and (ii) its export price (FOB price) is less than its domestic cost of production.

The valuation of non-tradables is done as per the principles of shadow pricing discussed earlier. On the output side, if the impact of the project is to increase the consumption of the product in the economy, the measure of value is the marginal consumers' willingness to pay; if the impact of the project is to substitute other production of the same non-tradable in the economy, the measure of value is the saving in cost of production. On the input side, if the impact of the project is to reduce the availability of the input to other users, their willingness to pay for that input represents social value; if the project's input requirement is met by additional production of it, the production cost of it is the measure of social value.

Externalities An externality, also referred to as an external effect, is a special class of good which has the following characteristics: (i) It is not deliberately created by the project sponsor but is an incidental outcome of legitimate economic activity. (ii) It is beyond the control of the persons who are affected by it, for better or for worse. (iii) It is not traded in the market place.

An external effect may be beneficial or harmful. Examples of *beneficial external effects* are:

- An oil company drilling in its own fields may generate useful information about oil potential in the neighbouring fields.
- The approach roads built by a company may improve the transport system in that area.
- The training programme of a firm may upgrade the skills of its workers thereby enhancing their earning power in subsequent employments.

Examples of *harmful external effects* are:

- A factory may cause environmental pollution by emitting large volumes of smoke and dirt. People living in the neighbourhood may be exposed to health hazards and put to inconvenience.
- The location of an airport in a certain area may raise noise level considerably in the neighbourhood.
- A highway may cut a farmer's holding in two, separating his grazing land and his cowsheds, thereby adversely affecting his physical output.

Since SCBA seeks to consider all costs and benefits, to whomsoever they may accrue, external effects need to be taken into account. The valuation of external effects is rather difficult because they are often intangible in nature and there is no market price which can be used as a starting point. Their value is estimated by indirect means. For example:

- The benefit of information provided by the oil field to neighbouring oil fields may be equated with what the neighbouring oil fields would have spent to obtain such information.
- The value of better transport provided by the approach roads may be estimated in terms of increased activities and benefits derived therefrom.
- The benefit from the training programme may be estimated in terms of the increased earning power of workers.
- The cost of pollution may be estimated in terms of the loss of earnings as a result of damage to health caused by it and the cost of time spent for coping with the unhygienic surroundings.
- The cost of noise may be inferred from the differences in rent between the noise-affected area and that of some other area which is comparable except for the level of noise.
- The harmful external effect of the highway may be measured by the consumer willingness to pay for the output of the farmer which has been reduced due to the highway.

The above examples serve to emphasise the difficulties in measuring external effects. In view of this, some economists have suggested that these effects be ignored. In order to justify their suggestion, they argue that since a project is likely to have both beneficial and harmful external effects, one may not err much in assuming that the net effect would be zero. This argument, seemingly a rationalisation for one's ignorance, lacks validity. External effects must be taken into account wherever it is possible to do so. Even if these effects cannot be measured in monetary terms, some qualitative evaluation must be attempted.

Labour Inputs The principles of shadow pricing for goods may be applied to labour as well, though labour is considered to be a service. When a project hires labour, it could have three possible impacts on the rest of the economy: (i) it may take labour away from other employments; (ii) it may induce the production of new workers; (iii) and it may involve import of workers.

When a project takes labour away from other employments, the shadow price of labour is equal to what other users of labour are willing to pay for this labour. In a relatively free market this will be equal to the marginal product of such labour.

The social cost associated with inducing 'additional' production of workers consists of the following: (i) the marginal product of the worker in the previous employment—if the worker is previously unemployed, this would naturally be zero; (ii) the value assigned by the worker on the leisure that he may have to forego as a result of employment in the project—the value of this leisure is reflected in his reservation wage[3]; (iii) the additional consumption of food when a worker is fully employed as opposed to when he is idle or only partly employed; (iv) the cost of transport and rehabilitation when a worker is moved from one location to another; (v) the increased consumption by the worker and its negative impact on savings and investment in the society when the worker is paid market wage rate by the project; and (v) the cost of training a worker to improve his skills.

[3] The reservation wage of a person depends on the following: (i) the income he already enjoys through transfer payments, (ii) his idea of what job is acceptable to him, and (iii) his preference for work and leisure.

The social cost associated with the import of foreign workers is the wage they command. In their case, however, a premium should be added on account of the foreign exchange remitted abroad by these workers from their savings.

Capital Inputs When a capital investment is made in a project two things happen: (i) Financial resources are converted into physical assets. (ii) Financial resources are withdrawn from the national pool of savings and hence alternative projects are foregone. Thus, shadow pricing of capital investment involves two questions:

- What is the value of physical assets?
- What is the opportunity cost of capital (which reflects the benefit foregone by sacrificing alternative project/s)?

The value (shadow price) of physical assets is calculated the way the value of other resources is calculated. If it is a fully traded good, its shadow price is equal to its border price. If it is a non-traded good its price is measured in terms of cost of production (if the project induces additional domestic production of the asset) or consumer willingness to pay (if the project takes the asset from other users).

The opportunity cost of capital depends on how the capital required for the project is generated. To the extent that it comes from additional savings, its opportunity cost is measured by the consumption rate of interest (which reflects the price the saver must be paid to sacrifice present consumption); to the extent that it comes from the denial of capital to alternative projects, its opportunity cost is the rate of return that would be earned from those alternative projects. This is also called the investment rate of interest. In practice, the consumption rate of interest may be used as the discount rate because in stage three of the UNIDO analysis all inputs and outputs are converted into their consumption equivalents.

There are, however, problems in determining the consumption rate of interest empirically. So the UNIDO approach recommends a 'bottom up' procedure. As per this procedure, the project analyst calculates the internal rate of return of a project and presents the project to the planners (or politicians) who are the decision makers. If the project is accepted, the analyst may assume that the planners judge the consumption rate of interest to be more than the interest rate of return. On the basis of a repetitive application of this process, the range for estimated consumption rate of interest can be sufficiently narrowed for practical use, provided, of course, the planners on the top are consistent.

Foreign Exchange The UNIDO method uses domestic currency as the numéraire. So the foreign exchange input of the project must be identified and adjusted by an appropriate premium. This means that valuation of inputs and outputs that was measured in border rupees has to be adjusted upward to reflect the shadow price of foreign exchange.

How is the shadow price of foreign exchange established? The *Guidelines* method determines the shadow price of foreign exchange on the basis of marginal social value as revealed by the consumer willingness to pay for the goods that are allowed to be imported at the margin. The shadow price of a unit of foreign exchange is equal to:

$$\sum_{i=1}^{n} F_i Q_i P_i \tag{14.1}$$

where F_i is the fraction of foreign exchange, at the margin, spent on importing commodity i, Q_i is the quantity of commodity i that can be bought with one unit foreign exchange (This will be equal to 1 divided by the CIF value of the goods in question), and P_i is the domestic market clearing price of commodity i

Example Commodities 1, 2, 3, and 4 are imported at the margin. The proportion of foreign exchange spent on them, the quantities that can be bought per unit of foreign exchange, and the domestic market clearing prices are as follows:

$F_1 = 0.3,$	$F_2 = 0.4,$	$F_3 = 0.2,$	$F_4 = 0.1$
$Q_1 = 0.6,$	$Q_2 = 1.5,$	$Q_3 = 0.25,$	$Q_4 = 3.0$
$P_1 = 16,$	$P_2 = 8,$	$P_3 = 40,$	$P_4 = 5$

The value of a unit of foreign exchange is:

$$(.3)\,(0.6)\,(16) + (0.4)\,(1.5)\,(8) + (0.2)\,(0.25)\,(40) + (.1)\,(3.0)\,(5) = ₹11.180.$$

The calculation of the shadow price of foreign exchange in terms of the consumer willingness to pay is based on the assumption that the foreign exchange requirement of a project is met from the sacrifice of others. The use of foreign exchange by a project, however, may also induce the production of foreign exchange through additional exports or import substitution. In such a case, the shadow price of foreign exchange would be based on the cost of producing foreign exchange, and not on consumer willingness to pay for foreign exchange. One of the best known approaches to determine the cost of producing foreign exchange is the domestic resource cost method proposed by Michael Bruno. Though this approach is oriented to estimate what is the cost of producing foreign exchange by a single project, its principles can be applied to estimate the cost of producing foreign exchange at the macro level.

Programming Approach Another approach for determining the value of foreign exchange is the programming approach. According to this approach, the shadow price of foreign exchange is obtained by solving the dual problem of an economy-wide optimising mathematical programming model. In the primal model, one of the constraints represents limited foreign exchange availability. (More than one constraint relating to foreign exchange may be introduced if it is necessary to distinguish various foreign currencies.) Hence the shadow price represents the contribution that unit of foreign exchange at the margin would make to the objective function.

Conceptually sound, the usefulness of this approach in practice depends on whether the model reflects economic realities and whether the required data are available. Since these conditions are not readily satisfied, caution should be exercised in employing this approach.

Bridge Project To illustrate the calculation of net economic benefit, two examples are given. The first example is that of a bridge project. The second example is that of a river valley project.

Presently, a ferry service, operated privately, is being used to cross a river. The ferry operator charges ₹3 per person. It costs him ₹2 per person. 50,000 persons use the ferry service. (This means that the number of persons crossing the river by ferry service throughout the year is 50,000.)

The government is considering construction of a bridge over the river. It is estimated that after the bridge is constructed 2,50,000 persons will cross the river on the bridge. The bridge is expected to cost ₹3 million initially and its annual maintenance cost would be ₹10,000. It has an indefinitely long life. Once the bridge is constructed the ferry operator is expected to close down the ferry service and sell the ferry boats for ₹100,000.

Required: Define the social costs and benefits of constructing the bridge, assuming that the monetary figures given in the problem represent economic values.

Solution: The social costs and benefits of bridge construction may be defined as follows:

Costs

These consist of the following:

1. Construction cost: ₹3,000,000 (This is a one-shot cost).
2. Maintenance cost: ₹10,000 (This is an annual cost).

Benefits

These consist of the following:

1. Value of ferries released: ₹100,000 (This is one-shot benefit).
2. Savings in the cost of ferry operation: ₹100,000 (This is an annual benefit).
3. Increase in consumer satisfaction: This is equal to willingness to pay of 200,000 additional persons who are expected to use the bridge. Since the first additional person is willing to pay almost ₹3 (the charge of the ferry operator) and the last person is willing to pay almost nothing (there is no toll for using the bridge) the average willingness to pay of additional users, assuming that the demand schedule is linear, is ₹1.50. So the willingness to pay of 200,000 additional persons is 200,000 × ₹1.50 = ₹300,000. (This is shown in Exhibit 14.2 by the triangle.)

Exhibit 14.2 ***Consumer Willingness to Pay***

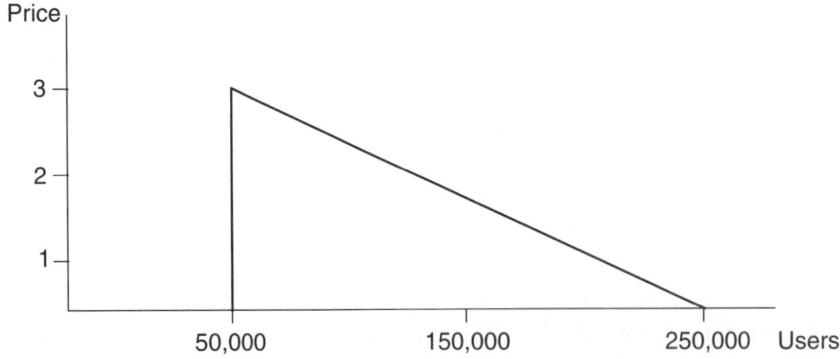

River Valley Project The government is considering a multi-purpose river valley project which would involve construction of a dam, a reservoir, a power house, and several irrigation canals. The project would supply water for irrigation, generate electricity, and provide a measure of protection against floods. The following information has been gathered by the project control board.

The project will require the following during the construction stage:

1. Indigenous power equipment costing ₹200 million.
2. Imported power equipment costing $10 million.
3. 20,000 tonnes of steel produced indigenously and made available to the project at ₹6000 a tonne.
4. 350,000 tonnes of cement produced indigenously and made available to the project at ₹800 a tonne.
5. Other construction materials (sand, bricks, etc.) costing ₹100 million.
6. 25 million mandays of unskilled labour for which the project control board has decided to pay a daily wage rate of ₹10.
7. Skilled labour costing ₹100 million.

Once commissioned, the operating and maintenance cost of the project would be ₹35 million per year.

The annual benefits expected from the project would be as follows:

1. 300,000 acres of land will be irrigated.
2. 120 million units of electricity will be generated for domestic use.
3. Flood damages to the extent of ₹10 million will be avoided annually.

The following additional information is available:

1. Power equipment produced indigenously is a tradable item whose FOB value is $ 15 million.
2. A gift of $ 10 million, available from a foreign agency, can be used for acquiring imported equipment. This gift, however, is not project-tied. Hence, if it is not assigned to the project, it can be used for some other purpose.
3. The shadow price per dollar is ₹12, though the official price is ₹10.
4. Steel is a tradable item whose FOB value is $ 400 per tonne.
5. Cement is not a tradable item. One-half of the cement required for the project will come from additional domestic production which has a cost of ₹700 per tonne; one-half of the cement required for the project will come from diversion from other consumers who are willing to pay, on average, ₹1,200 per tonne.
6. Other construction materials are non-tradable items. The requirement of the project will be met by way of additional production. The cost of this production will be ₹80 million.
7. The shadow price of unskilled labour is ₹5 per day.
8. The compensation paid to skilled labour reflects what others are willing to pay for their services.
9. The operating and maintenance cost of ₹35 million reflects economic value as well.

10. The water levy by the project control board would be ₹100 per acre. However, the value of additional output per acre, attributable to the water supplied by the project, will be ₹400 a year.
11. The electricity tariff charged by the project control board would be 30 paise per unit. The consumer willingness to pay, however, would be, on an average, 50 percent more than the tariff charged.
12. The project control board is not able to collect anything for the protection provided against floods.

Required: Define the costs and benefits from the private (project control board's) and the economic point of view.

Solution: The costs and benefits from the private and economic (social) angles are shown in Exhibit 14.3.

Exhibit 14.3 ***Costs and Benefits from the Private and Economic Angles***

Costs	*Nature*	*Private Angle (₹in million)*	*Economic Angle (₹in million)*	*Explanation for Economic Values*
1. Indigenous power equipment	One shot	200	180	This is a tradable item whose FOB value is $ 15 million. This is converted into rupees by applying the shadow price of foreign exchange.
2. Imported power equipment	One shot	-	120	The foreign exchange is converted into rupees by applying the shadow price foreign exchange.
3. Steel	One shot	120	96	This is a tradable item whose FOB value is $ 8 million. This is converted into rupees by applying the shadow price of foreign exchange.
4. Cement	One shot	280	332.5	This is a non-tradable item. 175,000 tonnes of cement required by the project is produced additionally in the country for which the cost of production ₹122.5 million. 1,75,000 tonnes of cement required for the project is diverted from other users who are willing to pay ₹210 million.
5. Other construction material	One shot	100	80	This is non-tradable item. The requirement of the project is met by additional domestic production costing ₹80 million.
6. Unskilled labour	One shot	250	125	25 million mandays are multiplied by ₹5, the shadow wage rate.

(*Contd.*)

Costs	Nature	Private Angle (₹ in million)	Economic Angle (₹ in million)	Explanation for Economic Values
7. Skilled labour	One shot	100	100	The compensation paid to skilled labour reflects what others are willing to pay for it.
8. Operating and maintenance cost	Annual	35	35	The annual operating and maintenance cost reflects economic value as well.
Benefits				
1. Irrigation	Annual	120	120	The value of additional agricultural output attributable to the water supplied by the project is ₹120 million.
2. Electricity	Annual	54	54	The consumer willingness to pay for the electricity provided by the project is, on average, 50 percent higher than the electricity tariff charged.
3. Flood relief	Annual	10	10	The value of savings due to flood relief benefit from the project is ₹10 million annually.

14.4 MEASUREMENT OF THE IMPACT ON DISTRIBUTION

Stages three and four of the UNIDO method are concerned with measuring the value of a project in terms of its contribution to savings and income redistribution. To facilitate such assessments, we must first measure the income gained or lost by individual groups within the society.

Groups For income distribution analysis, the society may be divided into various groups. The UNIDO approach seeks to identify income gains and losses by the following:

- Project
- Other private business
- Government
- Workers
- Consumers
- External sector

There can, however, be other equally valid groupings.

Measure of Gain or Loss The gain or loss to an individual group within the society as a result of the project is equal to the difference between the shadow price and the market price of each input or output in the case of physical resources or the difference between the price paid and the value received in the case of financial transactions.

Example 1 Farmers in a certain area use 1 million units of electricity generated by a hydroelectric project. The benefit derived by them, measured in terms of the willingness to pay, is equal to ₹0.4 million. The tariff paid by them to the electricity board is ₹0.25 million. So, the impact of the project on the farmers is a gain of ₹0.15 million.

Example 2 A mining project requires 1,000 labourers. These labourers are prepared to offer themselves for work at a daily wage rate of ₹40. (This represents their supply price.) The wage rate paid to the labourers, however, is ₹100 per day. So the redistribution benefit enjoyed by the group of 1,000 labourers is ₹60,000 (1,000 × (100 – 40)) per day.

14.5 SAVINGS IMPACT AND ITS VALUE

Most of the developing countries face scarcity of capital. Hence, the governments of these countries are concerned about the impact of a project on savings and its value thereof. Stage three of the UNIDO method, concerned with this, seeks to answer the following questions:

- Given the income distribution impact of the project what would be its effects on savings?
- What is the value of such savings to the society?

Impact on Savings The savings impact of a project is equal to:

$$\Sigma \Delta Y_i MPS_i \tag{14.2}$$

where ΔY_i is the change in income of group i as a result of the project, and MPS_i is the marginal propensity to save of group i

Example As a result of a project the income gained/lost by four groups is: Group 1 = ₹100,000, Group 2 = ₹500,000, Group 3 = – ₹200,000, and Group 4 = – ₹400,000. The marginal propensity to save of these four groups is as follows:

$$MPS_1 = 0.05,\ MPS_2 = 0.10,\ MPS_3 = 0.20, \text{ and } MPS_4 = 0.40.$$

The impact on savings of the project is:

$$100{,}000 \times 0.05 + 500{,}000 \times 0.10 - 200{,}000 \times 0.20 - 400{,}000 \times 0.40 = - ₹1{,}45{,}000.$$

Value of Savings The value of a rupee of savings is the present value of the additional consumption stream produced when that rupee of savings is invested at the margin. The additional stream of consumption generated by a rupee of investment depends on the marginal productivity of capital and the rate of reinvestment from additional income. If the marginal productivity of capital is r and the rate of reinvestment from additional income a, the additional stream of consumption generated by a rupee of investment can be worked out as shown in Exhibit 14.4.

Exhibit 14.4 ***Derivation of Additional Consumption Stream from a Rupee of Investment Now***

Year	0	1	2	3	...n...
Investment (cumulative)	1	1 + ar	$(1+ar)^2$		$(1+ar)^n$
Income		r	$r(1+ar)$	$r(1+ar)^2$	$r(1+ar)^{n-1}$
Additional investment		ar	$ar(1+ar)$	$ar(1+ar)^2$	$ar(1+ar)^{n-1}$
Consumption		$r(1-a)$	$r(1-a)$ $(1+ar)$	$r(1-a)$ $(1+ar)^2$	$r(1-a)$ $(1+ar)^{n-1}$

From this exhibit we find that the consumption stream starts with $r(1 - a)$ and grows annually at the rate of ar forever. Its present value when discounted at the social discount rate k is:

$$I = \frac{r(1-a)}{(1+k)} + \frac{r(1-a)(1+ar)}{(1+k)^2} + \ldots + \frac{r(1-a)(1+ar)n-1}{(1+k)^n} + \ldots$$

$$= \frac{\dfrac{r(1-a)}{(1+k)}}{1-\dfrac{(1+ar)}{(1+k)}} = \frac{r(1-a)}{(k-ar)} \tag{14.3}$$

where I is the social value of a rupee of savings (investment), r is the marginal productivity of capital, a is the reinvestment rate on additional income arising from investment, and k is the social discount rate.

The social value of savings (also called the shadow price of investment) for certain values of r, a, and k is given in Exhibit 14.5. The formula for the social value of savings is valid when the following conditions are satisfied: (i) The marginal productivity of capital and the reinvestment rate on additional income (marginal propensity to save) are constant over time. (ii) Savings rate in the society will not become optimal in the foreseeable future. While these conditions may seem somewhat restrictive, in practice, for want of better information, it is convenient to accept them.

Exhibit 14.5 ***Shadow Price of Investment***

		k = 0.08	k = 0.10	k = 0.12
r = 0.10	a = 0.20	1.33	1.00	0.80
	a = 0.30	1.40	1.00	0.77
	a = 0.40	1.50	1.00	0.75
	a = 0.50	1.67	1.00	0.71
r = 0.12	a = 0.20	1.72	1.26	1.00
	a = 0.30	1.91	1.31	1.00
	a = 0.40	2.25	1.38	1.00
	a = 0.50	3.00	1.50	1.00
r = 0.15	a = 0.20	2.40	1.71	1.33
	a = 0.30	3.00	1.91	1.40
	a = 0.40	4.50	2.25	1.50
	a = 0.50	15.00	3.00	1.67

14.6 INCOME DISTRIBUTION IMPACT

Many governments regard redistribution of income in favour of economically weaker sections or economically backward regions as a socially desirable objective. Due to practical difficulties in pursuing the objective of redistribution entirely through the tax, subsidy, and transfer measures of the government, investment projects are also considered as investments for income redistribution and their contribution toward this goal is considered in their evaluation. This calls for suitably weighing the net gain or loss by each group, measured earlier, to reflect the relative value of income for different groups and summing them.

How should the relative weights be determined? The *Guidelines* suggested that the weights, which essentially reflect political judgements, may be determined by an iterative process involving interaction between the analyst and the planners. To illustrate, consider a project:

Net present value of the project	– ₹2 million
Income gain to low income group as a result of the project	₹5 million

Suppose the project is accepted by the planners. This implies that the planners place a premium of at least 40 percent on income going to the poor. If the planners reject this project but accept some other project which requires a premium of at least 30 percent on the income going to the poor, the project analyst may infer that the premium placed by planners on income going to the poor lies between 30 percent and 40 percent.

This procedure works well if only two groups are involved (in the previous example it was assumed that the two groups were the poor and the others). Where more than two groups are involved the procedure breaks down because several unknown weights are involved. In such a situation, the analyst would not be able to figure out, given the preference of the planners, the relative weights assigned by them on income to the various groups. To tackle this problem, a single factor has to be found which determines the income distribution weights so that the 'bottom-up' approach becomes workable. This single factor, as economists suggest, is the elasticity of marginal utility of income.[4] This is defined as the rate at which the marginal utility of income falls with increases in the level of income. For example, if the marginal utility of income declines by 5 percent with a 5 percent increase in income, the elasticity of marginal utility of income is 5 percent/5 percent = 1[5]. Likewise, if the marginal utility of income declines by 10 percent with a 5 percent increase in income, the elasticity of marginal utility of income is 10 percent/5 percent = 2. If the elasticity of marginal utility is equal to 1.0, a 1 percent increase in the income of a person earning ₹1,000 a year is socially as valuable as a 1 percent increase in the income of a person earning ₹10,000 a year, or ₹100,000 a year, or for that matter any amount a year. This means that from the social point of view the following gains are equally valuable:

A gain of ₹10 to a person earning ₹1,000 a year.
A gain of ₹100 to a person earning ₹10,000 a year.
A gain of ₹1,000 to a person earning ₹100,000 a year.

[4] The marginal utility of income is the value derived from one more unit of income. This obviously depends on the present level of income.

[5] By convention, the negative sign is omitted.

This implies that if the weight at ₹1,000 is put at 1, the weight at ₹10,000 is 1/10, and the weight at ₹100,000 is 1/100.

In general, the weight attached to an income is given by the formula:

$$w_i = \left(\frac{b}{c_i}\right)^n \tag{14.4}$$

where w_i is the weight attached to income at c_i level, b is the base level of income that has a weight of 1, and n is the elasticity of the marginal utility of income.

Exhibit 14.6 shows the relative weights for different levels of income for values of n varying between 0 and 1, given a base level of income of ₹1,000 which has a weight of 1.

Exhibit 14.6 ***Relative Weights for Different Levels of Income for Values of n Varying between 0 and 1***

	Value of n				
Level of Income	*0.2*	*0.4*	*0.6*	*0.8*	*1.0*
500	1.15	1.32	1.52	1.74	2.00
1,000	1.00	1.00	1.00	1.00	1.00
5,000	0.72	0.53	0.38	0.28	0.20
10,000	0.63	0.40	0.25	0.16	0.10
20,000	0.55	0.30	0.17	0.09	0.05
30,000	0.51	0.26	0.13	0.07	0.03
50,000	0.46	0.21	0.10	0.04	0.02
100,000	0.40	0.16	0.06	0.03	0.01

14.7 ADJUSTMENT FOR MERIT AND DEMERIT GOODS

In some cases, the analysis has to be extended beyond stage four to reflect the difference between the economic value and social value of resources. This difference exists in the case of merit goods and demerit goods. A merit good is one for which the social value exceeds the economic value. For example, a country may place a higher social value than economic value on production of oil because it reduces dependence on foreign supplies. The concept of merit goods can be extended to include a socially desirable outcome like creation of employment. In the absence of the project, the government perhaps would be willing to pay unemployment compensation or provide mere make-work jobs.

In the case of a demerit good, the social value of the good is less than its economic value. For example, a country may regard alcoholic products as having a social value less than the economic value.

The procedure for adjusting for the difference between social value and economic value is as follows: (i) Estimate the economic value. (ii) Calculate the adjustment factor as the difference between the ratio of social value to economic value and unity. (iii) Multiply the economic value by the adjustment factor to obtain the adjustment. (iv) Add the adjustment to the net present value of the project as calculated in stage four.

To illustrate, consider a project for which the following information is available: (i) The present economic value of the output of the project is ₹25 million. (ii) The output of the project has a social value which exceeds its economic value by 20 percent. Given this information, the adjustment factor would be 0.2 (120 percent/100 percent – 1). Multiplying the present economic value by 0.2, we get an adjustment of ₹5 million. This, then, is added to the present economic value of ₹25 million.

When the socially valuable output of the project does not appear as an output in the economic analysis—as is the case when the project generates employment—the procedure is somewhat different. In such a case the output is treated like an externality and its valuation in social terms is the adjustment.

While the adjustment for the difference between the social value and economic value is seemingly a step in the right direction, it is amenable to abuse. Once the analyst begins to make adjustment for social reasons, projects which are undesirable economically may be made to appear attractive after such adjustment. Since the dividing line between 'political' and 'social' is rather nebulous, it becomes somewhat easy to push politically expedient projects, irrespective of their economic merit by investing them with social desirability. While there is no way to prevent such a manipulation, the stage-by-stage UNIDO approach mitigates its occurrence by throwing it in sharp relief.

14.8 LITTLE–MIRRLEES APPROACH

I.M.D. Little and J.A. Mirrlees have developed an approach (hereafter referred to as the L–M approach) to social cost benefit analysis expounded by them in the following works: *Manual of Industrial Project Analysis in Developing Countries, Vol. II* and *Project Appraisal and Planning for Developing Countries.*

There is considerable similarity between the UNIDO approach and the L–M approach. Both the approaches call for:

1. Calculating accounting (shadow) prices particularly for foreign exchange savings and unskilled labour.
2. Considering the factor of equity.
3. Using DCF analysis.

Despite considerable similarities there are certain differences between the two approaches:

1. The UNIDO approach measures costs and benefits in terms of domestic rupees whereas the L–M approach measures costs and benefits in terms of international prices, also referred to as border prices.
2. The UNIDO approach measures costs and benefits in terms of consumption whereas the L–M approach measures costs and benefits in terms of uncommitted social income.
3. The stage-by-stage analysis recommended by the UNIDO approach focuses on efficiency, savings, and redistribution considerations in different stages. The L-M approach, however, tends to view these considerations together.

14.9 SHADOW PRICES

The outputs and inputs of a project are classified into the following categories: (i) traded goods and services, (ii) non-traded goods and services, and (iii) labour.

Shadow Price of Traded Goods The shadow price of a traded good is simply its border price. If a good is exported, its shadow price is its FOB price and if a good is imported its shadow price is its CIF price. If foreign demand is not perfectly elastic, the marginal export revenue is substituted for the FOB price; similarly, if foreign supply is not perfectly elastic, the marginal import cost is substituted for the CIF price. The logic for using border prices for traded goods is fairly straight-forward: border prices represent the correct social opportunity costs or benefits of using or producing a traded good.

Accounting Price[6] of Non-Traded Goods Some goods and services like land, building, transportation, and electricity are not amenable to foreign trade. Hence, there is no border price observable for them. Accounting prices for non-traded items are defined in terms of marginal social cost and marginal social benefit.

The marginal social cost of a good is the value in terms of accounting prices of the resources required to produce an extra unit of the good. For example, the marginal social cost of a bus trip is roughly equal to the cost of material inputs (fuel, oil, wear and tear of the bus, etc.) evaluated at border prices plus the social wage of the driver and the conductor.

The marginal social benefit is the value of an extra unit of the good from the social point of view. When a good is not taxed and is consumed by only one income group, its marginal social benefit is equal to its market price multiplied by a factor which represents the value assigned to an increase in the income of that group vis-à-vis an equal increase in uncommitted social income.

To determine the accounting price of a non-traded input, one should estimate the proportion in which the demand for that input will be met from increased production and decreased consumption elsewhere in the economy. If the proportion of increase in production to decrease in consumption is, say, 2:1, the accounting price of the non-traded input will be:

$$\frac{2}{3}\text{ Marginal social cost} + \frac{1}{3}\text{ Marginal social benefit}$$

Use of Conversion Factors Ideally, the accounting price of a non-traded item is defined in terms of marginal social cost and marginal social benefit. In practice, the calculation of marginal social cost and marginal social benefit is often a difficult task. As a practical expedient, L–M suggest that the monetary cost of a non-traded item be broken down into tradable, labour, and residual components. The tradable and residual components may be converted into social cost by applying suitable social conversion factors; the labour component's social cost can be obtained by using shadow wage rate (which is discussed below).

Shadow Wage Rate The shadow wage rate is an important but difficult-to-determine element in social cost benefit analysis. It is a function of several factors: (i) the marginal

[6] The terms accounting price and shadow price are used interchangeably.

productivity of labour, (ii) the cost associated with urbanisation (cost of transport, urban overheads, etc.), and (iii) the cost of having an additional amount committed to consumption when the consumption of the worker increases as a result of the higher income he enjoys in urban employment.

L–M suggest the following formula for calculating the shadow wage rate:

$$SWR = c' - 1/s\,(c - m) \tag{14.5}$$

where SWR is the shadow wage rate, c' is the additional resources devoted to consumption, $1/s$ is the value of a unit of committed resource, c is the consumption of the wage earner, and m is the marginal product of the wage earner.

To understand clearly the components of SWR, Eq. (14.5) may be rewritten as follows:

$$SWR = m + (c' - c) + \left(1 - \frac{1}{s}\right)(c - m) \tag{14.6}$$

The first term, m, is the marginal product of labour; the second term, $(c' - c)$, represents the cost of urbanisation (it is the cost associated with providing the consumption level of c though it does not form part of it); the third term, $(1 - 1/s)\,(c - m)$, represents the cost of having an additional amount $(c - m)$ committed to consumption (it may be noted that 1 is the value of a unit of uncommitted resource and $1/s$ is the value of a unit of committed resource).

Accounting Rate of Return The accounting rate of return (interest) is the rate used for discounting social profits. In determining the accounting rate of return the following considerations should be borne in mind:

- The future social profit for all the projects must be discounted in the same way.
- The accounting rate(s) of interest should be such that all mutually compatible projects with positive present social value can be undertaken.
- The accounting rate of interest should maintain some kind of balance between investment and investible resources: too low an accounting rate of interest would lead to over-investment with inflationary effects and too high an accounting rate of interest would leave savings under-utilised and result in excessive unemployment.
- The rate of return currently being earned is a good guide to the accounting rate of interest when the following conditions are reasonably satisfied: (i) indirect taxes are fairly uniform with little discrimination between imported and exported commodities, and (ii) the social wage rate is close to the actual wage rate.
- The initial estimate of the accounting rate of interest should, in principle, be such that it would allow only a few of the best projects in the past.
- Experience is the best guide to the choice of accounting rate of interest: if the investment requirement of acceptable projects exceeds the availability of investible funds, increase the accounting rate of interest; if the investment requirement of acceptable projects is less than the availability of investible funds, decrease the accounting rate of interest. The adjustment in the accounting rate of interest, however, should be gradual over time.

14.10 SCBA BY FINANCIAL INSTITUTIONS

The all-India term-lending financial institutions—IDBI, IFCI, and ICICI[7]—appraise project proposals primarily from the financial point of view. However, they also scrutinise projects from the larger social point of view. ICICI was perhaps the first financial institution to introduce a system of economic analysis as distinct from financial profitability analysis. IFCI adopted a system of economic appraisal in 1979. Finally, IDBI also introduced a system for economic appraisal of projects financed by them. Though there are some minor variations, the three institutions follow essentially a similar approach which is a simplified version of the L–M approach. We shall describe the appraisal procedure followed by IDBI.

IDBI, in its economic appraisal of industrial projects, considers three aspects:

- Economic rate of return
- Effective rate of protection
- Domestic resource cost

Economic Rate of Return The method followed by IDBI to calculate the economic rate of return may be described as a 'Partial Little-Mirrlees' method because while international prices are used for valuation of tradable inputs and outputs, L–M method is not followed in its entirety. The significant elements of IDBI's method are described below:

1. International prices are regarded as the relevant economic prices and, hence, it is necessary to substitute market prices with international prices for all non-labour inputs and outputs.
2. For tradable items, where international prices are directly available, CIF prices are used for inputs and FOB prices are used for outputs.
3. For tradable items where international prices are not directly available and for non-tradable items (like electricity, transportation, etc.), social conversion factors are used to convert actual rupee cost into social cost. In some cases (like land), a social conversion factor is applied directly to the actual rupee cost. In other cases (like transport), the actual rupee cost is broken down into three components—tradable component, labour component, and residual component—and these components are valued in social terms. Generally, the social cost of the tradable component is obtained by multiplying it by a factor of 1/1.5; the social cost of labour component is obtained by multiplying it by a factor of 0.5 (shadow price of labour is considered to be 50 percent of the actual); the social cost of the residual component is obtained by multiplying it by a factor of 0.5. Exhibit 14.7 shows the social conversion factor/break-up into tradable, labour, and residual components for various items.

[7] IDBI and ICICI have now become universal banks.

Exhibit 14.7 ***Social Conversion Factor (SCF) or Proportions of Three Components, Tradable (T), Labour (L), and Residual (R)***

Item	*SCF or Proportions*
Land	*SCF* = 1/1.5
Buildings and construction	Proportions: *T* = 0.5, *L* = 0.25, *R* = 0.25
Indigeneous equipment	*SCF* = 0.70
Transportation	Proportions: *T* = 0.65, *L* = 0.25, *R* = 0.10
Engineering and know-how fees	*SCF* = 1.50
Bank charges	*SCF* = 0.02
Preoperative expenses	*SCF* = 1.00
Labour	*SCF* = 0.50
Salaries	*SCF* = 0.80
Repairs and maintenance	*SCF* = 1/1.5
Water, fuel, etc.	Proportions: *T* = 0.50, *L* = 0.25, *R* = 0.25
Electricity	Proportions: *T* = 0.71, *L* = 0.13, *R* = 0.16
Domestic stores	*SCF* = 0.80
Other overheads	*SCF* = 1/1.5

Illustration A new project for manufacturing a product which is currently being imported in the country is being appraised. The project would have a life of 15 years and it will lead to import substitution. The capital outlay on the project would be as follows:

	(₹ in million)
Land	0.2
Buildings	10.0
Imported equipment (CIF value: ₹6 million)	7.0
Indigenous equipment (CIF value of similar equipment: ₹40 million)	50.0
Transport	1.0
Engineering and know-how fees	5.0
Preoperative expenses	4.8
Bank charges	2.0
	80.0

The working capital requirement of the project, consisting only of imported raw materials, will be ₹16 million (CIF value: ₹12 million).

The estimated annual profitability of the project is as follows:

	(₹ in million)
Revenues	
Sales revenue (10,000 tonnes at ₹10,000 per tonne; CIF price is ₹7,000 per tonne)	100
Expenses	
Imported raw materials (CIF value: ₹8 million)	10
Indigenous raw materials and stores	40
Labour	5

(Contd.)

Salaries		3
Repairs and maintenance		1
Water, fuel, etc.		5
Electricity		5
Rate	3.015	
Duty	1.985	
Depreciation	–	4
Other overheads		7
Profit		
Taxable profit		20

For the sake of simplicity we may assume that capital costs are incurred at the beginning (i.e., at the end of year 0) and full production begins from year 1 itself.

Given the above information, let us convert the financial costs and benefits into social costs and benefits. We first begin with social costs associated with the initial outlay on the project which consists of capital outlay and working capital. These are shown in Exhibit 14.8. Based on this exhibit, the social cost of initial outlay is worked out as follows:

		(₹ *in million*)
Tradable value *ab initio*		70.473
Social cost of tradable component	$= 5.65/1.5$	3.767
Social cost of labour component	$= 2.75 \times 0.5$	1.375
Social cost of residual component	$= 2.60 \times 0.5$	1.300
Total social cost of initial outlay		76.915

Exhibit 14.9 shows the conversion of operating costs into social costs. Based on this exhibit, the annual social cost of operation is worked out as follows:

	(₹ *in million*)
Tradable value *ab initio*	= 50.234
Social cost of tradable component $= 4.63/1.5$	= 3.087
Social cost of labour component $= 1.642 \times 0.5$	= 0.821
Social cost of residual component $= 1.73 \times 0.5$	= 0.865
Annual social cost of operations	= 55.007

Exhibit 14.8 ***Social Costs Associated with the Initial Outlay***

(₹ *in million*)

Item	*Financial Cost*	*Basis of Conversion*	*Tradable Value ab initio*	*T*	*L*	*R*
Land	0.2	*SCF* = 1/1.5	0.133			
Buildings	10.0	*T* = 0.50, *L* = 0.25, *R* = 0.25		5.00	2.50	2.50
Imported equipment	7.0	*CIF* value	6.00			

(Contd.)

(₹ in million)

Item	Financial Cost	Basis of Conversion	Tradable Value ab initio	T	L	R
Indigeneous equipment	50.0	*CIF* value of similar equipment	40.0			
Transport	1.0	$T = 0.65$, $L = 0.25$, $R = 0.10$		0.65	0.25	0.10
Engineering and know-how fees	5.0	SCF = *1.50*	7.5			
Preoperative expenses	4.80	*SCF* = 1.0	4.80			
Bank charges	2.00	SCF = *0.02*	0.04			
Working capital requirement	16.0	*CIF* value	12.00			
Total	96.0		70.473	5.65	2.75	2.60

The annual value of output at CIF prices is ₹70 million. Hence, the social net benefit per year would be:

$$70 - 55.007 = ₹14.993 \text{ million.}$$

In addition to this annual net benefit for 15 years, there will be the recovery of working capital worth ₹12 million at the end of the 15th year. Other recoveries may be ignored.

Putting the above figures together, we find that the stream of costs and benefits associated with the project would be:

Year/s	*Net social benefit (₹in million)*
0	– 76.915
1–14	14.993
15	26.993

The economic rate of return for the project, which is the internal rate of return of the stream of social costs and benefits, is the value of r in the equation:

$$76.915 = \sum_{t=1}^{14} \frac{14.993}{(1+r)^t} + \frac{26.993}{(1+r)^{15}}$$

Solving this equation we find that the economic rate of return is about 19 percent.

Exhibit 14.9 ***Conversion of Financial Costs into Social Costs***

(₹ in million)

Item	*Financial Cost*	*Basis of Conversion*	*Tradable Value ab initio*	*T*	*L*	*R*
Imported raw material	10.00	CIF value	8.00			
Indigenous raw material and stores	40.00	SCF = 0.80	32.00			
Labour	5.00	SCF = 0.50	2.50			
Salaries	3.00	*SCF = 0.8*	2.40			
Repairs and maintenance	1.00	SCF = 1/1.5	0.667			
Water, fuel, etc.	5.00	*T* = 0.50, *L* = 0.25, *R* = 0.25		2.50	1.25	1.25
Electricity (Rate portion)	3.015	*T* = 0.71, *L* = 0.13, *R* = 0.16		2.13	0.392	0.48
Other overheads	7.00	*SCF* = 1/1.5	4.667			
Total	74.015		50.234	4.63	1.642	1.73

Effective Rate of Protection Tariffs, import restrictions, and subsidies are used to encourage domestic industries and protect them against international competition. The extent to which a project is sheltered is measured by the Effective Rate of Protection (*ERP*). It is calculated as follows:

$$\frac{\text{Value added at domestic prices} - \text{Value added at world prices}}{\text{Value added at world prices}}$$

This ratio is multiplied by 100 to express the *ERP* in percentage terms.

The data required for calculating the *ERP* may be arranged as follows:

	At domestic prices	**At world prices**
A. Selling price		
B. Input cost		
Traded		
Non-traded		
C. Value added		

The domestic selling price is net of taxes and excise duties but inclusive of a reasonable selling commission. The selling price at world price is the CIF price for imports and FOB for exports.

The input cost consists of the cost of the following inputs:

- Raw materials and stores
- Power, fuel, and water
- Repairs and maintenance
- Part of administrative overheads and expenses
- Selling expenses

The distinction between traded inputs (which are valued both at domestic and world prices) and non-traded inputs (which are valued at domestic price only) is made as follows:

1. *Raw Materials and Stores* In general these are taken as traded items and their value at domestic and world prices (CIF prices) are estimated. However, raw materials which have a low value-to-volume ratio and involve disproportionately high transport cost (like silica and pulp) and which are not imported are regarded as non-traded items.
2. *Power, Fuel, and Water* These are normally treated as 'non-traded' items. However, where fuel is in the form of oil and/or coal and fuel costs are significant, it should be regarded as a traded item and valued at both domestic and world prices.
3. *Repairs and Maintenance* This is a non-traded item. However, when this entails substantial consumption of spares and chemicals (not included in raw materials) it is regarded as a traded item and valued at both domestic and world prices.
4. *Selling Expenses* This is regarded as a non-traded item.
5. *Part of Administrative Overheads and Expenses* Administrative costs may be divided into two parts: labour costs and other expenses (like rent, insurance charges, telephone tariff, etc.). Since labour costs are part of value added, other expenses only are considered as input costs. These are regarded as non-traded items.

The difference between the selling price and input costs is the value added. This represents payment to labour and capital.

Illustration The calculation of *ERP* may be illustrated with the help of an example. The domestic prices and world prices of the inputs and outputs of a project in a normal year are given in Exhibit 14.10.

The *ERP* in this case is:

$$\frac{\text{Value added at domestic prices} - \text{Value added at world prices}}{\text{Value added at world prices}} = \frac{60 - 30}{30} = 1 \text{ (or 100\%)}$$

Exhibit 14.10 ***Domestic and World Prices***

(₹ in millions)

		Domestic prices	World prices
	Inputs		
■ Tradable Inputs			
Raw materials		300	250
Consumable stores		50	30
	Total	350	280
■ Non-tradable Inputs			
Power, fuel, and water		20	
Repairs and maintenance		15	
Administrative and other overheads		30	
Selling expenses		25	
	Total	90	90
■ Total Input Costs		440	370
	Output		
■ Sales Realisation		500	400
■ Value Added		60	30

It may be emphasised that when the value added at domestic prices is the same as the value added at world prices, the *ERP* is zero. In such a case, it implies that the project does not enjoy any protection from international competition. When the value added at domestic prices is higher than the value added at world prices, as is often the case, the *ERP* takes a positive value. Clearly, the higher the value of *ERP*, the higher the implied protection enjoyed by the project. It is generally agreed that the extent of protection given to a project should not exceed 30 percent.

Domestic Resources Cost Domestic resources cost (*DRC*) reflects the domestic cost incurred per unit of foreign exchange saved or earned. Financial institutions use the following formula to calculate *DRC:*

$$DRC = \frac{A + B + C}{P - (Q + R + S + T)} \times \text{Exchange rate}$$

where A is the annual charge on domestic capital calculated at the rate of 10 percent, B is the annual depreciation on domestic capital assets (other than land) calculated at the rate of 8 percent, C is the annual cost of non-traded inputs, P is the sales realisation at international prices, Q is the annual charge on imported capital assets at the rate of 10 percent, R is the annual depreciation on imported capital assets at the rate of 8 percent, S is the annual cost of imported inputs, and T is the annual cost of domestically procured, but tradable inputs.

A word about the various elements in the above formula is in order.

Domestic Capital This consists of the following: (i) Cost of domestically procured plant, machinery, and miscellaneous fixed assets, excluding excise duty and sales tax. (ii) Preliminary and preoperative expenses excluding interest during construction (iii) Clearing and local transportation cost of imported machinery. (iv) Working capital investment other than investment in imported and tradable raw material inventory.

Imported Capital This consists of the following: (i) Cost of imported plant, machinery, and miscellaneous fixed assets, excluding import duties. (ii) Working capital investment in imported and tradable raw material inventory, net of all taxes and duties.

Cost of Domestically Procured Operating Inputs Domestically procured operating inputs may be divided into two parts: (a) Traded/tradable inputs. There are items that can be traded in the international market. They are valued at international prices. (ii) Non-traded inputs. These are items that cannot be traded in the international market. They are valued at their domestic cost after excluding transfer payments like taxes, duties, and subsidies.

Sales Realisation at International Prices The output of the project is valued at international prices, also called as border prices. The border price means *CIF* (cost, insurance, and freight) price for an imported/importable/import substitute good and *FOB* (free on board) price for an exported/exportable good.

Cost of Imported Operating Inputs Imported operating inputs are valued at the actual price paid for them. Import duty is not considered. Local transportation cost is treated as a domestic cost.

Note that taxes, duties, and subsidies are excluded from the valuation of all items found in the *DRC* formula because they are mere transfer payments to or from the government and hence do not represent a cost or gain to the economy as a whole.

Illustration The capital employed in a project is estimated as follows:

Item	Total Cost (excluding taxes, duties, and subsidies)	₹ in million For DRC Calculation	
		Domestic Capital	Imported Capital
(1)	(2)	(3)	(4)
1. Land	15	15	
2. Buildings	10	10	
3. Plant and machinery			
(i) Imported	100	–	100
(ii) Indigenous	40	40	
4. Transportation and erection	5	5	
5. Miscellaneous fixed assets	30	20	10
6. Preliminary and pre-operative expenses (excluding interest during construction)	35	35	
7. Contingencies	15	5	10
8. Working capital requirement	55	45	10
9. Total capital employed	305	175	130
10. Charge on capital @ 10%		17.5	13.0
11. Depreciation on capital @ 8% (excluding land and working capital requirement)		9.2	9.6

The project is expected to achieve the normal level of production in the third year of operation when its output valued at border prices is estimated at ₹275 million.

The cost of traded/tradable inputs and non-traded inputs are expected as follows:

Item	Total Cost (excluding taxes, duties, and subsidies)	For DRC Calculation		
		Non-tradable component	Tradable component at border prices	Imported component
(1)	(2)	(3)	(4)	(5)
1. Raw materials and consumables	150	20	100	30
2. Utilities (power fuel, water, etc.)	25	20	5	–
3. Repairs and maintenance	10	10	–	–
4. Wages and salaries	20	20	–	–
5. Rent and insurance	3	3	–	–
6. Administrative expenses	5	5	–	–
7. Selling expenses	7	7	–	–
Total operating cost	220	85	105	30

The present exchange rate is ₹50 per dollar.

Given the above information, the *DRC* of the project is calculated below:

$$DRC = \frac{17.5 + 9.2 + 85.0}{275.0 - (13.0 + 9.6 + 30.0 + 105.0)} \times ₹50.0$$

$$= ₹47.6$$

Thus the domestic resource cost per US dollar saved is ₹47.6, which is lower than the present exchange rate. Hence it is desirable to manufacture the product in the country rather than import it.

14.11 PUBLIC SECTOR INVESTMENT DECISIONS IN INDIA

The public sector has been assigned an important role in the Indian economy. The government policy toward the public sector has been stated as follows:

> "Not only will it be a producer of important and strategic goods of basic nature, but it will also be used as a stabilising force for maintaining essential supplies for the consumer."

The public sector today commands a predominant position in many basic industries: coal, crude oil and refining, steel, power, fertilisers, locomotives, basic drugs, machine tools, and so on.

It is somewhat surprising that even though substantial investments were made in the public sector since independence, the mechanisms of appraisal and selection were rather primitive till the middle 1960s. For a long time the important proposals were appraised by the Expenditure Finance Committee that used procedures which were rather slip-shod. This is obvious from an examination of the memos of the Expenditure Finance Committee that clearly made a short shrift of economic considerations.

Initiatives to Improve the Quality of Investment Decisions The need for preparing feasibility studies was perhaps first highlighted by the committee on 'utilisation of external assistance' which observed that "the delay in foreign aid utilisation is due to the dearth of well conceived projects ready for immediate implementation". Triggered by this awareness and a felt need to improve the quality of project planning and strengthen the public investment decision making process in India, the following steps were taken:

- In 1965, the Government of India set up a separate Bureau of Public Enterprises (BPE, hereafter), with the objective of "integrating and strengthening the arrangement for economic coordination and evaluation of technical, economic, and financial aspects of projects and the working of public enterprises in India." The BPE is an autonomous organisation under the Ministry of Finance and is required to supervise and regulate all aspects of public sector projects.
- In 1965, the Planning Commission prepared and circulated a *Manual of Feasibility Studies for Public Sector Projects*. This manual outlines in detail the procedure required to be adopted for project formulation.
- In 1972, the Government of India set up a special division in the Planning Commission called the Project Appraisal Division (PAD, hereafter) to appraise the central sector projects from the national viewpoint and to make observations regarding the economic viability of investment projects whose capital cost exceeds a certain limit. The PAD has been entrusted with the work of developing a research methodology and other steps

required to evolve systematic project planning in India. The PAD has prepared and circulated the *Guidelines for the Preparation of Feasibility Reports for Industrial Projects.*

- In 1972, the Government of India set up a high-powered Public Investment Board (PIB, hereafter) with a view to evolve a scientific procedure for taking investment decisions. The functions assigned to the PIB are: (a) examination of the broad contours of investment proposals in the project formulation stage based on which a decision to prepare the feasibility report would be taken; (b) taking investment decisions on proposals for public investment to produce goods and services; and (c) consideration of proposals for revision of cost estimates which exceed those approved at the time of investment decisions.

Since the appraisal of the PAD and the recommendations of the PIB have an important bearing on public sector investments in India, we will examine their role in some detail. Before doing that, let us first look at the key steps in the public investment decision making process in India.

Key Steps in the Public Investment Decision Making Process in India Broadly the principal steps in the public investment decision making process in India are as follows:

1. The Planning Commission formulates the five-year plan indicating the broad strategy of planning, the role of each sector, the physical targets to be achieved by each sector, and the financial outlays to be made available for the development of each sector.
2. The administrative ministries develop sectoral plans. It is in these plans that the projects of the public sector enterprises are identified. The identification of a project provides the green signal for the preparation of its feasibility report.
3. The concerned public sector enterprise prepares the feasibility report and forwards it to its administrative ministry.
4. The administrative ministry carries out a preliminary scrutiny of the feasibility report and sends copies of the same to the various appraising agencies, namely, the Planning Commission, the Department of Economic Affairs and the Plan Finance Division of the Finance Ministry, and the Bureau of Public Enterprises for their comments.
5. The PAD of the Planning Commission carries out a detailed appraisal. The objective of its appraisal is not only to suggest whether to accept or reject the project but also to suggest how it may be re-formulated to enhance its technical, financial, commercial, and economic viability.
6. The Investment Planning Committee of the Planning Commission discusses the appraisal note of the PAD and recommends to the PIB the view of the Planning Commission on whether the project should be accepted, rejected, deferred, reformulated, or redesigned.
7. The PIB considers the (a) appraisal note of the PAD along with the view of the Planning Commission, (b) the comments of the BPE, (c) the comments of the plan finance division of the ministry of finance, and (d) the note of the administrative ministry. If the PIB clears the project, it sends it to the cabinet for its approval.
8. The cabinet generally accepts the recommendation of the PIB and approves its implementation.

Project Appraisal Division The Project Appraisal Division (PAD) of the Planning Commission was set up in 1972 and entrusted with the following functions:

(a) to suggest standard formats for submission of projects and procedures for their techno-economic evaluation;
(b) to conduct actual techno-economic evaluation of selected major projects and programmes submitted to the Planning Commission;
(c) to assist the state governments and central ministries in giving effect to standardised formats and procedures for project evaluation; and
(d) to undertake and support research leading to progressive refinement of methodology and procedure for project evaluation.

The appraisal notes of the PAD are fairly comprehensive and cover the following: (a) project description and background of the investment proposal, (b) plan and project, (c) justification for the project, (d) demand and market analysis, (e) choice of technology and proposed capacity, (f) gestation period, project life, capacity utilisation, production build-up, product-mix, infrastructural requirements and availability, (g) capital costs and norms, (h) operating costs and norms, (i) possibilities of cost minimisation, (j) possible alternatives and the least cost option, (k) financial analysis by DCF method and sensitivity analysis, and (*l*) social profitability analysis and sensitivity analysis.

In the economic appraisal (also referred to as social profitability analysis) of industrial projects[8], the methodology followed by the PAD is a modified version of the Little-Mirrlees approach. The key elements of the methodology adopted by the PAD are as follows:

1. All tradable inputs are valued at border prices.
2. Transfer cost items (taxes, duties, etc.) are ignored.
3. All non-tradable items, especially power and transport, are evaluated in terms of marginal cost.
4. Foreign exchange involved in the inputs and outputs are valued at specified premia.
5. Social wage rates (or shadow wage rates) are applied to the unskilled and semi-skilled labour.[9]
6. The numéraire is defined as savings in domestic rupees rather than foreign exchange (as recommended by the Little–Mirrlees approach).

Public Investment Board The Public Investment Board (PIB) is a committee of secretaries which appraises and recommends all central public sector projects[10] involving an outlay exceeding a certain amount[11]. Besides the Secretary, Expenditure, Ministry of Finance, who

[8] The projects forwarded to the PAD are divided into three broad categories: (i) industrial projects, (ii) infrastructural projects, and (iii) social projects. Our discussion focuses on the economic appraisal of industrial projects.

[9] Reflecting the employment and income generation aspect of the project, the social wage rate varies from state to state and from urban to rural location. In general, it ranges between 40 percent and 70 percent of the monetary wage rate.

[10] Other than the projects of departmental undertakings like the Railways and Ordnance Factories which have their own procedures for project evaluation and sanction.

[11] For projects involving smaller outlays, decision making powers have been decentralised as follows: (a) Public sector undertakings have complete autonomy for projects up to specified ceilings depending on their gross blocks. (b) Administrative ministries have complete or partial autonomy within certain ceilings. (c) Expenditure Finance Committee is empowered to decide for certain types of projects within specified cost ceilings.

serves as its chairman, the PIB has the following members: Secretary, Economic Affairs, Ministry of Finance, Secretary, Planning Commission, Secretary, Industrial Development, Secretary to the Prime Minister, and Secretary to the administrative ministry concerned with the investment proposal. The Director General of the BPE and the Adviser, PAD are permanent invitees to the PIB.

The PIB is assisted by various agencies. The Plan Finance Division of the Ministry of Finance, which functions as the secretariat of the PIB, scrutinises the proposals particularly with reference to budgetary and plan provisions. The BPE examines construction costs, technical aspects, and financial aspects. The PAD of the Planning Commission provides assistance in economic appraisal and examines critical assumptions underlying the project. The Integrated Financial Adviser in the sponsoring ministry furnishes the feasibility study and provides whatever additional information is called for by the PIB.

The guidelines followed by the PIB in appraising investment proposals are as follows:

- The contribution of the project to the economic and social objectives and adherence to the concerned policies of the government.
- The advisability of undertaking the project in the public sector or the joint sector or leaving it to the private sector.
- Availability of plan funds and desirability of diversion of plan funds to the new project from those already on hand.
- The plan capacity and the timing of investment in the light of supply and demand balance including export possibilities of the product/service.
- The economic benefits of the project as distinct from financial returns.
- Crucial assumptions in the feasibility report that are likely to affect the performance of the commissioned project in relation to the claims made thereon in the feasibility report.
- Major technological and constructional aspects which may have a bearing on the investment decision.

Lacunae The institution of the PIB (and its technical arm, the PAD) represents an important advance in the process of public investment decision making in India. It has (a) promoted a more scientific appraisal of investment projects, (b) provided a forum for bringing to bear an integrated approach to project appraisal and selection, (c) expedited the process of decision making, and (d) strengthened the hands of the government to resist pressures based on non-economic considerations to a certain extent.

Despite these improvements, public investment decision making in India, as the critics argue, suffers from the following deficiencies:

- Lack of detailed disaggregative sectoral planning.
- Pre-emptive advance commitments.
- Practice of submitting projects of the same sector/undertaking in a piecemeal manner.
- Insufficient generation and analysis of options.
- Preparation of feasibility reports without adequate studies/investigations.
- Avoidable overlap in the appraisal of several agencies.
- Tardy clearance procedures.
- Sacrifice of economic considerations at the altar of political expediency.
- Emphasis on procedures rather than substance.

SUMMARY

- Social Cost Benefit Analysis (SCBA) is a methodology for evaluating projects from the social point of view. In the context of planned economies, SCBA aids in evaluating individual projects within the planning framework.
- In SCBA the focus is on social costs and benefits of a project. These often tend to differ from the costs incurred in monetary terms and benefits earned in monetary terms by the project. The principal reasons for discrepancy are: (i) market imperfections, (ii) externalities, (iii) taxes, (iv) concern for savings, (v) concern for redistribution, and (vi) merit and demerit goods.
- Towards the end of 1960s and early 1970s two principal approaches for SCBA emerged: UNIDO approach and Little–Mirrlees approach.
- The UNIDO method of project appraisal involves five stages: (i) calculation of the financial profitability of the project measured at market prices; (ii) obtaining the net benefit of the project measured in terms of economic (efficiency) prices; (iii) adjustment for the impact of the project on savings and investment; (iv) adjustment for the impact of the project on income redistribution; and (v) adjustment for the impact of the project on merit and demerit goods.
- The measurement of financial profitability of the project in stage one is similar to the financial evaluation discussed at great length in the previous chapters of this book.
- Stage two is concerned with the determination of the net benefit of the project in terms of economic (efficiency) prices also referred to as shadow prices.
- A key issue in shadow pricing is whether a good is tradable or not. For a traded good, the shadow price is the border price, translated in domestic currency at market exchange rate. The shadow price of a non-traded good is measured in terms of consumer willingness to pay or cost of production depending on the impact of the project on the rest of the economy.
- Since SCBA seeks to consider all costs and benefits, to whomsoever they may accrue, external effects also need to be taken into account. The valuation of external effects is rather difficult because they are often intangible in nature and there is no market price which can be used as a starting point.
- The principles of shadow pricing for goods may be applied to labour as well, though labour is considered to be a service. When a project takes labour away from other employments, the shadow price of labour is equal to what other users of labour are willing to pay. The shadow price associated with inducing 'additional' production of workers consists of the marginal product of labour in previous employment plus certain other costs.
- The opportunity cost of capital depends on how the capital required for the project is generated. To the extent that it comes from additional savings, its opportunity cost is measured by the consumption rate of interest; to the extent that it comes from the denial of capital to alternative projects, its opportunity cost is the rate of return that would be earned from those alternative projects. In practice, the consumption rate of interest may be used as the discount rate because in stage three of the UNIDO method all inputs and outputs are converted into their consumption equivalents.

- The UNIDO method uses domestic currency as the numéraire. So the foreign exchange impact of the project must be identified and valued. The UNIDO method determines the shadow price of foreign exchange on the basis of marginal social value as revealed by the consumer willingness to pay for the goods that are allowed to be imported at the margin.
- Stage three of the UNIDO method seeks to answer the following questions: Given the income distribution impact of the project what would be its effect on savings? What is the value of such savings to the society? The savings impact of a project is equal to:

$$\Sigma \Delta Y_i MPS_i$$

The shadow price (value) of a rupee of savings, given certain simplifying assumptions, is equal to:

$$\frac{r(1-a)}{k-ar}$$

- Stage four of the UNIDO method is concerned with measuring the impact of the project on income redistribution. This calls for suitably weighting the net gain or loss to various groups in the society and summing them.
- The Little–Mirrlees (L–M) approach to SCBA has considerable similarity with the UNIDO approach. However, there are certain important differences as well.
- As per the L–M approach, the outputs and inputs of a project are classified into the following categories: (i) traded goods and services, (ii) non-traded goods and services, and (iii) labour.
- The shadow price of a traded good is simply its border price. If a good is exported its shadow price is its FOB price and if a good is imported its shadow price is its CIF price. The shadow prices for non-traded items are defined in terms of marginal social cost and marginal social benefit.
- The L–M approach suggests the following formula for calculating the shadow wage rate (*SWR*):

$$SWR = c' - \frac{1}{s}(c - m)$$

- While the financial institutions—IDBI, IFCI, and ICICI—approach project proposals primarily from the financial point of view, they also evaluate them from the larger social point of view.
- Though there are some minor variations, the three institutions follow essentially a similar approach which is a simplified version of the L–M approach.
- IDBI considers three aspects in its economic appraisal of industrial projects: economic rate of return, effective rate of protection, and domestic resource cost.
- The economic rate of return is simply the internal rate of return of the stream of social costs and benefits.
- The effective rate of protection is calculated as follows:

$$\frac{\text{Value added at domestic prices} - \text{Value added at world prices}}{\text{Value added at world prices}} \times 100$$

- Till the middle of 1960s the mechanism for appraisal and selection of public sector projects in India was rather primitive. To improve the quality of project planning and strengthen the public investment decision making process several steps were taken: creation of the Bureau of Public Enterprises; establishment of the Project Appraisal Division (PAD) in the Planning Commission; and institution of the Public Investment Board (PIB).
- In the economic appraisal (also referred to as social profitability analysis) of industrial projects, the PAD follows a modified version of the Little–Mirrlees approach.
- The PIB is a committee of secretaries which appraises and recommends all central public sector projects involving an outlay exceeding a certain amount. (For projects involving smaller outlays the decision making powers have been decentralised.)
- The institution of the PIB (and its technical arm, the PAD) represents an important advance in the process of public investment decision making in India. It has promoted a more systematic approach to public sector investment decision making. Yet, there are serious lacunae which have marred the quality of public investment decisions in India.

QUESTIONS

1. Discuss the principal sources of discrepancy between social costs and benefits on the one hand and monetary costs and benefits on the other.
2. What are the five stages of appraisal in the UNIDO method as described in the *Guide to Practical Project Appraisal*?
3. What questions are raised in defining the numéraire? How is the UNIDO numéraire specified?
4. Explain what is the consumer willingness to pay?
5. As per the UNIDO method, how are the following valued?
   (a) tradable inputs and outputs
   (b) non-tradable inputs and outputs
   (c) labour
   (d) foreign exchange
   (e) savings
6. What are the similarities and differences between the UNIDO approach and the Little–Mirrlees approach?
7. How are the following defined or determined in the Little–Mirrlees approach:
   (a) shadow price of traded goods
   (b) accounting price of non-traded goods
   (c) shadow wage rate
   (d) accounting rate of return
8. What are the key elements of the method used by IDBI to calculate the economic rate of return?
9. What is the 'effective rate of protection' and the 'domestic resource cost'? How are the two related?

10. Discuss the initiatives taken to improve the quality of public investment decision making in India.
11. What are the principal steps involved in the public investment decision making process in India?
12. Discuss the role of the PAD and the PIB.
13. What are the key elements of the methodology adopted by the PAD for economic appraisal?
14. What deficiencies characterise public investment decision making in India?

PROBLEMS

1. A government is considering building a tunnel across a sea channel which can currently only be crossed by ship. The following information is available.
   (i) The tunnel will consist of a two-track railway and cars and passengers will be carried by train. It will cut crossing time by two hours for cars and passengers.
   (ii) The relevant categories of traffic are:
      (a) cars (and their passengers)
      (b) passengers not in cars
      (c) freight
   (iii) The authorities who would operate the tunnel have decided to charge a toll which would maximise revenue. The toll that they have decided to charge is ₹160 per car which compares favourably with the charge by ship which is ₹200.
   (iv) Because of the quicker and cheaper journeys available, it is forecast that the following traffic per year for the foreseeable future will be diverted from the existing method of travel:
      75,000 cars (with an average of two passengers)
      50,000 passengers not in cars
      350,000 tonnes of freight
      In addition 50,000 extra car journeys (with two passengers each) will be made.
   (v) The average value of passenger time is ₹6 per hour.
   (vi) The diverted traffic will reduce the cost of operation of the existing ship by ₹40 million a year, while at the forecast levels of traffic, the maintenance and operating cost of the tunnel will be ₹3 million. Its capital cost will be ₹400 million. The life of the tunnel will be 50 years.
   (vii) Assuming that the monetary figures given above reflect social value, calculate the IRR of the stream of social costs and benefits.
2. A government is considering whether it should close down the branch line passenger services from station *A* to station *B*. No goods are currently carried by rail.
   The chief accountant of the government estimates the annual cost of train movement, track maintenance, signalling, and other expenses to be ₹1,520,000, including ₹120,000 toward depreciation and interest charges.
   If the line were closed at any time, the diesel train operating on it could be sold to another country for ₹240,000. Nothing else has any re-sale value. The line is used for 1,000 single journeys each day (250 days per year). The single fare is ₹4.00. So the line is losing money, a deficit met by taxation.
   If the line is closed, it is estimated that of the former journeys, 800 will be made by bus (at the same fare), and 200 will not be made. The bus fare is the same as the rail fare and the extra bus

fares exactly offset the bus operations' extra cost. Bus journey takes an average of 40 minutes longer than the rail journey. The average value of passengers' time is ₹2 per hour. Enumerate the social costs and benefits associated with the proposal.

3. The economic planning department of a state is considering a proposal to build an 80-mile road from a capital to a village which has hitherto only been accessible by river boat. The road will cost ₹24 million and the annual maintenance charges will be approximately ₹1 million. The social discount rate is 10 percent. Analysis suggests that the following effects are likely to result from the completion of the road:
   (i) A saving of ₹0.5 million per year on the cost of shipping agricultural produce from the village and its surrounding area.
   (ii) The opening up to development of an additional 50,000 acres of land. Development will cost ₹3,000 per acre and produce, after 5 years, crops worth ₹1,000 per acre per year. The land will be settled by small holders, who will move from other employments where their earnings average ₹1,500 per year. An estimated 8,000 small holdings will be provided. Land cleaning and drainage cost will be borne by the government, and each settlor will receive a grant of ₹5,000 to assist him in meeting relocation costs. Prior to the time the main crop becomes established, other crops yielding ₹200 per acre per year can be grown.
   (iii) The land after development will be worth ₹380 million whereas its present value as timber land is just ₹100 million.
   (iv) Tax revenue from the area will be increased by ₹1 million per year.
   (v) Value of timber output will be increased by ₹20 million in the first year, while the land is being cleared, but will be reduced by ₹4 million per year after the clearing.
   (vi) The income of boat operators on the river will be reduced by ₹0.5 million per year. Boats costing ₹3 million and scheduled for replacement in five years will not be replaced, and the labour displaced will be absorbed elsewhere at equivalent wages.

   Which of the effects listed above should be taken into account in the social cost benefit analysis? Should the road be built? Assume that the road's life is 30 years.

MINICASE

A project for manufacturing a product which is currently being imported in the country is being appraised. The project would have a life of 20 years and it will lead to import substitution. The capital outlay on the project is expected to be as follows:

	(₹ *in million*)
Land	0.30
Buildings	12.00
Imported equipment	15.00
(CIF value: ₹9 million)	
Indigenous equipment	80.00
(CIF value of similar equipment: ₹60 million)	
Transport	2.00
Engineering and know-how fees	6.00
Pre-operative expenses	6.00
Bank charges	3.70

The working capital requirement of the project, consisting only of domestic raw materials, will be ₹25 million.

The estimated annual profitability of the project is as follows:

Revenue	(₹ *in million*)
Sales revenues	150
(CIF value of the output is ₹110 million)	
Expenses	
Raw materials and stores (indigenous)	85
Labour	7
Salaries	5
Repairs and maintenance	1.2
Water, fuel, etc.	6
Electricity	7
Rate-5	
Duty-2	
Depreciation	4.8
Other overheads	10
Profit	
Taxable profit	24

For the sake of simplicity we may assume that capital costs are incurred at the beginning (i.e., at the end of year 0) and full production begins from year 1 itself. Using the social conversion factors employed by IDBI, calculate the economic rate of return for the project. After 20 years only working capital will be recovered.

APPENDIX 14A

SOCIAL IMPACT ASSESSMENT*

Projects have economic impacts, environmental impacts, social impacts, and biodiversity impacts. Since sustainable development is increasingly accepted as a fundamental objective for public policy and decision-making, all these impacts need to be considered.

Social impacts are defined as "the consequences to human populations of any public or private actions that alter the ways in which people live, work, play, relate to one another, organise to meet their needs, and generally cope as members of society." The main types of social impacts can be grouped into five overlapping categories: lifecycle impacts, cultural impacts, community impacts, quality of life impacts, and health impacts.

Social Assessment or Social Impact Assessment (SIA) provides a framework for considering the key relevant social aspects, involving the participation of a wide range of stakeholders, and formulating and implementing mitigative measures. Exhibit 14A.1 provides an overview of the social assessment process cycle.

* Venugopal Unni and Prasanna Chandra

Exhibit 14A.1 ***Social Assessment Process Cycle****

Key Principles of Social Impact Assessment

The key principles of Social Impact Assessment are as follows:

1. Achieve extensive understanding of local and regional settings to be affected by the action or policy.
2. Focus on key social and cultural issues related to the action or policy from the community and stakeholder profiles.
3. Identify research methods, assumptions and significance that are holistic, transparent and replicable.
4. Provide quality information that satisfy scientific norms for use in decision-making.
5. Ensure that any environmental justice issues are fully described and analysed by taking into consideration the vulnerable stakeholders and populations.
6. Undertake evaluation/monitoring and mitigation measures.

Important Aspects of Social Impact Analysis

For meaningful SIA, the following are important:

Public Participation The population group that would be affected beneficially or adversely by the project should be involved in the planning process.

Identification of Various Data Requirements The data requirements for the proposed action need to be identified. For a road project, for instance, the data would be the location, land

* Adapted from Rietberg – McCracken and Narayan 1998.

requirement, ancillary facilities, construction schedule, size of the workforce and its local content, institutional resources and social issues like poverty, age, ethnicity, gender, etc.

Profile of Baseline Condition The existing human environment and social conditions need to be documented. The human environment should cover gender, number of single-headed households, family size, occupation, income and asset levels, education, access to health services, etc. Social issues should include population details, factors affecting income and productivity such as risk aversion of the poorest groups, land tenure, access to productive inputs, markets, labour opportunities and migration, family composition, kinship reciprocity, organisation and capacity affecting participation in local level institutions and access to services and information, stakeholder attitudes and values towards the project, capacity to manage the project, and the incentives needed, etc.

Scoping of Impacts This involves identification and prioritisation of the range of likely social impacts by reviewing all of the available social science literature, public surveys and public participation techniques etc. Social analysis and participation methods include: (a) Stakeholder workshops with a trained facilitator to assess issues and design development projects collaboratively. (b) Field visits to local stakeholders and using participatory assessment methodologies such as participatory rural appraisal (PRA) or Beneficiary Assessment which provide tools for collaborating with local people in analysis and planning.

Analysis and Prediction of Social Impacts To analyse and predict social impacts, the following methods are used.

- *Comparative method* This method relies on past research and experiences in similar cases.
- *Straight-line trend projection* This method assumes that what has happened in the past will continue in the future. For example, the visitors coming for recreation will increase at the same rate as they did in the past.
- *Population multiplier methods* This method assumes that increase in population implies a commensurate increase in jobs, housing units, infrastructure needs, and so on.
- *Statistical significance analysis* This involves employing statistical techniques to determine whether there is a significant difference in appropriate SIA variables with and without the proposed action.
- *Scenario analysis* The impact of a project on various SIA variables may be assessed by developing alternative scenarios. Experts, local authorities, and knowledgeable citizens may be contacted to create scenarios.
- *Calculation of 'future foregone'* When a social assessment is done, it is important to ask: What options would be given up irrevocably as a result of the project? For example, the construction of a dam will preclude river recreation and submerge agricultural land.

Evaluation of Alternatives and Impact Modification It is worthwhile to evaluate, on a modest scale, alternatives or modifications to the project and their consequences for the affected parties. Also, a mitigation plan needs to be developed and implemented, in order of preference, to avoid, minimise and compensate for the adverse impacts. This could be done by modification or redesign of the project/policy or compensation through substitute facilities, resources and opportunities.

Monitoring Plan A monitoring plan should be implemented, by tracking and comparing, to identify deviations from the proposed plan and any important unanticipated impacts. It should spell out, to the degree possible, the nature and extent of additional steps needed in such events.

Biases SIA practitioners should guard against the following biases:

- *Spatial bias* Information may be gathered from accessible locations, overlooking remote areas or nomadic tribes.
- *Seasonal bias* SIA may be carried out at a time (such as harvesting time or hunting season) when it may be difficult to gain representative information.
- *Personal bias* Information may be gathered from influential people only.
- *Professional bias* There may be an inadequate interaction between disciplinary specialists, resulting in omission of important linkages.

*Source: *Impact Assessment and Project Appraisal*, Volume 21, Number 3, September 2003.

Chapter 15 Multiple Projects and Constraints

LEARNING OBJECTIVES

After studying this chapter you should be able to

- Discuss the nature of constraints which characterise capital budgeting.
- Explain the linear programming model.
- Discuss the integer linear programming model.
- Explain the goal programming model.

When investment projects are considered individually, any of the discounted cash flow criteria—net present value, internal rate of return, or benefit cost ratio—may be applied for obtaining a correct "accept or reject" signal. In an existing organisation, however, capital investment projects often cannot be considered individually or in isolation. This is because the pre-conditions for viewing projects individually—project independence, lack of capital rationing, and project divisibility—are rarely, if ever, fulfilled. Under the constraints obtaining in the real world, the so-called rational criteria *per se* may not necessarily signal the correct decision.

This chapter explains the nature of constraints which render "selection of projects in isolation" meaningless, discusses the problems with the method of ranking, and shows how the techniques of mathematical programming may be employed to select the capital budget in the face of constraints.

15.1 CONSTRAINTS

Project Dependence Projects *A* and *B* are economically independent if the acceptance or rejection of one does not change the cash flow stream of the other or does not affect the acceptance or rejection of the other. For example, an investment in a power press and an investment in a computer installation are economically independent. On the other hand, projects *A* and *B* are economically dependent if the acceptance or rejection of one changes the cash flow stream of the other or affects the acceptance or rejection of the other.

What kinds of economic dependency are found among projects? The most conspicuous kind of economic dependency occurs when projects are mutually exclusive. If two or more projects are mutually exclusive, acceptance of any one project out of the set of mutually exclusive projects automatically precludes the acceptance of all other projects in the set.

From an economic point of view, mutually exclusive projects are substitutes for each other. For example, the alternative possible uses of a building represent a set of mutually exclusive projects. Clearly if the building is put to one use, it cannot be put to any other use.

A second kind of economic dependency exists when projects, even though not mutually exclusive, negatively influence each other's cash flows if they are accepted together. Bierman and Smidt have given an excellent illustration of this kind of economic dependency: a project for building a toll bridge and a project for operating a toll ferry. These two projects are such that when they are undertaken together, the revenues of one will be negatively influenced by the other.

A third kind of economic dependency, which may be referred to as positive economic dependency, occurs when there is complementarity between projects. If undertaking a project influences favourably the cash flows of another project, the two projects are complementary projects. Complementarity may be of two types: asymmetric complementarity and symmetric complementarity. In asymmetric complementarity, the favourable effect extends only in one direction. For example, project *A* favourably influences the cash flows of project *B* whereas project *B*, in turn, has no influence on the cash flows of project *A*. In symmetric complementarity, the favourable effect extends in both directions: project *A* has a favourable influence on the cash flows of project *B* and, likewise, project *B* has a favourable influence on the cash flows of project *A*.

Capital Rationing Capital rationing exists when funds available for investment are inadequate to undertake all projects which are otherwise acceptable. (It may be recalled that a project is acceptable if the net present value is greater than zero or the internal rate of return is greater than the cost of capital or the benefit–cost ratio is greater than one.)

What are the sources of capital rationing? Capital rationing may arise because of an internal limitation or an external constraint. Internal capital rationing is caused by a decision taken by the management to set a limit to its capital expenditure outlays; or, it may be caused by a choice of hurdle rate higher than the cost of capital of the firm. Internal capital rationing, in either case, results in rejection of some investment projects which otherwise are acceptable.

External capital rationing arises out of the inability of the firm to raise sufficient amounts of funds at a given cost of capital. In a perfect market, a firm can obtain all its funds requirement at a given cost of capital. In the real world, however, the firm can raise only a limited amount of funds at a given cost of capital. Beyond a certain point, the cost of capital tends to increase as shown in Exhibit 15.1.

What is the implication of a capital supply curve of the kind shown in Exhibit 15.1? The implication of a rising capital supply curve is that some projects which would be acceptable if the cost of capital were constant will have to be postponed or abandoned.

Project Indivisibility Capital projects are considered indivisible, i.e., a capital project has to be accepted or rejected in toto—a project cannot be accepted partially.

Given the indivisibility of capital projects and the existence of capital rationing, the need arises for comparing projects. To illustrate this point, consider an example. A firm is evaluating three projects, *A*, *B*, and *C*, which involve an outlay of ₹5 million, ₹4 million,

Exhibit 15.1 ***Behaviour of Cost of Capital***

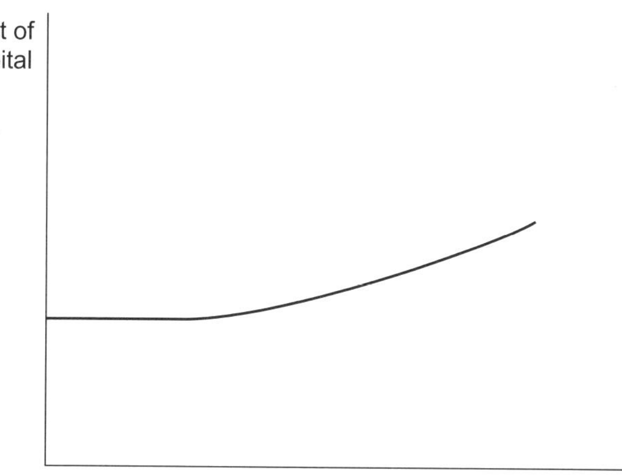

and ₹3 million respectively. The net present value of these projects are ₹2 million, ₹1.5 million, ₹1 million respectively. The funds available to the firm for investment are ₹7 million. In this situation, acceptance of project *A* (project with the highest net present value) which yields a net present value of ₹2 million results in the rejection of projects *B* and *C* which together would yield a combined net present value of ₹2.5 million. Hence, because of the indivisibility of projects, there is a need for comparing projects before the acceptance/rejection decisions are taken.

15.2 METHOD OF RANKING

Because of economic dependency, capital rationing, or project indivisibility, a need arises for comparing projects in order to accept some and reject others. What approaches are available for determining which projects to accept and which projects to reject? Basically, two approaches are available: (i) the method of ranking, and (ii) the method of mathematical programming. This section discusses the method of ranking; the following section discusses the method of mathematical programming.

Fairly simple, the method of ranking consists of two steps: (i) Rank all projects in a decreasing order according to their individual NPVs, IRRs, or BCRs (ii) Accept projects in that order until the capital budget is exhausted.

The method of ranking, originally proposed by Joel Dean[1] is seriously impaired by two problems: (i) conflict in ranking as per discounted cash flow criteria, and (ii) project indivisibility.

Conflict in Ranking In a given set of projects, preference ranking tends to differ from one criterion to another. For example, NPV and IRR criteria may yield different preference rankings. Likewise, there may be a discrepancy between the preference rankings of NPV and

[1] Joel Dean, *Capital Budgeting*, New York, Columbia University Press, 1951.

BCR (benefit cost ratio) criteria. When preference rankings differ, the set of projects selected as per one criterion tends to differ from the set of projects selected as per some other criterion. This may be illustrated by an example.

Consider a set of five projects, *A, B, C, D,* and *E,* for which the investment outlay, expected annual cash flow, and project life are as shown below:

Project	*Investment Outlay*	*Expected Annual Cash Flow*	*Project Life*
	(₹)	(₹)	(Years)
A	10,000	4,000	12
B	25,000	10,000	4
C	30,000	6,000	20
D	38,000	12,000	16
E	35,000	12,000	9

The NPV, IRR, and BCR for the five projects and the ranking along these dimensions are shown in Exhibit 15.2.

Exhibit 15.2 ***NPV, IRR, and BCR for the Five Projects***

Project (₹)	*NPV Ranking*	*NPV (Percent)*	*IRR Ranking*	*IRR*	*BCR*	*BCR Ranking*
A	14,776	4	39	1	2.48	1
B	5,370	5	22	4	1.21	5
C	14,814	3	19	5	1,49	4
D	45,688	1	30	3	2.20	2
E	28,936	2	31	2	1.83	3

It is clear that in the above case that the three criteria rank the projects differently. If there is no capital rationing, all the projects would be accepted under all the three criteria although internal ranking may differ across criteria. However, if the funds available are limited, the set of projects accepted would depend on the criterion adopted.

Sources of Conflicts Conflicts in project ranking may arise because of:

- Size disparity
- Time disparity
- Life disparity

Size Disparity A source of ranking conflict may be the disparity in the size of initial outlays. Such conflicts arise mainly because the NPV represents an absolute magnitude whereas the IRR and BCR are relative measures. To illustrate such conflicts consider two mutually exclusive projects, *A* and *B*, being analysed by a firm whose cost of capital is 10 percent.

	Project A	*Project B*
Original investment	₹4,00,000	16,00,000
Cash inflow per year	₹1,00,000	3,00,000
Useful life	10 years	10 years

The NPV, IRR, and BCR for projects *A* and *B* are shown below:

	Project A	*Project B*
Original investment	₹4,00,000	16,00,000
Present value of cash inflows	₹6,14,460	18,43,380
Net present value	₹2,14,460	2,43,380
Internal rate of return	about 22 percent	about 13 percent
Benefit cost ratio	1.536	1.152

The NPV of *B* is higher than the NPV of *A*, whereas the IRR and BCR of *A* are higher than the IRR and BCR of *B*. How can this conflict between the two be resolved? The resolution of conflict depends on the circumstances of the firm.

1. If the firm has enough funds available to it at a given cost of capital, project *B* is preferable to project *A* because it contributes more to the NPV of the firm.
2. If the firm has limited availability of funds and acceptance of project *B* means giving up project *A* (because projects *A* and *B* are mutually exclusive) and some other project(s) because of capital rationing, then the NPV of project *B* must be compared with the sum of NPV of project *A* and the NPV of other project(s) which may be sacrificed in order to choose project *B* in preference to project *A*. Suppose the adoption of project *B* means that project *A* and project *C*, which has the following characteristics, are sacrificed.

	Project C
Initial outlay	₹12,00,000
Net present value	1,00,000

In this case, given the limited availability of funds, it makes sense to choose projects *A* and *C* in preference to project *B* because the combined NPV of projects *A* and *C* is ₹3,14,460, whereas the NPV of project *B* is only ₹2,43,380.

Time Disparity Projects may differ with respect to the pattern of cash inflows associated with them. Such time disparities of cash inflows may lead to conflicts in ranking. To illustrate, consider two projects, *X* and *Y*, being evaluated by a firm whose cost of capital is 10 percent.

	Project X	*Project Y*
Initial outlay	₹1,10,000	₹1,10,000
Cash inflows		
Year 1	31,000	71,000
Year 2	40,000	40,000
Year 3	50,000	40,000
Year 4	70,000	20,000

The NPV, IRR, and BCR of these projects are shown below:

	Project X	*Project Y*
Initial outlay	₹1,10,000	₹1,10,000
Present value of cash inflows	1,46,613	1,41,314
Net present value	36,613	31,314
Internal rate of return	about 22 percent	about 25 percent
Benefit cost ratio	1.333	1.285

The NPV and BCR of project *X* are higher than that of project *Y*, whereas the IRR of project *X* is lower than that of project *Y*. This conflict occurs because the IRR method assumes that the intermediate cash inflows can be re-invested at the IRR and hence favours a project like *B* which has higher earlier cash inflows. The NPV and BCR methods, on the other hand, assume that the intermediate cash inflows can be re-invested at the firm's cost of capital (a lower rate) and hence do not discriminate much against a project which has larger cash flows later in its life.

How can a conflict arising due to time disparity be resolved? Such a conflict can be resolved by defining the re-investment rates that are applicable to the cash flows of the firm and calculating modified versions of NPV and BCR.

Life Disparity In some cases the mutually exclusive alternatives have varying lives: distemper painting versus plastic emulsion painting, re-building a plant versus replacing it. Life disparity may lead to conflict in ranking. To illustrate, consider two projects, *P* and *Q*, being evaluated by a firm which has a cost of capital of 12 percent:

	Project P	*Project Q*
Initial outlay	₹2,00,000	₹2,00,000
Cash inflows		
Year 1	3,00,000	80,000
Year 2	-	80,000
Year 3	-	2,80,000

The NPV, IRR, and BCR for projects P and Q are:

	Project P	*Project Q*
Initial outlay	₹2,00,000	₹2,00,000
Present value of cash inflows	₹2,67,857	₹3,34,512
NPV	₹67,857	₹1,34,512
IRR	50%	50%
BCR	1,339	1,673

Which project should be selected when there is a time disparity? One approach is to compare the alternatives on the basis of their equivalent annual benefit (EAB) and select the alternative with the highest EAB. The EAB of a project is equal to:

$$\text{Net present value} \times \text{Capital recovery factor}$$

To illustrate, the EAB of the projects *P* and *Q* are calculated below:

	Project P	*Project Q*
Net present value	₹67,857	₹1,34,512
Life	1 year	3 years
Capital recover factor[2] (given $k = 10\%$)	1.100	0.402
EAB	₹74,643	₹54,086

Project Indivisibility A problem in choosing the capital budget on the basis of individual ranking arises because of indivisibility of capital expenditure projects. To illustrate, consider the following set of projects (ranked according to their NPV) being evaluated by a firm which has a capital budget constraint of ₹2,500,000.

Project	*Outlay* (₹)	*NPV* (₹)
A	1,500,000	400,000
B	1,000,000	350,000
C	800,000	300,000
D	700,000	300,000
E	600,000	250,000

If the selection is based on individual NPV ranking, projects *A* and *B* would be included in the capital budget—these projects exhaust the capital budget. A cursory examination, however, would suggest that it is more desirable to select projects *B*, *C*, and *D*. These three projects can be accommodated within the capital budget of ₹2,500,000, and have a combined NPV of ₹950,000 which is greater than the combined NPV of projects *A* and *B*.

Feasible Combinations Approach The above example suggests that the following procedure may be used for selecting the set of investments under capital rationing:[3]

1. Define all combinations of projects which are feasible, given the capital budget restriction and project interdependencies.
2. Choose the feasible combination that has the highest NPV.

To illustrate this procedure, consider the following projects that are being evaluated by a firm which has a capital budget constraint of ₹3,000,000.

Project	*Outlay* (₹)	*NPV* (₹)
A	1,800,000	750,000
B	1,500,000	600,000
C	1,200,000	500,000
D	750,000	360,000
E	600,000	300,000

Projects *B* and *C* are mutually exclusive. Other projects are independent.

[2] It may be recalled that the capital recovery factor is simply the inverse of present value interest factor for annuity.

[3] This procedure can also take care of project interdependencies.

Given the above information, the feasible combinations and their NPVs are shown below:

Feasible Combination	*Outlay*	*NPV*
	(₹)	(₹)
A	1,800,000	750,000
B	1,500,000	600,000
C	1,200,000	500,000
D	750,000	360,000
E	600,000	300,000
A and *C*	3,000,000	1,250,000
A and *D*	2,550,000	1,110,000
A and *E*	2,400,000	1,050,000
B and *D*	2,250,000	960,000
B and *E*	2,100,000	900,000
C and *D*	1,950,000	860,000
C and *E*	1,800,000	800,000
B, *D* and *E*	2,850,000	1,260,000
C, *D* and *E*	2,550,000	1,160,000

The most desirable feasible combination consists of projects *B*, *D* and *E* as it has the highest NPV.

15.3 MATHEMATICAL PROGRAMMING APPROACH

The feasible combinations procedure described above becomes increasingly cumbersome as the number of projects increases and as the number of years in the planning horizon increases. To cope with a problem of this kind, it is helpful to use mathematical programming models. The advantage of mathematical programming models is that they help in determining the optimal solution (the most desirable combination of investments) without explicitly evaluating all feasible combinations.

A mathematical programming model is formulated in terms of two broad categories of equations: (i) the objective function, and (ii) the constraint equations. The objective function represents the goal or objective the decision maker seeks to achieve. Constraint equations represent restrictions—arising out of limitations of resources, environmental restrictions, and managerial policies—which have to be observed. The mathematical model seeks to optimise the objective function subject to various constraints.

The objective function and constraint equations are defined in terms of parameters and decision variables. Parameters represent the characteristics of the decision environment which are given. Decision variables represent what is amenable to control by the decision makers.

Out of the wide variety of mathematical programming models, we shall discuss three types:

- Linear programming model.
- Integer programming model.
- Goal programming model.

15.4 LINEAR PROGRAMMING MODEL

The most popular mathematical programming model, the linear programming model is based on the following assumptions:

- The objective function and the constraint equations are linear.
- All the coefficients in the objective function and constraint equations are defined with certainty.
- The objective function is unidimensional.
- The decision variables are considered to be continuous.
- Resources are homogeneous. This means that if 100 hours of direct labour are available, each of these hours is equally productive.

Linear Programming Model of a Capital Rationing Problem The general formulation of a linear programming model for a capital rationing problem is:

Maximise $$\sum_{j=1}^{n} NPV_j \, X_j \quad (15.1)$$

Subject to

$$\sum_{j=1}^{n} CF_{jt} \, X_j \leq K_t \; (t = 0, 1, ..., m) \quad (15.2)$$

$$0 \leq X_j \leq 1 \quad (15.3)$$

where NPV_j is the net present value of project j, X_j is the amount of project j accepted, CF_{jt} is the cash outflow required for project j in period t, and K_t is the capital budget available in period t.

The following features of the model may be noted.

1. All the input parameters - NPV_j, CF_{jt}, K_t - are assumed to be known with certainty.
2. The X_j decision variables are assumed to be continuous but limited by a lower restriction (0) and an upper restriction (1).
3. The *NPV* calculation is based on a cost of capital figure which is known with certainty.

Lorie and Savage Problem In their classic paper, "Three Problems in Rationing Capital," Lorie and Savage[4] discussed the following nine-project, two-period problem:

[4] J.H. Lorie and L.J. Savage, "Three Problems in Rationing Capital," *Journal of Business*, vol. 28 (Oct 1955).

Project	*Net Present Value (NPV_j)*	*Cash Outflow in Period 1 (CF_{j1})*	*Cash Outflow in Period 2 (CF_{j2})*
1	14	12	3
2	17	54	7
3	17	6	6
4	15	6	2
5	40	30	35
6	12	6	6
7	14	48	4
8	10	36	3
9	12	18	3

The linear programming formulation of this problem is as follows:

Maximise $14X_1 + 17X_2 + 17X_3 + 15X_4 + 40X_5 + 12X_6 + 14X_7 + 10X_8 + 12X_9$

Subject to

$$12X_1 + 54X_2 + 6X_3 + 6X_4 + 30X_5 + 6X_6 + 48X_7 + 36X_8 + 18X_9 + S_1 = 50 \quad \text{Funds constraint for year 1}$$

$$3X_1 + 7X_2 + 6X_3 + 2X_4 + 35X_5 + 6X_6 + 4X_7 + 3X_8 + 3X_9 + S_2 = 20 \quad \text{Funds constraint for year 2}$$

$$\left.\begin{array}{lll} X_1 + S_3 = 1 & X_4 + S_6 = 1 & X_7 + S_9 = 1 \\ X_2 + S_4 = 1 & X_5 + S_7 = 1 & X_8 + S_{10} = 1 \\ X_3 + S_5 = 1 & X_6 + S_8 = 1 & X_9 + S_{11} = 1 \end{array}\right] \text{Upper limit on project acceptance}$$

$$X_j \geq 0 \ (j = 1, 2, ..., 9)$$

$$S_i \geq 0 \ (i = 1, 2, ..., 11)$$

The linear programming solution for the above problem is shown in Exhibit 15.3. From Exhibit 15.3 we find that

1. The basic variables (variables which take a positive value in the optimal solution) are X_1, X_3, X_4, X_6, X_7, X_9, S_4, S_7, S_8, S_9, and S_{10}. Their values are shown in the last column of the tableau ($X_1 = 1.0$; $X_3 = 1.0$; $X_4 = 1.0$; $X_6 = .969697$, and so on).
2. The rest of the variables (X_2, X_5, X_8, S_1, S_2, S_3, S_5, S_6, and S_{11}) are non-basic variables, which means that they take a zero value. A value of zero for X_1, X_5, and X_8 means that these three projects are completely rejected in the optimal solution. A value of zero for S_1 and S_2 implies that the budgets of 50 in year 1 and 20 in year 2 are fully exhausted on the six accepted projects.

Extensions to Reflect Other Constraints The above linear programming model may be extended to incorporate other constraints. Two such extensions are described here.

Carry Forward of Cash The funds constraints embodied in Eq. (15.2) appears somewhat rigid. In practice, funds may be shifted from one period to another. Such a possibility may be reflected in the funds constraints. To illustrate, consider the funds constraints for the first two years.

$$\sum_{j=1}^{n} CF_{j1} X_j \leq K_1 \tag{15.4}$$

$$\sum_{j=1}^{n} CF_{j2} X_j \leq K_2 \tag{15.5}$$

Now, suppose surplus funds in year 1 can be shifted to year 2 and funds so shifted earn r percent return. This possibility calls for re-writing the above expressions as follows:

$$\sum_{j=1}^{n} CF_{j1} X_j + SF_1 = K_1 \tag{15.4a}$$

$$\sum_{j=1}^{n} CF_{j2} X_j \leq K_2 + SF_1 (1 + r) \tag{15.5a}$$

In these expressions, SF_1 represents surplus funds in year 1 transferred to year 2. Since a negative SF_1 tantamounts to borrowing (which is not possible), we may add the constraint

$$SF_1 \geq 0 \tag{15.6}$$

to the above constraints.

Non-Financial Constraints Besides funds, there may be other constraints pertaining to labour, material, and demand. These constraints can be readily incorporated in the linear programming model. An example of a material constraint is given below:

$$\Sigma\, m_j X_j \leq M \tag{15.7}$$

where m_j is the material required for project j, X_j is the proportion of project j accepted, and M is the total availability of material.

Illustration Consider a firm which is evaluating seven projects with the following characteristics:

Project	*Net Present Value* (NPV_j)	*Cash Outflow in Period 1* (CF_{j1})	*Cash Outflow in Period 2* (CF_{j2})
1	6	5	7
2	8	9	5
3	8	12	4
4	7	3	10
5	4	4	6
6	12	10	15
7	9	13	9

The budget available to the firm is limited to 35 in year 1 and 30 in year 2.

Exhibit 15.3 ***Optimal Tableau for Linear Programming Formulation of Lorie-Savage Nine-Project Problem***

Basic Variables	X_1	X_2	X_3	X_4	X_5	X_6	X_7	X_8	X_9	S_1	S_2	S_3	S_4	S_5	S_6	S_7	S_8	S_9	S_{10}	S_{11}	RHS
X_1	1.0											1.0									1.00
X_3			1.0											1.0							1.00
X_4				1.0											1.0						1.00
X_6		.455			5.91	1.0				–0.15	.1818	–.364			–.273					–.273	.96969
X_7		1.068			– .114		1.0	.75		–.023	–.023	– .205		–1.0	–.091					–.341	.04545
X_9									1.0											1.0	1.00
S_4		1.0											1.0								1.00
S_7					1.0											1.0					1.00
S_8		–.455			5.91					.015	.1818	.364		–1.0	.273	1.0				.273	.03030
S_9		–1.068			.114				.75	–.023	.023	.205		.091			1.0			.341	.95454
S_{10}									1.0									1.0			1.00
Z	0	3.41	0	0	29.32	0	0	50	0	.1364	1.864	6.77		0	5.0	10.45	0	0	0	3.95	70.273
	μ_1	μ_2	μ_3	μ_4	μ_5	μ_6	μ_7	μ_8	μ_9	ρ_1	ρ_2 γ_1	γ_2	γ_3	γ_4	γ_5	γ_6	γ_7	γ_8	γ_9	γ_9	

There are two additional constraints: power constraint and managerial constraint. The requirements and constraints applicable in this respect are shown below:

Project	*Power Requirement* (E_j)	*Managerial Requirement* (M_j)
1	2	6
2	4	5
3	5	7
4	3	2
5	4	4
6	7	8
7	6	3
	$\Sigma X_j E_j \leq 18$	$\Sigma X_j M_j \leq 20$

The linear programming formulation of the capital budgeting problem, under various constraints mentioned above, is as follows:

Maximise $\quad 6X_1 + 8X_2 + 8X_3 + 7X_4 + 4X_5 + 12X_6 + 9X_7$

Subject to

$$5X_1 + 9X_2 + 12X_3 + 3X_4 + 4X_5 + 10X_6 + 13X_7 + S_1 = 35 \quad \text{Funds constraint for year 1}$$

$$7X_1 + 5X_2 + 4X_3 + 10X_4 + 6X_5 + 15X_6 + 9X_7 + S_2 = 30 \quad \text{Funds constraint for year 2}$$

$$2X_1 + 4X_2 + 5X_3 + 3X_4 + 4X_5 + 7X_6 + 6X_7 + S_3 = 18 \quad \text{Power constraint}$$

$$6X_1 + 5X_2 + 7X_3 + 2X_4 + 4X_5 + 8X_6 + 3X_7 + S_4 = 20 \quad \text{Managerial constraint}$$

$$\left.\begin{array}{ll} X_1 + S_5 = 1 & X_5 + S_9 = 1 \\ X_2 + S_6 = 1 & X_6 + S_{10} = 1 \\ X_3 + S_7 = 1 & X_7 + S_{11} = 1 \\ X_4 + S_8 = 1 & \end{array}\right] \quad \text{Upper limits on project acceptance}$$

$$X_j \geq (j = 1, 2, ..., 7)$$

$$S_i \geq (i = 1, 2, ..., 11)$$

It may be noted that the approach taken in this formulation is similar to that represented in Eqs (15.1) through (15.3) above, except that 'slack variables' have been added to each inequality constraint to transform it into an equality constraint. Slack variables S_1 and S_2 represent the amounts unallocated in years 1 and 2; slack variable S_3 represents surplus power; slack variable S_4 represents surplus managerial capacity; slack variables S_5 through S_{11} represent the proportions of projects 1 through 7, respectively, which are not accepted.

15.5 INTEGER LINEAR PROGRAMMING MODEL

In his pioneering work on the application of mathematical programming to capital budgeting, Weingartner discussed the linear programming approach as well as the integer linear programming approach.[5] The principal motivation for the use of integer linear programming approach are: (i) It overcomes the problem of partial projects which besets the linear programming model because it permits only 0 or 1 value for the decision variables. (ii) It is capable of handling virtually any kind of project interdependency.

Integer Linear Programming Model for Capital Budgeting The basic integer linear programming model for capital budgeting under capital rationing is as follows:

Maximise

$$\sum_{j=1}^{n} X_j \, NPV_j \qquad (15.8)$$

Subject to

$$\sum_{j=1}^{n} CF_{jt} \, X_j \leq K_t \; (t = 0, 1, \cdots, m) \qquad (15.9)$$

$$X_j = (0, 1) \qquad (15.10)$$

It may be noted that the only difference between this integer linear programming model and the basic linear programming model discussed earlier is that the integer linear programming model ensures that a project is either completely accepted ($X_j = 1$) or completely rejected ($X_j = 0$).

Incorporating Project Interdependencies in the Model By constraining the decision variables to 0 or 1, the integer linear programming model can handle almost any kind of project interdependency. To illustrate, let us see how the following kinds of project interdependencies are incorporated in the integer linear programming model:

- Mutual exclusiveness
- Contingency
- Complementariness

Mutual Exclusiveness If two or more projects are mutually exclusive, acceptance of any one project out of the set of mutually exclusive projects, automatically precludes the acceptance of all other projects in the set. From an economic point of view, mutually exclusive projects are substitutes for each other. Mutual exclusiveness is reflected in the integer programming model by the following constraint:

$$\sum_{j \in J} X_j \leq 1 \qquad (15.11)$$

where J is the set of mutually exclusive projects under consideration, and $j \in J$ is an expression which means that project j belongs to set J.

[5] Martin H. Weingartner, *Mathematical Programming and Analysis of Capital Budgeting Problems*, Englewood Cliffs, N.J.: Prentice-Hall, 1963.

Constraint (15.11) means that the upper limit on the number of projects that can be selected from the set J is 1. This, of course, means that the firm may not select any project from the set J. If it is necessary to choose one project, but only one project, constraint (15.11) would become:

$$\sum_{j \in J} X_j = 1 \qquad (15.12)$$

An important variant of the mutual exclusiveness condition is one in which the firm may delay a project for one or more years. Consider, for example, project X:

Time	*Cash Flow*
0	– 10,000
1	3,000
2	3,000
3	3,000
4	3,000
5	3,000

The NPV of this project, given a cost of capital of 12 percent, is 814. If the firm can delay this project by 1 or 2 years, two new projects X' and X'' can be defined:

Time	*Cash Flow of X′*	*Cash Flow of X″*
0	–	–
1	– 10,000	–
2	3,000	– 10,000
3	3,000	3,000
4	3,000	3,000
5	3,000	3,000
6	3,000	3,000
7	–	3,000

The NPVs of projects X' and X'' to be included in the objective function are respectively 727 and 649. These values naturally differ from the NPV of X because of delays in cash flows associated with X' and X''. Since at best only one of the projects—X, X' and X''—can be accepted, the following constraint is incorporated in the integer linear programming model:

$$X + X' + X'' \leq 1 \qquad (15.13)$$

Contingency A contingency relationship between two or more projects implies that the acceptance of one project is contingent on the acceptance of some other project(s). For example, if project B cannot be accepted without accepting project A, we say that project B is contingent on project A. Put differently, project A is a prerequisite project for project B. Such a relationship is represented by the following constraint in the integer linear programming model:

$$X_B \leq X_A \qquad (15.14)$$

It may be noted that as per constraint (15.14), project *B* can be accepted only when project *A* is accepted; project *A*, however, can be accepted independently.

A project may be contingent on not one but two (or even more) projects. Suppose, the acceptance of project *R* is contingent on the acceptance of projects *P* and *Q*. Such a contingency relationship is reflected in the following constraint.

$$2X_R \leq X_P + X_Q \tag{15.15}$$

Mutual Exclusiveness and Contingency Project dependency may reflect both mutual exclusiveness and contingency requirements. Some examples are described below:

1. *M* and *N* are mutually exclusive projects; a third project, *P*, is contingent on the acceptance of either *M* or *N*. This condition is reflected in the following constraints:

$$X_M + X_N \leq 1 \tag{15.16}$$

$$X_P \leq X_M + X_N \tag{15.17}$$

2. Out of the set of projects, *A*, *B*, *C* and *D*, only three projects can be accepted. Further, for accepting project *E*, at least two projects out of the above set should be accepted. This condition is reflected in the following constraints:

$$X_A + X_B + X_C + X_D \leq 3 \tag{15.18}$$

$$2X_E \leq X_A + X_B + X_C + X_D \tag{15.19}$$

Complementariness If undertaking a project influences favourably the cash flows of another project, the two projects are complementary projects. To illustrate how complementarity is reflected in the integer linear programming model, consider two projects *R* and *S*. Either of them can be accepted individually. However, if both are accepted together the following benefits will accrue: (i) The cost will reduce by 5 percent. (ii) The net cash inflow will increase by 10 percent. To reflect a complementary relationship of this kind, a composite project *RS* representing the combination of *R* and *S* is set up; the cash inflows of *RS* would be 10 percent higher than the sum of the cash inflows of *R* and *S*. Further, since it is not possible to accept *R* and *S* as well as *RS*, because the latter is the composite project consisting of *R* and *S*, the following constraint is incorporated in the integer linear programming formulation:

$$X_R + X_S + X_{RS} \leq 1 \tag{15.20}$$

Illustration Consider the following nine projects.

Project	*Net Present Value* (NPV_j)	*Cash Outflow in Year 1* (CF_{j1})	*Cash Outflow in Year 2* (CF_{j2})
1	44	50	48
2	30	40	22
3	20	10	40
4	25	36	5
5	35	25	60

(*Contd.*)

Project	Net Present Value (NPV_j)	Cash Outflow in Year 1 (CF_{j1})	Cash Outflow in Year 2 (CF_{j2})
6	24	43	15
7	42	40	0
8	28	33	14
9	60	75	48

The budget constraints for the two years are 150 and 180 respectively. The following project interdependencies obtain:

1. Projects 1 and 2 are mutually exclusive.
2. Out of the set of projects 4, 5, and 6 at least two must be accepted.
3. Project 9 cannot be accepted unless projects 4 and 6 are accepted.
4. Project 7 can be delayed by one year. Such a delay would not change the cash outflows but reduce *NPV* to 35.
5. Projects 8 and 9 are complementary. If the two are accepted together, the total cash outflows will be less by 8 percent whereas the *NPV* will be more by 10 percent.

Given the nature of the problem, in addition to the decision variables X_1 through X_9 for the original 9 projects, a few additional decision variables are required as follows:

X_{10} is the decision variable to represent the delay of project 7 by one year.

X_{11} is the decision variable for the composite project which represents the combination of projects 8 and 9.

The integer linear programming formulation is as follows:

Maximise $44X_1 + 30X_2 + 20X_3 + 25X_4 + 35X_5 + 24X_6$
$+ 42X_7 + 28X_8 + 60X_9 + 35X_{10} + 96.8X_{11}$

Subject to

$$50X_1 + 40X_2 + 10X_3 + 36X_4 + 25X_5 + 43X_6$$
$$+ 40X_7 + 33X_8 + 75X_9 + 0X_{10} + 99.4X_{11} \leq 150$$
$$48X_1 + 22X_2 + 40X_3 + 5X_4 + 60X_5 + 15X_6$$
$$+ 0X_7 + 14X_8 + 48X_9 + 40X_{10} + 47.88X_{11} \leq 180$$
$$X_1 + X_2 \leq 1$$
$$2X_9 \leq X_4 + X_6$$
$$X_7 + X_{10} \leq 1$$
$$X_8 + X_9 + X_{11} \leq 1$$
$$X_j = \{0, 1\} j = 1, 2, \cdots, 11$$

Evaluation The principal strengths of the integer linear programming model, clearly demonstrated above, are:

1. It overcomes the problem of partial projects which besets the linear programming model.
2. It is capable of handling virtually any kind of project interdependency.

The major shortcomings of the integer linear programming model are:

1. The solution of an integer linear programming model takes considerably more time than the solution of the linear programming model. Pettway reported that for an integer linear programming model with 28 projects and 15 budget constraints, four out of six algorithms that he tried failed to reach an optimal solution in 5 minutes of CPU time on an IBM 360–65 system; the two algorithms which located the optimal solution took 118 seconds and 181 seconds. By contrast, the solution time for the linear programming model of the same problem would take just one to two seconds. Further, the solution time for integer linear programming tends to grow exponentially as the number of projects increases because of the combinatorial nature of the problem. Other frustrating aspects of the integer linear programming model are: (i) The solution time may be highly variable—a small problem may take much more time than a large problem. (ii) Minor variations in the problem may lead to significant increase in solution times. (iii) No single solution algorithm works best for all types of integer linear programming problems.
2. Meaningful shadow prices are not available for the integer programming formulation. This happens because the integer linear programming model permits only discrete variation, not continuous variation, of the decision variables. In the integer linear programming model, constraints which are not binding in the optimal solution are assigned zero shadow prices although the objective function would decrease when the availability of resources, representing non-binding constraints, is diminished. Gomory and Baumol summarise the problem of shadow prices in integer linear programming as follows:[6]

   In integer programming, inputs clearly must be thought of as coming in indivisible units. For that reason we cannot speak, e.g., of the marginal profit contribution of a small change in input, i.e., we must deal with $\Delta R/\Delta X$ rather than dR/dX (as we do in *LP*) where ΔX is an indivisible unit of input X and R is total profit. But a dual-price represents dR/dX which may change over the range of a unit change in X, and hence it may well give an incorrect evaluation of the marginal revenue of input X.

15.6 GOAL PROGRAMMING MODEL

Throughout this text we have assumed that the principal goal of financial management is to maximise the wealth of shareholders, which, under conditions of perfect capital market, can be realised by selecting the set of capital projects that maximise net present value.

However, in the real world, capital market imperfections (like capital rationing, differences in lending and borrowing rates, etc.) exist. Further, empirical observation show that managers pursue a multiple goal structure which includes, *inter alia*, the following:

- Growth in sales and market share.
- Growth and stability of reported earnings.
- Growth and stability of dividends.

[6] R.E. Gomory and W.J. Baumol, "Integer Programming and Pricing," *Econometrica*, September 1966.

Therefore, a realistic representation of real-life situations should reflect the multiple goals pursued by the management. The goal programming approach, a kind of mathematical programming approach, provides a methodology for solving an optimisation problem that involves multiple goals. This approach, originally proposed by Charnes and Cooper[7] in 1961, has been extended by Ijiri, Ignizio, and others.

To use the goal programming model, the decision maker must:

1. State an absolute priority order among his goals.
2. Provide a target value for each of his goals.

The goal programming methodology seeks to solve the programming problem by minimising the absolute deviations from the specific goals in order of the priority structure established. Goals at priority level one are sought to be optimised first. Only when this is done will the goals at priority level two be considered; so on and so forth. At a given priority level, the relative importance of two or more goals is reflected in the weights assigned to them.

Goal Programming Format In general, the goal programming format is as follows:

$$\text{Minimise} = \{P_1 [f_1 (d_1^+, d_1^-)] + P_2 [f_2(d_2^+, d_2^-)] + \cdots + P_m [f_m (d_m^+, d_m^-)]\} \quad (15.21)$$

Subject to

$$\Sigma a_{j1} X_j \le C_1 \quad (15.22a)$$
$$\Sigma a_{j2} X_j \le C_2 \quad (15.22b)$$

.

.

$$\Sigma a_{jk} X_j \le C_k \quad (15.22k)$$

.

$$\Sigma b_{j1} X_j + d_1^- - d_1^+ = G_1 \quad (15.23a)$$
$$\Sigma b_{j2} X_j + d_2^- - d_2^+ = G_2 \quad (15.23b)$$

.

.

.

$$\Sigma b_{jm} X_j + d_m^- - d_m^+ = G_m \quad (15.23m)$$
$$X_j, d_i^+, d_i^- \ge 0 \quad (15.24)$$

The goal programming model is formulated in terms of three principal components: (i) the objective function, (ii) the economic constraints, and (iii) the goal constraints.

Objective Function The objective function, expressed as Eq. (15.21), seeks to minimise the weighted deviation from the target levels of various objectives in accordance with a priority structure. A formal representation of the objective function calls for specifying the following:

---

[7] A. Charnes and W.W. Cooper, *Management Models and Industrial Applications of Linear Programming*, New York: John Wiley & Sons, 1961.

- The priority levels of goals.
- The relative weights attached to each goal where there are two or more goals at the same priority level.
- The relevant deviational variables which should be minimised with respect to each goal.

Economic Constraints The economic constraints embodied in Eqs (15.22a) through (15.22k) represent resource limitations or restrictions emanating from the decision environment which cannot be violated. Hence they are also referred to as 'hard constraints'. The economic constraints in a goal programming model are similar to the constraints found in a linear programming model. Hence, such constraints require the usual slack or surplus variables.

Goal Constraints The goal constraints, embodied in Eqs (15.23a) through (15.23m) represent target levels of various goals that are pursued by the decision maker. Defined as strict equalities, goal constraints contain, in addition to an expression showing the impact of decision variables on goal attainment, two deviational variables denoted by d^+_i and d^-_i. d^+_i indicates that the desired level of goal i has been over-achieved; d^-_i indicates that the desired level of goal i has been under-achieved. When the desired goal level has been over-achieved d^+_i is non-zero and d^-_i is zero; when the desired goal level has been underachieved, d^+_i is zero and d^-_i is non-zero; when the desired goal level is exactly achieved, both d^+_i and d^-_i are zero. The deviational variables tie the goal constraints and the objective function. For each goal, the appropriate deviational variable(s) is (are) placed in the objective function.

Illustration To illustrate the application of goal programming let us reconsider the example used in the context of our discussion on linear programming in which there were seven projects with the following characteristics:

Project	*Net Present Value* (NPV_j)	*Cash Outflow in Period 1* (CF_{j1})	*Cash Outflow in Period 2* (CF_{j2})	*Power Requirement* (E_j)	*Managerial Requirement* (M_j)
1	6	5	7	2	6
2	8	9	5	4	5
3	8	12	4	5	7
4	7	3	10	3	2
5	4	4	6	4	4
6	12	10	15	7	8
7	9	13	9	6	3
		$\Sigma X_j CF_{j1} \leq 35$	$\Sigma X_j CF_{j2} \leq 30$	$\Sigma X_j E_j \leq 18$	$\Sigma X_j M_j \leq 20$

The firm considering these projects now feels that in addition to the NPV objective, there are two other goals viz., net income objective and sales growth objective. The firm wants the net income from the set of projects selected to be 6 and 9 respectively in years 1 and 2. Further, the firm has set a sales growth target to 10 percent for the first two years.

The contribution of the projects to net income and sales growth is shown below:

Project	Net Income		Sales Growth	
	Year 1	*Year 2*	*Year 1*	*Year 2*
1	1.0	1.4	0.010	0.020
2	2.1	1.6	0.015	0.010
3	1.8	2.5	0.018	0.025
4	1.2	3.0	0.020	0.025
5	1.0	0.8	0.015	0.010
6	2.5	1.2	0.030	0.025
7	1.4	1.3	0.025	0.020

The priorities assigned to various goals are as follows:

Priority 1 : Net income
Priority 2 : Sales growth
Priority 3 : NPV

At priority level one, net income for year one is considered two times as important as the net income for year two; at priority level two, sales growth for year one is considered three times as important as the sales growth for year two.

The goal programming formulation of the above problem is given below.

Goal Function

$$\text{Minimise} = [P_1 (2d_1^- + d_2^-) + P_2 (3d_3^- + d_4^-) + P_3 (d_5^- - d_5^+)]$$

Economic Constraints

$$5X_1 + 9X_2 + 12X_3 + 3X_4 + 4X_5 + 10X_6 + 13X_7 + S_1 = 35 \quad \text{Funds constraint for year 1}$$

$$7X_1 + 5X_2 + 4X_3 + 10X_4 + 6X_5 + 15X_6 + 9X_7 + S_2 = 30 \quad \text{Funds constraint for year 2}$$

$$2X_1 + 4X_2 + 5X_3 + 3X_4 + 4X_5 + 7X_6 + 6X_7 + S_3 = 18 \quad \text{Power constraint}$$

$$6X_1 + 5X_2 + 7X_3 + 2X_4 + 4X_5 + 8X_6 + 3X_7 + S_4 = 20 \quad \text{Managerial constraint}$$

$$X_1 + S_5 = 1 \qquad X_5 + S_9 = 1$$

$$X_2 + S_6 = 1 \qquad X_6 + S_{10} = 1$$

$$X_3 + S_7 = 1 \qquad X_7 + S_{11} = 1$$

$$X_4 + S_8 = 1$$

$$X_j \geq 0 \ (j = 1, 2, ..., 7)$$

$$S_i \geq 0 \ (i = 1, 2, ..., 11)$$

Goal Constraints

$$1.0X_1 + 2.1X_2 + 1.8X_3 + 1.2X_4 + 1.0X_5 + 2.5X_6 + 1.4X_7 + d_1^- - d_1^+ = 6 \quad \text{Net income for year 1}$$

$$1.4X_1 + 1.6X_2 + 2.5X_3 + 3.0X_4 + 0.8X_5 + 1.2X_6 + 1.3X_7 + d_2^- - d_2^+ = 9 \quad \text{Net income for year 2}$$

$$0.01X_1 + 0.015X_2 + 0.018X_3 + 0.020X_4 + 0.015X_5 + 0.03X_6 + 0.025X_7 + d_3^- - d_3^+ = 0.10 \quad \text{Sales growth for year 1}$$

$$0.02X_1 + 0.01X_2 + 0.025X_3 + 0.025X_4 + 0.01X_5 + 0.025X_6 + 0.02X_7 + d_4^- - d_4^+ = 0.10 \quad \text{Sales growth for year 2}$$

$$6X_1 + 8X_2 + 8X_3 + 7X_4 + 4X_5 + 12X_6 + 9X_7 + d_5^- - d_5^+ = 50 \quad \text{NPV}$$

It may be noted that the goal constraint of *NPV* is arbitrarily set equal to 50. In the objective function, the NPV goal, set at priority level 3, is defined as

$$\text{Minimise } (d_5^- - d_5^+)$$

This has the effect of striving for the maximum possible deviation from the target value—this means NPV is sought to be maximised.

Appropriate Objective Function The decision maker may be interested in pursuing varied actions relative to different goals. The objective function term should reflect the character of the desired action. Here is a list of objective function terms corresponding to various desired actions.

Desired Action	Objective Function Term
■ Attain a minimum level of some goal	Minimise d^-
■ Do not exceed a given level of some goal	Minimise d^+
■ Minimise the deviation from a specified goal level	Minimise $(d^+ + d^-)$
■ Maximise the value achieved in relation to a given goal level	Minimise $(d^- - d^+)$
■ Minimise the value achieved in relation to a given level	Minimise $(d^+ - d^-)$

SUMMARY

- Because of constraints like project dependence, capital rationing, and project indivisibility, investment projects cannot be viewed in isolation.

- The types of economic dependency found among projects are: mutual exclusiveness, negative dependency, and positive dependency (complementariness).
- Capital rationing exists when funds available for investment are inadequate to undertake all projects which are otherwise acceptable. Capital rationing may arise because of an internal limitation or an external constraint.
- Capital projects are generally indivisible. This means that a capital project has to be accepted or rejected in total—a project cannot be accepted partially.
- Because of economic dependency, capital rationing, or project indivisibility, a need arises for comparing projects in order to accept some and reject others. Two approaches are available for this purpose: the method of ranking, and the method of mathematical programming.
- Fairly simple, the method of ranking consists of two steps: (i) Rank all projects in decreasing order according to their individual NPVs, IRRs, or BC₹(ii) Accept projects in that order until the capital budget is exhausted.
- The method of ranking is seriously impaired by two problems: (i) conflict in ranking as per discounted cash flow criteria, and (ii) project indivisibility.
- In a given set of projects, preference ranking tends to differ from one criterion to another. Ranking conflicts are traceable to size disparity, time disparity, and life disparity.
- A mathematical programming model is formulated in terms of two broad categories of equations: (i) the objective function, and (ii) the constraint equations.
- Out of the wide variety of mathematical programming models, three types have greater applicability to the capital budgeting problem: linear programming model, integer linear programming model, and goal programming model.

QUESTIONS

1. Discuss different kinds of project dependency.
2. Discuss the sources of capital rationing.
3. Construct a set of five projects for which there is conflict in ranking as per the NPV, IRR, and BCR criteria.
4. Describe the feasible combinations approach. Illustrate it with a numerical example.
5. What assumptions underlie the linear programming model?
6. Critically evaluate the integer linear programming model as a tool for capital budgeting.
7. Discuss the following in the context of a goal programming model: objective function, economic constraints, and goal constraints.

PROBLEMS

1. Consider a set of five projects:

Project	*Investment Outlay*	*Expected Annual Cash Inflow*	*Project Life*
	(₹)	(₹)	Years
M	50,000	18,000	10
N	100,000	50,000	4
O	120,000	30,000	8
P	150,000	40,000	16
Q	200,000	30,000	25

Rank the five projects on the dimensions of NPV, IRR, and BCR. The discount rate is 10%.

2. Give two hypothetical 3-year projects for which the NPV (at discount rate 10 percent) and IRR give different ranking.
3. Give two hypothetical 4-year projects for which the BCR and IRR criteria give different rankings. Assume that the discount rate is 12 percent.
4. Five projects, *A*, *B*, *C*, *D*, and *E* are available to a company.

	A	*B*	*C*	*D*	*E*
Initial investment	₹20,000	50,000	75,000	100,000	150,000
Annual cash inflow	₹6,000	8,000	15,000	15,000	25,000
Life	5 years	10	8	12	7
Salvage value	₹5,000	–	–	15,000	50,000

Project *B* is a prerequisite for project *E* and projects *C* and *D* are mutually exclusive. Otherwise the projects are independent. If the cost of capital for the firm is 10 percent, which projects should be chosen at the following budget levels: ₹200,000 and ₹250,000. Assume that the decision criterion is the net present value. Use the feasible combinations approach.

5. A firm is evaluating six investment opportunities:

Project (j)	*Net Present Value* (NPV_j)	*Cash Outflow in Period 1* (CF_{j1})	*Cash Outflow in Period 2* (CF_{j2})
	(₹)	(₹)	(₹)
1	10,000	15,000	5,000
2	15,000	12,000	13,000
3	25,000	8,000	40,000
4	40,000	35,000	25,000
5	60,000	100,000	10,000
6	100,000	50,000	110,000

The budget available is limited to ₹150,000 in year 1 and ₹200,000 in year 2. Any amount not spent in year 1 can be transferred to year 2. The amount so transferred will earn a post-tax return of 8 percent.

There are two additional constraints: working capital constraint and managerial constraint. The requirements and constraints applicable in this respect are:

Project (j)	*Power Requirement* (W_j)	*Managerial Requirement* (M_j)
1	5,000	15
2	6,000	20
3	5,000	30
4	10,000	35
5	12,000	40
6	40,000	60
	$\Sigma X_j W_j \le 60{,}000$	$\Sigma X_j M_j \le 120$

Develop a linear programming formulation of the above capital budgeting problem.

6. Consider the following ten investment projects.

Project (j)	*Net Present Value* (NPV_j)	*Cash Outflow in Period 1* (CF_{j1})	*Cash Outflow in Period 2* (CF_{j2})
	55	75	40
2	75	80	85
3	50	75	8
4	60	35	100
5	105	80	160
6	12	20	9
7	60	70	5
8	120	155	100
9	50	55	20
10	40	10	90

The budget constraints for years 1 and 2 are 400 and 350 respectively. The following project interdependencies exist:

(i) Projects 3 and 7 are mutually exclusive.

(ii) Out of the set of projects 5, 8, 9, and 10 at least two must be accepted.

(iii) Project 6 is a prerequisite for project 2.

(iv) Project 8 can be delayed by one year. Such a delay would shift the cash outflows by one year and reduce the NPV of project 8 by 20. No fund constraint applies to year 3.

(v) Projects 4 and 5 are complementary. If the two are accepted together, the total cash outflows will be less by 5 percent whereas the NPV will be more by 8 percent.

(vi) If project 8 is accepted, project 9 must also be accepted.

Develop the integer linear programming formulation of the above problem.

7. Delta International is considering seven projects with the following characteristics:

		Contribution to Net Income			*Contribution to Sales Growth (percentage)*			
Project	*Initial Outlay*	*Year 1*	*Year 2*	*Year 3*	*Year 1*	*Year 2*	*Year 3*	*NPV*
1	12	1.2	1.1	1.6	1.0	1.5	1.8	4
2	14	1.6	1.2	1.5	1.2	1.0	1.2	5
3	15	0.6	1.2	2.0	0.5	1.2	2.5	6
4	16	1.5	1.6	1.8	1.8	2.0	2.2	8
5	11	0.5	1.2	1.5	0.6	1.4	1.8	4
6	23	0.9	2.5	4.0	1.0	3.0	3.5	9
7	20	1.8	2.0	2.2	2.0	3.0	3.5	7

The capital budget constraint is 65. The goals sought by management are as follows: (i) maximisation of NPV, (ii) contribution to net income of 6.0, 8.0, and 10.0 in years 1, 2, and 3, and (iii) contribution to sales growth of 6, 8, and 10 percent in years 1, 2, and 3. The priorities assigned to various goals are as follows:

Priority 1	:	Net income
Priority 2	:	Sales growth
Priority 3	:	NPV

At priority level 1, the relative weights attached to the net income of years 1, 2, and 3 are 3, 2, and, 1 respectively. At priority level 2, the relative weights attached to the contribution to sales growth of years 1, 2, and 3 are 4, 2, and 1 respectively.

Formulate the above problem as a goal programming problem.

8. The Premier Company draws a two-year capital budget. The amount available for the next two years is ₹2.5 million, ₹2 million is on hand now and ₹0.5 million will be available after a year. Some projects can be undertaken now, some after a year. The BCR of the projects calculated at the point of investment is as follows:

					(in millions)
	Projects Available Now			*Projects Available After a Year*	
Number	*Initial investment*	*BCR*	*Number*	*Initial investment*	*BCR*
1	0.8	1.08	6	0.5	1.03
2	0.2	1.35	7	0.4	1.21
3	0.4	1.20	8	0.6	1.17
4	0.3	1.03	9	0.3	1.01
5	0.2	0.98			

The tax rate of the company is 60 percent and its post-tax cost of capital is 10 percent. One year bank deposit carries 8 percent of interest. Develop an integer linear programming formulation of the problem.

Valuation of Real Options

Learning Objectives

After studying this chapter you should be able to

- Describe options and their payoffs just before expiration.
- Discuss the key factors that determine the value of a call option.
- Compute the value of a call option using the binomial model.
- Compute the value of a call option using the Black-Scholes model.
- Describe the various types of real options.
- Explain how the binomial model and Black-Scholes model may be used for valuing real options.

The discounted cash flow (DCF) analysis has been the basic framework for valuing assets, real and financial, since the 1950s. Hence our discussion of capital budgeting focused on DCF techniques. In recent decades, however, a growing number of academicians and practitioners have argued that the traditional DCF model does not fully capture the value of a real project, as it does not reflect the options embedded therein.

The DCF model was initially developed for valuing financial securities like bonds and stocks. Investors in these securities are generally passive. Barring exceptional circumstances, they can hardly do anything to enhance the interest or dividend they get from such financial assets. However, real assets cannot be considered as passive investments because managers can, through their actions, influence the outcomes of such assets. As a capital expenditure unravels, chance plays an important role and managers can respond to changing conditions and actions of competitors. The opportunities that managers have are called managerial options or real options, as they involve real assets, not financial assets.

The important types of real options found in capital projects are the option to delay the project, the option to expand the project, the option to contract or abandon the project, and the option to change the outputs or inputs of the project. These options give managers flexibility to amplify gains or to reduce losses.

Given the fact that these options are found in most real projects, particularly strategic investments, finance theorists and practitioners argue that the strategic NPV of a project must be defined as:

Strategic NPV = Conventional NPV + Real option value (ROV)

The thrust of this chapter is on the valuation of real options with the help of the binomial model and the Black-Scholes model. Since these models were developed initially in the context of financial options, the chapter begins with a discussion on how financial options work and what their payoffs are.

16.1 HOW OPTIONS WORK

An option is a special contract under which the option owner enjoys the right to buy or sell something without the obligation to do so. Options have a special terminology associated with them.

- The option to buy is a *call option* (or just call) and the option to sell is a *put option* (or just put).
- The *option holder* is the buyer of the option and the *option writer* is the seller of the option.
- The fixed price at which the option holder can buy and/or sell the underlying asset is called the *exercise price* or *strike price.*
- The date when the option expires or matures is referred to as the *expiration date* or *maturity date.* After the expiration date, the option is worthless.
- The act of buying or selling the underlying asset as per the option contract is called *exercising the option.*
- A *European option* can be exercised only on the expiration date whereas an *American option* can be exercised on or before the expiration date.
- Options traded on an exchange are called *exchange-traded options* and options not traded on an exchange are called *over-the-counter options.*
- Options are said to be *at the money* (ATM) or *in the money* (ITM) or *out of the money* (OTM) as shown here:

	Call option	*Put option*
ATM:	Exercise price = Market price	Exercise price = Market price
ITM:	Exercise price < Market price	Exercise price > Market price
OTM:	Exercise price > Market price	Exercise price < Market price

Exchange-traded options are standardised in terms of quantity, trading cycle, expiration date, strike prices, type of option, and mode of settlement. For example, option contracts on individual securities on the National Stock Exchange shall have a maximum of three-month trading cycle, shall expire on the last Thursday of the month, shall be American style, and shall be cash settled. The lot size and the number of strike prices and stock specific.

Exhibit 16.1 shows the quotations for call options and put options on Reliance Industries Limited as on 13-12-2018 drawn from the publication *Bhavcopy* of NSE.

The value of an option, if it were to expire immediately, is called its *intrinsic value.* The excess of the market price of any option over its intrinsic value is called the *time value of the option.* To illustrate, suppose the market price of a share is ₹260, the exercise price of a call option on the share is ₹250, and the market price of the call option is ₹15. In this case, the intrinsic value of the option is ₹10 (₹260 – ₹250) and the time value of the option is ₹5 (₹15 – ₹10).

Exhibit 16.1 *Options on NSE*

Instrum-ent	Symbol	Expiry_Dt	Strike_Pr	Option_Typ	Open	High	Low	Close	Settle_Pr	Con-tracts	Val_In lakh	Open_Int	Chg_In_Oi	Time-stamp
OPTSTK	RELIANCE	27-Dec-18	980	CE	140	142.2	129.1	142.2	142.2	6	33.5	3000	–1000	13-Dec-18
OPTSTK	RELIANCE	27-Dec-18	1240	CE	2.5	2.5	1.45	1.8	1.8	853	5297	5E+05	10000	13-Dec-18
OPTSTK	RELIANCE	27-Dec-18	1400	CE	0.35	0.5	0.35	0.45	0.45	3	21	72500	–500	13-Dec-18
OPTSTK	RELIANCE	27-Dec-IS	980	PE	1.05	2.55	1.05	1.95	1.95	228	1119	3E+05	–7000	13-Dec-18
OPTSTK	RELIANCE	27-Dec-18	1240	PE	123.8	129.5	118.3	129.5	129.45	9	61.3	74500	500	13-Dec-18
OPTSTK	RELIANCE	27-Dec-18	1400	PE	277	277	277	277	277	1	8.38	31000	0	13-Dec-18
OPTSTK	RELIANCE	31-Jan-19	1080	CE	72.8	72.8	66.65	66.65	66.65	9	51.7	3000	–3500	13-Dec-18
OPTSTK	RELIANCE	31-Jan-19	1200	CE	21.55	22	16.75	18.7	18.7	102	622	59500	9500	13-Dec-18
OPTSTK	RELIANCE	31-Jan-19	1300	CE	8	8	4	5.55	5.55	111	725	63000	15000	13-Dec-18
OPTSTK	RELIANCE	31-Jan-19	1080	PE	26.5	35	26.5	30.65	30.65	95	527	41000	19000	13-Dec-18
OPTSTK	RELIANCE	31-Jan-19	1200	PE	92.95	96	92.95	96	96	6	38.8	10500	3000	13-Dec-18
OPTSTK	RELIANCE	31-Jan-19	1300	PE	0	0	0	152	188.8	0	0	10500	0	13-Dec-18
OPTSTK	RELIANCE	28-Feb-19	1000	CE	0	0	0	205.4	145.1	0	0	0	0	13-Dec-18
OPTSTK	RELIANCE	28-Feb-19	1180	CE	0	0	0	90.9	48.1	0	0	0	0	13-Dec-18
OPTSTK	RELIANCE	28-Feb-19	1380	CE	0	0	0	27.95	9.25	0	0	0	0	13-Dec-18
OPTSTK	RELIANCE	28-Feb-19	1000	PE	0	0	0	18.3	22.4	0	0	0	0	13-Dec-18
OPTSTK	RELIANCE	28-Feb-19	1180	PE	0	0	0	80.5	102.6	0	0	0	0	13-Dec-18
OPTSTK	RELIANCE	28-Feb-19	1380	PE	0	0	0	213.9	260.6	0	0	0	0	13-Dec-18

16.2 OPTIONS AND THEIR PAYOFFS JUST BEFORE EXPIRATION

This section looks at the features of call and put options and their payoffs just before expiration, from the point of view of the option holder as well as the option writer (option seller).

Call Option The most common type of option, the call option, gives the option holder the right to buy an asset at a fixed price during a certain period. While there is no restriction on the kind of asset, the most popular type of call option is the option on stocks. For example, investors can buy call options on Reliance Industries stock (and many other stocks) on the National Stock Exchange and Bombay Stock Exchange. A typical call option on Reliance Industries stock entitles the investor to buy 100 shares of Reliance Industries on or before say July 25, 200X at an exercise price of ₹Y. Such an option is valuable if there is some likelihood that the price of the common (equity) stock of Reliance Industries will rise above ₹Y on or before July 25, 200X. To provide protection to the option holder, the option contract generally specifies that the exercise price and the number of shares will be adjusted for stock splits and stock dividends. For example, if the Reliance Industries stock splits 4 to 1, the option contract will be for 400 shares at an exercise price of ₹Y/4. Of course, no adjustment is made for cash dividends, as the holder of a call option is not entitled to dividends.

Payoff of a Call Option What is the payoff of a European call option? To answer this question let us look at the possible payoffs of the call option just before expiration.[1] The payoff of the call option (C) just before expiration depends on the relationship between the stock price (S_1) and the exercise price (E). Formally,

$$C = S_1 - E \text{ if } S_1 > E \quad (16.1)$$

$$C = 0 \text{ if } S_1 \leq E \quad (16.2)$$

This means $C = \text{Max}(S_1 - E, 0)$. Exhibit 16.2 shows graphically the value of a call option. When $S_1 \leq E$, the call is said to be "out of money" and is worthless. When $S_1 > E$, the call is said to be "in the money" and its value is $S_1 - E$.

Exhibit 16.2 *Payoff of a Call Option*

Put Option The opposite of a call option is a *put option*. While the call option gives the holder the right to buy a stock at a fixed price, the put option gives the holder the right to sell a stock

[1] Recall that such an option can be exercised only on the expiration date, but not before.

at a fixed price. For example, a put option on the Reliance Industries stock may give its holder the right to sell 600 shares of Reliance Industries on or before a certain date at a price of ₹Y per share. Such an option is valuable if there is some possibility that the price of Reliance Industries stock will fall below ₹Y per share on or before a certain date.

Payoff of a Put Option The payoff of a put option just before expiration depends on the relationship between the exercise price (*E*) and the price of the underlying stock (S_1). If $S_1 < E$, the put option has a value of $E - S_1$, and is said to be "in the money". On the other hand, if $S_1 \geq E$, the put option is worthless, and is said to be "out of money". Thus the payoff of a put option just before expiration is:

	If $S_1 < E$	If $S_1 \geq E$
Value of the put option	$E - S_1$	0

Put differently, just before expiration the payoff of a put option is Max ($E - S_1$, 0).

Exhibit 16.3 plots the relationship between the value of the underlying stock and the payoff of the put option.

Exhibit 16.3 ***Payoff of a Put Option***

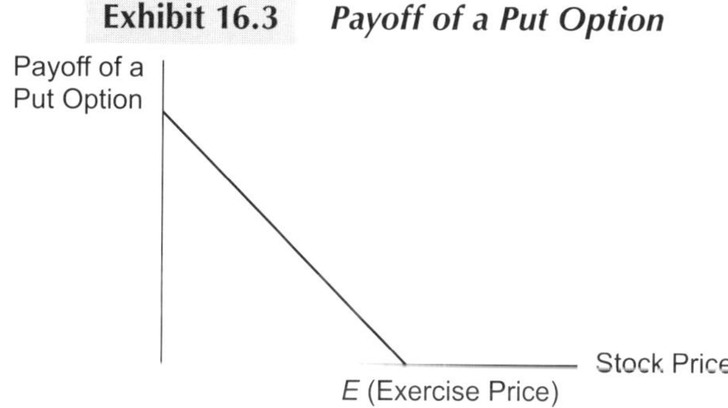

Seller's Position We discussed the payoff of call and put options from the point of view of the option buyer (or holder). Let us now look at the options from the point of view of the option writer (or seller).

A writer of a call option collects the option premium from the buyer (holder) of the option. In return, he is obliged to deliver the shares, should the option buyer exercise the option. If the stock price (S_1) is less than the exercise price (*E*) on the expiration date, the option holder will not exercise the option. In this case, the option writer's liability is nil. On the other hand, if the stock price (S_1) is more than the exercise price (*E*), the option holder will exercise the option. Hence the option writer loses $S_1 - E$.

What is the payoff from the point of view of the seller (or writer) of a put option? If the price of the stock (S_1) is equal to or more than the exercise price (*E*), the holder of the put option will not exercise the option. Hence the option writer's liability is nil. On the other hand, if $S_1 < E$, the holder of the put option will exercise the option. Hence the option writer loses $E - S_1$. The payoffs for "selling a call" and "selling a put" from the sellers' point of view are plotted in Exhibit 16.4.

Exhibit 16.4 ***Payoffs to the Seller of Options***

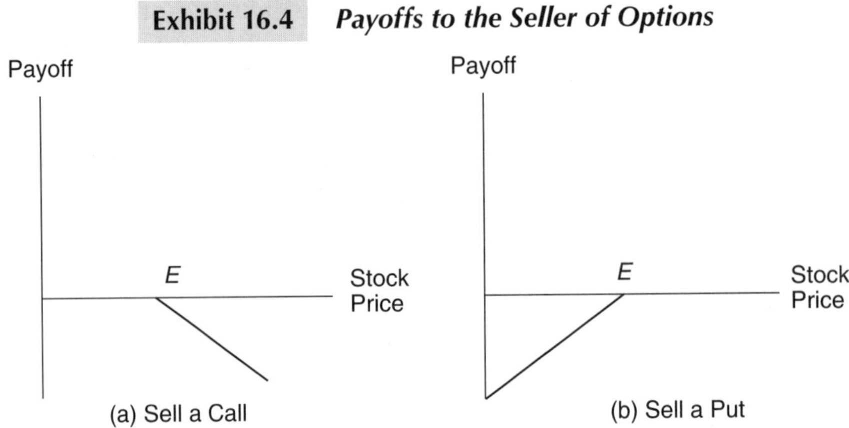

16.3 FACTORS DETERMINING OPTION VALUES

In the previous section, we looked at the payoffs of options just before the expiration date. Now, we determine the present value of options.

Boundaries Before we identify the factors determining option values, it is helpful to specify the boundaries within which the value of an option falls.

The minimum value at which a call option sells before the expiration date, say, at time zero, is Max $(0, S_0 - E)$. This means that C_0, the value of a call option, can never fall below zero (this happens when $S_0 < E$). Also, it means that the value of a call option cannot fall below $S_0 - E$ (this happens when $S_0 > E$). To see why this is so, consider a call option with $E = 150$, $S_0 = 250$, and $C_0 = 75$. In this case it pays an investor to buy the call option for 75, exercise it for 150, and finally sell the stock for 250. By doing so he earns a profit of:

$$S_0 - (C_0 + E) = 250 - (75 + 150) = 25$$

This profit, reflecting arbitrage profits, comes without incurring any risk or cost. Such a profit cannot occur in a well functioning financial market. Hence in such a market C_0 cannot sell for less than $S_0 - E$.

What is the upper limit for the option price? A call option entitles the holder to buy the underlying stock on payment of a certain exercise price. Hence its value cannot be greater than that of the underlying stock. If it were so, the investor would be better off by buying the stock directly. The upper and lower bounds for the value of a call option are shown in Exhibit 16.5.

Key Factors Driving Option Value As indicated above, the price of a call option must fall in the shaded region of Exhibit 16.5. Put formally,

$$\text{Max } (S_0 - E, 0) \leq C_0 \leq S_0 \tag{16.3}$$

Exhibit 16.5 ***Upper and Lower Bounds for the Value of Call Option***

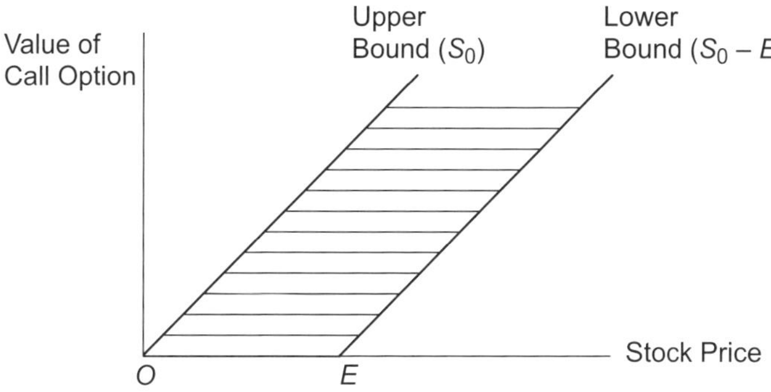

Where exactly in the shaded region will the value of a call option be? The precise location of the option value depends on five key factors:

- Exercise price
- Expiration date
- Stock price
- Stock price variability
- Interest rate

Exercise Price By now it is obvious that, other things being constant, the higher the exercise price the lower the value of the call option. Remember that the value of a call option can never be negative, regardless of how high the exercise price is set. Further it has a positive value if there is some possibility that the stock price will be higher than the exercise price before the expiration date.

Expiration Date Other things being equal, the longer the time to expiration date the more valuable the call option. Consider two American calls with maturities of one year and two years. The two-year call obviously is more valuable than the one year call because it gives its holder one more year within which it can be exercised.

Stock Price The value of a call option, other things being constant, increases with the stock price. This point is obvious from the figures showing the relationship between the stock price and the value of call option.

Variability of the Stock Price A call option has value when there is a possibility that the stock price exceeds the exercise price before the expiration date. Other things being equal, the higher the variability of the stock price, the greater the likelihood that the stock price will exceed the exercise price. This point is graphically illustrated in Exhibit 16.6.

In this figure the price distribution of two stocks, *A* and *B*, is given. While both *A* and *B* have the same expected value, A has a lower variance than *B*. Given an exercise price of *E*, a call option on *B* is more valuable than that on *A*. This is so because the holder of a call option gains when the stock price exceeds the exercise price and does not lose when the stock price is less than the exercise price.

Exhibit 16.6 ***Value of Call Options for Low Variability and High Variability Stocks***

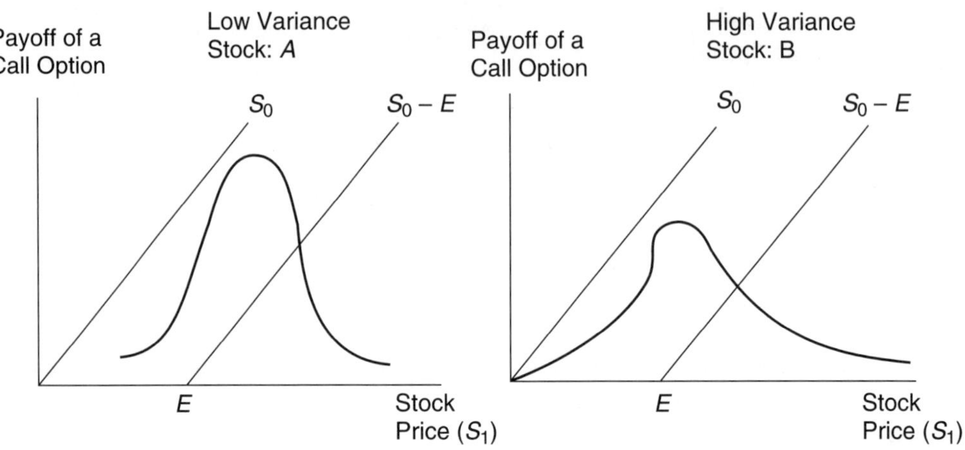

So fundamental is this point that it calls for another illustration. Consider the probability distribution of the price of two stocks, *P* and *Q*, just before the call option (with an exercise price of 80) on them expires.

P		*Q*	
Price	*Probability*	*Price*	*Probability*
60	0.5	50	0.5
80	0.5	90	0.5

While the expected price of stock *Q* is same as that of stock *P*, the variance of *Q* is higher than that of *P*. The call option, given an exercise price of 80, on stock *P* is worthless as there is no likelihood that the price of stock *P* will exceed 80. However, the call option on stock *Q* is valuable because there is a distinct possibility that the stock price will exceed the exercise price.

Remember that there is a basic difference between holding a stock and holding a call option on the stock. If you are a risk-averse investor you try to avoid buying a high variance stock, as it exposes you to the possibility of negative returns. However, you will like to buy a call option on that stock because you receive the profit from the right tail of the probability distribution, while avoiding the loss on the left tail. Thus, regardless of your risk disposition, you will find a high variance in the underlying stock desirable.

Interest Rate When you buy a call option you do not pay the exercise price until you decide to exercise the call option. Put differently, the payment, if any, is made in future. The higher the interest rate, the greater the benefit will be from delayed payment and vice versa. So the value of a call option is positively related to the interest rate.

Functional Relationship The manner in which the five variables discussed above influence the value of a call option is shown in the following relationship:

$$C_0 = f\,[\underset{+}{S_0}, \underset{-}{E}, \underset{+}{\sigma^2}, \underset{+}{t}, \underset{+}{r_f}] \tag{16.4}$$

where C_0 is the value of the call option, S_0 is the price of the underlying stock (or asset in general), E is the exercise price, σ^2 is the variance of the return on the underlying asset, t is the time left to expiration, and r_f is the risk-free interest rate.

The sign (+, –) put below a variable denotes the nature of its influence on the value of the call option. You must be eager to know the precise relationship between these variables and the value of call option. Black-Scholes developed their celebrated option pricing model which expresses this relationship. Before we look at their model, it is helpful to understand the two-state or binomial option valuation model.

16.4 BINOMIAL MODEL FOR OPTION VALUATION

The standard DCF (discounted cash flow) procedure involves two steps, viz. estimation of expected future cash flows and discounting of these cash flows using an appropriate cost of capital. There are problems in applying this procedure to option valuation. While it is difficult (though possible) to estimate expected cash flows, it is impossible to determine the opportunity cost of capital because the risk of an option is virtually indeterminate as it changes every time the stock price varies.

Since options cannot be valued by the standard DCF method, financial economists struggled to develop a rigorous method for valuing options for many years. Finally, a real breakthrough occurred when Fisher Black and Myron Scholes[2] published their famous model in 1973. The basic idea underlying their model is to set up a portfolio which imitates the call option in its payoff. The cost of such a portfolio, which is readily observed, must represent the value of the call option.

The key insight underlying the Black-Scholes model may be illustrated through a single-period binomial (or two-state) model. The following assumptions may be employed to develop this model.

- The stock, currently selling for S, can take two possible values next year, uS or dS ($uS > dS$).
- An amount of B can be borrowed or lent at a rate of r the risk-free rate. The interest factor $(1 + r)$ may be represented, for the sake of simplicity, as R.
- The value of R is greater than d but smaller than $u (d < R < u)$. This condition ensures that there is no risk-free arbitrage opportunity.
- The exercise price is E.

The value of the call option, just before expiration, if the stock price goes up to uS, is

$$C_u = \text{Max}\,(uS - E, 0) \tag{16.5}$$

Likewise, the value of the call option, just before expiration, if the stock price goes down to dS is

$$C_d = \text{Max}\,(dS - E, 0) \tag{16.6}$$

---

[2] Fisher Black and Myron Scholes, "The Pricing of Options and Corporate Liabilities," *Journal of Political Economy*, Vol. 81, May–June 1973.

Let us now set up a portfolio consisting of Δ shares of the stock and B rupees of borrowing. Since this portfolio is set up in such a way that it has a payoff identical to that of a call option at time 1 (next year), the following equations will be satisfied:

Stock price rises: $\Delta\, uS - RB = C_u$ (16.7)

Stock price falls $\Delta\, dS - RB = C_d$ (16.8)

Solving Eqs (16.7) and (16.8) for Δ and B, we get

$$\Delta = \frac{C_u - C_d}{S(u-d)} = \frac{\text{Spread of possible option prices}}{\text{Spread of possible share prices}} \quad (16.9)$$

$$B = \frac{dC_u - uC_d}{(u-d)\,R} \quad (16.10)$$

Δ is referred to as the option delta or hedge ratio.

Since the portfolio (consisting of Δ shares and B debt) has the same payoff as that of a call option, the value of the call option is

$$C = \Delta S - B \quad (16.11)$$

Note that the value of option is found out by looking at the value of a portfolio of shares and loan that imitates the option in its payoff. So this may be referred to as the option equivalent calculation.

To illustrate the application of the binomial model consider the following data for Pioneer's stock:

$$S = ₹200,\ u = 1.4,\ d = 0.9$$

$$E = ₹220,\ r = 0.10,\ R = 1.10$$

$$C_u = \text{Max}\ (uS - E, 0) = \text{Max}\ (₹280 - ₹220, 0) = ₹60$$

$$C_d = \text{Max}\ (dS - E, 0) = \text{Max}\ (₹180 - ₹220, 0) = 0$$

Given the preceding data, we can get the values of Δ and B by using Eqs (16.10) and (16.11).

$$\Delta = \frac{C_u - C_d}{(u-d)S} = \frac{60}{0.5\,(200)} = 0.6$$

$$B = \frac{dC_u - uC_d}{(u-d)R} = \frac{0.9\,(60)}{0.5\,(1.10)} = ₹98.18$$

Thus the portfolio consists of 0.6 of a share plus a borrowing of ₹98.18 (entailing a repayment of ₹98.18(1.10) = 108 after one year). The identity of the payoffs of the portfolio and call option is as follows:

	Portfolio	*Call Option*
When u occurs	$1.4 \times 200 \times 0.6 - 108 = 60$	$C_u = 60$
When d occurs	$0.9 \times 200 \times 0.6 - 108 = 0$	$C_d = 0$

Given the equivalence of the call option and the portfolio, the value of the call option is:

$$C = \Delta\, S - B = 0.6 \times 200 - 98.18 = ₹21.82$$

Note that we could establish the value of the call option without any idea about the probability that the stock would go up or come down. An optimistic investor may think that the probability of an upward move is high whereas a pessimistic investor may think that it is low. Yet the two will agree that the value of the call option is ₹21.82. Why? The answer lies in the fact that the current stock price of ₹200 already incorporates the views of the optimists as well as the pessimists. And the option value, in turn, depends on the stock price.

Risk-Neutral Valuation Why should the call option on Pioneer stock sell for ₹21.82? If the option price exceeds ₹21.82, you can make a certain profit by borrowing ₹98.18, selling a call option, and buying 0.6 of a share of Pioneer's stock. Likewise, if the option price is less than ₹21.82, you can make a certain profit by selling 0.6 of a share of Pioneer's stock, lending ₹98.18, and buying a call option. In either case you have an opportunity to make money without incurring any risk. Put differently, you have a money machine.

Since there cannot be a money machine, the equilibrium price of the call option is ₹21.82. Note that we established the equilibrium price of the call option without knowing anything about the attitude of investors toward risk. The price of the option does not depend on the investor attitude toward risk. It does not matter whether investors love risk or hate risk.

This suggests that there is an alternative method for valuing the option. In this alternative method, called the risk-neutral valuation method, we assume that investors are risk-neutral (indifferent to risk), calculate the expected future value of the option, and convert it into its present value by using the risk-free rate.

If investors are risk-neutral, the expected return on the equity stock of Pioneer must be equal to the risk-free rate.

Expected return on Pioneer's stock =10 per cent

Since Pioneer's stock can either rise by 40 percent to 280 or fall by 10 percent to ₹180, we can calculate the probability of a price rise in the hypothetical risk-neutral world.

Expected return = [Probability of rise × 40%] + [(1 – Probability of rise) × – 10%)] = 10%

Therefore the probability of rise is 0.40[3]. This is called the risk-neutral probability.

We know that if the stock price rises, the call option has a value of ₹60 and if the stock price falls the call option has a value of ₹0.

Hence, if investors are risk-neutral, the call option has an expected future value of:

$$[(\text{Probability of rise} \times ₹60] + [(1 - \text{Probability of rise}) \times ₹0]$$

$$= 0.40 \times ₹60 + 0.60 \times ₹0 = ₹24$$

The current value of the call option is the present value of the expected future value:

$$\frac{\text{Expected future value}}{1 + \text{Risk-free rate}} = \frac{₹24}{(1.10)} = ₹21.82$$

Not surprisingly, this is exactly the answer we got by using the option equivalent method. Thus, we have two ways of calculating the value of an option in the binomial world.

[3] Note that this is the probability of rise in our hypothetical risk-neutral world. Since real world investors are risk-averse and not risk-neutral, they will require a higher expected return from a risky stock. Hence the true probability of rise will be greater than 0.40.

Option Equivalent Method Find a portfolio of shares and loan that imitates the option in its payoff. Since the two alternatives have identical payoffs in the future, they must command the same price today.

Risk Neutral Method Assume that investors are risk-neutral, so that the expected return on the stock is the same as the risk-free interest rate. Calculate the expected future value of the option and discount it at the risk-free interest rate.

16.5 BLACK-SCHOLES MODEL

The above analysis was based on the assumption that there were two possible values for the stock price at the end of one year. If we assume that there are two possible stock prices at the end of each six-month period, the number of possible end-of-year prices increases. As the period is further shortened (from six months to three months or one month), we get more frequent changes in stock price and a wider range of possible end-of-year prices.

Eventually, we would reach a situation where prices change more or less continuously, leading to a continuum of possible prices at the end of the year. Theoretically, even for this situation we could set up a portfolio which has a payoff identical to that of a call option. However, the composition of this portfolio will have to be changed continuously as the year progresses.

Calculating the value of such a portfolio and through that the value of the call option in such a situation appears to be an unwieldy task, but Black-Scholes developed a formula that does precisely that. Their formula is:

$$C_0 = S_0\, N(d_1) - \frac{E}{e^{rt}}\, N(d_2) \tag{16.12}$$

where C_0 is the equilibrium value of a call option now, S_0 is the price of the stock now, E is the exercise price, e is the base of natural logarithm, r is the continuously compounded risk-free annual interest rate, t is the length of time in years to the expiration date, and $N(d)$ is the value of the cumulative normal density function

$$d_1 = \frac{l_n\left[\dfrac{S_0}{E}\right] + \left[r + \dfrac{1}{2}\sigma^2\right]t}{\sigma\sqrt{t}} \tag{16.13}$$

$$d_2 = d_1 - \sigma\sqrt{t} \tag{16.14}$$

where l_n is the natural logarithm and σ is the standard deviation of the continuously compounded annual rate of return on the stock.

Though one of the complicated formulae in finance, it is one of the most practical. The formula has great appeal because four of the parameters, namely, S_0, E, r, and t are observable. Only one of the parameters, namely, σ^2, has to be estimated. Note that the value of a call option is affected by neither the risk aversion of the investor nor the expected return on the stock.

Assumptions You may have guessed by now that the Black-Scholes model, like other models in economics and finance, is based on a set of simplifying assumptions. Yes, you are right. The assumptions underlying the Black-Scholes model are as follows:

- The call option is the European option
- The stock price is continuous and is distributed lognormally
- There are no transaction costs and taxes
- There are no restrictions on or penalties for short selling
- The stock pays no dividend
- The risk-free interest rate is known and is constant.

These assumptions may appear very severe. However when some of them do not hold, a variant of the Black-Scholes model applies. Further, empirical studies indicate that the Black-Scholes model applies to American options as well.

Applying the Black-Scholes Formula Although the Black-Scholes model appears difficult it is fairly easy to apply. This may be illustrated with an example.

Consider the following data for a certain stock

- Price of stock now = S_0 = ₹60
- Exercise price = E = ₹56
- Standard deviation of continuously compounded annual returns = $\sigma = 0.3$
- Years to maturity = $t = 0.5$
- Risk-free interest rate per annum = 0.14

Applying the Black-Scholes model involves four steps

Step 1: Calculate d_1 and d_2

$$d_1 = \frac{\left[l_n \frac{S_0}{E}\right] + \left[r + \frac{\sigma^2}{2}\right] t}{\sigma \sqrt{t}}$$

$$= \frac{.068993 + 0.0925}{0.2121} = \frac{0.161493}{0.2121} = 0.7614$$

$$d_2 = d_1 - \sigma\sqrt{t}$$

$$= 0.7614 - 0.2121 = 0.5493$$

Step 2: Find $N(d_1)$ and $N(d_2)$. $N(d_1)$ and $N(d_2)$ represent the probabilities that a random variable that has a standardised normal distribution will assume values less than d_1 and d_2. The simplest way to find $N(d_1)$ and $N(d_2)$ is to use the Excel function NORMSDIST. Alternatively, you can use Table A.5 in Appendix A at the end of book

$$N(d_1) = N\,(0.7614) = 0.7768$$

$$N(d_2) = N\,(0.5493) = 0.7086$$

Step 3: Estimate the present value of the exercise price, using the continuous discounting principle

$$\frac{E}{e^{rt}} = \frac{₹56}{e^{0.14\times0.5}} = ₹52.21$$

Step 4: Plug the numbers obtained in the previous steps in the Black-Scholes model

$$C_0 = ₹60 \times 0.7768 - ₹52.21 \times 0.7086$$
$$= ₹46.61 - ₹37.00 = ₹9.61$$

Replicating Portfolio Note that the principle of replicating portfolio used in the binomial model also undergirds the Black-Scholes model. Exhibit 16.7 shows the replicating portfolios for calls and puts, in the binomial and the Black-Scholes models.

Exhibit 16.7 ***Replicating Portfolio for Calls and Puts***

Option Position	***Replicating Portfolio*** *Binomial Model*	*Black-Scholes Model*
Buy Call Option	Borrow B Buy Δ shares of stock	Borrow $Ee^{-rt} N(d_2)$ Buy $N(d_1)$ shares of stock
Sell Call Option	Lend B Sell short Δ shares	Lend $Ee^{-rt} N(d_2)$ Sell short $N(d_1)$ shares
Buy Put Option	Lend B Sell short Δ shares	Lend $Ee^{-rt} (1- N(d_2))$ Sell short $(1- N(d_1))$ shares
Sell Put Option	Borrow B Buy Δ shares	Borrow $Ee^{-rt} (1- N(d_2))$ Buy $(1- N(d_1))$ shares

Adjustment for Dividends The Black-Scholes model given in Eq. (16.12) assumes that the stock pays no dividend. When dividend is paid the stock price diminishes. Hence, call options become less valuable and put options become more valuable. To reflect dividend payments, two adjustments are commonly made, one for options that have a short life and the other for options that have a long life.

Short-term Options When options expire in less than one year, the present value of dividends expected during the life of the option is subtracted from the current value of the stock to obtain a 'dividend-adjusted value', which is then used as the input for S in the Black-Scholes model.

$$\text{Adjusted stock price} = S' = S - \sum \frac{Div_t}{(1+r)^t} \qquad (16.15)$$

$$\text{Value of call} = S' N(d_1) - Ee^{-rt} N(d_2) \qquad (16.16)$$

where
$$d_1 = \frac{l_n\left[\frac{S'}{E}\right] + \left[r + \frac{\sigma^2}{2}\right]t}{\sigma\sqrt{t}}$$

$$d_2 = d_1 - \sigma\sqrt{t}$$

Long-term Options Computing the present value of dividends and adjusting for the same is tedious and difficult in the case of long-term options. If the dividend yield (y = dividend/current stock price) is expected to remain fairly stable during the life of the option, the Black-Scholes model can be modified to reflect dividend payment.

$$C = Se^{-yt} N(d_1) - Ee^{-rt} N(d_2) \tag{16.17}$$

where

$$d_1 = \frac{l_n \frac{S}{E} + \left[r - y + \frac{\sigma^2}{2} \right] t}{\sigma \sqrt{t}}$$

$$d_2 = d_1 - \sigma \sqrt{t}$$

This adjustment essentially does two things: (i) it discounts the value of the stock to the present at the dividend yield to reflect the expected drop in value on account of dividend payments, and (ii) it offsets the interest rate by the dividend yield to reflect the lower cost of carrying the stock (in the replicating portfolio).

16.6 TYPES OF REAL OPTIONS

A variety of options are embedded in real projects. They may be classified into four broad types: investment timing options, growth options, flexibility options, and abandonment options.

Investment Timing Options Traditional NPV analysis assumes that a project may be accepted or rejected, implying that it may be undertaken now or never. Often, however, the firm has the option of making the investment now or deferring the decision to future. The "wait and watch" option is a common real option.

Delaying the investment may help in resolving some uncertainty about the value of the project. The option to delay is more valuable to a firm which is protected by entry barriers like proprietary technology, patents, and licenses, as these factors diminish the threat of competition.

Growth Options A growth option allows a firm to grow in different ways. First, the firm may expand the capacity of an existing product line, if the market response to the product is favourable. Sometimes, capacity expansion can be achieved at a modest cost by making debottlenecking investments. Second, the firm may add new related products or newer versions of the original product. Michael Porter calls the original investment as a "beachhead" as it opens up new opportunities in future. For example, Proctor and Gamble acquired the Charmin Paper Company which served as a beachhead to launch a cluster of products like disposable diapers, paper towels, and bathroom tissues. Third, the firm may enter newer geographic markets. For example, Disneyland has successfully entered newer markets in Europe and Japan.

Flexibility Options Apart from the options that naturally exist in most projects, managers can incorporate flexibility in designing the project. The designed-in options may take the form of input flexibility options and output flexibility options.

An **input flexibility** option allows a firm to switch between alternative inputs. For example, an electric power plant may go for a flexible dual-fuel boiler which can switch between gas or oil as fuel, depending on which source of energy is cheaper at a given point of time.

An **output flexibility** option allows a firm to alter the product mix. Oil refineries, for example, are typically designed with this flexibility. This permits them to switch from one product mix to another, depending on which product mix is the most profitable at a given point of time.

Abandonment Options The DCF analysis assumes that a project will continue till the end of its specified economic life. While some projects may be somewhat irreversible in nature, others offer a possibility of premature abandonment. If a project does not perform well and there is very little promise for improvement, the firm can consider the exit option. The firm need not continue with an uneconomic activity indefinitely. An abandonment option reduces the downside risk of the project.

Some projects also provide the option of temporary closure. For example, an iron ore mining project may be closed for a while if the output price of the iron ore is depressed. In general, shut down options are more valuable when the variable costs are high.

Key Differences between Financial and Real Options

There are two key differences between financial and real options:

1. The information required for valuing options and making decisions about exercising them is more readily available for financial options than for real options. For example, a holder of call option on the stock of Reliance Industries can look at the current stock price and decide what to do. However, the value of an untested drug cannot be read off from the NSE screen.
2. While the right to exercise a financial option is unambiguous, the holder of a real option often is unclear what the precise right is and how long the same will last.

16.7 APPLICATIONS OF THE BINOMIAL MODEL

This section discusses two applications of the binomial model, one for valuing a vacant land, which can be developed now or in future, and the other for valuing an option to abandon.

Valuing a Vacant Land Vacant land has value because it can be used for a variety of purposes. For example, a particular plot of land may be used for building apartments or a shopping complex. Further, the construction can be done now or in future. The developer would like to develop the property now or in future so that the present value of the difference between benefits and costs is maximised. While the best possible use of land presently can be established easily, its best possible future use may not be known now.

The option valuation approach can be used to determine the value of a vacant land that provides the option to choose one of several possible uses now or in future. The procedure for doing so involves the following steps:

1. Compute the risk-neutral probabilities associated with various outcomes by observing the market prices of traded investments (price of apartments or office blocks and the risk-free rate of interest).
2. Calculate the expected cash flow next year. For this calculation use the risk-neutral probabilities and assume that the best alternative will be chosen under each outcome.
3. Compute the current value of land by discounting the expected cash flow at the risk-free interest rate.

Illustration A builder owns a plot of land that can be used for either eight or twelve apartment units. The construction cost for these two alternatives are ₹3.6 million and ₹6.2 million respectively. The current market price per apartment is ₹0.6 million. The yearly rental (net of expenses) per unit is ₹0.05 million and the risk-free interest rate is 12 percent per annum. If the market for apartments is buoyant next year, each apartment unit will sell for ₹0.75 million; if the market is sluggish each apartment unit will sell for ₹0.54 million. What is the value of the vacant plot? Assume that the construction cost will remain the same in year 1.

Presently, an eight unit building yields a profit of ₹1.2 million (= 8 × 0.6 – 3.6) and a twelve unit building yields a profit of ₹1.0 million (= 12 × 0.6 – 6.2). Hence an eight-unit building is the best alternative if the builder has to construct now.

However, if the builder waits for a year, his payoffs will be as follows:

	Market Condition	
Alternative	*Buoyant (apartment price: ₹0.75 million)*	*Sluggish (apartment price: ₹0.54 million)*
8-unit building	$0.75 \times 8 - 3.6 = 2.4$	$0.54 \times 8 - 3.6 = 0.72$
12-unit building	$0.75 \times 12 - 6.2 = 2.8$	$0.54 \times 12 - 6.2 = 0.28$

Thus, if the market turns out to be buoyant the best alternative is the 12-unit building (payoff: ₹2.8 million) and if the market turns out to be sluggish the best alternative is the eight-unit building (payoff: ₹0.72 million).

Given the preceding information, we can apply the binomial method for valuing the vacant land.

Step 1: *Calculate the risk-neutral probabilities* The binomial tree given in Exhibit 16.8 shows that a ₹0.6 million investment in an apartment this year yields a year end value of ₹0.80 million (₹0.75 million plus ₹0.05 million in rent) or ₹0.59 million (₹0.54 million plus ₹0.05 million in rent) depending on market conditions. Given a risk-free rate of 12 per cent, the risk-neutral probabilities must satisfy the following condition:

$$₹0.60 \text{ million} = [p \times ₹0.80 \text{ million} + (1 - p) \times ₹0.59 \text{ million}]/(1.12)$$

Solving this we get $p = 0.39$ and $1 - p = 0.61$

Step 2: *Calculate the expected cash flow next year* The expected cash flow next year is: $0.39 \times 2.8 + 0.61 \times 0.72 =$ ₹1.531 million

Step 3: *Compute the current value* The current value of land applying the risk-free rate of 12 percent is:

₹1.531/1.12 = ₹1.367 million

Since ₹1.367 million is greater than ₹1.2 million the profit from constructing an eight-unit building now, it is advisable to keep the land vacant. The value of the vacant land is ₹1.367 million.

Exhibit 16.8 ***Binomial Tree of Apartment Values***

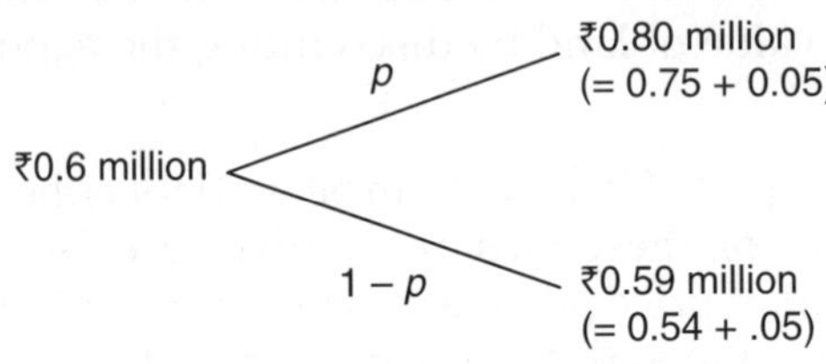

Valuing an Option to Abandon Your firm has decided to manufacture a new product labelled Titus. It is evaluating two alternative machines, both costing the same, to manufacture Titus.

Alternative *A*: A special purpose machine designed for Titus. While it reduces the cost of production, it does not have much resale value.

Alternative *B*: A general purpose machine. Though it involves a higher cost of production, it has a good resale value

The demand for Titus may be strong or weak. The payoffs (measured as the project's cash flow for the first year plus the present value of future cash flows evaluated as at the end of the first year) of the two alternatives under different market conditions will be as follows:

	Payoff (₹ in million)	
	Alternative A	*Alternative B*
Strong demand	30.0	28.0
Weak demand	14.0	12.0

From the DCF point of view, alternative *A* is clearly superior to alternative *B*. However, alternative *B* offers an advantage in the form of valuable flexibility. If the demand turns out to be weak, the general purpose machine can be sold for ₹16 million at the end of year 1, an amount that is greater than ₹12 million, the payoff associated with weak demand. Note that alternative *A* does not offer valuable flexibility because the special purpose machine can be sold for only ₹10 million at the end of year 1, an amount that is less than ₹14 million, the payoff associated with weak demand.

Given the option to sell the machine, the payoffs to alternative B are as follows:

Strong demand → Continue production → Own a project worth ₹28 million
Weak demand → Exercise the option to sell the machine → Receive ₹16 million

Value of the Abandonment Put Suppose the value of alternative B, ignoring the option of abandonment, is ₹18 million. This represents the value of the underlying asset today, assuming that your firm is obliged to continue producing Titus irrespective of how profitable it turns out to be. If the demand turns out to be strong, the value at year 1 rises to ₹28 million giving a return of 55.6 per cent; on the other hand, if the demand turns out to be weak, the value at year 1 falls to ₹12 million, giving a return of –33.3 percent.

Now let us introduce the put option. Clearly your company would like to continue with the project if the demand turns out to be strong. However, should the demand turn out to be weak, your company will be better off if it abandons the project and sells the machine. The put option in this case will have a value of ₹4 million (₹16 million – ₹12 million). The payoffs to the put option are summarised below:

	Year-end Values of the Project	*(₹ in million)*
	12	28
Value of put option	16–12 = 4	0

Exhibit 16.9 shows the present and future values of the underlying project. While the future values of the abandonment option are shown in the parenthesis, the present value of the abandonment option has yet to be calculated—it is shown as a question mark.

Exhibit 16.9 ***Binomial Tree***

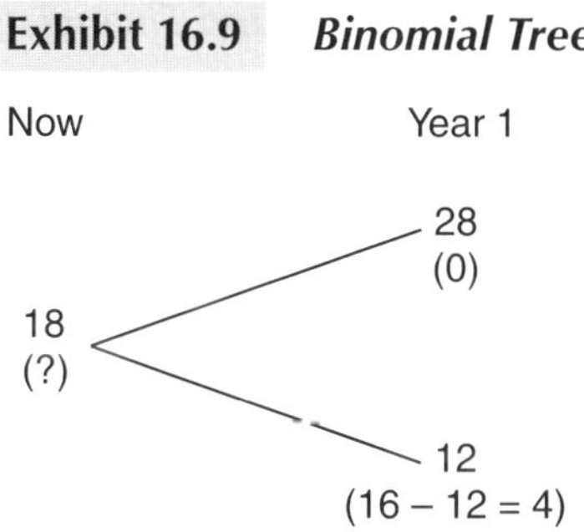

As the project has only two possible outcomes, we can apply the binomial model. Recall that there are two methods of applying the binomial model: option equivalent method and risk-neutral method.

For our purposes we will apply the risk-neutral method. The return on the proposed project will be 55.6 percent or –33.3 percent. Hence the expected return is:

$$\text{Expected return} = (\text{Probability of strong demand}) \times 55.6\% + (1 - \text{Probability of strong demand}) \times -33.3\%$$

The risk neutral method assumes that investors do not care about risk. So the return required by them is simply the risk-free return. Suppose the risk-free return is 6 per cent. Then the probability of strong demand in this hypothetical risk-neutral world can be calculated as follows:

$$\text{Expected return} = (\text{Probability of strong demand}) \times 55.6\% + (1 - \text{Probability of strong demand}) \times -33.3\% = 6\%$$

Probability of strong demand = 0. 44

Probability of weak demand = 1 – 0. 44 = 0. 56

The payoff to the put option at the end of year 1 will be either 0 or ₹4 million. Hence the expected payoff to the put option is:

Expected payoff to put option = (Probability of strong demand) × 0
+ (1 – Probability of strong demand) × 4
= 0. 44 × 0 + 0. 56 × 4 = ₹2.24 million

Discounting ₹2.24 million for one year at 6 percent gives a value of 2.24/1.06 = ₹2.11 million. Thus the abandonment option has a value of ₹2.11 million.

16.8 APPLICATIONS OF THE BLACK-SCHOLES MODEL

This section discusses two applications of the Black-Scholes model, one for valuing an option to make a follow on investment and the other for valuing a natural resource option.

Valuing an Option to Make a Follow on Investment Your firm is looking at a proposal to manufacture an electronic educational aid called Electriad-I. The projected cash flows for this proposal are shown in Exhibit 16.10.

Exhibit 16.10 ***Cash Flows and Financials for Electriad-I***

(₹ in millions)

	Year					
	0	*1*	*2*	*3*	*4*	*5*
Initial outlay	(150)					
After-tax operating cash flow		20	40	50	50	40
Terminal cash flow						30
Net cash flow	(150)	20	40	50	50	70
Present value at 18 per cent	(150)	16.9	28.7	30.5	25.8	30.6

Present value of cash inflows	= 16.9 + 28.7 + 30.5 + 25.8 + 30.6 = 132.5
Investment outlay	= 150
Net present value	= 132.5 – 150 = -17.5

Although the proposal has a negative NPV, the chief executive of your firm considers it worthwhile. He argues, "If we undertake Electriad-I now we will be in a position to make a follow on investment in an advanced version, Electriad-II, four years down the road. If conditions are favourable, such a follow on investment can be very profitable."

Sensing the possibility of applying the option pricing model for valuing the option to make the follow on investment, you request him to provide key financial estimates for the follow on investment opportunity. He furnishes the following information:

- Electriad-II will be double the size of Electriad-I. It will require an investment of ₹300 million (this is akin to the exercise price of a call option).
- The expected cash inflows of Electriad-II too will be twice those of Electriad-I. Hence, they will have a present value of ₹265 million as at the end of year four.

You need one more crucial piece of information: the degree of uncertainty characterising the cash inflows of Electriad-II. Your chief executive is not able to provide an estimate of this. You look at the stock price behaviour of your company and find that it has a standard deviation of 40 percent per year. In the absence of any other information, you assume that the cash inflows of Electriad-II too would have the same standard deviation. The risk-free interest rate is 12 percent per annum.

The preceding information may be cast in terms of the inputs required by the Black-Scholes model.

S_0 = present value of the asset = $265 \times e^{-.18\times4}$ = ₹129 million
E = exercise price = ₹300 million
σ = standard deviation of continuously compounded annual returns = 0.4
t = years to maturity = 4
r = risk-free interest rate = 12 percent

Step 1: Calculate d_1 and d_2

$$d_1 = \frac{l_n\left[\frac{S_0}{E}\right]+\left[r+\frac{\sigma^2}{2}\right]t}{\sigma\sqrt{t}} = \frac{-0.843+\left[.12+\frac{.16}{2}\right]4}{0.4\sqrt{4}} = -.05375$$

$$d_2 = d_1 - \sigma\sqrt{t} = -0.85375$$

Step 2: Find $N(d_1)$ and $N(d_2)$

$$N(d_1) = 0.4786$$
$$N(d_2) = 0.1966$$

Step 3: Estimate the present value of the exercise price

$$E\,.\,e^{-rt} = 300/1.6161 = ₹185.63 \text{ million}$$

Step 4: Plug the numbers obtained in the previous steps in the Black-Scholes model

$$C_0 = ₹129 \text{ million} \times 0.4786 - ₹185.63 \text{ million} \times 0.1966$$
$$= ₹61.74 \text{ million} - ₹36.49 \text{ million} = ₹25.25 \text{ million}$$

Based on this calculation you argue that a call value of ₹25.25 million more than offsets the negative NPV of ₹17.5 million and hence Electriad-I is a worthwhile proposition. Your chief executive too agrees with you because your quantitative evaluation squares with his intuitive reflection, though he is not sure how you came up with a value of ₹25.25 million for the call option. Of course, you have a different concern about that number because you are not sure whether the assumptions underlying the calculation are realistic.

Valuing a Natural Resource Option An important application of real option valuation has been to natural resources. In a natural resource investment, the underlying asset is the natural resource and the exercise price is the cost of development. If the estimated value of the natural resource is V and the cost of development X, the potential payoffs from a natural resource are:

When	*Payoff*
$V > X$	$V - X$
$V \leq X$	0

Thus, the payoff function of an investment in a natural resource option is similar to that of a call option.

To value a natural resource option, you have to estimate the following:

- Value of the available reserves of the resource
- Development cost
- Time to expiration of the option
- Variance in value of the underlying asset
- Dividend yield

Value of the Available Resources The value of the available resources (the asset under consideration) is a function of the quantity and price of the natural resource. For instance, geologists can provide reasonably reliable estimates of the quantity of oil in a particular oil basin and oil economists can provide forecast of oil price.

Development Cost The development cost represents the exercise price of the option. A knowledge of past costs and an understanding of the specifics of the investment is required to get a handle on the development cost.

Time to Expiration of the Option The life of a natural resource option is usually defined in two ways: (i) The period over which the natural resource can be exploited. For example, the government may grant a lease period of 20 years for an oil basin. (ii) The time taken to exhaust the inventory of the natural resource. For example, if a gold mine has an inventory of 900,000 ounces and the capacity output rate is 60,000 ounces per year, the inventory will be exhausted in 15 years and this represents the life of the natural resource option.

Variance in the Value of the Underlying Asset The variance in the value of the underlying asset depends on the variability in the estimate of available reserve and the variability in the price of the resource. If the quantity of the available reserve is known, the variance of the value of the asset depends on the variability of the price of the resource.

Cost of Delay Conceptually similar to the dividend yield in a stock, the cost of delay in a natural resource option represents the loss in production for each year of delay. It may be estimated as annual net production revenue as a percentage of the market value of the reserve.

For natural resource options, you have to consider the development lag as well. This is the time lag between the decision to extract the resource and the actual extraction. A simple way to adjust for this lag is to discount the value of the developed reserve for the time lag involved in development at the net production revenue/asset value ratio (or the dividend yield).

Valuing an Oil Reserve ONG, an oil major, is assessing the value of the option to extract oil from a particular oil basin. The following information has been gathered:

- The estimated oil reserve in the basin is 100 million barrels of oil. It may be assumed that there is no variability characterising this quantity.
- The development cost is $1 billion.
- The right to exploit the basin will be enjoyed for 25 years.

- The marginal value per barrel of oil presently is $20—this represents the difference between the price per barrel of oil and the marginal cost of extracting a barrel of oil. The standard deviation of l_n(oil price) is estimated to be 0.2.
- Once developed, the net production revenue each year will be 4 percent of the value of the reserve.
- The risk-free rate is 8 percent.
- The development lag is two years.

Given the preceding information, the inputs to the Black-Scholes formula can be estimated as follows:

S_0 = current value of the asset = value of the developed reserve discounted back for two years (the development lag) at the dividend yield = $\$20 \times 100/(1.04)^2 = \$\ 1849.11$ million
E = exercise price = development cost = $ 1000 million. This is assumed to be fixed over time.
σ = standard deviation of the l_n (oil price) = 0.2
t = life of the option = 25 years
r = risk-free rate = 8 percent
y = dividend yield = net production revenue/value of reserve = 4 percent

Given these inputs, the call option is valued as follows:

Step 1: Calculate d_1 and d_2

$$d_1 = \{l_n\ (1849.11/1000) + [.08 - .04 + (.04/2)]\ 25\} \div 0.2\sqrt{25}$$
$$= 0.6147 + 1.5 = 2.1147$$
$$d_2 = d_1 - \sigma\sqrt{t}$$
$$= 2.1147 - 1.000 = 1.1147$$

Step 2: Find $N(d_1)$ and $N(d_2)$

$$N(d_1) = N\ (2.1147) = 0.9828$$
$$N(d_2) = N\ (1.1147) = 0.8675$$

Step 3: Estimate the present value of the exercise price

$$E/e^{rt} = 1000/e^{.08 \times 25} = \$\ 135.33 \text{ million}$$

Step 4: Plug the numbers obtained in the previous steps in the Black-Scholes model

$$C = \$1849.11 \text{ million} \times 0.9828 - \$135.33 \text{ million} \times 0.8675$$
$$= \$1699.91 \text{ million}$$

16.9 STRATEGY AS A PORTFOLIO OF REAL OPTIONS[4]

Generally, a firm faces a wide range of investment opportunities that vary in terms of profitability, uncertainty, and time to expiration. What should be the investment strategy of the firm?

[4] This section is based on Timothy A. Luehrman, "Strategy as a Portfolio of Real Options," *Harvard Business Review*, Sept.–Oct. 1998.

Luehrman has proposed an approach to develop strategy using the real options. In this approach, potential projects are mapped on the basis of two option-value metrics, one representing a value based on NPV analysis and the other a volatility (risk) measure, as shown in Exhibit 16.11.

Exhibit 16.11 ***Real Option-Value Space***

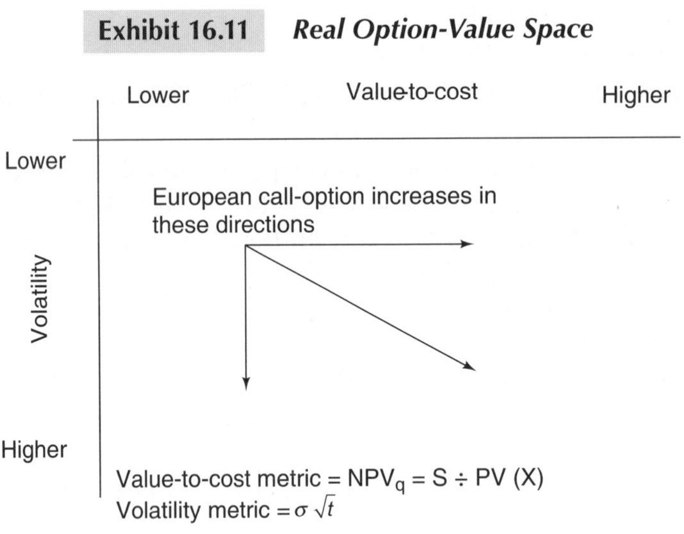

Source: Timothy A. Luehrman, op. cit.

He says that managing a portfolio of projects is similar to tending a garden of tomatoes. On any given day, the tomatoes in a garden (like projects in a business) have varying prospects for growth and value creation. An experienced gardener is able to distinguish between ripe tomatoes, rotten tomatoes, and the rest that fall somewhere "in-between". While the ripe tomatoes have to be harvested and the rotten tomatoes have to be discarded the choice with respect to the "in-between" ones is not very clear. It is helpful to divide the "in-between" ones into four groups for determining an appropriate course of action:

- Imperfect, but edible tomatoes: They can be picked now, but would ripen with more time on the vine. If left on vine, there is some risk that squirrels will get them first. It makes sense to allow them to ripen, unless the scavenger risk is high.
- Inedible, but very promising tomatoes: It does not make sense to pick them now, even though they are vulnerable to scavengers. With enough time left in the season, many of them will ripen beautifully and eventually be picked.
- Less promising green tomatoes: With sun, water, and a little luck some of them will ripen before the season is over. Allow them to remain on the vine and monitor their growth.
- Late blossoms and small green tomatoes: It is unlikely that they will be harvested in the season. So ignore them or prune them.

Using the metaphor of a tomato garden, Luehrman divides the option-value space of business opportunities into six distinct regions, numbered 1 through 6 clockwise, as shown in Exhibit 16.2. Each of these regions calls for a different strategy.

Exhibit 16.12 ***The Tomato Garden***

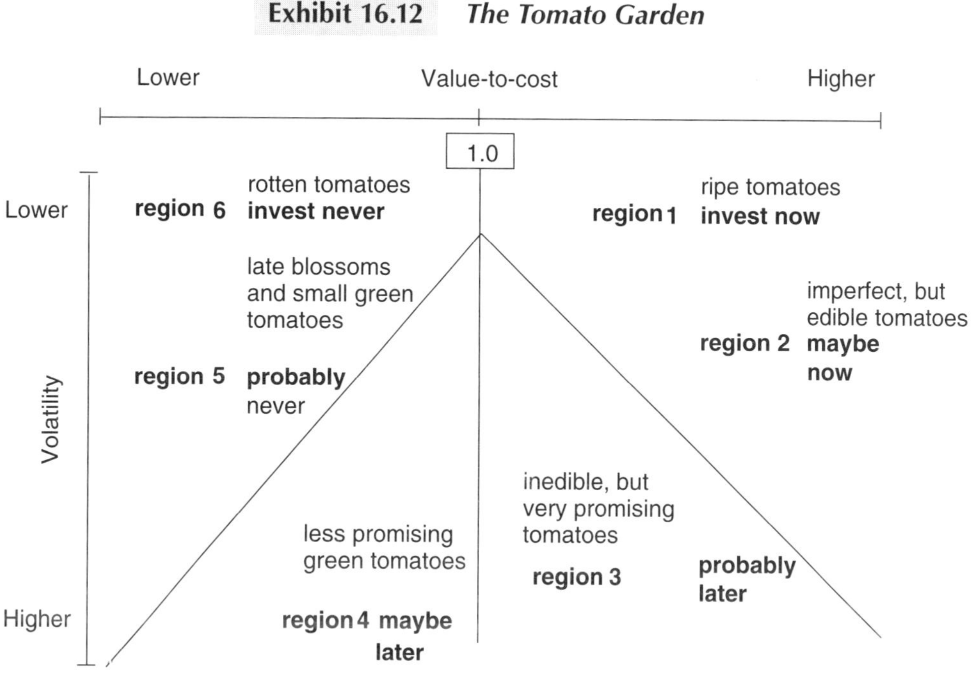

Source: Timothy A. Luehman op. cit.

Region 1: Businesses in this region have a value-to-cost ratio greater than 1 (which means a positive NPV). They have low uncertainty and short time to expiration. The optimal strategy in this region is to "invest now."

Region 2: Businesses in this region have positive NPV. They are characterised by some volatility and/or some time to expiration. So, it may make sense to wait for a while. However, if there is a possibility of preemption by competitors, the optimal strategy may be to exercise the option early.

Region 3: Businesses in this region too have a positive NPV. Further, they are characterised by high levels of uncertainty and/or time to expiration. Hence, they are likely to become more valuable in future, particularly with active management. So, the optimal strategy is to defer the exercise of option.

Region 4: Businesses in this region have a value-to-cost ratio of less than 1 (i.e. a negative NPV). They are characterised by high levels of remaining uncertainty and/or time to expiration. If harvested now, they will destroy value. However, depending on how uncertainty unravels there may be some possibility that these businesses may add value with time and active management. So, a "wait and watch" strategy makes sense.

Region 5: Businesses in this region have a negative NPV. Given their limited volatility and/or time to expiration, it makes sense to ignore them.

Region 6: Businesses in this region have a negative NPV. They are characterised by little uncertainty and/or will expire soon. The optimal strategy is never to invest in such businesses.

16.10 JUDGEMENTAL ASSESSMENT OF OPTIONS

Valuing the options embedded in real life projects with the help of Black-Scholes model often requires heroic assumptions. Yet the insights provided by this model can be combined with well-informed, experienced judgement to get a handle over option values. If you can identify the options and specify the circumstances under which they would be exercised, you can make an informed estimate of their values. The procedure for doing this, thus, would broadly involve three steps:

- Identify options
- Analyse environmental uncertainty
- Value options

Identify Options Options embedded in real life projects are basically of two types: incremental options and flexibility options. An *incremental option* provides the firm opportunities to make profitable investments in future. A *flexibility option* in a project gives the firm a wider latitude in manufacturing so that it can cope better with unexpected changes and exploit profitable opportunities that come its way.

Analyse Environmental Uncertainty Options are valuable in unpredictable environments. Uncertainty creates opportunities for exercising options. Incremental options multiply when future uncertainty increases. For example, most of the foreign investments made in Europe around 1990 were motivated by future uncertainty, not current profitability. Such investments provide the "thin end of the wedge" that facilitates the exploitation of opportunities that arise in an uncertain environment. By the same token, flexibility options tend to have greater value when the environment is more uncertain.

Value the Options Once the options provided by the project are compiled and the environmental uncertainties delineated, the value of options may be assessed. While the Black-Scholes model may not be readily applicable to options embedded in many real life projects because of the difficulty in quantitatively specifying the inputs, the key ideas of this model may be combined with the experience and judgement of managers to develop a practical procedure for valuing options. Bear in mind the following insights provided by the Black-Scholes model:

- The greater the uncertainty characterising a project, the higher the value of the options embedded in the project.

- The longer the duration of a project, the higher the value of the options inherent in it.

Exhibit 16.13 presents a matrix showing the combined effect of environmental uncertainty and project duration on the relative values of cash flows and options. The percentages shown, however, are merely suggestive. They have to be, of course, specified by the project evaluator to reflect his subjective assessment.

Exhibit 16.13 ***Relative Values of Cash Flows and Options***

Duration of the Project		Environmental Uncertainty: Low	Environmental Uncertainty: High
	Long	Cash flows: 75 Options: 25	Cash flows: 60 Options: 40
	Short	Cash flows: 95 Options: 5	Cash flows: 75 Options: 25

Examples of Real Options Analysis

Here are some examples of real options analysis.

- At Merck, R & D projects are analysed in the real options framework. An R & D project involves staged investments (which depend on the outcomes in previous stages) and hence is eminently suitable for real options analysis.
- Shell Oil evaluates capital projects and investment strategies using real options analysis. When Shell Oil acquires a license to develop an oil field, it has to decide when to start development, how much to spend on development, often in stages, and whether to seek an extension of the license.
- Intel uses real options analysis to evaluate its acquisitions. For example, when Intel purchased Level One Communications it really acquired the option to produce different types of chips than those it manufactured itself. The demand for the chips of level One Communications is linked to the growth of the Internet. Thus Intel acquired manufacturing capability in a complementary business.

16.11 MISTAKES MADE IN REAL OPTION VALUATION[5]

There are two important differences between financial options and real options. First, the underlying assets (such as stocks or currencies) of financial options are traded every minute whereas the underlying assets (such as land, buildings, factories) of real options are traded infrequently. Second, the exercise of choice is fairly straightforward for financial options but quite complicated for real options. The holder of a stock option has merely to decide whether to buy the stock at some predetermined price. It is not so simple for real options. For example, the owner of a vacant land must decide more than just whether he should build on his land. He has to decide what to build (apartments, independent villas, resort, and so forth) and how soon to build.

Given the difficulties in valuing and exercising real options, it is not surprising that mistakes are made in real option valuation. The more common mistakes characterising real option valuation in practice are described below:

Unthinking Application of the Black-Scholes Model Analysts often tend to "force-fit" the Black-Scholes model to real option problems, even when the realities of the situation are not consistent with the assumptions underlying the Black-Scholes model. (There is an old saying: "Give a little boy a hammer and he finds that everything that he comes across needs pounding.")

Use of Wrong Volatility To value the options embedded in natural resource investments, analysts often wrongly use the volatility of the commodity price rather than the volatility of the value of the underlying asset (like the oil field). In general, the volatility of the commodity price is greater than the volatility of the value of the underlying asset.

Assumption of a Fixed Exercise Price While the exercise price of a financial option is fixed, the exercise price of a real option may vary over time. For example, the cost of developing an oil field tends to increase over time. So, it is not correct to assume a fixed exercise price.

Overestimation of the Value of Flexibility Often there is a disconnect between the way real options are valued and the way they are managed. For example, management may delay expansion due to a procrastination tendency or fail to shut down an uneconomic facility in a timely manner due to inertia or emotional attachment. Hence, the value of options, which are exercisable in theory but often not exercised in practice, is likely to be overestimated.

Abuse of Real Options to Justify a Project on Strategic Grounds It is fairly easy for a project sponsor to invoke real options in defence of a pet project. He can spell out various options that are created by the initial investment and justify the project as having "strategic significance."

---

[5] Sheridan Titman, John D. Martin, and V. Ravi Anshuman, *Valuation*, Section 11.6, Pearson Education, Inc., 2008.

Failure to Consider Feedback Effects The actions of a firm can have an impact on the environment in which it operates. For example, power companies in the U.S. invest in "peaker plants" that are turned on in response to peak demand when electricity prices rule high. Peaker plants are valued as an option to sell power when electricity prices are very high. The emergence of many peaker plants in the late 1990s in the U.S., however, led to a higher availability of capacity during peak-load periods, leading to a reduction in the volatility of electricity prices. Failure to consider such feedback effects causes an overvaluation of options.

16.12 MANAGING REAL OPTIONS

Often there is a significant gap between the theoretical and realised values of real options because of a disconnect between the way options are valued and the way options are managed. This applies to financial options as well. As Thomas Copeland and Peter Tufano put it in a March 2004 *Harvard Business Review* article, "There is a long standing and mounting body of evidence showing that even financial options are exercised suboptimally. At times, holders are trigger-happy, exercising too soon; at other times, they fall asleep at the switch." Indeed, if holders of financial options behave suboptimally, we can't expect holders of real options to behave any better.

What can be done to promote a more timely and rational exercise of real options? The company's planning and budgeting system should reflect the decision trees constructed in developing the binomial model to value the project. More specifically, the planning and budgeting system should:

1. **Identify the trigger points** The trigger points tell the managers when there is a need to exercise options. They correspond to the nodes on a binomial decision tree.
2. **Specify the rules governing the exercise decisions** The rules governing the exercise decisions are specified by what academics call the optimal exercise boundaries for an option.
3. **Clearly assign responsibilities** Decisions don't occur on their own. Someone has to make them. So the firm must clearly identify in advance who will be responsible for acting on the trigger.
4. **Motivate people** The firm should ensure that people are motivated to act in a timely and rational manner through a system of rewards and penalties.

In essence, the planning and budgeting system should specify **when** the decisions will have to be taken, **what** the decision rules will be, **who** the decision makers will be, and **why** will the decision makers act rationally.

Firms that employ real options for strategic reasons must learn to manage them well. This applies more to large firms. As Thomas Copeland and Peter Tufano put it: "This is particularly urgent as companies grow, because experience suggests that manager's instinctive nimbleness and alertness diminish as their decisions grow in scale and impact. The pilot of 747 relies a lot more on instruments than does the pilot of a turn engine Cessna."

Managing Real Options Proactively

The key guidelines for managing real options proactively are as follows:

1. Extend the option duration by innovating to hold technological lead, by signaling the ability to exercise, and by maintaining regulatory barriers.
2. Increase the uncertainty of expected cash flows by developing innovative products, by extending opportunity to related markets, and by encouraging complementary products.
3. Increase the present value of expected cash flows by developing alliances with low-cost suppliers and by developing new marketing initiatives.
4. Reduce the value lost by waiting to exercise the option by locking up key resources and by creating implementation hurdles for competitors.
5. Reduce investment by leveraging economies of scale and by exploiting economies of scope.

SUMMARY

- The standard DCF analysis calls for evaluating a project on the basis of its cash flows over its economic life. Such an evaluation, however, does not capture the value of options embedded in the project.
- The strategic NPV of a project is defined as:
  Strategic NPV = Conventional NPV + Real Option Value (ROV)
- An option is a special contract under which the option owner enjoys the right to buy or sell something without the obligation to do so.
- There are two basic types of options: call options and put options. A call option gives the option holder the right to buy a stock (or asset) at a fixed price on or before a certain date. A put option gives the holder the right to sell stock (or some other asset) at a specified price on or before a certain date.
- The value of a call option depends on five factors: exercise price, expiration date, stock price, stock price variability, and interest rate.
- The key insight underlying the Black-Scholes model may be illustrated through a single-period binomial (or two-state) model.
- There are two ways of calculating the value of an option in the binomial world: (i) *Option Equivalent Method:* Find a portfolio of shares and loan that imitates the option in its payoff. Since the two alternatives have identical payoffs in the future, they must command the same price today. (ii) *Risk Neutral Method:* Assume that investors are risk-neutral, so that the expected return on the stock is the same as the risk-free interest rate. Calculate the expected future value of the option and discount it at the risk-free interest rate.

- Black-Scholes developed the following formula (referred to commonly as the Black-Scholes model) showing how the value of a call option is related to the basic factors:

$$C_0 = S_0 N(d_1) - \frac{E}{e^{rt}} N(d_2)$$

- The Black-Scholes model assumes that the stock pays no dividend. To reflect dividend payments, two adjustments are commonly made, one for options that have a short life and the other for options that have a long life.
- Options embedded in real life projects may be valued with the help of the binomial model or the Black-Scholes model, if suitable quantitative estimates can be defined.
- Where quantitative estimates cannot be defined with a measure of confidence, Black-Scholes model cannot be applied meaningfully. Yet, the insights provided by this model can be combined with well-informed, experienced judgement to get a handle over option values.
- The following are the common mistakes characterising real option valuation in practice: unthinking application of the Black-Scholes model; use of wrong volatility; assumption of a fixed exercise price; overestimation of the value of flexibility; abuse of real options to justify a project on strategic grounds; and failure to consider feedback effects.
- Firms that employ real options for strategic reasons must learn to manage them well.

QUESTIONS

1. What are the limitations of the DCF model?
2. Define the following terms: option holder, option writer, exercise price, maturity date.
3. What is the payoff of a European call option and put option?
4. Define the payoffs of a call option and a put option from the point of view of the option writer (or seller).
5. Specify the boundaries within which the value of a call option falls.
6. Discuss the key factors that have a bearing on the value of a call option.
7. Show why a higher variability of the stock price has a positive effect on the value of call option.
8. Derive the value of call option in the binomial world using the option equivalent method.
9. What is the value of a call option as per the Black-Scholes model?
10. State the assumptions underlying the Black-Scholes model.
11. Describe the risk-neutral valuation method.
12. Discuss the adjustments made for dividend payment in the Black-Scholes model.
13. What are the merits of the binomial option model?
14. Discuss how the value of options embedded in capital projects may be judgementally assessed.
15. What can be done to promote a more timely and rational exercise of options?
16. Discuss the common mistakes characterising real option valuation in practice.

PROBLEMS

1. Alpha Company's equity is currently selling for ₹100 per share. In a year from now it can rise to ₹150 or fall to ₹90. The risk-free interest rate is 15 percent. What is the value of a call option on Alpha Company's equity as per the Binomial model? The exercise price is ₹100.
2. Beta Company's equity is currently selling for ₹60. In a year from now it can rise or fall. On the downside it may fall to ₹45. The call option on Beta's equity has a value of ₹5. If the risk-free interest rate is 16 percent, to what level would Beta's equity rise on the upside? Assume that the excise price is ₹60.
3. The following information is available for Abhishek Industries:

$$S_0 = ₹70,\ E = ₹72,\ r_f = 0.12,\ \sigma = 0.30$$

   Calculate the price for a six month call option as per the Black-Scholes model.
4. What is the value of a European call option (no dividends) with an exercise price of ₹50 and an expiration date three months from now if the stock price is ₹40, the variance of the stock is 0.40, and the risk-free rate is 14 percent?
5. Your firm is looking at a proposal to manufacture a certain computer called Comp-I. The projected cash flows for this proposal are as follows:

			Year		*(₹ in millions)*
	0	*1*	2	3	4
Initial outlay	(100)				
After-tax operating cash flow		20	50	50	20
Terminal cash flow					10

   The discount rate applicable to this proposal is 20 percent.

   If your firm undertakes Comp-I proposal, it will be in a position to make a follow on investment in an advanced version, Comp-II, four years from now. Comp-II will be double the size of Comp-I in terms of investment outlay and cash inflows. The cash inflows of Comp-II would have a standard deviation of 30 percent per year.

   (a) What is the net present value of the cash flows of Comp-I?

   (b) What is the value of the option to invest in Comp-II?

   Assume that the risk-free rate is 12 percent.
6. A builder owns a plot of land that can be used for either nine or fifteen apartment units. The construction costs of these two alternatives are ₹9 million and ₹17 million respectively. The current price per apartment is ₹1.2 million. The yearly rental (net of expense) per unit is ₹0.10 million and the risk-free interest rate is 10 percent per annum. If the market for apartments is buoyant next year, each apartment unit will sell for ₹1.5 million; if the market is sluggish each apartment unit will sell for ₹1.1 million. What is the value of the vacant plot? Assume that the construction cost will remain unchanged.
7. Max Oil Limited is assessing the value of the option to extract oil from a particular oil basin. The following information has been gathered:
   - The estimated oil reserve in the basin is 100 million barrels of oil. Assume that there is no variability characterising this quantity.
   - The development cost is $600 million.

- The right to exploit the basin will be enjoyed for 20 years.
- The marginal value per barrel of oil presently is $22—this represents the difference between the price per barrel of oil and the marginal cost of extracting a barrel of oil. The standard deviation of l_n (oil price) is estimated to be 0.25.
- Once developed, the net production revenue each year will be 5% of the value of the reserve.
- The risk-free rate is 8%.
- The development lag is three years.

What is the value of the option to extract oil?

MINICASE

Your firm is looking at a proposal to manufacture a portable music system called Harmonica- I. The projected cash flows of this proposal are shown in the following table.

	0	1	2	3	4
Initial outlay	(550)				
After-tax operating cash flow		120	240	240	120
Terminal cash flow					50

The discount rate applicable to Harmonica-I is 18 percent.

Prima facie, the cash flows of the project do not suggest that the project is attractive. However, Laxman Rao, the chief executive of your firm, a scientist turned entrepreneur, is quite excited about the project. He believes that if the firm undertakes Harmonica-I proposal now, the firm will be in a position to make a follow on investment in an advanced version, Harmonica-II, four years from now. He is quite confident that the firm will have all the capabilities to do so, if it undertakes Harmonica-I initially.

In a recent meeting of the capital budgeting committee, Laxman Rao provided the following estimates:

- Harmonica-II will be twice the size of Harmonica-I. It will require an investment of 1100.
- The expected cash inflows of Harmonica-II will be twice those of Harmonica-I.
- The standard deviation of the cash inflows of Harmonica-II will be 30 percent.
- The risk free interest rate is 10 percent.

(a) What is the net present value of Harmonica-I?

(b) What factors will determine the value of the option to invest in Harmonica-II?

(c) What is the value of the option to invest in Harmonica-II?

(d) What are the differences between financial options and real options?

(e) What are the kinds of real options found in capital projects?

(f) What are the mistakes commonly characterising real option valuation in practice.

(g) What are the advantages of the binomial model?

(h) Discuss how the value of options embedded in capital projects may be judgementally evaluated.

APPENDIX 16A
SLOW ADOPTION OF REAL OPTIONS

In a 2002 survey of 205 Fortune 1,000 CFOs, Patricia A. Ryan found that real option analysis was trailing a field of 13 'Supplementary Capital Budgeting Tools'. As compared to 85.1 percent for sensitivity analysis and 66.8 percent for scenario analysis, only 11.4 percent of the respondents said that they used real option analysis. As far as the 'Basic Capital Budgeting Tools' are concerned, NPV topped the list with 96 percent. Champions of real option analysis who have touted it as the most important new development in capital budgeting in decades may find this sobering. Says Alexander J. Trantis, "It took decades for NPV to become widely accepted in practice. Real options is an even more sophisticated tool. It's going to take a few decades as well to be well integrated in corporations."

Here are some obstacles to the use of real option analysis:

1. Unlike financial options, most real options do not expire at a specific date. So managers are not likely to exercise the 'abandonment option' when they should.
2. Projects assume a life of their own. So, it is not easy to terminate them.
3. There is a love for the ideation of new projects. People are excited by all the options they are creating.
4. A manager is not likely to exercise growth option if he is being compensated.

Judgemental, Behavioural, Strategic, and Organisational Considerations

LEARNING OBJECTIVES

After studying this chapter you should be able to

- Discuss factors that influence managerial judgement.
- Show why a gulf exists between strategic planning and capital budgeting.
- Discuss how different types of informational asymmetries create distortions.
- Understand the earnings impact of investment proposals.
- Explain what is meant by reverse financial engineering.

So far we have discussed the framework for investment appraisal developed by financial economists. We assumed that cash flows and risks associated with a project can be estimated realistically; that a hurdle rate consistent with the risk exposure of the project can be established using a risk-return model; that the real options embedded in a project can be valued using the option pricing model; that the constraints characterising capital budgeting situations can be handled using mathematical programming models; that strategic planning and capital budgeting are reasonably well knit; that there is no informational asymmetry problem in organisations; that managers act to maximise the value of the firm; and that project sponsors develop unbiased forecasts. In essence we assumed that all the relevant facts of a project can be quantified and managers act as rational economic agents.

In the real world, however, many facets of a project are not or often cannot be quantified, managerial judgement is expressed in a somewhat qualitative manner, strategic planning and financial analysis are not properly woven together, informational asymmetry leads to agency problems, managers appear to be more concerned about the impact of a project on EPS and less bothered about its NPV, and a variety of organisational considerations are relevant for investment decision making. Put differently, judgmental, strategic, behavioural, and organisational considerations—all of which are difficult to quantify and incorporate in a rational, economic model—have an important bearing on capital budgeting.

Just because these issues cannot be expressed and handled quantitatively, we cannot ignore them and sweep them under the carpet. Doing so will lead to a 'what counts counts' bias.

This chapter looks at these dimensions of capital budgeting and explores ways and means of weaving together the quantitative and qualitative facets of investment decision making.

17.1 MANAGERIAL INTUITION AND JUDGEMENT

Strategic investment decisions involve major resource commitments and they have a significant impact on the firm. Meant to enhance the long-term competitive position of the firm, such investments are characterised by many uncertainties that cannot be fully quantified. In making such decisions, managers look at quantitative information like cash flows and rate of return—which may be based on highly uncertain assumptions—and combine them with their subjective judgement about competitive dynamics and prospects of success. Intuition and judgement are often as important as formal economic analysis. Indeed the use of intuition in major business decisions, including capital expenditure decisions, is far more common than people think. Many chief executives admit that ultimately their decisions are based on gut-feeling.

Robert Docktor conducted an experiment in which he wired up a group of chief executive officers to an electroencephalograph. He found that the brains of chief executive officers were more active in the right hemispheres, suggesting that they frequently relied on intuitive hunches to define complex problems in an open-ended state of ambiguity. Henry Mintzberg's study likewise showed that for making most of the strategic decisions, managers depend on the factor of judgement rather than explicit analysis. They are often guided by their intuition and are not able to explain adequately the how or why of their strategic decisions.

Bruce D. Henderson, a leading management expert, has expressed the importance of intuition as follows:

> The final choice in all business decisions is, of course, intuitive. It must be. Otherwise, it is not a decision, just a conclusion—a printout.[1]
>
> Intuition can be awesome in its value at times. It is known as good judgement in every day affairs. Intuition is in fact the subconscious integration of all the experiences, conditioning, and knowledge of a lifetime, including the emotional and cultural biases of that life time.[2]

Notwithstanding the supposed importance of intuition, do not take it at its face value because overconfidence is a powerful source of illusions. As Kahneman put it "If people can construct a simple and coherent story, they will feel confident regardless of how well grounded it is in reality." Consider your gut feeling as an important data point, but evaluate it consciously and deliberately to see if it makes sense in the context.

Factors Influencing Judgement Judgement is influenced by a variety of factors such as:

- Quality of information
- Track record of the sponsor
- Internal politics
- Intangible benefits

[1] Bruce D. Henderson, *Henderson on Corporate Strategy*, New York, The New American Library, 1979.

[2] Bruce D. Henderson op. cit.

- Opportunity cost
- Cost of reversing the decisions
- Superstition

Quality of Information Large amounts of information must be analysed to evaluate strategic investments that shape a firm's competitive position. These include economic forecasts, market and demand analysis, technical assessment, cash flow forecasts, risk analysis, rate of return, and so on. Discerning managers evaluate the quality of information and analysis done by their staff assistants and external consultants: Have they considered all the important variables and their interrelationships? Have they taken into account the potential reaction of competitors? Have they considered intangibles?

Almost invariably managers make judgemental adjustments to the numbers presented to them. The extent of adjustment depends on the degree of confidence they have in the quality of information and analysis submitted to them.

Track Record of the Sponsor A project cannot be divorced from its sponsor. Research on the decision making processes of the top management suggests that a decision at this level is likely to be a bet on the sponsor of the project. The facts, the projections, and even the project tend to be secondary in importance if the questions asked by the top management are: Who is the sponsor of the project? What is his commitment to the project? What is his track record? Will he be able to surmount obstacles on the way and deliver the goods?

Internal Politics Internal political elements often have an important bearing on capital budgeting decisions. Various levels of management tend to get divided into factions. Mutual loyalties among people belonging to the same faction may lead to acceptance of otherwise marginal or even sub-marginal projects. On the other hand, negative feelings among people belonging to different factions may lead to the rejection of otherwise promising projects. Put differently, internal political games can mar the quality of decision making and investment proposals may not be viewed in an unbiased and objective manner.

Intangible Benefits A capital project may generate some benefits that cannot be easily quantified. It may increase the flexibility available to the organisation; it may improve the attractiveness of the product; it may give the organisation a sense of pride; it may make the work environment more pleasing; it may strengthen the technological capability of the firm; it may enhance the morale of the firm. Referred to generally as intangibles, these benefits cannot be translated into monetary terms. Yet, they are relevant and cannot be ignored in investment decision making.

Opportunity Cost Every investment has an opportunity cost associated with it. While exercising their judgement, managers ask questions like: If resources are committed to this project which other projects will we have to sacrifice? If none of the current investment proposals is attractive should money be invested in mutual funds temporarily or even returned to shareholders through share buybacks?

Apart from looking at the opportunity cost of an investment, managers also consider the cost of inaction. If we do not make this investment will a competitor pre-empt us? If so, are we likely to forfeit valuable prime mover advantages to rivals?

The opportunity cost of investment as well as the risk of inaction have a bearing on judgement.

Cost of Reversing the Decision A strategic investment often commits the business to a course of action for years to come. Smart managers would seek answers to questions like: What happens if this investment sours? Can we reverse it or modify it to contain the damage? How much would the reversal cost? It makes sense to develop a plan to exit.

Superstition Many businessmen consult astrologers or depend on some other superstitious counsel. Wit the following statements of two businessmen:

- What do businessmen have to lose if, plain business sense apart, they also want to know if the planets are favourably disposed toward them.
- The more money a businessman makes, the more insecure he feels. Consulting an astrologer is a therapeutic experience. If you are going through a bad phase and are told that it has been caused due to the adverse effects of planets in your horoscope, you do not completely blame yourself. Moreover, most Indian businessmen are by nature religious.

The dependence on astrological advice or superstitious counsel is not confined to India. It is pervasive globally. In a profoundly insightful book, Kenneth Boulding writes:

> The persistence of superstition even into a supposedly scientific age is testimony to the power of traditional images in ambiguous situations. It is a curious fact, for instance, that even in the most advanced societies the daily paper frequently carries a column of astrological advice!![3]

Astrologers and psychologists have argued that magical rites and superstitious behaviour make the world look more deterministic and instill confidence in our ability to manage it. Superstitious beliefs seem to help in:

- Relieving anxiety.
- Imparting a sense of control.
- Encouraging necessary activity.

Hence, such beliefs persist. And the more unpredictable or uncertain the future appears to be, the greater may be the psychological urge to rely on superstitions.

17.2 MISSION, GOALS, STRATEGY, AND CAPITAL BUDGETING

The mission of a firm provides the overarching perspective for its activities which naturally cover strategy formulation and capital budgeting. Most firms state their mission in formal terms. Here are some examples of mission statements.

Merck	:	*To preserve and improve life.*
IBM	:	*To achieve value-added leadership position.*
McKinsey	:	*To help leading corporations and governments to be more successful.*
HDFC	:	*To develop close relationships with individual households; maintain position as the premier housing finance institution in the country; transform ideas into viable and creative solutions.*

[3] Kenneth Boulding, *The Meaning of the 20th Century*, New York: Harper & Row, 1964.

Firms may call their mission statements by different names such as credo or *raison détre* or statement of purpose. Irrespective of the label assigned, a mission statement is meant to communicate the larger purpose of the organisation, ignite the collective imagination and passion of its employees, and inspire them to achieve more.

With the mission of the firm as the backdrop, the management of the firm specifies its goals. Goals are generally expressed in quantitative terms. For example, the goals of a firm over the next five years may be to double its revenues, increase the proportion of international revenues to 40 percent, and raise the return on invested capital to 18 percent.

To accomplish its goals, the firm articulates its strategy. The word strategy is used in different ways. For our purpose, it is useful to look at the distinction between corporate strategy and business strategy.

Corporate strategy is concerned with where resources should be invested. The key corporate level resource allocation questions are: Which businesses should the firm invest in? What should be the allocation of the firm's resources across various businesses in its portfolio?

Business strategy by contrast is concerned with how the firm should compete in its chosen product markets. A firm may choose to follow a strategy of cost leadership or product differentiation or both.

The strategy of a business unit drives individual project decisions. While the bulk of this book has focused on evaluating individual projects, the analyst must recognise that individual projects subserve business strategy. Indeed, one can argue that a firm in a practical sense invests in a business strategy and hence projects that support the strategy are undertaken. Individually a project may be a negative-NPV project, yet it may be essential for implementing the chosen strategy.

Since what matters more is the worthwhileness of the investment strategy as a whole and not the attractiveness of individual projects per se, let us note the following characteristics of a good investment strategy:

- It enables the firm to build unique capabilities that cannot be easily imitated by competitors.
- It provides adequate flexibility to cope with changing economic conditions. This means that the strategy provides scope for scaling up in favourable times and scaling down in unfavourable times.

Strengthening the Links between Strategy and Capital Budgeting Capital budgeting is the principal instrument for implementing strategy. While well-managed firms align capital budgeting to strategy, in many firms the tie-in between strategy and capital budgeting is somewhat loose and tenuous. Wit the following:

- Investment proposals are often considered as self-contained projects and viewed more or less in isolation. The rationale proferred for this approach is that if individual proposals are sound, a collection of such proposals should represent a meaningful commitment of funds.
- The sponsors of proposals, particularly operating personnel, tend to, quite understandably, view the proposals from their limited perspective. An operating person, for example, may justify an investment in terms of increase in output and decrease in unit cost. The effect of the investment on the break-even point or inventory level may be beyond his concern.

- Many investment proposals, suggested by people down the line and apparently fulfilling certain standards of profitability, may be rejected by the capital budgeting committee because they conflict with the rationale of the firm's strategy. This may breed frustration and cynicism about the role of formal analysis.

In order to ensure that strategy and long-range plans firmly undergird the capital budgeting process, the following ought to be done:

- Long-range planning should precede capital budgeting.
- Long-range plans should be formalised and communicated to all persons involved in the process of capital budgeting.
- During the capital budgeting exercise, investment proposals should be viewed in the context of the critical premises of long-range plans.

A suggested time table linking business planning and capital budgeting is given in Exhibit 17.1.

Exhibit 17.1 ***Linkages between Business Planning and Capital Budgeting***

	Business Planning		*Capital Budgeting*
April-August	Several scenarios are explored		
September	Initial premises are agreed to	September	Initial capital budgeting guidelines are formulated
October-December	Work is continued toward developing a final formal business plan	October - January	Capital budget selection is carried out in divisions and departments
January	Final business plan is adopted	February	Capital budget is approved by the executive committee
		March	Capital budget is approved by the board

Missions and Funds Allocation In the context of our present discussion which is concerned with the linkage between strategy and capital budgeting, it is somewhat relevant to mention the use of strategic missions as the basis of funds allocation at the Department of Defence, US. Traditionally, the approach used for budgetary allocation at the Department of Defence, US, was to allocate the budgetary pie to the three services, Army, Navy, and Air Force. When Robert McNamara took office as Secretary, Department of Defence, he introduced, a new approach to budgetary allocation, which was based on nine program elements reflecting the major missions of the Department of Defence. Program Element No.1, for example, represented development of a "Strategic Retaliatory Force" and the budget for this program covered bombers, polaris submarines, and land-based intercontinental ballistic missiles.

The approach adopted by the Department of Defence, US can be meaningfully applied to a corporate entity. Determining corporate missions admittedly is a significant managerial challenge. Once the missions are delineated and communicated they serve as the base for resource allocation. If missions are not properly developed and communicated, funds allocation becomes, as Tilles puts it, "a gamesmanship rather than a rational matching of means and ends."

An Approach to Decision Making To determine whether a project is worthwhile or not, strategic factors, financial payoffs, and intangible benefits may be combined in the manner shown in Exhibit 17.2. The key guidelines underlying the approach displayed in this exhibit are:

- In a decision involving measurement as well as judgement, as far as possible, separate the quantifiable and intangible factors.
- Don't rely exclusively on measurable factors and spurious over-quantification. Put differently, avoid the 'what counts counts' bias.

Exhibit 17.2 ***An Approach to Decision Making***

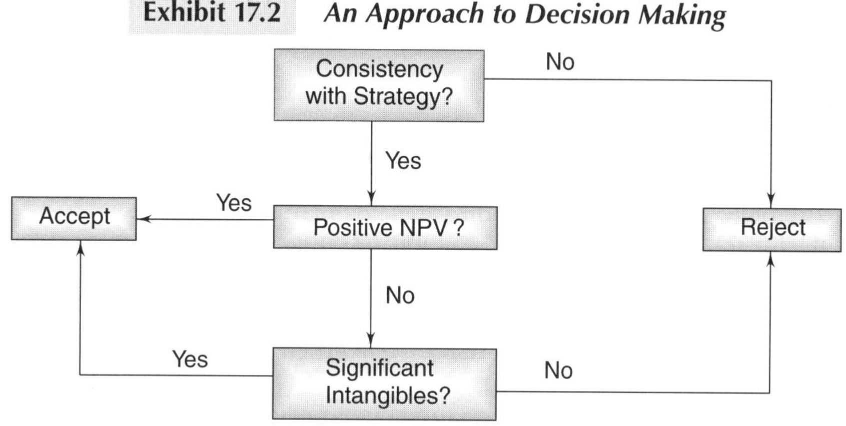

17.3 BRIDGING THE GULF BETWEEN STRATEGIC PLANNING AND FINANCIAL ANALYSIS

Strategic planning, among other things, is concerned with the issue of allocating a firm's resources across different lines of business. In this sense, strategic planning may be viewed as capital budgeting on a grand scale. Yet we find that strategic planning is often naïve from the financial point of view and/or the results of strategic planning and financial analysis are not properly reconciled.

This section explores why a gulf exists between strategic planning and financial analysis and shows how the differences between the two may be reconciled.

Different Frameworks The frameworks employed in strategic planning and financial analysis differ. The salient differences are highlighted below:

	Strategic planning	*Financial analysis*
Objective	Achieve a balanced goal structure	Maximise shareholder value
Responsibility		
– Internal	Corporate planning department	Finance department

– External	Consultant	Investment banker
Type of analysis	Primarily qualitative	Primarily quantitative
Advantage	Comprehensive qualitative assessment	Disciplined quantitative reasoning
Disadvantage	Lacking in rigour	Omission of hard-to-quantify factors

Mistakes Committed in Financial Analysis In applying DCF analysis the following mistakes are commonly committed[4]:

Mechanical Projection of Cash Flows Forecasting cash flows over an extended period of time (say 7 to 15 years, as is required in most DCF calculations) calls for incorporating the effects of factors like competition, technical change, inflation, and so on. This is an inherently difficult task. Hence, in practice, short-run forecasts are often mechanically extrapolated to get long-run forecasts.

Optimistic Bias in Cash Flows Knowledgeable observers of capital budgeting believe that profitability is overstated because the initial investment is understated and the operating cash flows are exaggerated. The principal reasons for such optimistic bias appear to be (i) intentional overstatement, (ii) lack of experience, (iii) myopic euphoria, and (iv) capital rationing.

Emphasis on IRR IRR is the most commonly used DCF criterion in practice. It is preferred because it is a relative measure and it seems more appropriate when the investment funds are limited. IRR, however, is biased against long-lived capital-intensive projects which may be of greater strategic significance to the firm. Ideally, NPV, conceptually superior to all other criteria, should be used as it has no bias against such projects.

Inconsistent Treatment of Inflation Often inflation is treated inconsistently in DCF analysis. While discount rates are defined in nominal terms to reflect the factor of inflation, cash flows are expressed in real terms or only partially adjusted for inflation. Such an inconsistency clearly discriminates against long-lived projects which may have substantially positive NPVs.

Unreasonably High Discount Rates Discount rates used in DCF calculations are sometimes set unrealistically high. This may be because of one or more of the following reasons: (i) Management may lack familiarity with what the normal returns in the capital market are. (ii) Premiums are asked for risk that can be easily diversified away. (iii) Required returns are raised to compensate for the optimism of project sponsors. Such an adjustment makes sense only if the sponsor bias increases geometrically over time. This, however, is rarely true.

Inadequacy of DCF Analysis Even if the mistakes alluded to in the preceding discussion are avoided, DCF analysis is deficient for evaluating projects which have options embedded in them. Consider a project which is in the nature of a "beach-head". If the firm succeeds in this project, it can make a follow on investment. In other words, there is a second-stage investment opportunity - indeed, there may be opportunities beyond the second-stage as well. The DCF method is not enough for evaluating a project like this because it does not

[4] S. C. Myers, "Finance Theory and Financial Strategy", *Interfaces*, January–February 1984.

take into account the value of the option(s) embedded in the project. DCF analysis must be combined with option valuation. Fortunately, option pricing models promise help in valuing options inherent in real life projects.

Financial Naïveté of Strategic Planning Strategic planning is often naïve from the financial point of view. Wit the following:

- Strategic analysis focuses on variables like earnings per share and book rate of return which are considered irrelevant by modern finance theory.
- Strategic planning is sometimes based on the premise that a firm should, by and large, depend on internally available funds. Put differently, the existence of the capital market is ignored.
- The hurdle rates applied in strategic planning are often not related to the opportunity cost of capital.
- Strategic planning typically emphasises a diversified business portfolio while the finance theory suggests that investors can resort to a more efficient "home made" diversification.

Reconciling the Differences To bridge the gap between strategic planning and financial analysis, a conscious effort is required on both the sides.

- Financial analysts must avoid the mistakes commonly committed by them and expand the scope of their work to reflect the values of options embedded in investments of strategic significance.
- Strategic planners must understand the logic of DCF analysis, acquire familiarity with the meaning of the capital market data, and calculate the NPVs, at least as a rough check on the results of their analysis.

While a complete reconciliation is not practical, a sincere attempt to see each other's point of view and to unearth hidden premises will facilitate better communication and understanding. This will ensure that strategic analysis is not financially naïve and financial analysis is not insensitive to strategic issues.

17.4 INFORMATIONAL ASYMMETRY AND CAPITAL BUDGETING

The conventional 'textbook' approach to capital budgeting is starkly simple: accept projects which have a positive NPV. It does not make any difference whether the investment decision making is centralised or decentralised; it is irrelevant whether the existing firm implements it or a newly set up firm executes it; it does not matter what mix of financing is employed.

The behaviour of firms, however, is not always in conformity with what has been said above. In the real world:

- Firms often ration capital and do not invest in all projects that have positive NPVs.
- A lot of attention is paid to the extent to which capital budgeting decisions are centralised.

- Often, new projects are organised as separate corporate entities.
- The mix of financing is considered to be very important.

Why does a discrepancy exist between what the conventional model says and how the real world firms behave? Informational asymmetries of various sorts seem to create such a hiatus. Informational asymmetry exists if the transacting parties have unequal information, *ex ante* or *ex post*.

We may classify informational asymmetry into three broad types:

- Informational asymmetry between shareholders and bondholders.
- Informational asymmetry between current shareholders and prospective shareholders.
- Informational asymmetry between managers and shareholders.

A brief discussion of the distorting effects of different types of informational asymmetries follows:[5]

Informational Asymmetry between Shareholders and Bondholders Informational asymmetry between shareholders and bondholders has two possible distorting consequences

Asset substitution moral hazard	:	Shareholders may prod management to substitute riskier assets for safer assets, at the expense of bondholders.
Underinvestment moral hazard	:	In firms with risky debt, shareholders have an incentive to avoid investing in new projects that have a positive NPV, because they would not like the cash flows of new projects to be diverted for servicing existing risky debt.

Informational Asymmetry between Current Shareholders and Prospective Shareholders When there is informational asymmetry between current shareholders and prospective shareholders, the latter will not fully appreciate the future payoffs of various resource commitments. As the firm's stock price may not fully reflect the benefits of such resource commitments, the new shareholders will not fully share the cost of resource commitments even though they partake in the benefits arising from them. If the firm is interested in maximising the wealth of present shareholders, it may choose projects that are likely to be different from those that would be chosen in a symmetric information setting. The common distortions resulting from such informational asymmetry are:

- Preference for projects with shorter payback period.
- A greater degree of capital rationing.
- Centralisation of capital budgeting.
- Accumulation of liquidity despite the existence of positive *NPV* projects.

Informational Asymmetry between Managers and Shareholders Managers are interested in maintaining and building their reputation. Since, as compared to shareholders, they

[5] See Anjan V. Thakor, "Corporate Investments and Finance", *Financial Management*, Summer 1993.

are typically better informed about the payoffs of projects, they can trade on the relative ignorance of the latter. This gives them latitude to choose investments aimed at building their reputation rather than enhancing the wealth of shareholders. As David Hirshleifer[6] has suggested, the concern for managerial reputation may lead to three kinds of distortions in investment decisions, namely:

Visibility Bias Managers seek to improve short-term indicators of performance.

Resolution Preference Managers attempt to advance the arrival of good news and delay the announcement of bad news.

Mimicry and Avoidance Managers try to imitate the actions of superior managers and avoid the actions of inferior managers.

These incentives may lead to the following investment biases:

- Squeezing of an investment to improve short-term cash flows.
- Premature liquidation of assets to show that they are worth a lot.
- Adoption of projects with earlier payoffs.
- Avoidance of worthwhile projects that carry risk of early failure to protect short-term reputation.
- Escalation of inferior projects to avoid admission of failure.
- Undertaking projects which are supposed to have benefits in the distant future to protect short-term reputation.
- Conformity with other managers to avoid the 'odd manager' label.
- Deviation from other managers to avoid seeming mediocre.

17.5 REVERSE FINANCIAL ENGINEERING

Most organisations use reasonably well-defined quantitative indicators (such as IRR being more than 20 percent or accounting rate of return being more than 25 percent) for approving or rejecting project proposals. Since a project sponsor is keen to get his project included in the capital budget, he is likely to massage the numbers and dress up his project proposal to satisfy the organisational norms. It is fairly easy to do so, by merely tweaking some assumption or the other. In most cases there are 8 to 10 assumptions (such as market size, market share, selling price, raw material cost, project life, growth trajectory, and so on) underpinning the financial projections. Often, the desired financial numbers can be obtained by modifying a few of these assumptions by just 1 to 3 percent. Thanks to informational asymmetry – project sponsors often know much more than project approvers – the project approvers may not be able to detect the nature of financial manipulation.

Is there some way by which such financial manipulation can be checked. Rita Gunter McGrath and Ian MacMillan have suggested a process they call *discovery-driven planning* that has the potential of improving the quality of anlaysis. Discovery-driven planning reverses the sequence of the steps in the stage-gate process. Its logic is fairly simple. Since the project

[6] David Hirshleifer, "Managerial Reputation and Corporate Investment Decisions", *Financial Management*, Summer 1993.

sponsors know how good the numbers should be to get the project approved, why go through the farce of making and revising assumptions to get the desired set of numbers? Instead, start with the minimal acceptable revenue, income, and cash flow statement and then ask "what assumptions must be fulfilled to get these numbers." The project sponsor is expected to develop an assumptions checklist – a list of assumptions that must be valid for the project to succeed. MCGrath and MacMillan refer to this as the "reverse income statement." If a critical assumption is not proved to be valid, the project sponsor must modify its strategy until all the underlying assumptions are valid. If no set of plausible assumptions supports the numbers, the project is rejected.

How is *discovery driven planning* better than the traditional method of project planning? The traditional method focuses the spotlight on financial projections, while obfuscating the assumptions. But there is no need to shine the spotlight on the numbers as the desirability of attractive numbers has never been questioned. By contrast, discovery-driven planning focuses the spotlight on the assumptions that reflect the key uncertainties, a place where senior managers need illumination.

Championing the cause of discovery-driven planning, Christensen *et.al* argue in a January 2008 HBR article: "Today, processes like discovery-driven planning are more commonly used in entrepreneurial settings than in the large corporations that desperately need them. We hope that by recounting the strengths of one such system, we'll persuade established corporations to reassess how they make decisions about investment projects."

17.6 GROUP PROCESS

Major investment and financing decisions take place in group settings, such as executive management meetings and board meetings.

In theory, a group decision is supposed to exploit the synergies arising from bringing together people with diverse skills, perspectives, and values. A constructive use of individual differences among group members is expected to produce process gains.

Many groups, however, are unable to achieve process gains. On the contrary, they experience process loss due to psychological reasons. Behavioural research has identified three important features of group behaviour.

- *Accuracy* In intellectual tasks, groups tend to outperform individuals – an intellectual task is a problem that has a correct answer which once identified is readily accepted by all group members as being correct. However, in judgemental tasks groups may tend to underperform individuals.
- *Polarisation* Groups tend to become polarised in respect to risk tolerance. Group discussions generally magnify risk-seeking behaviour.
- *Unwarranted Acceptance* As a result of group discussion, group members tend to readily accept a decision. Such acceptance, often unwarranted, creates an *illusion of effectiveness,* a kind of collective overconfidence.

Reasons for Group Errors Groupthink, poor information sharing, and inadequate motivation are the three main reasons for group errors.

Groupthink Just as an individual tends to overweight evidence that confirms a view and underweights evidence that disconfirms that view, groups are characterised by a collective form of confirmation bias called *groupthink.*

According to Hersh Shefrin, the following conditions are especially conducive for the emergence of groupthink:

- A strong, opinionated leader.
- The group dynamics.
- Group members function under stress.
- Group members have a strong desire for social conformity.
- There is no well-defined procedure for decision making.

Poor Information Sharing People often do not share relevant information with others in their group, even when the members of the group have a common goal.

Inadequate Motivation Some members of a group may not work hard and rely on others to produce group benefits. This leads to a free-rider agency conflict called *social loafing.*

Countering Groupthink Groupthink occurs because a desire for conformity leads to collective confirmation bias and group members are reluctant to share information or challenge proposals made by others.

According to Hersh Shefrin groupthink can be checked by:

- Asking group members to refrain from stating their positions at the beginning of the discussion.
- Explicitly encouraging debate, disagreement, and information sharing.
- Designating one member of the group to be a devil's advocate for each major proposal.
- Regularly inviting outside experts to attend meetings, with the charge that they challenge the group to refrain from meek conformism.

Using Premortem People prefer harmony over conflict. This leads to social biases like groupthink and sunflower management. Group think involves striving for consensus at the expense of a realistic evaluation of alternatives. Sunflower management is the tendency for groups to align with the opinions of their leaders.

Thanks to these social biases, people do not express their reservations candidly and forcefully. They do not want to disrupt harmony by trying to surface potential problems. As a result, an objective and balanced appraisal of decision alternatives is compromised.

How can people be encouraged to express contrary views freely? Psychologist Gary Klein suggests the use of the *premortem* technique. It is a sneaky way to get to motivate people to serve as a devil's advocate without encountering resistance. If a project turns sour, some lessons will be learned about why the project failed and what went wrong as in the case of a medical postmortem. Why don't we invert the process? Before the project starts, someone should say, "We have a crystal ball that can predict the future. Our crystal ball says that the project has failed. It has been a fiasco. Now everyone should take few minutes and write down all the reasons why he thinks the project failed." This will encourage people to think of insightful reasons why this project might fail. There will be an interesting competition among people to come up with potential problems that others many have overlooked. The entire dynamics would change. Instead of avoiding things that might disrupt harmony, people will try to surface potential problems.

Daniel Kahneman regards premortem as a great idea. He says "My guess is that, in general, doing a premortem on a plan that is about to be adopted won't cause it to be abandoned. But it will probably be tweaked in ways that everybody will recognise as beneficial. So the premortem is a low-cost, high-pay off kind of thing."

17.7 IMPACT ON EARNINGS

In theory, managers are supposed to maximise firm value by choosing projects on the basis of their NPVs. In practice, managers look at NPVs as well as the accounting implications of their investment decisions. In particular, they are concerned with the impact of investments on reported earnings in the short run.

A recent survey of CFOs suggests that capital market pressures induce decisions that at times sacrifice long-term value at the altar of short-term earnings. Nearly four-fifths of the respondents mentioned that they would reduce spending on research and development, brand promotion, and so on that are value-enhancing in the long run, in order to meet short-term earnings targets.

There are several reasons why managers care about short-term earnings. First, short-term incentive compensation of top management in many companies is linked, directly or indirectly, to earnings. Second, the value of stock options and stock grants (given as part of long-term incentive compensation) depends on corporate earnings, at least in the short run. Third, when reported earnings are good, the board of directors generally grants greater freedom to top management for pursuing their strategies and projects. Fourth, favourable earnings inspire greater confidence in capital providers, employees, customers, suppliers, and other stakeholders.

The emphasis on short-term earnings may lead to acceptance of projects that are earnings-accretive but NPV-negative and rejection of projects that are NPV-positive but earnings-dilutive.

To illustrate these possibilities, let us consider two situations:

Situation A: A Project that is Earnings-Accretive but NPV-Negative Alpha Limited is considering a project which requires an outlay of ₹100 million. The project is perpetual and is expected to produce a constant profit before interest and tax of ₹12 million per year. The investment will be financed with a perpetual debt of ₹100 million, carrying an interest rate of 8 percent per year. The tax rate applicable to Alpha Limited is 50 percent. The opportunity cost of capital for this project is 10 percent.

The impact of the project on profit after tax will be

■ PBIT	₹12 million
■ Interest on debt	₹8 million
■ PBT	₹4 million
■ Tax	₹2 million
■ PAT	₹2 million

The NPV of the project will be:

$$\frac{\text{PBIT}\,(1 - \text{Tax rate})}{\text{Opportunity Cost of capital}} - \text{Investment outlay}$$

$$\frac{12(0.5)}{0.10} - 100$$

$$60 - 100 = -\ ₹40 \text{ million}$$

Thus we find that the project is earnings-accretive but NPV-negative. Why is it so? The discrepancy arises because the earnings criterion does not consider the opportunity cost of capital properly.

Situation B: A Project that Is NPV-positive but Earnings-Dilutive Beta Corporation is considering a project that requires an outlay of ₹100 million, has a life of 5 years, and has an opportunity cost of capital of 10 percent. Rupees 40 million of loan, carrying an interest rate of 12.5 percent per annum, is taken for the project. The loan will be repaid at the end of 5 years in one lumpsum. The tax rate applicable to the project is 50 percent.

The expected cash flows of the project are given below:

(₹ *in millions*)

		0	*1*	*2*	*3*	*4*	*5*
A.	Investment	(100)					
B.	Revenues		80	100	200	300	500
C.	Costs		80	90	110	120	160
D.	Depreciation		20	20	20	20	20
E.	PBIT		(20)	(10)	70	160	320
F.	Interest		5	5	5	5	5
G.	PBT		(25)	(15)	65	155	315
H.	PAT		(12.5)	(7.5)	32.5	77.5	157.5
I.	PBIT (1–T)		(10)	(5)	35.0	80.0	160
J.	Operating Cash Flow (D+I)		10	15	55	100	180
K.	Net Salvage Value						20
L.	Net Cash Flow (A+J+K)	(100)	10	15	55	100	200

The NPV of the project is:

$$-100 + \frac{10}{(1.10)} + \frac{15}{(1.10)^2} + \frac{55}{(1.10)^3} + \frac{100}{(1.10)^4} + \frac{200}{(1.10)^5}$$

$$= +₹112.8 \text{ million}$$

Although the project has a positive NPV, it is earnings-dilutive (as measured by PAT) in the first two years.

17.8 ORGANISATIONAL CONSIDERATIONS

In order to be meaningful and viable, the capital budget of a firm must satisfy some conditions. These are:

- It must be compatible with the resources of the firm.
- It must be controllable.
- It must be endorsed by the executive management.

Compatibility with Resources The capital budget of a firm must be compatible with its resources—financial capacity and managerial capability.

Financial Capacity The financial capacity of a firm may be estimated as follows: operating cash flow – fixed funding requirements + potential funding sources.

The operating cash flow of a firm is defined as: profit after tax + depreciation + other non-cash charges – increase in working capital (or + decrease in working capital).

The fixed funding requirements are equal to: debt repayment obligation + preference capital repayment obligation + preference dividend + normal equity dividend.

The potential funding sources consist of: excess cash balance + saleable fixed assets + reserve borrowing capacity + new equity issue.

Managerial Capability The managerial capability of every organisation has its own limitation. Management competence in one industry does not necessarily imply competence in another industry. This sets a limit - which of course can be overcome over a period of time - on investment in unrelated lines of activity. Further, imbalances in organisational skills may be an inhibiting factor. A firm may have outstanding engineering and production expertise that may not be matched by marketing skills, which may be, at least in the short-run, a factor limiting growth.

Assessing the managerial capability is more difficult than estimating the financial capacity. The methods of evaluation in this area being weak, there may be a tendency to gloss over it or side-step it. However, the inability to identify critical managerial limitations and organisational imbalances can seriously vitiate funds allocation. Indeed, this is one of the most vulnerable facets of capital budgeting.

Controllability As the business environment is continually changing and evolving, even the best conceived business plans may turn out to be ill-advised and poorly timed. Hence, proper controls should be instituted in the process of capital budgeting. This involves the following:

- The base level spending and the expansion investments should be segregated.
- Sound profitability criteria should be applied to expansion investments.
- Projects included in the capital budget should be thoroughly reviewed prior to actual implementation.
- Major projects should be divided into sub-phases for the purpose of controlling expenditures.
- Actual costs must be periodically compared against planned costs.

Base Level Spending and Expansion Investments The segregation of base level spending and expansion investments, a major aspect of control, deserves some elaboration. Base level spending, representing outlays on 'required' investments (also referred to sometimes as 'maintenance' investments), should be carefully distinguished from expansion investments also referred to as 'discretionary' investments or 'growth' investments. Base level spending represents the minimum spending required for sustaining current operations. If the base level capital budget is not properly drawn up, current operations may be 'short-changed' or 'gold-plated'.

As against the base level spending, expansion projects are discretionary in nature. Selection of expansion projects is a test of managerial initiative, insight, imagination, and judgement. In view of the mistakes that can be made with respect to expansion investments, the capital budgeting process should give high visibility and prominence to such projects.

Executive Management Endorsement The capital budget of the firm should be fully backed by the executive management. Without the endorsement of the executive management, the capital budgeting process may lack meaning and usefulness. Endorsement of the executive management is required at all stages: long-range planning, funds planning, planning to strengthen managerial capabilities and rectify organisational imbalances, and development of budgetary controls.

Endorsement of executive management means (i) conviction in the long-range strategy of the firm, (ii) strong desire to implement the approved capital budget, and (iii) willingness to be subjected to the discipline of capital budgeting.

SUMMARY

- A mosaic of influences that can best be described qualitatively have an important bearing on capital expenditure decisions.
- Capital budgeting is the principal instrument for implementing a firm's strategy. Hence the two should be properly linked.
- In a decision involving measurement as well as judgement, as far as possible, separate the quantifiable factors and the intangible factors.
- Strategic planning, among other things, is concerned with the issue of allocating a firm's resources across different lines of business. In this sense, strategic planning may be viewed as capital budgeting on a grand scale.
- Strategic planning is often naïve from the financial point of view and/or the results of strategic planning and financial analysis are not properly reconciled.
- In applying DCF analysis, the following mistakes are commonly committed: mechanical projection of cash flows, optimistic bias in cash flows, emphasis on IRR, inconsistent treatment of inflation, and unreasonably high discount rates.
- To bridge the gap between strategic planning and financial analysis, a conscious effort is required on both the sides. Financial analysts must avoid the mistakes commonly committed by them and strategic planners must understand the logic of the DCF analysis.

- The behaviour of firms in the real world is often at variance with the textbook model. The discrepancy arises mainly because of informational asymmetries.
- In theory, a group decision is supposed to exploit the synergies arising from bringing together people with diverse skills, perspectives, and values. Most groups, however, experience process loss due to psychological reasons.
- In theory, managers are supposed to maximise firm value by choosing projects on the basis of their NPVs. In practice, managers look at NPVs as well as the accounting implications of their investment decisions. In particular, they are concerned with the impact of investments on reported earnings in the short run.
- Since a project sponsor is keen to get his proposal included in the capital budget, he is likely to massage the numbers to dress up his project proposal. Is there some way by which such financial manipulation can be checked? McGrath and MacMillan have suggested a process they call *discovery-driven planning* that has the potential of improving the quality of analysis.
- In order to be meaningful and viable, the capital budget of a firm must satisfy some conditions: (i) It must be compatible with the resources of the firm. (ii) It must be controllable. (iii) It must be endorsed by the executive management.

QUESTIONS

1. Discuss the influence of intuition and judgement in capital budgeting. What factors influence judgement?
2. "The tie-in between strategy and capital budgeting is often loose and tenuous." Comment.
3. Suggest ways and means of strengthening the linkage between long-range planning and capital budgeting.
4. What are the salient differences in the frameworks applied in strategic planning and capital budgeting?
5. Discuss the mistakes commonly committed in applying the DCF analysis.
6. What are the different kinds of informational asymmetries? What types of distortions do they introduce in project choices?
7. What factors contribute to group errors?
8. What is groupthink? How can groupthink be checked?
9. Why do managers care about the impact on projects on short-term reported earnings?
10. Give examples of projects that are earnings-accretive but NPV-negative and projects that are NPV-positive but earnings-dilutive.
11. What is reverse financial engineering?
12. Discuss how discovery-driven planning can improve the quality of analysis.
13. What conditions should the capital budget satisfy in order to be meaningful and viable?
14. How would you measure the financial capacity of the firm?
15. What should be done to ensure that proper controls are instituted in the process of capital budgeting?

Financing

CHAPTER 18

Financing of Projects

CHAPTER 19

Venture Capital and Private Equity

PART FIVE

Chapter 18 Financing of Projects

LEARNING OBJECTIVES

After studying this chapter you should be able to

- Explain the differences between investment decisions and financing decisions.
- Describe the key factors that have a bearing on the debt-equity ratio for a project.
- Discuss the features of various domestic sources of finance as well as their pros and cons.
- Compare the various methods of raising finance.
- Describe the features of eurocurrency loans and bonds.
- Distinguish between a full recourse structure and a limited recourse structure.
- Specify the kind of information lenders want for appraising term loan requests.
- Discuss how financial institutions appraise a project.

For pedagogic purposes we discuss project financing after project selection. In practice, however, project financing is considered in some way or the other right from the time of project conception. Indeed project financing is intertwined with project planning, analysis, and selection. As the project proposal progresses through the stages of planning, analysis, and selection, the contours of project financing become clearer.

A capital project entails investment in land, plant and machinery, miscellaneous fixed assets, technical know-how, distribution network, and working capital. Hence a capital project may be regarded as a mini-firm - after all when you look at the balance sheet of a firm you find that it has investments in similar assets.

So, the issues to be considered in financing a project are identical to those considered in financing a business firm. What is an appropriate capital structure? Which financing instruments make more sense? What are the pros and cons of public and private sources of capital? How much should the firm depend on domestic capital market and how much on the international capital market?

Note that when financial institutions look at a project, they may consider only the long-term sources of finance. We, however, prefer to look at all the sources of finance, long-term as well as short-term. In line with this perspective, this chapter discusses all the sources of finance required to set up a project.

Financing Decisions are Relatively Easier

The vocabulary of financing is confusing and the number of complex and exotic financing instruments is expanding. Yet, at a fundamental level, financing decisions, compared to investment decisions, are relatively easier to make and have a lesser impact on firm value, thanks to the following differences:

Financing Decisions	*Investment Decisions*
■ Financing decisions take place in capital markets which are approximately perfect.	■ Investment decisions take place in real markets which tend to be imperfect.
■ While making financing decision, decisions, you can observe the value of similar financial assets.	■ While making investment decisions, you have to estimate the value of the capital projects.
■ There are very few opportunities in the realm of financing that have an NPV that is significantly different from zero.	■ There are many opportunities in the realm of capital budgeting that have an NPV that is significantly different from zero.

Given the intense competition in capital market, financial economists argue that securities are fairly priced. Put differently, they believe that the capital market is efficient.

18.1 CAPITAL STRUCTURE

The two broad sources of finance available to a firm are: shareholders' funds and loan funds. Shareholders' funds come mainly in the form of equity capital and retained earnings and secondarily in the form of preference capital. Loan funds come in a variety of ways like debenture capital, term loans, deferred credit, fixed deposit, and working capital advance.

Ignoring preference capital (which is of minor significance), the basic differences between shareholders' funds (referred to as equity) and loan funds (referred to as debt) are as follows:

Equity	*Debt*
■ Equity shareholders have a residual claim on the income and the wealth of the firm.	■ Creditors (suppliers of debt) have a fixed claim in the form of interest and principal payment.
■ Dividend paid to equity shareholders is not a tax deductible payment.	■ Interest paid to creditors is a tax deductible payment.
■ Equity ordinarily has an indefinite life.	■ Debt has a fixed maturity.
■ Equity investors enjoy the prerogative to control the affairs of the firm.	■ Debt investors play a passive role—of course, they impose certain restrictions on the way the firm is run to protect their interest.

Key Factors in Determining the Debt-Equity Ratio

The key factors in determining the debt-equity ratio for a project are:

- Cost
- Nature of assets
- Business risk
- Norms of lenders
- Control considerations
- Market conditions

Cost Lenders require a lower rate of return compared to equity shareholders. This advantage gets magnified when the firm pays taxes, because the interest on debt is a tax-deductible payment whereas the dividend on equity is not. The lower cost of debt, however, is accompanied by a higher degree of risk. Put differently, debt is a cheaper but riskier source of finance, whereas equity is a costlier but safer source of finance.

Nature of Assets The nature of a firm's assets has an important bearing on its capital structure. If the assets are primarily tangible (plant and machinery and buildings) and have a liquid resale/secondary market, debt finance is used more. For example, electric utility companies use more debt because their assets are mainly tangible, physical in nature. On the other hand, if the assets are primarily intangible (brands and technical know how), debt finance is used less. For example, software companies use very little debt as their assets are mainly intangible.

What explains the link between the nature of assets and the use of debt finance? The major explanation is that lenders are more willing to lend against tangible assets and less inclined to lend against intangible assets.

Business Risk Business risk refers to the variability of earning power (defined as profit before interest and taxes/total assets). It is influenced, *inter alia*, by the following factors:

- *Demand Variability* Other things being equal, the higher the variability of demand for the products manufactured by the firm, the higher is its business risk.
- *Price Variability* A project which is exposed to a higher degree of volatility in the prices of its products is, in general, characterised by a higher degree of business risk in comparison with similar firms which are exposed to a lesser degree of volatility for the prices of their products.
- *Variability of Input Prices* When input prices are highly variable, business risk tends to be high.
- *Proportion of Fixed Operating Costs* If fixed costs represent a substantial proportion of total costs, other things being equal, business risk is likely to be high. This is because when fixed costs are high, PBIT is more sensitive to variations in demand.

Generally, the affairs of the firm are, or should be, managed in such a way that the total risk borne by equity shareholders, which consists of business risk plus financial risk, is not unduly high. This implies that if the firm is exposed to a high degree of business risk, its financial risk should be kept low. On the other hand, if the firm has a low business risk profile, it can assume more financial risk.

Norms of Lenders The norms employed by the lenders have a bearing on the capital structure. For example, financial institutions at one time permitted a debt-equity ratio of 2:1. At that time most of the projects had a debt-equity ratio close to 2:1. Now the general debt-equity ratio norm allowed by financial institutions is 1:1. Of course, for highly capital-intensive projects they permit a higher debt-equity ratio. For example, for a power generation project they permit a debt-equity ratio of 2.33:1.

Control Considerations The extent of equity stake that the promoters want to have in a project has an important bearing on its capital structure. Let us say that the cost of a project is 10,000 and the promoters of the project can invest 2,000. If they want to have a minimum stake of 50 percent in the equity of the project, the total equity cannot exceed 4,000. Hence the balance 6,000 has to be in the form of debt, leading to a debt-equity ratio of 1.5:1. On the other hand, if they want a minimum stake of 40 percent in the equity of the project, the total equity cannot exceed 5,000. So, the balance 5,000 has to be in the form of debt, leading to a debt-equity ratio of 1:1.

Market Conditions If the equity market is buoyant and equity shares can be issued at an attractive premium, the project may rely more on equity. On the other hand, if the equity market is depressed, the project may depend more on debt.

A Checklist

When should a project use more equity and when should a project use more debt. Here is a checklist:

Use more equity when

- The tax rate applicable is negligible.
- Business risk exposure is high.
- Dilution of control is not an important issue.
- The assets of the project are mostly intangible.
- The project has many valuable growth options.

Use more debt when

- The tax rate applicable is high.
- Business risk exposure is low.
- Dilution of control is an issue.
- The assets of the project are mostly tangible.
- The project has few growth options.

18.2 MENU OF FINANCING

Finance can be raised from a variety of sources that may be classified in different ways as shown in Exhibit 18.1. The various forms of financing are discussed in the following sections.

Exhibit 18.1 *Sources of Finance*

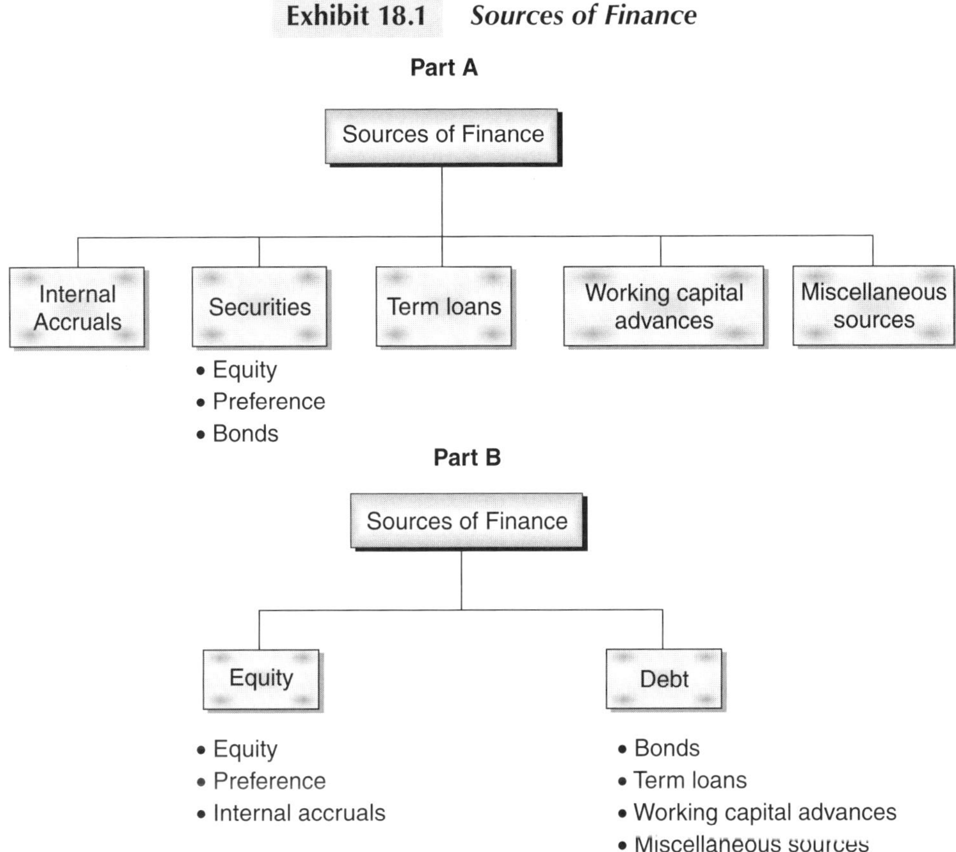

• Public and Private Sources of Capital

A firm can raise equity and debt capital from both public and private sources. Capital raised from public sources is in the form of securities offered to public through an offer document filed with the Securities Exchange Board of India[1]. These securities can be traded on public secondary markets like the National Stock Exchange or the Bombay Stock Exchange, which are recognised stock exchanges that facilitate the trading of public securities.

Private capital comes either in the form of loans given by banks and financial institutions or in the form of issue of securities like equity shares, preference shares, and debentures which are privately placed with a small group of sophisticated investors like private equity funds, venture capital firms, financial institutions, insurance companies, mutual funds, and wealthy individuals.

[1] This, however, does not apply when a firm raises fixed deposits or issues commercial paper.

• The Typical Pattern of Financing

When a company is formed, it first issues equity shares to the promoters (founders) and also, in most cases, raises loans from banks, financial institutions, and other sources. As the need for financing increases, the company may issue shares and debentures privately to promoters' relatives, friends, business partners, employees, financial institutions, banks, mutual funds, venture capital funds, and others - venture capital funds are likely to be an important source of finance for a nascent venture. Such investors are specific and small in number.

As the company grows further, it may have to raise capital from the public. The first issue of equity shares to the public by an unlisted company is called the initial public offering (IPO). Subsequent offerings are called seasoned offerings.

Apart from equity shares, a firm may issue preference shares[2] and debentures to the general investing public through a public issue.

18.3 INTERNAL ACCRUALS

The internal accruals of a firm consist of depreciation charges and retained earnings. Depreciation represents the allocation of capital expenditure to various periods over which the capital expenditure is expected to benefit the firm. Suppose a machine costs ₹100,000 and has an economic life of five years at the end of which its expected salvage value is 0. If the machine is depreciated using the straight line method the annual depreciation charge will be ₹20,000. Each year a depreciation cost of ₹20,000 is shown in the profit and loss account. This cost merely represents a periodic writeoff of a capital cost incurred in the beginning. Put differently, it is a non-cash charge. Hence, it is considered an internal source of finance.

Retained earnings are that portion of equity earnings (profit after tax less preference dividends) which are ploughed back in the firm. Because retained earnings are the sacrifice made by equity shareholders, they are referred to as internal equity. Companies normally retain 30 percent to 80 percent of profit after tax for financing growth. If you look at a sample of corporate balance sheets you will find that reserves and surplus (other than share premium reserve and revaluation reserve), which essentially represent accumulated retained earnings, are an important source of long-term financing. Even this is an understatement of the contribution of retained earnings to long-term financing because a portion of reserves and surplus would have been capitalised by the firm if it had issued bonus shares.

• Advantages and Disadvantages of Internal Accruals

Internal accruals are viewed very favourably by most corporate managements for the following reasons:

- Internal accruals are readily available. Management does not have to talk to outsiders (shareholders or lenders).
- Use of internal accruals, in contrast to external equity, eliminates issue costs and losses on account of underpricing.

[2] Over the years preference shares have declined in importance.

- There is no dilution of control when a firm relies on internal accruals.
- The stock market generally views an equity issue with skepticism. Internal accruals, however, do not carry such negative connotation.

The disadvantages of internal accruals include the following:

- The amount that may be available by way of internal accruals may be limited.
- The opportunity cost of retained earnings is quite high as it is equal to the cost of equity—remember that retained earnings, in essence, represent dividends foregone by equity shareholders.
- The opportunity cost of depreciation-generated funds is equal to the weighted average cost of capital of the firm.
- Many firms do not fully appreciate the opportunity costs of retained earnings and depreciation-generated funds. They tend to impute a low cost to internal accruals. Comforted by the easy availability of internal accruals and the notion that they have a low cost, managements may invest in sub-marginal projects that destroy shareholder value.

18.4 EQUITY CAPITAL

Equity capital represents ownership capital as equity shareholders collectively own the company. They enjoy the rewards and bear the risks of ownership. However, their liability, unlike the liability of the owner in a proprietary firm and the partners in a partnership concern, is limited to their capital contributions.

Some Terms

Let us look at some of the terms relating to equity capital.

Authorised, Issued, Subscribed, and Paid-up Capital The amount of capital that a company can potentially issue, as per its memorandum, represents the *authorised capital*. The amount offered by the company to the investors is called the *issued capital*. That part of issued capital which has been subscribed to by the investors represents the *subscribed capital*. The actual amount paid up by the investors is called the *paid-up capital*—typically the issued, subscribed, and paid-up capital are the same.

Par Value, Issue Price, Book Value, and Market Value The *par value* of an equity share is the value stated in the memorandum and written on the share scrip. The par value of equity shares is generally ₹10 (the most popular denomination) or ₹100. Infrequently, one comes across par values like ₹1, ₹2, ₹5, ₹50, and ₹1,000.

The *issue price* is the price at which the equity share is issued. Generally the issue price and par value are one and the same for new companies. An existing company may sometimes set its issue price higher than the par value. Sonata Software (India) Limited, for example, set its issue price at ₹80 per share as against the par value of ₹10 per share. When the issue price exceeds the par value, the difference is referred to as the share premium. It may be noted that the issue price cannot be, as per law, lower than the par value.[3]

[3] Technically, shares may be issued at a discount although procedural complexity makes it infrequent.

The *book value* of an equity share is equal to:

$$\frac{\text{Paid-up equity capital + Reserves and surplus}}{\text{Number of outstanding equity shares}}$$

Quite naturally, the book value of an equity share tends to increase as the ratio of reserves and surplus to paid-up equity capital increases.

The *market value* of an equity share is the price at which it is traded in the market. This price can be easily established for a company which is listed on the stock market and actively traded. For a company which is listed on the stock market but traded very infrequently, it is difficult to obtain a reliable market quotation. For such a company, the market quotation may reflect the sale of a few shares in a past period and hence may not reflect the current market value of the firm. For a company which is not listed on the stock market, one can merely conjecture as to what its market price would be if it were traded. The market price is determined by a variety of factors like current earnings, growth prospects, risk, and company size.

• Rights of Equity Shareholders

The rights of equity shareholders are as follows:

Right to Income The equity investors have a residual claim to the income of the firm. The income left after satisfying the claims of all other investors belongs to the equity shareholders. This income is simply equal to profit after tax minus preferred dividend.

The income of equity shareholders may be retained by the firm or paid out as dividends. The dividend decision is the prerogative of the board of directors.

Right to Control Equity shareholders elect the board of directors and have the right to vote on every resolution placed before the company. The board of directors, in turn, selects the management which controls the operations of the firm. Hence, equity shareholders exercise an indirect control over the operations of the firm. How effective is such indirect control? Often such indirect control is weak and ineffective because of the apathy and indifference of most of the shareholders who rarely bother to cast their votes, by post or through a proxy, let alone attend the annual general meetings. Scattered and ill-organised, equity shareholders fail to exercise their collective power effectively. Usually, the management of the firm, with the support of a well organised but not necessarily a very substantial group of shareholders, is able to hold the reins of control.

Pre-emptive Right The pre-emptive right enables existing equity shareholders to maintain their proportional ownership by purchasing the additional equity shares issued by the firm. The law requires companies to give existing equity shareholders the first opportunity to purchase, on pro rata basis, additional issues of equity capital. For example, if the company has 1,000,000 outstanding shares of equity stock and proposes to issue 200,000 additional equity shares, an equity shareholder owning 100 shares has the right to purchase 20 of the 200,000 new shares before those are offered to anyone else. The equity shareholders may, however, forfeit this right, partially or totally.

Right in Liquidation As in the case of income, equity shareholders have a residual claim over the assets of the firm in the event of liquidation. Claims of all others—debenture holders, secured lenders, unsecured lenders, other creditors, and preferred share-holders—are settled prior to the claim of equity shareholders. More often than not, equity shareholders do not get anything in the event of liquidation because the liquidation value of assets is not adequate to fully meet the claims of others.

• Advantages and Disadvantages of Equity Capital

An important source of long-term financing, equity capital offers the following advantages:

- There is no compulsion to pay dividends. If the firm has insufficiency of cash, it can skip equity dividends without suffering any legal consequences.
- Equity capital has no maturity date and hence the firm has no obligation to redeem.
- Because equity capital provides a cushion to lenders, it enhances the creditworthiness of the company.
- Presently, equity dividends are tax-exempt in the hands of investors.

The disadvantages of raising finances by issuing equity shares are as follows:

- Sale of equity shares to outsiders dilutes the control of existing owners.
- The cost of equity capital is high, usually the highest. The rate of return required by equity shareholders is generally higher than the rate of return required by other investors.
- Equity dividends are paid out of profit after tax, whereas interest payments are tax-deductible expenses. Partially offsetting this disadvantage is the fact that equity dividends are tax-exempt whereas interest income is taxable in the hands of investors.
- The cost of issuing equity shares is generally higher than the cost of issuing other types of securities. Underwriting commission, brokerage costs, and other issue expenses are high for equity issues.

18.5 PREFERENCE CAPITAL

Preference capital represents a hybrid form of financing—it partakes some characteristics of equity and some attributes of debentures. It resembles equity in the following ways: (i) preference dividend is payable only out of distributable profits; (ii) preference dividend is not an obligatory payment (the payment of preference dividend is entirely within the discretion of directors); and (iii) preference dividend is not a tax-deductible payment.

Preference capital is similar to debentures in several ways: (i) the dividend rate of preference capital is usually fixed; (ii) the claim of preference shareholders is prior to the claim of equity shareholders; and (iii) preference shareholders do not normally enjoy the right to vote.

• Types of Preference Shares

There are various types of preference shares, depending on the rights associated with them.

Cumulative and Non-cumulative Preference Shares Cumulative preference shares entitle the shareholders to receive dividends for previous year/s in which dividend was not paid. A company cannot declare equity dividends unless dividends on cumulative preference shares are paid with arrears.

Participating and Non-participating Preference Shares The holders of participating preference shares get a share in the profits of the company after a certain rate of dividend is paid to the equity shareholders of the company. This is in addition to the fixed rate of dividend declared on preference shares before any equity dividend is paid. The holders of non-participating preference shares can get only a fixed dividend and do not get any share in the surplus left after paying equity dividend.

Redeemable and Non-redeemable Preference Shares Redeemable preference shares are repayable at par or at premium after a specified period. Non-redeemable preference shares are not repayable, except when the company goes into liquidation. At present, companies in India can issue only redeemable preference shares where the redemption period does not exceed twenty years.

Convertible and Non-convertible Preference Shares Convertible preference shares can be converted into equity shares at the option of the preference shareholders in accordance with certain predetermined terms. Non-convertible shares do not carry such an option.

• Advantages and Disadvantages of Preference Capital

Preference capital offers the following advantages:

- There is no legal obligation to pay preference dividend. A company does not face bankruptcy or legal action if it skips preference dividend.
- There is no redemption liability in the case of perpetual preference shares. Even in the case of redeemable preference shares, financial distress may not be much because (i) periodic sinking fund payments are not required and (ii) redemption can be delayed without significant penalties.
- Preference capital is regarded as part of net worth, if its redemption is subordinated to repayment of debt.
- Preference shares do not, under normal circumstances, carry voting right. Hence, there is no dilution of control.
- No security of assets is provided to preference shareholders. Hence, the mortgageable assets of the firm are conserved.

Preference capital, however, suffers from some serious shortcomings:

- Compared to debt capital, it is a more expensive source of financing because the preference dividend is not, unlike debt interest, a tax-deductible expense. Further, there is a dividend distribution tax.
- Skipping preference dividend can adversely affect the image of the firm in the capital market.
- Compared to equity shareholders, preference shareholders have a prior claim on the assets and earnings of the firm.
- If a firm skips preference dividends for three years, it has to grant voting right to preference shareholders, on matters affecting them.

18.6 DEBENTURES (OR BONDS)

For large publicly traded firms, debentures are a viable alternative to term loans. Akin to promissory notes, debentures are instruments for raising debt finance. Debenture holders are the creditors of the company. The obligation of a company toward its debenture holders is similar to that of a borrower who promises to pay interest and principal at specified times. Debentures often provide more flexibility than term loans as they offer greater choice with respect to maturity, interest rate, security, repayment, and special features.

• Features

The important features of debentures are as follows:

- When a debenture issue is sold to the investing public, a trustee is appointed through a trust deed. The trustee, usually a bank or financial institution or insurance company, is supposed to ensure that the borrowing firm fulfills its contractual obligations.
- Debenture issues in India are typically secured by mortgages/charges on the immovable properties of the company and a floating charge on its other assets (subject to prior charges created in favour of the company's bankers over the current assets). However, the order of priority of mortgages/charges may vary across different debenture issues. Occasionally, companies issue unsecured debentures. These are debentures that are not backed by specific assets of the firm, but by its general credit.
- Corporate debt may be short-term, medium-term or long-term. Short-term corporate debt of less than one year is called commercial paper. Medium-term debentures may have a maturity of 1 year to 5 years. Long-term debentures typically have a maturity period of 5 to 12 years.
- Publicly issued debentures that have a maturity period of 18 months or more have to be compulsorily credit rated.
- Debentures are typically redeemable in nature. For all debenture issues with a maturity period of more than 18 months, a Debenture Redemption Reserve (DRR) has to be created. The company should create a DRR equivalent to at least 25 percent of the amount of issue before redemption commences.
- Debentures may carry a fixed rate of interest or floating rate of interest or zero rate of interest.
- Debentures may carry a 'call' feature, which provides the issuing company the option to redeem the debentures at a certain price before the maturity period. Sometimes debentures may have a 'put' feature which gives the holder the right to seek redemption at specified times at predetermined prices.

• Innovations in Debentures

Thanks to the latitude enjoyed by companies from early 1990s, a variety of debt instruments have been employed. Here is a sampling:

Deep Discount Bonds A deep discount bond does not carry any coupon rate but is issued at a steep discount over its face value. It is also referred to as a 'zero interest (coupon) bond' or just a zero. For example, in 1992 the Industrial Development Bank of India (IDBI) issued deep discount bonds. Each bond having a face value of ₹100,000 was issued at a deeply discounted price of ₹2500 with a maturity period of 25 years from the date of allotment (i.e. February 1, 1993). The investor as well as IDBI have the option to withdraw or redeem the bond respectively at the end of 5, 9, 12, 15, or 20 years from the date of allotment at the deemed value of ₹5300, ₹9600, ₹15,300, ₹25,000 and ₹50,000 respectively.

Deep discount bonds appeal to issuers interested in conserving their cash flows during the life of the bonds. On the other side of the market, they appear attractive to investors who want to protect themselves against the reinvestment rate risk. Remember that the imputed interest on a deep discount bond is automatically reinvested at a rate equal to its yield to maturity.

Convertible Debentures A convertible debenture, as the name suggests, is a debenture that is convertible, partially or wholly, into equity shares. As per SEBI guidelines, the provisions applicable to fully convertible debentures (FCDs) and partially convertible debentures (PCDs) are as follows:

- The conversion premium and the conversion timing shall be predetermined and stated in the prospectus. If the convertible portion exceeds ₹50 lakh and the issuer has not determined the conversion price at the time of issue, the holders of such convertible debt instruments shall be given the option of not converting the convertible portion into equity shares. However, where the upper limit on the conversion price is disclosed to the investors at the time of issue, such option need not be given, as long as the conversion price is within the said upper limit.
- Compulsory credit rating will be required for partly convertible debentures.

Convertible debentures are commonly used all over the world and are gaining currency in India as well. Why are they popular? The conventional explanations for their popularity are: (a) convertible debentures are a cheaper source of finance because interest rate on them is typically lower than that on straight debentures; (b) convertible debentures enable a company to effectively issue equity shares at a premium because the conversion price associated with a convertible debenture is typically higher than the price at which equity shares can be issued currently.

The conventional explanations have a "free lunch" flavour. So you should be suspicious of them.

Modern finance theory offers better explanations: (a) Convertible debentures improve cash flow matching. Firms prefer financing instruments that can be comfortably serviced. A growing but risky firm may find convertible debentures appealing because of a lower initial burden, though they may entail expensive dilution later. (b) Convertible debentures generate financial synergy. They make sense when it is very costly or difficult to assess the risk characteristics of the issuing firm. Remember that these instruments have two components, the straight debenture component and the call option component. If the company turns out to be risky, the debenture instrument will have a low value but the call option component will have a high value. On the other hand, if the company turns out to be relatively risk-free the debenture component will have a high value but the call option component a low value. Given this compensating behaviour of the two components, the required yield on the convertible debenture will not be very sensitive to default risk.

Floating Rate Bonds Conventional bonds carry a fixed rate of interest. Floating rate bonds, on the other hand, earn an interest rate that is linked to a benchmark rate such as the Treasury bill interest rate. For example, in 1993 the State Bank of India came out with the first ever issue of floating interest rate bonds in India. It issued 5 million (₹1000 face value) unsecured, redeemable, subordinated, floating interest rate bonds in the nature of promissory notes carrying interest at 3 percent per annum over the bank's maximum term deposit rate.

Floating rate bonds have been essentially a response to inflation risk. They make sense to a borrower whose assets earn returns that fluctuate with interest rates. Financial institutions and banks which give variable rate interest loans find such bonds appealing. Who is interested in buying floating rate bonds? Investors concerned about the stability of their principal find floating rate bonds attractive. The prices of these bonds tend to be fairly stable and close to par value compared to fixed interest bonds.

Indexed Bonds The payoff of a typical indexed bond consists of two parts. The first part represents a fixed amount and the second part represents a variable component whose value is dependent on some index. For example, ICICI issued Indexed Bonds in 1997 for ₹6000 each. It was a composite instrument comprising of two parts: a discount bond and a detachable index warrant. The face value of the discount bond was ₹22,000 and its redemption date was May 27, 2009. The detachable warrant had a payoff that was linked to BSE Sensex as follows: 2000 × BSE Sensex 2009/BSE Sensex 1997.

An indexed bond appeals to investors who are looking for an assured return along with capital appreciation that is linked to some index.

Strips GE Capital Services India issued India's first STRIP debentures (separately tradeable interest and principal debentures) in 1998. Each STRIP debenture consisted of seven detachable strips, one for the principal and six for interest coupons. Each strip was to be listed and traded separately on the National Stock Exchange.

Advantages and Disadvantages of Debt Financing

Term loans and debentures are two important ways of raising long-term debt. The advantages of debt financing are as follows:

- Interest on debt is a tax-deductible expense, whereas equity and preference dividends are paid out of profit after tax.
- Debt financing does not result in dilution of control because debt holders (term lending institutions and debenture-holders) are not entitled to vote.
- Debt holders do not partake in the value created by the company as payments to them are limited to interest and principal.
- Issue costs of debt are significantly lower than those on equity and preference capital.
- The burden of servicing debt is generally fixed in nominal terms. Hence debt provides protection against high unanticipated inflation.
- The maturity of a debt instrument can be tailored to the needs of the borrowing firm.

Debt financing is not an unmixed blessing. It has certain disadvantages associated with it:

- Debt financing entails fixed interest and principal repayment obligation. Failure to meet these commitments can cause a great deal of financial embarrassment and even lead to bankruptcy.

- Debt financing increases financial leverage which, according to CAPM, raises the cost of equity to the firm.
- Debt contracts impose restrictions that limit the borrowing firm's financial and operating flexibility. These restrictions may impair the borrowing firm's ability to resort to value-maximising behaviour.
- If the rate of inflation turns out to be unexpectedly low, the real cost of debt will be greater than expected.

Dominance of Straight Debt and Equity

Apart from straight debt and equity, firms can issue a variety of other securities. Theoretically, firms can issue an endless range of securities. However, the actual number of alternative securities used by firms in not very large and the proportion of financing raised through them is fairly small. Why? A plausible explanation why firms primarily use straight debt and equity is offered by Fama and Jensen*. According to them it makes sense to segregate the financial claims of the firm into only two parts: a relatively low-risk claim represented by debt and a relatively high-risk claim represented by equity. They argue that specialised risk bearing by residual claimants reduces contracting costs – the costs incurred to monitor contract fulfillment. Thanks to specialised risk bearing, shareholders and bondholders do not have to monitor each other. It is enough if debtholders monitor shareholders. This kind of one-way monitoring lessens the total cost of contracting than what it would otherwise be. Hence it makes sense for most firms to use only straight debt and equity.

* Fama, E.F., and M.C. Jenson, "Agency Problems and Residual Claims," *Journal of Law and Economics*, June 1983.

18.7 METHODS OF OFFERING

There are different ways in which a company may raise finances in the primary market: public offering, rights issue, and private placement.

Public Offering

A public offering or public issue involves sale of securities to the members of the public. The three types of public offering are: the initial public offering (IPO), the seasoned equity offering, and the bond offering.

Initial Public Offering The first public offering of equity shares of a company, which is followed by a listing of its shares on the stock market, is called the initial public offering (IPO).

Decision to Go Public The decision to go public (or more precisely the decision to make an IPO so that the securities of the company are listed on the stock market and are publicly traded) is a very important issue. It is a complex decision, which calls for carefully weighing the benefits against costs.

Benefits	*Costs*
■ Access to a larger pool of capital	■ Dilution
■ Respectability	■ Loss of flexibility
■ Lower cost of capital compared to private placement	■ Disclosures and accountability
■ Liquidity	■ Periodic costs

Eligibility for IPOs An Indian company, excluding certain banks and infrastructure companies, can make an IPO if it satisfies the following conditions.[4]

- The company has a certain track record of profitability and a certain minimum networth.
- The securities are compulsorily listed on a recognised stock exchange, which means that a certain minimum percent of each class of securities is offered to the public.
- The promoter group (promoters, friends, relatives, associates, etc.) is required to make a certain minimum contribution to the post-issue capital.
- The promoters' contribution to the equity is subject to a certain lock-in period.

The IPO Process From the perspective of merchant banking, the IPO process consists of four major phases: (a) hiring the merchant bankers, (b) due diligence and prospectus preparation, (c) marketing, and (d) subscription and allotment.

The company wishing to go public has to hire the merchant bankers to manage its offering. The selection of a merchant banker is usually referred to as a 'beauty contest'. Typically, it involves meeting different merchant bankers, discussing the plans for going public, and getting a valuation estimate. Understandably, the choice of the merchant banker is guided mainly by the valuation estimate offered. Often, a company going for an IPO selects two or more merchant bankers to manage the issue. The primary manager is called the "lead manager" and the other managers are called "co-managers".

Once the managers are selected, *due diligence and prospectus preparation* begin. The merchant bankers understand the company's business and plans, examine various documents and records, prepare the draft prospectus, file the same with the regulatory authorities, and arrange for its printing. Merchant bankers, lawyers, accountants, and company managers have to toil for countless hours to complete the legal formalities that finally culminate in the printing of the prospectus. Since book building is commonly used, the issue price is not fixed in advance, but a price band is given.

The next phase of an IPO is the *marketing phase*. After all the regulatory approvals are in place, the company embarks on a *road show* to promote the issue. A road show involves presentation by the management of the company to potential investors (mostly institutional) in different locations. Concurrently, the issue is advertised in various media primarily targeted at retail investors.

The final phase of the IPO involves receiving *subscription and allotment* of shares. The subscription is normally kept open for five to ten days. During this period, investors can submit their bid-cum-application forms. After the subscription is closed, the merchant bankers fix the final issue price, determine the pattern of allotment, complete the allotment of shares, and secure the listing on one or more recognised stock exchanges.

---

[4] The guidelines for making an IPO tend to change. Readers are advised to refer to the latest guidelines at www.sebi.com

Seasoned Equity Offering For most companies their IPO is seldom their last public issue. As companies need more finances, they are likely to make further trips to the capital market with seasoned equity offerings, also called secondary offerings.

While the process of a seasoned equity offering is similar to that of an IPO, it is much less complicated. The company may employ the merchant bankers who handled the IPO. Further, with the availability of secondary market prices, there is no need for elaborate valuation. Finally, prospectus preparation and road shows can be completed with less effort and time than that required for the IPO.

Bond Offering The bond offering process is similar to the IPO process. There are, however, some differences:

- The prospectus for a bond offering typically emphasises a company's stable cash flows, whereas the prospectus for an equity offering highlights the company's growth prospects.
- Pure debt securities are typically offered at a predetermined yield because the book building route is not considered appropriate for them.
- Debt securities are generally secured against the assets of the issuing company and that security should be created within six months of the close of the issue of debentures.
- A debt issue cannot be made unless credit rating from a credit rating agency is obtained and disclosed in the offer document.
- It is mandatory to create a debenture redemption reserve for every issue of debentures.
- It is necessary for a company to appoint one or more debenture trustees before a debenture issue.

Rights Issue

A rights issue involves selling securities in the primary market by issuing rights to the existing shareholders. When a company issues additional equity capital, it has to be offered in the first instance to the existing shareholders on a pro rata basis. This is required under Section 81 of the Companies Act, 1956. The shareholders, however, may by a special resolution forfeit this right, partially or fully, to enable a company to issue additional capital to the public.

Procedure for Rights Issue A company making a rights issue sends a letter of offer along with a composite application form consisting of four forms (A, B, C and D) to the shareholders. Form A is meant for the acceptance of the rights and application of additional shares. This form also shows the number of rights shares the shareholder is entitled to. It also has a column through which a request for additional shares may be made. Form B is to be used if the shareholder wants to renounce the rights in favour of someone else. Form C is meant for application by the renouncee in whose favour the rights have been renounced, by the original allottee, through Form B. Form D is to be used to make a request for split forms. The composite application form must be mailed to the company within a specific period, which is usually 30 days.

Rights Issue versus Public Issue A rights issue offers several advantages over a public issue. The floatation costs of a rights issue are significantly lower than those of a public issue.

Theoretically, the subscription price of a rights issue is irrelevant because the wealth of a shareholder who subscribes to the rights issue or sells the rights remains unchanged, irrespective of what the subscription price is. Hence, the problem of transfer of wealth from existing shareholders to new shareholders does not arise in a rights issue.

• Private Placement

A private placement is an issue of securities to a select group of persons not exceeding 200. Private placement of shares and convertible debentures by a listed company can be of two types.

Preferential Allotment When a listed company issues shares or debentures to a select group of persons in terms of the provisions of Chapter VII of SEBI (Issue of Capital and Disclosure Requirements) Regulations 2009, it is referred to as a preferential allotment. The issuer has to comply with various provisions, relating to pricing, disclosures, lock-in period and so on, apart from the requirements of the Companies Act.

Qualified Institutional Placement (QIP) A QIP is an issue of equity shares or convertible securities to Qualified Institutional Buyers in terms of the provisions of Chapter VII of SEBI (ICDR) Regulations.

Private Placement of Bonds From 1995 onwards private placement of debentures thrived, thanks to minimal regulation. Corporates, financial institutions, infrastructure companies, and others depended considerably on privately placed debentures which were subscribed to mainly by mutual funds, banks, insurance organisations, and provident funds.

Information and disclosures to be included in the Private Placement Memorandum were not defined, credit rating was not mandatory, listing was not compulsory, and banks and financial institutions could subscribe to these issues without too many constraints.

The regulatory framework changed significantly in late 2003 when SEBI and RBI tightened their regulations over the issuance of privately placed debentures and the subscription of the same by banks and financial institutions. The key features of the new regulatory dispensation are:

- The disclosure requirements for privately placed debentures are similar to those of publicly offered debentures under SEBI Regulations.
- Debt securities shall carry a credit rating of not less than investment grade from a credit rating agency registered with SEBI.
- Debt securities shall be issued and traded in demat form.
- Debt securities may be optionally listed.
- The trading in privately placed debt shall take place between QIBs and HNIs (High Networth Individuals) in standard denomination of ₹10 lakh.
- Banks should not invest in non-SLR securities of original maturity of less than one year other than commercial paper and certificates of deposits which are covered under RBI guidelines.
- Banks should not invest in unrated non-SLR securities.

• How Do the Various Methods of Offering Compare

How do the three methods compare broadly in terms of the amount that can be raised, the cost of issue, dilution of control, degree of underpricing, and market perception? Exhibit 18.2 presents a summary comparison for an equity issue. As far as a debt issue is concerned dilution of control is a non-issue and the market perception is positive under all the methods.

Exhibit 18.2 ***Summary Comparison of the Various Methods***

	Public Issue	*Rights Issue*	*Private Placement*
■ Amount that can be raised	Large	Moderate	Moderate
■ Cost of issue	High	Negligible	Negligible
■ Dilution of control	Yes	No	Yes
■ Degree of underpricing	Large	Irrelevant	Small
■ Market perception	Negative	Neutral	Neutral

18.8 TERM LOANS

Firms obtain long-term debt mainly by raising term loans or issuing debentures. We have discussed at length the features and types of debentures. Now we turn our attention to term loans.

Historically, term loans given by financial institutions and banks have been the primary source of long-term debt for private firms and most public firms. Term loans, also referred to as term finance, represent a source of debt finance which is generally repayable in less than 10 years. They are typically employed to finance acquisition of fixed assets and working capital margin. Term loans differ from short-term bank loans which are employed to finance short-term working capital need and tend to be self-liquidating over a period of time, usually less than one year.[5]

Features of Term Loans

The following features of term loans are discussed below:

- Currency
- Security
- Interest payment and principal repayment
- Restrictive covenants

Currency Financial institutions (hereafter, we will, for the sake of simplicity, use the term financial institution to refer to all financial intermediaries like development financial institutions, commercial banks, and insurance companies) give rupee term loans as well as foreign currency term loans. The most significant form of assistance provided by financial institutions, rupee term loans are given directly to industrial concerns for setting up new projects as well as for expansion, modernisation, and renovation projects.

These funds are provided for incurring expenditure on land, building, plant and machinery, technical know-how, miscellaneous fixed assets, preliminary expenses, preoperative expenses, and margin money for working capital.

[5] In practice, of course, due to the phenomenon of "roll over", their effective maturity may be longer.

Financial institutions provide foreign currency term loans for meeting the foreign currency expenditure towards import of plant, machinery and equipment, and payment of foreign technical know-how fees. The periodical liability for interest and principal remains in the currency/currencies of the loan and is translated into rupees at the prevailing rate of exchange for making payments to the financial institutions.

Security Term loans typically represent secured borrowing. Usually assets, which are financed with the term loan, provide the prime security. Other assets of the firm may serve as collateral security.

All loans provided by financial institutions, along with interest, liquidated damages, commitment charges, expenses, etc., are secured by way of:

1. First equitable mortgage of all immovable properties of the borrower, both present and future; and
2. Hypothecation of all movable properties of the borrower, both present and future, subject to prior charges in favour of commercial banks for obtaining working capital advance in the normal course of business.

Interest Payment and Principal Repayment The interest and principal repayment on term loans are definite obligations that are payable irrespective of the financial situation of the firm. To the general category of borrowers, financial institutions charge an interest rate that is related to the credit risk of the proposal, subject usually to a certain floor rate. Financial institutions impose a penalty for defaults. In case of default on payment of interest, the borrower is liable to pay further interest on interest (compound interest) at the document rate. For default in repayment of instalments of principal, the borrower is liable to pay by way of liquidated damages, additional interest at the rate of 2 percent per annum for the period of default on the amount of principal in default. In addition to interest, lending institutions levy an upfront fee on the sanctioned loan amount usually at the rate of one percent.

Institutions Providing Term Loans

Institutions that provide term loans in India may be divided into three broad categories as follows:

All India Financial Institutions These include IFCI, ICICI, and IDBI, the three oldest general term-lending institutions (ICICI and IDBI have been transformed into banks in recent years), and specialised institutions like Exim Bank, IL&FS, Power Finance Corporation, IDFC, and SIDBI, and insurance companies (LIC and GIC) with marginal exposure to term-lending.

State Level Financial Institutions Most of the states have a State Industrial Development Corporation (SIDC) and a State Financial Corporation (SFC).

Commercial Banks Historically, commercial banks were marginal players in the term-lending arena, as their main thrust was on providing working capital finance. In recent years, commercial banks have stepped up their term-lending activities.

The principal amount of a term loan is generally repayable over a period of four to seven years after an initial grace period of one to two years. Typically, term loans provided by financial institutions are repayable in equal semi-annual instalments or equal quarterly instalments.

Note that the interest burden declines over time, whereas the principal repayment remains constant. This means that the total debt servicing burden (consisting of interest payment and principal repayment) declines over time. This pattern of debt servicing burden, typical in India, differs from the pattern obtaining in western economies where debt is typically amortised in equal periodic instalments.

Restrictive Covenants In order to protect their interest, financial institutions impose restrictive conditions on the borrowers. While the specific set of restrictive covenants depends on the nature of the project and the financial situation of the borrower, loan contracts often require that the borrowing firm:

- Broad-base its board of directors and finalise its management set-up in consultation with and to the satisfaction of the financial institutions.
- Make arrangements to bring additional funds in the form of unsecured loans/deposits for meeting overruns/shortfalls.
- Refrain from undertaking any new project and/or expansion or make any investment without the prior approval of the financial institutions.
- Obtain clearances and licences from various government agencies.
- Repay existing loans with the concurrence of the financial institutions.
- Refrain from additional borrowings or seek the consent of financial institutions for additional borrowings.

Further, loan agreements impose restrictions on the transfer of shareholding by promoters/ associates.

Term Loan Procedure

The procedure associated with a term loan involves the following steps:

Submission of Loan Application The borrower submits an application form which seeks comprehensive information about the project. The application form covers the following aspects:

- Promoters' background
- Particulars of the industrial concern
- Particulars of the project (capacity, process, technical arrangements, management, location, land and buildings, plant and machinery, raw materials, effluents, labour, housing, and schedule of implementation)
- Cost of the project
- Means of financing
- Marketing and selling arrangements
- Profitability and cash flow
- Economic considerations
- Government consents

Initial Processing of Loan Application When the application is received, an officer of the financial institution reviews it to ascertain whether it is complete for processing. If it is incomplete, the borrower is asked to provide the required additional information. When the application is considered complete, the financial institution prepares a 'Flash Report' which is essentially a summarisation of the loan application. On the basis of the 'Flash Report', it is decided whether the project justifies a detailed appraisal or not.

Appraisal of the Proposed Project The detailed appraisal of the project covers the marketing, technical, financial, managerial, and economic aspects. The appraisal memorandum is normally prepared within two months after site inspection. Based on that a decision is taken whether the project will be accepted or not.

Issue of the Letter of Sanction If the project is accepted, a financial letter of sanction is issued to the borrower. This communicates to the borrower the assistance sanctioned and the terms and conditions relating thereto.

Acceptance of the Terms and Conditions by the Borrowing Unit On receiving the letter of sanction from the financial institution, the borrowing unit convenes its board meeting at which the terms and conditions associated with the letter of sanction are accepted and an appropriate resolution is passed to that effect. The acceptance of the terms and conditions has to be conveyed to the financial institution within a stipulated period.

Execution of Loan Agreement The financial institution, after receiving the letter of acceptance from the borrower, sends the draft of the agreement to the borrower to be executed by authorised persons and properly stamped as per the Indian Stamp Act, 1899. The agreement, properly executed and stamped, along with other documents as required by the financial institution must be returned to it. Once the financial institution also signs the agreement, it becomes effective.

Creation of Security The term loans (both rupee and foreign currency) and the deferred payment guarantee assistance provided by the financial institutions are secured through the first mortgage, by way of deposit of title deeds, of immovable properties and hypothecation of movable properties. As the creation of mortgage, particularly in the case of land, tends to be a time consuming process, the institutions permit interim disbursements.[6] The mortgage, however, has to be created within a year from the date of the first disbursement. Otherwise the borrower has to pay an additional charge of 1 percent interest.

Disbursement of Loans Periodically, the borrower is required to submit information on the physical progress of the projects, financial status of the project, arrangements made for financing the project, contribution made by the promoters, projected funds flow statement, compliance with various statutory requirements, and fulfillment of the pre-disbursement conditions. Based on the information provided by the borrower, the financial institution will determine the amount of term loan to be disbursed from time to time. Before the entire term loan is disbursed, the borrower must fully comply with all terms and conditions of the loan agreement.

---

[6] The interim security, prior to the creation of the final security, usually comprises all the stipulated security, but the mortgage.

Monitoring Monitoring of the project is done at the implementation stage as well as at the operational stage. During the implementation stage, the project is monitored through: (i) regular reports, furnished by the company, which provide information about placement of orders, construction of buildings, procurement of plant, installation of plant and machinery, trial production, etc, (ii) periodic site visits, (iii) discussion with promoters, bankers, suppliers, creditors, and others connected with the project, (iv) progress reports submitted by the nominee directors, and (v) audited accounts of the company.

During the operational stage, the project is monitored with the help of (i) quarterly performance reports on the project, (ii) site inspection, (iii) reports of nominee directors, and (iv) comparison of performance with promise.

The most important aspect of monitoring, of course, is the timely recovery of dues represented by interest and principal repayment.

Syndicated Loans Syndication is an arrangement wherein several banks participate in a single loan. The corporate seeking a syndicated loan chooses a lead bank to manage the same. The lead bank prepares an information memorandum which is sent to other banks potentially interested in participating in the syndicated loan. Based on the interest evinced by the participating banks, the lead bank works out the sharing arrangement.

While bilateral loans are preferred for small ticket loans, syndicated loans are becoming popular for large ticket loan. For example, IDBI Bank lead managed a ₹6,000 crore syndicated loan for HINDALCO in 2005. The loan has a tenor of 10 years with a re-set after five years. Thirty banks participated in this loan which was priced at five-year G-sec yield plus 65 basis points.

How is loan syndication different from consortium financing which was popular earlier? Consortium financing involved a presentation to be given by the company to a group of bankers and was more rule based. Further, under a consortium arrangement, participating banks offered other services like letter of credit, working capital credit, guarantees and so on and interacted regularly with the company.

18.9 WORKING CAPITAL ADVANCES

Working capital advance by commercial banks represents the most important source for financing current assets.

Forms of Bank Finance

Working capital advance is provided by commercial banks in three primary ways: (i) cash credits/overdrafts, (ii) loans, and (iii) purchase/discount of bills. In addition to these direct forms, commercial banks help their customers in obtaining credit from other sources through the letter of credit arrangement.

Cash Credits/Overdrafts Under a cash credit or overdraft arrangement, a pre-determined limit for borrowing is specified by the bank. The borrower can draw as often as required provided the outstanding does not exceed the cash credit/overdraft limit, subject to the availability of adequate security. The borrower also enjoys the facility for repaying the amount, partially or fully, as and when he desires. Interest is charged only on the running balance, and not on the limit sanctioned. A minimum charge may be payable irrespective of the level of borrowing, for availing of this facility. This form of advance is highly attractive from the borrower's point of view because while the borrower has the freedom of drawing the amount in parts as and when required, interest is payable only on the amount actually outstanding.

Loans These are advances of fixed amounts to the borrower. The borrower is charged with interest on the entire loan amount, irrespective of how much he draws. In this respect, this system differs markedly from the overdraft or cash credit arrangement wherein interest is payable only on the amount actually utilised. Loans are payable either on demand or in periodical instalments. When payable on demand, loans are supported by a demand promissory note executed by the borrower.

Purchase/Discount of Bills A bill usually arises out of a trade transaction. The seller of goods draws the bill on the purchaser. The bill may be either clean or documentary (a documentary bill is supported by a document of title to goods like a railway receipt or a bill of lading) and may be payable on demand or after a usance period. On acceptance of the bill by the purchaser, the seller offers it to the bank for discount/purchase. When the bank discounts/purchases the bill, it releases the funds to the seller. The bank presents the bill to the purchaser (the acceptor of the bill) on the due date and gets its payment.

Letter of Credit A letter of credit is an arrangement whereby a bank helps its customer to obtain credit from its (customer's) suppliers. When a bank opens a letter of credit in favour of its customer for some specific purchases, the bank undertakes the responsibility to honour the obligation of its customer, should the customer fail to do so.

• Application and Processing

A customer seeking an advance is required to submit an appropriate application form—there are different types of application forms for different categories of advances. The information furnished in the application covers, *inter alia*, the following: the name and address of the borrower and his establishment; the details of the borrower's business; the nature and amount of security offered. The application form has to be supported by various ancillary statements like the financial statements and financial projections of the firm.

The application is processed by the branch manager. This primarily involves an examination of the following factors: (i) ability, integrity, and experience of the borrower in the particular business, (ii) general prospects of the borrower's business, (iii) purpose of advance, (iv) requirement of the borrower and its reasonableness, (v) adequacy of the margin, (vi) provision of security, and (vii) period of repayment and repayment capacity.

• Sanction and Terms and Conditions

Once the application is duly processed, it is put up for sanction to the appropriate authority. The sanctioning powers of various officials—like Branch Manager, Regional Manager, General Manager, etc.—are defined by virtue of the position they occupy.

If the sanction is given by the appropriate authority, along with the sanction of advance, the bank specifies the terms and conditions applicable to the advance. These usually cover the following: (i) the amount of loan or the maximum limit of the advance, (ii) the nature of the advance, (iii) the period for which the advance will be valid, (iv) the rate of interest applicable to the advance, (v) the primary security to be charged, (vi) the insurance of the security, (vii) the details of the collateral security, if any, to be provided, (viii) the margin to be maintained, and (ix) other restrictions or obligations on the part of the borrower. It is a common banking practice to incorporate important terms and conditions on a stamped security document to be executed by the borrower. This helps the bank to create the required charge on the security offered and also obligates the borrower to observe the stipulated terms and conditions.

• Security

For working capital advances, commercial banks seek primary security either in the form of hypothecation or in the form of pledge.

Hypothecation Under this arrangement, the owner of the goods borrows money against the security of movable property, usually inventories. The owner does not part with the possession of property. The rights of the lender (hypothecatee) depend upon the arrangement between the lender and the borrower. Should the borrower default in paying his dues, the lender (hypothecatee) can file a suit to realise his dues by selling the goods hypothecated.

Pledge In a pledge arrangement, the owner of the goods (pledgor) deposits the goods with the lender (pledgee) as security for the borrowing. Transfer of possession of goods is a precondition for pledge. The lender (pledgee) is expected to take reasonable care of goods pledged with him. The pledge contract gives the lender (pledgee) the right to sell goods and recover dues, should the borrower (pledgor) default in paying debt.

• Margin Amount

Banks do not provide hundred percent finance. They insist that the customer should bring a portion of the required finance from other sources as margin amount. The margin amount is determined taking into account the type of security offered, the riskiness of the project, the value of business connection, and so on.

18.10 MISCELLANEOUS SOURCES

Apart from the sources of finance mentioned earlier, there are several other ways in which finance may be obtained. These include:

- Deferred credit
- Lease and hire purchase finance
- Unsecured loans and deposits
- Special schemes of institutions
- Subsidies and sales tax deferments and exemptions
- Short-term loans from financial institutions
- Commercial paper
- Factoring
- Securitisation

Deferred Credit

Many a time the suppliers of machinery provide deferred credit facility under which payment for the purchase of machinery is made over a period of time. The interest rate on deferred credit and the period of payment vary rather widely. Normally, the supplier of machinery, when he offers deferred credit facility, insists that a bank guarantee should be furnished by the buyer.

Lease Finance and Hire Purchase

Leasing and hire purchase are currently a supplementary form of debt finance.

Lease Finance A lease represents a contractual arrangement whereby the lessor grants the lessee the right to use an asset in return for periodic lease rental payments. While leasing of land, buildings, and animals has been known from times immemorial, the leasing of industrial equipments is a relatively recent phenomenon, particularly on the Indian scene.

There are two broad types of lease: finance lease and operating lease. A *finance lease* or capital lease is essentially a form of borrowing. Its salient features are:

- It is an intermediate term to long-term non-cancellable arrangement. During the initial lease period, referred to as the 'primary lease period', which is usually three years or five years or eight years, the lease cannot be cancelled.
- The lease is more or less fully amortised during the primary lease period. This means that during this period, the lessor recovers, through the lease rentals, his investment in the equipment along with an acceptable rate of return. Thus, a finance lease transfers substantially all the risks and rewards incident to ownership to the lessee.
- The lessee is responsible for maintenance, insurance, and taxes.
- The lessee usually enjoys the option for renewing the lease for further periods at substantially reduced lease rentals.

An *operating lease* can be defined as any lease other than a finance lease. The salient features of an operating lease are:

- The lease term is significantly less than the economic life of the equipment.
- The lessee enjoys the right to terminate the lease at a short notice without any significant penalty.
- The lessor usually provides the operating know-how and the related services and undertakes the responsibility of insuring and maintaining the equipment. Such an operating lease is called a 'wet lease'. An operating lease where the lessee bears the costs of insuring and maintaining the leased equipment is called a 'dry lease'.

From the above features of an operating lease it is evident that this form of a lease does not result in a substantial transfer of the risks and rewards of ownership from the lessor to the lessee. The lessor structuring an operating lease transaction has to depend upon multiple leases or on the realisation of a substantial resale value (on expiry of the first lease) to recover the investment cost plus a reasonable rate of return thereon. Therefore, specialising in operating lease calls for an in-depth knowledge of the equipments and the secondary (resale) market for such equipments. Of course, the prerequisite is the existence of a resale market.

Given the fact that the resale market for most of the used capital equipments in our country lacks breadth, operating leases are not in popular use. In recent years there have been attempts to structure car lease and computer lease transactions in the operating lease format.

At present, the following are the key features of lease finance in India:

- Most leases in India are finance leases, not operating leases
- Lease finance is available for identifiable performing assets
- Lease finance is available in small volume
- There is a great deal of flexibility in structuring lease finance
- Lease of immovable assets is not possible by banks
- Lease tenors up to eight years is available

Hire-Purchase Finance companies usually offer the facility of leasing as well as hire-purchase to its clients. What are the features of a hire-purchase arrangement? How are hire-purchase instalments split between interest and principal payments? How should the potential user of an asset choose between leasing and hire-purchase?

The main features of a hire-purchase arrangement are as follows:

- The hiree (the counterpart of lessor) purchases the asset and gives it on hire to the hirer (the counterpart of lessee).
- The hirer pays regular hire–purchase instalments over a specified period of time. These instalments cover interest as well as principal repayment. When the hirer pays the last instalment, the title of the asset is transferred from the hiree to the hirer.
- The hiree charges interest on a flat basis. This means that a certain rate of interest, usually around 8 percent, is charged on the initial investment (made by the hiree) and not on the diminishing balance.
- The total interest collected by the hiree is allocated over various years. For this purpose, the 'sum of the years digits' method is commonly employed.

The following differences between leasing and hire–purchase, from the point of view of the lessee (hirer), may be noted.

Leasing	*Hire-Purchase*
■ The lessee cannot claim depreciation	■ The hirer is entitled to claim depreciation.
■ The entire lease rental is a tax-deductible expense for the lessee.	■ Only the interest component of the hire-purchase instalments is a tax- deductible expense for the hirer.
■ The lessee, not being the owner of the asset, does not enjoy the salvage value of the asset.	■ The hirer, being the owner of the asset, enjoys the salvage value of the asset.

Instalment Purchase An instalment purchase is similar to hire purchase in the sense that the buyer pays for the purchase by way of instalments over a period of time. However, there is one important difference. In a hire purchase arrangements, the title of the asset is transferred from the hiree to the hirer when the hirer pays the last instalment. But, in an instalment purchase arrangement, the title of the asset is passed to the buyer on payment of the first instalment itself. In case of default, the seller can force the buyer to sell the asset and make good the remaining instalments.

• Unsecured Loans and Deposits

Unsecured loans are typically provided by the promoters to fill the gap between the promoters' contribution required by financial institutions and the equity capital subscribed to by the promoters. These loans are subordinated to the institutional loans. The rate of interest chargeable on these loans is required to be less than the rate of interest on the institutional loans. Finally these loans cannot be repaid without the prior approval of the financial institutions.

Deposits from the public, referred to as public deposits, represent unsecured borrowing of one to three years (five years in the case of non-banking finance companies) duration. Many existing companies prefer to raise public deposits instead of term loans from financial institutions because restrictive covenants do not accompany public deposits. However, it may not be possible for a new company to raise public deposits. Further, it may be difficult for it to repay public deposits within three years.

• Special Schemes of Institutions

Financial institutions have designed special schemes to serve the varied needs of industry. The important ones are:

Bill Rediscounting Scheme Operated by the IDBI, the bill rediscounting scheme is meant to promote the sale of indigenous machinery on deferred payment basis. Under this scheme, the seller realises the sale proceeds by discounting the bills or promissory notes accepted by the buyer with a commercial bank which in turn rediscounts them with the IDBI. This scheme is meant primarily for balancing equipment and machinery required for expansion, modernisation, and replacement schemes.

Suppliers' Line of Credit Administered by the ICICI, the Suppliers' Line of Credit is somewhat similar to the IDBI's Bill Rediscounting Scheme. Under this arrangement, ICICI directly pays to the machinery manufacturer against usance bills duly accepted or guaranteed by the bank of the purchaser.

• Subsidies and Sales Tax Deferments and Exemptions

Governments and development agencies may provide subsidies for certain kinds of projects. Of late, however, these have decreased in importance. Previously, the central government as well as the state governments provided subsidies to industrial units located in backward areas. The central subsidy has been discontinued but the state subsidies continue. The state subsidies vary between 5 percent to 25 percent of the fixed capital investment in the project, subject to a ceiling varying between ₹0.5 million and ₹2.5 million depending on the location.

To attract industries, the states provide incentives, *inter alia*, in the form of sales tax deferments and sales tax exemptions.

Under the sales tax deferment scheme, the payment of sales tax on the sale of finished goods may be deferred for a period ranging between five to twelve years. Essentially it implies that the project gets an interest-free loan, represented by the quantum of sales tax deferred, during the deferment period.

Under the sales tax exemption scheme, some states exempt the payment of sales tax applicable on purchases of raw materials, consumables, packing, and processing materials from within the state which are used for manufacturing purposes. The period of exemption ranges from three to nine years depending upon the state and the specific location of the project within the state.

• Short-term Loans from Financial Institutions

Financial institutions provide short-term loans to companies with a good track record. To be eligible for such a loan, a company must satisfy certain conditions relating to dividend track record, debt-equity ratio, current ratio, and interest coverage ratio.

Short-term loans provided by financial institutions have the following features:

- They are totally unsecured and are given on the strength of a demand promissory note.
- The loan is given for a period of one year and can be renewed for two consecutive years, provided the original eligibility criteria are satisfied.

• Commercial Paper

A commercial paper represents a short-term unsecured promissory note issued by firms which enjoy a fairly high credit rating. Generally, large firms with considerable financial strength are able to issue commercial paper. The important features of commercial paper are as follows:

- The maturity period of commercial paper ranges from 90 to 180 days.
- Commercial paper is sold at a discount from its face value and redeemed at its face value. Hence the implicit interest rate is a function of the size of the discount and the period of maturity.
- Commercial paper is directly placed with investors who mostly intend holding it till its maturity. Hence there is no well developed secondary market for commercial paper.

• Factoring

A factor is a financial institution which offers services relating to management and financing of debts arising from credit sales. While factoring is well-established in western countries, only two factors, the SBI Factoring and Commercial Services Limited and Canbank Factoring Limited, which have been mandated by the Reserve Bank of India to operate in the western region and the southern region respectively, have made some tangible progress. The Punjab National Bank and the Bank of Allahabad are expected to set up factoring agencies to serve northern region and the eastern region, respectively.

Features of a Factoring Arrangement The key features of a factoring arrangement are as follows:

- The factor selects the accounts of the client that would be handled by it and establishes, along with the client, the credit limits applicable to the selected accounts.
- The factor assumes responsibility for collecting the debt of accounts handled by it. For each account, the factor pays to the client at the end of the credit period or when the account is collected, whichever comes earlier.
- The factor advances money to the client against not-yet-collected and not-yet-due debts. Typically, the amount advanced is 70 to 80 percent of the face value of the debt and carries an interest rate which may be equal to or marginally higher than the lending rate of commercial banks.
- Factoring may be on a recourse basis (this means that the credit risk is borne by the client) or on a non-recourse basis (this means that the credit risk is borne by the factor). Presently, factoring in India is done on a recourse basis.
- Besides the interest on advances against debt, the factor charges a commission which may be 1 to 2 percent of the face value of the debts factored.

Securitisation

Securitisation involves packaging a designated pool of assets (mortgage loans, consumer loans, hire purchase receivables, and so on) and issuing securities which are collateralised by the underlying assets and their associated cash flow stream. Securitisation is originated by a firm that seeks to liquefy its pool of assets. Securities backed by mortgage loans are referred to as *mortgage backed securities;* securities backed by other assets are called *asset based securities.*

Key Steps in Securitisation Securitisation can take place in different ways and assume complex structures. Broadly, the following steps are involved in a securitisation programme:

1. **Seasoning** The originator (the firm that seeks to liquefy its assets) identifies the assets to be securitised and packages them in a pool.
2. **Credit Enhancement** The originator or some other agency may enhance the credit quality of the pool of assets to be securitised by providing insurance, often of a limited kind, to the investors.
3. **Transfer to a Special Purpose Vehicle** The pool of assets is transferred to a Special Purpose Vehicle (SPV), usually organised as a Trust, for valuable consideration. Once the transfer is completed, the assets are taken off the balance sheet of the originator.
4. **Issuance of Securities** The SPV issues securities backed by the pool of assets held by it. These securities are called Pass Through Certificates (PTCs) because the cash flows received from the pool of assets are transmitted (passed) to the holders of these securities on a pro-rata basis after deduction of service fee. There may be one or more classes of PTCs with differing priorities. Where there are two or more classes of PTCs, the rules for the distribution of interest and principal repayments, derived from the underlying pool of assets, among different classes of PTC holders are specified upfront.

18.11 RAISING VENTURE CAPITAL

A young company that is not yet ready or willing to tap the public financial market may seek venture capital. Such capital is provided by venture capital funds which are prepared to finance an untried company that appears to have promising prospects. Venture capital represents financial investment in a risky proposition made in the hope of earning a high rate of return.

Preparing a Business Plan

If you are approaching a venture capitalist to finance your project, how should you prepare your business plan? Here are some guidelines:

- Use simple and clear language. Avoid bombastic presentation and technical language.
- Focus on four basic elements, viz. people, product, market, and competition.
- Give projections for about two to five years with emphasis on cash flows.
- Identify risks and develop a strategy to cope with the same.
- Convince them that the management team is talented, experienced, committed, and determined.

18.12 RAISING CAPITAL IN INTERNATIONAL MARKETS

Thanks to the globalisation of capital markets, Indian firms can raise capital from euromarkets or from the domestic markets of various countries or from export credit agencies.

Euromarkets

The term euromarkets seems to be a misnomer because they do not have a physical location. *Euromarkets,* more accurately offshore markets, refer to a collection of international banks that help firms in raising capital in a global market which is beyond the purview of any national regulatory body.

An Indian firm can access the euromarkets to raise a eurocurrency loan or issue a euro bond or issue global depository receipts or issue eurocurrency convertible bonds.

Eurocurrency Loans Subject to certain terms and conditions, the Government of India permits Indian firms to resort to external commercial borrowings for the import of plant and machinery. The most common instrument of external commercial borrowing is the *eurocurrency loan.*

A eurocurrency is simply a deposit of currency in a bank outside the country of the currency. For example, a eurodollar is a dollar deposit in a bank outside the US. Likewise, a euroyen is a yen deposited in a bank outside Japan. How do eurocurrency deposits arise? This may be explained with an example. Suppose an American oil company buys oil from a Sheikh in the Middle East and pays US $10 million drawn on the Chase Manhattan Bank and the Sheikh deposits the cheque in his account with a Swiss bank. The dollar deposit, placed outside the United States, the country of the dollar currency, is a eurodollar deposit. The Swiss bank can use this deposit for granting eurodollar loans.

The main features of eurocurrency loans, which represent the principal form of external commercial borrowings are:

- Eurocurrency loans are often syndicated loans, wherein a group of lenders, particularly banks, participate jointly in the process of lending under a single loan agreement. The syndicate of lenders is represented by the lead bank. The borrower is required to pay a syndication fee, which is a front-end payment, usually ranging between ½ percent and 2 percent, to the lead bank. This represents the management fees payable to the lead bank, participation fee to the other banks, and other charges.
- The rate of interest on eurocurrency loans is a floating rate. It is usually linked to LIBOR (London Inter Bank Offer Rate) or SIBOR (Singapore Inter Bank Offer Rate). The spread over the LIBOR or SIBOR rate is mainly a function of the creditworthiness of the borrower and size of the loan. Air India International, for example, obtained a eurodollar loan of US $88 million in 1982, at an interest rate of 3/8 percent above the LIBOR. While the rate is determined at the beginning of each interest period, the interest is payable at the end of each period.
- The interest period may be 3, 6, 9, or 12 months in duration. It is largely left to the option of the borrower.
- The borrower often enjoys the multi-currency option which enables it to denominate the interest and principal in the new currency opted for. This option is exercisable at the end of each interest period.
- The eurocurrency loans are repayable in a bullet payment or in instalments, which are typically equal, over a period of time as agreed to by the parties. The borrower may prepay the loan after giving due notice to the lead bank. When prepayment is done, some premium is payable. The lender may also reserve the right to recall the outstanding loan under certain circumstances.

The features of eurocurrency loans are illustrated by the following example.

Syndicated Eurocurrency Loans Raised by Power Finance Corporation

	1st Issue (January 1997)	*2nd Issue (July 1998)*
Amount Initially Targeted	US $ 50 million	US $ 100 million
Amount Actually Collected	US $ 75 million	US $ 100 million
Actual Pricing	50 bp over LIBOR	115 bp* over LIBOR
Maturity	Average five years	Seven years put 5
Repayment Terms	Repayment in 5 equal installments after end of four years	Bullet
Other Costs (approx.)	0.07 bps annualised	0.20 bps annualised
Lenders Meet/Roadshows	Hong Kong, Singapore	Bombay, Bahrain, London, Singapore
Availability Period	60 days from date of signing	30 days from date of signing
Number of Participating Banks	Fourteen	Fourteen
Lead Manager	Nat West Markets	ANZ Investment Bank

* One basis point (bp) is one -hundredth of one percent.

Evaluation Overseas debt, particularly in the form of eurocurrency loans, offers the following advantages:

- Participating institutions have deep pockets and a very professional approach.
- There is a great deal of flexibility in structuring these loans.
- Tenors up to 10 years are easily available.

The disadvantages of overseas debt are:

- It is not economical for small projects due to high appraisal and syndication costs.
- Pricing of loans depends on risk perception.
- It may be difficult to negotiate changes with investors.

Eurocurrency Bonds Firms using the euromarkets for debt financing can take out loans (called eurocurrency loans) or sell bonds (referred to as eurocurrency bonds). The important features of a eurocurrency bond are:

- It is issued outside the country in whose currency it is denominated. For example, eurodollar bonds are sold outside the US and euroyen bonds are sold outside Japan.
- It is usually managed by a syndicate of investment banks and offered to investors in many countries.
- It is a bearer bond. This means that it is unregistered and payable to the person who carries it.
- The interest on it is usually paid annually or half-yearly.

While the eurocurrency loan is the most popular form of external commercial borrowing, some firms have raised money by issuing eurocurrency bonds (or eurocurrency notes). Power Finance Corporation, for example, raised overseas debt by issuing euronotes in 1997 that had the following features:

Power Finance Corporation Limited
Euro Notes Issue

- Amount : US $ 100 million
- Maturity Period : 12 years bullet
- Interest rate : 7.5% p.a. fixed (135 bp over US Treasury) payable half yearly
- Type of Instrument : Unsecured Global Bond Issue tradable in stock exchanges abroad.
- Other Costs (approx.) : .02 bp annualised
- Lenders Meet/Roadshows : Hong Kong, USA, UK
- Availability Period : On signing
- Lead Manager : ING Barings
- Other Agents : Paying agent, Listing agent, Trustee

Note that the lending rates in the eurodebt market tend to be lower than those in domestic markets. Why? There are several reasons. First, on eurodeposits, banks have no reserve requirements. Second, borrowers in eurocurrency market are typically large, reputed companies with good credit ratings. Third, banks price these loans aggressively as there are no regulators.

Global Depository Receipts From the early 1990s, Indian companies have issued global depository receipts (GDRs), which represent indirect equity investment, in the euromarkets.

In the depository receipts mechanism, the shares issued by a firm are held by a depository, usually a large international bank, who receives dividends, reports, etc. and issues claims against these shares. These claims are called depository receipts—in euromarkets they are called GDRs—with each receipt being a claim on a specified number of shares. The underlying shares are called *depository shares*. The GDRs are denominated in a convertible currency—usually US dollars. GDRs may be listed and traded on major stock exchanges or may trade in the OTC market. The issuer firm pays dividends in its home currency which is converted into dollars by the depository and distributed to the holders of GDRs. This way the issuing firm avoids listing fees and onerous disclosure and reporting requirements which would be obligatory if it were to be directly listed on the stock exchange. Holders of GDR can convert them into the underlying share by surrendering the depository receipts to the depository.

A company planning a GDR issue must obtain the approval from the Ministry of Finance as well as the FIPB (Foreign Investment Promotion Board) since GDR issues are deemed to be foreign direct investment. The government periodically issues guidelines for GDR issues. These guidelines set out the criteria a potential issuer must satisfy, the permissible uses of the funds raised, and the manner in which the funds are to be deployed till the issuing company is ready to use them. The custodian is required to be an Indian institution.

• Foreign Domestic Markets

A second way to raise money internationally is to sell securities directly in the domestic capital markets of foreign countries. This is referred to as direct issuance. For example, a British firm may issue dollar-denominated equity stocks in the US capital market or a German firm may issue yen-denominated bonds in the Japanese capital market. A foreign issuer has to satisfy all regulations applicable to domestic firms. In addition, it may be required to fulfill certain special obligations applicable to foreign issuers.

Indian firms can also issue bonds and equities in the domestic capital market of a foreign country. In recent years, Indian firms have tapped the domestic capital markets of countries like the US, Japan, UK, and Switzerland.

US Capital Market The US capital market is the largest national capital market, complemented by a very active derivatives market. The most prestigious funding option in the US market is a public issue of *Yankee Bonds* (dollar denominated bonds issued in the US capital market by foreign borrowers). A public issue of Yankee bonds has to comply with stringent listing requirements of the SEC in the US. Yankee bonds can also be offered on a private placement basis to QIBs (qualified institutional buyers) under what is popularly known as rule 144A. Such bonds do not have to comply with the stringent listing requirements under the Securities Act, 1933. Reliance Industries Limited was perhaps the first Indian company to issue Yankee bonds in the US.

Apart from tapping the US bond market, Indian companies can raise funds in the US equity market by issuing American Depository Shares (ADSs). Like GDRs, ADSs represent claims on a specific number of shares. The principal difference between the two is that the GDRs are issued in the euromarket whereas ADSs are issued in the US domestic capital market.

Other Markets Besides the US domestic capital market, Indian companies have tapped the domestic capital markets of other countries such as Japan and UK, issuing mainly debt instruments such as *Samurai Bonds* (publicly issued bonds in the Japanese market), *Shibosai Bonds* (privately issued bonds in the Japanese market), *Bulldog Bonds* (UK market), and *Rembrant Bonds* (Dutch market).

Export Credit Schemes

Export credit agencies have been established by the governments of major industrialised countries for financing exports of capital goods and related technical services. The prominent export credit agencies are US EXIM, JEXIM, HERMES, and COFACE. These agencies follow certain consensus guidelines for supporting exports under a convention known as the Berne Union. As per these guidelines, the interest rate applicable for export credits to Indian companies for various maturities are regulated. Two kinds of export credit are provided: buyer's credit and supplier's credit.

Buyer's Credit Under this arrangement, credit is provided directly to the Indian buyer for purchase of capital goods and/or technical services from the overseas exporter. The buyer's credit facility operates as follows:

- The overseas exporter and the Indian buyer negotiate a contract.
- An application for the buyer's credit facility is made to the export credit agency of the exporter's country along with relevant details (like the types of goods/services to be exported, approximate value of the contract, terms of payments, schedule of projected shipment of goods or provision of services, percentage of financing required, etc.).
- The buyer's credit facility is approved by the export credit agency of the exporter's country.
- A loan agreement delineating the terms and conditions of the buyer's credit is negotiated between the overseas exporter's bank, the Indian borrower, and where applicable the Indian guarantor.

Supplier's Credit This is a credit provided to the overseas exporters so that they can make available medium-term finance to Indian importers. The supplier's credit facility operates as follows:

- The overseas exporter notifies his bank and the export credit agency of a potential export order of an Indian buyer who requires medium-term finance.
- The export credit agency communicates to the bank its willingness to provide the facility.
- The terms of the facility are incorporated in the contract between the overseas exporter and the Indian buyer.

Salient Features The salient features of finance provided by export credit agencies are:

- The finance is tied to import of goods and services
- Up to 85 percent of the value of imports is available as finance.
- The finance is available for long tenors at reasonable cost.
- Export credit agencies insist on a bank guarantee.

Financing of Non-Manufacturing Businesses

Non-manufacturing businesses, such as trading and service businesses, do not normally, in their earlier stages, involve investment in real estate. They tend to be essentially working capital intensive and/or knowledge intensive. Hence they are financed mainly by way of equity and working capital borrowings. In addition, their requirements of assets such as furniture and office equipment, vehicles, and material handling systems are met through asset financing arrangements such as leasing, hire purchase, and instalment purchase.

As these businesses expand, on the strength of profitable performance, they may invest in land, buildings, warehouses, and other fixed assets. To support such investment they may rely on long-term borrowings as well.

18.13 PROJECT FINANCING STRUCTURES

Two principal project financing structures have evolved over the years: full recourse structure and limited recourse structure.

• Full Resource Structure

Traditionally, project financing involved "full recourse" asset-backed lending. The salient features of a "full recourse" financing structure are as follows:

- If a new company is set up for implementing the project, the proposed borrowings for the project are fully secured by a first charge on all the existing and future assets of the borrowing company, by way of mortgage of immovable assets and hypothecation of current assets. If the project is implemented as an expansion or diversification project of an existing company, which already has lenders with charges on assets, the lenders for the new project get a *pari passu* charge on the entire block of assets, including the assets of the new project. Put differently, the existing and proposed assets are thrown into a common pool on which new and existing lenders acquire rights that are proportional to the amounts financed by them.
- Although the viability of the proposed project is assessed on a stand-alone basis, the cash flows from the existing as well as proposed activities are considered to judge whether the existing as well as the proposed debt can be serviced.
- Apart from the charge on the assets, the project sponsors provide personal guarantee for debt servicing. Further, in some cases the lenders may insist on a corporate guarantee from a group company.

• Limited Recourse Structure

Private sector participation in infrastructure projects, a relatively new phenomenon on the Indian scene, has been accompanied by a limited recourse, cash-flow based financing structure, in line with international practice. The salient features of this structure are as follows:

- The project is set up at as a separate company, called a Special Purpose Vehicle (SPV). The SPV is not supposed to handle any other business activity without the prior approval of the lenders.
- The private sector promoter who sponsors the project usually takes a substantial stake in the equity of the project and enjoys the over-all responsibility for running the project.
- The sponsor provides standby support for cost overruns in the project, provided the quantum of such support is crystallised prior to the financial closure.
- The security package for the lenders includes a registered mortgage/hypothecation of all assets, a pledge of sponsor holdings in the SPV, an assignment of all project contracts and documents, and a charge on future receivables.
- The cash flow of the SPV is handled by an independent agent (acting on behalf of the security trustee). The cash flow is allocated in a pre-determined manner to various requirements including debt servicing. After all the requirements are met, the residual cash flow is available to the project company.
- In some cases, the payment risk is mitigated by a state or central government guarantee.
- Lenders do not have recourse to the sponsors and their other businesses.
- Being a separate entity, the SPV is bankruptcy remote from the other businesses of the sponsor.

18.14 FINANCIAL CLOSURE

Financial closure means that all the sources of funds required for the project have been tied up. A key milestone in project implementation, financial closure may take a long time, particularly for infrastructure projects, because several things have to be sorted out to make the project structure fundable. For example, it took about three years to hammer out a model power purchase agreement to be signed by the independent power producers with the respective state electricity boards.

In general, financial closure is achieved soon when:

- Suitable credit enhancement is done to the satisfaction of lenders.
- Adequate underwriting arrangements are made for market-related offerings.
- The resourcefulness of the promoters is well established.
- The process is started early and concurrent appraisal is initiated if several lending agencies are involved.

18.15 FINANCIAL INSTITUTIONS: WHAT INFORMATION THEY WANT AND HOW THEY APPRAISE

This section describes the information sought by financial institutions and the dimensions along which financial institution appraise a project.

• Information to be Furnished for Term Loan Appraisals Along With the Project Report/Information Memorandum[7]

Most of the financial institutions both at the state and national level have very detailed application forms which seek elaborate details of various aspects of the borrowing company, the promoters, and the project. The loan application can be prepared by attaching additional enclosures wherever necessary or by preparation of a separate Project Report. The standard information to be furnished by the borrowing company is as follows:

Particulars	*Enclosures*
(a) Name of the company, constitution, registered office, list of the promoters, shareholding pattern, paid up capital, licensed and installed capacity, name of auditors, bankers, location and particulars of production facilities, number of employees etc.	1. Memorandum & Articles 2. List of Directors 3. IT and WT returns for the past three years of the company and promoters 4. Bankers' references 5. Board resolution 6. Shareholder resolutions for 239(1) (d)
(b) Details of the present activities of the company, past financial performance, details of associated companies and their performances.	1. Past audited accounts for three years of the company and associated entities. 2. Details of existing term loans, unsecured loans and existing charge holders. 3. Group company details with Annual Reports. 4. Banker's Report on the company and the main promoters 5. Copies of income tax returns filed by main promoters 6. NOC for ceding exclusive/pari passu charge from the existing charge holders
(c) Promoters and management structure and profiles of whole time directors and key management personnel	1. Details of Shareholders Agreement and copies thereof. 2. Details of Board of Directors, management and organisational set-up. 3. Copies of Joint Venture/technical collaboration agreement, if any 4. Banker's report on Foreign Collaborator 5. Employment contracts with MD/ Whole time directors

(*Contd.*)

[7] This section has been extracted from the book *Investment Banking* by Pratap Subramanyam, published by Tata McGraw-Hill Publishing Company.

Particulars	*Enclosures*
	6. Documents to substantiate the proposed promoter's contribution 7. Names of promoters who would furnish personal guarantees and net worth statement of promoters
(d) Particulars of the project 1. Cost break-up 2. Proposed financing pattern 3. Products and uses 4. Key raw materials and sourcing arrangements 5. Location and justification 6. Technology arrangements and equipment sourcing 7. Manpower requirement and availability 8. Details of utilities and arrangements 9. Schedule of implementation 10. Statutory approvals obtained and to be obtained	1. Copies of Statutory approvals such as RBI/FIPB approval, industrial license if required. 2. Clearance from the Ministry of Environment and Forests for larger projects costing above ₹1500 crore 3. Other regulatory clearances from CEA/TRAI/ERC or other such authorities 4. State level government approvals and application for NOC from Pollution Control Board 5. Key documents such as copies of title deeds of land, location map, copies of key project contracts, collaboration or technology agreements 6. Back-up documents justifying the estimation of cost of the project such as civil work estimates, quotations for machinery, etc. 7. In case of second hand machinery, a chartered engineer's certificate regarding the residual life of the machines 8. Fuel supply/raw material sourcing agreement 9. Details of tie-up for marketing, firm enquiries if any and buy-back agreements 10. Sources of market information 11. Details of orders on hand, supply schedules, etc. 12. Details of effluents produced and measures for treatment and discharge
(e) Financial workings for the project justifying the viability of the project.	1. Detailed bases of assumptions made for the workings and back-up statements.

• Project Appraisal

Financial institutions appraise a project from the marketing, technical, financial, economic, and managerial angles. The principal issues considered and the criteria employed in such appraisal are discussed below.

Market Appraisal The importance of the potential market and the need to develop a suitable marketing strategy cannot be over-emphasised. Hence efforts are made to:

- Examine the reasonableness of the demand projections by utilising the findings of available surveys, industry association projections, and independent market surveys (which may sometimes be commissioned).
- Assess the adequacy of the marketing infrastructure in terms of promotional effort, distribution network, transport facilities, stock levels, etc.
- Judge the knowledge, experience, and competence of the key marketing personnel.

Technical Appraisal The technical review done by the financial institutions focuses mainly on the following aspects:

- Product mix
- Capacity
- Process of manufacture
- Engineering know-how and technical collaboration
- Raw materials and consumables
- Location and site
- Building
- Plant and equipments
- Manpower requirements
- Break-even point

The technical review is done by qualified and experienced personnel available in the institutions and/or outside experts (particularly where large and technologically sophisticated projects are involved).

Financial Appraisal The financial appraisal seeks to assess the following:

Reasonableness of the Estimate of Capital Cost While assessing the capital cost estimates, efforts are made to ensure that (a) padding or under-estimation of costs is avoided, (b) specification of machinery is proper, (c) proper quotations are obtained from potential suppliers, (d) contingencies are provided, and (e) inflation factors are considered.

Reasonableness of the Estimate of Working Results The estimate of working results is sought to be based on (a) a realistic market demand forecast, (b) price computations for inputs and outputs that are based on current quotations and inflationary factors, (c) an approximate time schedule for capacity utilisation, and (d) cost projections that distinguish between fixed and variable costs.

Adequacy of Rate of Return The general norms for financial desirability are as follows:

- Internal rate of return : 15% or 3–5% more than WACC
- Return on investment : 20–25 percent after tax
- Debt-service coverage ratio : 1.5 to 1.75

In applying these norms, however, a certain degree of flexibility is shown on the basis of the nature of the project, the risks inherent in the project, and the status of the promoter.

Appropriateness of the Financing Pattern The institutions consider the following in assessing the financing pattern:

- A general debt-equity ratio norm of 1 : 1
- A requirement that promoters should contribute a certain percentage of the project cost (30-50 percent)
- Stock exchange listing requirements
- The means of the promoter and his capacity to contribute a reasonable share of the project finance

Economic Appraisal The economic appraisal looks at the project from the larger social point of view. The methodology adopted by the financial institutions for the purpose of economic appraisal (also referred to as social cost benefit analysis) is labeled as 'Partial Little Mirrlees' approach. In addition to the calculation of the economic rate of return as per this approach, they also look at two other economic indicators: (i) effective rate of protection, and (ii) domestic resource cost. Admittedly, the economic appraisal done by financial institutions is not very rigorous and sophisticated. Also, the emphasis placed on this appraisal is rather limited.

Managerial Appraisal In order to judge the managerial capability of the promoters, the following questions are raised:

How resourceful are the promoters?
How sound is the understanding of the project by the promoters?
How committed are the promoters?

Resourcefulness This is judged in terms of the prior experience of the promoters and the progress achieved in organising various aspects of the project.

Understanding This is assessed in terms of the credibility of the project plan (including inter alia, the organisation structure, the staffing plan, the estimated costs, the financing pattern, the assessment of various inputs, and the marketing programme) and the details furnished to the financial institutions.

Some Norms of Financing

While hammering out the financing structure of a business, the following norms should generally be borne in mind.

1. Generally, the debt–equity ratio should not exceed 1:1 for service companies, 2:1 for manufacturing companies, and 4:1 for infrastructure companies.
2. Secured loans should normally have a fixed assets coverage ratio (FACR) of 1.25:1.
3. The annual debt-service coverage ratio (DSCR) should be at least 1.5.
4. The 'total outside liabilities' to 'total net worth,' i.e., TOL/TNW, ratio should not exceed 3:1.
5. Current liabilities including working capital borrowings are not more than 75 percent of current assets.

Commitment This is gauged by the resources (financial, managerial, material, and other) applied to the project and the zeal with which the objectives of the project, short-term as well as long-term, are pursued. Managerial appraisal also involves an assessment of the calibre of the key technical and managerial personnel working on the projects, the schedule for training them, and the remuneration structure for rewarding and motivating them.

18.16 CREDIT RISK RATING[8]

Credit risk rating is a rating assigned by a bank to its borrowers based on an analysis of their ability and willingness to repay the debt. It covers various parameters like financials, management, business and industry.

RBI guidelines require banks to have a comprehensive risk rating system that serves as a single point indicator of diverse risk factors. Such a system calls for substantial degree of standardisation in ratings across borrowers. Also, subjectivity, which is an unavoidable factor in any lending decision, is sought to be kept at a minimum in credit risk rating systems. Banks can use the rating for taking credit decisions in a consistent manner, as a valuable/primary input in pricing of loans and for purposes of review by management, Basel II accord also mandates that banks desirous of minimising their capital adequacy requirements should have a proper credit risk rating system in place.

The rating models followed by different banks vary in details and possibly on the emphasis laid on the different risk factors. Also, over time, the models will undergo changes in the light of new experiences, changes in assessment methodology in response to regulatory requirements, and so on. For instance, large banks in India will eventually incorporate factors like the probability of default to comply with the requirements of the latest Basel accord.

Salient Features

The salient features of the rating systems presently followed by banks in India are as follows:

1. For large loans, companies usually submit detailed actual and projected operating and financial data in a set of forms called the CMA format. A detailed analysis of this data together with all other needed information is then done and scores are awarded on various risk parameters.
2. To qualify for rating, the company will have to first come clean on certain aspects: the conduct of the account should be satisfactory; there should not be instances of wilful default; there should not be any corporate governance or environmental issues; the management should possess the minimum needed commitment and competence; there should be no audit remarks casting aspersion on integrity and so on.
3. The rating is usually done across the following dimensions.
   - *Financial risk*: For existing borrowers financial risk carries nearly 50 percent of the total weightage, whereas for new borrowers it carries nearly 25 to 40 percent of

[8] This section has been contributed by Pradip Lath.

the total weightage. Assessment of financial risk relies mainly on financial ratio analysis. In addition, future prospects of the borrower as well as risk mitigation by way of collateral security or financial standing are considered.

- *Business and industry risk*: This usually gets about half the weightage given to financial risk for existing borrowers while for new businesses, understandably, the weightage is on par with financial risk. Product quality and acceptance, cash flow pattern, capacity utilisation, competition, industry outlook, regulatory issues, and the impact of WTO are some of the factors considered.
- *Management Risk*: For new borrowers this is the major risk, carrying a weightage of nearly fifty percent. It is evaluated in terms of management's integrity, credibility, competence, commitment, structure, and so on. Existing borrowers with good track record, experience, and so on will normally get a higher score.

4. A minimum fifty percent score is generally set as the hurdle rate for sanction of new credit facilities or for continuation of existing ones. The rating exercise is an ongoing one and the RBI guidelines want the banks to do this on a half yearly basis quite independent of the ritual of periodic renewal of credit facilities. In practice though, it is, at best, an annual exercise.

• Key Financial Ratios

For evaluating financial risk, the following ratios are most commonly considered.

For Working Capital Loans	***For Term Loans***
■ Current ratio	■ Project debt-equity ratio.
■ Total outside liabilities / Tangible net worth (TOL/TNW)	■ TOL / TNW
■ Profit after tax / Net sales	■ Gross average debt service coverage ratio of project and all loans separately.
■ Profit before depreciation interest and tax / Interest	■ Term of payments in years
■ Return on capital employed	■ Return on capital employed
■ Current assets turnover	■ Fixed asset coverage ratio

In addition, there are other financials like the availability of collaterals and guarantees which are common to all credit facilities including non-fund based support.

SUMMARY

- A capital project may be regarded as a mini-firm. So the issues to be considered in financing a project are identical to those considered in financing a business firm.
- Although the number of complex and exotic financing instruments is expanding, the financing decision, compared to the investment decision, is relatively easier to make and has a lesser impact on value.

- The two broad sources of finance available to a firm are: shareholders' funds (equity funds) and loan funds (debt funds).
- The key factors in determining the debt-equity ratio for a project are: cost, nature of assets, business risk, norms of lenders, control considerations, and market conditions.
- A firm should use more equity when the corporate tax rate is negligible, the business risk exposure is high, the dilution of control is not an important issue, the assets of the firm are mostly intangible in nature, and the firm has many valuable growth options. The firm should use more debt under opposite circumstances.
- When a company is formed, it first issues equity shares to the promoters (founders) and also, in most cases, to a select group of investors. As the company grows, it may rely on the following methods of raising equity capital: initial public offering, seasoned offering, rights issue, and private placement.
- The internal accruals of a firm consist of depreciation charges and retained earnings.
- Equity and debt come in a variety of forms and are raised in different ways.
- Equity capital represents ownership capital as equity shareholders collectively own the firm. Equity shareholders enjoy the rewards as well as bear the risk of ownership.
- The rights of equity shareholders consist of: (i) the right to residual income, (ii) the right to control, (iii) the pre-emptive right to purchase additional equity shares issued by the firm, and (iv) the residual claim over assets in the event of liquidation.
- The first public offering of equity shares of a company, which is followed by a listing of its shares on the market, is called an initial public offering (IPO). A public issue by a listed company is called a seasoned offering. A rights issue involves selling securities in the primary market by issuing rights to the existing shareholders. Private placement involves sale of securities to a limited number of sophisticated investors such as financial institutions, mutual funds, venture capital funds, banks, and so on.
- Preference capital represents a hybrid form of financing—it partakes some characteristics of equity and some attributes of debentures.
- For large firms, debentures are a viable alternative to term loans. Debentures are instruments for raising debt finance. Debentures often provide more flexibility than term loans as they offer greater choice with respect to maturity, interest rate, security, repayment, and special features.
- Thanks to the latitude enjoyed by companies, a variety of debt instruments like deep discount bonds, convertible debentures, floating rate bonds, secured premium notes, and indexed bonds have been employed.
- Term loans represent a source of debt finance which is generally repayable in less than 10 years. They are typically employed to finance acquisition of fixed assets and working capital margin.
- Financial institutions give rupee term loans as well as foreign currency term loans. Term loans represent secured borrowing. Usually assets, which are financed with the term loan, provide the prime security. Other assets of the firm or promoters may serve as collateral security. The principal amount of a term loan is generally repayable over a period of four to seven years after an initial grace period of one to two years. In order to protect their interest, financial institutions impose restrictive covenants on the borrowers.

- Financial institutions appraise a project from the marketing, technical, financial, economic, and managerial angles.
- Working capital advance by commercial banks represents the most important source for financing current assets. Working capital advance is provided by commercial banks in three primary ways: (i) cash credits/overdrafts, (ii) loans, and (iii) purchase/discount of bills.
- Apart from the principal sources like equity, internal accruals, term loans, debentures, and working capital advance there are several other ways in which finance may be obtained. These include deferred credit, lease finance, hire purchase, unsecured loans and deposits, special schemes of institutions, subsidies, sales tax deferments and exemptions, commercial paper, factoring, and securitisation.
- A young company that is not yet ready or willing to tap the public financial market may seek venture capital which represents financial investment in a risky proposition made in the hope of earning a high rate of return.
- Thanks to globalisation of capital markets, Indian firms can raise capital from euromarkets or from the domestic markets of various countries or from export credit agencies.
- Euromarkets refer to a collection of international banks that help firms in raising capital in a global market which is beyond the purview of any national regulatory body.
- An Indian firm can access the euromarkets to raise a eurocurrency loan or issue a eurobond.
- Eurocurrency loans, which represent the principal form of external commercial borrowings are syndicated loans carrying a floating rate generally linked to LIBOR.
- While the eurocurrency loan is the most popular form of external commercial borrowing, Indian firms also raise money by issuing eurocurrency bonds (or notes).
- From early 1990s, Indian companies have issued global depository receipts (GDRs), which represent indirect equity investment, in the euromarkets.
- Indian firms can also issue bonds and equities in the domestic capital market of a foreign country.
- Export credit agencies have been established by the governments of major industrialised countries for financing exports of capital goods and related services. Two kinds of export credit are provided: buyer's credit and supplier's credit.
- Two principal project financing structures have evolved over the years: full recourse structure and limited recourse structure.
- Financial closure means that all the sources of funds required for a project are tied up.
- Financial institutions appraise a project from the marketing, technical, financial, economic, and managerial angles.
- Credit risk rating is a rating assigned by a bank to its borrowers based on an analysis of their ability and willingness to repay the debt.

QUESTIONS

1. Discuss the key considerations in determining the debt-equity ratio of a firm.
2. When should a firm use more equity and when should a firm use more debt?
3. Discuss the rights of equity shareholders.
4. What are the pros and cons of going public?
5. List the principal steps involved in a public issue.
6. Describe briefly a rights issue and a private placement.
7. How do the three methods of raising finance, viz. public issue, rights issue, and private placement differ.
8. What are the advantages and disadvantages of equity capital?
9. What are the advantages and disadvantages of internal accruals?
10. Discuss the key features of term loans.
11. Describe the procedure involved in obtaining a term loan.
12. Discuss the key issues considered by financial institutions while appraising a project for term financing.
13. What are the features of debentures?
14. Describe the important innovations in debenture.
15. Discuss the conventional and modern finance explanations for convertible debentures.
16. Why is private placement of debentures so common in India?
17. What are the advantages and disadvantages of debt financing?
18. Describe the various ways in which banks provide working capital advance.
19. What are the salient features of a finance lease and an operating lease?
20. Discuss the features of hire purchase. How does it differ from leasing?
21. What are the features of commercial paper? factoring?
22. Discuss the guidelines for preparing a business plan to be given to a venture capitalist.
23. What are the main features of eurocurrency loans and eurobonds?
24. What is a GDR?
25. Discuss how the export credit schemes operate.
26. Describe the salient features of: (a) full recourse structure, and (b) limited recourse structure in project financing.
27. What are the principal issues considered and the criteria employed by financial institutions in appraising projects.
28. Discuss the salient features of the rating systems presently followed by banks in India.

MINICASE

Consider the following situations.

A. Vikram, Naresh, and Ravi worked in the R&D centre of a multinational company in Bangalore for about five years. Bitten by the entrepreneurial bug, they quit their jobs recently and set up a company called VNR Informatics Private Limited with the immediate object of developing a software product for the telecom sector. At present the company has an equity capital of ₹1.5 crore contributed equally by the three promoters. According to the business plan for the proposed software product, the company needs additional financing of ₹1.5 crore.

B. Manas Textiles, a leading producer of cotton fabrics, is based in Ahmedabad. Nearly three-fourths of its production is exported to customers in the U.S. The company's plant and equipment have been financed to the extent of 50 percent by a consortium of lenders, who are not inclined as of now to increase their exposure to the company as the company went through debt restructuring sometime back. The company buys its inputs in cash but offers 90 days credit to its customers in the U.S. Thanks to a recent spurt in export sales, the company needs ₹50 crore of additional financing.

C. Bharat Oil Company needs ₹150 crore for doing test drilling in a certain block awarded to it by the Government of India. If the outcome of the test drilling is favourable, Bharat Oil Company will require ₹350 crore for developing the site. As per the latest balance sheet, the total assets of Bharat Oil Company are ₹2500 crore. The market price per share of the company is ₹270 and the earnings per share are ₹30. Other firms in the oil industry sell at an earnings multiple between 11 and 13. Bharat Oil Company's debt-equity ratio is 30 percent, compared to the industry's average of 40 percent.

D. ADCL is a movie production company set up by three persons with experience in the movie industry about six years ago. One of them is a leading star and he owns 50 percent equity of ADCL; the other two own 25 percent each. ADCL's recent movie, *The Indian Dream* turned out to be a blockbuster at the box office. Enthused by this success, the promoters want to double the number of movies produced by the company. To achieve this goal the company plans to raise ₹50 crore from external sources.

E. Tasty Foods Private Limited runs a chain of food stores in western India. It is owned by three Patil brothers each of whom holds one-third equity in the company. Though profitable, the company is experiencing financial strain due to its rapid growth rate. Its real estate is mortgaged, its inventories are hypothecated, and its debtors are largely factored. Presently the company has ₹20 crore of total assets. It needs equipment costing ₹2 crore for its shipping department.

Required

Suggest the financing method that seems most appropriate for each situation and give your reasons for the same.

APPENDIX 18A

TYPES OF CHARGES CREATED ON ASSETS FOR SECURING ADVANCES

The types of charges created on assets for securing advances are as follows:

- Pledge
- Hypothecation
- Mortgage
- Assignment of debt
- Lien

Pledge The salient features of a pledge are:

(i) The ownership of the asset remains with the borrower (pledger) but the possession of the asset is in the hands of the lender (pledge).

(ii) The lender hands over the possession of the asset to the borrower when the loan is fully repaid.

(iii) The lender enjoys the "right of sale" if the loan is not repaid, after giving proper notice to the borrower.

(iv) The lender is expected to take care of the asset pledged. The borrower is required to execute an "Agreement to Pledge."

Hypothecation Under hypothecation, the possession of the asset remains with the borrower. In case the borrower defaults, the lender has the right to take possession of the hypothecated asset and sell it to realise the dues. However, before doing that the lender has to, unlike in the case of pledge, file a suit and take the permission of the court. The hypothecation charge is created by the borrower by executing a "Deed of Hypothecation" in favour of the lender.

Mortgage While movable assets can be pledged or hypothecated, immovable assets such as land and buildings can only be mortgaged. As in the case of hypothecation, the ownership and possession remain with the borrower (mortgagor) but the lender (mortgagee) gets the right to take possession and sell the mortgaged property after filing a suit and getting permission from the court. If the mortgage deed expressly authorises the mortgagee to sell the property without filing a suit, the mortgagee can sell the property without the intervention of court. Although there are many types of mortgage, the most common ones are the registered mortgage and the equitable mortgage.

A **registered mortgage** is one which is registered with the Registrar of Properties. The Registrar will record the mortgage in the land records which is made known to anyone who checks the land records. While the registered mortgage is the most secure way of creating a charge over an immovable property, it entails stamp duty, payable by the borrower, which can be a substantial sum. The lender should satisfy himself that the property is not charged to anyone else, by requesting the Registrar of Properties to issue a Non-Encumbrance Certificate. The Non-Encumbrance Certificate issued by the Registrar states all the subsisting chargers created on the property during the past 30 years. The lender should also ensure that the property is registered in the name of the owner in the records of the municipality/panchayat and property taxes have been paid up to date.

Under **equitable mortgage** (EM), no stamped deed of mortgage is prepared or registered. The mortgage is created by the borrower by handing over the title deed, katha (or a document evidencing that the name of the owner is recorded in the municipal or panchayat records), and the latest tax paid receipt. Of course, the bank will have to get the title verified and get a Non-Encumbrance Certificate, before accepting the documents in creation of the mortgage. The advantage of an EM is that it can be easily executed on plain paper and it does not involve stamp cost. The disadvantage is that the creation of mortgage is not noted in the land records maintained by the Registrar of Properties and the future buyers of the property will not be aware of the existence of mortgage in favour of the bank.

Assignment of Debt While tangible assets are pledged or hypothecated or mortgaged, "actionable claims" are charged to a lender through a "Deed of Assignment." An "actionable claim" represents a right to claim an amount from another person. Examples of actionable claims are (a) debts or receivables, (b) amounts receivable under an Insurance Policy, (c) amounts receivable under a legally valid contract such as a guarantee or indemnity, and (d) subsidies or duty drawbacks or any other amount receivable from the government.

The person who assigns the actionable claim is called the assignor and the person in whose favor the actionable claim is assigned is called the assignee. The assignor retains the ownership and possession of the actionable claim. The assignee gets the right to recover the same.

There are two types of assignment: legal assignment and equitable assignment. In a *legal assignment*, the assignor executes a deed of assignment in favour of the assignee. Banks create such a charge when they give loans against life insurance policies. In an *equitable assignment*, the assignor executes an irrevocable power of attorney (POA) in favor of the assignee (say a bank) to collect payment. For example, in bill purchase and bill discounting the invoice is accompanied by a bill of exchange which gives the bank the authority to demand payment from the drawee.

Lien A "lien" is the right to hold another's property till the debt is repaid. Banks enjoy the right of general lien, meaning that in the absence of any specific document or charge, banks can exercise the right of lien on any asset of the borrower which comes into their possession. According to section 171 of the Indian Contract Act, 1872 "Bankers may, in the absence of a contract to the contrary retain as a security for a general balance of account any goods bailed to them".

APPENDIX 18B

DUE DILIGENCE REVIEW

Due diligence has been defined as "a measure of prudence, activity, or assiduity, as is properly to be expected from, and ordinarily exercised by, a reasonable and prudent person under the particular circumstances, not measured by any absolute standard but depends on the relative facts of the special case".

For corporate investments, a due diligence review (DDR) involves a comprehensive examination of the representations and affairs of the company by potential investors so that an informed decision can be taken. DDR is normally broken down into three parts: (a) Business, commercial, and technical DDR; (b) Financial DDR; and (c) Legal DDR.

The business, commercial, and technical DDR is generally conducted by the potential investors themselves, thanks to their in-house expertise and industry network. Occasionally, they may engage technical consultants.

The financial DDR involves verifying the books of account, financial statements, and business transactions of the company to determine how true and fair are the financial statements of the company and how accurate are the oral and written representations (as given in the information memorandum and other literature) of the company. The financial DDR may almost tantamount to the financial audit of the firm and is carried out for the past three years or so. In some cases, financial DDR may also involve vetting the financial forecast of the company as provided in the information memorandum. The financial DDR is carried out by an accounting firm or an investment bank, on behalf of the potential investor.

The legal DDR covers the legal aspects of the business and includes, *inter alia*, the IPRs of the company, material contracts and agreements of the companies with third parties and the legal implications thereof, statutory compliance under various laws and defaults, if any, and outstanding litigations and their possible consequences. The legal DDR is generally conducted by a law firm—a part of the work may be contracted out to a practising company secretary or covered in the financial DDR.

Based on the DDR report that the potential investor typically regards as a confidential report, the investor may seek clarifications or explanations from the company.

The company that seeks finance from a potential investor has to provide information for the DDR exercise. Typically, it sets up a 'Data Room,' where all the information required by the agency conducting the DDR is made available. Nowadays, companies set up a 'Virtual Data Room' which gives a web-enabled access to DDR information and documents to the authorised agencies. The information to be furnished by a company for financial and legal due diligence will, inter alia, cover the following: capital and shareholding, details of the group, details of promoters and directors, details of secured and unsecured borrowings, minutes of board and general meetings, books of account, financial statements, and audit reports, direct and indirect taxes, capital WIP and capitalisations, HR, labour law compliance and retirement benefits, other statutory compliances, outstanding litigations, material agreements and contracts, and financial forecasts. Naturally, a company contemplating a transaction has to be well prepared for a DDR exercise.

Chapter 19 Venture Capital and Private Equity[1]

LEARNING OBJECTIVES

After studying this chapter you should be able to

- Distinguish between VC financing and conventional financing.
- Discuss how a VC assesses the business and management.
- Explain how a VC values the equity shares of the investee company.
- Compare VC with private equity.
- Describe the key elements of regulation of VC industry in India.
- Discuss the current concerns of the Indian VC industry.

A young private company that is not yet ready or willing to tap the public financial markets may seek venture capital (VC) or private equity (PE). While there are some differences between VC and PE, there is considerable overlap between the two in practice. So much so, in most countries these terms are used interchangeably. Hence most of the discussion of this chapter will apply to VC as well as PE, though for the sake of convenience the term VC will be used frequently. Such capital is provided by VC or PE funds, which are prepared to finance risky projects that have promising prospects.

While the concept of VC is many centuries old, the practice of VC remained somewhat fragmented and individualised throughout the long history. Only in the last six decades or so, the field of VC has acquired a certain degree of coalescence, maturity and sophistication, particularly in the USA.

VC is a relatively recent phenomenon on the Indian scene and has emerged as one of the much talked about financing alternatives in India over the past two decades.

This chapter discusses various aspects of VC. Throughout the discussion the VC investor is referred to as the "investor," the company that receives VC funding as the "investee" or, simply, the "company," the management of the company as "management" or "management-team" and the portfolio of investments of the VC investor as the "portfolio."

19.1 VC INVESTORS

A variety of financial institutions, corporations, and individuals provide venture capital. The most significant among these investors are VC funds.

[1] This chapter has been contributed by Professor G. Sabarinathan of IIM, Bangalore.

VC funds may be described as funds constituted into distinct pools of capital for investment in relatively high-risk opportunities in anticipation of potentially high rates of return. These funds are usually committed for predefined and limited periods of time, ranging from seven to twelve years. At the end of the period the investments are liquidated and the capital is returned to the investor, with any capital appreciation thereon. Investors in these funds are usually interested in long-term capital appreciation and not short-term gains or periodic returns by way of dividend or interest. Most VC funds are not listed on any exchange; nor do they have an alternate secondary market mechanism worth mentioning. Investments in these funds are therefore usually illiquid in the initial years. Investors in VC funds are institutional investors and high net worth individuals who have the ability and the preparedness to accept the illiquidity. VC funds are usually mostly *independent* in the sense that they do not represent or subserve the strategic interests of any of the investors in these funds. Their primary objective is to produce a financial return for the investors in the fund. This last criterion is important as it helps companies who raise capital from VC funds to be sure that they can function independently, without the fear of being "controlled" by another business interest group.

Managers of VC funds charge investors a fixed annual fee, usually 2% of the capital under management. Further, fund managers retain 20% of the capital gain (carried interest) realised from the investments.[2] The share of the capital gain provides an incentive to the fund manager to maximise the value of the portfolio and aligns the interests of the fund manager with that of the investors in the fund.

The constitution of VC funds and the unique compensation mechanism for managers of these funds, as outlined above, considerably influence the investment strategy of VC funds.

19.2 WHAT IS A VC INVESTMENT

The popular impression is that VC is synonymous with the financing of technology centric businesses or innovative and hitherto untried business ideas. In reality VC is a broader and much more flexible form of financing business enterprises. A better understanding of the broad scope of VC could be conveyed by the following examples of some typical VC investments that have been made in different countries in the past.

- A national or regional chain of stores across India, based on a new retailing concept such as retailing of office supplies.
- A company which produces programmes for television channels.
- A Chinese manufacturer of hand tools who competes in the international market on the basis of operational efficiencies and low cost, without compromising on quality.
- An African exporter of processed horticultural produce.
- A popular India retail brand of groceries.
- An Indian manufacture of industrial products primarily for high voltage applications.
- An auto ancillary engaged in manufacture of forged and machined components.

Common to these examples are exceptional growth prospects and a sustainable competitive advantage that helps maintain growth in sales and profitability, which could potentially result in superior returns to the investor.

A survey of the literature on VC, including practitioner accounts, industry association definitions and academic publications, indicates that VC investments usually involve:

- Businesses with high growth potential in terms of sales and profitability.
- Medium to long term investment horizons or holding periods ranging from two to ten years.
- Risk levels higher than those inherent in debt financing or investment in equities of well-established firms with a history of profitable operations.
- Equity or quasi-equity financing instruments which enable the investor to participate in the risk and the financial upside of the enterprise.
- Active investor involvement in the management of the investee after the funding.

19.3 WHAT MAKES A VC INVESTMENT DIFFERENT

VC investments differ from traditional loan transactions or investments in the equity of a well-established firm, listed on a stock exchange. In this section we examine some of the more important distinguishing features.

High Uncertainty Levels VC investors usually fund companies that are exposed to higher degrees of uncertainty. Resolving the uncertainty affecting these firms is rendered more complex by the absence of historical information on the operations of the enterprise.

The sources of risk and uncertainty in a venture investment are many more and complex than in most other investment opportunities. These risks include:

1. *Technology risk:* The risk that a product, process or service based on a hitherto untried technology may fail to perform as expected.
2. *Product market risk:* The risk that sales volume or price realisation of a product may be lower than expected due to poor customer acceptance of the product or unforeseeable competitive conditions.
3. *Management risk:* The risk that the management team may not have the capability to deliver the results projected in the business plan. Historically, from practitioner accounts, management failure appears to have been the single most important reason for failure of VC backed enterprises. In turn, the failure of the management could be due to a host of reasons ranging from just lack of competence to more serious issues such as the inability of the team members to stick together in running the business or even lack of integrity.
4. *Liquidity risk*: The risk that the VC investor may not be able to encash his investment. VC funds mostly invest in unlisted companies. Unless the shares of these companies are successfully listed and traded on a stock exchange, or the companies are acquired, the investment in these companies could turn out to be illiquid. Illiquidity risk emanates from weak conditions in the capital market, or because investors do not consider the company or industry to be financially attractive.

Information Disclosure Public companies in India whose shares are listed on a stock exchange are mandated to disclose copious amounts of information under the Companies Act 2013 as well as by the Securities and Exchange Board of India (SEBI, hereafter) Regulations. Unlisted companies, which VC investors fund, are subject to the disclosure requirements under the Indian Companies Act 2013. These disclosures are less frequent than those required in the case of listed enterprises and cover a smaller gamut of information. Further, companies in the early stage of evolution are not organisationally equipped to provide all the financial and business information that investors may wish to have.

19.4 THE VC INVESTMENT APPRAISAL PROCESS AND MANAGEMENT

We look at the key elements of the investment management process within a VC fund as a transaction evolves through the various stages of a deal.

Assessment of Business and Management The VC investment process commences with a meeting with the promoters and the key members of the management team of the company. This is followed by a critical evaluation of the business plan by the personnel of the fund. The plan articulates the vision of the promoters and top management of the company over the investment horizon. It spells out the firm's strategy in much greater detail.[2]

The emphasis in the evaluation process is on the following aspects.

Management Team VC fund managers realise that the key to building a successful company is an effective and top class management team. The VC investor's appraisal process lays considerable emphasis on the evaluation of the management team of the company for its leadership ability, integrity, completeness in terms of skills to manage various functional areas, and their cohesiveness as a team. As the company develops, VC investors prepare themselves to even bring about changes in the management team if and when the incumbent team fails to deliver. At the same time, experienced investors also recognise that such changes are painful to bring about; as such, it is well worth the effort to ensure that the company has the right management team to start with.

Business Strategy VC investors spend a great deal of time seeking answers to broad strategic questions such as:

- What is the value proposition that the company's product or service offers? Can it be understood by the end user in simple terms?
- Is there a felt long term need for the company's product? Is there a sizeable market?
- Does the investee firm have a sustainable competitive advantage? What is the source of the competitive advantage?
- What is the revenue model of the company?

[2] In more recent times the business plan has morphed into various different formats. Entrepreneurs present the essential elements of an idea in high powered presentations that make more active use of contemporary audio visual and digital communication technologies. An even more contemporary alternative to the business plan is the Lean Canvas. The Lean Canvas builds on the idea of Lean Startups. More on Lean Startups at http://www. http://theleanstartup.com

- What are the operating economics of the business? Is it a scalable business?
- Is the investment opportunity consistent with the VC fund's investment philosophy and strategy? Can the partners in the fund add value to the investee company?
- How valuable will the company in question be over the investor's holding period?

It may be observed that the common drift among the questions above is an attempt to assess whether the company, over a three to five year period, will have a sizeable share of a large market, based on an unassailable, competitive position, and consequently produce a super normal growth in profit and shareholder wealth.

Given the levels of uncertainty surrounding a VC backed company and the lack of quality data, VC investors do not place much emphasis on complex quantitative analyses of the prospective financial position of a VC backed company. The VC investor develops a set of several broad business – and corresponding financial – scenarios such as a base case and one optimistic and pessimistic scenario. He then applies his judgement to form a view on the most likely financial picture of the company over the expected investment horizon.

Exit Focus Most VC investors manage funds with a limited life, as mentioned earlier. That limits them to look at investments with finite holding periods. (The common means of disinvestment are discussed later in this note.). The VC investor tends to assess the prospects of and the likely means to liquidate his investment, right at the time of committing the investment. Absent a clear path to liquidity, the VC investor is reluctant to commit capital to the company.

Valuation of a VC Transaction All aspects of the VC transaction process are equal in importance; but it would be fair to argue that valuation is more equal than the others in terms of importance. Valuation is the process by which the investor decides the price he wishes to pay for the equity shares of the investee company. (For the purposes of this discussion we assume that the deal is being structured as subscription to equity shares.)

The most commonly used method of valuation used by VC funds involves the following steps:

1. Identify the amount of capital to be invested by the investor.
2. Identify the target rate of return expected by the investor. These rates are usually based on rough-and-ready return estimates, taking into account the stage of investment (such as seed, startup, etc.), the expected holding period, and the level of risk perceived in the investment by the investor.
3. Estimate the multiple of the original investment that will fetch the required rate of return over the anticipated holding period. For example, a 25% compounded annual rate of return over a four year holding period would translate into a multiple of 2.44 times the original investment.
4. Project the market value of the firm based on performance expected in the targeted year of exit. This involves multiplication of an appropriate metric such as Earnings Per Share (EPS) or Earnings Before Interest Depreciation, Tax and Amortisation (EBIDTA) by a multiple number that reflects the valuation that investors may be willing to pay (or may have paid) in other recent transactions.

5. Estimate the percentage of the projected value of the equity of the firm that the investor needs to own in order to achieve his return objective. This will also be the percentage of the company's equity that the investor would needs to own at the time of exiting from the investment in order to realise his return objectives.

Illustration SVC Capital is considering an investment of ₹20 million in Vidya Technologies, an educational venture. SVC Capital has a target rate of return of 30 percent per annum from this venture and its planned holding period is 4 years. Vidya Technologies has projected a PAT of ₹15 million for year 4, which SVC Capital finds reasonable. SVC Capital believes that a P/E multiple of 12 for year 4 to be reasonable. What percentage of the equity of Vidya Technologies should SVC Capital own at the time of exit to realise it return objective?

- SVC Capital's investment in Vidya Technologies should grow to:
  ₹20 million $(1.30)^4$ = ₹87.12 million
- The projected value of Vidya Technologies at the end of the 4-year holding period is:
  ₹15 million × 12 = ₹180 million
- The percentage of the equity of Vidya Technologies that SVC Capital must own at the time of exit is: ₹57.12 million/ ₹180 million = 32 percent.

The following observations are worth noting regarding the valuation approach described above:

1. The above approach assumes that the firm is all equity financed.
2. The valuation of the transaction can vary considerably depending on the choice of value for Profit After Tax (PAT), EBIDTA, Price/Earnings (P/E) ratio, P/E BIDTA ratio and choice of comparable firms, etc.
3. Investors in an earlier round of financing end up with a lower percentage shareholding than they start off with, as the firm issues new equity in subsequent rounds of financing. This phenomenon is known as dilution of share ownership. This does not mean that the value of the investment goes down. Early stage investors start with a higher percentage of equity so as to provide for such potential dilution. Estimating such dilution involves estimating the amount of capital the company is likely to raise in future and the price at which these rounds of financing would be raised and requires a large dose of judgment.

The valuation of deals is influenced by the following factors.

Outlook for the Economy Other things being equal, a positive outlook for the overall economy influences investors to pay a higher price for a given investment opportunity. A healthy economy helps companies do well and also leads to higher valuations at the time of exit and therefore higher valuations at the time of making the investment.

Capital Market Conditions A buoyant stock market appears to influence investors to pay liberal valuations because it suggests better prospects for higher exit valuations for the VC investor. Equally, in some markets buoyant stock markets could also end up financing companies that are ideally candidates for growth capital funding from VCs and PE investors.

Thus buoyant stock markets can increase valuations at the time of entry by playing the role of a substitute for VC.

Industry Related Factors From time to time investors seem to prefer certain sectors over others. Such preference is reflected in the price that shares of companies in that sector command. This trend has been observed across many VC markets, including the American market.

Deal Related Factors The specifics of the investment opportunity in question also influence the valuation of the investment opportunity. Such factors will include the stage of investment, the sources of risk, product or service differentiation and other factors that could affect the company's competitive position.

Demand for and Supply of Capital Many analysts and practitioners seem to believe that excessive liquidity or supply of capital can push valuations up to unhealthy levels, resulting in low portfolio returns for VC funds. The exuberance of VC investors in India in 1999–2000, in 2008–09, and more recently in 2015–16 could be attributed, among other factors, to a similar situation in supply of capital in India.

Deal Structuring Most VC transactions are structured as equity or equity linked instruments because of the elegance of equity shares as an instrument and their risk reward sharing features. However, structuring funding as equity subscription exposes the investor to liquidity risk. Further, equity investors also run the risk of getting locked into investments at a fixed price, arrived at on the basis of some anticipated financial performance. In case the company does not deliver the anticipated performance the VC investor will have overpaid for the investment. To avoid such a risk, investors structure their funding as convertible instruments. The price at which these instruments are converted into equity is often linked to the actual performance of the company, measured in terms of appropriate metrics such as EPS or EBIDTA that is agreed upon right in the beginning. The conversion mechanism provides an incentive to the management team to deliver projected, or even better-than-projected, performance since higher performance leads to a higher price paid by the investor (at the time of conversion) for the company's shares. The investor, in turn, gets to subscribe to shares at a price linked to the performance of the company.

While structuring a deal VC investors also build in performance incentives for management. These incentive mechanisms usually have one or more of the following features.

- Options to subscribe to additional equity shares in the company at attractive, low valuations or for consideration other than cash, so that founders and members of the management team may build up a sizeable share ownership in return for technological and/or managerial contribution.
- The incentives are tied to unambiguous pre-identified performance milestones such as profit measures, market value of the firm, or measures of operational performance such as successful product or technology development.

This powerful combination of incentive compensation and post financing involvement by the VC investor is considered to be key to the effectiveness of VC investors in building valuable portfolios. (We discuss post-financing involvement in a later section).

Stages of Pre-IPO Financing

There are various stages of pre-IPO financing for a business undertaking. A well-accepted classification of these stages is as follows:

1. **Seed money financing** A small amount of financing required to prove a concept or develop a product. It does not cover marketing.
2. **Start-up financing (Angel funding)** Financing for less than one-year old firms, mainly to meet marketing and product development expenditures.
3. **First-round financing (Venture funding)** Financing needed to begin sales and manufacturing after the start-up funds are exhausted.
4. **Second-round financing (Venture/PE funding)** Working capital funds required for a firm that is selling its product but still incurring losses.
5. **Third-round financing (PE funding)** Financing required by a firm that has already crossed the break-even point and is planning an expansion. This is also called growth funding.
6. **Fourth-round financing (PE funding)** Financing of a firm that is reached a size and stature that makes it a likely candidate to go public in 1–2 years time. It is also called late stage funding.

Generally, seed money financing is provided by the entrepreneur and his friends, start-up financing is provided by angel investors, first round financing is provided by venture capital funds, and subsequent round financing is largely provided by private equity funds. Generally, before the private equity investor steps in the funding is also known as early stage funding.

The Nature and Governance of Investor-Investee Relationship Once the investment has been made the VC investor spends considerable time supporting the management team of the investee. The VC industry refers to this as "value addition". The investor and investee are bound by the potential for mutual economic benefit: capital gain for the investor and funding and value addition for the investee. This post financing engagement helps in another way. Over time, the interests or motivation of the entrepreneur may diverge from that of the investor. For example, the investor will usually seek a timely exit through an IPO or trade sale. The entrepreneur may be keen to ensure his continued role in the management of the company. In the event of such divergence of interests, the investor may like to ensure that his interests prevail. Lastly, the high degree of uncertainty and riskiness of a VC transaction require the investor to respond to many exigencies in the company as it develops after the investor has disbursed the funds. All these eventualities cannot be envisaged at the time of or prior to the commitment of funds, despite the most thorough due diligence and appraisal process. Post financing engagement enables the investor to be equipped with the ability and the authority to be able to respond to these eventualities in the investee company.

The VC investor also recognises that the entrepreneur has an important advantage. As an "insider" he has a deeper insight into the business than the investor. Economists refer to this situation as information asymmetry. Information asymmetry increases the probability of wrong investment decisions by the investor. Unlike in a lending situation, where the loan is most of the time secured by some assets which the lender can dispose of to recover the loan dues in case of a default by the borrower, the VC investor's only option is to ensure that the company stays on track. The VC investor ensures that he has the contractual right to protect his interests in these situations by entering into an appropriate contract with the investee.

Post Financing Relationship The purposes of post financing engagement by the VC are twofold. First, to support the management team with strategic and managerial inputs so as to make the enterprise more valuable. Second, to provide oversight to ensure that the company is managed in line with the contracts governing the investment.

The investor accomplishes these through three levers of control. First, the investor contributes to strategic decisions such as constitution of the board, appointment of key managers, and strategy formulation and implementation. Further, he brings his understanding of the financial market to help the company with its financial strategy. As part of this engagement, the VC plays an active part in planning the Initial Public Offering (IPO) of the company's shares, wherever a company is likely to make an IPO. In many markets, including India, a reputed VC investor's share ownership of a company is viewed as a "certification" of the quality of the issuing company.

Second, VC investors write detailed investment agreements that allow them to control key areas of decision making such as expansion or restructuring of the capital base of the company (equity as well as debt), declaration of dividend, business expansion and diversification, formation of strategic partnerships, restructuring of the business in terms of hiving off or divesting existing businesses and so on. The investor participates in these decisions by nominating one or more directors to the Board of the company. In addition, the partner in a VC fund, who is responsible for the post investment engagement with the company, typically spends some time every month meeting with the CEO of the portfolio company and key members of the management team and discussing matters of strategic importance. The investor also reviews periodic financial information from the company. In some instances the partner from the VC fund assumes even executive responsibility as the CEO or Chairman of the Board.

Third, the VC investor wields considerable influence over the entrepreneur's conduct by influencing or controlling the continued availability of funds. If the VC investor threatens to cut off supply of funds, other VC investors would hesitate to invest in the company too, essentially choking the company of any VC funding.

It must however be pointed out that the style and extent of post financing involvement tends to vary across investment situations and funds. Interestingly, certain styles appear to be more widely prevalent in particular markets. These styles in turn appear to change or evolve over time. For example, in the Indian context, in the early years of the industry, investor's involvement appears to have been largely to protect the interests of the investor. Investor's nominees on the investee's board of directors appear to have engaged themselves in strategy formulation or key recruitments in a limited way. In recent years investment professionals who have had prior experience in building businesses either as managers or as entrepreneurs have been actively investing in the market. They, in turn, appear to take a more active part in managing the affairs of investee companies.

Exiting from Investments 'Exiting' from an investment is an important consideration for the investor.

The two most common exit routes for VC investors are disposal of shares on a stock exchange, once the shares are listed; and sale of the portfolio company or its assets to a strategic acquirer (also known as a "trade sale"). In a few instances, the investor sells his shares back to the founders or other incumbent principal shareholders of the company. Selling back to the promoters however is a less popular option among investors, given the limited capital appreciation that it can provide.

VC investors ensure at the time of committing the investment that there are one or more potential paths to exit from the investment. The investor may even articulate his exit expectations to the entrepreneur in some detail, right in the beginning. Further, investors provide for adequate measures to influence exit related decisions in the investment agreements.

19.5 VC AND PE – A COMPARISON

As noted earlier, there are several common characteristics between the institutions of VC and PE. Both of them invest in companies that would not be able to attract capital from public securities markets. They are both constituted as independent pools of capital, managed by fund management teams which have considerable financial incentives tied into the overall objective of maximising investor wealth. The investors in these funds are either large institutions such as pension funds or high net worth individuals who can afford to absorb the risk and illiquidity. Finally, both VC and PE believe in active oversight of their investments, armed with tightly written investment agreements that give them the contractual right to ensure good governance of the firms.

There are several differences however. PE investors, in contrast to VC, mostly invest in later stage opportunities. They invest in companies which have a substantial operating history in mature industries. These companies may often times have sizeable cash flows. They fund buyouts of companies from existing owners either to facilitate the retirement of the incumbent owners or to help rejuvenate the company's operations under a new management team. Quite often, irrespective of whether there is an ownership change or not, private equity investments are used to effect financial or operational restructuring of companies. Since they involve later stage businesses with large cash flows, PE investment packages may involve secured or unsecured debt, which is rare in VC transactions. These loans, which are often not investment grade, provide a higher yield than investment grade debt and are retired using the company's operating cash flows.

The extent and nature of risks in PE investments are understandably different from those in the case of VC. Product market risks in PE investments are limited to sales and profitability of the business and do not extend to such basic sources of risk such as non-performance of the product in the market or the acceptance of the product by customers. PE funded enterprises have full-fledged management teams and usually are not vulnerable to significant operational or manufacturing risks. Given these differences, the nature of involvement of the investor in the post investment phase is limited to oversight at the Board level, unlike the VC investor whose involvement is far more hands-on.

Finally, it must be noted that some of these distinctions are not as sharp as they may appear to be. Further, companies that raise their first round of funding from typical VC investors eventually raise their subsequent rounds from PE investors. Sometimes the VC investors who backed the enterprise in its earlier round participate in later rounds of funding alongside the new PE investors. Flipkart, the popular e-commerce enterprise raised a small first round of VC funding from Accel Partners, a typical VC fund. It went through many more rounds of follow on funding before it was eventually acquired by retailing giant Walmart. The large later rounds of funding were provided by typical later stage, PE style investment funds like Softbank and Tiger. Similarly Policybazaar, an online aggregator of insurance policies, was initially funded by Inventus, a typical early stage VC fund, while investors in its later rounds included large institutional investors like Temasek who are known to back more mature enterprises.

These distinctions between PE and VC are summarised in the table below.

Feature	*VC*	*PE*
Investment Target	■ Early stage businesses, expansion ■ Innovative products, services, technologies ■ Heavily dependent on external financing ■ Unlisted companies	■ Later stage businesses, involves operational or financial restructuring, with or without management team and /or ownership changes ■ Mature products, services ■ Generally have large cash flows ■ May be listed or unlisted
Horizon	Medium- to long-term: Three–eight years	Medium-term: Two–five years
Risks	May be one or more of technology, product development, market response to product/ service, management, operational and illiquidity	Usually limited to product–market risks; does not involve the other elements listed in the case of VC of investment
Structure	■ Equity or equity-type instruments such as convertible debt or preference shares ■ Syndication of investment, if any, among fellow VCs.	■ Equity and debt combinations. Debt is usually high risk, of speculative grade. ■ Syndicate may include institutions such as insurance companies and banks, who are primarily lenders.
Post Financing Engagement	Active, as it encompasses board composition, top management team recruitment, strategy formulation and internal systems processes and controls.	Active, but less than their VC counterparts. Involvement mainly limited to ensuring high quality governance.

Investment Management Team	Former managers and entrepreneurs with tremendous experience and vast, powerful networks in professional and industrial circles, primarily keeping in mind the post financing engagement needs	Primarily former financial market professionals.
Prevalence	Largely in US and to some extent in the UK, Canada, Singapore, Israel and Japan. What goes on in the name of VC elsewhere in the world is largely PE. Started as VC in India, evolved into distinct activities from late nineties.	Prevalent in the US, Continental Europe, Asia Pacific, Japan and many emerging markets.

PE has emerged as a significant constituent of the financial markets in the USA and Europe. It has played an important part in the restructuring of these economies. In the USA it helped restore profitability to many poorly run companies. In Europe, where PE has been much more common than VC, it helped ageing owners to find owner-management teams. Given the large size of transactions, it is much larger than VC in terms of capital under management.

PE and the Hedge Funds Industry A discussion on the PE industry would be incomplete without a brief mention of the emerging participation of hedge funds in PE transactions. Given the large variety among hedge funds in terms of their strategy and style and given their flexibility in pursuit of investment returns it was but inevitable that some of the hedge funds would eye the attractive returns in PE investments. A precise estimate of the amount of capital invested by hedge funds in PE transactions is not available. Such an estimate is made all the more difficult by the fact that many hedge funds make opportunistic PE investments while some set aside designated sums of money specifically for PE investments. But it does appear that participation levels are no longer trivial.

The approach of hedge funds to appraisal, structuring, contracting, post financing engagement, and holding periods varies from that of PE funds and is possibly influenced by their primary interest in investing in listed securities. The fact that hedge funds normally provide a liquidity option to investors in their funds, albeit such options may be limited, may likely influence their approach to investing.

It appears reasonable to expect that in the foreseeable future the participation of hedge funds in PE funds is all set to increase.

Term Sheet

Private equity funding has been gaining importance in the last few years. The starting point of PE funding is a 'term sheet' which reflects the understanding reached between the PE fund (the investor), the promoters, and the company. It summarises the terms and conditions for the proposed investment in the company. It is followed by due diligence and then by the Shareholders' Agreement and /or Share Subscription Agreement. Finally, the provisions of the Shareholders' Agreement are included in the Articles of Association of the Company.

The standard 'term sheet' covers the following:

- Company
- Promoters
- Investor
- Quantum of investment
- Investment instruments
- Pricing of instruments
- Conditions precedent
- Deployment of funds
- Conditions subsequent
- Shareholding pattern
- Board representation by the investor
- Pre-emptive rights of the investor
- Promoter lock-in and investor's Right of First Refusal (ROFR)
- Investor's veto rights
- Investor's exit rights
- Non-compete and non-solicit clauses
- Representations and warranties
- Auditors
- Due diligence
- Definitive documentation
- Confidentiality
- Exclusivity
- Validity
- Governing law

19.6 THE INDIAN VC INDUSTRY

Evolution The Indian VC industry is of relatively recent origin. Prior to the establishment of VC institutions, Indian development financial institutions provided risk capital to enterprises in the form of subscription to equity, seed capital to first generation entrepreneurs, and other similar forms of risk capital.

ICICI Ventures (formerly TDICI Ltd.) was the first VC institution and was promoted as a joint venture between ICICI Ltd. and Unit Trust of India (UTI) in 1988. Several other commercial banks and development financial institutions followed, with their own VC subsidiaries. With the de-regulation of foreign investment into Indian companies, from the mid nineties international investors emerged as more significant players in the Indian VC industry.

Foreign investors brought with them the lessons they had learned in various other developed as well as emerging markets. They introduced Western investment management styles and processes into their transactions in India. Rigorous due diligence, robust contracting, active post financing involvement, and a sharp focus on timely and profitable exit are among their more important contributions to the VC industry in India.

Investment Activity Levels Venture Intelligence, a provider of VC and PE industry data, indicates that the number of companies funded increased from 76 deals in 2001 to 186 deals in 2005 to 507 deals in 2007.[3] Investment activity slowed down in 2009 to 289 deals because of the global financial crisis of 2008, but picked up again to 490 deals in 2011 and reached an all time high in 2015 of 723 investments. Many of these companies received more than one round of funding. Thus the number of investment deals consummated were 5455 respectively, representing 3499 enterprises. These transactions represent funds invested in excess of US $ 140 billion (₹998,060 crores at current exchange rates). The volume of funds committed are quite close to the $ 251 billion of foreign portfolio investments that had flowed into the Indian stock and bond markets as of December 2017.

Early stage investments accounted for 34% of the number of all deals funded through the period. Later stage investments require large sums of funding compared to early stage deals. Hence later stage investments would account for a larger share of the funds committed.[4]

About 37% of all deals were in enterprises located in the southern states while about 34% of the deals in enterprises in the western states. The concentration of deals was much higher when measured in terms of cities. The five cities of Delhi and the surrounding areas of the National Capital Region, Mumbai, Chennai, Bangalore, and Hyderabad accounted for around 80% of the deals, suggesting a strong agglomeration effect.

Over the past thirty years the investment preferences of the industry have been shifting. In the years preceding the economic reforms of 1991, the VC and PE industry concentrated on export oriented enterprises and businesses that involved substitution of imports. Post 1991 investment preferences have shifted over the years as new sectors and opportunities emerged. Funds evaluate the prospects for exits when they choose new sectors. During the period from 2000 to 2017 five sectors accounted for the highest number of deals. These are

[3] Early stage companies receive more than one round of funding from VC investors. However, each round of funding requires more or less the same rigour of evaluation, negotiation and contracting as the first investment in the enterprise. Each such financing round is termed a deal and treated as though it was a new investment. The number of deals reported here is greater than the number of companies funded through this period.

[4] The discussion in this section is based on Sabarinathan, G., Aditya Muralidhar and Ahana Shetty (2017), Venture Capital Industry in India: An Exploratory Study, IIMB Working Paper No 542. Readers who are interested in further details may refer to the working paper downloadable at http://www.iimb.ac.in/sites/default/files/2018-06/WP%20No.%20542_0.pdf

online services (22.6% of the deals), financial services (9.1%), mobile services (8.0%), enterprise software (6.4%), and information technology products and services other than enterprise products and services (6.1%). Investor interest in these sectors persisted during the entire period even as interest in other sectors fluctuated. For example, business process outsourcing companies appeared to have been popular in the early 2000s but went out of favour thereafter. At the same time interest in sectors like health care and educational technology has been growing during the past five years.

The important message from these trends is that investors in PE and VC are careful in allocating their capital to sectors where they can look forward to exits with high rates of return over a limited period of five to seven years. Their challenge is to identify these sectors before competition intensifies with the entry of a large number of players. The corollary for entrepreneurs is that investors' interest at a certain point in time does not mean that the interest will persist at all time in future.

The other important point to note is that the VC and PE industry is now involved in financing a wide range of sectors and industries in India. Apart from the well-known role in financing technology and other high growth sectors, VC and PE funded enterprises touch nearly every aspect of our lives from real estate to general and sector specific retailing of various goods, many of the personal care products in daily use, healthcare, education, transportation and financial services, to name just a few. The impact of VC and PE on our modern life is thus far more than we might imagine.

More than 930 VC and PE funds participated in the Indian market during this period. Considering the number of investments and the volume of capital committed this was a large number of players. The low average number of deals per fund is the result of close to 600 of the funds having made less than five investments. This may have been so because they may be regional funds and India must be one of the countries in the region that they may have been investing in. So also the rate at which funds seemed to cease investing in India was high. Around 300 of the 937 funds had not made a fresh investment for a period of two years or more as of 2013, suggesting that they may have ceased investment activity in India.

About 34% of the 5455 deals were follow on investments. The data shows a sharp increase in follow on financing from 2007, further indicating that as investors as well as entrepreneurs gained more experienced in VC and PE funding, the industry as a whole matured. The provision of follow-on funding is viewed as a sign of the maturing of the VC industry for two reasons. First, the increase in follow on funding indicates that funds have sufficient capital to support its portfolio enterprises. Second, it shows that the industry is capable of meeting the critical growth funding needs of enterprises before they can be financially self-reliant or access public equity markets.

VC and PE funds investing in India exited from 971 companies. Some of these were complete while a large number were partial too. These comprised 143 public offerings and 828 trade sales. Between the two trade sales have been growing in number over the years while IPOs have remained constant. More recently, a third exit route known as secondary sales has been gaining in popularity. This involves a VC or PE fund buying out the stake of another VC or PE fund. One of the commonly voiced concerns about the VC and PE industry in India has been that exits are difficult. The data suggests that the rate of exit is not as low as popular media analyses might suggest. Further the rate of exits appears to have been improving over time, pointing to yet another dimension of maturity of the Indian industry.

Important Trends Beyond the story of growth in the Indian VC and PE industry, the available data point to three important trends that suggest a substantial shift in the nature of operations of the industry.

First, the VC and PE industry has been investing significant amounts of capital in an endeavour to create enterprises that can even be market leaders and can even take on global players who have large balance sheets from which they can support their Indian operations. The case of Flipkart and ANI Technologies (ANI, hereafter), the company that operates the Ola cab hailing service are two visible examples. While Flipkart was battling Amazon in the online marketplace till it got acquired by Walmart in 2018, Ola continues to battle global ride hailing leader Uber. At last count Flipkart had raised $7.3 billion as of August 2017 from 18 rounds of funding while ANI had raised $3.30 billion in 16 rounds as of September 2018.

This development has many implications. It tells us that global VCs and PEs believe that Indian entrepreneurs can quickly build large businesses that can compete against large global competitors. These high growth enterprises are referred to as unicorns when their value reaches the US $ 1 billion mark, which at current rates of exchange amounts to ₹7000 crores. Flipkart, ANI Technologies (owner of Ola), Paytm, a payment processing enterprise are three examples of around twenty enterprises from India that are said to have attained "unicorn" status.

Second, a related trend that has made it possible for enterprises like Flipkart and Ola to grow so rapidly has been their timely acquisition of smaller competitors, essentially leaving just one or two leading players in almost every online business. Sometimes referred to as a "winner take all" trend it is important for VC investors to identify those entrepreneurs who have the capability to outgrow competition and then acquire smaller competitors. Having identified them they need to back them up with the large amounts of capital that is required to support an acquisition-led growth strategy.

Third, there has been a significant growth in angel financing activity. In a related development a number of angel networks have emerged in the past decade. Angel networks are a formal association of individual angel investors. Between individual angels and angel networks, the entire spectrum of early stage funding is now covered in India, from as little as ₹25 lakhs going up to ₹10 crores. In the years to come angels and angel networks are expected to form an important source of early stage equity funding for Indian enterprises.

19.7 REGULATORY FRAMEWORK

The VC and PE industries are subject to relatively lower levels of regulation across the world since they manage capital provided by institutional investors and high net worth individuals who are presumed to be capable of arriving at informed decisions. The Indian VC and PE industries are governed by a somewhat complex institutional and regulatory framework. A brief discussion on the framework follows.

The regulatory framework governs the industry at four levels. Right at the top is the set of regulations affecting the creation of the investment vehicle and the inward remittance of funds and outward remittance of disinvestment proceeds. At the next level is the Indian Companies Act 2013 which relates to issuance of securities by companies in India and the governance of companies. The Companies Act 2013 also regulates the starting up of enterprises, their conduct of businesses and shutting down. The third set of regulations are the laws governing the listing and trading of enterprises on public securities exchanges. Finally, there are the regulations governing the taxation of gains and income from investment activities.

Regulations of VC Funds Registered in India Investment fund management organisations that are established in India are governed by the Alternate Investment Fund Regulations, 2012, (AIF Regulations, hereafter), promulgated by Securities and Exchange Board of India (SEBI hereafter). These regulations recognise four broad types of investment funds covering VC and PE funds, hedge funds and social impact investment funds and angel investment funds. In order to effectively regulate these investment vehicles, the regulations require all alternate investment funds to register with SEBI. Funds established in India that do not register with SEBI may not engage in the VC and PE business. Needless to state, such funds will not be able to avail of tax incentives provided to VC and PE funds. By stipulating a high minimum subscription amount for investors and placing a limit on the maximum number of subscribers to a fund the regulations seek to ensure that VC and PE funds which invest in high risk opportunities are not retailed to investors for whom such funds may not be appropriate avenues for investment. The regulations also have broad restrictions on the investments that these funds can make.

Regulation of VC Funds Registered Outside India VC and PE funds that are organised as investment entities registered outside India are not subject to the regulations of AIF. They may however have to comply with regulations that apply to the country in which they are registered as well as the countries from which they raise capital. Their investments from offshore vehicles are governed by the foreign direct investment (FDI, hereafter) regulations of India. Over the years these regulations have been liberalised considerably to permit unrestricted foreign ownership in nearly all sectors. Under the liberalised environment, most VC and PE investments are subject to an automatic approval to be accorded by the Reserve Bank of India. There are certain restrictions on the types of financial instruments that VC and PE funds can employ while structuring a deal for an Indian company. For example, overseas VC and PE funds cannot structure their deals only as instruments that are compulsorily convertible into equity shares in the investee company. This takes away an important means of managing liquidity risk for VC and PE investors. These restrictions change from time to time. Investors therefore need to watch out for these changes in regulations while investing in India.

Finally, there are the regulations governing the taxation of gains and income from investment activities which are governed by the Indian Income Tax Act, 1961. Capital gains in excess of ₹1 lakh from securities and other assets that have been owned for more than 12 months, known as long term capital gains, are taxed at 10%. Capital gains from assets that have been held for a shorter period are subject to a tax rate of 15%. Section 10(23FB) of the Indian Income Tax Act, 1961 exempts from tax the income and long term capital gains of VC and PE funds. In order to avail of the tax exemption the VC fund will have to register with the SEBI as noted earlier. Most private equity funds comprising foreign capital are located in tax efficient jurisdictions that benefit from the double tax avoidance agreements (DTAAs) that the Government of India has in force with 85 countries across the world. These DTAAs ensure that investors would not pay higher taxes by investing through the fund than they would have if they had invested directly

Businesses in India are also governed by laws specific to various industries. Investors need to be mindful of the prevalence of these regulations while evaluating investments. For example laws governing restaurants can be local to the city or state in which the restaurant operates.

19.8 CURRENT CONCERNS OF THE INDIAN VC INDUSTRY

Considering the potential for the various sectors in a rapidly growing economy, the Indian market should provide many attractive investment opportunities for VC investors. However there appear to be numerous issues that could cause concern to potential investors. Some of them are discussed briefly below.

1. The common refrain among VC investors has been the *lack of deal flow* of an acceptable "quality". This could be, *inter alia,* due to a complex interaction of social, cultural, and economic issues that could possibly be inhibiting the growth of entrepreneurship. For example, a McKinsey report estimated that India had 10,440 enterprises that would be considered attractive investment opportunities compared to 16,700 in Russia and 41,150 in China.
2. There is very little data on the performance of Indian VC portfolios. There have been individual instances of spectacular investment successes. But it remains to be seen if they have resulted in the success of an entire portfolio in terms of a competitive rate of return, adjusted for risk, fees and costs. The growing volume of capital committed to Indian VC and PE suggests that investors see the potential for attractive returns.
3. Contract enforcement in India takes far too long and is fraught with too much uncertainty. This, combined with the relatively low levels of awareness of and commitment to sound corporate governance practices, appears to heighten anxiety about protecting investor's interests in a company.
4. The regulatory regime is said to make entry into and exit from investments complex, time consuming, and costly for foreign investors. The extant regime that provides for exemption of the profit and capital gains of VC funds from income tax are considered to be too restrictive to permit a healthy development of the business.

19.9 HOW TO APPROACH A VC FUND

Most of the discussion above has been from the VC's viewpoint of the business. It would be useful for an entrepreneur, who proposes to raise VC, to keep some of the following considerations in mind.

Select the VCs you want to dialogue with VC funds have distinct investment focus areas in terms of industry sectors, the stage of evolution of the companies in which they would like to invest, the amount of financing, and the extent of post financing involvement that the investor wishes to adopt. The entrepreneur would need to choose the VC fund, taking into account the fund's investment focus, before he sets out to have a serious discussion. This information can be acquired from brochures of various funds or their web sites or by availing of the services of investment bankers who specialise in VC and PE funding.

Given the trends of investment preferences that we noted earlier, the entrepreneur may even need to think of approaching a few angel investors who are active in the investment market. Since their activities are not widely known or publicised, entrepreneurs may need to contact intermediaries who specialise in raising capital for early stage investments from these various sources.

Present an exciting and convincing story VC fund managers select a small number of companies to fund from a large number of investment proposals they receive. In order to catch the investors' attention, the entrepreneur must therefore have a business plan package that presents an exciting and convincing business story, laying out the potential size of the market for the product or service, the firm's competitive strategy, the financial return potential, and last but not the least, the competence of the management team to deliver these results.

Choose the right investment partner VC involves a closer relationship between the investor and the investee than between a lender and a borrower. So, the entrepreneur must ensure that the VC fund:

- Develops a productive and harmonious relationship with the investee firm.
- Has the organisation and personnel, with the necessary skills and experience to contribute post financing value in areas such as business strategy, marketing, and finance. A similar consideration applies to angel investors and angel investment networks too.
- Has enough capital to meet the continuing financing needs of the investee firm.

In the case of an angel investor, the motives and the motivations of the investor also need to be understood clearly.

Clear expectations and flexible approach Given that VC and PE investors provide more than just capital it is important for the entrepreneur to have a clear expectation of what he expects from the partnership with the capital provider. Expectations could cover a wide gamut of aspects of the relationship, such as the nature of engagement between the investor and the management team, performance and return expectations, and exit horizon to name a few. If both the investor and the investee articulate and agree on these at the start of the relationship it can help avoid subsequent disappointments. At the same time, it is important for both parties to recognise that not all aspects of this relationship can be identified upfront. The two parties need to have an open attitude towards resolving amicably issues that could not be foreseen upfront as they emerge.

Be prepared for an open relationship VC and PE investors engage more closely with the managements of enterprises they fund than lenders. The relationship between the investor and the investee is most productive when the entrepreneur and investee approach the relationship in a transparent manner and accommodate each other's reasonable business expectations. The entrepreneur has to be clear that he is prepared for such an open relationship with his financing partner when he raises VC.

Conclusion

Even after three decades of funding more than four thousand enterprises, it is still early days for the VC and PE industry in India. But that is hardly surprising. The American VC industry which everyone looks up to as a role model today did not achieve the kind of depth, breadth, or sophistication it can boast of today for nearly thirty years after the first initiatives took off. The industry began to take off only after the landmark amendment to what was known as the Prudent Man Rule in the Employee Retirement Income Security Act in 1979. This key amendment led to the flow of institutional capital into VC and PE funds, which in turn led to the rapid growth of the industry thereafter. Given the growth prospects for the Indian economy and the increasing selectivity of Indian stock exchanges in serving as a source of equity, companies are increasingly turning to VC and PE as a source of financing. Entrepreneurship has been receiving encouragement and attention from a number of different sources such as the government, educational institutions, centres of excellence in research, large corporate organisations, and so on. With the increase in entrepreneurial activity and the maturing of the entrepreneurial ecosystem, the level of VC and PE investing in India is all set to increase even further in the years to come. This augurs well for the industry, entrepreneurs, and professionals who seek to engage with the entrepreneurial ecosystem.

SUMMARY

- A company which is in the early stages of development may not often be ready or willing to tap the public financial market. Such a company could benefit from VC.
- VC funds are freestanding pools of capital, raised mostly from institutional investors and high net worth individuals who have the ability to provide long term capital.
- VC investments typically fund businesses with potential for high growth in sales and profitability, equity or quasi-equity financing instruments, medium to long term investment horizons, above average investment risks and returns, and active post financing involvement between investor and investee.
- Exceptionally high risks in terms of technology, management, product market and achieving liquidity increase the overall uncertainty underlying VC investments. VC investors also face the added problem of having to seek out information that they need, since unlisted firms are subject to less demanding and less frequent disclosure obligations, unlike their listed counterparts.
- The VC investment evaluation process is different from that of appraising a term loan opportunity. VC investors place considerable emphasis on assessing the capability of the management team, analysing the strategic strengths of the business under consideration and on whether, how and over what time frame investors will achieve liquidity on the investment.
- The process of assigning a monetary value to the equity shares of the prospective investee is known as valuation. VC investors convert the valuation estimate to arrive at a percentage of the equity that they seek for the amount of capital they propose to invest. The valuation of the firm, dependent as it is on several critical assumptions such as projected financial performance of the investee and choice of P/E or P/EBIDTA

multiple, tends to be influenced by factors such as the outlook for the economy and capital market, industry and deal related factors, and demand and supply for capital.

- VC investors put a great deal of effort into structuring the deal, which comprises choosing the instruments for funding the company and defining the terms of the instrument such as yield, redemption or conversion as the case may be. The choice takes into account the investor's concern about liquidity and the need for influence in the management of the company, post financing.
- The relationship between the investor and the investee is governed through a set of agreements between the investor and the investee. These agreements define the rights of the investor and provide the levers of control to the investor so long as the investor holds a financial stake in the investee enterprise.
- The extent and style of post financing involvement adopted by VC fund managers varies from one fund to another. Through their nominees on the Board of Directors, VC investors participate in organisation building and ensure that key business decisions at the investee firm do not adversely affect the investor's interests.
- VC investors exit from their investments by selling their shares on a stock exchange once the shares are listed or by selling their stake to a strategic investor.
- The Indian VC industry is young by international standards but has evolved rapidly over the past decade. Foreign investors who entered the Indian industry after the de-regulation of foreign investment brought in their international fund management practices. Investment preferences of VC funds in India seem to have evolved in response to changes in the economy and the industrial sector, brought about by the economic reform process.
- The Indian VC industry is regulated by the Securities and Exchange Board Of India (SEBI). Funds which are registered with SEBI and fulfill criteria laid down in the Indian Income Tax Act 1961 enjoy exemption from income and capital gain tax. Foreign investors who invest through investment companies registered outside India, are subject to investment regulations governing foreign direct investments and are not subject to the regulatory oversight of SEBI.
- Notwithstanding these points of concern, the potential for industrial growth in the Indian economy should make the Indian VC industry attractive to foreign investors.

QUESTIONS

1. Define a venture capital investment.
2. How does a venture capital investment differ from an investing in the equity of an established firm listed on a stock exchange?
3. How does venture capital differ from private equity?
4. How do venture capital investors value their investment in a company? What are some of the factors that could influence this valuation?
5. Discuss the salient aspects of the VC industry in India.
6. What are the current concerns of the Indian VC industry?

7. Discuss the considerations that an entrepreneur should be in mind while approaching a VC fund.

MINICASE

Praveen Bhargava, a Ph.D. in molecular biology, is working as a professor in the International Science Institute. Based on this research work, he has developed an enzyme which he believes has commercial potential. Praveen Bhargava has set up Enzy Laboratories to commercially develop the product.

Enzy Laboratories has approached Gamma Venture Capital with a funding request for ₹200 million by way of equity. Gamma requires a rate of return of 30 percent from its equity investment in Enzy and its planned holding period is 5 years. Enzy has projected an EBITDA of ₹300 million for year 5, which Gamma considers to be credible. Gamma believes that an EBITDA multiple of 6 for year 5 to be reasonable. At the end of year 5, Enzy is likely to have a debt of ₹200 million and a cash balance of ₹80 million.

(a) What share in equity of Enzy will Gamma ask for?
(b) What factors generally influence valuation of VC deals?
(c) Discuss the considerations an entrepreneur like Praveen Bhargava should bear in mind while approaching a VC fund.

Some Useful Websites and Data Sources

- www.sebi.gov.in is the official website of SEBI. It provides the SEBI guidelines on alternate investment funds, SEBI's official circulars, list of registered VC funds and so on.
- https://www.bvca.co.uk/ is the official website of the British Private Equity and Venture Capital Association. Apart from data on the UK VC industry it also has interesting articles and reference material such as accounting standards for the VC industry.
- https://nvca.org/ is the official website of the National Venture Capital Association (NVCA) of the USA. Provides summary data on the US VC industry and templates for standard documents like term sheets.
- https://www.investeurope.eu/ is the official website of the Invest Europe, formerly known as European Venture Capital Association. Provides data on the European VC industry and interesting articles and reference material on the VC industry in Europe.
- https://ivca.in/ is the official website of the Indian Private Equity and Venture Capital Association.

Data Sources

This is a list of a few sources. There are many more sources of data available. Data on the Indian VC industry is just beginning to be available. Questions about the accuracy of the data aside the data is not comprehensive; nor does it cover all the transactions. Some of the more company used data sources are: Venture Intelligence, VC Circle, Prequin, and Pitch book

Infrastructure Projects

PART SIX

Chapter 20

Infrastructure Projects and Public-Private Partnership

LEARNING OBJECTIVES

After studying this chapter you should be able to

- Describe the characteristics of an infrastructure project.
- Explain the features of a public-private partnership.
- Discuss the structures of public-private partnership.
- Explain the typical configuration of an infrastructure project.
- Describe the role and responsibilities of various project parties.
- Discuss the contents of key project contracts.
- Discuss the features of a typical power purchase agreement (PPA).
- Describe the ways of managing risk in infrastructure projects.
- Identify the shortcomings of infrastructure management and ways to mitigate them.

Infrastructure includes the capital required to produce economic services from utilities (like electricity, gas, telecommunications, and water) and transport works (like roads, bridges, urban transit systems, seaports, and airports) and is central to promoting economic activity. Good infrastructure helps in providing economic services efficiently, promotes competitiveness, and supports high productivity. Poor infrastructure, on the other hand, impedes economic growth and can be seriously detrimental to the efficient use of scarce resources.

Infrastructure projects, which typically provide essential services, have one or more of the characteristics mentioned below:

- They are highly capital-intensive.
- They involve huge sunk costs.
- They have a long operating life.

The vital role of infrastructure in the economy, the essential nature of its services, the size of individual projects, and its important social dimensions call for governmental role in planning and promoting, and in ensuring independent regulation that provides a level playing field for both public and private sector enterprises. When projects are operational, the role of the government will be determined by the ownership and the operational structure of the project concerned.

Traditionally, infrastructure projects in India were owned and managed by the government or government undertakings. Given the massive investments required in infrastructure, there is now a broad consensus that private sector participation in this activity must be encouraged.

Private initiative in infrastructure projects can take many forms, ranging from contracted operation of public utilities to full ownership, operation, and maintenance of these facilities. Some of the principal objectives of promoting private investment in the development and operation of infrastructure projects are ensuring greater economic efficiency and better availability of the facility itself. Depending on their nature, however, infrastructure projects are either more or less suitable for private participation and the level of such participation can be varied to reflect the same. Projects that are designed to provide significant social benefits such as low cost urban transportation systems may be more suited to traditional government ownership, whereas projects that have strong commercial attraction, like telecommunication, are more suited for private sector involvement.

20.1 CHARACTERISTICS OF INFRASTRUCTURE PROJECTS

Infrastructure projects, which typically provide essential services, have one or more of the following characteristics.

- *High Capital Costs* Infrastructure projects such as airports, ports, roads, and telecommunication have high capital costs, but relatively low operating costs.
- *Long Gestation Period* Typically, ports, airports, metro railways, and so on have long gestation period.
- *Steady Cash Flows* Barring some exceptions like telecommunications, most infrastructure projects generate steady cash flows, with relatively low upsides.
- *High Entry Barriers* When the government grants a concession or license for an infrastructure project, it usually grants it monopoly, at least for some length of time.
- *Need for High Government Support* Since most infrastructure projects involve public-private partnership, they need high government support.
- *High Regulation* Given the monopoly or quasi-monopoly they enjoy, infrastructure projects are highly regulated and the stress is on independent regulators like TRAI (Telecom Regulatory Authority of India) and CERC (Central Electricity Regulatory Commission).
- *Highly "Contractual" Project Structures* The project is structured in such a way that there are several contracts.
- *Multiple Risks* Infrastructure projects are characterised by multiple risks. Through various contracts an effort is made to achieve proper risk sharing.

20.2 PUBLIC-PRIVATE PARTNERSHIP

Committed to raise the investment in infrastructure from the current level of less than 5 percent of the Gross Domestic Product to 8 percent, the Government of India is keen on involving the private sector through public-private partnerships (PPPs) which have been used in many countries.

What is a PPP? Broadly, a PPP refers to a contractual partnership between the public and private sector agencies in which the private sector is entrusted with the task of providing infrastructure facilities and services that were traditionally provided by the public sector. An example of a PPP is a toll expressway project financed, constructed, and operated by a private developer.

According to the Government of India, a PPP project is a project based on a contract or concession agreement between a government or statutory entity and a private sector company for delivering an infrastructure service on payment of user charges. A private sector company is a company in which 51 percent or more of equity is owned and controlled by a private entities.

A PPP does not mean that the government is absolved of its responsibility. Ultimately the government remains accountable for the quality of service and reasonableness of price. Under a PPP arrangement, the role of the government is to facilitate, enable, and monitor the service whereas the role of the private partner is to finance, build, and operate the service.

The basic characteristics of a PPP project are: (i) The project stems from a government-led planning and prioritisation process. (ii) There is a genuine sharing of risks between the government and the private sector. This means that the government accepts some risks and does not transfer the entire risk to the private sector and vice versa.

The process of finalising a PPP involves detailed cost and risk appraisal, complex and time-consuming bidding procedure, difficult stakeholder management, and long-drawn negotiations before reaching financial closure. Hence PPPs critically depend on sustained and explicit support of the sponsoring government. To deal with the complexities of PPPs, the government should have the ability to handle the legal, regulatory, policy, and governance issues.

Relevance of PPPs for India India, the second fastest growing and the fourth largest economy of the world (in terms of PPP), faces huge gaps between the demand and supply of essential social and economic infrastructure and services. There is a shortage of power, roads, ports (airports and seaports), irrigation facilities, water and sanitation services, and so on. The deficient infrastructure is a major constraint in sustaining, deepening, and expanding India's economic growth and competitiveness. It also impedes inclusive growth and poverty alleviation.

Recognising the importance of infrastructure, the Government of India (GOI) has stepped up its spending on infrastructure through a series of national programmes such as the National Highway Development Programme (NHDP), Bharat Nirman, Providing Urban Services in Rural Areas (PURA), Jawaharlal Nehru National Urban Renewal Mission (JNNURM), the Prime Minister's Rural Road Programme, National Rail Vikas Yojana, National Maritime Development Programme (NMDP), airport expansion programme, and so on. However, the estimated investment requirements are far greater than governmental resources. So, the Approach Paper to the Eleventh Plan had argued for reaching out to the private sector and private savings and aggressively promoting private partnership in infrastructure development. The National Development Council (NDC) has passed a resolution which says that "increased private sector participation has now become a necessity" for mobilising the resources required for infrastructure expansion and upgradation.

Status of PPPs and Key Government Initiatives India had some PPPs like The Great Indian Peninsular Railway Company (operating between Bombay and Thane) and the Bombay Tramway Company as early as the 19th century. Since the opening of the economy in 1991, the government has initiated the process of partnering with the private sector. While not much progress was made in the initial years, in recent years the momentum has picked up in sectors such as roads, ports (seaports and airports), telecommunication, and power. The Delhi-Noida Bridge Project, the Tirupur Water Supply Project, NHAI, ports at Mundra and Pipavav, and airport projects at Mumbai and Delhi are some conspicuous examples. To give impetus to PPPs, several initiatives have been taken. The GOI has established a Cabinet Committee on Infrastructure (COI), a high-level Committee of Secretaries, a PPP Apraisal Committee (PPPAC) on the model of the Public Investment Board (PIB), and several task forces to streamline decision making and operationalise PPPs. It has established the Viability Gap Funding (VGF) scheme and the India Infrastructure Finance Company Limited (IIFCL) to provide long-term finance to PPP projects. The GOI is working on several initiatives to assist and encourage capacity building at the state and central levels. It is providing assistance for creating state level PPP cells as nodal agencies, streamlining their approval process, and developing PPP toolkits (model concession agreements, project manuals, bidding documents, and project preparation manuals).

The Way Forward In order to accelerate PPPs, the following are needed:

- A stronger policy and regulatory framework has to be created, both at the centre and the states. The US-India CEO forum has called for a policy and regulatory framework that fosters efficiency and transparency in the bidding process, ensures sanctity of contracts, encourages competition, promotes market-driven tariffs, and separates regulatory and adjudication authorities.
- The availability of long-term equity and debt for PPPs has to be augmented through suitable instruments and mechanisms.
- The shelf of bankable PPP projects has to be expanded.
- The capacity of the government to manage PPP projects has to be substantially strengthened.
- The government should expeditiously award contracts, facilitate land acquisition, and ensure better coordination between the centre and states. In particular, large size PPP projects may be put out for bidding after obtaining mandatory clearances and approvals, preferably through a Shell Company/Special Purpose Vehicle as was done recently in the case of Ultra Mega Power Projects.

Some Observations from the Report of the Committee on Revisiting and Revitalising the PPP Model of Infrastructure The Government of India set up a committee under the chairmanship of Vijay Kelkar for suggesting ways of revitalising the PPP model of infrastructure. Here are some of its observations:

- India today offers the world's largest market for PPPs.
- India's success in deploying PPPs as an important instrument for creating infrastructure here will depend on a change in attitude and in the mindset of all authorities dealing with PPPs, including public agencies partnering with the private sector, government

departments supervising PPPs, and auditing and legislative institutions providing oversight of PPPs.

- The Government may take early action to amend the Prevention of Corruption Act 1988 which does not distinguish between genuine errors in decision making and acts of corruption.
- Inefficient and inequitable allocation of risk in PPPs can be a major factor in PPP failures.
- Typically, infrastructure PPP projects span over 20-30 years and a developer often loses bargaining power related to tariffs and other matters in case there are abrupt changes in the economic or policy environment which are beyond his control. The committee feels strongly that the private sector must be protected against what has been called an 'Obsolescing Bargain'.

20.3 TYPICAL STRUCTURES

A PPP is organised as a special purpose vehicle that has relationships with various parties as shown in Exhibit 20.1.

Exhibit 20.1 ***Infrastructure Projects: Typical Structure***

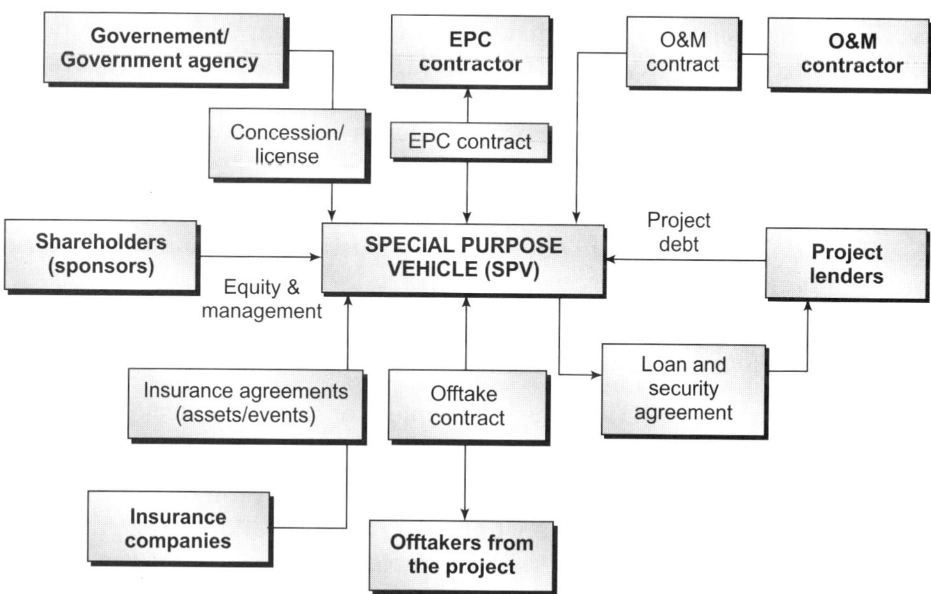

20.4 STRUCTURES OF PPP

The commonly used structures of public-private partnership are:

- Build-operate-transfer (BOT)

- Build-own-operate-transfer (BOOT)
- Build-own-operate (BOO)
- Build-lease-transfer (BLT)
- Lease-develop-operate (LDO)
- Rehabilitate-operate-transfer (ROT)
- Design-build-finance-operate-transfer (DBFOT)

Build-operate-transfer (BOT) BOT is used extensively in the infrastructure sector for effecting public-private partnership. In a BOT structure, the government or a public entity delegates to a private sector entity the task of designing, building, operating, and maintaining the infrastructure facility for a certain period (the concession period). During this period, the private entity is responsible for raising the finance for the project and is entitled to retain the revenues generated by the project. At the end of the concession agreement, the facility is transferred to the government or a public entity, without any compensation to the private entity involved.

Build-own-operate-transfer (BOOT) A BOOT structure differs from BOT in that the private entity owns the facility during the concession period.

Build-own-operate (BOO) In a BOO structure, the private entity retains the ownership of the project. Hence, it gets the benefits of any residual value of the project. What is the justification of a BOO company to retain the assets of the project after the concession period? Typically the project tariff is fixed in such a way that it includes four components as compensation for providers of capital: cost of equity, cost of debt, return of equity, and return of debt. In the case of a BOO company, the return of equity does not take place during the concession period. So, the company can retain the assets of the project after the concession period.

Build-lease-transfer (BLT) Under the BLT structure, the private entity designs and builds a complete project or facility (such as a seaport), sells to the government, simultaneously leases it back (usually for 15 to 30 years) to operate it as a business, and finally transfers it to the government at a pre-determined price.

Lease-develop-operate (LDO) The government or the public sector entity retains the ownership of the newly created infrastructure facility that it leases to a private promoter.

Rehabilitate-operate-transfer (ROT) The government or the public sector entity allows the private promoter to rehabilitate and operate a facility during a concession period.

Design-build-finance-operate-transfer (DBFOT) The private promoter assumes the entire responsibility for the design, construction, financing, and operation of the project during the concession period. At the end of that period, the project is transferred to the government.

The most common structures used in India are BOO and BOOT. Typically, electricity generation using coal or gas are BOO projects and hydro-electric or road projects are BOOT projects. The concept here seems to be that if a company uses public resources or needs extensive Government support even to come into being, such projects are set up as BOOT projects. In the case of a hydro-electric project, the company uses water which is a public resource (strictly speaking, it uses gravity and not water, to turn the turbines!). In the case of road projects, the company needs the Government to use its power of 'eminent domain' to acquire land to construct the road.

The term 'transfer' in this context needs an explanation. It is not that the firm literally hands over the company to the Government. What is transferred is the stream of profits beyond the concession period till the end of the project's physical life. Therefore, the Government auctions those projects/assets at the end of the concession period to capture the present value of the profit stream.

20.5 TYPICAL PROJECT CONFIGURATION

Given the complexity of risks that need to be managed during the construction and operations phase of an infrastructure project, project sponsors have tended to follow some simple arrangements while implementing these projects:

- Projects are typically implemented in a Special Purpose Vehicle ("SPV"), which is a distinct corporate entity incorporated with the objective of implementing and operating the project. This ensures that the risks associated with the project are "ring-fenced" and do not flow back to the sponsor entities.
- Project sponsors take an equity stake in the SPV; depending on the project cost, sponsors' ability and objectives as well as project lenders' requirements, the minimum stake could be in the range of 15–30 percent of the project cost and is referred to as the "Sponsors' Contribution".
- The SPV enters into contractual arrangements with project contractors, offtakers, operators, government, and project lenders (together referred to as "Project Parties"). In non-recourse project financing, project lenders would not have any fall-back on the resources/assets of the sponsors if the SPV fails to meet debt servicing obligations; however, in the case of limited-recourse financing, under certain circumstances, project sponsors would have certain contractual obligations towards project lenders. In most cases of project financing, other project parties would have no recourse to the project sponsors.
- Infrastructure projects can be financed at a relatively higher gearing (i.e. debt-equity) ratio vis-à-vis conventional projects, especially if offtake is assured by bankable entities. For example, in Indian road projects, where private enterprise would construct, operate, and maintain the road during the Concession Period and would earn an assured annuity from the National Highways Authority of India (NHAI) irrespective of the actual level of traffic, lenders may be willing to consider higher gearing of up to 4:1. In power projects where offtake was assured to the extent of a certain Plant Load Factor (PLF) by the SEBs concerned, lenders have traditionally financed on a debt-equity ratio (DER) of 2.33:1. For large conventional projects, where the project and hence the lenders are exposed to pure market risks, the DER would rarely exceed 2:1.

In infrastructure projects, the effort on the part of the different project parties is to ensure that contracts are as ironclad as possible and as less left to subjective interpretation. The objective of the contracts is to establish project related obligations for each project party and ensure that certain risks are allocated to those parties who are in the best position to manage the risk. At the project development and financing stages, it is therefore important to have experienced financial and legal advisors who will advise the SPV and the sponsors on appropriate risk allocation and ensure that the legal and structural framework to enable the risk allocation is correctly defined.

20.6 KEY PROJECT PARTIES

As the project moves from the developmental stages to financing and thereafter to construction and finally to operations, several project parties get involved with the project. Some, like the financial advisors, exit once the financing is fully tied up and the project has drawn down loans from the lenders and equity from the investors, while others like the EPC contractor are extensively associated with the project during the construction phase and by contract during the "Defect Liability Period" post commercial operations. A brief description of each of the project parties and their typical role is given below.

Project Sponsors Project sponsors are responsible for converting a concept into a project and having a role in setting up a project vehicle, identifying and recruiting right managerial talent to implement and run the project, providing a clear mandate to such management on their expectations, and finally subscribing to a significant proportion of equity in the project vehicle.

Project Vehicle The SPV is responsible for delivering a bankable project during the financing phase, implementing the project, and thereafter operating it in a manner that is financially viable. It selects and appoints all the project contractors, negotiates and executes the contracts, arranges the financing, supervises construction and commissioning, and operates the project either directly or through an Operations and Maintenance (O&M) Contractor.

Project Lenders Project lenders provide debt to finance the construction of the project. Typically a consortium of project lenders, led by a "Lead Bank", ascertains a bankable project cost and in consultation with the SPV and the project sponsors develops the pattern of financing the same, disburses debt, and performs a monitoring role during the construction phase, and on commissioning monitors the performance and operation of the project till all debt is repaid. Project lenders are secured by project assets and do not normally interfere in the day-to-day operations of the SPV. However, under conditions of default, the project lenders' rights increase substantially and in extreme cases of default, and if provided for in the Project Loan Documents, project lenders can take over the management of the project as well as the sponsors' equity.

EPC Contractor Typically an EPC contractor designs the project, procures all the engineering skills and equipment to construct the project, erects all the project facilities, ensures that test and trial-runs are completed, and finally commissions the project, all on a turnkey basis. The EPC contractor's key objective is to deliver a project, as per pre-defined specifications, within a certain cost and time frame. It also provides performance guarantees to the SPV. It may choose to sub-contract certain portions of the assignment to other contractors but such sub-contracting does not relieve it from its sole responsibility of delivering a constructed project to the SPV.

O&M Contractor As the name indicates, the O&M contractor is responsible for operating and maintaining the plant in line with industry best practices. Performance parameters that need to be achieved during operations are pre-defined in an O&M contract and the O&M contractor provides managerial skills and operations experience to achieve and possibly surpass the agreed parameters.

Government The government is a key project party. It provides a concession to the SPV to set up the project and ensures that a proper legislative and regulatory framework exists that allows the SPV concerned to compete on a "level-playing field" along with existing, possibly government-owned entities, in the same field. In some cases, like in the electricity generation sector, state governments have counter-guaranteed the performance of offtake obligations of the SEBs and in certain cases, the central government has counter-guaranteed the performance of the state governments.

20.7 PROJECT CONTRACTS

A project company is unusual in the sense that it is set up to undertake a single project. However, there is nothing unusual about the parties that participate in the project. All companies have equity shareholders, lenders, contractors, suppliers, and customers, and all deal with the government. The key differentiating feature of project finance is the manner in which project risks are allocated to various parties involved in a project.

Through a comprehensive web of contracts, every major risk inherent in the project is allocated to the party/parties that is best able to assess and manage that risk. Since a party to a project will agree to assume risk at a reasonable price only if it understands that risk clearly, project finance is appropriate only for projects like power stations, roads, railway lines, airports, and telecom networks that involve established technologies. Project finance is not suitable for projects that involve complex or unproven technologies, as suggested by the inability of the U.K. government to arrange project finance for research and development projects.

Provisions of Key Project Contracts Some of the fundamental provisions of key project contracts are given below:

Project Contract	*Contents*	*Final Objective*
Shareholders' Agreement	An agreement between all of SPV's shareholders, including Project Sponsors that establishes: 1. Shareholding pattern 2. Shareholders' representation in management 3. Minority protection rights, if any 4. Decision making process in certain reserved matters	■ Ensures that equity funding is fully tied up and available to the SPV as per its financing requirements ■ Attempts to ensure a smooth functioning of the SPV; ensures that certain decisions are made with the concurrence of all shareholders as opposed

Project Contract	*Contents*	*Final Objective*
	5. Proposed pattern of cash calls and remedies available against funding defaults by one share holder 6. Shareholders' Exit Process and Right of First Refusal (ROFR) to other shareholders	to a simple majority of the SPV's Board ■ Lays down an unambiguous process by which a shareholder can monetise its shareholding and the right of other shareholders in such an event
EPC Contract	An agreement between the SPV and the EPC contractor that establishes: 1. The EPC contractor's sole responsibility in designing, procuring, constructing, testing, and finally commissioning the plant/facility according to specifications laid down in the contract within a specified date and certain cost 2. Guaranteed and Minimum Performance parameters. 3. Responsibility of the contractor to rectify the plant if it fails to meet Guaranteed Performance Parameters and Penalities/Liquidated Damages (LDs) payable if the plant fails to meet Minimum Performance Parameters. Typically maximum LDs are capped at 20–30 percent of the EPC contract value[1]	■ Reduces the risk of time and cost escalations for the SPV ■ By selecting a properly qualified contractor, the SPV can mitigate, to a large extent, non-performance risks ■ By seeking warranties from the contractor the SPV ensures that for an adequate "Defects Liability Period", spare parts are available and repairs are carried out by experienced personnel at zero or low cost

[1] It has been argued that Contractors' liability should be capped at much higher levels say 50–75 percent of the Contract Value. However, this is not very common, as inevitably in such events, Contractors attempt to balance out the risk by inflating the Base Contract Price itself. The Project, by trying to insulate itself from a potential non-performance risk, may actually find itself priced out of the market on account of a higher capital cost. A better way to negotiate is to ensure that EPC contract price is competitive and once the price has been negotiated, try and convince the contractor to subscribe to some equity in the project, in which case the Contractor is incentivised to implement the project with great diligence.

Project Contract	*Contents*	*Final Objective*
Project Loan Agreements	An agreement between the SPV and the project lenders that establishes: 1. Certain Conditions Precedent ("CPs") on fulfillment of which an approved loan is drawable by the SPV 2. The amount of loan approved 3. Loan tenor, moratorium, repayment obligations, interest rates, and up-front/management fees 4. Security and Credit Enhancements 5. Events of Default and Remedies available to lenders under conditions of default 6. Sponsor covenants in full recourse/limited recourse financing conditions	▪ Ensures that conditions under which the loan is drawable is clear to the SPV as well as the lenders ▪ Ensures that the security and credit enhancement mechanisms are documented and therefore enforceable by contract ▪ Ensures that lenders have additional rights in the operation and management of the company under conditions of default and can accelerate loan repayments, if required
O&M Contract	An agreement between the SPV and the O&M contractor that establishes 1. Responsibility of the O&M contractor to operate the plant/facility to ensure the project/facility's availability 2. Maintenance obligations that will ensure that the project/facility is maintained as per industry best practices 3. Bonus payments to the O&M contractor, for exceeding pre-determined performance parameters and penalties for under achievement	▪ Ensures certain level of mitigation of operating and performance risks

20.8 FINANCIAL STRUCTURE AND CORPORATE GOVERNANCE

Many argue that the essence of project finance is the web of contracts meant to ensure that all parties work in concert for the success of the project, to distribute risks efficiently, and to prevent the abuse of monopoly power.

This argument is valid but incomplete as it does not explain the organisational structure, the ownership structure, and the financial leverage of the project. Put differently it does not explain why the project is handled as a separate company, why operators, contractors, suppliers, and consumers typically participate in the equity of the project company, and why the project company relies heavily on debt in the form of non-recourse financing or limited recourse financing. Indeed a government interested in a certain infrastructure project can raise money on its own and enter into contracts with various parties.

Separate SPVs ensure that multiple concessions with different or conflicting terms are not imposed on the same SPV. It also enhances the tradeability of these SPVs. As it is not possible to write comprehensive contracts (which can envisage every possible contingency) and monitor them effectively, equity participation of various stakeholders makes them more committed to the project. For example, when the operator and the main contractor have a significant stake in the equity of the project, they have an incentive to be more efficient. Finally, separately identifiable and assured cash flows facilitate a greater reliance on debt in the form of non-recourse financing or limited recourse financing.

20.9 AN ILLUSTRATION: A POWER PROJECT

An electricity generation project is an example of an infrastructure project. In such a project the SPV owns the generation assets and enters into a Power Purchase Agreement (PPA) with the State Electricity Board (SEB). Since the SEB purchases all the power generated by the SPV, the PPA, which establishes the conditions under which electrical energy would be sold by the SPV and purchased by the SEB and conditions by which payments would be secured, is amongst the most important contracts that need to be negotiated and executed. By means of a contract, the state government guarantees the payment obligations of the SEB.

A typical structure of such a project is shown in Exhibit 20.2.

Exhibit 20.2 ***Parties in a Power Project***

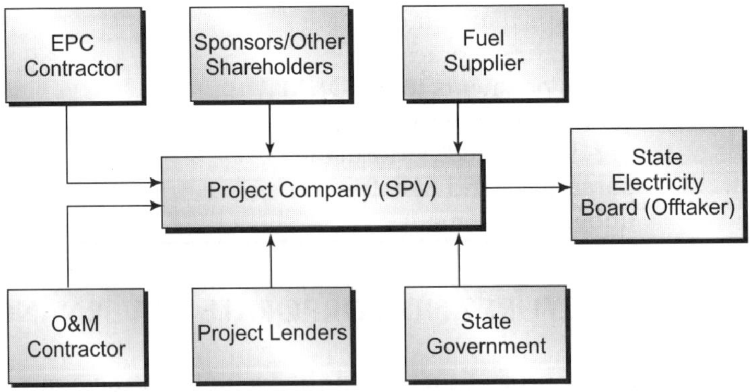

EPC Contractor
Sponsors/Other Shareholders
Fuel Supplier
Project Company (SPV)
State Electricity Board (Offtaker)
O&M Contractor
Project Lenders
State Government

Features of a Power Purchase Agreement (PPA) The salient characteristics of a typical PPA would be as follows:

- The PPA establishes the conditions under which the SPV would sell power to the SEB and the SEB would buy power from the SPV.
- Under the PPA, the SEB guarantees a minimum offtake from the SPV or, if it fails to do so, a minimum payment. Typically the minimum payment would cover all the fixed charges incurred by the project including depreciation, interest on term loans, fixed O&M expenses, and return on equity.
- A payment mechanism and a security mechanism that ensures availability of payments on time is established. In India, several large power projects have been financed on the basis of a 3-tier security mechanism depicted in Exhibit 19.2. At the first level, the SEBs open and continue to keep open a letter of credit (LC) from an acceptable bank in favour of the SPV. The LC typically covers about 30-45 days of average billing. The second tier comprises an escrow account where the receivables of the SEB itself are escrowed in favour of the SPV. In the event the SPV has invoiced for energy sold and the SEB has not made payment and the LC has also become inoperable, collections that are captured in the escrow are first released to the SPV and thereafter the remaining escrow balances can be released to the SEB. In the event both the LC and the escrow are inoperable, the third tier of the security mechanism, viz. an irrevocable guarantee of the state government that owns the SEB, can be enforced[2].
- The PPA also lays down the formula for computing tariffs, which in addition to the fixed charges, also includes variable costs such as fuel cost and also an incentive for performance.
- The responsibilities of the SEB include construction of interconnection facilities to ensure that the energy generated by the SPV can be sold through the state electricity grid. If the cost of interconnection facilities is high and its construction is likely to be time-consuming, it may be viewed as a serious risk by project lenders, especially given the precarious financial condition of most Indian SEBs. If the interconnection facilities are not ready on time, the project, even though it is ready to generate power, will not be in a position to sell power.
- The PPA also envisages termination under conditions of sustained default by either the SPV or the SEB in performing their respective obligations or under conditions of Force

[2] The 3-tier security structure has not worked in the practical environment as LCs may not always be opened by the SEB's bank if the SEB continues to be default grade; the escrow account may not be meaningful in the event there are multiple projects feeding the same SEB and the SEB is run on non-commercial lines such that the cost of power from the SPVs is higher than the revenues earned by the SEB and finally, in most cases, the state government guarantees may not be bankable given the large continuing commitments of the SEBs and the not so good financial positions of the states themselves. Lenders are therefore proposing to assist projects in states which have agreed to reform the SEBs and lay down the commercial principles under which power would be metered, sold and tariffs recovered from consumers. Such reforms linked financing is also likely to be linked to milestones with lenders disbursing debt on being satisfied with the state's progress in reforming the SEB along commercial lines.

Majeure. The PPA also allows an exit to the project's shareholders and lenders in the event it is terminated by providing for an SEB buyout of the facilities and laying down different buyout prices that would be payable by the SEB under different termination conditions. It also ensures that appropriate remedy periods are available prior to effecting a termination.

When financing a power project, lenders consider the PPA as an important project document and evaluate the sufficiency of negotiated tariffs, especially if the "fixed charges" element is pre-determined and not "cost-based". Lenders also evaluate the requirement of interconnection facilities and take a view on the ability of the SEB to complete the same prior to Commercial Operations Date ("CoD") of the project. Amongst the key provisions of the PPA is the security and credit enhancement mechanism and lenders also need to be satisfied with the same. Project lenders also ensure that under different events of termination and consequent SEB buyout, the committed buyout price includes outstanding debt and interest.

In addition to the risks mitigated through the PPA, the project is also exposed to certain construction and additional operating risks. Operating risks cover (a) the inability of the O&M operator to run the plant to ensure the required level of availability for reasons attributable to material defects in the plant for which the EPC contractor can be held liable during the

Exhibit 20.3 ***Tier Payment and Security Mechanism***

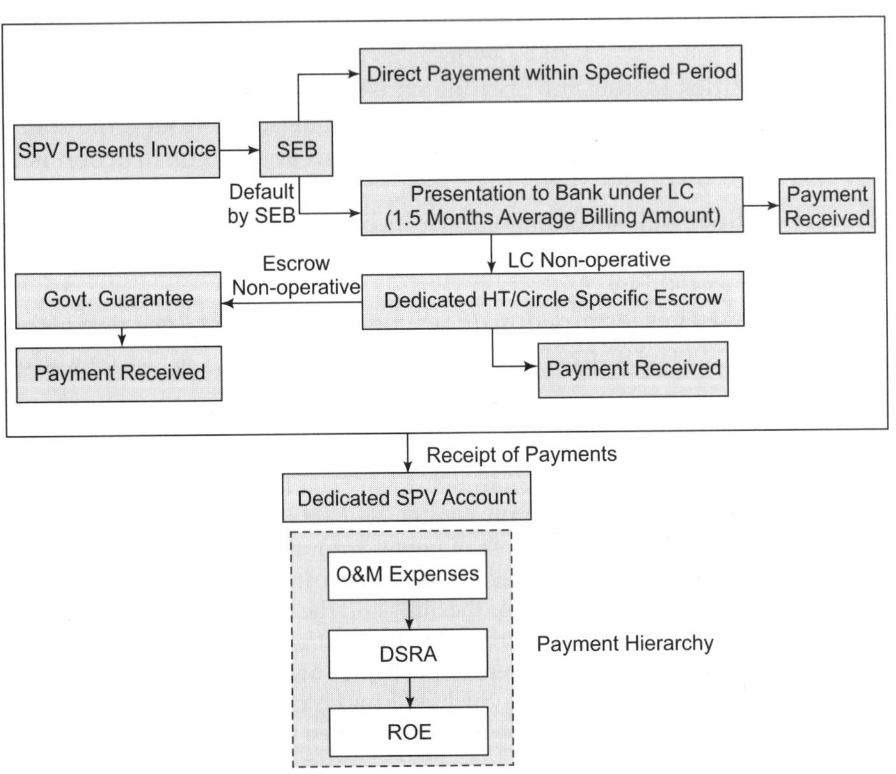

Defects Liability Period and (b) the inability of the fuel supplier to supply adequate quality/ quantity of fuel leading to lower plant availability. A Fuel Supply Agreement (FSA), between the fuel supplier and the SPV, that is structured properly ensures that the risks associated with inadequate quality/quantity of fuel are passed on to the fuel supplier and the fuel supplier compensates the SPV for any alternate fuels that may need to be purchased by it or pays "Consequential Damages" to the SPV, which are essentially all the losses suffered by the SPV under the PPA and other project documents on account of a default by the fuel supplier under the FSA. As before, the guiding objective in such contracting is to ensure that the risks are substantially mitigated for the SPV by allocation to parties that are in the best position to manage these risks. It is entirely feasible that an O&M contractor or a fuel supplier or an EPC contractor may agree to bear only a part of the Consequential Damages resulting on account of their non-performance and the SPV is therefore exposed to certain residual risks under certain events of non-performance. Under such situations, lenders need to carefully evaluate these residual risks, the qualifications of the project parties whose non-performance may expose the SPV to such risks and thus arrive at the probability of such risks actually materialising. If lenders are not completely satisfied, they may seek some form of back-stopping by sponsors and therefore change the flavour of the financing from non-recourse to "limited" or "full" recourse.

Risk Mitigation Mechanisms In a way, mitigation of the project's construction and operating risks are fundamental to the process of financing. The key risks and how they are mitigated are shown below.

Key Risks	*Mitigation Mechanisms*	*Project Parties Expected to Bear the Risk*
Project Cost Overrun	▪ Fixed Price, Date Certain EPC Contract ▪ Project cost to include sufficient contingency provisions to cover physical contingencies, cost escalations on account of adverse exchange rate fluctuations, cost escalations on account of change orders/ design modifications during implementation etc. ▪ Careful evaluation of EPC contractor's qualifications. ▪ Cost comparison with similar projects ▪ Loan disbursements allowed only after all statutory approvals for construction have been received by SPV	▪ EPC Contractor/Project Sponsors

Key Risks	*Mitigation Mechanisms*	*Project Parties Expected to Bear the Risk*
Shortfall in Financing	■ Undertaking from Sponsors to fund cost overruns (may be capped) ■ Draw down allowed only on financial closure ■ Undertaking from Sponsors to finance shortfalls, if any	Sponsors
Commercial Risks	■ Careful evaluation of the electricity demand supply scenario in the state ■ A view on the ability of the SEB to meet committed offtake targets	SEB, State Government and Lenders[3]

Once the lenders are satisfied with the risk allocation mechanism, a project cost and a financing structure is finalised. The lenders then approve the debt facilities to the project, which become drawable at the time of "financial close", which is defined as a time when the SPV has met all the CPs associated with the approved loans. Some typical CPs in power project financing are as under:

- Completion of acquisition of land for the project
- Complete tie-up of the project equity, identification of project sponsors, and execution of a satisfactory Shareholders' Agreement
- Completion of Front End Engineering Design by reputed engineering consultants and finalisation of a technical configuration for the project
- Execution of a bankable (what banks find worthy of lending against) EPC contract
- Completion of Environmental Impact Assessment studies and receipt of clearances from the Ministry of Environment and Forests and from the State Pollution Control Board
- Execution of a bankable PPA
- Execution of a bankable O&M agreement
- Execution of a bankable FSA
- Equity subscription by sponsors at least to the extent of 20-30 percent of their final estimated contribution[4]
- Tie-up of all debt, execution of loan documentation with all project lenders
- Creation of security (mortgage of land/hypothecation of assets)
- Assignment of all project contracts to lenders
- Execution of all documents by the SEB to facilitate the credit enhancement process

[3] Under certain conditions of limited recourse financing, lenders may require Sponsors to provide cash deficit supports or other forms of credit enhancements.

[4] Negotiable, typically about 50 percent; in certain cases lenders have also sought entire sponsors' contribution to come in upfront, prior to any loan disbursements.

The CPs form part of Term Sheet that is issued by the lenders to the SPV. In addition to the CPs, the Term Sheet also contains applicable commercial terms and security and credit enhancement requirements, if any. A typical credit enhancement that most power projects (and infrastructure projects) provide to lenders is creation of a 6-month forward Debt Service Reserve Account (DSRA), which is a special account administered by a lender's representative and funded directly from the payments made by the SEB (through a Trust and Retention Account) in such a manner so as to ensure that the account always contains funds sufficient to service the following 6 months' debt service obligations. In addition, project lenders would also want all the project contracts, including, inter alia, the PPA, O&M, EPC and Insurance Agreements to be assigned to the lenders. In limited recourse financing, lenders may insist that sponsors pledge their shareholding in the SPV to project lenders, provide certain cash deficit support undertakings to lenders, provide certain funding in the event there are cost overruns and also undertake not to exit the project/or even reduce their initial shareholding unless all loans are fully repaid. In most such financing, lenders also reserve the right to nominate a Director on the Board of the SPV.

20.10 MANAGING RISKS IN PRIVATE INFRASTRUCTURE PROJECTS

While all projects are risky, private infrastructure projects in developing countries seem to be characterised by a higher degree of risk. Investors perceive greater risk in these projects partly because these projects are undertaken by special purpose companies and not by established utility companies with strong balance sheets.

To ensure that such projects are financeable, the sponsors must carefully assess various risks and take appropriate risk mitigation measures. The major risks involved and the methods for managing them are described below.

Construction Risk Due to unexpected developments during the construction period, there may be time and cost overruns or the completed project may have shortfall in performance parameters. Construction risk tends to be more in sectors such as transportation and power and less in sectors such as telecommunications and urban services.

Construction risk can be shifted to a certain extent to the EPC (engineering, procurement, and construction) contractor who is given turnkey responsibility with suitable penalties for delays and performance shortfall. However, since the penalties for non-performance are typically capped, the construction risk cannot be eliminated completely. The residual risk has to be borne by investors.

Operating Risk The performance of the project may be below the projected level of performance. Operating risk tends to be lower when the project uses a tested technology (as in the case of a power project or a road project) and higher when the technology is changing rapidly (as in the case of a telecom project).

Operating risk can be mitigated by entrusting the operations to an experienced and competent O&M (operations and maintenance) contractor with provisions for liquidated damages and taking appropriate insurance covers.

Market Risk The actual market and demand conditions may turn out to be very different from what was assumed in determining the viability of the project.

When the private producer sells to a monopoly purchaser (as in the case of an independent power producer selling to a monopoly distributor), market risk may be mitigated by entering into an agreement that guarantees a minimum level of purchase. When the private producer sells directly to individual users who have multiple options (as in the case of roads), the project sponsors may ask the government to guarantee a certain minimum payment if the tariff falls below a certain level. To ensure symmetry, such a guarantee may be balanced by sharing a portion of revenue when the tariff exceeds a certain level.

Interest Rate Risk The project company often borrows money at a floating interest rate. Hence, the changes in interest rate during the life of the project cause interest rate risk. This risk is particularly pronounced for infrastructure projects because of high capital intensity, long payback periods, and high levels of gearing.

Interest rate risk may be mitigated by transferring it to consumers through a tariff formula that treats interest cost as a pass-through cost. Alternatively, interest rate risk may be hedged through devices like interest rate swaps and interest rate caps and collars.

Foreign Exchange Risk When a project relies on foreign currency debt, unfavorable variation in the exchange rate results in a higher debt servicing burden in terms of domestic currency. Foreign exchange risk may be managed by shifting it to consumers through a tariff formula that automatically provides adjustment for exchange rate changes. Alternatively, the project company may resort to currency swaps.

Payment Risk An infrastructure project may face the risk of not being paid for services provided. This risk is more pronounced when the project company sells to a monopoly buyer as in the case of an independent power producer (IPP) supplying power to a monopoly public sector distributor; it is less severe when the project company sells to a multitude of customers as in the case of a telecom operator or a toll road.

Payment risk may be mitigated by a mechanism such as letter of credit, government guarantee, and escrow arrangement.

Regulatory Risk Infrastructure projects are subject to regulation that covers, among other things, tariff determination. Arbitrary changes in the regulatory framework are a source of risk.

The onus of mitigating regulatory risk seems to lie with the government. As Montek Ahluwalia put it: "In general, regulatory risk is best handled by establishing strong and independent regulatory authorities that operate with maximum transparency of procedures within a legal framework that provides investors with credible recourse against arbitrary action."

Political Risk Infrastructure projects are highly visible and touch the lives of public in basic areas. This makes them vulnerable to populist political action that can jeopardise their financial viability – in the extreme case, political action can lead to cancellation of license or nationalisation.

Political risk can be partially mitigated through political risk insurance offered by multilateral organisations, such as the Multilateral Investment Guarantee Agency, or bilateral investment protection agreements. It can also be reduced by incorporating into the project agreement a suitable provision for compensation against arbitrary action, subject to international arbitration. Yet another instrument is the World Bank's new partial risk guarantee instrument which covers debt service payments if they are interrupted because the government does not fulfil its specific obligations.

20.11 SOME SHORTCOMINGS IN INFRASTRUCTURE MANAGEMENT[5]

Infrastructure has become a "thorn in development flesh," particularly in South Asia. This was primarily due to the following factors.

1. *A rigid bureaucracy* Many bureaucrats believed that infrastructure is the absolute monopoly of the government.
2. *A lack of ability or willingness to pay for good infrastructure* This view is shared by the public as well as the authorities at large.
3. *A lack of understanding of how to create a "viable infrastructure model"* A viable infrastructure model is a model that gives the investor (including the Government) a reasonable return and at the same time does not overcharge the users.
4. *Unwillingness to pay for specialised knowledge* There has been very little appreciation that better technologies and expertise bring enormous improvements and these have to be adequately compensated.
5. *Inadequate training of operating personnel* While it is common for the top brass of infrastructure projects (who usually have a short tenure) to receive some training, the middle and lower level executives who do the actual work day after day hardly receive any training.
6. *Lack of process and method* Proper manuals of operation and structured process for running infrastructure projects are rarely developed.
7. *Inappropriate sharing of risks* Infrastructure projects usually carry twice as many risks as industrial projects. These risks have to be properly shared by the government and various parties involved in the infrastructure project.

Some Solutions Here are some solutions to address the problems mentioned above:

1. *Focus on utilising existing projects rather than announcing new projects* This option is generally not explored because of the political compulsion to unveil big projects and an unwillingness to let the private sector in for technology and operation.
2. *Handover public assets on long-term lease* Using a system of transparent tendering or bidding, lease out infrastructure assets to private sector players, while retaining the ownership with the government.
3. *Build management capacity* The managerial and operating staff of infrastructure projects must be trained regularly. In addition, more courses on infrastructure management must be introduced in engineering colleges and business schools.
4. *Create public awareness to pay for good infrastructure* The public must be sensitised that good infrastructure costs money and users must pay for it.

[5] Contributed by Padmanabhan Nair.

5. *Strengthen the regulatory structure* A regulatory structure must be created that provides a satisfactory return to the investor while protecting the users.
6. *Deepen the debt market* While the government provides "viability gap funding" by way of equity to strategically important projects, infrastructure requires huge amounts of debt financing. There is an urgent need to deepen the debt market.

20.12 MEASURES OF SAVINGS IN INFRASTRUCTURE COSTS

According to the McKinsey Global Institute report on *Infrastructure Productivity: How to Save $1 Trillion* (released in January 2013), $57 trillion of infrastructure investment will be required between 2013 and 2030, just to keep up with the projected global GDP growth. The monumental size of infrastructure deficit and the daunting task of financing it will dominate political and public discussion. This focus, however, diverts attention from the compelling and urgent issue of how to raise the productivity of infrastructure investment by a substantial margin. According to McKinsey if the proven best practices are scaled up, it is possible to achieve savings of 40 percent or $ 1 trillion a year. Three main levers can deliver the potential savings: improving project selection and optimising infrastructure portfolios; streamlining delivery; and making the most of existing infrastructure projects.

Improving Project Selection and Optimising Infrastructure Portfolios By selecting the right combination of projects, a significant amount ($ 200 billion annually) can be saved. As the McKinsey report put it: "To achieve these savings, owners must use precise selection criteria that ensure proposed projects meet specific goals; develop sophisticated evaluation methods to determine costs and benefits; and prioritise projects at a system level, using transparent, fact-based decision making."

Streamlining Delivery Streamlining project delivery can save up to $ 400 billion annually, while accelerating timelines significantly. Adequate investment in early-stage project planning and design is a key source of savings in project delivery. According to the McKinsey report, "This can reduce costs significantly by preventing changes and delays later on in the process when they become even more expensive." The report adds, "Owners can structure contracts to encourage cost-saving approaches, including design-to-cost principles that ensure the development of 'minimal technical solutions'—the lowest-cost means of achieving a prescribed performance specification, rather than mere risk avoidance."

Making the Most of Existing Infrastructure Assets By getting more out of existing capacity, some infrastructure needs can be met. The McKinsey report estimates that savings up to $ 400 billion a year can be achieved by increasing asset utilisation, optimising maintenance planning, and deploying better demand-management measures. To secure the savings identified above, the infrastructure governance and delivery system has to be upgraded by (a) improving coordination between the infrastructure authorities responsible for the different types of infrastructure, (b) clearly separating political and technical responsibilities for infrastructure, (c) dividing roles and responsibilities between public and private sectors, establishing clarity on market structure, regulation, pricing and subsidies, ownership and financing, (d) creating reliable data on which to base day-to-day oversight and long-term planning, and (e) building strong public-sector capabilities across the value chain of planning, delivery, and operations.

SUMMARY

- Infrastructure projects have the following characteristics: they are highly capital-intensive, they involve huge sunk costs, and they have a long operating lives.
- Traditionally infrastructure projects in India were owned and managed by the government or government undertakings. Given the massive investments required in infrastructure, there is a broad consensus now that private sector participation in this activity must be encouraged in the form of public-private partnerships (PPPs).
- A PPP project is a project based on a contract or concession agreement between a government or statutory entity and a private sector entity for delivering infrastructure service on payment of user charges.
- A PPP project is a special purpose vehicle that has relationships with various partners.
- The commonly used structures of PPP are build-operate-transfer (BOT), build-own-operate-transfer (BOOT), build-own-operate (BOO), build-lease-transfer (BLT), lease-develop-operate (LDO), rehabilitate-operate-transfer (ROT), and design-build-finance-operate-and transfer (DBFOT).
- The key project parties are project sponsors, project vehicle, project lenders, EPC contractor, O&M contractor, and government. Through a comprehensive web of contracts, every major risk inherent in the project is allocated to the party/ parties that is best able to assess and manage that risk.
- The major risks involved in PPPs are: construction risk, operating risk, market risk, interest rate risk, foreign exchange risk, payment risk, regulatory risk, and political risk.
- There are several deficiencies in infrastructure management, particularly in developing countries.
- The three main levers to save on infrastructure costs are: improving project selection and optimising infrastructure portfolios; streamlining delivery; and making the most of the existing infrastructure projects.

QUESTIONS

1. Discuss the characteristics of infrastructure projects.
2. What is a public-private partnership (PPP)?
3. Discuss the relevance of PPPs in India and how they can be taken forward.
4. Describe the typical configuration of a PPP.
5. What are the commonly used structures of a PPP?
6. Briefly describe each of the project parties and their responsibilities.

7. What are the important contents and objectives of the Shareholders' Agreement?
8. What are the important contents and objectives of the EPC Contract?
9. What are the important contents and objectives of the Project Loan Agreement?
10. What are the important contents and objectives of the O&M Contract?
11. Show diagrammatically the parties in a power project.
12. What are the salient features of a Power Purchase Agreement (PPA)?
13. Discuss the major risks in PPSs and the ways to manage them.
14. What are the shortcomings in infrastructure management in India? What can be done to overcome them?
15. Discuss the measures of savings in infrastructure projects.

APPENDIX 20A
THE CONCESSION AGREEMENT[6]

The Concession Agreement is an agreement between the Government which is the grantor of Concession – (the word concession means leave of permission to operate) and the Project Company (which is the Grantee or beneficiary of the concession) to construct and implement a project.

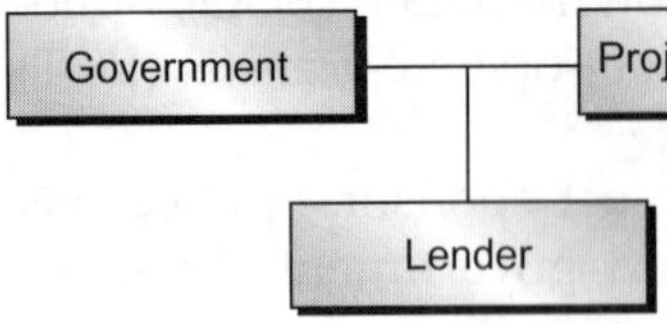

Government — Project Company

Lender

The lender is a party to the Concession Agreement (CA), since without the debt and the consequent covenants which are laid out by the lender, the CA will be an incomplete document. Considering the low share of equity compared to debt, and the promoter's contribution in it itself a fraction of it, it can be inferred that the promoter project company mainly plays the role of a conductor of a band, and its critical function is one of coordination between various players. In this context, there is goal congruence between the Government and the lender, in the sense both want to ensure that the project is a success. Thus, the Government has an ally in the form of the lender in these projects.

The CA broadly covers two very different aspects, viz., commercial terms and financial terms, which are described below:

Commercial Terms

Commercial terms include the following:

1. **Obligation to construct a project by a certain date and to certain specifications**: These will require back-to-back agreements with suppliers and EPC contractors. For instance, if a private Power Generation Company gives a guarantee that it will pay ₹X as penalty for delay for every day of delay from the deadline of say October 1, then it may have another contract with its EPC with a deadline of September 15, and a penalty of ₹1.5X

[6] Contributed by Dr. V. Ranganathan, former professor, IIMB.

for every day of delay. These clauses bring in the discipline of completing the projects on time.

Similarly, there is an obligation to ensure quality because there are tight legal clauses about the consequences (in terms of penalties) in case of non-compliance to quality. The downside is that the legal costs are huge.

2. **Mechanism by which the specification may be varied:** Often times, for complex projects, many of which are the first time they are undertaken, it is not possible to draw up a correct and flawless specification in the beginning itself. Therefore it is important to have a common understanding between the Government and the Project Company on how the specifications will be varied, more specifically which changes will be paid for and which changes will have to be accommodated as part of the process itself. There is information asymmetry between the Government and the Project Companies, and often the Project Company may quote a low expenditure to secure the contract and make up the money by charging for change in specification. Government must consciously try to minimise this.
3. **Warranties to the standard of construction:** A third party consultant is to be appointed by the Project Company who will certify the quality and warranties have to be given for specific number of years of trouble-free operation.
4. **Completion and testing procedures:** When a project is ready to give steady state output or service level is to be clearly determined by a standard set of completion and testing procedures so that the commercial operation date, the date from which revenue stream will start coming, is determined in an unambiguous manner.
5. **Operation, maintenance and improvement procedures:** Clear establishment of these procedures will make sure of efficient and safe operations.
6. **Accounting and reporting procedures:** These have to be in conformity with the standard GAAP.
7. **Payment of a concession fee:** Government typically charges a concession fee for giving the license to operate, which is included in the CA.
8. **Tariffs and revisions:** This is regarding the tariffs set for the sale of output or service provided by the Project Company. It may relate to toll charges for a toll road or bridge crossing, cost of power for a power generating company, though in the latter case it may be covered by a detailed power purchase agreement (PPA), or aeronautical and non-aeronautical charges for an airport. The tariff may be a number like ₹X per kwh of electricity or it may be a formula like how the gas price is determined based on various other prices. Sometimes they are left to the regulator to be determined. But some World Bank professionals have suggested a concept called *"Regulation by contract"* where the tariff is set in the CA itself for the initial two tariff periods, to remove regulatory risk faced by the private sector Project Company[7].

---

[7] Manish Agarwal, Bernard Tenenbaum and Alexander, "Delhi Discom Privatisations" World Bank, 2003.
http://www.energytoolbox.org/library/incentive-based_operating_contracts/reference+background_documents/The_Delhi_Electricity_Discom_Privatizations_Observations_and_Recommendations.pdf

9. **Termination rights and consequences:** The CA may be terminated by the host Government for a variety of reasons. The Airport modernisation CA with GMR group was terminated by the Government of Maldives on the grounds that it was void from the outset[8]. GMR claimed ₹5,000 crores for the abrupt and unilateral termination. In the Enron-MSEB Dabhol contract, both Enron and the State of Maharashtra issued notices to end the contract[9]. The lender and the Project Company should provide for such eventualities and safeguard their interest in the event of such unpleasant occurrence.
10. **Transfer of assets and personnel at the commencement and expiry of concession period**: The operation in the host country may require the bringing in of assets and expert expatriate personnel from the home country of the MNC. The personnel must get easy visa and they should be able to remain with the SPV as long as they are required. Similarly, there should be clarity as to how the assets and personnel will be taken back or redeployed after the end of the concession period. These issues arise because a project company is not like a *going concern* which will remain indefinitely till liquidation.

Financial Terms

Financial terms are meant to satisfy the lenders about the safety of monies due to them. These cover the following:

- Assets on which the lenders will have a security charge.
- Nature of security charge.
- Negative pledges.
- Direct agreement with third parties.
- Right to acquire management control.

Assets Covered by Security Charge The lenders generally ask for a security charge on the following:

- Concession agreement
- Operating agreement
- Physical assets
- Sales contracts
- Insurance covers
- Production proceeds

Nature of Security Charge The nature of security can be fixed or floating. Fixed charge refers to the charge that can be ascertained with a specific asset, while creating it. Floating charge is a charge created on assets of uncertain magnitude at the time of creation, like oil in the ground. The conversion of floating charge into fixed charge is known as crystallisation, as a result of it the security is no more a floating security. This occurs upon acceleration of a loan repayment, when the company is about to wind up.

---

[8] http://www.livemint.com/Companies/VxYsszdFG0HXa0WVjVscUJ/GMR-claims-Rs5000-crore-from-Maldives-govt-for-terminating.html

[9] http://edition.cnn.com/2001/BUSINESS/asia/05/25/india.dabhol/

Negative Pledge A negative pledge in an unsecured loan agreement is a provision that prevents the borrower from obtaining any secured loan without the consent of the unsecured lender.

Direct Agreement with Third Parties Suppose the SPV has signed a contract with a coal supplier to supply coal for electricity production. For some reason, the coal supplier is not paid and he may stop supplying coal. To prevent such a possibility, the lender signs a direct agreement with the coal supplier stipulating that the latter should continue to supply coal and the payment for the same will be made by the lender.

Right to Acquire Management Control In the event of imminent default, the lender will have the right to acquire management control. This means that the lender can:

- Take charge over the company's shares
- Have a golden share (meant for the purpose of management control, but not for dividend)
- Step into the shoes of the promoter and run the company.

Support of the Host Government

In order to ensure the viability and bankability of the infrastructure project, the host government may provide financial and non-financial support. The important ways in which it provides support are as follows.

Capital Subsidy or Revenue Subsidy The host government may give capital subsidy or revenue subsidy if the tariffs have to be set lower to maximise the use of the asset.

Infrastructure Act To mitigate uncertainty over future government policy, the government may pass an Infrastructure Act.

Comfort Letters These letters may be given by the sponsors or the host government to the lenders to assuage their feeling of discomfort!

Chapter 21

Evaluation and Financing of Infrastructure Projects

LEARNING OBJECTIVES

After studying this chapter you should be able to

- Identify the key issues addressed in technical feasibility studies of public-private partnership projects.
- Understand the salient differences between the appraisal of capital investment projects and infrastructure projects.
- Appreciate the key challenges in infrastructure financing.
- Describe the features of project financing versus direct financing.
- List the sources of infrastructure financing.
- Discuss the key recommendations of the Committee on Infrastructure Financing.
- Enumerate the efforts of the government and RBI to attract investment in infrastructure.
- Describe some arrangements that are especially relevant to infrastructure financing.

There is a massive need for infrastructure investments. SBI Capital Markets Research has projected infrastructure investments for FY 2018–FY 2022 as follows.

Future Projections (FY 18–22)

Sector	*Investments (₹ lakh Cr)*	*Investments (USD trillion)*	
Power	14.5	0.223	Renewables, Transmission network
Roads	10.0	0.154	Mega plans in roads
Railways	8.0	0.123	Enhanced budget
Airports & Ports	1.0	0.015	Non-metro airports
Urban Development	5.5	0.085	Major focus
Others	11.0	0.169	
Total	50.0	0.769	

Units: 1 lakh crore = 1 trillion /USD 1 = INR 65
Source: SBI Capital Markets Research

Traditionally, private infrastructure investment relied mainly on bank financing and on capital market to some extent. Going forward it will be necessary to tap other sources of finance and design more innovative ways of financing.

This chapter discusses various aspects of evaluation and financing of PPP projects.

21.1 TECHNICAL FEASIBILITY OF INFRASTRUCTURE PROJECTS

Infrastructure projects are highly capital intensive, have long economic life, and have a significant impact on the lives of people. Given the massive investments in infrastructure proposed by the government, a great thrust is being given on the PPP (public-private partnership) model. A PPP is a contractual arrangement between a government or statutory entity on the one side and a private sector company on the other side, for delivering an infrastructure service.

The different stages of a PPP project development lifecycle are as follows.

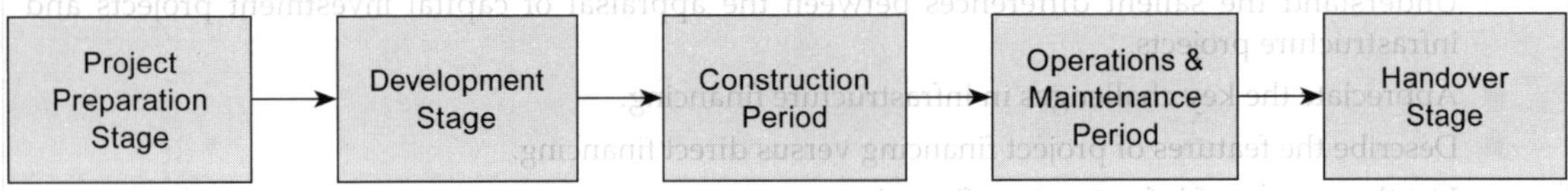

The project preparation stage involves identifying the project need by the government. The development stage comprises activities such as project feasibility study, project structuring, bid documentation, and selection of a private partner. The private partner then has the responsibility for the construction and operation and maintenance (O&M). The last stage involves handing over of the project facilities from the private partner to the public entity after the expiry of the agreement period.

It is crucial to justify infrastructure projects from technical, financial, economic, social, and environmental angles.

The technical feasibility of an infrastructure project to be undertaken under the PPP model is generally done by the public entity once a project is identified and prior to project structuring stage.

According to the *PPP Guidelines for Practitioners* prepared by the Ministry of Finance, Government of India, technical feasibility studies should address the following questions:

- What are the various engineering/design options and the optimum option?
- What is the cost associated with and service levels expected of the various engineering/design options?
- Which of the engineering/design options would be amenable for implementation by the private sector?
- How does each of the options affect environment and the society?
- What could be the public entity's extent of involvement in land acquisition and associated infrastructure creation, such as connectivity, water supply, power, etc?

21.2 SALIENT DIFFERENCES BETWEEN THE APPRAISAL OF CAPITAL INVESTMENT PROJECTS AND INFRASTRUCTURE PROJECTS[1]

For the purpose of this note, projects may be classified as follows:

A. A capital investment project set up within an existing company.
B. A capital investment project set up as a separate company which is a subsidiary or associate of an existing company (parent company)
C. An infrastructure project set up as a special purpose vehicle (a separate company) by sponsoring companies.

The manner in which these projects are appraised by the investors and lending institutions is shown below.

	A. Capital Investment Project Within an Existing Company.	B. Capital Investment Project Set up as a Separate Company.	C. Infrastructure Project Set up as a Special Purpose Vehicle (Separate Company).
Appraisal by the Investors			
Cash Flows	■ Cash flows are defined as incremental project cash flows.	■ Cash flows are identified from the point of new of the separate entity.	■ Project cash flows as well as equity cash flows are considered.
	■ Cash flows are generally considered for a period of 10 years or the loan repayment period.	■ Cash flows are generally considered for a period of 10 years or the loan repayment period.	■ Cash flows are considered for the entire project life or 30 years whichever is lesser.
	■ There is usually a salvage value which is positive	■ Since the new entity is regarded by the parent as a 'going concern' with indefinite life, no salvage value is considered.	■ There may or may not be any salvage value. Sometimes, there may be outlays incurred for dismantling or winding up the project.

[1] Contributed by Vivek Date

Appraisal Criteria	■ The commonly used appraisal criteria are NPV, IRR, payback period, and accounting rate of return.	■ Considering the indefinite life of the business entity the parent company may use accounting rates of return such as ROE and ROI.	■ NPV and IRR are calculated from the project point of view (PNPV and PIRR) and the equity point of view (ENPV and EIRR).
	■ A shorter payback period is used because firms do not want to take the risk of uncertainties in volume of sales, competition, input costs, and so on.	■ A little longer payback period is used depending upon the magnitude of investment and the nature of business.	■ An even longer payback period is acceptable because the outputs of services have an assured take off and competition is restricted.
Benchmark Rate	■ Weighted average cost of capital (WACC) is the most commonly used discount rate for calculating the NPV or evaluating the IRR.	■ A risk-adjusted return on equity (ROE) is generally used for assessing the new entity.	■ Weighted average cost of capital (WACC) is used to calculate PNPV and judge the PIRR. The cost of equity is used to calculate EPNV and judge the EIRR.
Appraisal and Requirements of Lending Institutions			
Debt Service Coverage ratio	■ A debt service coverage ratio of 1.5 is required.	■ A debt service coverage ratio of 1.5 is required.	■ A slightly lower debt service coverage ratio of 1.35 is acceptable.
Recourse	■ Entire company cash flows are relevant even though only incremental cash flows are considered for calculating NPV and IRR.	■ Cash flows of only the new entity are relevant. Sometimes guarantees are sought from the sponsors.	■ Cash flows of only the SPV are relevant, as loans are typically non-recourse based.

Loan Security/ Guarantee	■ Primary and collateral security from the company are insisted upon.	■ Over and above the primary and collateral securities, guarantees from promoters are insisted upon.	■ Movable assets are hypothecated. In addition, escrow accounts, assignment of all contracts, pledge of shares of sponsors, and step-in agreement are insisted.
Lenders' Control	■ Lenders are not much concerned with the agreements between the company and its buyers and suppliers.	■ Lenders are not much concerned with the agreements between the company and its buyers and suppliers.	■ Lenders examine the agreements between the SPV and all the contracting parties.

Financial Evaluation of an Infrastructure Project

The financial evaluation of a real life infrastructure project is discussed below. In this example, for the sake of simplicity, we look at pre-tax project cash flows (PBIDT) and pre-tax weighted average cost of capital.

Narmada Infrastructure Limited was set up as a Special Purpose Vehicle to build the Narmada bridge on a build, operate, and transfer (BOT) basis. The construction period of the bridge was supposed to be three years, 1998 through 2000. The Special Purpose Vehicle would enjoy a Concession Period of 15 years, 2001–2015, and after this period the bridge would be transferred to the government.

The project cost (including interest during the construction period) was estimated at ₹144 crore. It would be financed by ₹48 crore of equity and ₹96 crore of debt. For the first year of operation, viz., 2001, the projected revenue per day was as follows:

Cars:	3916 × ₹11	=	₹43,076
LCVs:	3578 × ₹28	=	₹100,184
Buses:	2565 × ₹33	=	₹84,645
Trucks:	21305 × ₹33	=	₹703,065
			₹930,975

Keeping a margin of 10 percent for maintenance and other factors, the revenue for 2001 was estimated as: ₹930975 × 365 × 0.90 = ₹30,58,25,288. The operating and maintenance expenses for year 2001 were estimated as ₹2,75,24,276.

Hence, the projected operating surplus (PBDIT) for year 1 (2001) was: ₹30,58,25,288 – ₹2,75,24,276 = ₹27,83,01,012. This may be approximated as ₹27.8 crore. It was assumed that this would grow at a rate of 8 percent per year over the Concession Period. The project may be evaluated at the beginning of 2001 (that is, year 1 of operation). To calculate the NPV of the project at that point of time, assume the following: (i) the imputed cost of equity during the construction period is ₹16 crore, (ii) the periodic cash flow is PBIDT, and (iii) the pre-tax WACC is 18 percent.

Given the above assumptions, the NPV of the project is:

$$NPV = \frac{27.8}{(1.18)} + \frac{27.8(1.08)}{(1.18)} + \cdots \frac{27.8(1.08)^{14}}{(1.18)^{15}} - 160$$

The benefit stream is a growing annuity. The present value of a growing annuity (PVGA) is:

$$PVGA = \frac{A}{r-g}\left(1 - \frac{(1+g)^n}{(1+r)^n}\right)$$

Applying this formula to our case, we find that the present value of benefits (PVB) is:

$$PVB = \frac{27.8}{0.18-0.08}\left(1 - \frac{(1.08)^{15}}{(1.18)^{15}}\right) = ₹204.4 \text{ crore}$$

$$NPV = 204.4 - 160 = ₹44.4 \text{ crore}$$

21.3 CHALLENGES IN INFRASTRUCTURE FINANCING

The first wave of private investment in infrastructure in India was largely supported by bank lending. This is not sustainable because of the asset-liability mismatch for banks.

Reliance on foreign capital for the scale of infrastructure required in India is not feasible. So we have to rely largely on domestic savings. Fortunately, India has a high rate of domestic savings. What is required is a sophisticated system of financial intermediation that can channel domestic savings into infrastructure in a way that does not create unmanageable risk.

Infrastructure financing presents a number of challenges:

- The scale of investment is large.
- Investors have to be prepared for a long horizon for debt repayment and return on equity.
- The output is not tradable, so the revenues occur in domestic currency. Hence infrastructure projects should generally be domestically financed to avoid high foreign exchange risk (although there are financial instruments to mitigate such risks in well-developed financial markets).
- The non-recourse nature of infrastructure financing, the unique risks associated with infrastructure, and the complex contracting arrangements that go with infrastructure projects call for special appraisal skills.

As a country's financial system matures and becomes more sophisticated, it can respond to these challenges in innovative ways. As Rajiv Lal and Ritu Anand observed, "It can bring a range of investors at various stages of the project. Investors with the requisite skills and risk appetite are needed to provide the initial financing, but should be able to offload the assets to other investors when the projects start yielding revenues, thus moving on to invest in new projects."

The principal sources of debt financing for infrastructure in India so far have been commercial banks, non-banking finance companies, external commercial borrowings, and insurance companies.

21.4 PROJECT FINANCING VERSUS DIRECT FINANCING

Infrastructure projects under the PPP model are almost invariably financed using the project financing approach.

Project financing involves raising funds for a capital investment project that can be economically separated from its sponsor. As against this, direct financing involves raising funds on the sponsor's general credit. It is instructive to compare the two.

Direct Financing	*Project Financing*
Cash flows from different assets and businesses of the sponsor are commingled.	Project-related assets and cash flows are segregated from the other activities of the sponsor.
Creditors have full recourse to the project sponsor. So, they look at the sponsor's entire portfolio for debt service.	Creditors generally have limited, or even no, recourse to the project sponsor. So, they look at project-related assets and cash flows for debt service.
Financing can be arranged fairly quickly.	Financing is time-consuming and involves higher information, contracting, and transaction costs.
Managers have considerable discretion in allocating free cash flow between dividends and re-investment. So, equity investors are exposed to the agency costs of free cash flow.	Managers have limited or no discretion with respect to free cash flow. Hence, the agency costs of free cash flow are mitigated.
Sponsor's debt capacity may be somewhat limited.	Sponsor's debt capacity is effectively enhanced.
Direct monitoring by investors is rather limited.	Investors do closer monitoring than in a typical company.

21.5 FINANCING SOURCES FOR PPP PROJECTS

The various sources for financing PPP projects are listed below:

Financing Sources for PPP Projects

Domestic Sources	*External Sources*
Equity	
■ Domestic developers (independently or in collaboration with international developers). ■ Public utilities (taking minority holdings). ■ Other institutional investors (likely to be very limited).	■ International developers (independently or in collaboration with domestic developers). ■ Equipment suppliers (in collaboration with domestic or international developers). ■ Dedicated infrastructure funds. ■ Other international equity investors. ■ Multilateral agencies (IFC, ADB).
Debt	
■ Domestic commercial banks (3–5 years). ■ Domestic term lending institutions (7–10 years). ■ Domestic bond markets (7–10 years). ■ Specialised infrastructure, financing institutions.	■ International commercial banks (7–10 years). ■ Export credit agencies (7–10 years). ■ International bond markets (10–30 years). ■ Multilateral agencies (15–20 years). ■ Bilateral aid agencies.

Source: Planning Commission, GoI

Key Considerations in the Financing and Planning Process

1. **Tailor the financing choice to the needs of the project:** There are a variety of ways of financing the debt component of infrastructure finance the principal ones being bank loans, privately placed debt, and publicly issued debt.
2. **Anticipate the ratings required by lenders or investors and the need for credit enhancement:** Since many institutional investors have a mandate to invest in investment grade assets, an investment grade rating helps in broadening the investor base. To achieve such a grade, a public guarantee and/ or credit enhancement-partial or full-may be used.
3. **Anticipate the need for usage guarantees:** Some transactions may not be financeable unless there is a certain level of public sector usage guarantee.
4. **Consider possible adverse impact of post-closing changes in laws and regulations:** Review the record of regulators and public sector authorities in respect of tariff revision and compensation in the wake of regulatory or contractual changes.

Each mode of financing has its inherent features, making it more or less suitable for a given infrastructure project. The criteria used for evaluating a mode of financing for its suitability are: tenor, interest rate structure, flexibility to accommodate changes in circumstances over the life of the project, confidentiality, all-in cost effectiveness. For example, a loan from a small group of relationship banks or private placement with a small number of investors may offer confidentiality and flexibility in terms of drawdown schedules, a simple process for amendments and waivers to the financing terms. A public market transaction might offer a longer tenor than a bank loan and a lower interest rate, but lesser confidentiality and flexibility in amending the terms during the life of the transaction.

21.6 RECOMMENDATIONS OF THE COMMITTEE ON INFRASTRUCTURE FINANCING

The Committee on Infrastructure Financing, chaired by Deepak Parekh, set up by the Ministry of Finance, submitted its report in May 2007. The recommendations of the committee are as follows:

1. Develop a deep and robust corporate debt market by (a) consolidating all the regulations relating to issuance of corporate debt securities under the aegis of SEBI to minimise the multiplicity of regulators, (b) removing TDS on corporate bonds in line with GOI securities, (c) reducing the stamp duty on issuance of debt instruments and making it uniform across the country, (d) allowing repo transactions on corporate bonds in inter-bank repo market through a specialised clearing and settlement platform, (e) increasing the efficiency of the private placement market for debt by confining it to only QIBs without number restrictions and developing an OTC market for privately placed debt securities, (f) removing regulatory asymmetry between loans and bonds, and (g) introducing credit derivatives.
2. Tap the potential of insurance sector by (a) widening the scope of infrastructure financing by insurance companies in terms of sectors, (b) liberalising the investment guidelines in terms of quality and types of eligible instruments, while relying more on management decisions, and (c) harmonising the definition of infrastructure under various regulations (such as those relating to banks and insurance).
3. Enhance the participation of banks, financial institutions, and large NBFCs in infrastructure financing by (a) promoting securitisation of loans, (b) modifying the exposure norms of NBFCs, (c) rationalising the exposure norms of financial intermediaries, (d) allowing banks, financial institutions and NBFCs to raise foreign currency borrowings for on-lending to infrastructure projects, (e) doing away with SLR norms on banks for the resources, domestic or foreign, raised by banks for a long-tenor (say at least 10 years) by way of bonds/term deposits for investment in infrastructure assets, and (f) permitting banks to issue fixed tenor long-term gold deposit certificates and using the proceeds of the same for financing infrastructure projects.
4. Provide fiscal incentives by (a) exempting infrastructure companies or project SPVs from withholding taxes on their foreign borrowings, (b) rationalising the dividend distribution tax, (c) providing tax rebate on investment in ultra mega power projects, and (d) giving investment in unlisted capital of infrastructure companies (operating or holding company) the same tax treatment as that given to a listed equity investment.

5. Facilitate equity flows into infrastructure by (a) liberalising buyback regulations for infrastructure companies, (b) permitting the change of bidders, and (c) allowing SEBI registered venture funds/private equity funds as bidding partners.
6. Induce foreign investments into infrastructure by (a) relaxing rules for FPI participation in 100 percent debt schemes of mutual funds, (b) according separate treatment for infrastructure holding companies (such as L&T Infrastructure Development Project Limited and GMR Infrastructure Limited) which are presently treated as NBFCs and hence subject to severe restrictions, and (c) removing the all-in-price ceiling on ECBs for senior, subordinated and mezzanine foreign debt for infrastructure projects.
7. Utilise a small portion of foreign exchange reserves for infrastructure development by (a) setting up a company in a foreign country which borrows a small fraction of India's foreign exchange reserves to invest in infrastructure development outside India meant to augment India's infrastructure needs or help in sourcing raw materials/importing machinery for India's development, and (b) creating monoline credit insurance company in a foreign country with RBI backing that can provide credit wrap to Indian infrastructure projects for raising resources from international markets.

21.7 EFFORTS OF THE GOVERNMENT AND RBI TO ATTRACT INVESTMENT

As per the Twelfth Plan, out of total $ 1 trillion, nearly 48 percent is estimated to come from private sector led by Public Private Partnerships. The balance 52 percent is expected to be made by the government through budgetary support and debt finance.

The Government and the RBI have made the following efforts to attract investment into the sector:

1. Setting up of India Infrastructure Finance Company Limited (IIFCL).
2. Extension of equity support to infrastructure Non-Bank Financial Companies (NBFC) by the National Investment and Infrastructure Fund (NIIF).
3. Issue of rupee denominated bonds in overseas markets, popularly called masala bonds.
4. Infrastructure bonds to be issued by IFCI (Industrial Financial Corporation Limited), LIC, and IDFC (Infrastructure Development Finance Corporation) with tax deduction incentives for individual tax payers.
5. Promotion of FDI in the infrastructure sector: To facilitate infrastructure financing 100 percent FDI is allowed under the automatic route in some of the sectors such as mining, power, civil aviation sector, construction and development projects, industrial parks, petroleum and natural gas sector, telecommunications, railways and special economic zones.
6. Viability gap funding.
7. Liberalised ECB (External Commercial Borrowings) regime for infrastructure companies. Companies can avail upto $ 750 million for infrastructure projects.
8. Use of foreign exchange reserves for infrastructure projects through (IIFCL).
9. Categorisation of infrastructure lending NBFCs into a special category by RBI and concessional assistance to them.

10. Issue of tax free infrastructure bonds for rail, road and irrigation programmes.
11. Allowing foreign portfolio investors to invest in infrastructure debt funds. Besides, QFIs are also encouraged to make investment in the sector especially through financing of bonds.
12. Take out financing scheme.
13. Green bond scheme.
14. Shift to hybrid annuity model.
15. Introduction of Infrastructure Investment Trusts (InvITs).

Key Challenges in Infrastructure Financing

Infrastructure sector in India is currently grappling with the following challenges.

1. Uncertainty and fluidity with regard to the policy and regulatory framework.
2. Subdued investments in PPP projects. This has resulted in a higher dependence on the government by way of EPC and other annuity based models.
3. Limited appetite for equity investment because the experience of equity investors in the infrastructure sector so far has not been very encouraging in general.
4. Negative sentiment in the lending community because of significant levels of non-performing assets.
5. Aggressive bidding in the reverse bidding process that threatens the long-term economic viability of the project.

21.8 SOME ASPECTS OF INFRASTRUCTURE FINANCING

It is instructive to look at the following aspects that are especially relevant to infrastructure financing: viability gap funding, hybrid annuity model, takeout financing, securitisation, zero coupon bonds, InvIT and India Infrastructure Finance Company Limited.

Viability Gap Funding

A major constraint for India's infrastructure sector is inadequate finance. Apart from the overall difficulty in raising funds, some projects, though economically worthwhile and necessary, may not be financially viable.

To promote such projects, the government has designed Viability Gap Funding (VGF). It represents a grant to support projects that are economically justified but not financially viable. The VGF scheme was launched in 2004 to support PPP projects. VGF is administered by the Ministry of Finance and a provision for it is made in the budget on a year-to-year basis.

VGF grants are given only for infrastructure projects where the selection of the private sector sponsors is through a process of competitive bidding. The VGF grant is disbursed during the construction stage but only after the private sector sponsor makes the equity contribution required for the project.

VGF is usually limited to 20 percent of the total capital cost of the project. VGF is generally provided from the government's budgetary allocation. Sometimes, it is provided by the statutory authority owning the project asset. If the sponsoring Ministry/ State Government/

statutory entity wants to provide assistance in addition to the stipulated amount under VGF, the same will be restricted to a further 20 percent of the total project cost.

The lead financial institution for the project is entrusted with the responsibility for periodic monitoring of the project against agreed milestones and performance levels for the purpose of disbursing the VGF grant.

Hybrid Annuity Model

In 2011–12, more than two-thirds of infrastructure projects were under the PPP mode. For large road projects, the PPPs became the default option. But difficulties in land acquisition, environment clearances, and inadequate equity base of concessionaires caused delays and litigation, casting a shadow over the PPP model.

PPPs now seem to have gained their relevance again, at least in the roads sector, thanks to a change in the terms of business between the government and the concessionaires. From a build operate transfer (BOT) model, most road projects are now being executed under the hybrid annuity model (HAM).

The HAM is a hybrid of BOT annuity and EPC models. Its salient features are as follows:

- The government contributes 40 percent of the project cost in the first five years through equal annual payment. The remaining 60 percent is paid as variable annuity amount after the completion of the project, based on the value of the asset created.
- The developer has to raise the balance 60 percent of the project cost in the form of equity and loans.
- The developer does not have the toll right. The National Highways Authority of India (NHAI) has the responsibility for revenue collection.

Thus, under the HAM model, while the private partner bears the construction and maintenance risk as in the case of BOT (toll) model, the government shares a portion of financing risk.

Delhi-Meerut Expressway Delhi-Meerut Expressway (Delhi Section) is India's first infrastructure project under the Hybrid Annuity Model, built by the Welspun Group. Inaugurated by Narendra Modi on May 27, 2018, it is India's first 14 lane expressway completed within 18 months. It is a green expressway with vertical gardens and solar panels and has coloured cycling track and coloured footpath.

Takeout Financing

Banks have played a pivotal role in financing infrastructure projects in India. However, for a sustained cycle of infrastructure financing, completed projects should attract alternate funding as shown below.

Project stage-Bank Financing → Post completion → Refinancing → Released funds → Fresh funding.

Takeout financing is a mechanism for financing longer duration projects by banks which are primarily interested in granting medium-term loans of 5–7 years. The longer-duration loan is taken out of the books of the financing bank within a pre-determined period by another institution, thus preventing asset-liability mismatch for the bank. After taking out the loan from the bank, the institution could offload it to another bank or keep it on its books.

Securitisation

Securitisation involves packaging a designated pool of assets (mortgage loans, consumer loans, hire purchase receivables, and so on) and issuing securities which are collateralised by the underlying assets and their associated cash flow stream. Securitisation is originated by a firm that seeks to liquefy its pool of assets. Securities backed by mortgage loans are referred to *as mortgage backed securities;* securities backed by other assets are called *asset based securities.*

Securitisation offers the following benefits:

1. It enables a lender (a bank or financial institution) to liquefy the receivables on its balance sheet. Apart from providing liquidity, it helps the lender in improving its asset-liability management.
2. For investors, securitisation provides an additional avenue of investment in quality paper backed by cash flow.
3. From the point of the financial system, securitisation links the capital market with the banking system. By converting loans into tradable debt securities, it improves the depth and liquidity in the debt market. It also spreads credit risks better in the financial system.

Zero Coupon Bonds (ZCB)

India needs to deepen its debt market so that infrastructure projects can tap a wide variety of bonds. One such instrument that needs fillip is the zero coupon bond (ZCB).

A deep discount bond does not carry any coupon rate but is issued at a steep discount over its face value. It is also referred to as 'zero interest (coupon) bond' or just a 'zero'. For example, the Industrial Development Bank of India issued deep discount bonds in 1996 which had a face value of ₹2 lakh and a maturity period of 25 years. The bonds were issued at ₹5300.

Deep discount bonds appeal to issuers interested in conserving their cash flows during the life of the bonds. On the other side of market, they appear attractive to investors who want to protect themselves against the reinvestment rate risk. Remember that the imputed interest on a deep discount bond is automatically reinvested at a rate equal to its yield to maturity. As Finnerty says: "With zeros, interest is effectively reinvested and compounded over the life of the debt issue at the yield to maturity at which the investor purchased the bond." This feature of deep discount bonds may be used by financial institutions in managing their liabilities.

A major disadvantage of deep discount bonds is that they entail a balloon payment at maturity. The issuer may experience difficulty in arranging for such a large payment and hence investors may be expected to bear a higher risk.

InvIT

InvIT, or Infrastructure Investment Trust, works like a mutual fund. An InvIT is designed to pool small sums of money from a number of investors to invest in infrastructure assets that generate cash flows over a period of time, a portion of which is distributed as dividend to investors.

InvITs are regulated under the SEBI Infrastructure Investment Trust Regulation, 2014. There are four parties to an InvIT—sponsors, investment managers, project managers, and the trustee. The infrastructure company interested in raising funds from the public will form the InvIT as the sponsor and appoint an investment manager to manage the assets and investments of the InvIT. The investment manager oversees the project manager who executes the project. Finally, the sponsor will also appoint a trustee.

India Infrastructure Finance Company Limited (IIFCL)

Set up by Government of India, IIFCL provides long-term finance for viable infrastructure projects through the following modes:

- Long-term debt
- Refinance to banks and financial institutions for loans with tenors exceeding 10 years
- Any other mode approved by the government. IIFCL's mandate is to give overriding priority to PPP projects.

The present offerings of IIFCL are as follows:

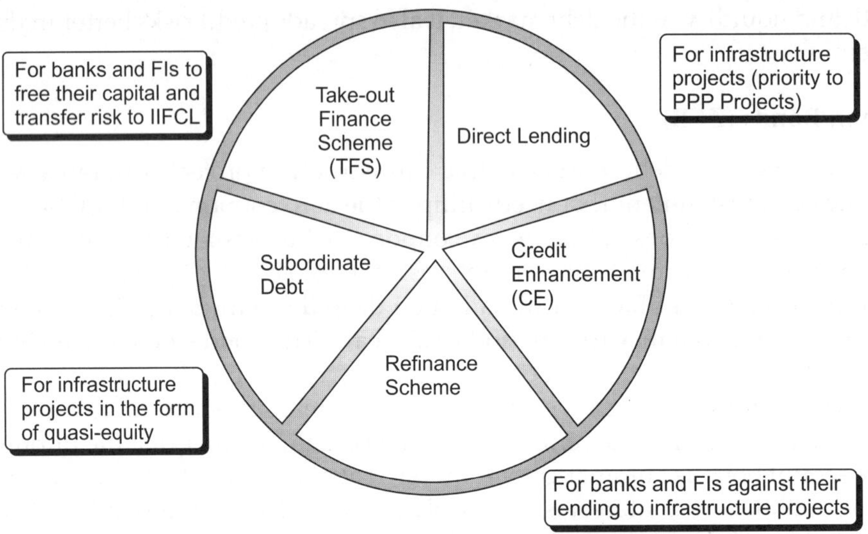

SUMMARY

- There is a massive need for financing infrastructure projects.
- There are important differences between the appraisal of capital investment projects and infrastructure projects.
- Infrastructure financing presents a number of challenges.

- Infrastructure projects under the PPP model are almost invariably financed using the project financing approach. Project financing involves raising funds for a project that can be economically separated from the sponsor.
- The key features of project finance which appear to be the principal arrangement for private sector participation in infrastructure projects are as follows:
  (a) The project is set up as a separate company which is granted a concession by the government.
  (b) The sponsor company which promotes the project usually takes a substantial stake in the equity of the project and enjoys the overall responsibility for running the project.
  (c) The project company enters into comprehensive contractual arrangements with various parties like contractors, suppliers, and customers.
  (d) The project company employs a high debt-equity ratio, with lenders having no recourse or only limited recourse to the sponsor company or to the government in the event of default.
- The Committee on Infrastructure Financing has made several recommendations:
  (a) Develop a deep and robust corporate debt market.
  (b) Tap the insurance companies.
  (c) Enhance the participation of banks, financial institutions, and large NBFCs.
  (d) Provide fiscal incentives.
  (e) Facilitate greater equity flows.
  (f) Induce foreign investments.
  (g) Utilise a small portion of foreign exchange reserves for infrastructure developments.
- The government and RBI have made many efforts to attract private sector investment in infrastructure.
- To promote projects which are economically worthwhile and necessary, but not financially viable, the government has designed the Viability Gap Funding scheme.
- To promote PPPs in the road sector, most road projects are now being executed under the hybrid annuity model (HAM).
- Takeout financing is a mechanism for financing longer duration projects by banks which are primarily interested in granting medium-term loans of 5–7 years. The longer-duration loan is taken out of the books of the financing bank within a pre-determined period by another institution, thus preventing asset-liability mismatch for the bank.
- Securitisation involves packaging a designated pool of assets (mortgage loans, consumer loans, hire purchase receivables, and so on) and issuing securities which are collateralised by the underlying assets and their associated cash flow stream.
- An InvIT, or Infrastructure Investment Trust, works like a mutual fund to pool savings of many investors for an infrastructure project.
- India Infrastructure Finance Company Limited (IIFCL) provides long-term finance for viable infrastructure projects.

QUESTIONS

1. What are the key issues raised in doing the technical feasibility study of a PPP project?
2. Discuss the salient differences between the appraisal of a capital investment project and an infrastructure investment project.
3. What are the key challenges in infrastructure financing?
4. Discuss the major differences between direct financing and project financing.
5. What are the key considerations in the financing and planning of infrastructure projects?
6. Discuss the recommendations of the Committee on Infrastructure Financing.
7. What efforts have the Government and RBI made to attract investment in infrastructure?
8. Discuss the following: viability gap funding, hybrid annuity model, takeout financing, securitisation, zero coupon bonds, and Inv IIT.
9. What are the present offerings of India Infrastructure Finance Company Limited (IIFCL)?

APPENDIX 21A

A CASE STUDY OF INDIRA GANDHI INTERNATIONAL DELHI AIRPORT*

For modernising the Delhi airport, the Airport Authority of India initiated the process to involve private sector through global competitive bidding. The GMR Consortia emerged as the successful bidder.

Delhi International Airport Limited (DIAL) was incorporated as a private limited company under the Companies Act 1956 on March 1, 2006, as the Special Purpose Vehicle to operate, maintain, develop, and modernise the Delhi Airport. Initially, the equity contributions were as follows: GMR group (50.1%), Airport Authority of India (26%), Fraport AG (10%), Eraman Malaysia Airports (10%), and India Development Fund (3.9%). In May 2006, the management of the airport was handed over to the DIAL. Construction started in 2007 and Phase 1A of the construction was commissioned in 2008. The initial term of the concession is 30 years and it is extendable for another 30 years.

DIAL decided to award the contract for constructing the Terminal Runway and other associated works on 'Design and Build' basis using 'Cost Plus' basis to meet stiff time lines—it may be mentioned that 42 months were available for the entire construction but the project was completed in 37 months. Under the 'Design and Build' approach both design and construction proceed parallely. It is meant to fast track the project.

The bids for construction were invited from reputed construction companies in December 2006 on 'Open Book' concept which envisages design, specification, review and finalisation and bid procurement parallely to save time. Out of fifteen respondents, Larsen and Toubro was chosen on the basis techno-commercial evaluation. It was awarded both the design and construction jobs for unity of command and better coordination.

* Adapted from Chapter 11 of Nand Dhameja and Sarika Dhameja *Infrastructure Development and Financing*, Viva Books, 2016.

For Phase-1, DIAL Board approved a project cost estimate of ₹8975 crore. The estimate was simply a 'guesstimate' based on available cost design which lacked reliable information and was meant to achieve financial closure. Exhibit 21A shows the project cost break-up and sources of finance. The firmed up cost estimate, however, was ₹12718 crore. The increase in project cost estimate and its financing is shown in Exhibit 21B.

Exhibit 21A ***Project Cost Break-up and Sources of Finance: Basis of Financial Closure***

Cost Break-up		*Sources of Finance*	
Description	*Amount (₹ crore)*	*Sources*	*Amount (₹ crore)*
T1, T2 and Initial CWIP	762	Equity	1,250
Runway / Taxiway / Apron / Lighting	1,765	Debt Domestic	3,650
Terminal 3 and Associated Building	4,669	ECB*	1,336
Preliminary, Preoperative and IDC	1,279	Lease Deposits / Trade Deposits	912
Delhi Metro	350	Development Fee (DF) – Funding Gap	1,827
Upfront Payment to AAI	150		
TOTAL	8,975	TOTAL	8,975

*External Commercial Borrowing

Exhibit 21B ***Increase in Project Cost Estimate and its Financing***

(Figure in ₹ crores)

Particulars		*Amount*
Project Cost Revised		12718
Initial		8975
Increase in Project Cost		3743
Sources to Finance Increase		
Additional Development Fee (DF)		1654
Other Sources:		
Additional Equity Contribution	1250	
Lease Deposit	559	
ECB	280	2089
Total Additional Means of Finance		3743

The contract with Larsen and Toubro was on Cost plus Basis and the estimated contract sum was ₹5,400 crore which included a fee @20.2%. The Operation, Management and Development Agreement (OMDA) had stiff penalties for delays as the project had to be completed before the Commonwealth Games to be held in New Delhi.

• KPMG Comments

In May 2010, the Government appointed Engineers India Limited (EIL) and KPMG as auditors to audit the project cost.

The important observations of KPMG are described below.

- The key reason behind the increase in the project cost estimate was the design-build approach adopted by DIAL, and also due to unforeseen scope additions (Delhi Metro, ATC tower etc).
- On the issue of risk mitigation, steps undertaken by DIAL to prevent cost escalation were not entirely compliant with international best practices and at no stage was the project cost capped and the risk of escalation shared with the Engineering Procurement and Commissioning (EPC) contractor.
- The contract terms with the EPC contractor did not have any incentives and penalties to enable better control on cost and the PMC did not look at the cost escalation aspect with reference to initial estimate of project costs.
- The increase in project cost was not communicated to the Ministry of Civil Aviation (MoCA) and AAI on a regular and proactive basis.
- The Gross Floor Area (GFA) exceeded the mandated one and no prior approval was taken from the DIAL Board for the same. Further, the GFA per Peak Hour Passenger (PHP) of T3 was higher than most leading airports in the Asia Pacific region.

Implementation

CHAPTER 22

Project Management

CHAPTER 23

Network Techniques for Project Management

PART SEVEN

Chapter 22 Project Management

LEARNING OBJECTIVES

After studying this chapter you should be able to

- Describe different forms of project organisation.
- Discuss the tools of project planning.
- Explain how performance analysis is done.
- Discuss the human aspects of project management.
- Specify the pre-requisites for successful project implementation.

The basic building blocks of the traditional form of organisation are a functional division of management and a well-defined hierarchical structure. Typically, a firm is organised into various departments, such as production, purchasing, marketing, finance, personnel, engineering, and research and development. Some of these departments have a line function and the others a staff function. Line managers have the principal responsibility for achieving the goals of the firm and are vested with decision making authority. Staff managers primarily serve in an advisory capacity - of course, within the staff departments they enjoy administrative powers.

The traditional form of organisation is quite appropriate for handling established operations which are characterised by a continuous flow of repetitive work, with each department attending to its specific functions – in such a setting, relatively stable inter-departmental and inter-personal relationships emerge. However, the traditional form of organisation is not suitable for project management. Why? There are several reasons: (i) a project is a non-routine, non-repetitive undertaking often plagued with many uncertainties; (ii) the relationships in a project setting are dynamic, temporary, and flexible; and (iii) a project requires a coordination of the efforts of persons drawn from different functional areas and contributions of external agencies. Due to these reasons, project management calls for a different form of organisation, sharper tools of planning and control, and improved means of coping with human problems.

This chapter discusses various issues relating to project management.

22.1 FORMS OF PROJECT ORGANISATION

The traditional form of organisation is not suitable for project work for the following reasons: (i) it has no means of integrating different departments at levels below the top management, and (ii) it does not facilitate effective communication, coordination, and control when several functional departments, with different professional backgrounds and orientations are involved in the project work under time and cost pressures, which often involves overlap, at least partial, of the development, design, procurement, construction, and commissioning work.

Hence there is a need for entrusting an individual (or group) with the responsibility for integrating the activities and functions of the various departments and external organisations involved in the project work. Such an individual may be called the project manager or project coordinator. Depending on the authority that is given to the person responsible for the project, the project organisation may take one of the following three forms:

- Line and staff organisation.
- Divisional organisation.
- Matrix organisation.

Line and Staff Organisation In this form of project organisation, a person is appointed with the primary responsibility of coordinating the work of the people in the functional departments. Such a person, referred to commonly as the project coordinator, acts essentially in a staff position to facilitate the coordination of line management in functional departments. The project coordinator does not have authority and direct responsibility of the line management. He serves as a focal point for receiving project-related information and seeks to promote the cause of the project by rendering advice, sharing information, and providing assistance. He may gently coax line executives to strive for the fulfillment of project goals. Deprived of formal organisational authority, he may find it difficult to exert leadership and feel unsure of his role. His influence would depend on his professional competence, closeness to top management, and persuasive abilities. Clearly, this is a weak form of organisation which may be employed mostly for small projects – it is certainly not suitable for large projects.

Divisional Organisation Under this form of project organisation, a separate division is set up to implement the project. Headed by the project manager, this division has its complement of personnel over whom the project manager has full line authority. In effect, this form of organisation implies the creation of a separate goal-oriented division of the company, with its own functional departments. While the project manager still has the problem of coordinating the inputs of other organisations involved in the project, he has total formal control over the division he heads.

A very strong form of project organisation, the divisional project organisation facilitates the process of planning and control, brings about better integration of efforts, and strengthens the commitment of project-related personnel to the objectives of the project. It considerably improves the prospect of fulfilling the time and budget targets.

This form of organisation, however, may entail an inefficient use of the resources of the firm. It may result in an unnecessary duplication of specialists in the company, because of the necessity to allocate them in total to each project. Further, it may be difficult to achieve a higher degree of specialisation of expertise because the divisional project organisation may have to manage with, say, one mechanical engineer, rather than two specialists.

Matrix Organisation The line and functional form of organisation is conducive to an efficient use of resources but is not suitable for an effective realisation of project objectives.

The divisional form of organisation, on the other hand, is suitable for effective realisation of project objectives but is not conducive to an efficient use of resources. The matrix form of organisation, the third form of project organisation, seeks to achieve the twin objectives of efficient use of resources and effective realisation of project objectives—at the cost of greater organisational complexity, of course.

In a matrix organisation, the personnel working on the project have a responsibility to their functional superior as well to the project manager. This means that the authority is shared between the project manager and the functional managers. The authority and influence of the project manager cut across the traditional vertical line of command. Exhibit 22.1 shows the organisation chart for a typical matrix organisation. As is evident from this exhibit, the project manager integrates the contributions of personnel in various functional departments toward the realisation of project objectives. While the personnel maintain their departmental affiliation and are responsible to their functional superiors, they are responsible to the project manager as well.

The matrix form of organisation is incongruent with the traditional organisation theory: there is dual subordination; responsibility and authority are not commensurate; the hierarchical principle is ignored. This clearly implies that the matrix form of organisation involves greater organisational complexity and creates an inherently conflictful situation. Yet it seems to be a better vehicle for the simultaneous pursuit of the twin objectives – efficient utilisation of resources and effective attainment of project objectives – which were discussed earlier.

22.2 PROJECT PLANNING

Projects involving a few activities, resources, constraints, and inter-relationships can be visualised easily by the human mind and planned informally. However, when a project crosses a certain threshold level of size and complexity, informal planning has to be substituted by formal planning. The need for formal planning is indeed much greater for project work than for normal operations. Without effective planning, there may be chaos.

Functions of Planning Planning, a vital aspect of management, serves several important functions:

- It provides a basis for organising the work on the project and allocating responsibilities to individuals.
- It is a means of communication and coordination between all those involved in the project.
- It induces people to look ahead.
- It instills a sense of urgency and time consciousness.
- It establishes the basis for monitoring and control.

Areas of Planning Comprehensive project planning covers the following:

- *Planning the project work* The activities relating to the project must be spelt out in detail. They should be properly scheduled and sequenced.

Exhibit 22.1 ***Matrix Organisation***

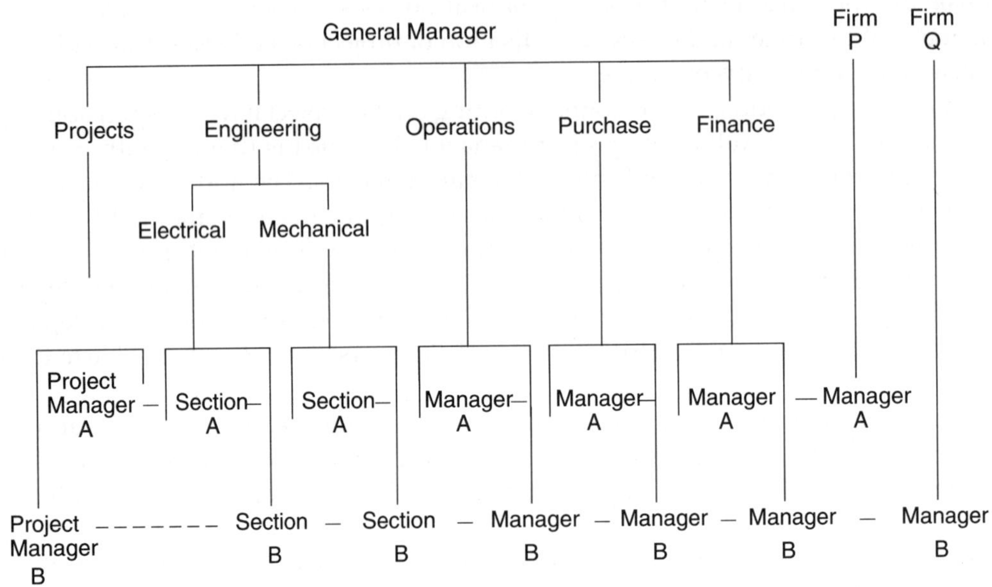

- *Planning the manpower and organisation* The manpower required for the project (managers, technologists, operators, and others) must be estimated and the responsibility for carrying out the project work must be allocated.
- *Planning the money* The expenditure of money in a time-phased manner must be budgeted.
- *Planning the information system* The information required for monitoring the project must be defined.

Project Objectives and Policies Often, the focus of project planning is on questions like who does what and when. Before such operational planning is done, the objectives and policies guiding the project planning exercise must be articulated. The questions to be answered in this context are: What are the technical and performance objectives? What are the time and cost goals? To what extent should the work be given to outside contractors? How many contractors should be employed? What should be the terms of contract?

Well-defined objectives and policies serve as the framework for the decisions to be made by the project manager. Throughout the life of the project, he has to seek a compromise between the conflicting goals of technical performance, cost standard, and time target. A clear articulation of the priorities of management will enable the project manager to take expeditious actions.

Work Breakdown Structure The work breakdown structure, as its name suggests, represents a systematic and logical breakdown of the project into its component parts. It is constructed by dividing the project into its major parts, with each of these being further divided into sub-parts. This is continued till a breakdown is done in terms of manageable units of work for which responsibility can be defined. Thus the work breakdown structure helps in:

- Effective planning by dividing the work into manageable elements which can be planned, budgeted, and controlled.
- Assignment of responsibility for work elements to project personnel and outside agencies.
- Development of control and information system.

Work Breakdown Structure and Project Organisation The project organisation represents formally how the project personnel and outside agencies are going to work. The work breakdown structure defines the works to be done in a detailed manner. To assign responsibility for the tasks to be done, the work breakdown structure has to be integrated with the project organisation structure. This calls for blending the vertical breakdown of the work (as arrived in the work breakdown structure) with the project organisation structure. This results in delineation of project tasks which are the specific responsibilities of organisational units/ managers. The technical name given to such a project task is *cost account*. A cost account represents a unit of work (i) which is defined in fairly concrete terms, (ii) for which a single person is responsible, and (iii) for which a budget of expenditure and manpower requirement can be prepared meaningfully.

Life Cycle of a Project The important stages in the life cycle of a project are:

- Project development and preliminary engineering
- Bidding and contract negotiation
- Engineering design
- Purchase and procurement
- Construction
- Commissioning

In planning these stages, one has to bear in mind two concepts: the rolling wave concept and the integration concept. According to the rolling wave concept, when detailed planning is done for project development and preliminary engineering, summary planning would be done for the remaining steps. When the actual work on project development and preliminary engineering commences, detailed planning would be done for the next stage which is concerned with bidding and contract negotiation, and so on. According to the integration concept, planning for all stages must be integrated, even though detailed planning would be done in accordance with the rolling wave concept. The need for integrative planning stems from the inter-relationship among various stages of project work. This need is further reinforced when the compulsion to reduce the project duration leads to overlap, at least partial, of various stages of the project.

Tools of Planning The oldest formal planning tool is the bar chart, also referred to as the Gantt chart or the multiple activity chart. In the last seven decades, network techniques have received considerable attention. This section briefly describes the nature of these tools of planning. (Network techniques, which warrant a detailed discussion, are covered at length in the following chapter.)

Bar Chart This is a pictorial device in which the activities are represented by horizontal bars on the time axis. The left-hand end of the bar shows the beginning time, the right-hand end the ending time. The duration of the activity is indicated by the length of the bar. The manpower required for the activity is shown by a number on the bar. An illustrative bar chart is shown in Exhibit 22.2.

Exhibit 22.2 ***An Illustrative Bar Chart***

	Time in Weeks from Project Start				
	10	20	30	40	50
Design	7				
Purchase of parts		12			
Fabrication		16			
Assembly				4	

The advantages of the bar chart are: (i) it is simple to understand; (ii) it can be used to show progress; and (iii) it can be used for manpower planning. The bar chart, however, suffers from some disadvantages which limit its usefulness: (i) it cannot show interrelationship among activities in large, complex projects; (ii) there may be a physical limit to the size of the bar chart, which may limit the size of the project that can be planned with this technique; and (iii) it cannot easily cope with frequent changes or updating.

Network Techniques These are more sophisticated than the traditional bar chart. In these techniques, the activities, events, and their inter-relationships are represented by a network diagram, also called an arrow diagram. Exhibit 22.3 shows an illustrative network diagram.

Exhibit 22.3 ***An Illustrative Network Diagram***

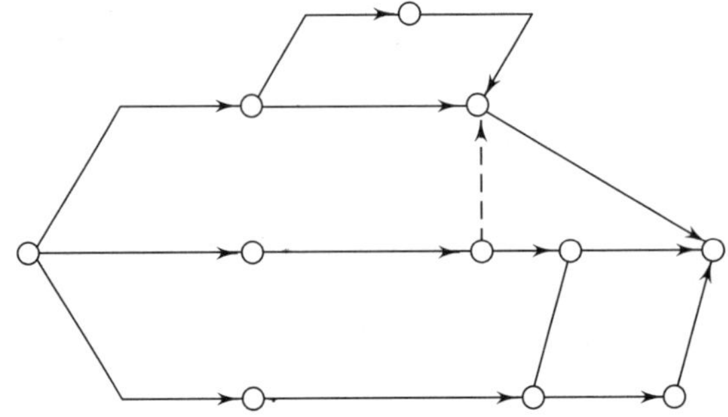

The advantages of network techniques are: (i) they can effectively handle inter-relationships among project activities; (ii) they identify the activities which are critical to the completion of the project on time and indicate the float (or spare time) for other activities; (iii) they can handle very large and complex projects; and (iv) they can be easily computerised and updated.

While the network techniques are a superior tool for project planning, they suffer from several drawbacks: (i) being more complicated than the traditional bar chart they are not easily understood by the project personnel; and (ii) they do not define an operational schedule which tells who does what and when.

Hierarchy of Plans A large project may consist of thousands (or even tens of thousands) of activities. A project plan consisting of such a large number of activities cannot be comprehended and visualised by the human mind. Hence, the global plan of so many activities may be held in a computer memory and structured on a hierarchical and modular basis in terms of plans of much smaller size, consisting of, say, 30 to 150 activities. Thus, for a large project a hierarchy of plans, having varying levels of detail, as illustrated by Exhibits 22.4 and 22.5 need to be prepared.

Exhibit 22.4 ***A Hierarchy of Bar Charts***

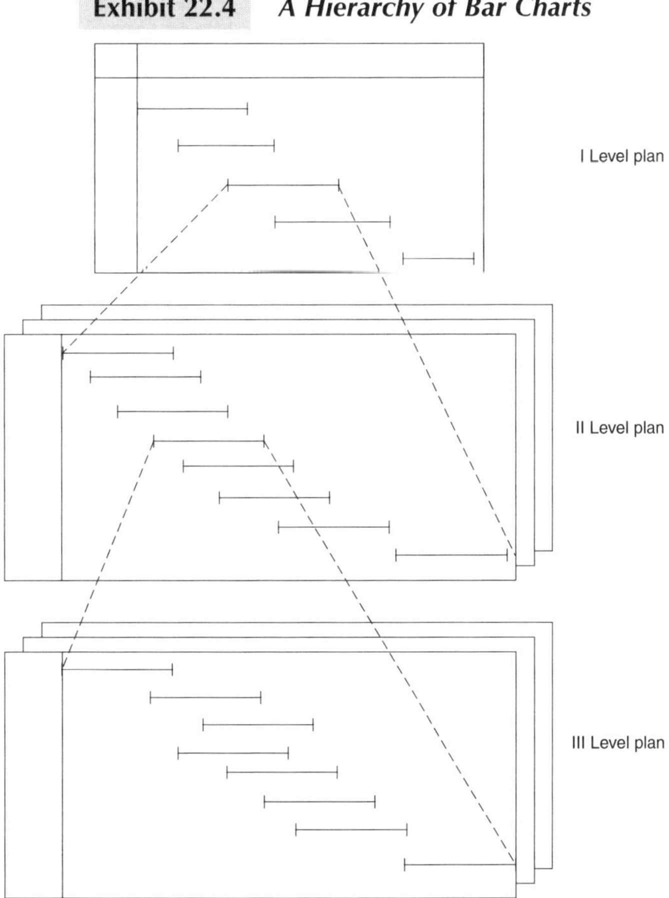

I Level Plan A highly summarised plan, the I level plan shows the broad activities of the project, such as engineering design, contract negotiation, procurement, construction, and commissioning with very elementary breakdown. It may serve as the basis for making rough estimates for overall resources and outlays. It would indicate the major inter-relationships in the project and suggest what could be the critical phases of the project. Such a plan is useful for strategic planning and establishing project objectives and policies. It serves as a tool for top management review.

II Level Plan The activities in the summary plan (at the I level) are shown in greater detail in the II level plan. This permits a more detailed examination of various stages of the project, so that inter-relationships can be properly established. The II level plan is essentially a tool of middle management planning, decision making, and control. It facilitates (i) identification of individuals responsible for various work packages,[1] (ii) aggregative manpower planning, and (iii) broad scheduling of project work.

III Level Plan This is the plan constructed in terms of cost accounts. It is useful for lower levels of management. It helps them in week to week, or even day to day, planning and control. Such a plan is based on a very detailed estimate of resource requirement, funds availability, project inter-relationships, and time targets.

Exhibit 22.5 ***A Hierarchy of Network Plans***

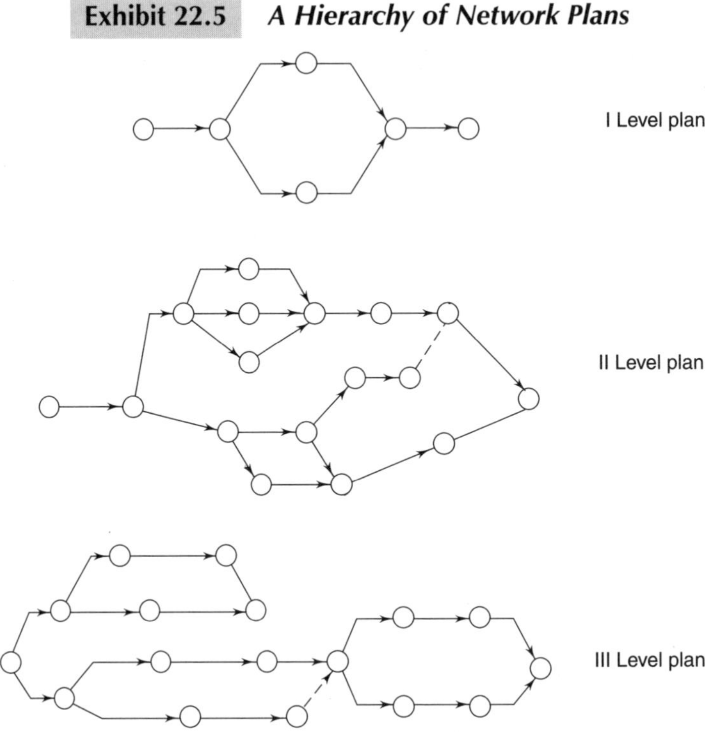

[1] A work package represents a higher element than the cost account in the work breakdown structure.

22.3 PROJECT CONTROL

No sooner is the project launched, control becomes the dominant concern of the project manager. Indeed, once the launch phase is over, planning and control become closely intertwined in an integrated managerial process.

Project control involves a regular comparison of performance against targets, a search for the causes of deviation, and a commitment to check adverse variances. It serves two major functions: (i) it ensures regular monitoring of performance, and (ii) it motivates project personnel to strive for achieving project objectives.

Reasons for Ineffective Control Effective control is critical for the realisation of project objectives. Yet, control of projects in practice tends to be ineffective. Why? There seem to be three reasons for poor control of projects.

Characteristics of the Project Most of the projects are large, complex undertakings involving many organisations and people. This renders the task of control difficult because:

- Keeping track of physical performance and expenditure on hundreds or thousands (or tens of thousands) of activities which are often non-routine is a stupendous task.
- Coordination and communication problems multiply when several organisations are involved in the project.

People Problems To control a non-routine project, a manager requires an ability to monitor a wide range of disparate factors, a sensitivity to symptoms indicative of potential problems, and a faculty for comprehending the combined effect of multiple forces. Naturally, most of the operational managers, used to the steady rhythm of normal operations and routine work, lack the experience, training, competence, and inclination to control projects.

Poor Control and Information System One of the factors which inhibits effective control is the poor quality of control and information system. Some of the weaknesses observed in the control and the information system are:

- *Delay in reporting performance* Often there is a delay in the reporting of performance. This prevents effective monitoring of the project and initiation of timely action to check adverse developments.
- *Inappropriate level of detail* Generally, cost information for control is collected in terms of cost codes found in the company's cost accounting system, irrespective of the level of detail employed for project planning and budgeting. Consider an extreme example wherein cost and value of work done are reported for the project as a whole. What is the value of such information for identifying where slippages are occurring and who is responsible for them?
- *Unreliable information* One of the major problems in project control is unreliable and inaccurate data and information. Often project managers receive reports which suggest that "everything is okay" or things are "reasonably within control" when the reality is otherwise. Further, for months after the project is completed, costs dribble in to change a favourable variance into an unfavourable one or to aggravate an unfavourable variance.

Variance Analysis Approach The traditional approach to project control involves a comparison of the actual cost with the budgeted cost to determine the variance. An example of variance analysis follows:

	Activity A	*Activity B*
Budgeted cost in the period	50,000	30,000
Cumulative budget to date	200,000	75,000
Actual cost in the period	55,000	28,000
Cumulative actual cost to date	240,000	80,000
Variance for the period	(5,000)	2,000
Cumulative variance to date	(40,000)	(5,000)

The variance analysis approach is inadequate for project control for the following reasons:

1. *It is backward looking rather than forward looking* It tells only what happened in the past but does not answer the following questions: What will happen in future? Is the rate of work accelerating or decelerating?
2. *It does not use the data effectively to provide integrated control* The traditional variance analysis shows whether in the time period under analysis more or less resources were expended than budgeted. However, it does not indicate the value of work done. This information is vital for purposes of control.

Performance Analysis: A Better Approach to Control Effective control over a project requires systematic 'performance analysis'. This calls for answering the following questions:

- Is the project as a whole (and its individual parts) on schedule, ahead of schedule, or behind schedule? If there is a variation, where did it occur, why did it occur, who is responsible for it, and what would be its implications?
- Has the cost of the project as a whole (and its individual parts) been as per budget estimates, less than the budget estimates, or more than the budget estimates? If there is a variation, where did it occur, why did it occur, who is responsible for it, and what would be its implications?
- What is the trend of performance? What would be the likely final cost and completion date for the project and its individual parts?

For small and simple projects, the project managers would do performance analysis for the project as a whole, or for its major components. As the project becomes larger and more complex, performance analysis needs to be done for individual segments of the projects which are referred to as 'cost accounts.' As we have seen earlier, a 'cost account' is a logical management centre.

Method of Analysis For analysing the performance at cost account and higher levels of the work breakdown structure, we employ a method of analysis which takes into account the value of work that has been done. In the traditional method of analysis, the project manager measured the actual progress against the predetermined schedule and the actual cost against the budget estimate. This did not enable him to know systematically whether the expenditure incurred was commensurate with progress. He perhaps relied on subjective estimates.

Performance analysis seeks to remove this subjectivity by employing an analytical framework based on the following terms:

- *BCWS* (Budgeted cost for work scheduled): It represents the total of three components: (i) budgets for all work packages, scheduled to be completed, (ii) budgets for the portion of in-process work, scheduled to be accomplished, and (iii) budgets for the overheads for the period.
- *BCWP* (Budgeted cost for work performed): This is equal to the sum of three components: (i) budgets for work packages actually completed, (ii) budgets applicable to the completed in-process work, and (iii) overhead budgets.
- *ACWP* (Actual cost of work performed): This represents the actual cost incurred for accomplishing the work performed during a particular time period.
- *BCTW* (Budgeted cost for total work): This is simply the total budgeted cost for the entire project work.
- *ACC* (Additional cost for completion): This represents the estimate for the additional cost required for completing the project.

Given the above terms, the project may be monitored along the following lines:

Cost variance	:	*BCWP – ACWP*
Schedule variance in cost terms	:	*BCWP – BCWS*
Cost performance index	:	*BCWP/ACWP*
Schedule performance index	:	*BCWP/BCWS*
Estimated cost performance index	:	*BCTW/(ACWP + ACC)*

Performance Analysis: An Illustration A project was begun on 1st January 20X0 and was expected to be completed by 30th September 20X0. The project is being reviewed on 30th June 20X0 when the following information has been developed.

			(₹)
Budgeted cost for work scheduled	(*BCWS*)	:	1,500,000
Budgeted cost for work performed	(*BCWP*)	:	1,400,000
Actual cost of work performed	(*ACWP*)	:	1,600,000
Budgeted cost for total work	(*BCTW*)	:	2,500,000
Additional cost for completion	(*ACC*)	:	1,200,000

Analysis

(₹)

- Cost variance : *BCWP – ACWP* = (1,400,000 – 1,600,000)
  = – 200,000
- Schedule variance in cost terms : *BCWP – BCWS* = (1,400,000 – 1,500,000)
  = – 100,000
- Cost performance index : *BCWP/ACWP* $= \frac{1,400,000}{1,600,000}$
  = 0.875

- Schedule performance index : $BCWP/BCWS = \dfrac{1,400,000}{1,500,000}$ $= 0.933$
- Estimated cost performance index : $BCTW/(ACWP + ACC) = \dfrac{2,500,000}{(1,600,000 + 1,200,000)} = 0.893$

22.4 HUMAN ASPECTS OF PROJECT MANAGEMENT

A satisfactory human relations system is essential for the successful execution of a project. Without such a system, the other systems of project management, however sound they may be by themselves, are not likely to work well. While technical problems can often be solved with additional investment of resources, people's problems may not be amenable to a satisfactory solution in the short span of the project life.

To achieve satisfactory human relations in the project setting, the project manager must successfully handle problems and challenges relating to:

- Authority
- Orientation
- Motivation
- Group functioning

Authority Except in the divisional organisation, the project manager, whose activities cut across functional lines of command, lacks the desired formal authority over project-related personnel. Without the conventional leverage of hierarchical authority, the project manager has to coordinate the efforts of various functional groups (within the organisation) and outside agencies. While he often has formal control emanating from contracts and agreements, as far as outside agencies involved in the project work are concerned, in his own organisation he has to contend with split authority and dual subordination.

Since the project manager works largely with professionals and supervisory personnel, the basis of the authority would be different from that found in simple superior–subordinate relationships. For exercising leadership and influence over professional people, he has to explain the logic and rationale for the project activities; show receptivity to the suggestions made by others; avoid unilateral imposition of decisions; eschew dogmatic postures; and search for areas of agreement which can be the basis of acceptable solutions.

His effective authority would stem from his ability to develop a rapport with the project personnel, his skill in resolving conflicts among various people working on the project, his professional reputation and stature, his skills in communication and persuasion, and his ability to act as a buffer between the technical, engineering, financial, and commercial people involved in the project.

Orientation Most of the managers working for a project are usually engineers (or technologists). Typically, an engineer:

- Works with physical laws, characterised by mathematical precision, as his tools.

- Adopts a structured, mechanical approach to his problems.
- Seeks an enduring solution to his problem.
- Attaches a high value on technical perfection.

When an engineer assumes managerial responsibilities, he faces a very different world in which he is supposed to:

- Perform the tasks of planning, organising, directing, and controlling the resources of the firm in a world of uncertainty.
- Adopt a more creative approach to solve non-programmed and unstructured problems.
- Attach greater importance to efficient utilisation of resources and resolution of human relation problems.

Thus the project manager has to strengthen the managerial orientation of project personnel so that the project goals and objectives can be efficiently achieved within the constraints of time and budget. Clearly for achieving this task he must himself be an accomplished engineer–manager.

Motivation The project manager functions within the boundaries of a socio-technical system. Most of the factors of this system—organisational structure, technical requirements, competencies of project personnel—are more or less 'given' for him. The principal behavioural factor which he can influence is the motivation of the project personnel. In this context, he should bear in mind the following:

- Human beings are motivated by a variety of needs: physiological needs, social needs, recognition needs, and self-actualisation needs. Individuals differ greatly in the importance they attach to various need satisfactions. Further, their attitudes tend to change with time and circumstances, and are significantly influenced by their peers and superiors.
- The traditional approach to management was based on the assumption that human beings regard work as unpleasant, shirk responsibility, and ordinarily employ inefficient and wasteful methods. Such a conception of human behaviour suggests that a great deal of pressure has to be applied. Behavioural research, however, has shown that while some pressure is beneficial, an excess of it is undesirable. Beyond a certain point, pressure is dysfunctional.
- Motivation tends to be strong when the goal set is challenging, yet attainable. If the goal is too demanding, it results in frustration and conflict; if too lax, it induces complacency.
- Expectation of reward, rather than fear of punishment, has a greater bearing on individual behaviour. Further, the effectiveness of reward or punishment depends on how quickly it is administered.
- In a project setting where hygiene factors (like pay, physical working conditions, etc.) are reasonably taken care of, the principal motivators would be a sense of accomplishment and professional growth. In this setting, the project manager should rely more on participative methods of management.

In order to succeed in motivating project personnel, the project manager must be a perceptive observer of human beings, must have the ability to appreciate the variable needs of human beings, must have skill in several styles of management suitable to different situations, and must be sensitive to the reactions of people so that he can act supportively rather than threateningly.

Understandably, the project manager has a difficult task. In this endeavour, he can, however, count on one blessing: the stimulating and satisfying nature of project work. In established organisations many professional and supervisory personnel find it difficult to see how their efforts redound to the realisation of organisational goals. Separated from top management by several layers of organisational hierarchy, they may not be able to relate their work meaningfully to the missions of the firm (which themselves often may be blurred to them). In addition, the jobs in established organisations are somewhat dull and routine. All this creates a sense of alienation and frustration which dampens motivation. Fortunately, in a project setting, where the superordinate goals are clearly defined and visible to all involved, where there is usually a great emphasis on participative style of management, where the layers in the organisational hierarchy are few, and where the jobs are more challenging, project personnel tend to have greater commitment. Being able to relate their work easily to the goals of the project, their motivation is usually high.

Project Manager Par Excellence

In our country, can anyone complete within time and budgeted cost, a large government urban transport project involving award of many contracts, land acquisition and recruitment, right under the very noses of top politicians? And without any major traffic jams or demolitions? Yes, E. Sreedharan has done just that with the Delhi Metro project in 2005. The media now famously calls him the Metro man.

Sreedharan joined Railways as an engineer and after a long meritorious stint there, retired in 1990. He was then asked to take up the first large BOT project, the Konkan Railway project. This work, earlier considered by many as impossible, involved construction of 150 bridges and 93 tunnels through soft soil. He successfully completed the project without any significant cost and time overrun. Again at the age of 66, instead of allowing him to retire, he was asked to head the Delhi Metro project in 1997. What followed is a masterpiece in project implementation. Delhi Metro project with an outlay of about two billion dollars is one of the fastest implemented projects of its kind in the world. And that too with high technology standards, safety, construction quality etc. Why politicians do not try their tricks on him? What sets him apart as an outstanding project manager?

It is his very high integrity, single minded commitment to work, managerial acumen and punctuality. He has a simple lifestyle and he considers work as a service to God. He creates a conducive and professional work culture, picking up the right people, motivating and rewarding them. This, along with the freedom to innovate and no punishment for unintentional mistakes, make the employees put up their best show even with governmental salaries.

Group Functioning In a large complex project, many persons drawn from different functions, departments, and organisations are involved. This leads to formation of groups, formal and informal. According to Rensis Likert, organisations may be considered as systems of interlocking groups. Thus, in a typical project organisation, many interlocking and interdependent groups are formed.

The groups formed in a project setting may be of three types: vertical groups, horizontal groups, and mixed groups. A *vertical group* consists of people drawn from different levels in the same department, or function, or company. A *horizontal group* consists of people drawn from different functions, departments, and companies, but occupying similar hierarchical positions. A *mixed group* consists of people drawn from different levels from various functions, departments, and companies.

A vertical group tends to form most naturally because of departmental/functional/organisational affinities. However, the existence of such groups may lead to a pronounced "we/they" attitude and accentuate conflicts. A horizontal group is a useful instrument in linking the overall project organisation. The members of the horizontal group, occupying key positions in their respective fields, serve as channels of communication. By their influence, they can strengthen the commitment to the project. The mixed group tends to promote greater cohesion of the total project organisation. It is very conducive to creating a 'project' attitude and developing an overriding commitment for the project. Hence the project manager should strive to establish a mixed group as the principal group of the project. However, it is difficult to establish such a group because of the temporary nature of a project—when members of a group know that the group would be dissolved sooner or later, they retain strong links with their parent company or department.

Building Effective Groups An effective group consists of members who are satisfied and committed and who strive for the attainment of project objectives, without dissipating their energies in inter-personal and inter-group conflicts. The manifest signs of an effective group are: *esprit de corps*, pride in the project, supportive behaviour, coordinated endeavour, mutual respect, and resilience during trying periods. An ineffective group, on the other hand, consists of disgruntled members who are more involved in inter-personal and inter-group rivalries and less concerned about project goals. Such a group is characterised by apathy, animosity, mutual bickering, disjointed efforts, cynical attitudes, and low morale.

How can effective groups be established? Studies in group dynamics suggest several stages, which are partially overlapping, in the formation of an effective group:

- Development of mutual trust
- Diminution of defensive behaviour
- Openness and candour in communication
- Cooperation and supportive behaviour
- Resolution of differences by mutual negotiation

For building an effective group, the firm must pursue a genuinely participative style of management. With this managerial philosophy, the project manager can facilitate the development of mutual trust and acceptance, open communication, cooperation, and project attitude. In this task, he needs leadership capabilities, sensitivity to human nature, perceptiveness, concern for welfare of others, maturity, and impartial approach. Clearly this is a difficult and challenging task.

22.5 PRE-REQUISITES FOR SUCCESSFUL PROJECT IMPLEMENTATION

Time and cost over-runs of projects are very common in India, particularly in the public sector. Due to such time and cost over-runs, projects tend to become uneconomical, resources are not available to support other projects, and economic development is adversely affected.

What can be done to minimise time and cost over-runs and thereby improve the prospects of the successful completion of projects? While a lot of things can be done to achieve this goal, the more important ones appear to be as follows:

- Adequate formulation
- Sound project organisation
- Proper implementation planning
- Advance action
- Timely availability of funds
- Judicious equipment tendering and procurement
- Better contract management
- Effective monitoring

Adequate Formulation Often project formulation is deficient because of one or more of the following shortcomings:

- Superficial field investigation
- Cursory assessment of input requirements
- Slip-shod methods used for estimating costs and benefits
- Omission of project linkages
- Flawed judgements because of lack of experience and expertise
- Undue hurry to get started
- Deliberate over-estimation of benefits and under-estimation of costs

Care must be taken to avoid the above deficiencies so that the appraisal and formulation of the project is thorough, adequate, and meaningful.

Sound Project Organisation A sound organisation for implementing the project is critical to its success. The characteristics of such an organisation are:

- It is led by a competent leader who is accountable for the project performance.
- The authority of the project leader and his team is commensurate with their responsibility.
- Adequate attention is paid to the human side of the project.
- Systems and methods are clearly defined.
- Rewards and penalties to individuals are related to performance.

Proper Implementation Planning Once the investment decision is taken—and often even while the formulation and appraisal are being done—it is necessary to do detailed implementation planning before commencing the actual implementation. Such planning should, *inter alia*, seek to:

- Develop a comprehensive time plan for various activities like land acquisition, tender evaluation, recruitment of personnel, construction of buildings, erection of plant, arrangement for utilities, trial production run, etc.
- Estimate meticulously the resource requirements (manpower, materials, money, etc.) for each period to realise the time plan.
- Define properly the inter-linkages between various activities of the project.
- Specify cost standards.

Advance Action When the project appears *prima facie* to be viable and desirable, advance action on the following activities may be initiated: (i) acquisition of land, (ii) securing essential clearances, (iii) identifying technical collaborators/consultants, (iv) arranging for infrastructure facilities, (v) preliminary design and engineering, and (vi) calling of tenders.

To initiate advance action with respect to the above activities, some investment is required. Clearly, if the project is not finally approved, this investment would represent an infructuous outlay. However, the substantial savings (in time and cost) that are expected to occur, should the project be approved (a very likely event, given the *prima facie* desirability of the project) often amply justify the incurrence of such costs.

Timely Availability of Funds Once a project is approved, adequate funds must be made available to meet its requirements as per the plan of implementation—it would be highly desirable if funds are provided even before the final approval to initiate advance action. Piecemeal, ad-hoc, and niggardly allocation, with undue rigidities, can impair the manoeuvrability of the project team. It is a common observation that firms which have a comfortable liquidity position are, in general, able to implement projects expeditiously and economically. Such firms can initiate advance actions vigorously, negotiate with suppliers and contractors aggressively, organise input supplies quickly, take advantages of opportunities to effect economies, support suppliers in resolving their problems so that they can in turn redound to the successful completion of projects, and sustain the morale of project-related personnel at a high level.

Judicious Equipment Tendering and Procurement To minimise time over-runs, it may appear that a turnkey contract has obvious advantages. Since these contracts are likely to be bagged by foreign suppliers, when global tenders are floated, a very important question arises. How much should we rely on foreign suppliers and how much should we depend on indigenous suppliers? Over-dependence on foreign suppliers, even though seemingly advantageous from the point of view of time and cost, may mean considerable outflow of foreign exchange and inadequate incentive for the development of indigenous technology and capability. Over-reliance on indigenous suppliers may mean delays and higher uncertainty about the technical performance of the project. A judicious balance must be sought which moderates the outflow of foreign exchange and provides reasonable fillip to the development of indigenous technology. In any case, the number of contract packages should be kept to a minimum in order to ensure effective coordination.

Better Contract Management Since a substantial portion of a project is typically executed through contracts, the proper management of contracts is critical to the successful implementation of the project. In this context, the following should be done:

- The competence and capability of all the contractors must be ensured—one weak link can jeopardise the timely performance of the project.
- Proper discipline must be inculcated among contractors and suppliers by insisting that they should develop realistic and detailed resource and time plans which are congruent with the project plan.
- Penalties—which may be graduated—must be imposed for failure to meet contractual obligations. Likewise, incentives may be offered for good performance.
- Help should be extended to contractors and suppliers when they have genuine problems—they should be regarded as partners in a common pursuit.
- Project authorities must retain the latitude to transfer contracts (partially or wholly) to other parties well in time where delays are anticipated.

Effective Monitoring In order to keep a tab on the progress of the project, a system of monitoring must be established. This helps in:

- Anticipating deviations from the implementation plan.
- Analysing emerging problems.
- Taking corrective action.

In developing a system of monitoring, the following points must be borne in mind:

- It should focus sharply on the critical aspects of project implementation.
- It must lay more emphasis on physical milestones and not on financial targets.
- It must be kept relatively simple. If made over-complicated, it may lead to redundant paper work and diversion of resources. Even worse, monitoring may be viewed as an end in itself rather than as a means to implement the project successfully.

22.6 ESSENCE OF PROJECT MANAGEMENT

Project Management Institute (PMI), the US-based institute, has certified over 200,000 project management professionals (PMPs) worldwide.

PMI has developed a body of knowledge termed the project management book of knowledge (PMBOK), that identifies and describes the best practices in project management. The PMBOK describes project management under nine areas as follows:

Project integration: This covers the integration of the three main project management processes, viz., planning, execution, and control.

Project scope management: This includes the processes meant to ensure that the project includes all the work, without any redundancy, to complete the project successfully.

Project time management: This covers the process required to ensure timely performance. It focuses on activity definition and activity sequencing.

Project cost management: This includes resource planning, cost estimation, cost budgeting, cash flow planning, and cost control.

Project quality management: This focuses on quality planning, quality assurance, and quality control.

Project human resource management: This covers organisation planning, staff acquisition, team development, and career planning.

Project communications management: This focuses on communication planning, information management, and progress reporting follow up.

Project risk management: This is concerned with risk identification and risk control.

Project procurement planning: This covers planning the panoply of procurement contracts, which are characteristic of project management.

22.7 ANALYSIS OF PROJECT RISK

The basic project cycle (identification, preparation, appraisal, implementation, and post-audit) provides a useful framework for analysing project risks. As time passes risks and uncertainties diminish. In a way, the project cycle represents a progress toward greater certainty. As suggested by A. O. Hirschman in his book *Development Projects Observed* (published by the Brookings Institution, Washington D. C. in 1976), risk diminishes over different stages of the project as follows.

Stage of Project Sequence	*Type of Estimate*	*Expected Accuracy %*
Identification		
(a) Project profile	Guesstimate	± 100
(b) Prefeasibility	Order of magnitude	± 50
Preparation		
(a) Feasibility study	Factorial	± 25
(b) Detailed design	Quantification	± 10
Implementation		
(a) Tender	Bid evaluation	± 7 ½
(b) Construction	Cost control	± 5

SUMMARY

- The traditional form of organisation is not very suitable for project work because it has no means of integrating different departments at levels below the top management and it does not facilitate effective communication, coordination, and control.
- Project organisation may take one of the following three forms: line and staff organisation, divisional organisation, and matrix organisation.
- In the line and staff form of project organisation, a person is appointed with the primary responsibility of coordinating the work of the people in the functional departments. Under the divisional form of project organisation, a separate division headed by the project manager is set up to implement the project. In a matrix organisation, the personnel working on the project have a responsibility to their functional superior as well as to the project manager.

- The line and functional form of organisation is conducive to an efficient use of resources but is not suitable for an effective realisation of project objectives. The divisional form of organisation, on the other hand, is suitable for an effective realisation of project objectives but not conducive to an efficient use of resources. The matrix form of organisation seeks to achieve the twin objectives of efficient use of resources and effective realisation of project objectives, at the cost of greater organisational complexity, of course.
- Comprehensive project planning covers the following areas: project work, manpower and organisation, money, and information systems.
- The important stages in the life cycle of a project are: project development and preliminary engineering, bidding and contract negotiation, engineering design, purchase and procurement, construction, and commissioning.
- The two important tools of planning are the bar chart and the network techniques. The bar chart is a pictorial device in which the activities are represented by horizontal bars on the time axis. In network techniques, the activities, events, and their inter-relationships are represented by a network diagram.
- For large projects, a hierarchy of plans showing various levels of detail may be prepared.
- The traditional approach to project control, involving a comparison of the actual cost with the budgeted cost, is referred to as variance analysis. This approach is inadequate for project control for the following reasons: (i) it is backward-looking rather than forward-looking, and (ii) it does not use the data effectively to provide integrated control.
- The modern approach to project control, referred to as performance analysis, involves monitoring the project along the following lines:

Cost variance	:	Budgeted cost of work performed—Actual cost of work performed.
Schedule variance in cost terms	:	Budgeted cost of work performed—Budgeted cost of work scheduled.
Cost performance index	:	Budgeted cost of work performed/Actual cost of work performed.
Schedule performance index	:	Budgeted cost of work performed/Budgeted cost of work scheduled.
Estimated cost performance index	:	Budgeted cost for total work—(Actual cost of work performed + Additional cost for completion).

- To achieve satisfactory human relations in the project setting, the project manager must successfully handle problems and challenges relating to (i) authority, (ii) orientation, (iii) motivation, and (iv) group functioning.
- Often, the project manager has to coordinate the efforts of various functional groups (within the organisation) and outside agencies without the leverage of hierarchical authority. His effective authority depends largely on his professional stature and inter-personal skills.

- The project manager has to strengthen the managerial skills of project personnel, particularly technical and engineering personnel.
- In order to succeed in motivating personnel, the project manager must be a perceptive observer of human beings, must have the ability to appreciate the variable needs of human beings, must have skills in several styles of management suitable to different situations, and must be sensitive to the reactions of people so that he can act supportively rather than threateningly.
- There are several stages, partially overlapping, in the formation of an effective group: development of mutual trust, diminution of defensive behaviour, openness and candour in communication, cooperation and supportive behaviour, and resolution of differences by mutual negotiation.
- Time and cost over-runs of projects are very common in India, particularly in the public sector. Hence, projects tend to become uneconomical and economic development is adversely affected.
- The important pre-requisites for successful completion of projects are: (i) adequate formulation, (ii) sound project organisation, (iii) proper implementation planning, (iv) advance action, (v) timely availability of funds, (vi) judicious equipment tendering and procurement, (vii) better contract management, and (viii) effective monitoring.
- The Project Management Institute (PMI) has developed a body of knowledge termed the Project Management Book Of Knowledge (PMBOK). The PMBOK describes project management under nine areas as follows: project integration, project scope management, project time management, project quality management, project human resource management, project communications management, project risk management, and project procurement planning.

QUESTIONS

1. "The traditional form of organisation is not suitable for the management of projects." Comment.
2. Describe and evaluate the various forms of project organisation.
3. What is a bar chart? What are its advantages and limitations?
4. Discuss the notion of hierarchy of plans.
5. Why does the control of projects in practice tends to be ineffective mostly?
6. Discuss and evaluate the variance analysis approach to project control.
7. What is 'performance analysis'? What are the dimensions along which monitoring is done in 'performance analysis'?
8. Discuss the authority and orientation problems in a project setting.
9. What considerations should the project manager bear in mind with respect to motivation of the project personnel?
10. What types of groups may be formed in a project setting?
11. What is an effective group? What are the stages in the formation of an effective group?
12. Discuss the pre-requisites for successful project implementation.
13. Describe the nine areas of project management identified in the PMBOK.

PROBLEMS

1. A project has begun on 1st April 200X and was expected to be completed by 31st December 200X. The project is being reviewed on 30th September 200X when the following information has been developed:
   - Budgeted cost for work scheduled (BCWS) : ₹6,000,000
   - Budgeted cost for work performed (BCWP) : ₹5,500,000
   - Actual cost of work performed (ACWP) : ₹5,800,000
   - Budgeted cost for total work (BCTW) : ₹10,000,000
   - Additional cost for completion (ACC) : ₹5,000,000

   Determine the following: (i) cost variance, (ii) schedule variance in cost terms, (iii) cost performance index, (iv) schedule performance index, and (v) estimated cost performance index.

Network Techniques for Project Management

LEARNING OBJECTIVES

After studying this chapter you should be able to

- Explain how a project network is developed.
- Discuss how the time for project activities is estimated.
- Explain the procedure for determining the critical path.
- Show how scheduling is done when resources are limited.
- Compute the probability of completing a project by a specified date.
- Discuss the procedure for CPM analysis.
- Explain how cost projection and cost analysis is done under the network cost system.

Once a project is selected, the focus shifts to its implementation. This involves the completion of numerous activities (project components) by employing various resources—men, materials, machine, money, and time—so that a project on paper is translated into a concrete reality.

The activities of a project have inter-relationships arising from physical, technical, and other considerations. For proper planning, scheduling, and control of the activities of a project, given their inter-relationships and constraints on the availability of resources, network techniques have been found quite useful. It may be noted that financial institutions and the Government of India insist that a network plan should accompany feasibility reports.

There are two basic network techniques: PERT and CPM. PERT, an acronym for *Program Evaluation Review Technique*, was originally developed to facilitate the planning and scheduling of the Polaris Fleet Ballistic Missile Project of the US government. Designed to handle risk and uncertainty, PERT is eminently suitable for research and development programmes, aerospace projects, and other projects involving new technology. In such projects the time required for completing various jobs or activities can be highly variable. Hence the orientation of PERT is 'probabilistic'.

CPM, an acronym for *Critical Path Method*, is akin to PERT. It was developed independently in 1956-57 by the Du Pont Company in the US to solve scheduling problems in industrial settings. CPM is primarily concerned with the trade-off between cost and time. It has been applied mostly to projects that employ a fairly stable technology and are relatively risk free. Hence its orientation is 'deterministic'.

Widely diverse projects like the following are amenable to analysis by PERT and CPM:

- Launching a spaceship
- Research and development programme
- Construction of a plant
- Building a river valley project
- Overhaul of an organisation
- Training of manpower
- Starting a new venture
- Adult literacy programme

The common characteristics of the above projects which make them amenable to analysis by PERT or CPM are:

1. The project can be broken down into a well-defined set of jobs or activities.
2. The activities must be performed in a certain sequence which is technologically ordered.
3. Within a defined sequence, the activities may be started and stopped in an independent manner.

This chapter discusses the basics of PERT, CPM, and network cost system.

23.1 DEVELOPMENT OF PROJECT NETWORK

Basic to PERT as well as CPM is the network diagram. The network diagram, also referred to as the project graph, shows the activities and events of the project and their logical relationships. A simplified network diagram for a dinner project is shown in Exhibit 23.1.

The network diagram is constructed in terms of activities and events. An activity is a definite task, job, or function to be performed in a project. For example, 'prepare dinner' (see Exhibit 23.1) is an activity. An activity is represented by an arrow. The head of the arrow marks the completion of the activity and the tail of the arrow marks its beginning. (The length and 'compass' direction of the arrow have no significance.) An event is a specific point in time indicating the beginning or end of one or more activities. It represents a milestone and does not consume time or resources. For example, event 2 in Exhibit 23.1 marks completion of the activity 'send invitation'.

Exhibit 23.1 ***Network Diagram for a Dinner Project***

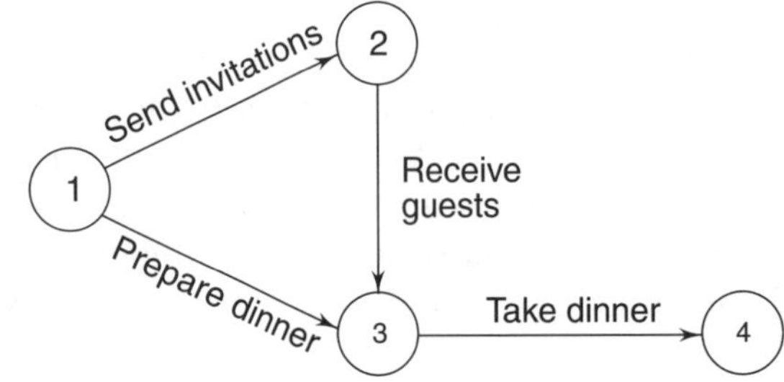

Since activities are the basic building blocks of a network diagram, it is necessary to enumerate all the activities of the project. For this purpose, it is helpful to break the project into several steps. The number of steps, of course, would depend on the magnitude and complexity of the project. For industrial projects, generally a two-step procedure could suffice. In the first step, the major parts of the project are identified and in the second step the activities of each major part are delineated. Activities should be so defined that they are distinct, reasonably homogeneous tasks for which time and resource requirement can be estimated.

Once the activities are enumerated it is necessary to define for each activity, the activities which precede it, the activities which follow it, and the activities which can take place concurrently. Given this information, the network diagram, showing the logical relationship between activities and events may be developed following either the *forward method* or the *backward method.*

The forward method begins with the initial event, marking the beginning of the project, and proceeds forward till the end event is reached. The backward method begins with the end event and works backwards till the beginning event is reached.

Rules for Network Construction The rules to be observed in constructing the network diagram are discussed below:

1. Each activity must have a preceding and a succeeding event. An activity is numerically denoted by the pair of preceding and succeeding events. In the dinner project, for example, the activity 'send invitations' is designated as (1–2).
2. Each event should have a distinct number. The number given to an event can be chosen in any way, provided this condition is satisfied. In practice, however, events are so numbered that the number at the head of the arrow is greater than that at its tail.
3. There should be no loops in the project network. A situation like the one shown in Exhibit 23.2 is not permissible.
4. Not more than one activity can have the same preceding and succeeding events. This means that each activity is represented by a uniquely numbered arrow and a situation like the one shown in Exhibit 23.3 is not permissible.

Exhibit 23.2 ***A Loop***

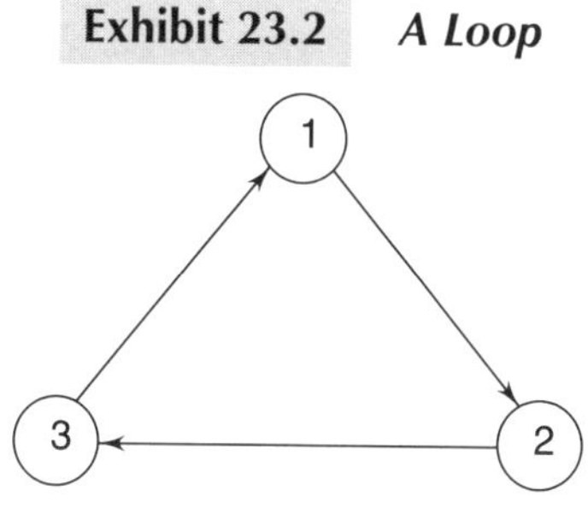

Exhibit 23.3 *A Network Diagram*

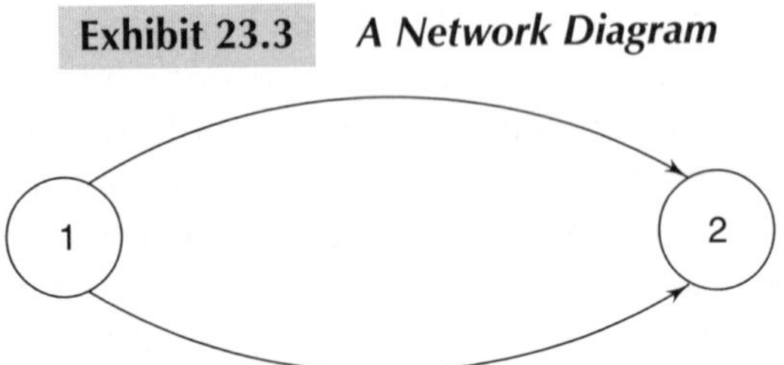

To ensure that each activity is uniquely numbered it may be necessary sometimes to introduce dummy activities. A dummy activity is an imaginary activity which can be accomplished in zero time and which does not consume resources. It is represented by a dashed arrow. Exhibit 23.4 shows a variant of Exhibit 23.3 with a dummy activity (3–2) introduced to conform to the rules of network construction.

Exhibit 23.4 *A Dummy Activity*

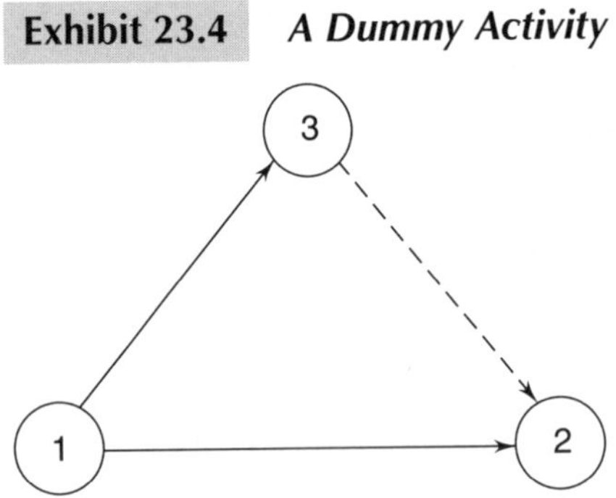

A dummy activity may also be used to represent a constraint, necessary to show the proper relationship between activities. Exhibit 23.5 shows part of a network diagram having a dummy activity.

In Exhibit 23.5, *X*, represented as (7–6), is a dummy activity showing a certain logical relationship. According to this figure, activities *P*(4–6) and *Q*(5–7) must be completed before activity *R* (6–8) can start.

Exhibit 23.5 *A Dummy Activity*

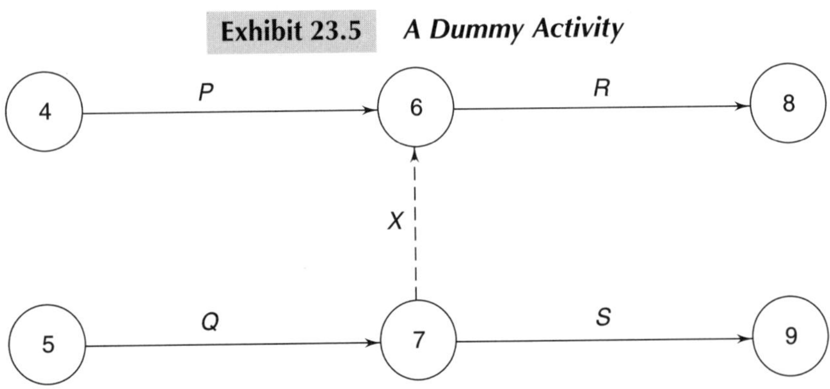

Illustration A building project consists of the following activities:

A = Lay foundation
B = Erect framework
C = Install millwork
D = Install wiring
E = Install plumbing
F = Plaster walls
G = Install siding
H = Decorate the interior
I = Finish the exterior

The interrelationship among these activities is as follows:

1. A should precede B.
2. B should precede C, D, E, F, and G.
3. C, D, E, and F should precede H.
4. G should precede I.

Given the above interrelationship the network diagram for the project is developed, in several steps, using the forward method, as shown in Exhibit 23.6.

Exhibit 23.6 ***A Network Diagram***

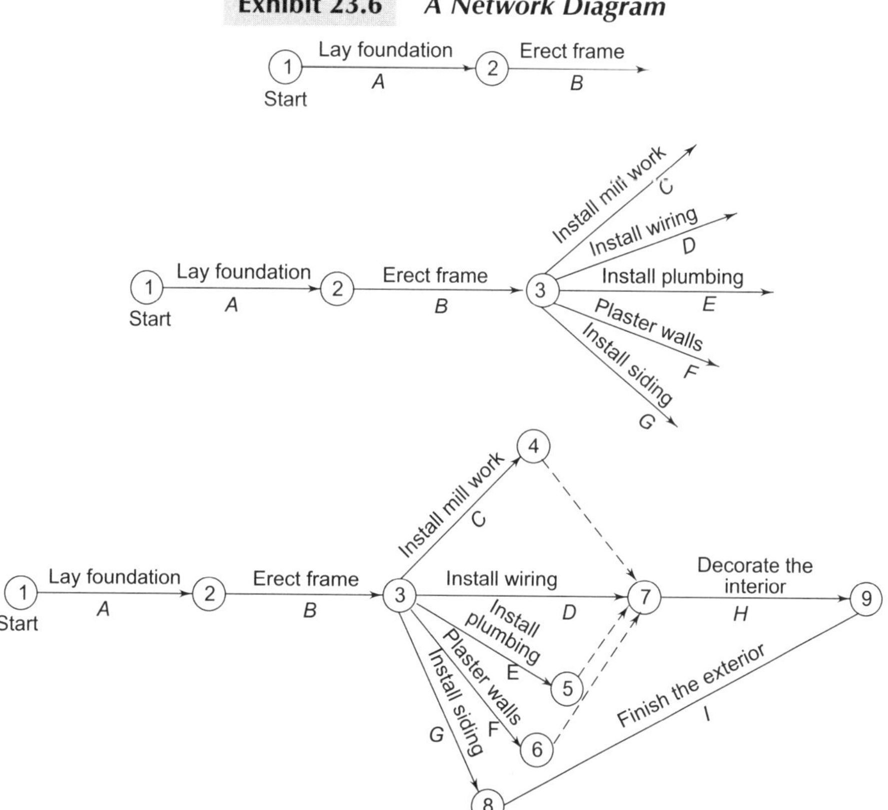

23.2 TIME ESTIMATION

Once the logic and detail of the network have been established, time estimates must be assigned to each activity. Generally, three time values are obtained for each activity:

1. Optimistic time (t_o)
2. Most likely time (t_m)
3. Pessimistic time (t_p)

The optimistic time, t_o, is the time required if no hurdles or complications arise. The most likely time, t_m, is the time in which the activity is most likely to be completed. This estimate takes into consideration normal circumstances, making allowance for some unforeseen delays. The pessimistic time, t_p, is the time required if unusual complications and/or unforeseen difficulties arise.

For discussing other aspects of PERT analysis a simple project shown in Exhibit 23.7 shall be used.

Exhibit 23.7 ***A Network Diagram***

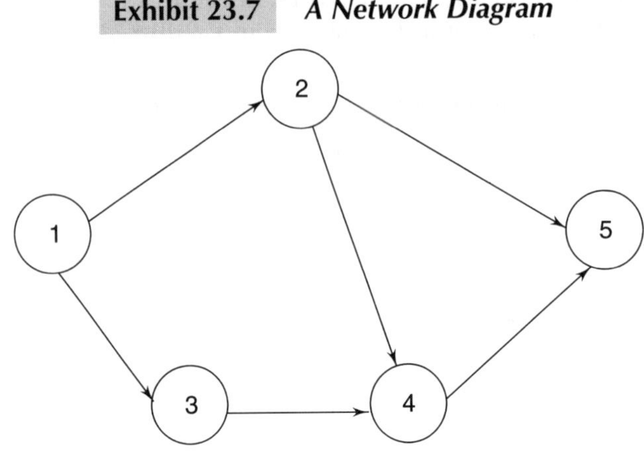

Obtaining Time Estimates Time estimates should be obtained by the PERT planner from persons who are responsible for estimation. The following points should be borne in mind while obtaining time estimates:

1. Time estimates should be obtained by skipping around the network rather than by following a specific path. If estimates are obtained by following one path, there is a tendency for the person providing the estimates to add them mentally and compare them with a previously conceived notion of the time of the total path.
2. The estimates of t_o, t_m, and t_p should be defined independently of each other.
3. The time available for completing the project should not influence the estimates of t_o, t_m, and t_p.
4. It should be made known that t_o, t_m, and t_p are estimates and not schedule commitments.

5. The estimates of t_o, t_m, and t_p should include allowances for occurrences which are generally considered as random variables (weather conditions, administrative delays, etc.) but not for occurrences that are normally not considered as random variables (flood, wars, etc.)

Average Time Once the three time estimates for each activity are obtained, the expected value of activity durations is calculated. The expected value, t_e, is usually obtained by the formula:

$$t_e = \frac{t_o + 4\,t_m + t_p}{6} \tag{23.1}$$

where t_e is the weighted arithmetic average time, t_o is the optimistic time, t_m is the most likely time, and t_p is the pessimistic time.

The time estimates for various activities in our illustrative project are shown in Exhibit 23.8.

Exhibit 23.8 ***Time Estimates***

Activity	*Time Estimate*	*Optimistic* t_e	*Most Likely* t_m	*Pessimistic* t_p	*Average* $t_e = \frac{t_o + 4t_m + t_p}{6}$
Numerical Description					
a	1-2	9	12	21	13
b	1-3	6	12	18	12
c	2-4	1	1.5	5	2
d	3-4	4	8.5	10	8
e	2-5	10	14	24	15
f	4-5	1	2	3	2

The network diagram with average time estimates is shown in Exhibit 23.9.

Exhibit 23.9 ***A Network Diagram***

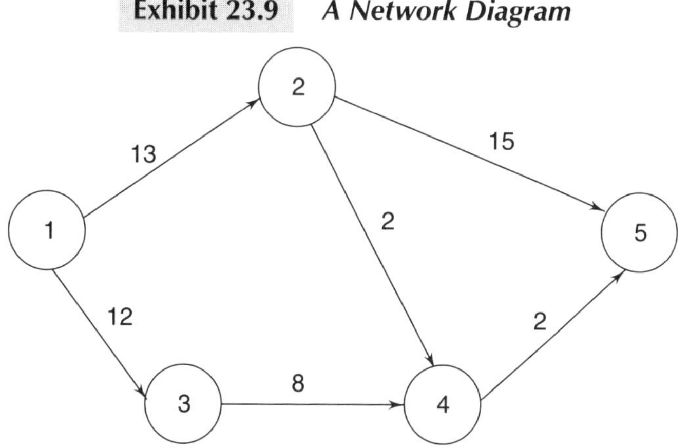

23.3 DETERMINATION OF THE CRITICAL PATH

Once the network diagram with single time estimates has been developed, the following computational procedure may be employed for determining the critical path/s, event slacks, and activity floats.

1. Calculate the Earliest Occurrence Time (EOT) for Each Event An event occurs when all activities leading to the event have been completed. In the network diagram shown in Exhibit 23.9, for example, event 4 occurs when activities (2–4) and (3–4) are completed. Obviously activity (2–4) cannot begin unless event 2 occurs, which in turn requires the completion of activity (1–2). Likewise, activity (3–4) cannot begin unless event 3 occurs which in turn requires the completion of activity (1–3). Thus we find that event 4 occurs when activities (1–2), (2–4), (1–3), and (3–4) are completed. In other words, event 4 occurs when paths (1–2–4) and (1–3–4) are completed.

The *EOT* of an event refers to the time when the event can be completed at the earliest. Looking at event 4 we find that since the paths leading to it, viz., (1–2–4) and (1–3–4) take 15 weeks and 20 weeks, respectively, the *EOT* of event 4 is 20 weeks. In general terms, the *EOT* of an event is the duration of the longest path (from the beginning event whose *EOT* is set at 0) leading to that event. The *EOTs* of various events in our illustrative project are shown in Exhibit 23.10. It may be noted that in Exhibit 23.10 and subsequent figures an event is represented by a circle. The upper half of the circle denotes the event number, the left quarter in the lower half denotes the *EOT*, and the right quarter in the lower half denotes the latest occurrence time, a term described later.

Exhibit 23.10 ***A Network Diagram***

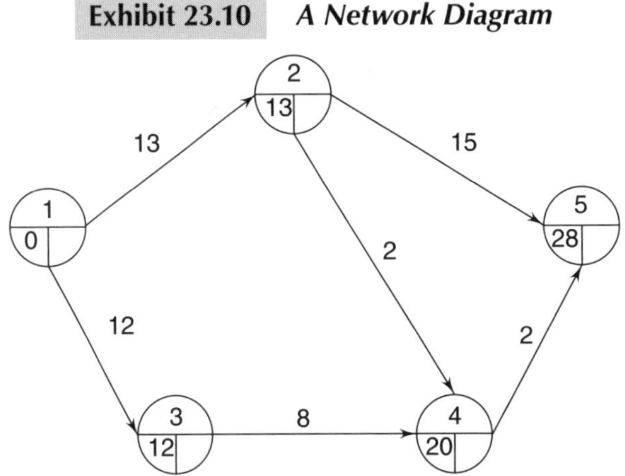

The *EOT* of the end event obviously represents the minimum time required for completing the project. To obtain the *EOT* of various events we start from the beginning event and move forward towards the end event. This computational procedure is referred to as the forward pass. In this computation we assume that each activity starts immediately on the occurrence of the event preceding it. Hence the starting and finishing time for various activities obtained from this computation are the earliest starting time (*EST*) and the earliest finishing time (*EFT*).

The general formula for *EOT* is:

$$EOT\ (i) = \text{Max}\ [EOT\ (k) + d(k, i)] \tag{23.2}$$

where *EOT* (*i*) is the earliest occurrence time of event *i*, *EOT* (*k*) is the earliest occurrence time of event *k* (*k* precedes *i*,and there may be several *k*s), and *d* (*k*, *i*) is the duration of activity (*k*, *i*).

The maximisation shown is done considering all activities (*k*, *i*) leading to event node *i*.

The formulae for *EST* and *EFT* are:

$$EST\ (i,j) = EOT\ (i) \tag{23.3}$$

$$EFT\ (i, j) = EOT\ (i) + d(i, j) \tag{23.4}$$

where *EST* (*i*, *j*) is the earliest starting time for activity (*i*, *j*), *EOT* (*i*) is the earliest occurrence time of event (*i*), *EFT* (*i*, *j*) is the earliest finishing time for activity (*i*, *j*), and *d*(*i*, *j*) is the duration of activity (*i*, *j*).

2. Calculate the Latest Occurrence Time (LOT) for Each Event The *LOT* for an event represents the latest allowable time by which the event can occur, given the time that is allowed for the completion of the project (occurrence of end event). Normally, the time allowed for the completion of the project is set equal to the *EOT* of the end event. (In other words, the project is supposed to be completed at the earliest possible time.) This means that for the end event the *LOT* and *EOT* are set equal. The *LOT* for various events is obtained by working backward from the end event. This procedure is known as the backward pass. The *LOT* for event 4 in our illustrative project, for example, is equal to the *LOT* for event 5, the end event, minus the duration of the activity (4–5) which connects event 4 with 5. Since the *LOT* for event 5 is 28 weeks and the duration of activity (4–5) is 2 weeks the *LOT* for event 4 is 26 weeks (28–2). This represents the latest time by which event 4 should occur to enable the project to be completed in 28 weeks. Likewise, the *LOT* for other events can be calculated by moving backward. The *LOT* for various events is shown (in the right quarter of the lower half of event nodes) in Exhibit 23.11.

Exhibit 23.11 ***A Network Diagram***

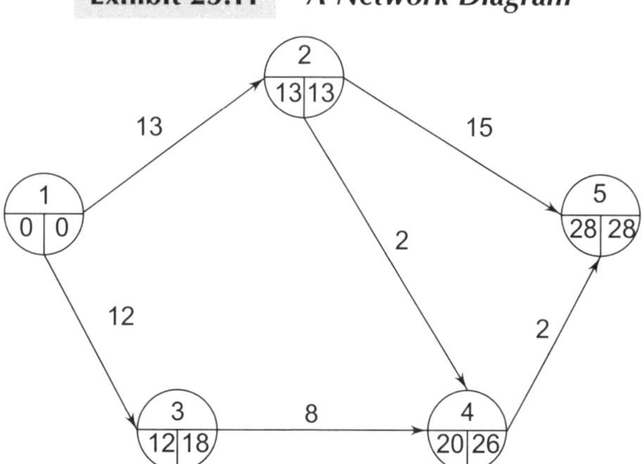

The general formula for *LOT* is:

$$LOT\,(i) = \text{Min}\,[LOT\,(j) - d(i, j)] \tag{23.5}$$

where *LOT* (*i*) is the latest occurrence time for *i*, *LOT* (*j*) is the latest occurrence time for *j*, (*j* follows *i* and there may be several *j*s), and *d*(*i*, *j*) is the duration of activity (*i*, *j*)

The minimisation shown here is done with respect to all activities (*i*, *j*) starting from *i*.

Given the *LOT* for various events we can calculate the latest finishing time (*LFT*) and latest starting time (*LST*) for various activities using the formulae:

$$LFT\,(i, j) = LOT\,(j) \tag{23.6}$$

$$LST\,(i, j) = LFT\,(i, j) - d(i, j) \tag{23.7}$$

where *LFT* (*i*, *j*) is the latest finishing time for activity (*i*, *j*), *LOT* (*j*) is the latest occurrence time for event *j*, *LST* (*i*, *j*) is the latest starting time for activity (*i*, *j*), and *d*(*i*, *j*) is the duration of activity (*i*, *j*).

3. Calculate the Slack for Each Event The slack for an event is the difference between its *LOT* and *EOT*. The slacks for various events of our illustrative project are shown in Exhibit 23.12.

Exhibit 23.12 ***Event Slack***

(in weeks)

Event	*LOT*	*EOT*	Slack = LOT – EOT
5	28	28	0
4	26	20	6
3	18	12	6
2	13	13	0
1	0	0	0

4. Obtain the Critical and Slack Paths The critical path starts with the beginning event, terminates with the end event, and is marked by events which have a zero slack. This is obviously the path on which there is no slack, no cushion. Other paths are slack paths with some cushion. The critical path for our illustrative project is (1–2–5). It is indicated by doubled arrows in Exhibit 23.13.

The critical path is the longest path from the beginning event to the end event. Since the end can be reached, i.e., project completed, only when this longest path is traversed, the minimum time required for completing the project is the duration on the critical path. The duration on the critical path of our project is 28 weeks; this is the minimum time required for completing the project. (It is already indicated by the *EOT* of event 5, the end event.)

Exhibit 23.13 ***A Network Diagram***

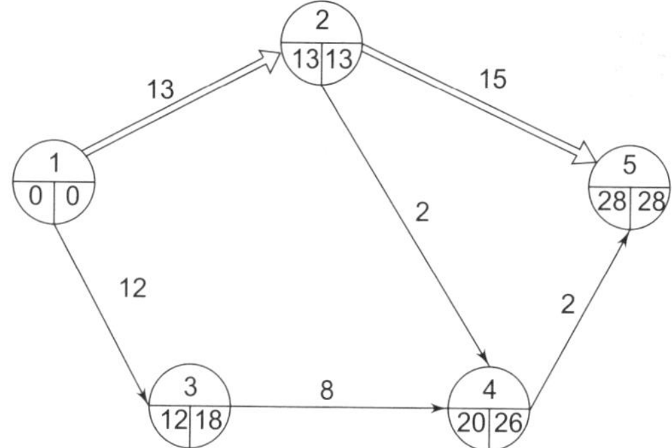

5. Compute the Activity Floats Given the estimates of activity time and event slacks, activity floats can be calculated. There are three measures of float: (i) total float; (ii) free float; and (iii) independent float. For illustrating these measures, let us consider activity (2–4) of our illustrative project. Activity (2–4) is shown in Exhibit 23.14.

In Exhibit 23.14, *EOT, LOT,* and *d* represent respectively, earliest occurrence time, latest occurrence time, and duration.

Exhibit 23.14 ***EOT and LOT***

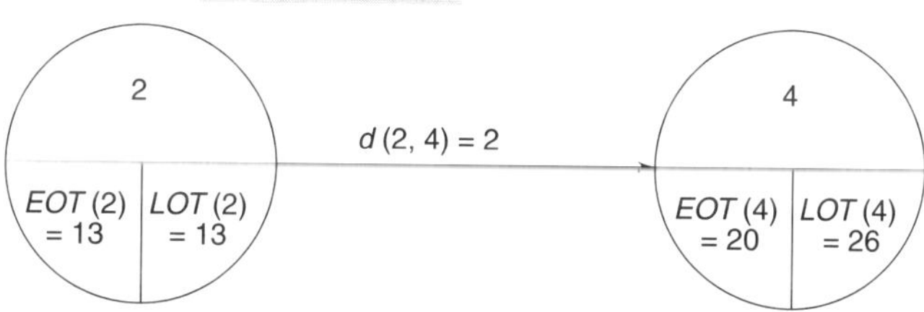

The *total float* of an activity is the extra time available to complete the activity if it is started as early as possible, without delaying the completion of the project. The total float for activity (2–4) is equal to:

	Latest occurrence time for event 4	– Earliest occurrence time for event 2	– Duration of activity (2–4)
=	26 weeks	– 13 weeks	– 2 weeks
=	11 weeks		

The *total float* represents the float under the most favourable conditions. This is so because the activity can be started at the earliest (the *EOT* of the preceding event) and completed at the latest (the *LOT* of its succeeding event). Obviously, activities which do not have a float even under these conditions, the most favourable ones, are critical to the project and hence lie on the critical path.

The *free float* of an activity is the extra time available to complete the activity when the activity is started at the *EOT* of its preceding event and completed by the *EOT* of its succeeding event. The free float for activity (2–4) is:

	Earliest occurrence time for event 4	– Earliest occurrence time for event 2	– Duration of activity (2–4)
=	20 weeks	– 13 weeks	– 2 weeks
=	5 weeks		

The *independent float* of an activity is the extra time available to complete the activity when the activity is started at the *LOT* of its preceding event and completed by the *EOT* of its succeeding event. The independent float for activity (2–4) is:

	Earliest occurrence time for event 4	– Latest occurrence time for event 2	– Duration of activity (2–4)
=	20 weeks	– 13 weeks	– 2 weeks
=	5 weeks		

The independent float represents the float under the most adverse conditions. Hence when an activity has a positive independent float it means that the activity has a cushion (equal to its independent float) irrespective of what happens elsewhere. (It may be noted that the independent float of an activity may be negative but the total float and free float cannot be negative.)

More generally, floats may be represented by the following equations:

$$TF\ (i, j) = LOT\ (j) - EOT\ (i) - d\ (i, j) \tag{23.8}$$

$$FF\ (i, j) = EOT\ (j) - EOT\ (i) - d\ (i, j) \tag{23.9}$$

$$IF\ (i, j) = EOT\ (j) - LOT\ (i) - d\ (i, j) \tag{23.10}$$

where *TF* (i, j) is the total float of activity (i, j), *LOT* (j) is the latest occurrence time for event j, *EOT* (i) is the earliest occurrence time of event i, $d\ (i, j)$ is the duration of activity (i, j), *FF* (i, j) is the free float of activity (i, j), *EOT* (j) is the earliest occurrence time of event j, *IF* (i, j) is the independent float of activity (i, j), and *LOT* (i) is the latest occurrence time of event i

The floats for various activities of our illustrative project are shown in Exhibit 23.15.

Exhibit 23.15 ***Activity Floats***

(in weeks)

Activity (i,j)	*Duration*	*Earliest Start Time (i,j) = EST (i)*	*Earliest Finish Time (i,j) = EFT (j)*	*Latest Start Time (i,j) = LST (i)*	*Latest Finish Time (i,j) = LFT (j)*	*Total Float*	*Free Float*	*Independent Float*
a (1-2)	13	0	13	0	13	0	0	0
b (1-3)	12	0	12	6	18	6	0	0
c (2-4)	2	13	15	24	26	11	5	5
d (3-4)	8	12	20	18	26	6	0	(6)
e (2-5)	15	13	28	13	28	0	0	0
f (4-5)	2	20	22	26	28	6	6	0

23.4 SCHEDULING WHEN RESOURCES ARE LIMITED

From Exhibit 23.15, we find that critical activities (1–2) and (2–5) have no float associated with them. This means that there is no flexibility whatsoever in scheduling these activities - the earliest starting time is the same as the latest starting time and the earliest finishing time is the same as the latest finishing time. For non-critical activities, however, some float is available and this provides flexibility in scheduling them. The choice available in this respect is bounded by two schedules: the early start schedule and the late start schedule.

The Bounding Schedules: Early Start Schedule and Late Start Schedule The early start schedule refers to the schedule in which all activities start as early as possible. In this schedule (i) all events occur at their earliest because all activities start at their earliest starting time and finish at their earliest finishing time; (ii) there may be time lags between the completion of certain activities and the occurrence of events which these activities lead to; and (iii) all activities emanating from an event begin at the same time.

The early start schedule suggests a cautious attitude towards the project and a desire to minimise the possibility of delay. It provides a greater measure of protection against uncertainties and adverse circumstances. Such a schedule, however, calls for an earlier application of resources.

The late start schedule refers to the schedule arrived at when all activities are started as late as possible. In this schedule (i) all events occur at their latest because all activities start at their latest starting time; (ii) some activities may start after a time lag subsequent to the occurrence of the preceding events; and (iii) all activities leading to an event are completed at the same time.

The late start schedule reflects a desire to commit resources late—as late as possible. However, such a schedule provides no elbow room in the wake of adverse developments. Any unanticipated delay results in increased project duration.

The early start schedule and the late start schedule for our illustrative project are shown in Exhibit 23.16. Here the project schedules are shown as graphs with a horizontal time scale.

Exhibit 23.16 ***Early and Late Start Schedules***

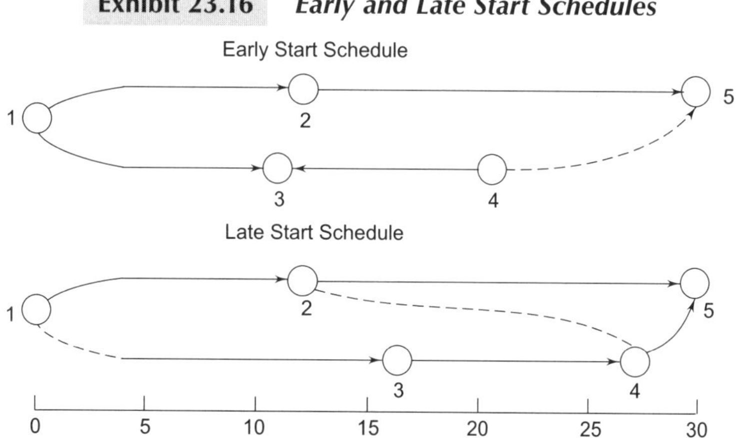

Choice of a Schedule in View of Resource Constraints In our discussion so far we have assumed that any schedule which is technologically feasible—which does not violate the logical relationship among activities as shown in the network diagram—can be adopted. For generating various schedules, the early start schedule, the late start schedule, or any other schedule lying between these two bounds, information was required regarding only network logic and activity durations.

This approach to scheduling implicitly assumes that adequate resources are available so that each activity can be scheduled anywhere between its earliest starting time and latest starting time. In real life situations, however, there may be restrictions on the availability of resources. For example, manpower supply may be limited or funds made available period-wise may be rigidly budgeted. When restrictions exist, various schedules may have to be considered to find out which one is the most appropriate in the light of these restrictions. We shall discuss two examples to indicate the broad approach to scheduling in the face of resource constraints.

Example 1: Scheduling to Match Availability of Manpower Let us consider a small project for which the network diagram is shown in Exhibit 23.17.

In Exhibit 23.17 activity duration is shown above the activity arrow and manpower requirement is shown below the activity arrow. Only 12 men are available for the project (a manpower resource constraint). The early start schedule of this project is shown as a graph on the horizontal time scale in Exhibit 23.18.

Looking at the manpower requirement for the early start schedule we find that it is 20 for the first day, 14 for the second day, 15 for the third day, 5 for the fourth day, and 5 for the fifth day. Obviously, this schedule is unacceptable in view of the manpower constraint. So, we explore the possibility of shifting activities. Our efforts at shifting activities, keeping the project duration at five days, soon reveal that no schedule is feasible with only 12 men. So we extend the duration of the project by one day and try various schedules to see whether we can find a feasible schedule. A little juggling of activities shows that a schedule like the one shown in Exhibit 23.19 is feasible—this is the best we can do.

Exhibit 23.17 ***Activity Durations and Manpower Requirements***

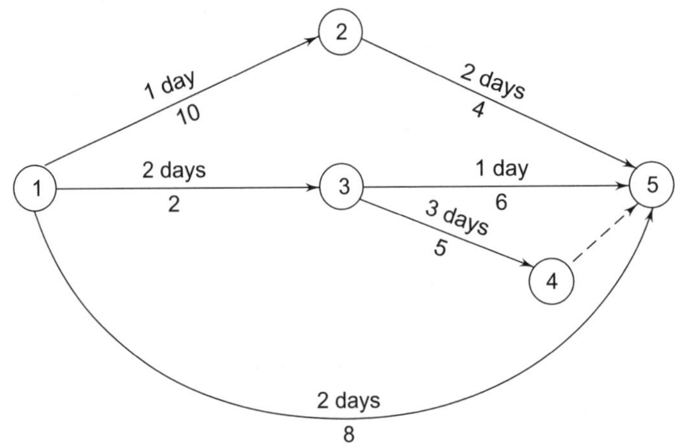

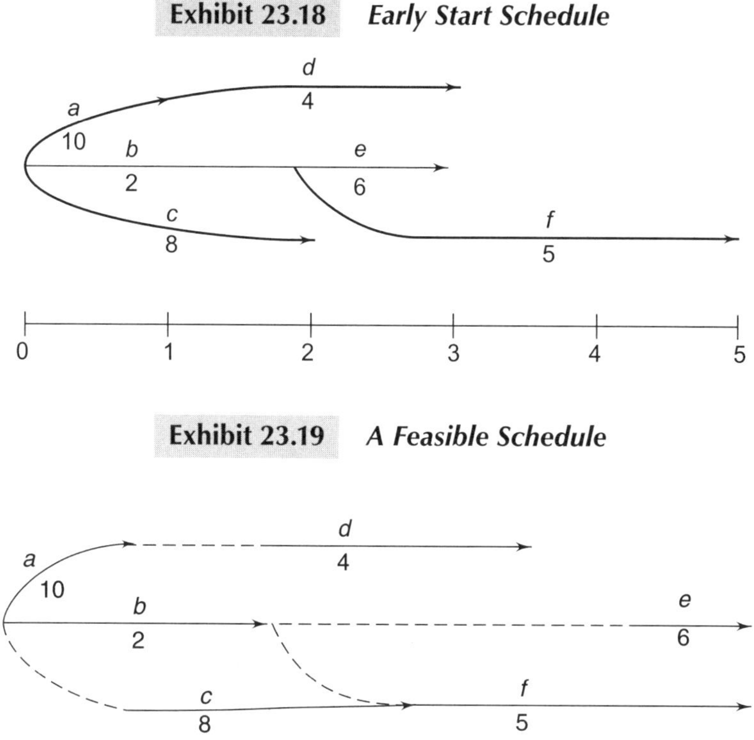

Exhibit 23.18 *Early Start Schedule*

Exhibit 23.19 *A Feasible Schedule*

Example 2: Scheduling to Match the Release of Funds The cost estimates for various activities of our illustrative project (see Exhibit 23.8) are given in Exhibit 23.20. For our discussion here, *weeks* have been changed to *months*.

Exhibit 23.20 *Cost Estimates*

Activity	*Duration in Months*	*Cost per Month (₹)*	*Cost (₹)*
(1-2)	13	200,000	2,600,000
(1-3)	12	500,000	6,000,000
(2-4)	2	1,000,000	2,000,000
(3-4)	8	250,000	2,000,000
(2-5)	15	100,000	1,500,000
(4-5)	2	750,000	1,500,000
		Total =	15,600,000

The government has decided to release ₹15,600,000, required for the project, in the following manner:

₹6,900,000 in the first year; ₹6,800,000 in the second year; and ₹1,900,000 in the third year. It has also stipulated that the unspent amount would lapse and hence cannot be carried forward.

Before we develop the project schedule, a preliminary question may be asked: Is it possible *prima facie* to schedule this project without extending its duration beyond 28 months, which is the minimum time required given the network logic and activity durations? To answer this question let us look at the funds requirement for the early start schedule and late start schedule. This is shown in Exhibit 23.21.

Exhibit 23.21 ***Funds Requirements for Different Schedules***

EARLY START SCHEDULE

Activities	1	2	3	4	5	6	7	8	9	10	11	12	13	14	15	16	17	18	19	20	21	22	23	24	25	26	27	28
(1.2)	2	2	2	2	2	2	2	2	2	2	2	2	2															
(1.3)	5	5	5	5	5	5	5	5	5	5	5	5																
(2.4)														10	10													
(3.4)													2.5	2.5	2.5	2.5	2.5	2.5	2.5	2.5								
(2.5)														1	1	1	1	1	1	1	1	1	1	1	1	1	1	1
(4.5)																					7.5	7.5						
Project Requirement Monthly	7	7	7	7	7	7	7	7	7	7	7	7	4.5	13.5	13.5	3.5	3.5	3.5	3.5	3.5	8.5	8.5	1	1	1	1	1	1
Project Requirement Cumulative	7	14	21	28	35	42	49	56	63	70	77	84	88.5	102	115.5	119	122.5	126	129.5	133	141.5	150	151	152	153	154	155	156

Month 0 5 10 15 20 25 28

LATE START SCHEDULE

Activities	1	2	3	4	5	6	7	8	9	10	11	12	13	14	15	16	17	18	19	20	21	22	23	24	25	26	27	28
(1.2)	2	2	2	2	2	2	2	2	2	2	2	2	2															
(1.3)							5	5	5	5	5	5	5	5	5	5	5	5										
(2.4)																									10	10		
(3.4)																			2.5	2.5	2.5	2.5	2.5	2.5	2.5	2.5		
(2.5)														1	1	1	1	1	1	1	1	1	1	1	1	1	1	1
(4.5)																											7.5	7.5
Project Requirement Monthly	2	2	2	2	2	2	7	7	7	7	7	7	7	6	6	6	6	6	3.5	3.5	3.5	3.5	3.5	3.5	13.5	13.5	8.5	8.5
Project Requirement Cumulative	2	4	6	8	10	12	19	26	33	40	47	54	61	67	73	79	85	91	94.5	98.0	101.5	105	108.5	112	125.5	139	147.5	156

In this exhibit activities are represented by bars. The length of the bar corresponds to activity duration.

The monthly fund requirement for each activity is shown above its bar. (Here it is assumed that expenditure on an activity is uniformly spread over its duration.) The project requirements, month-wise and cumulative, are shown along the time axis. The cumulative project requirements for the early start schedule and the late start schedule are also shown in the form of cost curves in Exhibit 23.22.

Exhibit 23.22 ***Cost Curves***

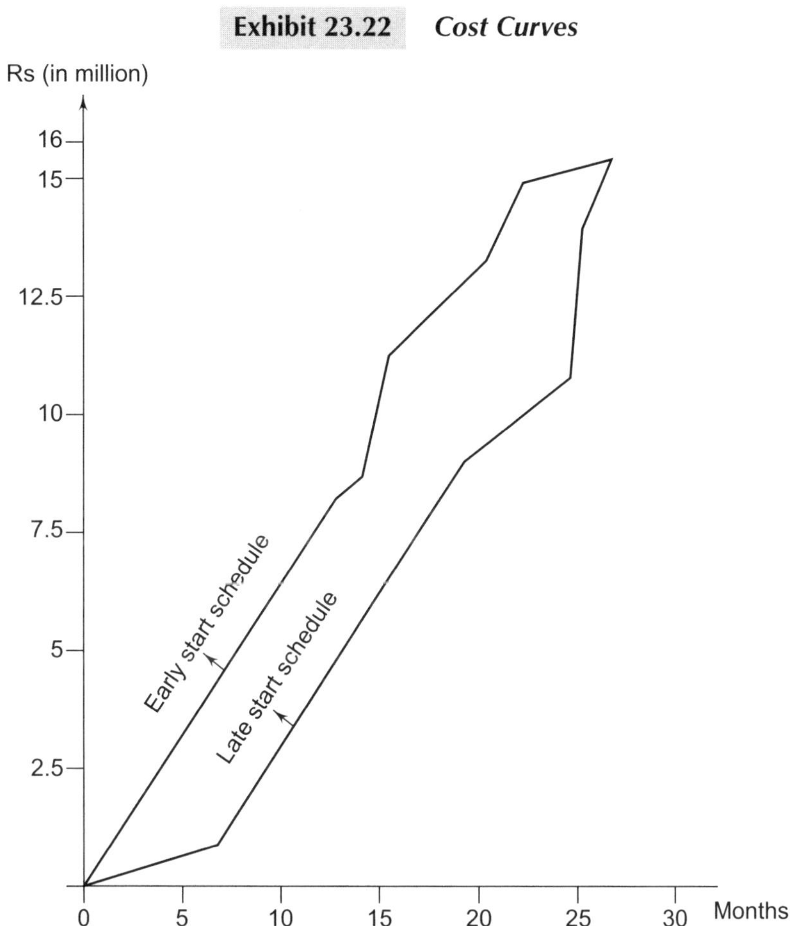

From Exhibits 23.21 and 23.22 we find that:

1. The rate of expenditure is relatively higher in the earlier stages for the early start schedule and is relatively higher in the later stages for the late start schedule.
2. A rate of spending greater than that of the early start schedule is not possible. (This is so because in the early start schedule all activities start as early as possible.) Any release of funds above the early start schedule requirement curve is beyond the capacity of the project to spend.

3. The rate of spending corresponding to the late start schedule is the absolute minimum necessary to complete the project on time. If the rate of spending is less than that corresponding to the late start schedule the project duration will have to be necessarily extended.
4. A pattern of funds release lying between the two bounds, early start schedule requirement and late start schedule requirement, *prima facie* suggests that a schedule can be worked out without extending project duration.

Let us now look at the cumulative funds release pattern for our illustrative project. This lies between the early start schedule requirement and the late start schedule requirement. So *prima facie* it suggests that a feasible schedule without extending the project duration can be developed. Let us proceed further and consider scheduling year by year. The activities that begin in year 1 according to the early start schedule are (1–2) and (1–3). If both these activities are commenced as early as possible, the fund requirement for year 1 would be ₹8.4 million. Since this amount exceeds ₹6.9 million, the amount to be released in year 1, the expenditure in year 1 has to be reduced by ₹1.5 million. For this we consider the possibility of shifting activities to subsequent periods. Looking at activities (1–2) and (1–3) we find that (1–2) is on the critical path, so there is no flexibility available with respect to it. Activity (1–3), however, can be shifted as it is not on the critical path. Since activity (1–3) requires ₹0.5 million per month it has to be shifted by three months so that the amount spent in year 1 is equal to the amount released in year 1. Since there is a free float of six months for activity (1–3), we shift it by three months.

We now go to year 2. The effects of shifting activity (1–3) by three months are as follows: (i) The funds requirement for year 2 on account of activity (1–3) increases by ₹1.5 million over and above what it is for the early start schedule. (ii) The earliest starting time for activity (3–4) moves to 15 months from 12 months and the earliest finishing time moves to 23 months from 20 months. Since this shift occurs within year 2, there is no change in funds requirement on account of activity (3–4). (iii) The earliest starting time for activity (4–5) moves to 23 months from 20 months and the earliest finishing time for activity (4–5) moves to 25 months from 23 months. This decreases the funds requirement for year 2 by ₹0.75 million. The net effect, therefore, is to increase funds requirement by ₹0.75 million over and above what it is for the earliest starting schedule. Hence the total requirement becomes ₹6.8 million + ₹0.75 million = ₹7.55 million. However, the funds budgeted for year 2 are only ₹6.8 million. So we consider the possibility of shifting some activities to year 3. We find that by shifting activity (4–5) to year 3 the expenditure in year 2 can be reduced to ₹6.8 million, the budget of that year. As a result of this shifting, the expenditure for year 3 (first four months of it) equals the budgeted funds release for year 3. The schedule arrived at finally is shown in Exhibit 23.23.

Problems in Scheduling Real Life Projects In the above discussion we have considered simple examples comprising a few activities and one constraint, to indicate the broad approach. In real life projects activities run into hundreds and there may be several constraints. The problem of scheduling in such cases tends to become very complex. For solving such problems the technique of linear programming may be used. Linear programming can be informationally intensive and computationally intensive. If linear programming is not feasible for some reason, some heuristic programme may be used.

Exhibit 23.23 ***The Selected Schedule***

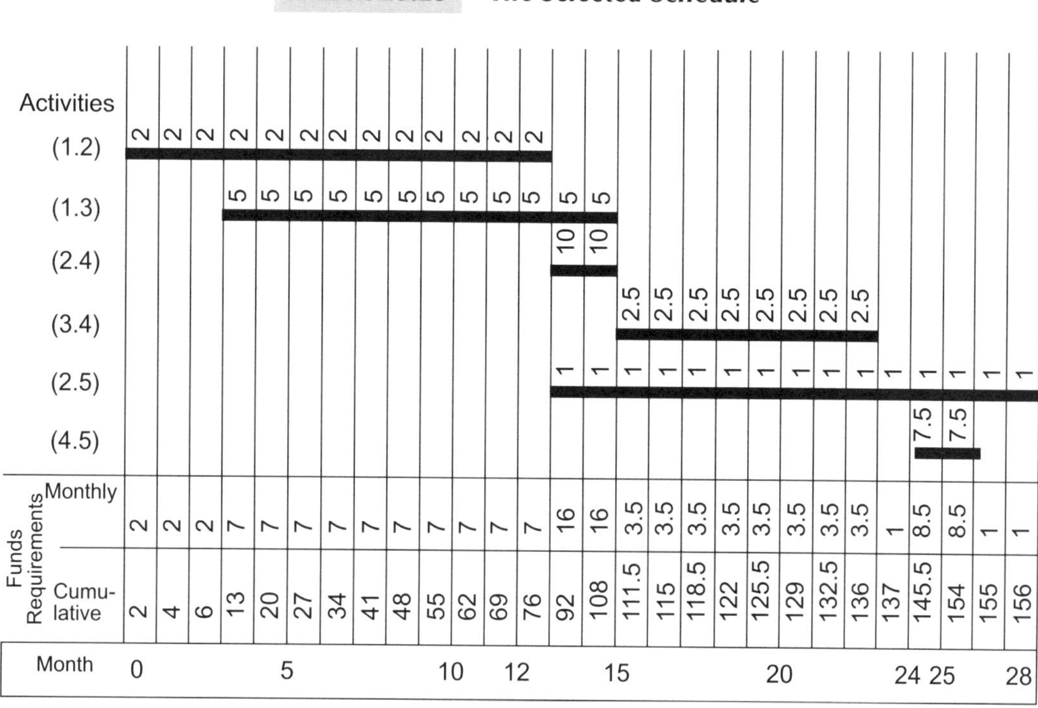

A heuristic is a rule of thumb like 'schedule critical activities first' or 'schedule the activity which has the largest independent float in the end'. A heuristic programme consists of a collection of such heuristics. In recent years, many heuristic programmes have been developed - they are formulated usually as computer programmes. These programmes may be broadly divided into two types: resource levelling programmes and resource allocation programmes. A resource levelling programme seeks to level resource requirements, given a constraint on project duration. A resource allocation programme tries to find the shortest project schedule, given fixed resource availabilities.

23.5 PERT MODEL

So far the analysis was focused on the determination of the critical path, event slacks, and activity floats. For this purpose we used single time estimates of activity duration though initially three-time estimates were developed for each activity. Now we consider the variability of project duration.

Measures of Variability Variability in PERT analysis is measured by variance or its square root, standard deviation. Variance of a set of numbers is the average squared difference of the numbers in the set from their arithmetic average. A simple example may be given to illustrate the calculation of variance. Let a series consist of numbers 4, 6, and 8. The average of this series is 6. The differences of various numbers in the series from this average are –2, 0, and 2. Squaring them we get 4, 0 and 4. Hence variance[1], the average of squared difference, is 8/3 and standard deviation is $\sqrt{8/3}$.

The steps involved in calculating the standard deviation of the duration of critical path are as follows:

1. Determine the standard deviation of the duration of each activity on the critical path.
2. Determine the standard deviation of the total duration of the critical path on the basis of information obtained in step 1.

For determining the standard deviation of the duration of an activity we require the entire probability distribution of the activity distribution. We, however, have only three values from this distribution: t_p, t_m, and t_o. In PERT analysis, a simplification is used in calculating the standard deviation. It is estimated by the formula[2].

$$\sigma = \frac{t_p - t_o}{6} \tag{23.11}$$

where σ is the standard deviation, t_p is the pessimistic time, and t_o is the optimistic time.

Variance is obtained by squaring σ.

The standard deviations and variances of the activities on the critical path of our illustrative project are shown in Exhibit 23.24.

Assuming that the probability distribution of various activities on the critical path are independent, the variance of the critical path duration is obtained by adding variances of activities on the critical path.[3]

---

[1] In this example we assumed that the three values 4, 6 and 8 had the same probability of occurrence (1/3) and hence we did not consider probabilities explicitly. Where the values have different probabilities associated with them, probabilities are considered explicitly. Variance is calculated by the formula $\Sigma p_i(X_i - \overline{X})^2$ where X_i is a possible value, p_i is the probability associated with it, and $\overline{X}$ is the weighted arithmetic average of X_is. This means $\overline{X} = \Sigma p_i X_i$.

[2] In this formula σ is one-sixth of the difference between the two extreme time estimates, t_p and t_o. It is based on the fact that nearly all the distribution of a single-peaked distribution falls within three standard deviations of the mean. For a normal distribution, 99.8 percent of the distribution lies within this interval and for no single-peaked distribution is it less than 89 percent according to Tchebycheff's inequality. This means that t_o and t_p are not necessarily the end points of the range of possible values but points beyond which the probability of occurrence is very small.

[3] This is based on an elementary theorem in statistics which says that when $X_1, X_2, X_3, \cdots, X_n$ are independent variables the following holds true:

$$\begin{aligned}\text{Variance}(X_1 + X_2 \cdots + X_n) = {} & \text{Variance}(X_1) \\ + {} & \text{Variance}(X_2) \\ & \vdots \\ + {} & \text{Variance}(X_n)\end{aligned}$$

Exhibit 23.24 ***Standard Deviation and Variance of Activity Duration on Critical Path***

Activity	t_p	t_o	$\sigma = t_p - t_o/6$	Variance = σ^2
(1-2)	21	9	2	4.00
(2-5)	24	10	2.33	5.43

Variance (critical path duration) = Sum of variances of activity durations on the critical path

This means

Standard deviation (critical path duration) = $\left(\text{Sum of variances of activity durations on the critical path}\right)^{1/2}$

The standard deviation of the critical path duration for our illustrative project is

$$(4 + 5.43)^{1/2} = 3.07$$

Now we know that the mean[4] and standard deviation of the critical path duration for our project are 28 weeks and 3.07 weeks, respectively.

For real life projects which have a large number of activities on the critical path we can reasonably assume that the critical path duration is approximately normally distributed[5], with mean and standard deviation obtained by the method described above.

A normal distribution looks like a bell-shaped curve as shown in Exhibit 23.25. It is symmetric and single peaked and is fully described by its mean and standard deviation. The probability of values lying within certain ranges is as follows:

Range	*Probability*
Mean ± One standard deviation	0.682
Mean ± Two standard deviations	0.954
Mean ± Three standard deviations	0.998

Exhibit 23.25 ***Normal Distribution***

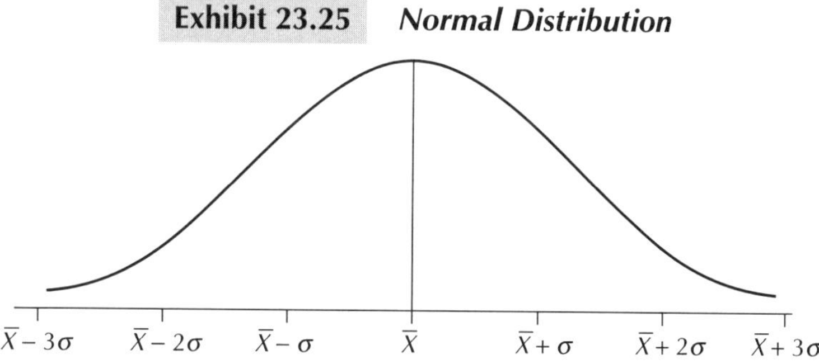

[4] The mean length of the critical path is simply the sum of the mean values of activity durations on the critical path. This is based on an elementary theorem in statistics which says:

$$E\,(X_1 + X_2 \cdots + X_n) = E\,(X_1) + E\,(X_2) \cdots E(X_n)$$

E stands for expected value or the mean value.

[5] This assumption is based on the central limit theorem, a fundamental theorem in statistics, which says that the sum of a large number of independent random variables is approximately normally distributed, irrespective of how the individual random variables are distributed.

Probability of Completion by a Specific Date Armed with information about mean (T) and standard deviation (σ) for critical path duration, which is normally distributed, we can compute the probability of completion by a specified date (D) as follows:

1. Find $Z = \frac{D - T}{\sigma}$
2. Obtain cumulative probability up to Z[6] by looking at the probability distribution of the standard normal variate. This is shown in Exhibit 23.26.

Exhibit 23.26 ***Cumulative Probability up to Z for Standard Normal Distribution***

Z	*Cumulative probability*
-3.0	0.001
-2.8	0.003
-2.6	0.005
-2.4	0.008
-2.2	0.014
-2.0	0.023
-1.8	0.036
-1.6	0.055
-1.4	0.081
-1.2	0.115
-1.0	0.159
-0.8	0.212
-0.6	0.274
-0.4	0.345
-0.2	0.421
0.0	0.500
0.2	0.579
0.4	0.655
0.6	0.726
0.8	0.788
1.0	0.841
1.2	0.885
1.4	0.919
1.6	0.945
1.8	0.964
2.0	0.977
2.2	0.986
2.4	0.992
2.6	0.995
2.8	0.997
3.0	0.999

[6] Z represents the number of standard deviations by which D, the specified date, exceeds T, the mean critical path duration. Determining Z is equivalent to converting our specific normal distribution (with mean T and standard deviation σ) into standard normal distribution. The mean and standard deviation of standard normal distribution are 0 and 1 respectively.

The above procedure may be illustrated for our project[7], which has $T = 28$ and $\sigma = 3.07$. The probability of completing this project by certain specified dates is shown in Exhibit 23.27.

Exhibit 23.27 ***Probability of Completion by the Specified Date***

Specified Date (D)	*Z*	*Probability of Completion by D*
20	$\frac{20-28}{3.07} = -2.6$	0.005
25	$\frac{25-28}{3.07} = -1.0$	0.159
30	$\frac{30-28}{3.07} = 0.6$	0.726

23.6 CPM MODEL

The PERT model was developed for projects characterised by uncertainty and the CPM model was developed for projects which are relatively risk-free. While both the approaches begin with the development of the network and a focus on the critical path, the PERT approach is 'probabilistic' and the CPM approach is 'deterministic'. This does not, however, mean that in CPM analysis we work with single time estimates. In fact, the principal focus of CPM analysis is on variations in activity times as a result of changes in resource assignments. These variations are planned and related to resource assignments and are not caused by random factors beyond the control of management as in the case of PERT analysis. The main thrust of CPM analysis is on time–cost relationships and it seeks to determine the project schedule which minimises total cost.

Assumptions The usual assumptions underlying CPM analysis are:

1. The costs associated with a project can be divided into two components: direct costs and indirect costs. Direct costs are incurred on direct material and direct labour. Indirect costs consist of overhead items like indirect supplies, rent, insurance, managerial services, etc.
2. Activities of the project can be expedited by crashing which involves employing more resources.
3. Crashing reduces time but enhances direct costs because of factors like overtime payments, extra payments, and wastage. The relationship between time and direct activity cost can be reasonably approximated by a downward sloping straight line. A typical cost-time line is shown in Exhibit 23.28.

[7] It may be noted that in our illustrative project there are only two activities on the critical path and hence the assumption that the project duration is approximately normally distributed may not be realistic. However, as real life projects have a large number of activities on their critical paths, the procedure illustrated here is useful for them.

4. Indirect costs associated with the project increase linearly with project duration. A typical line for indirect costs is shown in Exhibit 23.29.

Exhibit 23.28 ***Cost-Time Line***

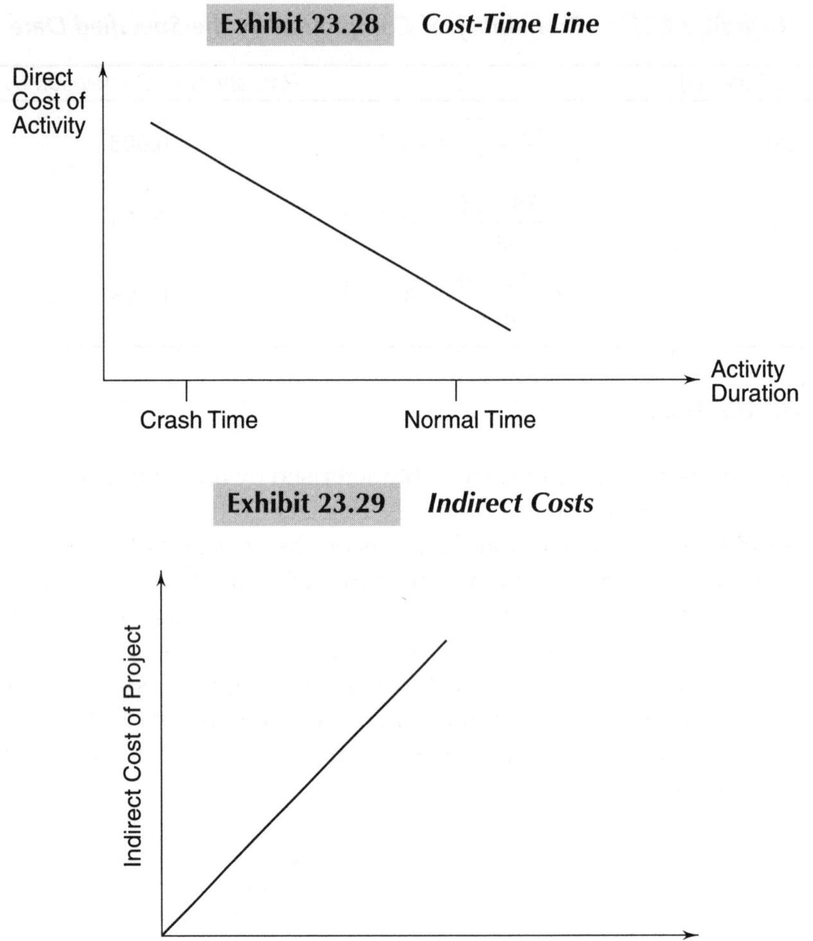

Exhibit 23.29 ***Indirect Costs***

Procedure Given the above assumptions, CPM analysis seeks to examine the consequences of crashing on total cost (direct cost plus indirect cost). Since the behaviour of indirect project cost is well defined, the bulk of CPM analysis is concerned with the relationship between total direct cost and project duration. The procedure used in this respect is generally as follows:

1. Obtain the critical path in the normal network. Determine the project duration and direct cost.
2. Examine the cost–time slope of activities on the critical path obtained and crash the activity which has the least slope.[8]

[8] If there is more than one critical path, one activity on each of the critical paths should be crashed. The activity crashed on each critical path, of course, will have the lowest cost–time slope on that path.

3. Construct the new critical path after crashing as per step 2. Determine project duration and cost.
4. Repeat steps 2 and 3 till activities on the critical path (which may change every time) are crashed.

Illustration The above procedure may be illustrated with an example. The activities, durations, and direct activity costs of a project are shown in Exhibit 23.30. The indirect cost is ₹2,000 per week.

Exhibit 23.30 ***Normal and Crash Time and Cost***

	Time in Weeks		*Cost*		*Cost to Expedite Per Week*
Activity	Normal	Crash	Normal	Crash	
			₹	₹	₹
1-2	8	4	3,000	6,000	750
1-3	5	3	4,000	8,000	2,000
2-4	9	6	4,000	5,500	500
3-5	7	5	2,000	3,900	950
2-5	5	1	8,000	12,000	1,000
4-6	3	2 ½	10,000	11,200	2,400
5-6	6	2	4,000	6,800	700
6-7	10	7	6,000	8,700	900
5-7	9	5	4,200	9,000	1,200
			45,200	71,100	

The project network with normal duration is shown in Exhibit 23.31.

Exhibit 23.31 ***Project Network***

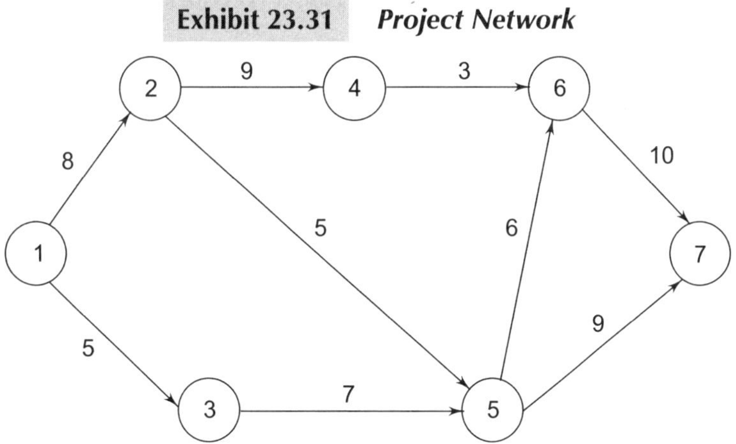

The critical path in the all-normal network is (1–2–4–6–7). The project duration is 30 weeks and the total direct cost is ₹45,200.

Examining the time–cost slope of activities on the critical path we find that activity (2–4) has the lowest slope; in other words, the cost to expedite per week is the lowest for activity (2–4). Hence activity (2–4) is crashed. The project network after such a crashing is shown in Exhibit 23.32.

Exhibit 23.32 ***Project Network***

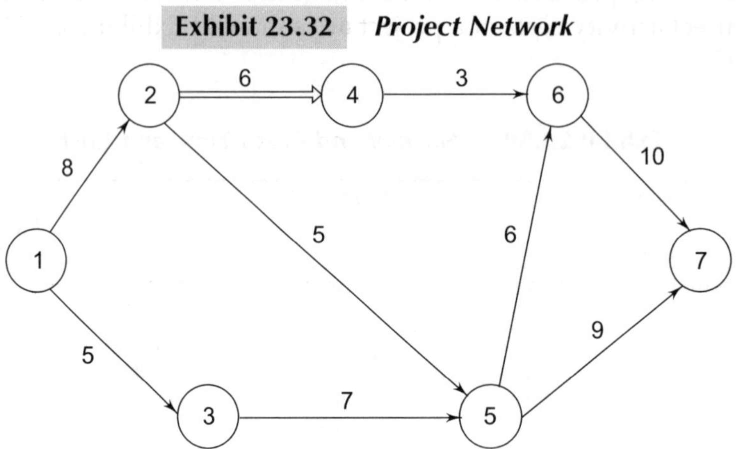

As per Exhibit 23.32 the critical path is (1–2–5–6–7), with a length of 29 weeks, and the total direct cost is ₹46,700.

Looking at the time–cost slope of the activities on the new critical path (1–2–5–6–7), we find that the activity (5–6) has the lowest slope. Hence this activity is crashed. The project network after such crashing is shown in Exhibit 23.33. As per this figure, the critical path is (1–2–4–6–7) with a length of 27 weeks and the total direct cost is ₹49,500.

Exhibit 23.33 ***Project Network***

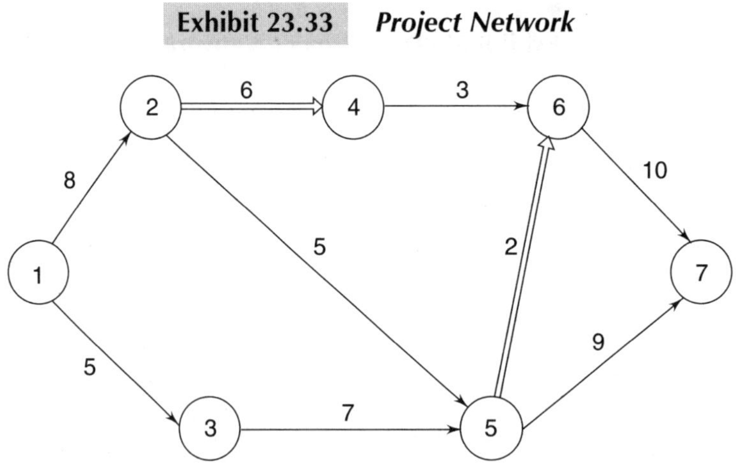

Comparing the time-cost slope of the non-crashed activities on the new critical path (1–2–4–6–7), we find that the activity which costs the least to crash is (1–2). Hence this is crashed. The project network after such a crashing is shown in Exhibit 23.34. As per this figure the critical path is (1–3–5–6–7) with a length of 24 weeks and the total direct cost is ₹52,500.

Exhibit 23.34 ***Project Network***

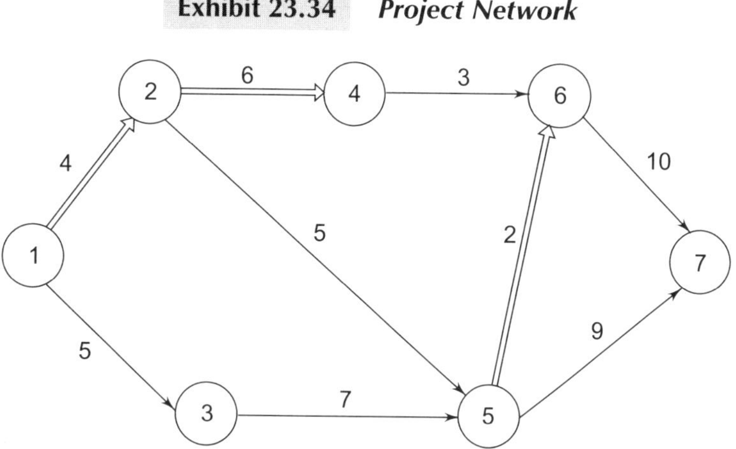

Looking at the time–cost slope of the non-crashed activities on the new critical path (1–3–5–6–7), we find that activity (6–7) has the lowest slope. Hence it is crashed. The project network after such a crashing is shown in Exhibit 23.35. As per this figure there are two critical paths (1–3–5–6–7) and (1–3–5–7), both with a length of 21 weeks, and the total direct cost is ₹55,200.

Exhibit 23.35 ***Project Network***

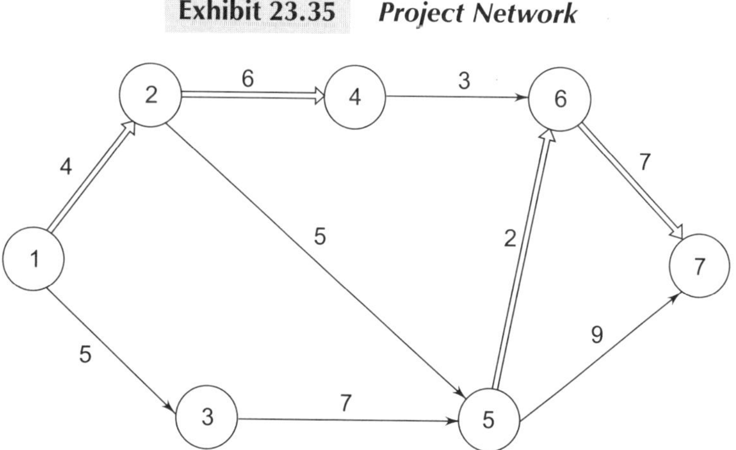

Considering the time-cost slope of non-crashed activities on critical paths (1–3–5–6–7) and (1–3–5–7), we find that activity (3–5) which is common to both the critical paths is the least costly to crash. Hence, it is crashed. The project network after this crashing is shown in Exhibit 23.36. As per this figure, the critical path is (1–2–4–6–7) with a duration of 20 weeks and the total direct cost is ₹57,100.

Exhibit 23.36 ***Project Network***

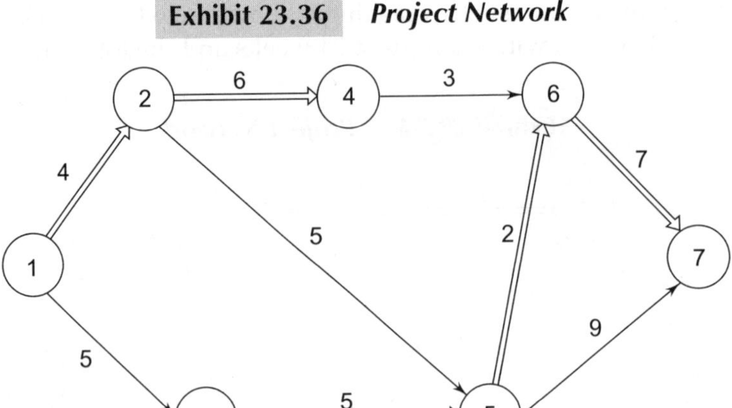

Looking at the new critical path (1–2–4–6–7) we find that the only non-crashed activity is (4–6). Crashing this gives us the project network shown in Exhibit 23.37. As per this figure, the critical path again is (1–2–4–6–7) with a duration of 19½ weeks and the total direct cost is ₹58,300.

Exhibit 23.37 ***Project Network***

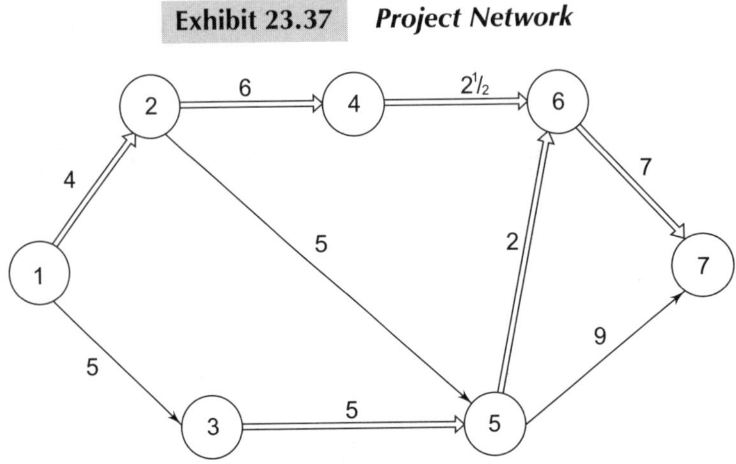

Since all the activities on the critical path (1–2–4–6–7) are crashed, there is no possibility of further time reduction. Hence let us now look at the time-cost relationship. Exhibit 23.38 shows this[9].

[9] At this stage, we look at the crashed activities on the non-critical paths to find out whether they can be de-crashed without increasing the project duration as indicated by the critical path (1–2–4–6–7). If this is possible, we begin with the activity which has the highest time–cost slope and proceed in the order of the decreasing time-cost slope. In our project, however, there is no scope for de-crashing on the non-critical path because it is not possible to do so without increasing the project duration.

From Exhibit 23.38, we find that the total cost is minimised for the project schedule represented by Exhibit 23.36 in which the activities crashed are (1–2), (2–4), (3–5), (5–6), and (6–7). The information provided in Exhibit 23.38 is useful for decision making.

Exhibit 23.38 ***Project Duration and Total Cost***

Exhibit	*Activities Crashed*	*Project Duration in Weeks*	*Total Direct Cost* (₹)	*Total Indirect Cost* (₹)	*Total Cost* (₹)
22.31	None	30	45,200	60,000	105,200
22.32	(2-4)	29	46,700	58,000	104,700
22.33	(2-4) and (5-6)	27	49,500	54,000	103,500
20.34	(1-2), (2-4) and (5-6)	24	52,500	48,000	100,500
22.35	(1-2), (2-4), (5-6) and (6-7)	21	55,200	42,000	97,200
22.36	(1-2), (2-4), (3-5), (5-6) and (6-7)	20	57,100	40,000	97,100
22.37	(1-2), (2-4), (3-5), (5-6), (4-6) and (6-7)	19 ½	58,300	39,000	97,300

If the objective is to minimise the total cost of the project, the pattern of crashing suggested by Exhibit 23.36 is optimal. If the objective is to minimise the project duration then the pattern of crashing suggested by Exhibit 23.37 is optimal. In real life situations, however, both the factors may be important. In addition, factors like strain on resources and degree of manageability are also important. The final decision would involve a careful weighing and balancing of these diverse factors, some quantitative, some qualitative. In any case, information along the lines provided in Exhibit 23.38 provides useful input for decision making.

23.7 NETWORK COST SYSTEM

The techniques of PERT and CPM discussed above are essentially time-oriented. They seek to answer questions like:

- What is the most desirable time schedule of activities?
- How much time would it take, on an average, to complete the project?
- What is the probability of completing the project in a specified time? (It may be noted that in CPM analysis, the primary objective is to develop a time schedule in view of time–cost tradeoff and not to develop a detailed budget of costs, activity-wise and time-wise. Similarly, when scheduling is done under funds constraint, the primary objective is to establish a time schedule consistent with funds constraint and not to develop a system for cost planning and control.)

Such analysis largely overlooks the cost aspect which is usually as important as the time aspect and sometimes even more. To provide a vehicle for cost planning and control of projects, the network cost system was developed. This represents a very useful supplement to the traditional time-oriented network analysis. Let us look at cost projection and cost analysis and control under the network cost system.

Cost Projection The basic principle of the network cost system is fairly simple: costs are planned, measured, analysed, and controlled in terms of project activities. Though simple, this principle represents a departure from the conventional cost accounting system where costs are generally planned, measured, analysed, and controlled in terms of functions or organisational divisions.

Once costs are estimated in terms of activities, cost projections can be made for any chosen schedule. For cost projection it is usually assumed that the expenditure for any activity is incurred evenly over the duration of the activity. Where this assumption does not appear valid, the activity should be divided into two or more sequential components, such that for each of the components the expenditure occurs uniformly over its duration. The projected cost curve for a given schedule and activity-wise cost estimates can be readily obtained.

Analysis and Control of Costs As the project progresses, the following may be measured/ estimated periodically for purposes of monitoring and control.

1. *Costs incurred to date* In a network cost system, costs are recorded activity-wise. Costs incurred to date can be obtained by summing up costs for various activities.
2. *Budgeted costs to date* Budgeted costs to date can be readily obtained from the cost projections made at the beginning.
3. *Value of work done to date* When costs are measured, an estimate should also be made of the extent of work accomplished. The value of work done can then be obtained as follows: budgeted costs × percentage work accomplished. This may be illustrated by an example. A certain activity has a budgeted cost of ₹80,000 and at the time of the periodic progress review it is estimated that 60 percent of the work has been accomplished. So the value of work done is put at ₹80,000 × 60 percent = ₹48,000.
4. *Cost over-run (under-run) to date* There is cost over-run when the cost incurred is more than the value of work done. Similarly, there is cost under-run when the cost incurred is less than the value of work done. Cost over-run (under-run) is usually expressed in percentage terms. It is defined as follows:

$$\frac{\text{Actual cost} - \text{Value of work completed}}{\text{Value of work completed}} \times 100$$

5. *Time over-run (under-run) to date.* There is time over-run if the project is behind schedule. Likewise, there is time under-run if the project is ahead of schedule. Time over-run (under-run) is usually defined in terms of months behind or months ahead.

Graphic Display The above information may be displayed graphically as shown in Exhibit 23.39.

Exhibit 23.39 has three graphs. The first graph shows budgeted costs (curve *A*), actual costs (curve *B*), and value of work (curve *C*). The second graph shows percentage cost over-run or under-run (curve *D*). It may be noted that curve *D* is derived from curves *B* and *C*. The vertical distance between curves *B* and *C* is divided by the height of curve *C* and multiplied by 100 to get curve *D*. The third graph shows the number of months by which the project is behind or ahead of the schedule (curve *E*). Curve *E* is derived from curves *A* and *C*. The months behind/ahead at any particular point of time is simply the horizontal distance (measured in months) of curve *C* at that point of time from curve *A*. Exhibit 23.39 provides information about time and cost, budget and actual, at one place and is a very useful device for monitoring and control.

Exhibit 23.39 ***Time and Cost, Budget and Actual***

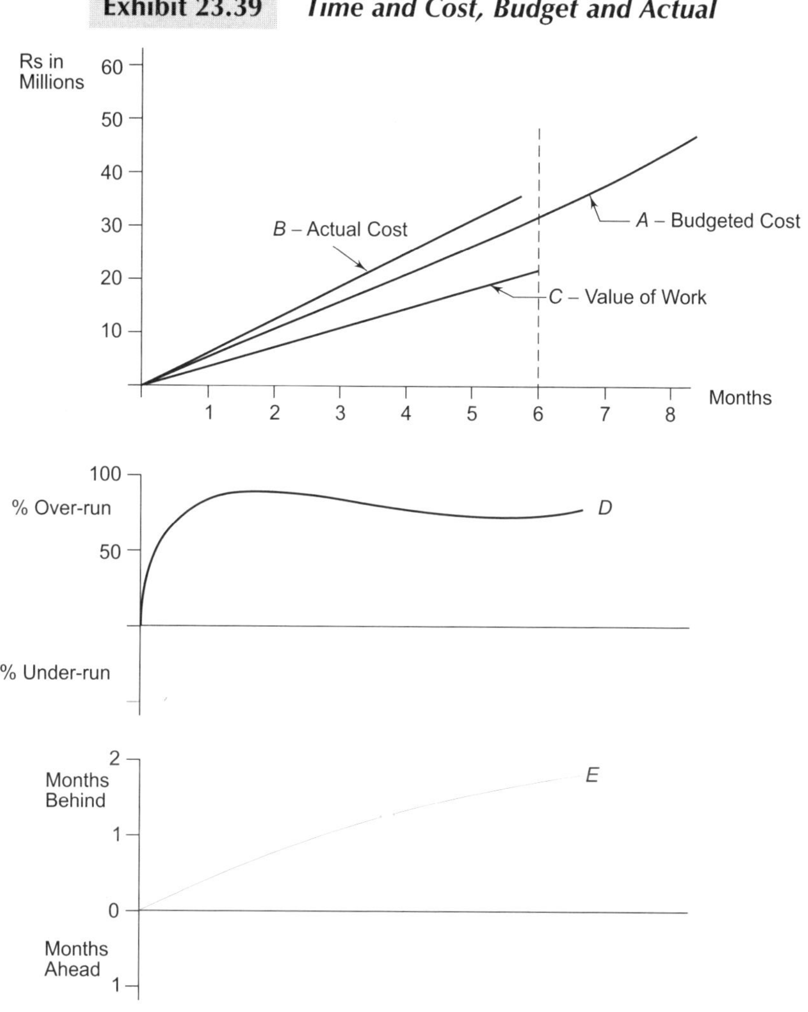

SUMMARY

- For proper planning, scheduling, and control of the activities of a project, given their interrelationships and constraints on the availability of resources, network techniques have been found quite useful.
- There are two basic network techniques: PERT and CPM. PERT is applied mostly to projects characterised by uncertainty; its orientation is probabilistic. CPM is applied to projects which are relatively risk-free; its orientation is deterministic. Widely diverse projects are amenable to analysis by PERT and CPM.
- The steps involved in PERT analysis are: (i) development of project network, (ii) time estimation, (iii) determination of critical path, event slacks, and activity floats, (iv) development of project schedule, and (v) calculation of the variability of project duration and the probability of completion in a given time.

- The network diagram is constructed in terms of activities and events. An activity is a definite task, job or function to be performed in a project. An event is a specific point of time indicating the beginning or end of one or more activities.
- The rules to be observed in constructing the network diagram are: (i) Each activity must have a preceding and succeeding event. (ii) Each event should have a distinct number. (iii) There should be no loops in the project network. (iv) Not more than one activity can have the same preceding and succeeding events.
- To ensure that each activity is uniquely numbered, it may be necessary to introduce dummy activities. A dummy activity is an imaginary activity which can be accomplished in zero time and which does not consume resources. A dummy activity may also be used to represent a constraint necessary to show the proper relationship between activities.
- Once the logic and detail of the network have been established, time estimates may be assigned to each activity. Generally, three time values are obtained for each activity: optimistic time (t_o), most likely time (t_m), and pessimistic time (t_p). The average time (t_e) is obtained by the formula:

$$t_e = \frac{t_o + 4t_m + t_p}{6}$$

- Once the network diagram with single time estimates has been developed, the following computational procedure may be employed for determining the critical path/s, event slacks, and activity floats: (i) Calculate the earliest occurrence time for each event. (ii) Calculate the latest occurrence time for each event. (iii) Calculate the slack of each event. (iv) Obtain the critical and slack paths. (v) Compute the activity floats.
- The early start schedule refers to the schedule in which all activities start as early as possible. The late start schedule reflects a desire to commit resources late—as late as possible.
- In real life situations there may be restrictions on the availability of resources. In the face of these, various schedules may have to be considered to find out which one is most appropriate in the light of these restrictions.
- Variability in PERT analysis is measured by variance or its square root, standard deviation.
- The steps involved in calculating the standard deviation of the duration of the critical path are as follows: (i) Determine the standard deviation of the duration of each activity on the critical path. (ii) Determine the standard deviation of the total duration of the critical path on the basis of information obtained in step (i).
- Armed with information about the mean and standard deviation of critical path duration, we can compute the probability of completion by a specified date.
- The usual assumptions underlying CPM analysis are: (i) The costs associated with a project can be divided into two components: direct costs and indirect costs. (ii) Activities of the project can be expedited by crashing which involves employing more resources. (iii) Crashing reduces time but enhances direct costs. (iv) Indirect costs associated with the project increase linearly with project duration.
- Given the above assumptions, CPM analysis seeks to examine the consequences of crashing on total cost (direct cost plus indirect cost). The procedure used in this respect is generally as follows: (i) Obtain the critical path in normal network. Determine the project duration and direct cost. (ii) Examine the cost-time slope of activities on the critical path obtained and crash the activity which has the least slope. (iii) Construct

the new critical path after crashing as per step (ii). Determine project duration and cost. (iv) Repeat steps (ii) and (iii) till all activities on the critical path (which may change every time) are crashed.

- To provide a vehicle for cost planning and control of projects, the network cost system was developed. This represents a very useful supplement to the traditional time-oriented network analysis.
- The basic principle of network cost system is fairly simple: costs are planned, measured, analysed, and controlled in terms of project activities.
- As the project progresses, the following may be measured/estimated periodically for purposes of monitoring and control: (i) costs incurred to-date, (ii) budgeted costs to-date, (iii) value of work done to-date, (iv) cost over-run (under-run) to-date, and (v) time over-run (under-run) to-date.

QUESTIONS

1. What is the basic difference between PERT and CPM?
2. What steps are involved in PERT analysis?
3. Discuss the rules for network construction.
4. What considerations should be borne in mind in time estimation?
5. What is the procedure for determining the critical path?
6. What are *EOT* and *LOT*?
7. Discuss the difference between total float, free float, and independent float.
8. What is an early start schedule and a late start schedule?
9. Illustrate the problem of scheduling in view of resource constraints with the help of an example.
10. How would you calculate the variability of project duration and probability of completion at a specified time? Illustrate with an example.
11. What are the usual assumptions underlying CPM analysis?
12. Discuss the procedure of CPM analysis with the help of a simple example.
13. Discuss the basic principle of network cost system.
14. What kind of periodic monitoring is done in a network cost system?

PROBLEMS

1. Draw the network diagram for an industrial project with which you are familiar.
2. A project consists of the following activities represented in terms of preceding and succeeding events. Draw its network diagram.

Activity	*Mean time (weeks)*
(1, 2)	4
(1, 3)	2
(1, 4)	3
(2, 4)	5
(3, 4)	6
(4, 5)	2
(5, 7)	3
(2, 5)	1
(4, 7)	5

3. A project consists of 12 activities and their time estimates are shown below:

Activity	*Time (in weeks)*		
	t_o	t_m	t_p
(1–2)	4	6	10
(1–3)	3	7	12
(1–4)	5	6	9
(1–7)	2	4	6
(2–4)	6	10	20
(2–6)	3	4	7
(2–7)	5	9	15
(3– 4)	3	7	12
(4– 5)	2	4	5
(5– 6)	1	3	6
(3–7)	2	5	8
(6–7)	1	2	6

(a) Draw the network diagram.
(b) Determine the critical path.
(c) Calculate event slacks and activity floats.
(d) Find the standard deviation of the critical path duration.
(e) Compute the probability of completing the project in 30 weeks.

4. The normal and crash times and direct costs for the activities of a project are shown below:

Activity	*Time*		*Cost*	
	Normal	*Crash*	*Normal*	*Crash*
(1–2)	5	2	6000	9000
(2–4)	6	3	7000	10,000
(1–3)	4	2	1000	2000
(3–4)	7	4	4000	8000
(4–7)	9	5	6000	9200
(3–5)	12	3	16,000	19,600
(4–6)	10	6	15,000	18,000
(6–7)	7	4	4000	4900
(7–9)	6	4	3000	4200
(5–9)	12	7	4000	8500

(a) Draw the network diagram.
(b) Determine all normal and critical paths.
(c) Find the minimum cost project schedule if the indirect costs are ₹1000 per week.

Review

CHAPTER 24

Project Review and Administrative Aspects

PART EIGHT

Chapter 24 Project Review and Administrative Aspects

LEARNING OBJECTIVES

After studying this chapter you should be able to

- Distinguish between economic rate of return and book return on investment.
- Discuss how a project must be reviewed for possible abandonment.
- Explain the difference between economic accounting and mental accounting.
- Discuss the administrative aspects of capital budgeting.
- Understand the agency problem and the devices for mitigating the same.
- Describe briefly the criteria for evaluating the capital budgeting system

The last phase of capital budgeting is concerned with the review of the projects undertaken. A project is monitored during the implementation phase so that time and cost over-runs are minimised. Further, after a project is commissioned its performance is periodically reviewed to see whether the same is in line with expectations. If things turn sour, the question of abandonment may also have to be examined.

The focus of this book has been mainly on the techniques of project analysis and selection and the supporting theoretical constructs. Capital budgeting, however, does not occur in a vacuum. Rather, it takes place in a real organisation with its attendant complexities such as compartmentalised thinking, multi-layered decision making, uneven knowledge of finance, bureaucratic red tape, and agency problems. To cope with these problems, firms develop suitable administrative procedures and try to mitigate agency problems through a combination of monitoring and incentives.

This chapter examines various facets of project review. It also discusses administrative aspects of capital budgeting and the devices for mitigating agency problems.

24.1 CONTROL OF IN-PROGRESS PROJECTS

Though a lot of effort is expended in selecting capital projects, things often go wrong in the implementation phase. This is evident from the frequent cost and time over-runs witnessed in practice. Hence it is necessary to exercise strict control on in-progress capital projects. There are two aspects of controlling in-progress capital projects.

Establishment of Internal Control Procedures For every in-progress capital project, proper control accounts are setup. These are charged with all relevant expenditures, which are further classified into capital and revenue items. These accounts reflect out-of-pocket payments as well as allocated expenses. The project-by-project segregation of costs ensures that proper attention can be directed to projects as they approach various milestones.

Use of Regular Progress Reports Periodic progress reports compare actual expenditures against estimates. They offer several benefits: (a) They provide timely information so that corrective action can be initiated to tackle potential problems. (b) They generate inputs for cash budgeting and fund raising. (c) They serve as the basis for calculating variances and explaining variances.

24.2 THE POST-AUDIT

Post-audit involves comparing actual results with predicted results and explaining the differences, if any. Many firms require the operating divisions to report on a monthly basis for six months or so after a project goes into operation. Thereafter, the project's performance is reviewed on a periodical basis like those of other operations.

The post-audit serves three purposes, in the main:

- *Improvement of forecasts* People tend to forecast better when they know that the actual results will be compared with forecasted results.
- *Improvement in operations* The project team will strive hard to improve operations so that they are in line with or even better than the forecasts. As one executive said: "You academicians worry about making good business decisions. In business, we also worry about making decisions good."
- *Identification of termination opportunities* If the post- audit reveals that the performance falls short of expectations, it may be worthwhile to terminate, rather than continue, the project.

The post-audit is not a simple process as several factors can complicate it.

1. Since there is a great deal of uncertainty characterising the future, a portion of projects undertaken by any fairly aggressive firm will necessarily fail to meet expectations.
2. Projects sometimes fail due to factors beyond the control of the operating managers – factors no one could realistically anticipate.
3. Due to interaction effects, it may be difficult to separate the results of a project from those of the larger system.
4. The executives responsible for initiating a given project would have moved on when the results are known. So, it may not be possible to shower praise or hand out blame.

Empirical evidence on post-audits suggests that, in general, cost reduction projects fall slightly below expectations, expansion projects fall slightly below expectations, and new product and new market projects fall short of expectations by a relatively larger margin. Well-run, successful organisations put a lot of emphasis on post-audits. Hence, the post-audit must be regarded as an important facet of the capital budgeting system.

Criteria for Periodic Evaluation It is a common practice to use book ROI defined as

$$\frac{\text{Cash flow} + \text{Change in book value}}{\text{Book value at the beginning of the year}}$$

for evaluating existing businesses and projects on a continuing basis. Though widely used, the book ROI has two serious flaws:

- Even though a project may earn a constant economic rate of return, its book ROI displays wide variation across time.
- There is an upward bias in the book ROI of a business which has substantial investment in intangible assets.

Constant Economic Rate of Return but Variable Book ROI Performance evaluation may be done in terms of economic rate of return or book return on investment:

Economic rate of return for a given year

$$= \frac{\text{Cash flow} + \text{Change in Present value}}{\text{Present value at the beginning of the year}}$$

Book return on investment for a given year

$$= \frac{\text{Cash flow} + \text{Change in book value}}{\text{Book value at the beginning of the year}}$$

The calculation of these measures may be illustrated with an example. Modern Enterprises Limited is considering an investment of ₹100 million in a new electronics unit which has an economic life of 7 years. The projected cash flows are as follows:

Year	1	2	3	4	5	6	7
Cash flow (*₹ in million*)	14	16	17	29	29	29	29

If the opportunity cost of capital is 12 percent, the *NPV* of the project turns out to be zero.

$$\text{NPV} = \frac{14}{(1.12)} + \frac{16}{(1.12)^2} + \frac{17}{(1.12)^3} + \frac{29}{(1.12)^4} + \frac{29}{(1.12)^5} + \frac{29}{(1.12)^6} + \frac{29}{(1.12)^7} - 100 = 0$$

The economic rate of return and the book return on investment (assuming a straight line depreciation over the 7-year life) for the electronics project are shown in Exhibits 24.1 and 24.2 respectively.

Exhibit 24.1 *Calculation of Economic Rate of Return*

	Year					(₹ in millions)	
	1	2	3	4	5	6	7
1. Cash flow	14	16	17	29	29	29	29
2. Present value at the beginning of the year, 12 percent discount rate	100	98	93.8	88.1	69.7	49.0	25.9
3. Present value at the end of the year, 12 percent discount rate	98	93.8	88.1	69.7	49.0	25.9	0
4. Change in value during the year (3-2)	-2	-4.2	-5.7	-18.4	-20.7	-23.1	-25.9
5. Economic income (1+4)	12	11.8	11.3	10.6	8.3	5.9	3.1
6. Economic rate of return (5/2)	.12	.12	.12	.12	.12	.12	.12
7. Economic depreciation	2	4.2	5.7	18.4	20.7	23.1	25.9

Exhibit 24.2 *Calculation of Book Return on Investment*

	Year					(₹ in millions)	
	1	2	3	4	5	6	7
1. Cash flow	14	16	17	29	29	29	29
2. Book value at the beginning of the year, straight line depreciation	100	85.7	71.4	57.1	42.9	28.6	14.3
3. Book value at the end of the year, straight line depreciation	85.7	71.4	57.1	42.9	28.6	14.3	0
4. Change in book value during the year (3-2)	-14.3	-14.3	-14.3	-14.3	-14.3	-14.3	-14.3
5. Book income (1+4)	-0.3	1.7	2.7	14.7	14.7	14.7	14.7
6. Book return on investment(5/2)	-0.003	0.020	0.038	0.257	0.343	0.514	1.028
7. Book depreciation	14.3	14.3	14.3	14.3	14.3	14.3	14.3

The economic rate of return shown in line 6 of Exhibit 24.1 remains constant at 12 percent throughout the life of the asset. This is a true measure of the project's profitability. The book ROI shown in line 6 of Exhibit 24.2 is very low in the initial years and rises rapidly from year 4 onwards. It becomes as high as 1.028 or 102.8 percent for year 7. Thus we find that the book ROI typically misrepresents true profitability, understating it in the earlier years and overstating it in the later years.

The popularity of book ROI, a flawed measure, seems to impair the quality of capital budgeting decisions. If managers are evaluated on the basis of book ROI they are likely to pay lip service to net present value. They may salute net present value but walk in the direction of book ROI. As the American Accounting Association Committee on Managerial Decision Models observed:

"The use of traditional accrual accounting methods for evaluating performance is a critical roadblock to implementation of present value models. Clearly, there is an inconsistency between citing present value models as being superior for capital budgeting decisions and then using entirely different concepts for tallying performance. As long as such practices persist, managers will often be tempted to make decisions which may be non-optimal under the present value criterion but optimal, at least over short or intermediate spans of time, under conventional accounting methods of evaluating operating performance."

Bias in Book ROI Book ROIs are biased upwards for businesses that make substantial intangible investments in R&D, brand building, and so on, simply because these outlays are not reflected on the balance sheet.

To illustrate this point let us compare two companies, a pharmaceutical company and a steel company. The pharmaceutical company invests mostly in R&D whereas the steel company invests mostly in plant and equipment. For the sake of simplicity, assume that both are mature firms which are not growing. However, they require investments to maintain the present level of business.

Exhibit 24.3 ***Financial Profiles of the Pharmaceutical and Steel Companies***

		(₹ in millions)
	Pharmaceutical	*Steel*
1. Revenues	2,000	2,000
2. Operating costs, excluding depreciation	1,000	1,000
3. Operating cash flow (1-2)	1,000	1,000
4. Investment in plant and equipment	200	600
5. Investment in R&D	600	200
6. Annual cash flow (3-4-5)	200	200

Exhibit 24.3 shows the financial profiles of the two companies. In order to maintain its existing business each company must invest ₹800 million annually. The only difference is that the pharmaceutical company invests mostly in R&D whereas the steel company invests mostly in plant and equipment.

The fixed assets of both the companies have an economic life of 5 years and are depreciated at a rate of 20 percent per annum as per the straight line method. Exhibit 24.4 shows the book asset values and annual depreciation for the two companies. Note that the sum of R&D and depreciation is the same for the two companies.

Exhibit 24.4 ***Book Asset Values and Annual Depreciation and R&D Outlays***

(₹ in millions)

	Pharmaceutical		Steel	
Age (years)				
investment	*Original of investment*	*Net book value investment*	*Original of investment*	*Net book value*
0 (New)	200	200	600	600
1	200	160	600	480
2	200	120	600	360
3	200	80	600	240
4	200	40	600	120
	Net Book Value	600		1800

	Pharmaceutical	*Steel*
Annual depreciation	200	600
R&D outlay	600	200
Total	800	800

The book ROIs for the two companies are calculated in Exhibit 24.5. Although the two companies have identical cash flows, profitability, and present values, the pharmaceutical company's book ROI is three times the steel company's. The difference arises because the value of the pharmaceutical company's assets are understated relative to the steel company's assets.

The point of this story is that a business with a high book ROI need not necessarily be performing better. It may simply have more hidden assets which are not reflected on the balance sheet.

Exhibit 24.5 ***Book ROI***

(₹ in millions)

	Pharmaceutical	*Steel*
1. Revenues	2,000	2,000
2. Operating costs, excluding depreciation	1,000	1,000
3. R&D expense	600	200
4. Depreciation	200	600
5. Net income	200	200
6. Net book value	600	1800
7. Book ROI (5/6)	33.3%	11.1%

A Possible Way Out The problem with book ROI stems from using book depreciation rather than economic depreciation. Why not then switch to economic depreciation? This is difficult because it calls for reestimating each asset's present value each year. No wonder accountants set up a depreciation schedule right in the beginning, however arbitrary it may be, and adhere to it.

One solution may be to use a depreciation schedule that conforms to the *expected* economic depreciation which is known right in the beginning. This way you do not have to restate each asset's present value every year. Despite forecasting inaccuracies this may be better than the accounting depreciation.

24.3 ABANDONMENT ANALYSIS

Capital expenditure management is a dynamic process. A capital investment cannot be regarded as a commitment till the end of the project life. As time rolls on, changes occur which can alter the attractiveness of projects or even entire divisions. Hence capital investments must be reappraised periodically to determine whether they should be continued or terminated or divested.

The techniques used to analyse a new project can also be used to analyse whether an existing project should be continued or terminated. However, there are some differences between an existing project and a new project:

- Most of the investment in a new project is still to be made and hence is a relevant cash outflow. By contrast, much of the investment in an existing project represents a sunk cost, which is not relevant for project analysis.
- In the case of a new project, the estimates of cash flows are likely to be more uncertain. On the other hand, thanks to the experience that the firm has with an existing project, the estimates of its future cash flows are likely to be more precise.
- The discount rate to be used for reappraising an existing project is likely to be different from that used to analyse the same project when it was initiated.

Once you estimate the incremental cash flows on an existing project and establish an appropriate discount rate, you can decide whether the project should be continued, terminated, or divested. To illustrate, assume that you are analysing an 8-year project three years into its life. The cash flows are as shown in Exhibit 24.6.

Exhibit 24.6 ***Analysis of an Existing Project***

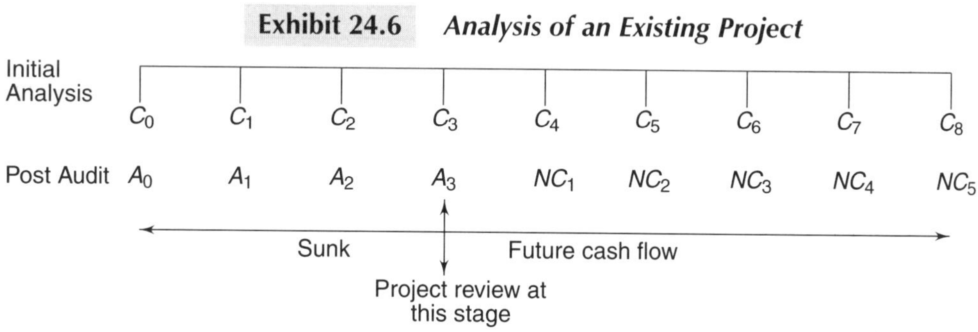

C_t is the forecast of cash flow for period t in the initial analysis ($t = 0...8$), A_t is the actual cash flow in period t ($t = 0...3$), and NC_n is the new forecast of cash flow in period n assessed at the end of year 3 ($n = 1...5$).

To decide whether the project should be continued or terminated or divested, the following information is required:

- *Present value of the expected cash flows (PVCF)* This is defined as:

$$PVCF = \sum_{n=1}^{m} \frac{NC_n}{(1+r)^n}$$

where m is the balance life of the project at the time of review and r is the appropriate discount rate.

- *Salvage value (SV)* This is the value expected to be realised from terminating the project and selling its assets.
- *Divestiture value (DV)* This is the price offered by a third party to buy the project.

Given the values of *PVCF, SV,* and *DV,* the following are the decision rules:

If	*Action*
$PVCF < SV < DV$	Divest
$PVCF < DV < SV$	Terminate
$SV < DV < PVCF$	Continue
$SV < PVCF < DV$	Divest
$DV < SV < PVCF$	Continue
$DV < PVCF < SV$	Terminate

Illustration Suppose you are analysing a call centre opened by Global Enterprises three years ago, which has a remaining life of five years. Exhibit 24.7 presents the initial forecast of cash flows, the actual cash flow upto the end of the third year, and the revised forecast for the balance five years.

The present value of expected cash flow (*PVCF*) at the end of year 3 works out to ₹253.1 million.

Exhibit 24.7 ***Analysis of an Existing Call Centre of Global Enterprises***

	Initial Analysis			*Analysis in Year 3*		
Year	*Initial forecast of cash flow*	*Present value at 12%*	*Year*	*Actual cash flow*	*Forecast in year 3*	*Present value of cash flow at 11%*
0	(250)	(250)		(230)		
1	30	26.8		20		
2	50	39.9		30		
3	80	56.9		65		
4	100	63.6	1		80	72.1
5	100	56.7	2		90	73.1
6	80	40.6	3		70	51.2
7	60	27.1	4		50	33.0
8	50	20.2	5		40	23.7
	Initial *NPV* = 81.8			*PVCF* at the end of year 3 = 253.1		

The salvage value (*SV*) at the end of year 3 is ₹175 million. A third party has offered to buy the call centre for ₹260 million.

What should Global Enterprises do? Since *DV* (260) > *PVCF* (253.1) > *SV* (175), the recommended course of action is to divest the call centre.

Behavioural Issues in Project Abandonment A basic rule of capital budgeting says that investment decisions should be guided by the net present value criterion. Applied to a project 'continuation versus abandonment' decision, this rule says the project must be abandoned if the net present value associated with abandonment is greater than the net present value associated with continuation. By the same logic, the project should be continued if the present value associated with continuation is greater than the net present value associated with abandonment.

Do managers follow the logic of net present value calculations in evaluating continuation versus abandonment decisions? It appears that they often overlook this logic. They have a tendency to get entrapped into losing projects and, in their attempts to rescue them, throw good money after bad. Why does this happen? While there can be several reasons, it happens mainly because sunk costs, which are irrelevant for economic accounting, are often not ignored in mental accounting.

To illustrate the difference between economic accounting and mental accounting, consider the example of a person who having already lost ₹20,000 in a business venture is confronted with a choice between two alternatives, *A* and *B*. Alternative *A* would yield a certain gain of ₹10,000 whereas alternative *B*, akin to a gamble, has two equiprobable payoffs, 0 and ₹20,000. If he employs the rules of economic accounting, he will form two accounts. The first contains a loss of ₹20,000 and it is closed. The second involves a choice between *A* and *B* in which he would obviously choose *A* (as the expected value of *A* is same as that of *B* without the dispersion characterising the latter). Put differently, a person who employs "economic accounting" will ignore sunk costs.

If he is guided by "mental accounting" he sees only one account that is open with an existing loss of ₹20,000. Put in other words, he does not ignore sunk costs. Hence he views alternatives *A* and *B* as follows:

A. Closing the account with a loss of ₹10,000. (The previous loss of ₹20,000 less the gain of ₹10000.)

B. Closing the account with a loss of ₹20,000 (if the pay-off of the gamble is zero) or a loss of nil (if the payoff of the gamble is ₹20,000).

Daniel Kahneman and Amos Tversky argue that people, confronted with a choice between a sure loss and a gamble which offers some prospect of reducing their loss to zero or so, tend to display risk-seeking behaviour.

A person who uses "mental accounting" does not adapt his asset position to losses and hence is likely to be entrapped in continuing the project. He distinguishes between unrealised 'paper losses' and 'realised losses' and adapts his asset position only after the losses are realised. Since realisation of losses induces regret, he is reluctant to realise them and resorts to procrastination as a way to defer the attendant pain. Of course, he may even deepen his commitment to the project further in the hope of finally emerging as a 'winner' and avoiding the ignominy of failure. In this context, note that commitment has a positive side as well as a negative side. On the positive side, it helps people to work harder, surmount obstacles, and scale great heights. On the negative side, it entraps people into negative NPV projects, induces them to throw good money after bad, and impairs their judgement.

Overcoming Resistance Since the NPV prescription is clear, there is no intellectual difficulty in distinguishing projects where commitment is worthwhile from projects where it is not. The difficulty seems to arise because of a 'self control' problem. While the rational internal "principal" may understand the benefits of terminating a losing project, it may find it difficult to persuade the internal "agent" to take the desired action because termination means that a mental account has to be closed and the accompanying loss realised. To overcome this tendency the following measures may be used.

Follow Certain Rules Rules are useful in exercising self-control. Two rules that may be considered in the present context are:

- Evaluate the projects in conformity with the principles of economic accounting.
- Review all projects periodically to determine whether they should be terminated or continued in accordance with the NPV rule.

Develop Proper Rewards and Penalties If there are high rewards for success and high penalties for failure, project managers (or sponsors) may have a tendency to deepen their commitment (which may lead to entrapment) and also delay disclosure of bad news about the project. To counter such tendencies, the performance evaluation system of the company should (a) reward project managers who disclose bad news early and penalise project managers who withhold bad news, and (b) convey a message to project managers that some failure is normal in business and early steps should be initiated to cut losses.

Institute Relatively Independent Reviews Companies can develop formal structures whereby projects are periodically reviewed by people who are not members of the project team to determine whether they should be continued or terminated in accordance with the principles of economic accounting. Such reviews are likely to be more objective and unbiased.

Managing Divestments Since divestments are becoming commonplace, corporates should approach them systematically and rationally. Here are some basic guidelines for managing divestments:

Regard Divestments as a Normal Part of Business Life Divestments are motivated *inter alia* by the following features of business life: (a) A company's disposition towards a given activity may change over its life cycle. What may appear as highly desirable and appealing at one stage may strike as unattractive and unappealing at another stage. (b) Decisions are based on judgements which are sometimes right and sometimes wrong—this is a fact of business life.

Hence, regard divestments as a normal process for all organisations, not just sick and unsuccessful organisations. As Leonard Vignola, Jr. says: "A company lives by expanding and contracting, by growing and changing, by acquiring and divesting. These are the actions of a healthy, vital company, not a sick, dying company.[1]"

---

[1] Leonard Vignola, Jr., *Strategic Divestment*, Amacom, New York: 1974.

Consider Divestment as One of the Many Responses to a Situation There are several options available when a business or project is under-performing. It may be continued as it is; it may be shut down till business conditions improve; new product lines may be added; an aggressive cost reduction programme may be initiated; manufacturing and/or distribution arrangements may be strengthened. When none of these alternatives seem feasible or desirable, consider divestment seriously.

Since divestment is one of the many responses, it must be considered as an integral part of the regular planning process. The planning group should be assigned responsibility for initiating divestment moves.

Approach Divestments Positively View a divestment as an opportunity, not a catastrophe. As Leonard Vignola, Jr. says:

"Difficulties abound and optimum divestment is not overly easy to accomplish. Yet divestment ought to be viewed as a chance to turn a less than favourable situation into a future benefit to the divesting company.[2]"

Announce divestment decisions candidly and create an impression that the company has the ability to deal with a problem realistically and sensibly. As Leonard Vignola, Jr. says:

"The decision to divest should be presented as a firm, aggressive, positive step on the part of the divesting company.[3]"

24.4 ADMINISTRATIVE ASPECTS OF CAPITAL BUDGETING

The discussion on administrative aspects of capital budgeting has been organised as follows:

- Identification of promising investment opportunities
- Classification of investments
- Submission of proposals
- Decision making
- Preparation of capital budget and appropriation
- Implementation
- Performance review

Identification of Promising Investment Opportunities Often firms have an abundance of investment proposals but a dearth of really worthwhile proposals. For identifying promising investment opportunities the following points should be borne in mind:

1. Monitor changes in market demand, sources of supply, profitability, competition, governmental policies, economic conditions, and technological developments.
2. Formulate long-range plans and perspectives based on analysis of opportunities and threats in the environment and assessment of internal strengths, weaknesses, capabilities, and limitations.
3. Communicate long-range plans and corporate perspectives to all persons who are likely to be involved in capital budgeting.

[2] Vignola *op. cit*

[3] Vignola *op. cit*

4. Encourage employees to make suggestions and reward them suitably for valuable suggestions.

In short, the relationship between the firm and its environment should be regularly analysed, corporate plans and perspectives must be widely shared, and the creativity and imagination of the employees must be tapped.

With regard to tapping the imagination of employees, it may be noted that in most organisations personnel at middle and lower levels do not contribute much to the pool of investment proposals. This is often due to the failure of the management to cull out good ideas emanating from different echelons of the organisation. To generate ideas, suggestion schemes are usually recommended. Suggestion schemes by themselves, however, cannot achieve the objective. According to John B. Mathews, Jr.:

"The solution seems to lie in that intangible thing known as 'climate', meaning in this case a receptivity to suggestions at all company levels and a pervading opinion that management has no monopoly on ideas and welcomes them from any and all sources."[4]

Classification The classification of capital expenditure proposals refers to the grouping of similar proposals into separate categories. Classification helps in decision making, budgeting, and control.

Investment proposals may be classified in many ways. We suggest below a scheme of classification which can, with minor modification, be adopted for most manufacturing enterprises:

1. *Replacement Investments* These represent capital expenditures for the replacement of existing fixed assets—this may become necessary because of the expiry of normal life or because of a change in technology.
2. *Modernisation and Rationalisation Investments* These comprise capital expenditures for improving productivity, increasing efficiency, reducing costs, and ensuring greater reliability.
3. *Expansion Investments* These represent capital expenditures for increasing capacity.
4. *New Product Investments* These represent capital expenditures to manufacture new products.
5. *Research and Development Investments* These represent capital expenditures on basic research and development.
6. *Obligatory and Welfare Investments* These represent expenditures on facilities which are obligatory and/or conducive to employee welfare.

Submission of Proposals To ensure that all relevant information for proposals is gathered systematically, a standardised proposal form may be used by all the sponsors of investment projects. A suggested proposal form is shown in Exhibit 24.8.

[4] J.B. Mathews, Jr. "How To Administer Capital Spending," *Harvard Business Review*, March–April, 1959.

Exhibit 24.8 ***Capital Investment Proposal Form***

(Useful particularly for replacement, modernisation, rationalisation, expansion, and new product investments.)

Sponsor's Name: Date:
Sponsor's Signature: Code No.:
(To be given by the capital budgeting committee)

Department:
Proposal:

A. *Project Features and Nature of Benefits*
(Describe the nature of the project and the kinds of benefits, both quantitative and qualitative, that are likely to accrue from it.)

B. *Cash Flow Summary Data*
(Give most probable values for cash flows. Cash flows must be defined consistently with the concept of funds employed. Show details of the cash flow calculation in an appendix.)

Period	Outlay for assets	Cash flow from operations	Cash flow from disposal of assets	Net cash flow
0				
1				
2				
3				
4				
5				
6				
7				
8				
9				
10				

C. *Risk Characteristics of the Project*
(Describe the uncertainties relating to factors which have an important bearing on the project.)

D. *Project Worthwhileness Measures*
(Several criteria of project worthwhileness are given below. It may not be necessary to calculate all criteria of worthwhileness in every case. However, at least one discounted cash flow method should be given.)

1. (i) Net present value at average cost of capital (r = *12% say*)
   (ii) Net present value at cost of capital adjusted for risk (r = 15% say)
2. Internal rate of return
3. Profitability index
4. Accounting rate of return
5. Cash payback period
6. Undiscounted benefit cost ratio

(Contd.)

E. *Comments of Reviewing Officers*
(Reviewing officers are expected to give their frank and candid opinion about the project.

	Reviewing Officer	*Initials*	*Date*
1.			
2.			
3.			
4.			

Space for Comments

	Reviewing Officer 1
	Reviewing Officer 2
	Reviewing Officer 3
	Reviewing Officer 4

To help the sponsor of the project in filling and submitting the form:

1. A procedures manual setting forth in detail the firm's capital budgeting policy and techniques may be prepared and widely disseminated.
2. Short duration training programmes may be organised.
3. The help of a staff person may be made available to the sponsor of the project.

The proposal form, before it reaches the capital budgeting committee, should normally be routed through persons who can comment on the estimates furnished by the sponsor. The routing channel, however, cannot be standardised. It will vary from one organisation to another and, perhaps, from one proposal to another.

Routing a proposal through several persons provides a mechanism for obtaining the views and judgements of others. For example, a proposal submitted by the plant superintendent may be routed through the production manager, sales manager, and engineering manager for their comments on different aspects of the project. This also facilitates coordination of inter-related activities. Obviously this system would yield benefits only when the persons through whom the proposal is routed give thought to it rather than merely forward it in a routine manner.

Decision Making It may be argued that the optimal capital budget for the firm as a whole can be drawn up only when capital investment decisions are completely centralised. This, however, is not desirable in most cases because some decentralisation is required to facilitate quick decisions, develop executives, and conserve top management time for important matters. That is why most of the companies empower executives at different levels to take investment decisions involving outlays up to certain limits. In one company, for example, the plant superintendent can okay investment outlays up to ₹500,000, the factory manager up to ₹1,000,000, the capital budgeting committee up to ₹5,000,000, and the managing director up to ₹10,000,000. Investments involving larger outlays need the consent of the board of directors.

While the system of rupee gateways has considerable merit, there may be certain pitfalls. Managers may break a project into several parts so that no decision at a higher level becomes necessary. For example, a production manager who is empowered to undertake a project up to ₹100,000 may split a project involving an outlay of ₹150,000 into two parts of ₹80,000 and

₹70,000 so that it is not sent upwards for review. This tendency can be countered by asking managers, when they seek budgetary appropriations, to indicate the additional investment required in related areas in the future.

Another problem in the delegation of capital investment decision making arises from differences in risk attitudes. Managers at lower levels tend to be more averse to risks than top management. They may discard projects which top management may approve. This tendency can be overcome to some extent by communicating corporate strategy and risk disposition of top management to all those who are involved in capital budgeting. In addition, lower level executives should be encouraged to take risks consistent with corporate policy by designing an appropriate system of rewards and punishment.

Preparation of Capital Budget and Appropriation Smaller projects which can be approved at lower levels may be covered by a blanket appropriation so that they can be undertaken expeditiously. Since these projects require small outlays, no elaborate funds planning is required for them. Projects of larger magnitude (which generally require the approval of the capital budget committee or managing director or the board of directors) may be included after approval in the tentative capital budget. The final capital budget, which serves as the basis of budgetary appropriations, should be drawn up after the availability of funds is ensured. Often careful planning of funds is required before budgetary appropriations are made.

While the capital expenditure budget is usually drawn up for one to two years, it is desirable to have a perspective plan ranging from 3 to 5 years. In some cases it may even be of a longer duration.

The capital expenditure budget, though it is based on a careful review of various factors, should not be regarded as inviolate. Changes in circumstances may warrant changes in the budget not originally contemplated. This is perhaps the reason why a final sanction is required before actual expenditure in many companies.

The coordination of the capital expenditure budget should preferably be done by a financial officer of the firm. In firms where a financial officer is not in charge of coordination, the budgetary process and the analysis of individual projects tend to be somewhat loose and sloppy.

Implementation Delay in implementation and the consequent increase in the project cost are very common. Cases are not infrequent where the actual time for execution has exceeded planned time by 50 percent. Cost over-runs are also very common. In many cases over-runs have been between 30 percent and 100 percent. These facts emphasise the need for expeditious implementation at a reasonable cost. For this the following are helpful:

1. *Adequate Formulation of Projects* Often delays occur because of insufficient preliminary studies and inadequate formulation of the project. Cases have come to notice where due to inadequate or limited investigation in regard to suitability of site, availability of required natural resources, other raw materials, etc. the execution of project has subsequently been delayed considerably resulting in substantial increase in cost and adversely affecting their economies.

   Such delays can be mitigated by bestowing greater care and attention on preliminary investigations and project formulation. The responsibility for investigation should be properly determined.

2. *Use of the Principle of Responsibility Accounting* By assigning definite responsibilities to project managers for completing the project on time, a sense of time consciousness can be instilled. This helps in expeditious implementation.
3. *Use of Network Techniques* Network techniques like PERT (Programme Evaluation Review Technique) and CPM (Critical Path Method) are helpful in project planning and control. With the help of these techniques, progress reporting becomes rather easy. Precise, prompt, and brief reports aid the management in appraisal and corrective action to ensure the successful completion of projects.
4. *Exercise of Proper Control* Once an appropriation is established, the sponsor (or manager) of the project is authorised to incur expenditure. Proper control over this expenditure needs to be exercised. Periodical reports on expenditure along with information on the degree of physical completion are helpful in this respect. Note that unless information regarding physical completion is available control becomes difficult.

Performance Review Performance review is meant for evaluating actual performance vis-à-vis projected performance. It is concerned with the verification of assumptions regarding both revenues and costs. In scope, it is broader than the popularly used accounting review which is concerned only with costs.

Despite its importance, performance review is one of the most neglected aspects of capital budgeting. The reasons seem to be:

- It is difficult to isolate the cash flows attributable to individual investments from financial accounts which are compiled for the firm as a whole and which are based on the accrual principle.
- There is an apprehension that a performance review may be used for punitive purposes.

The first problem can be overcome largely by using estimates and approximations wherever it is not possible to obtain accurate data. For example, if costs relating to a project have not been recorded separately, a reasonable estimate can usually be made on the basis of information relating to total costs and the activities of the firm. Likewise, cash flows from sales arising from a project can be roughly estimated by looking into the collection pattern of receivables as a whole.

The second problem can be overcome by making it clear to all project sponsors that the purpose of post-audit is to promote learning and not to penalise the persons involved. It provides feedback that is necessary for future improvements.

24.5 AGENCY PROBLEM

In theory, managers as agents of shareholders are supposed to take actions that maximise the welfare of the shareholders (the principals). In practice, managers enjoy substantial autonomy and have a natural inclination to pursue their own goals. This is the agency problem. To prevent from being dislodged from their position, managers may try to achieve some acceptable level of performance as far as shareholder welfare is concerned. However, beyond that their personal goals may acquire priority. *Inter alia*, they may seek to:

- Preside over a big empire that gives them power, stature, and higher compensation.
- Pursue pet projects that draw on their special skills and competencies so that their position in the organisation is entrenched.
- Enjoy generous compensation and lavish perquisites.
- Shirk efforts because identifying and implementing high-NPV projects is a very demanding proposition.
- Avoid risks because acceptance of high firm-specific risks, although quite acceptable to diversified shareholders, can threaten the security of their job and the growth prospects with the firm.

Agency costs can be mitigated by monitoring the actions and behaviour of the managers and by offering them right incentives that motivate them to maximise value.

Monitoring Monitoring helps in checking more visible agency problems like empire building, excessive perquisites, managerial absenteeism, and frauds. However, monitoring costs time and money and may not be worthwhile beyond a point. The law of diminishing marginal returns applies to monitoring as it does elsewhere.

Even with tight and expensive monitoring, certain kinds of agency costs cannot be prevented. Suppose shareholders want to monitor the investment decisions of the firm. How can they be sure that the capital budget finalised by the top management includes all positive-NPV investment opportunities available to the firm? Or, how can they be sure that project sponsors have not massaged the cash flow forecasts to get their favourite projects included? After all, managers know more about the prospects of the firm than the shareholders. The informational advantage enjoyed by managers gives them a lot of latitude to pursue their interests at the expense of the shareholders.

Incentive Compensation Because monitoring has its imperfections and limitations, suitable compensation plans must be designed to give managers the right incentive. A well-conceived incentive compensation plan goes a long way in aligning the interests of managers and shareholders. Bear in mind the following guidelines in designing the incentive compensation plan.

Integrate the Incentive Plan into the Total Compensation Architecture The compensation package of a firm seeks to reward executives in a variety of ways: base salary, perquisites, retirement benefits, incentive compensation, promotion, and so on. The incentive compensation cannot be designed in isolation. As it has a bearing on the overall risk-reward structure of the compensation scheme, it has to be fitted into the same.

Select the Right Set of Performance Measures The incentive compensation plan must be linked to performance measures that are consistent with the responsibilities of the executives. Alfred Rappaport recommends the following hierarchy of performance measures:

Level	*Measure*
CEO and corporate level executives	Total return to shareholders
Operating unit executives	Shareholder value added
Frontline employees and managers	Leading indicators of value like time to market new products and customer retention ratio.

Use Objective Criteria As far as possible the incentive compensation plan must be based on criteria that are easily observable by all parties and not amenable to manipulation. Use of objective criteria imparts credibility to the incentive plan and reduces subjectivity.

Reward Relative Performance Incentive compensation should be based on performance relative to that of some peer group rather than absolute performance. This ensures that the general market influences or industry-specific influences are abstracted from the performance measure, thereby providing the distinctive contribution made by the executive(s) to the wealth or profitability of the firm.

Lengthen the Decision Making Horizon of the Executives One possible solution to mitigate the short-term decision making horizon of executives is to adopt 'performance plans' which provide deferred compensation when certain 'long-term' (ranging, say, over a period of 3 to 7 years) goals are achieved.

24.6 EVALUATING THE CAPITAL BUDGETING SYSTEM OF AN ORGANISATION

The soundness of the capital budgeting system of an organisation may be evaluated in terms of the following criteria:

Results	Are the results of the capital budgeting system consistent with the goals of the organisation?
Techniques	Are efficient techniques being employed for purposes of capital expenditure planning, decision making, and control?
Communication	Are the premises underlying capital budgeting communicated to those who participate in this process?
Decentralisation	Is there meaningful delegation and decentralisation which permits decision making at appropriate levels?
Intelligibility	Are the policies, methods of analysis, and procedures understood by different segments of the organisation which are involved in capital budgeting?
Flexibility	Does the system have sufficient flexibility to respond to the dynamic changes in the environment and to permit variations in approaches for projects with differing characteristics?
Control	Are adequate controls being exercised in the implementation phase to ensure that slippages are mitigated?
Review	Is there a systematic review of capital investments which permits meaningful feedback for improving the system and its effectiveness?

24.7 DISCIPLINING THE CAPITAL BUDGETING PROCESS FOR SMALL TICKET ITEMS[5]

Tom Copeland argues that a company can reduce its capital expenditure and create sustainable value by conducting a rigorous evaluation of small-ticket items that are often unnecessary or wasteful. Yet, usually they get rubber-stamped by senior managers, who focus more on big-ticket investments.

Rubber-stamping, however, causes problems because people who prepare small-item capital budgeting proposals, generally lack the experience or understanding to properly think through them. Further, they have a natural inclination to ask for more.

Senior managers can bring discipline to the capital budgeting by asking the following questions.

1. **Is this your investment to make?** Sometimes a unit manager may request for an investment that is someone else's responsibility. By asking unit managers to explain why they, not others, need to make those investments, senior managers can check a lot of unnecessary spending.
2. **Does it really have to be now?** Managers have a natural inclination to ask for new machines on the grounds that the old ones require a lot of maintenance. To check this tendency, senior managers should require unit managers to consider various alternatives such as maintaining the existing machines or buying used ones.
3. **How are our competitors meeting compliance needs?** When making investments meant to comply with environmental, health, and safety regulations, managers tend to gold plate their investment requests. They don't want to be blamed for underspending, should something go wrong. A good way to check this tendency is to ask unit mangers to compare their proposals with what competitors are doing.
4. **Is the left hand duplicating investments already made by the right?** Telecom companies, banks, and other big organisations with far-flung and complicated operations tend to build excess capacity. To curb this tendency, various managers involved with the same item (such as servers) must regularly exchange information and communicate with one another.
5. **Are the trade-offs between profits and capital spending well understood?** In a company that emphasises profit above other performance measures, managers would request for more capital investment because the opportunity cost of equity is ordinarily not considered in calculating profit. For a proper evaluation of capital investment, the opportunity cost of equity must be taken into account while calculating profit.
6. **Are there signs of budget massage?** In large companies, senior managers generally monitor a unit's capital budget by mainly comparing a unit's spending with its forecasts. This provides unit managers with a lot of scope for massaging the capital budget. They may shuffle expenditures between capital and revenue to ensure that the capital budget rises gradually over time; they may resort to year-end loading

[5] This section is based on Tom Copeland, "Cutting Costs without Drawing Blood" *Harvard Business Review*, September-October 2000.

to protect their annual allocations. By querying unit managers throughout the year about their capital spending decisions, senior managers can check units from massaging their budgets.

7. **Are we using shared assets fully?** Networked businesses like telecoms, Internet service providers, airliners, electric utilities, and car-rental companies use a lot of shared assets. Bureaucratic procedures may lead to capital spending by some units while there may be excess capacity in others. Senior managers should check how fully shared assets are utilised.

By searchingly raising the above questions, senior managers can inject greater discipline in budget supervision. In addition, they must carry out regular audits of capital spending by units. Such audits must have a clear goal (such as reducing a unit's capital budget by at least 10 percent to 20 percent) and be inclusive (audit team must include a representative of the department being reviewed).

SUMMARY

- It is necessary to exercise a strict control on in-progress projects. There are two aspects of controlling in-progress capital projects: (a) establishment of internal control procedures, and (b) use of regular progress reports.
- An audit of a project after it has been commissioned is referred to as post-audit or post-completion audit. It is a useful feedback and review tool.
- Performance evaluation may be done in terms of economic rate of return or book return on investment (ROI):

  Economic rate of return for a given year =

  $$\frac{\text{Cash flow} + \text{Change in present value}}{\text{Present value at the beginning of the year}}$$

  $$\text{Book ROI for a given year} = \frac{\text{Cash flow} + \text{Change in book value}}{\text{Book value at the beginning of the year}}$$

- It is a common practice to use book ROI for evaluating existing businesses and projects on a continuing basis.
- Although widely used, the book ROI has two serious flaws: (a) Even though a project may earn a constant economic rate of return, its book ROI displays wide variation across time. (b) There is an upward bias in the book ROI of a business which has substantial investment in intangible assets.
- A capital investment cannot be regarded as a commitment till the end of the project life. Hence it has to be periodically reappraised to determine whether it should be continued or terminated or divested.
- The techniques used to analyse a new project can also be used to analyse whether an existing project should be continued or not.

- To decide whether a project should be continued or terminated or divested, calculate *PVCF* (present value of expected cash flows), *SV* (salvage value), and divestiture value (*DV*). Choose the option that has the highest value.
- It appears that managers often overlook the logic of net present value in evaluating "continuation versus abandonment" decisions and have a tendency to get entrapped into losing projects. To overcome this tendency, the following measures may be used:(i) follow certain rules, (ii) develop proper rewards and penalties, and (iii) institute relatively independent reviews.
- For identifying promising investment opportunities, the relationship between the firm and its environment should be regularly analysed, corporate plans and perspectives must be widely shared, and the creativity and imagination of the employees must be tapped.
- Investment proposals may be classified in many ways. The following scheme of classification can with minor modification be adopted for most manufacturing enterprises: (i) replacement investments, (ii) modernisation and rationalisation investments, (iii) expansion investments, (iv) new product investments, (v) research and development investments, and (vi) obligatory and welfare investments.
- To ensure that all relevant information for proposals is gathered systematically, a standardised proposal form may be used by all the sponsors of investment projects.
- Some decentralisation of capital budgeting is required to facilitate quick decisions, develop executives, and conserve top management time for important matters. That is why most companies empower executives at different levels to take investment decisions involving outlays up to certain limits.
- While the capital expenditure budget is usually drawn up for one to two years, it is desirable to have a perspective plan ranging from three to five years. In some cases it may even be of a longer duration. The coordination of the capital expenditure budget should preferably be done by a financial officer of the firm.
- For timely implementation of projects within reasonable costs, the following are helpful: adequate formulation of projects; use of the principle of responsibility accounting; use of network techniques; and exercise of proper control.
- Despite its importance, performance review tends to be one of the most neglected aspects of capital budgeting.
- Managers enjoy substantial autonomy and have a natural inclination to pursue their own goals. This is the agency problem. Agency costs can be mitigated by monitoring the actions and behaviour of the managers and by offering them right incentives that motivate them to maximise value.
- The soundness of the capital budgeting system of an organisation may be evaluated in terms of the following criteria: results, techniques, communication, decentralisation, intelligibility, flexibility, control, and review.
- A company can reduce its capital expenditure by conducting a rigorous evaluations of small-ticket items that are often unnecessary or wasteful.

QUESTIONS

1. Why should post-audit be done?
2. What is the difference between economic rate of return and book return on investment?
3. Explain the bias in book ROI.
4. Discuss the procedure for determining whether a project should be continued, terminated, or divested.
5. What is the difference between economic accounting and mental accounting?
6. Discuss measures for injecting greater rationality in project termination decisions.
7. What needs to be done to identify potential investment opportunities?
8. Suggest a scheme for classifying capital expenditure proposals in a manufacturing concern.
9. "The optimal capital budget for the firm as a whole can be drawn up only when capital investment decisions are completely centralised." Comment.
10. What are the advantages of conducting a performance review? What problems are encountered in performance review and how can they be overcome?
11. How would you evaluate the capital budgeting system of an organisation?
12. What questions should senior managers ask for disciplining the capital budgeting process for small ticket items?

PROBLEMS

1. Prabhat Limited is considering a project involving an outlay of ₹150 million. The projected cash inflows of this project over its 6-year life are as follows:

Year	1	2	3	4	5	6
Cash inflow (₹ in million)	25	30	40	45	50	30

This investment is a zero-NPV investment. Calculate the economic rate of return and the book return on income (assuming a straight line depreciation over the 6-year life) for the above project.

2. Matrix Limited had set up a project 4 years ago. The project has a remaining life of 6 years. The cash flow forecast for the balance life is as follows:

Year	1	2	3	4	5	6
Cash flow forecast (₹ in million)	30	35	45	50	30	25

The salvage value of the project if terminated immediately is ₹120 million. A third party has offered to buy the project for ₹175 million. The discount rate is 12 percent. What should Matrix do?

Tables

Table A.1 *Future Value Interest Factor*
FVIF (r, n) = $(1 + r)^n$

Period n	1%	2%	3%	4%	5%	6%	7%	8%	9%	10%	11%	12%	13%
0	1.000	1.000	1.000	1.000	1.000	1.000	1.000	1.000	1.000	1.000	1.000	1.000	1.000
1	1.010	1.020	1.030	1.040	1.050	1.060	1.070	1.080	1.090	1.100	1.110	1.120	1.130
2	1.020	1.040	1.061	1.082	1.102	1.124	1.145	1.166	1.188	1.210	1.232	1.254	1.277
3	1.030	1.061	1.093	1.125	1.158	1.191	1.225	1.260	1.295	1.331	1.368	1.405	1.443
4	1.041	1.082	1.126	1.170	1.216	1.262	1.311	1.360	1.412	1.464	1.518	1.574	1.630
5	1.051	1.104	1.159	1.217	1.276	1.338	1.403	1.469	1.539	1.611	1.685	1.762	1.842
6	1.062	1.126	1.194	1.265	1.340	1.419	1.501	1.587	1.677	1.772	1.870	1.974	2.082
7	1.072	1.149	1.230	1.316	1.407	1.504	1.606	1.714	1.828	1.949	2.076	2.211	2.353
8	1.083	1.172	1.267	1.369	1.477	1.594	1.718	1.851	1.993	2.144	2.305	2.476	2.658
9	1.094	1.195	1.305	1.423	1.551	1.689	1.838	1.999	2.172	2.358	2.558	2.773	3.004
10	1.105	1.219	1.344	1.480	1.629	1.791	1.967	2.159	2.367	2.594	2.839	3.106	3.395
11	1.116	1.243	1.384	1.539	1.710	1.898	2.105	2.332	2.580	2.853	3.152	3.479	3.836
12	1.127	1.268	1.426	1.601	1.796	2.012	2.252	2.518	2.813	3.138	3.498	3.896	4.335
13	1.138	1.294	1.469	1.665	1.886	2.133	2.410	2.720	3.056	3.452	3.883	4.363	4.898
14	1.149	1.319	1.513	1.732	1.930	2.261	2.579	2.937	3.342	3.797	4.310	4.887	5.535
15	1.161	1.346	1.558	1.801	2.079	2.397	2.759	3.172	3.642	4.177	4.785	5.474	6.254
16	1.173	1.373	1.605	1.873	2.183	2.540	2.952	3.426	3.970	4.595	5.311	6.130	7.067
17	1.184	1.400	1.653	1.948	2.292	2.693	3.159	3.700	4.328	5.054	5.895	6.866	7.986
18	1.196	1.428	1.702	2.026	2.407	2.854	3.380	3.996	4.717	5.560	6.544	7.690	9.024
19	1.208	1.457	1.754	2.107	2.527	3.026	3.617	4.316	5.142	6.116	7.263	8.613	10.197
20	1.220	1.486	1.806	2.191	2.653	3.207	3.870	4.661	5.604	6.728	8.062	9.646	11.523
25	1.282	1.641	2.094	2.666	3.386	4.292	5.427	6.848	8.623	10.835	13.585	17.000	21.231
30	1.348	1.811	2.427	3.243	4.322	5.743	7.612	10.063	13.268	17.449	22.892	29.960	39.116

(Contd.)

Period n	14%	15%	16%	17%	18%	19%	20%	24%	28%	32%	36%	40%
0	1.000	1.000	1.000	1.000	1.000	1.000	1.000	1.000	1.000	1.000	1.000	1.000
1	1.140	1.150	1.160	1.170	1.180	1.190	1.200	1.240	1.280	1.320	1.360	1.400
2	1.300	1.322	1.346	1.369	1.392	1.416	1.440	1.538	1.638	1.742	1.850	1.960
3	1.482	1.521	1.561	1.602	1.643	1.685	1.728	1.907	2.097	2.300	2.515	2.744
4	1.689	1.749	1.811	1.874	1.939	2.005	2.074	2.364	2.684	3.036	3.421	3.842
5	1.925	2.011	2.100	2.192	2.288	2.386	2.488	2.392	3.436	4.007	4.653	5.378
6	2.195	2.313	2.436	2.565	2.700	2.840	2.986	3.635	4.398	5.290	6.328	7.530
7	2.502	2.660	2.826	3.001	3.185	3.379	3.583	4.508	5.629	6.983	8.605	10.541
8	2.853	3.059	3.278	3.511	3.759	4.021	4.300	5.590	7.206	9.217	11.703	14.758
9	3.252	3.518	3.803	4.108	4.435	4.785	5.160	6.931	9.223	12.166	15.917	20.661
10	3.707	4.046	4.411	4.807	5.234	5.695	6.192	8.549	11.806	16.060	21.647	28.925
11	4.226	4.652	5.117	5.624	6.176	6.777	7.430	10.657	15.112	21.199	29.439	40.496
12	4.818	5.350	5.936	6.580	7.288	8.064	8.916	13.215	19.343	27.983	40.037	56.694
13	5.492	6.153	6.886	7.699	8.599	9.596	10.699	16.386	24.759	36.937	54.451	79.372
14	6.261	7.076	7.988	9.007	10.147	11.420	12.839	20.319	31.961	48.757	74.053	111.120
15	7.138	8.137	9.266	10.539	11.974	13.590	15.407	25.196	40.565	64.359	100.712	155.568
16	8.137	9.358	10.748	12.330	14.129	16.172	18.488	31.243	51.923	84.954	136.969	217.795
17	9.276	10.761	12.468	14.426	16.672	19.244	22.186	38.741	66.461	112.139	186.278	304.914
18	10.575	12.375	14.463	16.879	19.673	22.901	26.623	48.039	85.071	148.023	253.338	426.879
19	12.056	14.232	16.777	19.748	23.214	27.252	31.948	59.568	108.890	195.391	344.540	597.630
20	13.743	16.367	19.461	23.106	27.393	32.429	38.338	73.864	139.380	257.916	468.574	836.683
25	26.462	32.919	40.874	50.658	62.669	77.388	95.396	216.542	478.905	1033.590	2180.081	4499.880
30	50.950	66.212	85.850	111.065	143.371	184.675	237.376	634.820	1645.504	4142.075	10143.019	24201.4

Table A.2 *Future Value Interest Factor for an Annuity*

$$FVIFA\ (r,\ n) = \frac{(1+r)^n - 1}{r}$$

Period n	1%	2%	3%	4%	5%	6%	7%	8%	9%	10%	11%	12%	13%
1	1.000	1.000	1.000	1.000	1.000	1.000	1.000	1.000	1.000	1.000	1.000	1.000	1.000
2	2.010	2.020	2.030	2.040	2.050	2.060	2.070	2.080	2.090	2.100	2.110	2.120	2.130
3	3.030	3.060	3.091	3.122	3.152	3.184	3.215	3.246	3.278	3.310	3.342	3.374	3.407
4	4.060	4.122	4.184	4.246	4.310	4.375	4.440	4.506	4.573	4.641	4.710	4.779	4.850
5	5.101	5.204	5.309	5.416	5.526	5.637	5.751	5.867	5.985	6.105	6.228	6.353	6.480
6	6.152	6.308	6.468	6.633	6.802	6.975	7.153	7.336	7.523	7.716	7.913	8.115	8.323
7	7.214	7.434	7.662	7.898	8.142	8.394	8.654	8.923	9.200	9.487	9.783	10.089	10.405
8	8.286	8.583	8.892	9.214	9.549	9.897	10.260	10.637	11.028	11.436	11.859	12.300	12.757
9	9.369	9.755	10.159	10.583	11.027	11.491	11.978	12.488	13.021	13.579	14.164	14.776	15.416
10	10.462	10.950	11.464	12.006	12.578	13.181	13.816	14.487	15.193	15.937	16.722	17.549	18.420
11	11.567	12.169	12.808	13.486	14.207	14.972	15.784	16.645	17.560	18.531	19.561	20.655	21.814
12	12.683	13.412	14.192	15.026	15.917	16.870	17.888	18.977	20.141	21.384	22.713	24.133	25.650
13	13.809	14.680	15.618	16.627	17.713	18.882	20.141	21.495	22.953	24.523	26.212	28.029	29.985
14	14.947	15.974	17.086	18.292	19.599	21.015	22.550	24.215	26.019	27.975	30.095	32.393	34.883
15	16.097	17.293	18.599	20.024	21.579	23.276	25.129	27.152	29.361	31.772	34.405	37.280	40.417
16	17.258	18.639	20.157	21.825	23.657	25.673	27.888	30.324	33.003	35.950	39.190	42.753	46.672
17	18.430	20.012	21.762	23.698	25.840	28.213	30.840	33.750	36.974	40.545	44.501	48.884	53.739
18	19.615	21.412	23.414	25.645	28.132	30.906	33.999	37.450	41.301	45.599	50.396	55.750	61.725
19	20.811	22.841	25.117	27.671	30.539	33.760	37.379	41.446	46.018	51.159	56.939	63.440	70.749
20	22.019	24.297	26.870	29.778	33.066	36.786	40.995	45.762	51.160	57.275	64.203	72.052	80.947
25	28.243	32.030	36.459	41.646	47.727	54.865	63.249	73.106	84.701	98.347	114.413	133.334	155.620
30	34.785	40.568	47.575	56.805	66.439	79.058	94.461	113.283	136.308	164.494	199.021	241.333	293.199

(Contd.)

Period n	14%	15%	16%	17%	18%	19%	20%	24%	28%	32%	36%	40%
1	1.000	1.000	1.000	1.000	1.000	1.000	1.000	1.000	1.000	1.000	1.000	1.000
2	2.140	2.150	2.160	2.170	2.180	2.190	2.200	2.240	2.280	2.320	2.360	2.400
3	3.440	3.473	3.506	3.539	3.572	3.606	3.640	3.778	3.918	4.062	4.210	4.360
4	4.921	4.993	5.066	5.141	5.215	5.291	5.368	5.684	6.016	6.362	6.725	7.104
5	6.610	6.742	6.877	7.014	7.154	7.297	7.442	8.048	8.700	9.398	10.146	10.946
6	8.536	8.754	8.977	9.207	9.442	9.683	9.930	10.980	12.136	13.406	14.799	16.324
7	10.730	11.067	11.414	11.772	12.142	12.523	12.916	14.615	16.534	18.696	21.126	23.853
8	13.233	13.727	14.240	14.773	15.327	15.902	16.499	19.123	22.163	25.678	29.732	34.395
9	16.085	16.786	17.518	18.285	19.086	19.923	20.799	24.712	29.369	34.895	41.435	49.153
10	19.337	20.304	21.321	22.393	23.521	24.709	25.959	31.643	38.592	47.062	57.352	69.814
11	23.044	24.349	25.733	27.200	28.755	30.404	32.150	40.238	50.399	63.122	78.998	98.739
12	27.271	29.002	30.850	32.824	34.931	37.180	39.580	50.985	65.510	84.320	108.437	139.235
13	32.089	34.352	36.786	39.404	42.219	45.244	48.497	64.110	84.853	112.303	148.475	195.929
14	37.581	40.505	43.672	47.103	50.818	54.841	59.196	80.496	109.612	149.240	202.926	275.300
15	43.842	47.580	51.660	56.110	60.965	66.261	72.035	100.815	141.303	197.997	276.979	386.420
16	50.980	55.717	60.925	66.649	72.939	79.850	87.442	126.011	181.868	262.356	377.692	541.988
17	59.118	65.075	71.673	78.979	87.068	96.022	105.931	157.253	233.791	347.310	514.661	759.784
18	68.394	75.836	84.141	93.406	103.740	115.266	128.117	195.994	300.252	459.449	700.939	1064.697
19	78.969	88.212	98.603	110.285	123.414	138.166	154.740	244.033	385.323	607.472	954.277	1491.576
20	91.025	102.44	115.380	130.033	146.628	165.418	186.688	303.601	494.213	802.863	1298.817	2089.206
25	181.871	212.793	249.214	292.105	342.603	402.042	471.981	898.092	1706.803	3226.844	6053.004	11247.199
30	356.787	434.745	530.321	647.439	790.948	966.712	1181.882	2640.916	5873.231	12940.859	28172.276	60501.081

Table A.3 *Present Value Interest Factor*
PVIF (r, n) = $(1 + r)^{-n}$

Period n	1%	2%	3%	4%	5%	6%	7%	8%	9%	10%	11%	12%	13%
0	1.000	1.000	1.000	1.000	1.000	1.000	1.000	1.000	1.000	1.000	1.000	1.000	1.000
1	0.990	0.980	0.971	0.962	0.952	0.943	0.935	0.926	0.917	0.909	0.901	0.893	0.885
2	0.980	0.961	0.943	0.925	0.907	0.890	0.873	0.857	0.842	0.826	0.812	0.797	0.783
3	0.971	0.942	0.915	0.889	0.864	0.840	0.816	0.794	0.772	0.751	0.731	0.712	0.693
4	0.961	0.924	0.889	0.855	0.823	0.792	0.763	0.735	0.708	0.683	0.659	0.636	0.613
5	0.951	0.906	0.863	0.822	0.784	0.747	0.713	0.681	0.650	0.621	0.593	0.567	0.543
6	0.942	0.888	0.838	0.790	0.746	0.705	0.666	0.630	0.596	0.564	0.535	0.507	0.480
7	0.933	0.871	0.813	0.760	0.711	0.665	0.623	0.583	0.547	.0.513	0.482	0.452	0.425
8	0.923	0.853	0.789	0.731	0.677	0.627	0.582	0.540	0.502	0.467	0.434	0.404	0.376
9	0.914	0.837	0.766	0.703	0.645	0.592	0.544	0.500	0.460	0.424	0.391	0.361	0.333
10	0.905	0.820	0.744	0.676	0.614	0.558	0.508	0.463	0.422	0.386	0.352	0.322	0.295
11	0.896	0.804	0.722	0.650	0.585	0.527	0.475	0.429	0.388	0.350	0.317	0.287	0.261
12	0.887	0.788	0.701	0.625	0.557	0.497	0.444	0.397	0.356	0.319	0.286	0.257	0.231
13	0.879	0.773	0.681	0.601	0.530	0.469	0.415	0.368	0.326	0.290	0.258	0.229	0.204
14	0.870	0.758	0.661	0.577	0.505	0.442	0.388	0.340	0.299	0.263	0.232	0.205	0.181
15	0.861	0.743	0.642	0.555	0.481	0.417	0.362	0.315	0.275	0.239	0.209	0.183	0.160
16	0.853	0.728	0.623	0.534	0.458	0.394	0.339	0.292	0.252	0.218	0.188	0.163	0.141
17	0.844	0.714	0.605	0.513	0.436	0.371	0.317	0.270	0.231	0.198	0.170	0.146	0.125
18	0.836	0.700	0.587	0.494	0.416	0.350	0.296	0.250	0.212	0.180	0.153	0.130	0.111
19	0.828	0.686	0.570	0.475	0.396	0.331	0.276	0.232	0.194	0.164	0.138	0.116	0.098
20	0.820	0.673	0.554	0.456	0.377	0.312	0.258	0.215	0.178	0.149	0.124	0.104	0.087
25	0.780	0.610	0.478	0.375	0.295	0.233	0.184	0.146	0.116	0.092	0.074	0.059	0.047
30	0.742	0.552	0.412	0.308	0.231	0.174	0.131	0.099	0.075	0.057	0.044	0.033	0.026

(Contd.)

Period *n*	*14%*	*15%*	*16%*	*17%*	*18%*	*19%*	*20%*	*24%*	*28%*	*32%*	*36%*	*40%*
0	1.000	1.000	1.000	1.000	1.000	1.000	1.000	1.000	1.000	1.000	1.000	1.000
1	0.877	0.870	0.862	0.855	0.847	0.840	0.833	0.806	0.781	0.758	0.735	0.714
2	0.769	0.756	0.743	0.731	0.718	0.706	0.694	0.650	0.610	0.574	0.541	0.510
3	0.675	0.658	0.641	0.624	0.609	0.593	0.579	0.524	0.477	0.435	0.398	0.364
4	0.592	0.572	0.552	0.534	0.516	0.499	0.482	0.423	0.373	0.329	0.292	0.260
5	0.519	0.497	0.476	0.456	0.437	0.419	0.402	0.341	0.291	0.250	0.215	0.186
6	0.456	0.432	0.410	0.390	0.370	0.352	0.335	0.275	0.227	0.189	0.158	0.133
7	0.400	0.376	0.354	0.333	0.314	0.296	0.279	0.222	0.178	0.143	0.116	0.095
8	0.351	0.327	0.305	0.285	0.266	0.249	0.233	0.179	0.139	0.108	0.085	0.068
9	0.308	0.284	0.263	0.243	0.226	0.209	0.194	0.144	0.108	0.082	0.063	0.048
10	0.270	0.247	0.227	0.208	0.191	0.176	0.162	0.116	0.085	0.062	0.046	0.035
11	0.237	0.215	0.195	0.178	0.162	0.148	0.135	0.094	0.066	0.047	0.034	0.025
12	0.208	0.187	0.168	0.152	0.137	0.124	0.112	0.076	0.052	0.036	0.025	0.018
13	0.182	0.163	0.145	0.130	0.116	0.104	0.093	0.061	0.040	0.027	0.018	0.013
14	0.160	0.141	0.125	0.111	0.099	0.088	0.078	0.049	0.032	0.021	0.014	0.009
15	0.140	0.123	0.108	0.095	0.084	0.074	0.065	0.040	0.025	0.016	0.010	0.006
16	0.123	0.107	0.093	0.081	0.071	0.062	0.054	0.032	0.019	0.012	0.007	0.005
17	0.108	0.093	0.080	0.069	0.060	0.052	0.045	0.026	0.015	0.009	0.005	0.003
18	0.095	0.081	0.069	0.059	0.051	0.044	0.038	0.021	0.012	0.007	0.004	0.002
19	0.083	0.070	0.060	0.051	0.043	0.037	0.031	0.017	0.009	0.005	0.003	0.002
20	0.073	0.061	0.051	0.043	0.037	0.031	0.026	0.014	0.007	0.004	0.002	0.001
25	0.038	0.030	0.024	0.020	0.016	0.013	0.010	0.005	0.002	0.001	0.000	0.000
30	0.020	0.015	0.012	0.009	0.007	0.005	0.004	0.002	0.001	0.000	0.000	0.000

Table A.4 *Present Value Interest Factor for an Annuity*

$$PVIFA\ (r, n) = \frac{1 - \dfrac{1}{(1+r)^n}}{r}$$

Period n	1%	2%	3%	4%	5%	6%	7%	8%	9%	10%	11%	12%	13%
0	1.000	1.000	1.000	1.000	1.000	1.000	1.000	1.000	1.000	1.000	1.000	1.000	1.000
1	0.990	0.980	0.971	0.962	0.952	0.943	0.935	0.926	0.917	0.909	0.901	0.893	0.885
2	1.970	1.942	1.913	1.886	1.859	1.833	1.808	1.783	1.759	1.736	1.713	1.690	1.668
3	2.941	2.884	2.829	2.775	2.723	2.673	2.624	2.577	2.531	2.487	2.444	2.402	2.361
4	3.902	3.808	3.717	3.630	3.546	3.465	3.387	3.312	3.240	3.170	3.102	3.037	2.974
5	4.853	4.713	4.580	4.452	4.329	4.212	4.100	3.993	3.890	3.791	3.696	3.605	3.517
6	5.795	5.601	5.417	5.242	5.076	4.917	4.766	4.623	4.486	4.355	4.231	4.111	3.998
7	6.728	6.472	6.230	6.002	5.786	5.582	5.389	5.206	5.033	4.868	4.712	4.564	4.423
8	7.652	7.325	7.020	6.733	6.463	6.210	5.971	5.747	5.535	5.335	5.146	4.968	4.799
9	8.566	8.162	7.786	7.435	7.108	6.802	6.515	6.247	5.995	5.759	5.537	5.328	5.132
10	9.471	8.983	8.530	8.111	7.722	7.360	7.024	6.710	6.418	6.145	5.889	5.650	5.426
11	10.368	9.787	9.253	8.760	8.306	7.887	7.499	7.139	6.805	6.495	6.207	5.938	5.687
12	11.255	10.575	9.954	9.385	8.863	8.384	7.943	7.536	7.161	6.814	6.492	6.194	5.918
13	12.134	11.348	10.635	9.986	9.394	8.853	8.358	7.904	7.487	7.103	6.750	6.424	6.122
14	13.004	12.106	11.296	10.563	9.899	9.295	8.745	8.244	7.786	7.367	6.982	6.628	6.302
15	13.865	12.849	11.938	11.118	10.380	9.712	9.108	8.559	8.060	7.606	7.191	6.811	6.462
16	14.718	13.578	12.561	11.652	10.838	10.106	9.447	8.851	8.312	7.824	7.379	6.974	6.604
17	15.562	14.292	13.166	12.166	11.274	10.477	9.763	9.122	8.544	8.022	7.549	7.120	6.729
18	16.398	14.992	13.754	12.659	11.690	10.828	10.059	9.372	8.756	8.201	7.702	7.250	6.840
19	17.226	15.678	14.324	13.134	12.085	11.158	10.336	9.604	8.950	8.365	7.839	7.366	6.938
20	18.046	16.351	14.877	13.590	12.462	11.470	10.594	9.818	9.128	8.514	7.963	7.469	7.025
25	22.023	19.523	17.413	15.622	14.094	12.783	11.654	10.675	9.823	9.077	8.422	7.843	7.330
30	25.808	22.397	19.600	17.292	15.373	13.765	12.409	11.258	10.274	9.427	8.694	8.055	7.496

(*Contd.*)

Period n	14%	15%	16%	17%	18%	19%	20%	24%	28%	32%	36%	40%
0	1.000	1.000	1.000	1.000	1.000	1.000	1.000	1.000	1.000	1.000	1.000	1.000
1	0.877	0.870	0.862	0.855	0.847	0.840	0.833	0.806	0.781	0.758	0.735	0.714
2	1.647	1.626	1.605	1.585	1.566	1.547	1.528	1.457	1.392	1.332	1.276	1.224
3	2.322	2.283	2.246	2.210	2.174	2.140	2.106	1.981	1.868	1.766	1.674	1.589
4	2.914	2.855	2.798	2.743	2.690	2.639	2.589	2.404	2.241	2.096	1.966	1.849
5	3.433	3.352	3.274	3.199	3.127	3.058	2.991	2.745	2.532	2.345	2.181	2.035
6	3.889	3.784	3.685	3.589	3.498	3.410	3.326	3.020	2.759	2.534	2.339	2.168
7	4.288	4.160	4.039	3.922	3.812	3.706	3.605	3.242	2.937	2.678	2.455	2.263
8	4.639	4.487	4.344	4.207	4.078	3.954	3.837	3.421	3.076	2.786	2.540	2.331
9	4.946	4.772	4.607	4.451	4.303	4.163	4.031	3.566	3.184	2.868	2.603	2.379
10	5.216	5.019	4.883	4.659	4.494	4.339	4.193	3.682	3.269	2.930	2.650	2.414
11	5.453	5.234	5.029	4.836	4.656	4.486	4.327	3.776	3.335	2.978	2.683	2.438
12	5.660	5.421	5.197	4.988	4.793	4.611	4.439	3.851	3.387	3.013	2.708	2.456
13	5.842	5.583	5.342	5.118	4.910	4.715	4.533	3.912	3.427	3.040	2.727	2.469
14	6.002	5.724	5.468	5.229	5.008	4.802	4.611	3.962	3.459	3.061	2.740	2.478
15	6.142	5.847	5.575	5.324	5.092	4.876	4.675	4.001	3.483	3.076	2.750	2.484
16	6.265	5.954	5.669	5.405	5.162	4.938	4.730	4.033	3.503	3.088	2.758	2.489
17	6.373	6.047	5.749	5.475	5.222	4.990	4.775	4.059	3.518	3.097	2.763	2.492
18	6.647	6.128	5.818	5.534	5.273	5.033	4.812	4.080	3.529	3.104	2.767	2.494
19	6.550	6.198	5.877	5.584	5.316	5.070	4.844	4.097	3.539	3.109	2.770	2.496
20	6.623	6.259	5.929	5.628	5.353	5.101	4.870	4.110	3.546	3.113	2.772	2.497
25	6.873	6.464	6.097	5.766	5.467	5.195	4.948	4.147	3.564	3.122	2.776	2.499
30	7.003	6.566	6.177	5.829	5.517	5.235	4.979	4.160	3.569	3.124	2.778	2.500

Table A.5 *Normal Distribution*

(Area of the Normal Distribution, that is, Z Standard Deviations to the Left or Right of the Mean)

Number of Standard Deviations from Mean, (Z)	*Area to the Left or Right (One tail)*	*Number of Standard Deviations from Mean (Z)*	*Area to the Left or Right (One tail)*
0.00	0.5000	1.70	0.0446
0.05	0.4801	1.75	0.0401
0.10	0.4602	1.80	0.0359
0.15	0.4404	1.85	0.0322
0.20	0.4207	1.90	0.0287
0.25	0.4013	1.95	0.0256
0.30	0.3821	2.00	0.0228
0.35	0.3632	2.05	0.0202
0.40	0.3446	2.10	0.0179
0.45	6.3264	2.15	0.0158
0.50	0.3085	2.20	0.0139
0.55	0.2912	2.25	0.0122
0.60	0.2743	2.30	0.0107
0.65	0.2578	2.35	0.0094
0.70	0.2420	2.40	0.0082
0.75	0.2264	2.45	0.0071
0.80	0.2119	2.50	0.0062
0.85	0.1977	2.55	0.0054
0.90	0.1841	2.60	0.0047
0.95	0.1711	2.65	0.0040
1.00	0.1587	2.70	0.0035
1.05	0.1469	2.75	0.0030
1.10	0.1357	2.80	0.0026
1.15	0.1251	2.85	0.0022
1.20	0.1151	2.90	0.0019
1.25	0.1056	2.95	0.0016
1.30	0.0968	3.00	0.0013
1.35	0.0885	3.05	0.0011
1.40	0.0808	3.10	0.0010
1.45	0.0735	3.25	0.0006
1.50	0.0668	3.50	0.00023
1.55	0.0606	4.00	0.00003
1.60	0.0548	4.99	0.0000003
1.65	0.0495		

Appendix B Assessing the Tax Burden*

Preparation of project profitability involves computing the expected tax burden for the forecast period. This calls for familiarity with the provisions of the Income Tax Act that are relevant for determining the magnitude and timing of the tax burden for a new project. This appendix seeks to provide help in this respect. It is organised into four sections. The first section discusses the broad framework for deriving the taxable income; the second dwells on some important provisions relevant for computing the taxable income; the third focuses on the determination of tax burden and payment of tax; and finally, the fourth presents a comprehensive illustration of tax calculation. It should be emphasised here that taxation is a complex and specialised field that is best handled by experts. Our purpose here is to build a basic understanding of the tax framework relevant for financial appraisal of projects and not to provide a detailed exposition of the field.

1. FRAMEWORK FOR DERIVING TAXABLE INCOME

Income tax is a charge calculated by applying the rates prescribed annually in the Finance Act on the base called the total income. The total income, also known as taxable income, is computed with reference to a period defined as the previous year. Exhibit B.1 shows the schematic diagram for determining the total income of a corporate assessee under the Income Tax Act (Act hereafter). As a part of the rationalisation and simplification process,

Exhibit B.1 *Schematic Diagram for Determining the Total Income for Corporate Assessees*

Income from Business
+
Income from Other Heads under Tax Law
=
Gross Total Income
–
Deductions from Gross Total Income
=
Total Income

* This appendix has been contributed by Prof. Padmini Srinivasan, Associate Professor, Indian Institute of Management Bangalore. This appendix is updated with reference to the Assessment Year 2020–21.

many of the incentive schemes have been done away with, at the same time reducing the overall corporate income tax rates. By this, the Government hopes to reduce the complexities involved in the calculation of tax, and the administration of tax law would become easier.

Income from Business

This broadly consists of receipts less deduction associated with activities which can be attributed to the character of business/profession. The principal sources of receipts are sale proceeds, professional fees, and labour charges.

The deductions can be classified as follows:

1. *Actual business expenses incurred* The major items included under this head are: (i) rent, rates, taxes, insurance, repairs and maintenance in respect of premises used for business (Section 30)[1]; (ii) repairs, maintenance and insurance in respect of plant and machinery (Section 31); (iii) expenditure on scientific research not being in the nature of capital expenditure related to the business of the assessee (Section 35); (iv) expenditure on scientific research by certain notified businesses get weighted deductions; (v) insurance premium paid in respect of insurance of stock or stores of the business; bad debt etc. (Section 36); (vi) any other expenditure (not being in the nature of capital expenditure or personal expenses of the assessee) laid out or expended wholly and exclusively for the purposes of the business/profession (Section 37).
2. *Amortisation of certain expenses* Certain expenses are incurred at one time and a percentage of such expenses is allowed to be deducted against the income over a number of years by way of amortisation. These include: (i) outlays on fixed assets which are depreciated at the rates prescribed under rule 5 of the Income Tax Rules (Section 32); (ii) expenditure on patents and copyrights (Section 35A); (iii) expenditure for acquiring know-how (Section 35AB); (iv) preliminary expenses (Section 35D); (v) expenditure on prospecting of minerals (Section 35E); (vi) expenditure incurred by an Indian Company, for amalgamation or demerger of a company (Section 35 DD); and (vii) capital expenditure on family planning of employees (Section 36).
3. *Capital expenditures of certain types* Though capital expenditures are not normally allowed as a deduction in computing the business income, the following capital expenditures can be deducted by virtue of certain provisions of the Act: (i) capital expenditures on scientific research (other than land) related to the business carried on by the assesse [Section 35(1) (iv)]; (ii) capital expenditure incurred in connection with the business consisting of prospecting for or extraction or production of mineral oils (Section 42); and (iii) capital expenditure incurred in connection with acquiring any rights to operate telecommunication services (Section 35ABB).
4. *Certain contributions/payments* made to (a) certain recognised scientific research institutions / or to notified institutions [Section 35(1)(ii) and 35(1)(iia)]; (b) certain recognised institutions to be used for research in social science or statistical research [Section 35(1)(iii)]; (c) approved public sector companies and institutions for promoting the social and economic welfare of, or the uplift of, the public (Section 35AC); and

[1] Sections refer to the Sections of the Income Tax Act, 1961 as amended by Finance Act 2008.

(d) certain associations and institutions for carrying out programmes of conservation of natural resources (Section 35CCB) can be deducted for tax purposes.

In respect of contributions made to approved National Laboratories or a University or an Indian Institute of Technology with a specific direction that the amounts be used for scientific research undertaken under an approved programme, an amount equal to 200% of the contribution is allowed as deduction subject to conditions (Section 35 2AA).

5. *Carried forward losses and allowances* In computing the business income, losses and allowances carried forward from the previous years can be deducted subject to compliance with certain conditions.

Income from Other Heads Under Tax Law

The various other heads, the nature of income, and the deductions allowed under these heads by the Act are shown below.

Head	Nature of Income	Deductions Allowed
Income from house property	Income arising from building and land appurtenant thereto owned by the assessee	Deductions are specified under Sections 23 and 24 of the Act
Capital gains	Full value of consideration on transfer of capital assets	(a) Indexed cost of acquisition of the assets (b) Indexed cost of improvements (c) Expenses on transfer (d) Certain exemptions
Income from other sources	Interest and other incomes which cannot be taken under any other head	Expenses incurred to earn the income and depreciation where applicable

Gross Total Income This represents the summation of income from business and income from other heads under the Act as described above. This aggregation process involves setting-off negative figures in the manner as prescribed in the Act. Such set-off is done at two levels as follows:

(a) Setting-off negative figures under any source against positive figures under any other source within the same head of income; and

(b) Setting-off negative figures under any head of income against positive figures under any other head of income.

These provisions are discussed separately in the next section.

Exemptions/Deductions from Gross Total Income Certain incomes enjoy special exemptions under Chapter III, and do not form part of the total income.

The important exemptions are:

(1) Profits or gains arising from the export of articles or things or services of an assessee being an entrepreneur from the Special Economic Zone and has commenced business before 1st April, 2021 (Sec 10 AA).

(2) 100% of profits and gains derived from exports for a period of five years beginning from the year in which the goods are manufactured or services are provided, followed by 50% of profits and gains for the next consecutive 5 years thereafter.

Deductions from Gross Total Income Chapter VI A of the Act deals with various deductions that are allowed from the gross total income. The deductions under this chapter are allowed irrespective of the source of income and are akin to incentives. They are different from other deductions discussed earlier which are related to a specific head of income. If the gross total income is negative than no deduction under Chapter VI A is allowable. These deductions cannot make a gross total income negative.

The important deductions under chapter VI A are as follows:

1. Deduction in respect of profits and gains from new industrial undertaking providing infrastructure facility after a certain date (Section 80IA)
2. Deduction in respect of profits and gains derived from certain housing projects (Section 80IBA)
3. Deduction in respect specific business being eligible start-up (Section 80 IAC)
4. Deductions in respect of profits and gains from business of collecting and processing bio-degradable waste (Section 80JJA)
5. Deduction in respect of employment of new workmen (Section 80 JJAA)

Total Income This represents the difference between the gross total income and the deductions from the gross total income and is the base on which the tax rate is applied to arrive at the tax liability.

2. IMPORTANT PROVISIONS AND CONSIDERATIONS RELEVANT FOR DERIVING TAXABLE INCOME

In applying the framework for deriving the taxable income, discussed in the preceding section, the following provisions must be considered:

- Expenses incurred during construction period
- Depreciation
- Deduction in respect of expenditure on scientific research
- Deduction in respect of certain capital expenditure
- Exemptions in respect of profits and gains of newly setup industrial undertakings in free trade zone and Special Economic Zone
- Deduction in respect of profits and gains from newly setup industrial undertakings engaged in infrastructure development
- Deduction in respect of profits and gains derived from certain housing projects
- Deduction in respect specific business being eligible start-up
- Deductions in respect of profits and gains from business of collecting and processing bio-degradable waste

- Deduction in respect of employment of new workmen
- Disallowances
- Set-off, carry forward, and order of deduction for computing income from business

Expenses Incurred During Construction Period The first question that needs to be answered is what is construction period or what is the date from which the computation of profits and gains of the business should be reckoned for the purpose of income tax. Section 3 of the Act dealing with the definition of previous year (the period with reference to which total income is computed) provides a clue in the matter. According to this Section, the previous year in respect of any business commences from the date on which it is 'set up'. In the case of a factory, the date of 'set up' will be the date on which the unit is 'ready' to commence production after trial run, etc., though the actual commercial production may not start due to various reasons such as non-availability of raw material, power supply etc. This date of 'set up' is the cut-off date and all the expenditures incurred after this date are to be treated as revenue expenditure deductible in computing the income from business. It may not matter at this stage whether the unit is effecting sales or not for computing income under the head 'Profits and Gains of Business or Profession' for the purposes of income tax.

Once the date of 'set up' of business is determined, the treatment of various expenses incurred up to the date of the setting-up of the unit (other than direct expenses relating to construction) may be discussed.

During the construction stage of a project, a new company incurs various expenses. These expenses can be broadly classified as: (a) direct expenses relating to construction and (b) expenses other than direct expenses.

The expenses, which are directly related to construction, are considered as part of plant, machinery, building etc. The expenses incurred must be made through cheque/bank draft or electronic transfer if the payment exceeds ₹10000 in a day. The treatment of other expenses needs some elaboration. These expenses (other than direct) may be classified as follows: (i) preliminary expenses, (ii) indirect expenditure relating to construction, (iii) indirect expenditure not relating to construction, (iv) expenditure relating to technical know-how, (v) expenditure relating to a new project of an existing company, and (vi) income earned during the construction period.

Preliminary Expenses Preliminary expenses consist of the following: (a) expenditure in connection with preparation of feasibility report, preparation of project report, engineering services, market survey or any other survey necessary for the business of the assessee; (b) legal charges for drafting any agreement between the assessee and any other person for any purpose relating to the setting up or conduct of the business of the assessee; (c) legal charges for drafting the memorandum and articles of association, fees for registration of the company under the provisions of the Companies Act, cost of issue for public subscription of shares and debentures of the company; (d) such other items of expenditure (not being expenditure eligible for any allowance or deduction under any other provision of this Act) as may be prescribed. Deduction for specified preliminary expenses, which are incurred after the commencement of business for an extension of an undertaking or setting-up of a new unit is also available to service sector.

According to Section 35D of the Act, 20 percent of the preliminary expenses can be claimed as deduction for each of the five successive previous years beginning with the previous year in which the business commences or the extension of the undertaking is completed. The maximum amount of preliminary expenses that can be amortised is five percent of the cost of the project or capital employed (as defined in Section 35D) whichever is more.

Indirect Expenditure Relating to Construction These consist of expenses like financial charges, remuneration of various personnel engaged in construction activity, travelling and other expenses incurred for the purpose of implementing the project, depreciation on various assets used for the purpose of construction and trial production expenses. These expenses are allowed to be capitalised, i.e., added to the value of various assets setup by allocating them over the items of plant, machinery, buildings, etc., on some reasonable basis. The unit is permitted to claim depreciation on the enhanced value of these assets arrived at after such allocation and this value is referred to as the 'actual cost' of the assets. Such actual cost is reduced by that portion, if any, as has been met directly or indirectly by any other person or authority [Section 43 (1)].

Indirect Expenditure not Relating to Construction There are several expenses incurred during the construction period which are not in any way related to construction. Examples: expenses on the marketing department, expenses incurred due to the corporate status of the unit. Such expenses are not allowed to be capitalised nor are they allowed to be deducted from the income of the subsequent years. In the financial accounting these may be charged to the profit and loss account. From the income tax point of view, however, the company does not derive the benefit of charging these expenses against revenue. Hence, it is preferable that such expenses are incurred, as far as possible, after the date of setting up of the unit. Interest paid on borrowed funds for the acquisition of assets will not be allowed as expenses till the date on which the asset is first put to use.

Expenditure on Technical Know Capital expenditure incurred on technical know-how, incurred after 1st April, 1998, can be capitalised as direct expenditure related to construction or can be by itself treated as an intangible asset, on which depreciation can be claimed under Section 32. Revenue expenditure on technical know-how can be claimed as expenses under Section 37 (1).

Income Earned During Construction Period Income earned during the construction period which is attributable to construction activity can be reduced from the construction cost of the asset itself. Examples of such income are sale of products produced during trial run, sale of packing material used for machinery, hire charges received for plant and machinery which was given to the sub-contractor, sale of packing material used of machinery etc. Other types of incomes like interest received and share transfer fees received are normally treated as income (income from other source) for the purpose of Income tax Act.

Depreciation According to Section 32(1) of the Income Tax Act, depreciation at prescribed rates on the actual cost (as determined in the manner stated in the preceding heading) in respect of (i) buildings, plant and machinery and furniture and fittings being tangible assets and (ii) know-how, patents, copyrights, trademarks, licences, franchises or other business other business or commercial rights being intangible assets used for business/professional purposes is a tax deductible expense. For claiming the depreciation allowance the assets should be owned and used for the purpose of business by the assessee.

When a capital asset is imported by incurring a liability in foreign exchange and the rupee equivalent of such liability is outstanding at the end of each year or at the time of repayment increases/decreases due to fluctuation in rates of exchange then such increases/decreases are adjusted against the actual cost (Section 43A). The actual cost so adjusted at the end of each year is treated as if it was the actual cost from the date of acquisition of the asset. This necessitates adjustment toward depreciation in each year in respect of earlier years.

Depreciation is charged on blocks of assets which represent a group of assets, within the broad class of assets, of buildings, plant, machinery, and furniture, for which a common rate of depreciation is applicable. Depreciation will be calculated by applying the prescribed rate (which varies between 5% and 100%) on the written down value (WDV) of the entire block.

'Block of assets' means a group of assets falling within a class of assets comprising:

(a) tangible assets, being buildings, machinery, plant or furniture;

(b) intangible assets, being know-how, patents, copyrights, trademarks, licences, franchises or any other business or commercial rights of similar nature

Recent case laws have indicated that in infrastructure projects, particularly in Build Operate Transfer projects, certain rights acquired to operate can be treated as intangible assets and can be amortised at 25%.

When an asset is sold the amount realised from the sale of such asset (after deducting expense on sales) will simply be deducted from the WDV of that block. If the amount realised is greater than the WDV of the block, the difference will be treated as short-term capital gain. In a case where all the assets in the block are disposed off and there is still a balance in the account of the block, such amount will be treated as short-term capital loss.

Additionally, under Section 32AD, investment allowance can be claimed on investment made in new plant and machinery (other than ships, aircraft, vehicle and office appliance etc.) if manufacturing is setup in notified backward states. The plant should be acquired and installed before April 1, 2020.

To illustrate the above provisions, let us consider an example. A block of assets consisting of 10 items acquired during 2007 to 2017 has a written down value of ₹3 million as on 1st April 2017. During 2017–18, the assessee sells an asset for ₹2 million (on which an expense of ₹0.1 million is incurred on sale) and acquires an asset for ₹0.5 million.

The net block of assets for depreciation purposes at the end of 2017–18 will be:

Opening WDV	₹3.0 million
Value of addition during the year	₹0.5 million
	₹3.5 million
Less	
Sale proceeds (after deducting selling expense) for the asset sold	₹1.9 million
Net block for purposes of depreciation	₹1.6 million

In the above example, if the sale proceeds (after deducting selling expense) had been ₹5 million, the difference between this amount and ₹3.5 million should be treated as short-term capital gain and the net block for purposes of depreciation will be zero. Suppose, all the assets in the block (including the assets acquired during the year) are sold for ₹3.2 million (after deducting selling expense), the balance of ₹0.3 million remaining in the block amount will be treated as short-term capital loss.

It may be noted that when any asset is acquired and put to use during the previous year for a period less than 180 days then depreciation will be allowed only to the extent of 50 percent of the prescribed rate for that asset in respect of the year of acquisition.

In case any new machinery or plant (other than ship and aircraft) acquired by a manufacturer or an assessee who produces articles are things, a further sum of twenty percent of the actual cost will be allowed as deduction as additional depreciation subject to other conditions laid in Section 32 (1) (iia). Further, if the undertaking is setup in states of Andhra Pradesh, Telangana, Bihar or West Bengal, a further sum of 35 percent of the actual cost will be allowed as deduction as additional depreciation.

Deduction in Respect of Expenditure on Scientific Research Under Section 35, the following expenses relating to scientific research incurred during the previous year are allowed as deduction in computing the income from business:

- All expenses, both revenue and capital (other than cost of land) incurred on scientific research relating to the business of the assessee. Such expenditures incurred within three years before the commencement of business shall also be deemed to be incurred in the year of commencement of business and accordingly deductible in that year.
- Contributions to approved scientific research associations/institutions, university/college, and to be used for scientific research are eligible for deduction of 150% of the contribution made. From the assessment year beginning 1st April 2021, the deduction is the actual amount only. [Section 35(1)(ii)]
- Contribution paid to a company registered in India, and has a main object of scientific research and development and to be used by it for scientific research. Subject to other conditions prescribed. [Section 35(1 (iia)]
- Contributions to approved institutions to be used for research in social science or statistical research whether related to business or not are eligible for a deduction of 125% of the contribution. [Section 35(1)(iii)]
- In respect of contributions made to approved National Laboratories or University or Indian Institute of Technology, with a specific direction that the amounts be used for scientific research undertaken under an approved programme, an amount equal to 150% of the contribution is allowed as a deduction. From the assessment year beginning 1st April 2021, the deduction is restricted to the actual amount incurred only. [Secion35 (2AA)]
- A weighted deduction of 150% on revenue and capital expenditure (other than land and building) incurred on approved in-house research and development, of companies engaged in manufacturing and production of bio-technology or in manufacturing business (other than those mentioned in the Eleventh Schedule). From the assessment year beginning 1st April 2021 the deduction is restricted to the actual amount incurred only. [Section 35(2AB)(1)]
- Expenditure in the nature of capital expenditure incurred for acquiring any right to operate telecommunication services (spectrum or licence fees), either before the commencement of business or thereafter. A deduction can be claimed starting from

the year in which the payment is made (or the business has commenced), in equal instalments and ending in the year in which the licence comes to an end. [Section 35ABA, Section 35ABB]

- Expenditure made in the nature of capital expenditure (other than land, goodwill and financial instruments) for specified business are allowed as deduction in the year in which the business commences operations subject to certain conditions. Specified businesses include, laying and operating natural gas pipeline, building and operating new hotel of two star category or more, cold chain facility, hospital with at least one hundred beads, laying and operating slurry pipelines for transporting iron ores, setting up semiconductor wafer fabrication manufacturing unit, developing and building under a scheme for slum redevelopment, production of fertilizers, business in the nature of developing or operating and maintaining or developing, operating and maintaining any infrastructure facility. [Section 35AD]

Exemptions in Respect of Profits and Gains of Newly Established Units in Special Economic Zones [Section 10AA] This exemption is provided to an assessee, being an entrepreneur as referred to in clause (j) of Section 2 of the Special Economic Zone Act, 2005 from the unit which begins to manufacture or produce articles or things or provides services in a special economic zone after 1st April, 2006 and before the assessment year starting from 1st April, 2021. The exemption is available for 15 years as follows: A 100% deductions for the first 5 years and 50% for the next 5 years. Thereafter another 50% for the next consecutive 5 years or the amount transferred to SEZ reinvestment reserve account whichever lower will be allowed as exemption. The amount of profit that is eligible for exemption is calculated in the ratio as follows:

$$\text{Eligible profit} = \text{Profit of the business} \times \frac{\text{Export turnover of manufactured goods}}{\text{Total turnover of the business}}$$

There are other conditions attached to the exemptions.

Deductions in Respect of Profits and Gains on Newly Setup Industrial Undertaking Deduction in respect of profits and gains from newly setup industrial undertakings engaged in infrastructure development under Section 80-IA, Deduction in respect of profits and gains from certain industrial undertaking other than infrastructure development undertakings under Section 80IB and Deduction in respect of profits and gains from undertaking in North Eastern states under Section 80IE are available only if the unit is setup before 1st April, 2017.

Deduction in Respect of Profits and Gains from Specified Business Section 80-IAC allows 100% deduction of profits and gains derived from eligible business, subject to certain conditions. Eligible start-up business is engaged in innovation, development or improvement of products or processes or services or a scalable business with high potential employment generation or wealth creation. The deduction can be claimed for three consecutive assessment years out of seven years beginning from the year in which the business is incorporated. The turnover of the business does not exceed twenty-five crores in the previous year in which the deduction is claimed.

Disallowances The Income Tax Act provides that though certain expenses are incurred by the assessee during the previous year, they will not be allowed as a deduction (partly or fully) in computing the income under the head 'Profits and Gains of Business or Profession' under certain circumstances. The more important of these items are mentioned below:

1. Advertisement expenditure in the material published by any political party is disallowed in full [Section 37 (2B)].
2. Any expenditure incurred by the assessee that is prohibited by law, will not be allowed as deduction. (Section 37)
3. Expenditure on account of supply of goods, services, or facilities by certain specified related persons/organisations, which in the opinion of the assessing officer is excessive or unreasonable can be disallowed unless they are transactions done at arm lengths price [Section 40A (2)(a)].
4. Expenditure in respect of which payment is made in a sum exceeding ₹10,000, (to a person in a day/at a time), otherwise than by crossed cheque or bank draft or through electronic clearing system through a bank (except in certain exempted cases) is disallowed in full. Further, if expenses have been allowed as deduction and are later paid otherwise by a cheque or a bank draft, or through electronic clearing system of a bank, then such expenses will be treated as incomes [Section 40A(3)].
5. Contributions to unapproved gratuity or other funds of employees are disallowed in full [Section 40 A (7 and 9)].
6. Expenditures of the following kind are disallowed if they are not paid for within the previous year or within a stipulated time after the previous year: (a) expenses on account of tax, duty, or fees, (b) contributions to any provident/superannuation/gratuity/other welfare fund of employees, (c) payment of bonus or commission to employees, and (d) interest on any loan or borrowing from public financial institution, (e) interest payable on loans or advances from scheduled bank, (f) provision made for amount payable as in lieu of any leave (leave encashment) (as defined in Section 4A of the Companies Act, 1956) (Section 43B)[2].

Set-off, Carry Forward, and Order of Deduction for Computing Income from Business Various deductions and allowances are considered in computing the income from business as discussed in the first section. If the result after providing for such deductions and allowances is a negative figure in any year, this is allowed to be set-off against income from other heads and the remaining unabsorbed amount, if any, can be carried forward to the next year and set-off against the income of that year and so on. The provisions relating to set-off of negative income and aggregation and the order of deduction for computing income from business are as follows:

- The first step in the aggregation process is the determination of income under each head by setting-off losses against incomes under different sources. The rules for such set-off are as follows:

[2] It may be noted that this section makes an exception to the general principle of allowing expenditures as a deduction in the previous year in which they are incurred, irrespective of whether they are paid or not.

(a) Losses from any source under a given 'head of income' can be set-off only against income from any other source under the same 'head of income', with expectations noted in (b) below.

(b) Losses from long-term capital gains can be set-off from long-term capital gains only. Losses from speculation business (which falls under the head of income 'profits and gains of business or profession') can be set-off only against profits from speculation business. Likewise losses from owning and maintaining race horses can be set-off against profits from similar activity.

- Aggregation of income from all heads of income is done by setting-off losses from one head of income against income from other head/s. The rules regarding set-off and carry forward are as follows:

  (a) Subject to (i) above losses under any head of income other than the head capital gains can be set-off against the income under any other head of income. Losses under the head house property to the extent it relates to the interest on loan taken for construction, purchase or repair of such property can be set-off against income from any other head. In the subsequent year the carried forward loss should be set-off against income from house property and the balance loss can be carried forward for a period of eight subsequent years from the year in which the loss was first computed.

  (b) Losses that remain under the head capital gains (other than long-term capital gains) can be carried forward and set-off against income under the head capital gains (other than long-term) of subsequent years and so on. Long-term capital loss can be carried forward and set-off against long-term capital gains only. Such carry forward can be done for a period of eight subsequent years from the year in which the loss was computed.

  (c) Unabsorbed business loss (other than speculation business loss) of any year can be carried forward and set-off against income under the head of business of subsequent years, provided the business under which the loss was originally computed is continued to be carried on in the year in which the set-off is sought. Such carry forward can be done for eight subsequent years from the year in which the loss was computed.

  (d) Unabsorbed loss from speculation business can be carried forward and set-off against income from speculation business. Such carry forward can be done for eight subsequent years.

- Unabsorbed depreciation can be carried forward and set-off against the income from any other head of subsequent years without any limitation as to the number of years.
- Capital expenditure on scientific research which is not absorbed by available current profits is treated in the same way as unabsorbed depreciation.
- A recent CBDT circular has clarified that after giving effect to the provisions of Sections 70 and 71 there is any *income* (where there is no brought forward loss to be set-off in accordance with the provisions of Section 72 of the Act) and the same is eligible for deduction in accordance with the provisions of Chapter VI-A or Sections 10A, 10B, etc., the same shall be allowed in computing the total income of the assessee.

Order of Deduction for Computing Income from Business For the purposes of carry forward and set-off, the unabsorbed benefits from an earlier year are divided into various categories and are considered for set-off, along with certain current allowances, in the order given below in computing the income from business of the current year:

- Current scientific research capital expenditure
- Current depreciation
- Carried forward business loss
- Unabsorbed depreciation and unabsorbed capital expenditure on scientific research

A loss cannot be carried forward unless the return of Income Tax is filed within the time allowed under Section 139 (1) of the Act.

3. DETERMINATION OF THE TAX BURDEN AND PAYMENT OF TAX

Once the taxable income of the company is derived, the next step is the determination of the tax burden and its payment. For this purpose, we need to know: (i) tax rates for companies, (ii) calculation of minimum alternate tax, (iii) provisions for payment of advance tax, and (iv) provisions for payment of tax along with the filing return, (v) fringe benefit tax.

Tax Rates for Companies For tax purposes, companies are classified as domestic companies and foreign companies and are generally taxed at 30% and 40% respectively.

The tax rate for a domestic company would be 25% if turnover or gross receipt of the company does not exceed ₹25 crore in the previous year.

Additional components applicable to Domestic Entity Companies are:

(a) Surcharge: The amount of income tax shall be increased by a surcharge at the rate of 7% of such tax, where total income exceeds one crore rupees but not exceeding ten crore rupees and at the rate of 12% of such tax, where total income exceeds ten crore rupees.

However, the surcharge shall be subject to marginal relief, which shall be as under:

(i) Where income exceeds one crore rupees but not exceeding ten crore rupees, the total amount payable as income tax and surcharge shall not exceed total amount payable as income tax on total income of one crore rupees by more than the amount of income that exceeds one crore rupees.

(ii) Where income exceeds ten crore rupees, the total amount payable as income tax and surcharge shall not exceed total amount payable as income tax on total income of ten crore rupees by more than the amount of income that exceeds ten crore rupees.

(b) Health and Education Cess: "Education Cess" and "Secondary and Higher Education Cess" will be replaced by "Health and Education Cess" at the rate of 4%, on the amount of tax computed, inclusive of surcharge.

Foreign companies are levied a surcharge of 2% of tax where total income exceeds ₹1 crore and 5% of tax where total income exceeds ₹10 crore. The education cess is 3% of tax plus surcharge.

Though the rates of income tax are prescribed annually in the Finance Act, the Income Tax Act itself stipulates the rates of income tax in respect of certain types of incomes and these generally relate to foreign companies in respect of incomes of the nature of royalties, technical know-how fees, interest and dividends. In respect of long-term capital gains, the Act prescribes rates of tax both for domestic and foreign companies.

Such incomes are taxed at rates mentioned in the Act and the remaining total income is taxed at the rates stated above.

Minimum Alternate Tax In the case of an assessee, being a company, if the income tax is payable on the total income as computed under the Act, is less than 18.5% of its book profit, the tax payable for the relevant previous year shall be deemed to be 18.5% of such book profit. This tax is called Minimum Alternate Tax (MAT). That is, every company will now be paying at least 18.5% of the book profits as tax [Section 115JB(1)]. MAT credit entitlement is available for ten years. The annual accounts prepared are in accordance with Part II and III of Schedule VI of the Companies Act using the accounting policies, accounting standards and methods of depreciation and which are presented before the annual general meeting of the company.

In addition, a report in the prescribed format, from the accountant certifying that the book profit has been computed in accordance with the provisions of this section must be filed along with the return of income.

There are few items that are adjusted to the book profits to arrive at the final book profits on which MAT will be charged.

The following amounts have to be added back if debited to profit and loss account:

- The amount of provision for income tax and tax paid
- The amount carried to any reserve
- The amount set aside for unascertained liabilities
- The provision for losses of subsidiary companies
- The amounts paid or proposed as dividends
- Amount of expenditure related to exempt income
- The amount of depreciation excluding the amount of depreciation on account of revaluation of assets
- The amount of deferred tax and the provision thereof and amounts set aside for provision in diminution in the value of assets

Similarly, the following should be deducted from the profit and loss account:

- The amount withdrawn from any reserves or provision credited to profit and loss account
- The amount of loss brought forward or unabsorbed depreciation whichever is less as per books of accounts
- Income exempt from tax
- The net amount of income as reduced by expenses included in the profit and loss account which is exempt from tax under Section 10 shall be excluded
- The amounts of profit which are eligible for deduction under Section 80 HHC, or 80 HHE or 80 HHF and is also excluded for the purposes of calculation of MAT.
- The amount of deferred tax credited to the profit and loss statement

Provision for Advance Tax Advance tax is payable on the current income of the company in four instalments during the financial year as follows:

On or before	*Advance tax that should have been paid by the due date (as a percentage of the estimated total tax liability)*
15th June	15
15th September	45
15th December	75
15th March (succeeding)	100

For practical purposes, these provisions mean that income tax is payable along with the earnings. Thanks to this 'pay as you earn' principle, there is hardly any lag between earnings and tax payment.

Payment of Taxes At the time of filing return, the assessee is required to compute the tax liability based on the income stated in the return of income. If there is a shortfall between this tax liability and the sum of the advance tax paid and the tax deducted at source on incomes due to the company, then such shortfall is required to be paid before the return is filed. Such tax is referred to as self-assessment tax. Along with such shortfall in tax the assessee is also required to pay interest on (a) the shortfall in the advance tax payable in any instalment and (b) the self-assessment tax, if the return is filed beyond the due date. The due date for filing of return for companies is 31st October of the relevant assessment year.

4. ILLUSTRATION OF TAX CALCULATION

Bolt Infra Ltd., engaged in manufacturing of infrastructure projects starts its operation on 10.10.2018. The following details are available:

(All figures in ₹ millions)

1. The balance sheet of the company as on 10.10.2018 is as follows:

Liabilities		**Assets**	
Share capital	8.00	Plant and machinery	7.00
Central subsidy	1.50	Building	9.00
Term loan	10.50	Current assets, loans and advances etc.	1.00
Deposits	3.00	Preliminary and preoperative expenses	6.00
	23.00		23.00

2. The projected revenues and expenses for eight years ending 31st March are:

Revenues:

1	2	3	4	5	6	7	8
15.00	27.00	40.00	55.00	65.00	75.00	85.00	100.00

Expenses:

1	2	3	4	5	6	7	8
20.00	23.04	30.00	40.00	50.00	60.00	70.00	80.00

3. The company has projected to add equipment for carrying out scientific research relating to their business @ ₹0.01 million for each of the eight years.
4. Expenses include provision for retirement of employees in the 6th, 7th and 8th years at ₹0.3 million, ₹0.4 million and ₹0.5 million respectively.
5. Details of preliminary and preoperative expenses are as follows:
   ₹1.5 million – Indirect expenses relating to construction – Plant and Machinery;
   ₹1.0 million – Indirect expenses relating to construction – Buildings;
   ₹1.0 million – Preliminary expenses;
   ₹2.5 million – Indirect expenses not relating to construction.
6. Rate of Depreciation: 15% for plant and machinery and 10% for buildings.
   Required: Compute the total income and total tax liability for each of the eight years. Assume a tax rate of 30% and a surcharge of 7% on income tax (if income is above ₹1 crore) and an education cess of 4%.

The computation of tax liability is shown in Exhibit B.2.

Exhibit B.2 ***Bolt Infra Limited Computation of Tax Liability***

(₹ *in million*)

	Yr.1	*Yr.2*	*Yr.3*	*Yr.4*	*Yr.5*	*Yr.6*	*Yr.7*	*Yr.8*
REVENUE	15	27	40	55	65	75	85	100
Less: EXPENSES (See Note 1):	19.83	22.87	29.83	39.83	49.83	59.35	69.25	79.15
Profit before set-off	–4.83	4.13	10.17	15.17	15.17	15.65	15.75	20.85
Less:								
1. Current Depreciation (See Note 2)	1.14	2.13	1.86	1.62	1.42	1.24	1.08	0.95
2. Current Capital Expenditure on Scientific Research	0.1	0.1	0.1	0.1	0.1	0.1	0.1	0.1
	–6.07	1.9	8.21	13.45	13.65	14.31	14.57	19.8
Less:								
1. Carried Forward Business Loss	-	1.9	2.93					
2. Unabsorbed Depreciation	-	0	1.14					
3. Unabsorbed Capital Expenditure on Scientific Research	-	0	0.1					
Gross Total Income (G.T.I)	-	0	4.04	13.45	13.65	14.31	14.57	19.8
Less: Deductions from G.T.I	-	-	-	-	-	-	-	-
TOTAL INCOME	**-**	**-**	**4.04**	**13.45**	**13.65**	**14.31**	**14.57**	**19.8**
Income Tax								
Mat Tax (Note 3)		0.133	1.35	2.57				
(1) Basic Tax @ 30% of Total Income	-	-	1.21	4.04	4.10	4.29	4.37	5.94
(2) Surcharge @ 7% of Basic Tax	-	-		0.28	0.29	0.30	0.31	0.42
(3) Education Cess @ 4% of 1 & 3	-	-	0.05	0.17	0.18	0.18	0.19	0.25
Total	**-**		**1.26**	**4.49**	**4.56**	**4.78**	**4.86**	**6.61**

(*Contd.*)

	Yr.1	Yr.2	Yr.3	Yr.4	Yr.5	Yr.6	Yr.7	Yr.8
MAT Credit set-off				0.22				
Net Tax payable		0.133	1.35	4.27	4.56	4.78	4.86	6.61
Benefits Carried Forward								
(1) Business Loss	4.83	2.93						
(2) Unabsorbed Depreciation	1.14	1.14						
(3) Unabsorbed Capital Expenditure on Scientific Research	0.1	0.1						
(4) MAT Credit		0.13	0.09					

Note: In the above example we assume there are no deductions available.

Working Notes

1. Expenses under the head 'Business' before depreciation and capital expenditure on scientific research:

	Yr.1	Yr.2	Yr.3	Yr.4	Yr.5	Yr.6	Yr.7	Yr.8
Expenses as per statement	20.00	23.04	30.00	40.00	50.00	60.00	70.00	80.00
*	0.35	0.35	0.35	0.35	0.35	0.35	0.35	0.35
	19.65	22.69	29.65	39.65	49.65	59.65	69.65	79.65
**	0.18	0.18	0.18	0.18	0.18			
	19.83	22.87	29.83	39.83	49.83	59.65	69.65	79.65
Less:								
Provision for Gratuity not allowed U.S.40 A(7)	-	-	-	-	-	0.30	0.40	0.50
	19.83	22.87	29.83	39.83	49.83	59.35	69.25	79.15

**Less:* Preliminary Expenses Amortised under financial accounting (1.0 + 2.5 = 3.5) over 10 years.

***Add:* Preliminary Expenses allowed under Section 35D @ 20% of (5% of Capital employed of ₹18.5 million).

2. Depreciation

Actual Cost:

Plant and Machinery: 7.0 + 1.5 = 8.5 million

Buildings: 9.0 + 1.0 = 10.0 million

Rate of Depreciation: @ 15% for Plant and Machinery and 10% for Building. Since these assets were used for less than 180 days during the first year of operation, depreciation @ 50% of normal allowance is available for this year.

Schedule of Depreciation

	Yr.1	Yr.2	Yr.3	Yr.4	Yr.5	Yr.6	Yr.7	Yr.8
Plant and Machinery	0.64	1.18	1.00	0.85	0.72	0.62	0.52	0.44
Building	0.5	0.95	0.85	0.77	0.69	0.62	0.56	0.51
Total	1.14	2.13	1.86	1.62	1.42	1.24	1.08	0.95

Note 3: Computation of Minimum Alternate Tax

	Yr.1	Yr.2	Yr.3	Yr.4
Book Profits				
Income	15.00	27.00	40.00	55.00
Expenses as per statement	20	23.04	30	40
Less: Depreciation	1.14	2.13	1.86	1.62
Book Profit/(Loss)	(6.14)	1.83	8.14	13.38
Profit as per books		1.83	8.14	13.38
Less: C/o book loss or Depreciation which ever lower.		1.14	1.14	0.00
Book profit on which MAT is calculated		0.69	7.00	13.38
MAT Tax Payable		0.13	1.30	2.48
MAT including cess		0.13	1.35	2.55

Appendix C

Environmental Impact Assessment[1]

The goal of Environmental Impact Assessment (EIA) and Strategic Environmental Analysis (SEA) is to ensure environmentally sound and sustainable development. According to the United Nations Environment Program, "Formally, EIA/SEA are structured approaches for obtaining and evaluating environmental information prior to its use in decision-making in the development process. This information consists basically of predictions of how the environment is expected to change if certain alternative actions are implemented and advice on how best to manage environmental changes if one alternative is selected and implemented. EIA focuses on proposed physical developments such as highways, power stations, water resource projects and large-scale industrial facilities. SEA focuses on proposed actions at a "higher" level such as new or amended laws, policies, programmes and plans. Often, physical developments and projects are the result of implementation of a policy or plan, for example an extended highway network may be an outcome of a new transport policy."

Providing the basics of EIA, this appendix is organised as follows.

- Flow chart of EIA
- General procedure for EIA
- Impact Identification, Prediction, Evaluation, and Mitigation
- EIA methods
- Checklist for reviewing an EIA report

Flow Chart of EIA

The flow chart of EIA is given in Exhibit C.1.

[1] This appendix has been contributed by Dr. T.V. Ramachandra of Indian Institute of Science.

Exhibit C.1 ***Flow Chart of EIA Process***

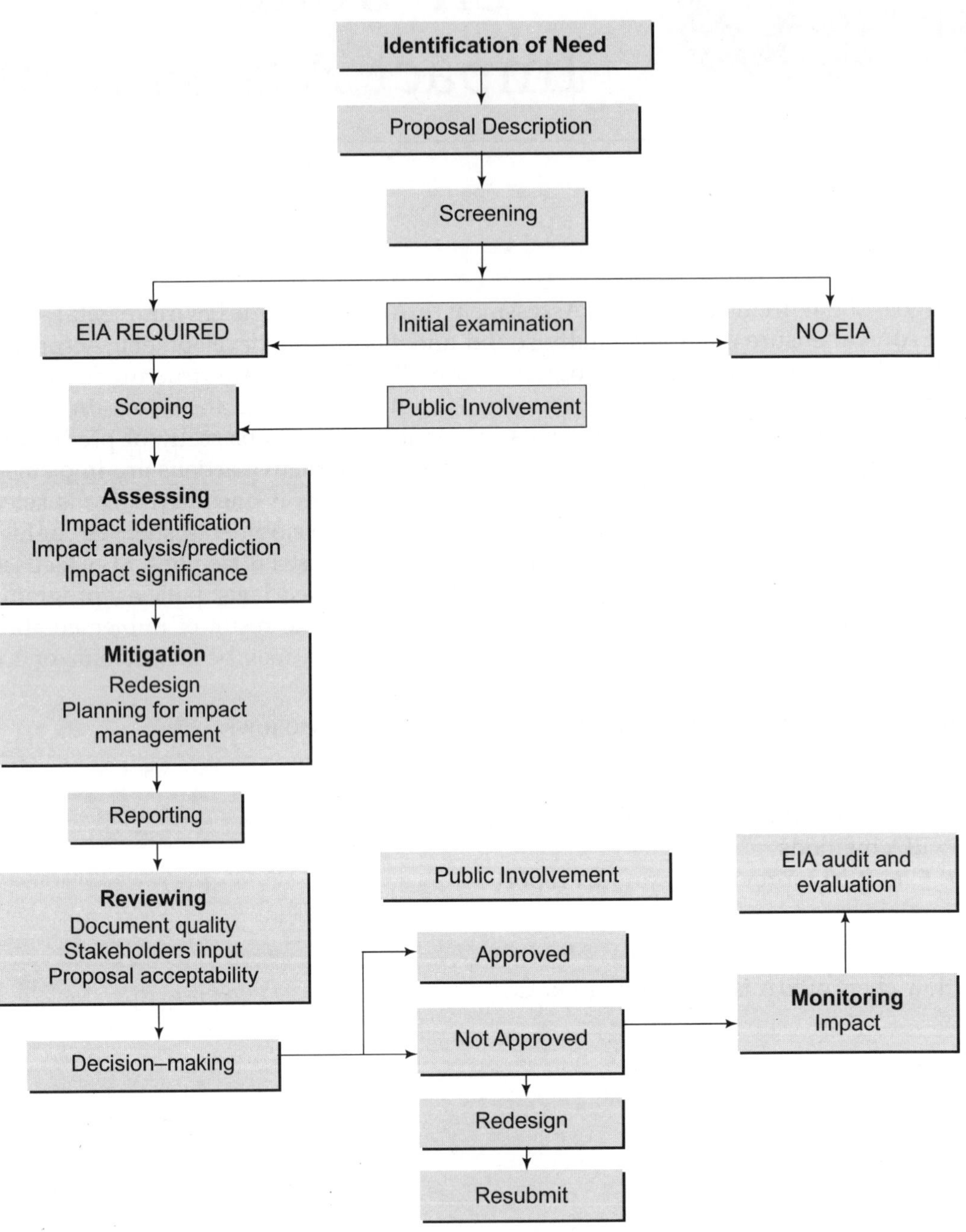

Source: E/A TRM, UNEP, 1996

General Procedure for EIA

The procedural aspects of EIA involve a wide range of activities carried out in the assessment. According to the laws and local practices, EIA process differs from country to country, but the general framework remains the same.

- *Project Screening:* It narrows the application of EIA to those projects that may have significant environmental impacts. Screening may be partly determined by the EIA regulations operating in a country at the time of assessment.
- *Scoping:* It seeks to identify key and significant issues at an early stage, from all of a project's possible impacts and from all the alternatives that could be addressed.
- *Consideration of Alternatives:* It seeks to ensure that the proponent has considered other feasible approaches, including alternative project locations, scales, processes, layouts, operating conditions, and the "no action" option.
- *Description of the Project/Development Action:* It includes a classification of the purpose and rationale of the project, and an understanding of its various characteristics including stages of development, location and processes.
- *Description of the Environmental Baseline:* It includes the establishment of both the present and future state of the environment, in the absence of the project, taking into account changes resulting from natural events and from other human activities.
- *Identification of Key Impacts:* It brings together the previous steps with the aim of ensuring that all potentially significant environmental impacts (adverse and beneficial) are identified and taken into account in the process.
- *The Prediction of Impacts:* It aims to identify the magnitude and other dimensions identified and changes in the environment with a project/action, by comparison with the situation without that project/action.
- *Evaluation and Assessment of Significance:* It seeks to assess the relative significance of the predicted impacts to allow a focus on key adverse impacts.
- *Mitigation:* It involves the introduction of measures to avoid, reduce, remedy or compensate for any significant adverse impacts.
- *Public Consultation and Participation:* It aims to assure the quality, comprehensiveness and effectiveness of the EIA, as well as to ensure that public's views are adequately taken into consideration in the decision making process.
- *Environmental Impact Statement (EIS) Presentation:* It is a full disclosure document; that details the process through which the project is developed including a number of alternatives, potential impacts of alternatives and its compliance with laws and order. It is a vital step in the process. If done badly, much good work in the EIA may be neglected.
- *Review:* It involves a systematic appraisal of the quality of the EIS, as a contribution to the decision-making process.
- *Decision-Making:* Decision-making on the project involves a consideration by the relevant authority of the EIS (including consultation responses) together with other material considerations.
- *Post Decision Monitoring:* It involves the recording of outcomes associated with development impacts, after a decision to proceed. It can contribute to effective project management.

- *Auditing:* It follows monitoring. It can involve comparing actual outcomes with predicted outcomes, and can be used to assess the quality of predictions and the effectiveness of mitigation. It provides a vital step in the EIA learning process.

Impact Identification, Prediction, Evaluation, and Mitigation

Environmental impact is any alteration of environmental conditions or creation of a new set of environmental conditions–adverse or beneficial–caused or induced by the project under consideration. The impact depends on the nature, scale, and location of the proposed activity, and it includes the effect on the natural resource base (i.e., the quality of air, water, noise, biological) and socio-economic components of the environment management. The impacts can be classified as primary, which can be attributed directly to the project, and secondary, which are indirect changes and typically include the changed patterns of socio-economic activities likely to be stimulated or induced by the proposed activity.

Inter alia, EIA involves identifying, predicting, evaluating, and mitigating environmental impact.

Identification Identification includes the following:

(i) Compile a candidate list of key impacts such as changes in air quality, noise levels, wildlife habitats, species diversity, landscape views, social and cultural systems, settlement patterns and employment levels. This data is drawn from as many EIA studies carried out on similar projects as possible.

(ii) Name all the project's *sources* of impacts (e.g., smoke emissions, water consumption, construction jobs) using checklists or questionnaires and then list possible *receptors* in the environment (e.g., crops, communities using the same water for drinking, migrant labourers) by surveying the existing environment and consulting with interested parties. Where the sources affect the receptors, a potential impact is suspected.

Prediction After identifying the environmental components likely to be impacted by the proposed activities the next logical step is impact prediction, which answers the question: What will be the extent of the changes? Prediction scientifically characterises the impact's causes and effects, and its secondary and synergistic consequences for the environment and the local community. It follows an impact within a single environmental parameter (e.g., a toxic liquid effluent) into its subsequent effects in many disciplines (e.g., reduced water quality, adverse impacts on fisheries, economic effects on fishing villages and resulting socio-cultural changes). Prediction draws on the physical, biological, socio-economic and anthropological data and techniques. In quantifying impacts, it may employ various tools such as mathematical models, photomontages, physical models, socio-cultural models, economic models, experiments, expert judgment, etc.

To prevent unnecessary expenses, the sophistication of the prediction methods used should be kept in proportion to the scope of the EIA. For instance, a complex mathematical model of atmospheric dispersion should not be used, if only a small amount of relatively harmless pollutant is emitted. Simpler models are available and are sufficient for the purpose. Also, it is unnecessary to undertake expensive analysis, if they are not required by the decision-makers for whom the EIA is being done.

All prediction techniques, by their nature, involve some degree of uncertainty. So, along with each attempt to quantify an impact, the study team should also quantify the prediction's uncertainty in terms of probabilities or margins of error.

One of the criticisms against EIA is that it does not give the prominence the social and cultural impacts deserve in describing the extent of changes expected to result from a major development project. Socio-cultural impacts should be integrated into every discussion of physical/biological change.

Evaluation This step evaluates the predicted adverse impacts to determine whether they are significant enough to warrant mitigation. In other words, evaluation attempts to find an answer for the question: Do the changes matter? The judgment of significance can be based on one or more of the following:

- Comparison with laws, regulations or accepted standards.
- Consultation with the relevant decision-makers.
- Reference to pre-set criteria such as protected sites, features or species.
- Consistency with government policy objectives.
- Acceptability to the local community or the general public.

Mitigation If the answer to the evaluative question (i.e., Do the changes matter?) is in the affirmative, i.e., the changes do matter, then the EIA proceeds to find an answer to the question: What can be done about them? In this phase, the study team formally analyses mitigation, and a wide range of measures is advanced to prevent, reduce, remedy or compensate for each of the adverse impacts evaluated as significant. Since all mitigation measures cost, it must be quantified.

The possible mitigation measures include:

- Changing project sites, routes, processes, raw materials, operating methods, disposal routes or locations, timing, or engineering designs.
- Introducing pollution controls, waste treatment, monitoring, phased implementation, landscaping, personnel training, special social services or public education.
- Offering (as compensation) restoration of damaged resources, money to affected persons, concessions on other issues, or off-site programmes to enhance some other aspect of the environment or quality of life for the community.

Once these measures are compared, and trade-offs between them weighed, the EIA study team proposes one or more action plans, usually combining a number of measures. The action plan may include technical control measures, an integrated management scheme (for a major project), monitoring, contingency plans, operating practices, project scheduling, or even joint management (with affected groups). The study team should explicitly analyse the implications of adopting different alternatives to help make the choices clearer for decision-makers. Several analytical techniques including the following are available for this purpose:

- Cost/benefit analysis, in which all quantifiable factors are converted to monetary values and actions are assessed for their effect on project costs and benefits. (Note, however, that the unquantifiable and qualitative aspects can be equally important, and often need to be taken into account in the decision-making process.)

- Explaining what course of action would follow from various broad value judgments (e.g., that social impacts are more important than resources).
- A simple matrix of environmental parameters versus mitigation measures, containing brief descriptions of the effects of each measure.
- Pair-wise comparisons, whereby the effects of an action are briefly compared with the effects of each of the alternative actions, one pair at a time.

The mitigation plan should be supplemented with an environmental management plan (EMP) to guide the proponent towards environmental improvements. The EMP is a crucial input to monitoring the clearance conditions and, therefore, the details of monitoring should be included in the EMP.

EIA Methods

The methods prescribed by the NEPA to carryout EIA include *ad hoc* approach, checklists, matrices, network and modeling. They are briefly discussed in the following paragraphs.

- ***Ad hoc approach:*** The most primitive method in EIA studies is the *ad hoc* approach. This crude method provides little guidance for assessing impacts on specific parameters beyond suggesting impacts on broad areas like impact on land, forests, populations, water, wildlife etc. It does not address secondary impacts.
- ***Checklist:*** Considering the environmental attributes involved in the project, checklists are improved version of *ad hoc* approach. The evaluator marks against each attribute considering its adverse, beneficial, or no effects by proposed project activities. This method defines parameters, but it is usually very large, subjective, and provides little guidance in decision-making process.
- ***Matrix method:*** Leopold's matrix is used to relate proposed actions and environmental components. It is composed of a matrix, based on project actions in columns against environmental components in rows. Based on the magnitude and importance of the impact, the appropriate cell is scored with positive sign for beneficial impacts and negative for deleterious impacts. Row totals provide impacts of all project actions on one environmental component whereas column totals provide the impacts of one project action on all environmental components. The matrix total provides the total environmental impact of the proposed project. This method does emphasise secondary impacts but is non-mathematical and hence its application becomes arbitrary.
- ***Mathematical matrices:*** Peterson's matrix is an improvisation over Leopold's method. It involves three matrices; the first is based on impacts of environmental action on various physical components of the environment on a scale of +3 to –3. The second matrix depends on impacts of affected physical components on human environment. Later these two matrices are multiplied to provide a third matrix that gives the effect of actions on human environment. A vector of relative weight of human impacts operates this third matrix. The weighted vector is then summed up to result in a total value of the project impact.
- ***Computer aided EIA:*** The highlight of this method is the use of air, water, and noise models for prediction of environmental parameters. In recent times, Geographic

Information System (GIS) has emerged as a very effective spatial analysis and presentation tool, enabling the identification of the impacted zones by using the overlay technique.

- ***Modeling approach:*** A large number of mathematical models have been developed for the assessment and simulation of a number of environmental attributes like air quality, water quality, noise, and behavior of biological systems. The approaches aim at modeling the environmental parameters for future prediction of impacts in quantitative terms. Key feature of this approach include the ability to give the non-mathematical experts the capacity to model complex, and non-linear feedback systems.

Checklist for Reviewing an EIA Report

(i) Executive summary

- An adequate summary of the significant findings of the EIA report.
- A sufficiently detailed description of how significant environmental issues will be resolved.
- A presentation of the study's conclusions.
- Effective, simple, visual presentations of the type and magnitude of the impacts.

(ii) Introduction

- Description of project rationale.
- Consideration and evaluation of project alternatives.
- Methods used to identify, predict and assess impacts.

(iii) Project description

- A listing of project activities that are likely to cause significant impacts to environmental resources.
- A listing of mitigation measures to be incorporated into the project.
- The location, scale, and scheduling of activities.
- Potential accident or hazard scenarios covered in the risk assessment are based on the characteristics of the project and the history of accidents at similar types of facilities.
- Information should match the expected operations according to the feasibility study.

(iv) Description of the baseline environment

- A description of the environmental components that may be significantly affected by the project.
- An explanation of the derivation of environmental indicators chosen to represent environmental components.
- Base maps for spatial data.

- Baseline values, or some other appropriate form of quantitative and qualitative information, for environmental components/resources that may be affected either directly or indirectly by project activities.

(v) Prediction/assessment of impacts

- A description of the major issues.
- Documentation of the cause and effect relationships between planned project activities and the environmental components.
- Identification of secondary or higher order effects with clearly defined pathways of impacts from higher order effects.
- Impact prediction includes a number of stated assumptions that affect the predicted impacts, their probability of occurrence, and degree of impact.
- Methods used to predict impacts.
- An assessment of the significance of predicted impacts, methods or approaches to assigning impact significance.
- Justification for the choice of methods used to predict environmental impacts.

(vi) Development of mitigation measures

- A description of all the environmental protection measures considered to mitigate or offset damaging environmental impacts from project activities.
- A description of the costs and benefits for each recommended environmental protection option developed to resolve a significant environmental issue, as well as a comparison of each option to the other options.
- Appropriateness and cost effectiveness of environmental protection measures.
- A description of the technology used in each environmental protection measure, including information regarding its prior effective use, the range of environmental conditions under which it is effective, and the level of skill required to operate or maintain the technology.
- A time schedule for implementation of the environmental protection measures, showing that they will be in use before the project impacts are felt.
- A drawing or table that illustrates how the mitigation measures address the significant environmental issues.

(vii) Public consultation and participation

- Description of strategy and approach.
- Chronology of individuals and groups consulted.
- Descriptions of methods used to consult with public.
- Summary of information obtained during consultations and how it was used in preparation of the EIA report.
- A sampling programme design (frequency, intensity) sufficient to provide the information necessary to answer questions.
- Analytical system quality assurance and quality controls are effective.
- Information for reporting monitoring results.

(viii) Environmental management plan and institutional arrangements

- Detailed descriptions of the environmental protection measures, the monitoring program, and follow-up activities.
- Monitoring requirements.
- Allocation of responsibilities and tasks.
- Staffing requirements.
- Budgets and schedules.
- Administrative arrangements.
- Administrative mechanisms for enforcement and taking corrective action are in place.

(ix) Summary and conclusions

- Net benefits which justify the project.
- Explanation of how adverse effects have been mitigated.
- Explanation of use or destruction of any irreplaceable components.
- Provisions for follow-up surveillance and monitoring.

Regulatory Aspects of EIA in India

Till the mid-1970s, EIA hardly received any attention in India. In 1976–77 EIA was considered for large scale river valley projects because of their serious socio-cultural and ecological consequences. The Department of Environment, that came up in 1980, established environmental information system and a few environmental appraisals for development projects. The creation of the Ministry of Environment and Forests in 1985–86 laid the foundation for many legislative provisions to protect environment and forests in India (http://envfor.nic.in/). As the concern over environment and ecosystem grew in 1980s (Chipko Andolan, Silent Valley agitation, Western Ghats movement, and Bhopal gas tragedy), India brought strict provision for EIA and made it statutory on 27th January 1994 under the provision of the Environment (Protection) Act of 1986.

EIA Notification 1994 This notification mandates a public hearing and requires the project proponent to submit an EIA report, an environmental management plan, details of the public hearing and a project report to the impact assessment agency for clearance, with further review by a committee of experts (in certain cases). Initially the impact assessment agency was the Ministry of Environment and Forests, Government of India. The EIA Regulations were applied to 29 designated projects/industries, which are enlisted in Schedule I of the notification. Any member of the public can have access to the summary of the project report and the details of the Environment Management Plan.

Several amendments were made to this original notification in 1997, 2002, 2003, 2004 and 2005, some diluting while others strengthening the environmental clearance process.

EIA Notification 2006 The Union Ministry of Environment and Forest (MEF) notified the new EIA Notification in September 2006 (http://envfor.nic.in/rules-regulation/environment-protection) after putting up the draft notification for public comment for a year. The objective of EIA Notification 2006 was to address the limitations in the old EIA Notification (1994).

Therefore, various modification have been incorporated in the old Notification, taking into account the feedback from the different stakeholders. Though there have been some improvements in the new notification over the previous one, it has failed to meet the expectations of the various stakeholders, especially members of the civil society, NGOs and local community.

Projects seeking environment clearance have been divided into two categories, Category A and B. The categorisation of the developmental projects / activities is specified in the Schedule to EIA notification 2006 (http://envfor.nic.in/legis/eia/so1533.doc).

- Category A: All projects and activities (major activities such as river valley projects, nuclear, thermal power projects, mining, etc.) require EIA study and clearance from central government.
- Category B: Environment clearance is accorded by the State Environmental Impact Assessment Authority (SEIAA), constituted by Govt. of India based on the appraisal and recommendation by the State Level Expert Appraisal Committee (SEAC). Category B is further divided into two categories-B1 (which will require EIA study) and B2, which does not require EIA study.

EIA Notification, 2009 Issued on January 19, 2009, this notification enhances the powers of the state authorities for certain types of clearances. Its key provisions are as follows:

- The project proponent has to compulsorily make public at their own cost the terms of the environmental clearances obtained by advertising it in two local newspapers of the district/state where the project is located.
- Copies of the environmental clearances will also have to be made available to the local bodies (Panchayats/ Municipal bodies).
- A self certification stating that the proposal shall not involve any additional pollution load, waste generation, or water requirement has be submitted to the regulatory authority by the project proponent.
- In the absence of a duly constituted SEAC/SEIAA a Category B project shall be treated as a Category A project.
- In case of expansion projects involving enhancement of production by more than 50%, holding of public constitution shall be essential and no exemption in this regard shall be provided.
- Irrigation projects not involving submergence or inter-state domain shall be appraised by the SEIAA as Category B project.
- Environmental clearances are also required for Thermal Power Plant > 50 MW (based on Biomass as fuel) and it falls in Category A.
- Any project or activity specified in Category B will be treated as Category A, if located in whole or in part within 10 kilometers from the boundary of protected areas (as per Wildlife Protection Act, 1972), critically polluted area (notified by CPCB), eco-sensitive regions (under Section 3 of Environment Protection Act 1986), or inter-state/ international boundaries.

Appendix D Detailed Project Report*

A detailed project report (DPR) is a business information document prepared in connection with a proposed project. It seeks to provide information for obtaining regulatory clearances and raising capital (primarily long-term debt capital).

While most lenders do not prescribe a specific format for preparing a DPR, they do specify the kind of information a DPR should provide. Typically, a DPR consists of the following:

- Business and management section
- Technical and marketing section
- Financial section
- Annexures

Business and Management Section

The business and management section covers the following:

1. A business history of the project company along with details of major projects undertaken in the past.
2 A financial history of the project company along with details of past and present lenders, credit facilities, shareholding pattern, listing status, market performance data, and details of financial performance for the past five years.
3. History and details of project sponsors (natural persons or juridical persons) in terms of personal information, previous experience, business and financial track record, net worth, existing banking relationships, list of individuals or entities forming part of the promoter group, and so on.
4. Business and operating environment in terms of the government regulation and key statutory approvals the industry and operating environment, nature of competition, critical success factors, pricing structure, inert- firm comparison, and so on.
5. Core management team in terms of the profile of directors (or partners or proprietor), resume of top management team and business heads, compensation structure of top management, key appointments and resignations in the past three years, and so on.

---

* Adapted from Annexure 1 of Chapter 6 of the following book: Pratap G. Subramanyam, *Strategic Corporate Finance*, Mumbai: Snowwhite®, 2011.

6. Organisation structure in terms of business divisions, department, personnel, and so on.

• Technical and Marketing Section

The technical and marketing section covers the following:

1. Details of the present project proposal in terms of location, land acquisition, installed capacity, products, manpower requirements and availability, project logistics, key project contracts, current status of the project, project implementation schedule, list of key approvals required and status thereof, and so on.
2. Details of the present and proposed technology in terms of the source of technology and details of the collaborator (if any), terms of collaboration and technology transfer, assessment of alternative technologies, technical description of the manufacturing process, list of key equipments required and equipment sourcing, cost parameters for technology and equipment, cost comparisons and competitive quotes, time elements in equipment sourcing, erection and commissioning, and so on.
3. Details of inputs required for the project and arrangements in terms of raw materials, water, power, effluent treatment and disposal, steam and compressed air, feedstock/ fuel supply. Transportation of raw materials and finished goods, supply chain management, technology and IT backbone for the business processes, international quality assurance standards such as ISO 9001, FDA, cGMP, star certification, and so on.
4. Market aspects and marketing arrangements in terms of potential users and market segments, distribution methodology, key marketing contracts, structure of the marketing chain, demand-supply analysis vis-a-vis capacity, competitor analysis, pricing strategy and other key marketing strategies, core competence in marketing the products, customer relations management, and so on.

• Financial Section

The financial section has to furnish adequate information on the financial viability of the project. This section covers the following:

1. Estimated project cost broken under the following broad heads: land and site development, buildings and civil works, plant and machinery, technical know-how, intangible asset costs, miscellaneous fixed assets, preliminary and pre-operative expenses, provision for contingencies (generally not exceeding 10 percent of non-firm cost), and margin money for working capital.
2. Proposed means of financing broken into equity capital and debt capital. Equity capital includes promoters' contribution, internal accruals, contribution of collaborator/ JV partner, private placement, rights issue, public issue, and subsides or grants. Debt capital includes long term loans, deferred payment obligations, development loans/ soft loans, and unsecured/ subordinated loans.
3. The projected financial statements consist of the projected profit and loss account, projected cash flow statement, and projected balance sheet. The projected financial

statements are prepared by developing the financial model of the project using spreadsheets. The key inputs required for developing the projected financial statements are: (a) project cost estimate and proposed means of finance, (b) estimates of quantity and prices of outputs and inputs leading to estimates of revenues and costs, (c) depreciation and loan amortisation schedules, (d) estimates of interest and financial costs, and working capital needs, and (e) estimates of income tax burden.

While developing financial projections, the following assumptions are generally made:

- Prices of finished products and raw materials are estimated by extrapolating the prevailing prices over the time frame required for commencement of commercial production, taking into account the price behaviour in the past three to five years. Once the prices are determined in his manner, they are held constant over the entire forecast period.
- Operating costs are estimated by taking the prevailing costs and applying a suitable escalation factor per year over the forecast period.
- For profitability projections, depreciation is calculated on a straight line basis and for tax estimation depreciation is calculated as per the written down value method.
- Interest costs on term loans and working capital loans are estimated taking into account the risk assessment of the project and prime lending rates of the relevant institutions.
- Working capital estimates are developed taking into account the appropriate holding periods for various working capital components. The bank finance for working capital is estimated as per the second method of lending prescribed under Tandon Committee norms.
- For preparing the projected profitability statement, no adjustment is made for closing and opening stocks.
- For preparing the projected cash flow statement, it is necessary to show suitable deployment of the excess cash that is generated year after year.

4. The key financial indicators used for judging the project are:
   - Profitability Indicators: Gross profit margin, net profit margin, earnings per share, cash earnings per share, return on capital employed, and return on net worth.
   - Financial Indicators: Debt-equity ratio, net worth, book value per share, total tangible net worth to total outside liabilities, current ratio, and interest cover.
   - Viability Indicators: Debt service coverage ratio, internal rate of return, weighted average cost of capital, and break-even point.

• Annexures Forming Part of DPR

The standard documents and material contracts included here are:

1. Loan application duly filled in with all relevant particulars.
2. DPR prepared by the borrower, if any.

3. Certified copies of Memorandum and Articles of Association and other important documents associated with the incorporation/constitution of the company.
4. Annual Reports/Financial Statements for the past three years in the case of existing companies.
5. Details of existing term loans, unsecured loans, and existing charge holders.
6. Financial statements of group companies or other promoter businesses. In case of SPV projects, the financials of the sponsoring companies for the past three years need to be furnished.
7. Banker's Report on main promoters and borrowing company.
8. Networth statements certified by Chartered Accountant for the project sponsors/ promoters and all entities forming part of the promoter group/sponsors.
9. Copies of latest IT/WT return/assessment orders for the company and promoters/ sponsors.
10. Copies of Shareholder Agreements if any for the project company.
11. Copies of JV/Technology transfer/Collaboration agreements if any.
12. Banker's report on foreign collaborator. JV partner.
13. All key quotations for equipment and other fixed assets.
14. Reasons for expansion/diversification where applicable.
15. Details of present installed capacity and capacity utilisation.
16. Quotations/orders for purchase of plant and machinery and other fixed assets.
17. In case of second-hand machinery, a chartered engineer's certificate regarding the residual life of the machines.
18. Technical certificates/warranties from chartered engineer/technical agency/ manufacturer for key equipment.
19. Fuel supply/Raw material agreements where applicable.
20. Marketing/buy-back agreements if any.
21. Reports/secondary data on market information.
22. Location diagrams, technical details and drawings.
23. Product endorsements from existing customers if any.
24. Copies of statutory approvals from FIPB/SIA/RBI/Commerce Ministry/In principle clearance of Ministry of Environment and Forests/State Industry Department. If all clearances are not yet available, relevant applications filed for pending approvals need to be furnished.
25. Copies of land allotment letter/sale deed/lease deed.
26. Details of effluents produced and measures for treatment and discharge.
27. State level government approvals and application for NOC from Pollution Control Board.
28. NOC from existing lenders/lessors for creation of charge/pari passu charge.
29. Copies of loan agreements/charge creation on existing assets of the company that are subsisting on the company.
30. Compliance certificate from a company secretary in practice or whole time secretary of the company.
31. Search report of a company secretary in practice on the company law filings and charges registered by the company.

Bibliography

Amran M. and N. Kulatilalka, *Real Options: Managing Strategic Investment in an Uncertain World*, Harvard Business School Press, Boston, 2000.

Bierman, H., Jr., and S. Smidt, *The Capital Budgeting Decision*, (7th ed.), Macmillan, New York, 1990.

Bower, J.L., *Managing the Resource Allocation Process*, Division of Research, Graduate School of Business Administration, Harvard University, Boston, 1970.

Bussey, L.E., *The Economic Analysis of Industrial Projects*, Prentice-Hall, Englewood Cliffs, N.J., 1978.

Charnes, A. and W.W. Cooper, *Management Models and Industrial Applications of Linear Programming*, John Wiley & Sons, New York, 1961.

Dean, J., *Capital Budgeting*, Columbia University Press, New York, 1951.

Ehrhardt M.C., *The Search for Value: Measuring the Company's Cost of Capital*, Harvard Business School Press, Boston 1998.

Grayson, C.J. Jr., *Decisions Under Uncertainty: Drilling Decisions by Oil and Gas Operators*, Division of Research, Harvard Business School, Boston, 1960.

Ignizio, J.P., *Goal Programming and Extension*, Lexington Books, D.C. Heath and Company, Lexington, Mass., 1976.

Little, I.M.D. and J.A. Mirrlees, *Project Appraisal and Planning for Developing Countries*, Hienemann Educational Books, London, 1974.

Markowitz, H.M., *Portfolio Selection: Efficient Diversification of Investments*, Cowles Foundation Monograph 16, John Wiley & Sons, New York, 1959.

Massee, P., *Optimal Investment Decisions: Rules of Action and Criteria for Choice*, Prentice-Hall, Englewood Cliffs, N.J., 1962.

Mize, J.H. and J.G. Cox, *Essentials of Simultation*, Prentice-Hall, Englewood Cliffs, N.J., 1968.

OECD, *Manual of Industrial Project Analysis in Developing Countries—Methodology and Case Studies*, OECD, Paris, 1972.

Planning Commission, *Guidelines for the Preparation of Feasibility Reports of Industrial Projects*, Controller of Publications, New Delhi, 1970.

Pouliquen, L.Y., *Risk Analysis in Project Appraisal*, Johns Hopkins Press, Baltimore, California, 1970.

Quirin, D.G., *The Capital Expenditure Decisions*, Richard D. Irwin, Homewood, Ill., 1967.

Raghuram G., et al., *Infrastructure Development and Financing*, Macmillan India, Delhi, 1999.

Raiffa, H., *Decision Analysis*, Addison-Wesley, Reading, Mass., 1968.

Reutlinger, S., *Techniques for Project Appraisal Under Uncertainty*, Baltimore, California, Johns Hopkins Press, 1970.

Sheridman, T., J. D. Martin and V. R. Anshuman, *Valuation: Analyzing Global Investment Oppurtunities*, Pearson Addison Wesley, Boston, 2007.

Subramanyam, P., *Investment Banking*, Tata McGraw-Hill, New Delhi, 2004.

Trigerogis, L., *Real Options*, MIT Press, Cambridge, 1996.

UNIDO, *Guidelines for Project Evaluation*, United Nations, 1972.

________, *Guide to Practical Project Appraisal*, United Nations, New York, 1978.

UNO, *Manual on Economic Development Projects*, United Nations, New York, 1958.

Weingartner, M.H., *Mathematical Programming and Analysis of Capital Budgeting Problems*, Prentice-Hall, Englewood Cliffs, N.J., 1963.

Weist, J.D. and F.K. Levy, *A Management Guide to PERT/CPM*, Prentice-Hall of India, New Delhi, 1974.

Index

R

S

T

U

V

W

Z

CFM-MHE Professional Series in Finance

Honorary Consulting Editor: Dr. Prasanna Chandra

The CFM-MHE Professional Series in Finance, a joint initiative of the Centre for Financial Management and McGraw Hill Education (India), seeks to synthesise the findings of financial research with the concerns of practitioners. The aim of the books in this series is to convey the important developments in the theory and practice of finance in a rigorous, but relatively non-technical manner for the benefit of: (a) finance practitioners and (b) students of MBA.

Titles in the Series

- *Financial Management: Theory and Practice, 10/e* — **Prasanna Chandra**
- *Projects: Planning, Analysis, Selection, Financing, Implementation and Review, 9/e* — **Prasanna Chandra**
- *Finance Sense: Finance for Non-finance Executives, 5/e* — **Prasanna Chandra**
- *Investment Analysis and Portfolio Management, 5/e* — **Prasanna Chandra**
- *Corporate Valuation: A Guide to Analysts, Managers, and Investors* — **Prasanna Chandra**
- *Strategic Financial Management: Managing for Value Creation* — **Prasanna Chandra**
- *Investment Game: How to Win, 7/e* — **Prasanna Chandra**
- *International Financial Management, 8/e* — **Prakash G Apte, Sanjeevan Kapshe**
- *Investment Banking: Concepts, Analyses and Cases, 3/e* — **Pratap G Subramanyam**
- *Macroeconomic Policy Environment, 2/e* — **Shyamal Roy**

CFM Quarterly in Finance

Centre for Financial Management brings out an e-journal called ***CFM Quarterly in Finance*** edited by Dr. Prasanna Chandra.

Written in a relatively non-technical manner, ***CFM Quarterly in Finance*** has three sections. The first section, the principal section, carries short articles and cases to discuss important ideas, concepts, and state-of-the-art practices in the broad fields of finance and investments. The second section carries snippets that provide useful insights. Finally, the third section provides some wit and wisdom.

CFM Quarterly in Finance is designed for two categories of readers: finance educators and finance practitioners. ***Finance educators*** will find the material useful to enrich the courses taught by them. ***Finance practitioners*** will get valuable insights and perspectives to handle their professional challenges.

You can access the ***CFM Quarterly in Finance*** at www.cfm-india.com